DAVID BOWIE
ALL THE SONGS

BENOÎT CLERC

DAVID BOWIE
ALL THE SONGS

The Story Behind
Every Track

BLACK DOG
& LEVENTHAL
PUBLISHERS
NEW YORK

CONTENTS

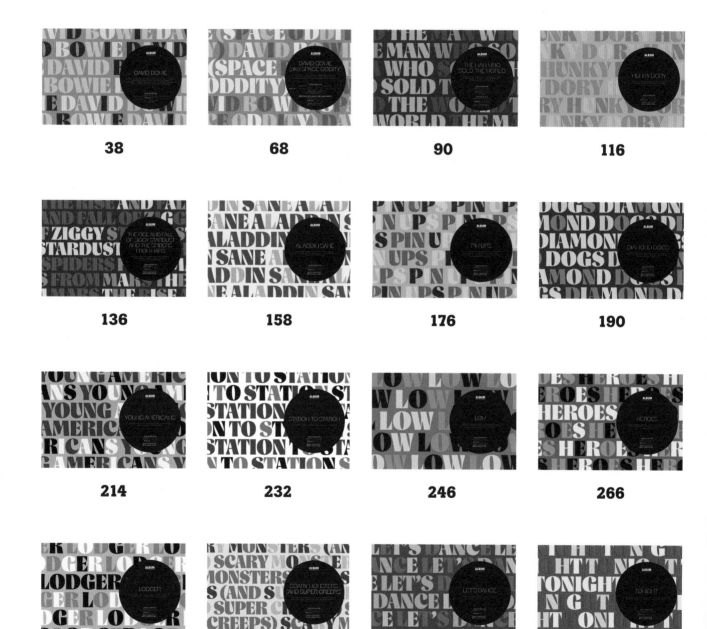

364

380

396

414

432

442

462

484

506

524

542

562

588

David Bowie launched his
triumphant Serious Moonlight
Tour at the Forest National arena
in Brussels, Belgium.

FOREWORD

It never fails: Mention David Bowie, and your listener's face lights up with a big smile. David Bowie, we love him, even if we sometimes know only a handful of his recordings. How do you explain this *strange fascination?* Is it his unique voice? His androgynous beauty? Or is it simply that his songs speak to the heart? It's difficult to say because it's hard to pin down the reasons for the admiration—a better word might be *love*—that fans have felt for David Bowie since the mid-1970s, when he rose to international rock stardom.

Who was this man, hiding behind the characters of Rainbow Man, Ziggy Stardust, the Thin White Duke, and Nathan Adler? Interviews with the singer himself—frequently described as a chameleon—and the observations of those who worked with him all point to a single truth: This was a man who was generous, accessible, and responsive to others. An (almost) normal man, in his personal life he was far removed from the alien-like image that he sometimes projected for public consumption. His career was quite unusual, though. From the very beginning, in 1964, until his death in 2016, David Bowie worked incessantly, constantly creating new works, adopting new musical trends, and reinventing himself with each new album. He never stopped surprising his fans with his risk-taking.

By establishing the chronology of an extraordinary life and career, *David Bowie All The Songs* sets out to unravel the mystery of this intriguing singer, tracing the recording sessions of his twenty-six studio albums, as well as his side adventure with Tin Machine, and his many collaborations with various contemporaries in the recording industry. Out of respect for the work created by this demanding artist, only songs recorded and published according to his wishes are discussed in this book. This is why, as connoisseurs will not fail to notice, we have omitted many compositions that never progressed past early demo stages ("Bars of the County Jail," "That's Where My Heart Is," "I'll Follow You," "I Want My Baby Back"), songs sung by other artists ("Rupert the Riley," recorded by Nick King All Stars in 1971) or those published in unorthodox ways ("Ching-A-Ling," "When I'm Five," from the promotional film *Love You till Tuesday).*

From "Liza Jane" to "Lazarus," David Bowie's 456 songs tell us more about the man than any traditional biography ever could. A detailed look at his discography sheds light on the lasting legacy of an unforgettable artist. *David Bowie All the Songs* is a listener's perfect companion to the catalog of one of the most important recording artists of the last hundred years.

A Note on the Text

In the interest of consistency, compilation albums and box sets featuring Bowie's works are listed at the end of this book. Only works issued by record labels in Europe, the United Kingdom, and the United States are included.

Titles issued solely in the maxi 45 rpm format are not considered singles.

The chart listings referenced throughout *David Bowie All the Songs,* are:

– For the UK: The Official Charts Company

– For the US: The Billboard Hot 100 (singles), The Billboard 200 (albums).

Unless otherwise stated, the references and rankings included herein relate only to a specific album's first edition.

BEGINNINGS

Born in Brixton, South London, on January 8, 1947, David Robert Jones emerged into a Britain that was still recovering from the effects of the war years. Clement Attlee was the prime minister, and it was a time of deep social and economic hardship that saw rationing of food after a winter with unusual amounts of snow and freezing temperatures caused significant damage to agriculture across the country. David's father, Haywood Stenton Jones, better known as John, had worked since 1935 as a public relations officer for the children's charity Dr. Barnardo's Homes. Praiseworthy as this type of work was, his past was rather murky. Earlier in his life, David's father had been the owner of two clubs and it was in one of them, the Boop-a-Doop club, that he met a singer named Hilda Louise Sullivan, who was to become his first wife in 1933. A few years later, Hilda adopted a little girl, Annette, who was the result of John's liaison with another woman. John's marriage to Hilda ended in 1945 when he met Margaret "Peggy" Mary Burns, who was an employee at the Ritz, a cinema in Tunbridge Wells, which is a small town in western Kent, located about thirty miles to the south of London. Even before his divorce to Hilda had been finalized, John went to live with his new partner in Kentish Town, moving not long afterward to Brixton. John and Peggy officially married in 1947.

Elvis, Dean Moriarty, and Little Richard: David's Early Influences

In 1953, the Jones family moved to Bromley in South London. The household expanded rapidly when Annette came to live with her father, soon to be joined by Terry, a second child born to Peggy shortly before the war. Terry's father was a Frenchman who quickly disappeared from Peggy's life, and this new half brother was to play an important role in young David's artistic development. In particular, Terry gave David a copy of Jack Kerouac's *On the Road*, thereby introducing David to the countercultural movement emerging on the other side of the Atlantic, as personified by Kerouac's character Dean Moriarty, who became the standard bearer of the Beat Generation. The young David Jones's introduction to rock 'n' roll also came through Terry, who played him Elvis Presley's early singles, including the famous "That's All Right," which was itself a cover of blues musician Arthur Crudup's original. But it was not only Elvis and the advent of this new music from America that was exciting for young David; indeed, he was fascinated by everything about the United States.

In 1955, Terry joined the Royal Air Force while David started at Burnt Ash Junior in Bromley, which was a school where music had an important place. Here he met Geoffrey MacCormack, someone who was to be one of his best friends and later a close artistic collaborator.

In 1957, the ten-year-old David discovered the musician who was to change his life: singer and pianist Little Richard, who had recently starred in two films from the United States. In Charles S. Dubin's movie *Mister Rock and Roll*, this extraordinary musician with the narrow mustache performed his single "Lucille" with a backing group that included three saxophones accompanying him in synchronized movements. It was an image that stayed with David Jones, who would reveal years later that Little Richard had immediately inspired him to play the sax in a group of his own one day. Little Richard also performed

A class photo from Bromley Technical High School, where David was introduced to practical music and joined his first bands.

"The Girl Can't Help It" in Frank Tashlin's movie of the same name, a number that immediately became an American rock 'n' roll classic.

In the autumn of 1958, David started at Bromley Technical High School (Bromley Tech) where the curriculum included fashion and art. It was here that he wrote his first songs. Like many young musicians, he started out with a cheap ukulele. Skiffle was a popular musical genre of the day; it was often played on improvised instruments while standing up, and it was inspired by blues, jazz, and American folk music. David made himself a double bass with a tea chest, a broom handle, and a piece of string. By varying the tension on the string, it was possible to modify the pitch of the notes. Now officially a bass player, he formed a duo with George Underwood, his new guitar-playing friend whom he had gotten to know the previous year through the Scout Group at St. Mary's Church in Bromley. In the summer of 1959, while spending a weekend on the Isle of Wight, Bowie played his first concert, performing classics like "Puttin' on the Style" (recorded by Vernon Dalhart in 1925 and popularized in Britain by Lonnie Donegan in 1957). The very successful B-side of Donegan's skiffle single "Gamblin' Man" was also covered by the duo. It was also around this time that Terry returned from his stint in the army, but he came back a very different person: He was withdrawn and often sullen. It was not long before he was diagnosed as bipolar, which forced David to reflect on some troubling aspects of the family's past. His maternal grandmother had also shown signs of psychological disturbance, as had his aunt Nora, who was eventually lobotomized.

Bromley Tech: David Jones's First Playground

Wanting to know more about the roots of an American culture that had begun to obsess him, David was soon exploring jazz and jazz's pioneering players, including Charles Mingus, Charlie Parker, and King Curtis. The influence of these last two, in particular, was to prove crucial in the young man's artistic evolution. His love of the saxophone, the instrument that crops up throughout his career and featured in a significant number of his songs, dates back to this formative time.

Returning to school after the summer of 1960, David Jones and George Underwood found themselves assigned to the same class. The new term also marked the arrival of a new art teacher, Owen Frampton. He encouraged amateur projects and invited his pupils to bring their musical instruments to school. His son, Peter Frampton, also attended Bromley Tech beginning in 1962, and he went on to become a British rock star in his own right, with hits including "Baby, I Love Your Way" and "Show Me the Way." Recalling those years spent alongside the future Bowie, Frampton later said: "My dad would hide the guitars in the office that we'd brought to school, and at lunchtime we'd get them out and that was when I learned my first Eddie Cochran song, 'C'mon Everybody,' which was taught to me by David."[1]

But to return to 1960: David was beginning to develop a taste for fashion and aesthetic excesses of every kind. "His appearance was always a little bit out of the way from the point of view of normal school dress,"[2] Owen Frampton was to say, having recognized the boy as someone very original, who was endowed with an artistic sense that

One of the scenes from *Mister Rock and Roll*, directed by Charles S. Dubin (1957), with the eccentric Little Richard and accompanied by a brass section that was the stuff of the young David Jones's dreams.

needed to be nurtured. David was also interested in the bizarre and esoteric novels of Frank Edwards and the unusual figures featuring in his 1961 book, *Strange People*. H. G. Wells, who coincidentally also grew up in Bromley, was also a favorite author of young David, who tore through such masterpieces as *The Invisible Man* and *The War of the Worlds*, published in 1897 and 1898, respectively. The mysterious, almost phantasmagoric universes and larger-than-life characters that sprang forth from these classic texts had a lasting influence on the budding artist, one that would manifest itself in the composition of many of his later hits.

While his best friend, George Underwood, had just set up the Kon-rads, a fledgling group that performed cover versions of rock numbers, David was busy discovering the saxophone. For Christmas in 1961, his father gave him an acrylic Grafton model that was molded out of plastic. Though grateful, only a month later David managed to persuade his father to get him a brass model, this time a Conn, which was made in America and produced a fuller and far more professional sound. Around the same time, David also discovered that an up-and-coming saxophonist named Ronnie Moss was listed in the phone book and lived in Orpington, which wasn't too far from the center of Bromley. The young musician plucked up his courage and called Moss on the phone, quickly asking about taking private lessons. The saxophone eventually became closely associated with the man who was to become David Bowie, even if his teacher would later comment with amusement on his pupil's less than impressive early ability: "I showed him how to blow, how to breathe and a little about how to read music. I told him that sax playing was all about the sound you had in your mind, not just reproducing notes on a paper. [...] He had

about eight lessons, one every two weeks. [...] He came for about sixteen weeks [...] and then he disappeared. [...] I don't know if he ever played much after that, but from the dreadful noise he makes on Lulu's record 'The Man Who Sold the World' I shouldn't think he did."[3]

The Kon-rads and Stage Baptism

On February 12, 1962, a fight broke out between David and George on the grounds of Bromley Tech. The cause of the quarrel was a certain Carol Goldsmith, who had caught the attention of both boys. An unlucky punch from Underwood wounded his rival's left eye and the fight was quickly broken up. Two days later, realizing that his eye was not improving, David went to Moorfields Eye Hospital in London, where he underwent an operation. Attempts to repair a torn retina were unsuccessful and his left pupil was to remain permanently dilated, giving the impression, often repeated in the press, that his eyes were different colors. In fact, this was just an illusion created by his permanently dilated retina. From that time, David suffered from anisocoria (pupils of differing sizes). Despite this incident, he never blamed Underwood or held the injury against him. Indeed, this unfortunate experience seems to have brought the two boys closer together. History does not relate what happened to the lovely Carol Goldsmith...

In June 1962, George Underwood invited David to play the saxophone in his group, the Kon-rads. On June 16, David took part in a concert on the steps of Bromley Tech as part of a festival organized by the school. The group played cover versions of songs by the Shadows, which were well received, and the musicians making up the group—Underwood on vocals, Neville Wills and Alan Dodds on guitars, Rocky "Shahan" Chaudhari on bass, and Dave Crook on drums—were happy to welcome their newest member. During the summer of 1962, the Kon-rads performed locally, gradually becoming better known. Their set list consisted mostly of covers (including Little Richard's "Lucille," Bruce Channel's "Hey Baby," and Chuck Berry's classic hit "Johnny B. Goode") and a few original compositions. It was at this time that David took on his first stage name: Dave Jay. Soon after adopting this new moniker, and when he wasn't playing his favorite instrument on the cover version of Glenn Miller's famous "In the Mood," Dave Jay began taking up the mic and doing the vocals for two other numbers: Curtis Lee's "A Night at Daddy Gee's" and Joe Brown's "A Picture of You."

On October 13, 1962, David and his friend George spent an unforgettable evening at the Granada Theatre in Woolwich, England, where their idol Little Richard was performing alongside the Tridents, Gene Vincent, and Sam Cooke. Blues, rock 'n' roll, and soul music came together in a concert that had a lasting effect on the two friends. Underwood remembers: "When Little Richard was performing, we thought he'd had a heart attack. [...] He did this amazing thing where he stood on this white grand piano, and then started to make groaning sounds and holding his heart. [...] So he fell onto the stage, lying there with the microphone right by his side. [...] All of a sudden Little Richard lifted his head up and shouted

'Awapbopaloobop Alopbamboom!' and the crowd went mad. David was flabbergasted, and he obviously never forgot it."[1] At the same time, the concert presented the young David Jones with a dilemma. With the humor and self-deprecation that became a leading characteristic of the man he would become, Bowie would later say: "I couldn't decide whether I wanted to play jazz or rock 'n' roll. And as I wasn't very good at jazz and I could fake it pretty well on rock 'n' roll, I played rock 'n' roll."[4]

As the Kon-rads became more ambitious, some changes were made to the group. The drummer, Dave Crook, was ousted and replaced by a newcomer, Dave Hadfield. This decision enraged George Underwood, who decided to

hand over the mic to Roger Ferris. Two additional singers also joined the group: sisters Stella and Christine Patton. The Kon-rads were now complete.

Those fans who have devoured the many biographies devoted to David Robert Jones will have noticed how "Kon-rads" is sometimes hyphenated and sometimes not. We know that the hyphen should be there since, as can be seen in group photos, the face of Dave Hadfield's bass drum displays the words "The Kon-rads." It appears again with the hyphen on all the publicity material produced by the musicians in 1962 (including on a Christmas card signed by all the members of the band and giving the address of their manager and drummer, Dave Hadfield).

Davie Jones and his King Bees
showing off the emergent mod look
in 1964: Roger Bluck and George
Underwood (standing), Robert Allen
and Dave Howard (seated).

In February 1963, the group's new lineup was captured in a photo session organized by David's father on the stage of a hall adjacent to the Dr. Barnardo's offices in central London at 18-26 Stepney Causeway. The official Dr. Barnardo's photographer, Roy Ainsworth, was requisitioned for the occasion. Now a stable and professional group, the photos show the musicians holding their instruments and standing proudly behind their elegant lead singer and two backing singers—all three of whom are dressed in white.

Discovering the Blues

In July 1963, David left Bromley Tech with a diploma in art in his pocket. He found a job as a junior paste-up artist with the advertising agency Nevin D. Hirst on New Bond Street in London. By now, David was concentrating fully on his rock group, and this day job did not suit his ambitions. It had certain advantages, however, chief among them the fact that the offices were situated in the heart of a fast-changing city. The neighborhood shop windows displayed all the latest fashions, there were art galleries nearby, and David's kindly employer regularly sent him out to buy discs at Dobells, a shop in the Charing Cross section of London that was famous for its stock of rare imports from the United States. Specializing in jazz and folk, the shop enabled the young graphic designer to discover American artists like John Lee Hooker, Dr. John, and Bob Dylan, and Bowie was quick to share his enthusiasm with George Underwood, with whom he was still very close. During the summer, the two friends formed a short-lived group with a drummer named Viv. His surname is not known, although numerous sources assert that he was Viv Andrews, the first drummer with Pretty Things. The trio performed a few concerts under the names of Dave's Reds & Blues, and then the Hooker Brothers.

On September 21, 1963, the Kon-rads gave a concert in the Orpington Civic Hall, near Bromley. Their singer, Roger Ferris, was violently attacked by leather-jacketed youths who were heavily influenced by American culture and images of biker gangs. Without a moment's hesitation, David, who was already confident behind a mic, took over on vocals. Ferris had this to say about the new division of labor: "He was already doing two or three numbers on his own. I remember he used to do 'Lucille,' the Little Richard song, because there was no way I could get my voice up to that point."[5] Among the audience that evening was Bob Knight, who was working as the assistant to Eric Easton, the manager of an up-and-coming group called the Rolling Stones. Knight admired the Kon-rads and introduced them to his boss. Fortune smiled on the musicians who were quickly booked to audition at Decca Studios for Decca Records. The audition took the form of a performance in a TV talent show *Ready, Steady, Win*. The prize for the winner was a contract with the prestigious Decca label. Easton and Knight were present but were not impressed by the group's rendering of their new song, "I Never Dreamed." An acetate recording was made at the time, but it didn't resurface until 2018, when its owner, Dave Hadfield, offered it for sale in an auction of his collection. This failed audition led to an impasse within the Kon-rads. The group refused to incorporate David's taste in music, as he was increasingly leaning toward Detroit soul music from the Motown label. The singer-saxophonist felt he had no choice, and so in October he left the Kon-rads to pursue new musical avenues.

Leslie Conn and the King Bees Adventure

At the beginning of 1964, David got to know a trio from Fulham in West London. The group called themselves the King Bees, and they consisted of drummer Robert Allen, guitarist Roger Bluck, and bass player Dave Howard. Fans of American blues music, the group had taken its name from the song "I'm a King Bee" written by singer and harmonica player Slim Harpo. Harpo also served as a major influence on the Rolling Stones, who covered "I'm a King Bee" on their first album. David joined the trio, taking his role as lead singer very seriously and changing his stage name once again—this time to Davie Jones. It was not long before he recruited his friend George Underwood as co-singer and guitarist, and soon concert posters were plastered all over the city announcing "Davie Jones with the King Bees." Davie Jones's preferred musical style was now the blues, and the set list included standard blues numbers such as Muddy Waters's "Got My Mojo Working" and "Hoochie Coochie Man," and, of course, the famous "I'm a King Bee," with Underwood on the harmonica.

The number of small concerts the group performed steadily increased, but they only made a few pounds for each performance, and that was on a good day. The group's front man was nevertheless optimistic. In March 1964, David decided to approach John Bloom, a media-friendly businessman who owned a laundry empire. Without Bloom's financial backing, the group

Davie Jones onstage with the King Bees. Left to right: George Underwood, Roger Bluck, Robert Allen, Davie Jones, Dave Howard.

could not survive. So, with the help of his father, David wrote a letter to Bloom that bore all the marks of bold and insolent youth: "With your money you could do for us what Brian Epstein has done for the Beatles and you would make another million for yourself."[3] Intrigued by this missive, but aware that he was no great expert in matters of rock 'n' roll, Bloom turned down the request. What he did do, however, was send his young correspondent a telegram with the phone number of a valuable contact in the music industry: Leslie Conn. Conn was the British manager of Doris Day's recordings, and he agreed to meet Davie Jones and his King Bees. Impressed by the singer's energy, a rather unusual audition was arranged. Leslie Conn suggested to the King Bees that they come to play at John Bloom's wedding anniversary at the Jack of Clubs in Soho. The performance was badly received: All those present seemed to disapprove of this amateurish and uncertain blues-rock. Bloom shouted: "Get 'em off! They're ruining my party!"[3] David ended up in tears and was consoled by Conn, who assured him that even if the guests were skeptical, he himself had been very impressed by their performance. Soon after, Leslie Conn became David "Davie" Jones's manager. But while he agreed to work with the King Bees, the group was never named in the contract.

"Liza Jane," Davie Jones's First Single

In May 1964, Conn engineered the much-coveted entrée with Decca Studios for Davie Jones and the King Bees. The manager had negotiated a contract for the recording of a single plus a B-side. The group recorded "Liza Jane" and "Louie, Louie Go Home," and the disc came out on June 5, 1964, on Vocalion Pop, which was one of Decca's many labels. It should be noted that the score of "Liza Jane" was published at the same time under Vocalian as the result of a typo. Another interesting point about this early recording is that although the group performed their own arrangement of an earlier blues song, it was credited to Leslie Conn. Business is business, it seems, and so the manager registered the title in his own name. Focused on taking on rock critics and the public at large, David chose to see beyond quarrels about author's rights and opted to overlook this matter.

Probably aware of John Bloom's patronage of the group—even if he had gotten angry with them on his wedding anniversary—the press reception was enthusiastic. However, the disc's first airing on the BBC, on the program *Juke Box Jury*, was panned by a jury consisting of comedian Charlie Drake, actors Diana Dors and Jessie Matthews, and music producer Bunny Lewis. They all, with the exception of Drake, voted "Liza Jane" a "flop"! On June 19, David and his

March 8, 1965: Davie Jones and the Manish Boys preparing to perform "I Pity the Fool" on the set of *Gadzooks! It's All Happening* for the BBC.

group appeared on the stage at Television House, Kingsway, as part of *Ready Steady Go!*, the great rival of the BBC's *Top of the Pops*. This was the first time the group had played live on television, and this much-longed-for day was made unforgettable by the guest appearance of John Lee Hooker, whom both Jones and Underwood fervently idolized.

David's motivation was in no way dented by the lukewarm reception given to the "Liza Jane" single and the harsh judgment of *Juke Box Jury*. Heedless of perceived failure or disappointment, he decided it was time to leave his job at Nevin D. Hirst. He had made up his mind: From now on he would devote himself to his musical career. He moved from the suburbs to London. Years later he gave a graphic description of suburban life: "You find yourself in the middle of two worlds: there's the extreme values of people who grew up in the countryside and the very urban feel of the city. In suburbia, you're given the impression that nothing culturally belongs to you, that you are sort of in this wasteland."[7] Although still benefiting from the moral and financial support provided by his father, David was determined to provide for himself as best he could in order to achieve his dreams. Unable to offer any lucrative recording contracts, Leslie Conn hired him to do some painting and decorating at his offices on Denmark Street. David went along with this, and he was helped by another artist in the Conn stable:

Mark Feld. David seemed to enjoy the company of this lively and original young man. Their paths would soon cross again when Feld appeared onstage under a new name: Marc Bolan, before going on to become one of the icons of the glam rock scene with his group, T. Rex.

The Manish Boys, the First Backing Band

Taking advantage of his newly acquired freedom now that he lived in the city, David could usually be found recording his first demos in his bedroom, or wandering around Denmark Street, which was known as "Tin Pan Alley." Here he could meet the denizens of so-called Swinging London, including musicians, designers, and artists of every kind. It was not unusual to see him in La Gioconda, a café next to the Central Sound Recording Studios. Young people gathered in this cramped space to discuss ideas in the hopes of remaking the world and planning the imminent British Invasion.

In July 1964, the young singer met members of the Manish Boys, a group consisting of Johnny "Edward" Flux on guitar, Bob Solly on keyboards, Johnny Watson on bass, and Mick White on drums. A brass section completed the lineup, with Paul Rodriguez playing tenor sax and Woolf Byrne playing baritone sax. Originally formed in Maidstone, which was about an hour's drive to the southeast of the

Shown here in 1965, Davie Jones was proud of his long blond hair, which proved to be a source of interest for journalists.

La Gioconda restaurant, the key meeting place on Denmark Street in London during the swinging sixties.

capital, the group was proud of their origins. David was attracted to their serious approach to music, as well as to their growing fame. Their skillful playing had already resulted in invitations to play at popular clubs like the Marquee and the Flamingo, two places that the King Bees had failed to penetrate. The group's sound was unashamedly influenced by soul music, and this helped them stand out in 1964 London, where rock 'n' roll was all the rage. This was a sound that David could relate to, having become a passionate fan of James Brown's album *Live at the Apollo*, which had been released the previous year. The Manish Boys had signed a commissioning contract with a well-known music publisher named Dick James, and they were in need of a front man to replace the bass player John Watson, who was acting temporarily as lead singer.

An audition arranged by Leslie Conn (who also worked with Dick James) took place on July 19 in a garage in Coxheath, Kent, that belonged to Paul Rodriguez. Bob Solly recalled how David "walked into the living room where we were all rehearsin', and instantly we said 'Okay, that's fine, he doesn't have to sing even.' He just looked the part, and he was dressed in buckskin, and thigh-high boots. [...] He did sing, but we weren't so interested in the singing as we were in his appearance basically."[8] The group decided to try David out, and six days later, on July 26, the new lineup of the Manish Boys gave their first concert at the Chicksands American airbase near Shefford. Although David's long and dazzlingly blond hair made him the target of a few homophobic comments, the concert was a success and other dates were planned. At this point, David Jones left the King Bees, and the group itself broke up shortly thereafter. Now the concert posters all around London were advertising "Davie Jones and the Manish Boys." From August 1964, the group made appearances in many different venues. Their set list was made

up of a number of covers of blues numbers, including Solomon Burke's "Can't Nobody Love You" and Jimmy Reed's "I Ain't Got You," as well as soul numbers like the Drifters' "If You Don't Come Back" and James Brown's "Try Me." Other titles performed were the King Bees' "Liza Jane," and some more overtly rock-tinged numbers such as "You Really Got Me," the Kinks' big hit that had been released on August 4 that very same summer.

In Defense of "Animal Filament"

On September 25, 1964, the group played for Mike Smith, who was Decca's artistic director and best known for having declined to sign up the Beatles after their famous audition on January 1, 1962. On October 6, 1964, Smith—who was now determined not to let another goose laying golden eggs slip through his fingers—invited Davie Jones and the Manish Boys to record three numbers at Regent Sounds Studio, which was located at 4 Denmark Street in London. The titles chosen were "Hello Stranger" by Barbara Lewis, Gene Chandler's "Duke of Earl," and "Love Is Strange," which had been composed by Bo Diddley in 1956 for the duo Mickey & Sylvia. Smith was not impressed, and after thanking the group, he let them go. In other words, Davie Jones and the Manish Boys left the studios without a contract. But David had a trick up his sleeve: If his music was not going to bring the fame he so eagerly sought, maybe his long hair might do it.

On November 2, 1964, an article by the journalist Leslie Thomas appeared in the *Evening News and Star*. Taking its headline from the successful comic review *Beyond the Fringe*, the article was titled "For Those Beyond the Fringe," and it introduced a society (invented by David) called "the International League for the Preservation of Animal Filament." Identified as the group's president, David set out the league's objectives over the course of

18 A FEW NOTES BEFORE GLORY

An Agreement made the 25th day of October 19 65

Between........Marquee Club Ltd........hereinafter referred to as the "Management"
of the one part and....Ralph Horton Esq.......hereinafter referred to as the "Artiste"
of the other part.

Witnesseth that the Management hereby engages the Artiste and the Artiste accepts an

engagement to } present....David Bowie & The Lower Third.

appear as

(or in his usual entertainment) at the Dance Hall/Theatre or other Venue and from the dates and for the
periods and at the salary stated in the Schedule hereto.

SCHEDULE

The Artiste agrees to appear at....one....Evening and....-....Matinee performances

at a salary of } £.20.0.0. Per Night....% of the gross advance and door takings. The Management guarantees a minimum
of £.........

....1....day(s) at Marquee Club, London, W.1. on Fridays 5th, 19th November
........day(s) at.................................on.................
........day(s) at.................................on.................

SPECIAL STIPULATIONS

1. The Artiste shall not, without the written consent of the Management, appear at any public place of entertainment within a radius of........miles of the venue during a period of........weeks immediately prior to and........weeks immediately following the engagement.

2. The Management shall, at their own expense, provide (a) first-class Amplification and Microphone equipment (b) Grand Piano and (c) (at dances only) Relief Band or music.
The Management agrees that any other bands performing the engagement(s) shall be composed of members of the Musicians' Union, and in the event of Musicians' Union action arising from the engagement of non-Unionists, the Management will be responsible for payment of the full fees as stated in the agreement; also that the playing of Recorded music shall not exceed Twenty minutes during the performance.

3. The price of admission to be not less than........per person in advance and........at the door.

4. The Orchestra/Band shall play for a maximum of........hours in separate sessions. Dance to commence at....7.30....and terminate at....11.00.... Approximate playing times for Artiste, ...to....and....
to........

5. Salary payable by....cash....to....group....
on/with....night of engagement....

6. The Artiste shall supply, without charge, photographs, wording for publicity and programme details (when required) to ....for receipt not later than........days before the commencement of the engagement.

7. ....shall appear personally throughout the performance.

We have to draw to your attention the fact that Directors of this Agency are also Directors of the company referred to as "Management".

This Agency is not responsible for any non-fulfilment of Contracts by Proprietors, Managers or Artistes but every reasonable safeguard is assured.

Signature........
Address........

Artistes representation and management 18 Carlisle Street Soho Square London west 1
Licensed annually by the L.C.C. telephone GERrard 6601/2

A big moment for David
Bowie and the Lower Third:
an engagement contract for
the Marquee, in London,
dated October 25, 1965.

the interview: "It's really for the protection of pop musicians, and those who wear their hair long. [...] It's time we united and stood up for our curls. Screaming Lord Sutch, P.J. Proby, The Pretty Things and, of course, The Stones and The Beatles—we want them all as members. You've no idea the indignities you have to suffer just because you've got long hair."[9] The article struck a chord, and just over a week later, on November 12, David appeared on the BBC2 news program *Tonight*, hosted by Cliff Michelmore. David joined the program to speak up for his association, which had now been renamed as the Society for the Prevention of Cruelty to Long-Haired Men. Appearing alongside David were George Underwood, John Watson, Paul Rodriguez, and Woolf Byrne. During the interview, Bowie explained: "We're all fairly tolerant, but for the last two years we've had comments like 'Darling' and 'Can I carry your handbag?' thrown at us. And I think it just has to stop now!"[10]

Whether it was thanks to David, "Davie" Jones's growing fame as a speechmaker, or the result of the endless gigs they had played around London, the Manish Boys signed up with the Arthur Howes Agency not long after the interview aired, and the tour organizers quickly got them six dates fronting for a group called Gerry and the Pacemakers.

At the beginning of 1965, Leslie Conn decided to take a new approach with Davie Jones and his group. He was able to pique the interest of an American producer named Shel Talmy, who was the producer responsible for the colossal success of "You Really Got Me" by the Kinks, who also happened to be signed with the Arthur Howes Agency. Talmy agreed to produce a single with Davie Jones and the Manish Boys, and Leslie Conn negotiated a contract with Parlophone, the EMI label that had previously signed up the Beatles in July 1962. On January 15, 1965, the group recorded two tracks at IBC Studios in Portland Place (where the Kinks' hit had also been recorded): "I Pity the Fool" and "Take My Tip," the latter of which was composed by David. It was an enriching experience but, when the single came out a few months later on March 5, David saw that his name was not credited and that instead the artist was listed simply as *the Manish Boys*. He discovered that the other members of the group had insisted Leslie Conn attribute the record to the entire band. The singer was furious and, despite a successful performance with the group on the March 8 episode of the BBC2 program *Gadzooks! It's All Happening*, David was beginning to lose interest in the group. Luckily for him, Conn had more faith in his blond protégé than in his backing band.

The Lower Third: The Last Stage Before Recognition?

In May 1965, David Jones left the Manish Boys to devote himself to a new musical project. An audition at a Soho club called La Discotheque on May 17, 1965, introduced him to the Lower Third, which was a group consisting of guitarist Denis "Tea-Cup" Taylor, bass player Graham

The "typically English" elegance and phlegm of the Lower Third, in 1965.

"Death" Rivens, and drummer Les Mighall; although Mighall would shortly be replaced by Phil Lancaster. This trio represented an ideal backing group for the up-and-coming star David "Davie" Jones. Abandoning long hair and the speeches supporting it, David now adopted the mod look, which consisted of short hair and a fitted jacket. He combined this look with a deliberately mysterious expression. While waiting for concert dates with the group to be fixed up, David persuaded Leslie Conn that a new single would help get things moving. In July 1965, Shel Talmy agreed to produce two additional recordings for Parlophone. Distribution of the disc— which included "You've Got a Habit of Leaving" on the A-side and "Baby Loves That Way" on the B-side—did not take place until August. This slight delay, combined with Conn's flagrant inactivity, irritated Jones (credited as "Davy" on the disc jacket), who believed his public was out there waiting to be conquered. He decided of his own accord to meet with the famous agent Terry King and presented himself at the Kings Agency offices, which was also located on Denmark Street. David got to know one of King's assistants, Ralph Horton, with whom he had an instant rapport. Horton knew the trade—he had worked as road manager for the Moody Blues in 1964—and now he devoted all his attention to this new singer. It was immediately clear to both men that they should collaborate. Despite what he had done for David's career thus far, Conn's recent inactivity led to his being dropped by the

singer. In September 1965, Horton officially took over as David Jones's manager.

Horton had a plan: In order to maximize their chances of success, he sought the support of a colleague named Kenneth Pitt. At the time, Pitt was the manager of a band called Manfred Mann, and he'd also made a name for himself after overseeing the organization of Bob Dylan's British tour in 1964. Pitt was busy with other projects, but he was able to offer a valuable piece of advice: David should change his stage name. Davie Jones was not a very original name in 1965. Another Jones (also David, but soon to call himself Davy) had recently gained fame in London for his performance in the successful musical *Oliver!* and his first single "What Are We Going to Do?" was just out on Colpix Records, Columbia Pictures' new label. (A few years later, Jones would go on to become the lead singer in the famous group the Monkees.) A name change was definitely needed.

David looked back to his first enthusiasms and recalled the admiration he'd felt for a soldier who had distinguished himself at the Battle of the Alamo in Texas. The exploits of this famous colonel had been featured in the popular TV series *The Adventures of Jim Bowie*, which aired in the United States from 1956 to 1958 but had not been shown on television in Britain. However, a 1960 movie about the battle, *The Alamo*, which starred John Wayne and featured Richard Widmark as Bowie, left a lasting impression on Jones. The hero had an

unusual weapon, a double-sided knife called a "Bowie knife." That was all the singer needed to make up his mind. He would take his name from this sharp weapon; from now on he would be David Bowie.

The Birth of Bowie

For the moment, David had to keep the name Davie Jones because he still had a large number of engagements to play with the Lower Third. It would be inconceivable to change the various types of publicity and advertising the group had undertaken for their upcoming concerts. On November 2, 1965, they took part in a BBC audition where they performed three numbers: "Baby That's a Promise," a new composition by David; James Brown's "Out of Sight"; and a rearranged version of "Chim Chim Cher-ee" from the movie *Mary Poppins*, which had been released in

1964. David Jones was a fan of musicals and had liked the song by Robert B. Sherman and Richard M. Sherman, but the BBC jury was unenthusiastic to say the least. Their judgment was damning: "Strange choice of material. Amateur sounding vocalist who sings wrong notes and out of tune."[11] It continued: "I don't think the group will get better with more rehearsal—what we heard will always be the product."[11]

Not put off, Ralph Horton continued to believe in his protégé and contrived to attract the attention of Tony Hatch, who was famous for composing and producing Petula Clark's hit song "Downtown," which hit number one in the United States in January 1965. Hatch was also behind the success of Sandie Shaw, one of the few women to feature in the British Invasion and the wave of British hits that reached America around this same time. Horton

David Bowie and the Buzz onstage at the Marquee Club in London, April 1966.

style, Pye insisted that the group record two more numbers. "Can't Help Thinking About Me" and "And I Say to Myself" were deemed safer and, important, easier to sell.

At the end of December, David Bowie and the Lower Third crossed the Channel to give three concerts in Paris. Two performances were given at the Golf Drouot nightclub on December 31 and January 2. On the evening between these two dates, the band performed a high-octane set at the Bus Palladium on the Rue Pierre-Fontaine, located near the Moulin-Rouge. Ralph Horton and David Bowie then flew back to London, leaving the members of the Lower Third to make their way back in a van—or, in fact, in an ambulance, which was what their tour van had originally been used for. The "van" still had its original lettering and a siren. This difference in treatment unsurprisingly led to feelings of inequality within the group. On January 6, 1966, the group launched their single with an event at the Victoria Tavern in London, and Horton introduced David to photographers without even mentioning the names of the other musicians. The members of the Lower Third knew their time was up.

A Made-to-Measure Group for David Bowie

When the single "Can't Help Thinking About Me" came out, it was credited to David Bowie with the Lower Third. However, no mention of the rest of the group was made in the accompanying publicity materials, which included a half page in the January 16 edition of *New Musical Express*. Keen to speed up their plans, at the beginning of February Bowie and Horton organized auditions at the Marquee, a famous club located at 165 Oxford Street. Their goal was to find a new backing band for the rising star. An advertisement placed in *Melody Maker* invited applications and, on the appointed day, Horton, Bowie, and the recently hired road manager Spike Palmer interviewed the candidates. John "Hutch" Hutchinson, a guitarist who had begun his career in music with a Scarborough group called the Tennesseans, recalled his arrival at the Marquee: "Spike gave me my instructions, 'When it's your turn up there, just play some rhythm and blues licks.' [...] I played a bit, and then a voice from the darkness shouted, 'Play some Bo Diddley.' [...] I thought it sounded a bit weak in the [...] silent club so I was relieved to hear another shout from the darkness, between riffs: 'Okay, that's fine, thank you.' I left the stage and put my Telecaster in its case and [...] Spike walked over [...] and told me, 'David says you're in.'"[12]

The other musicians hired to form David's new group, which was to be called the Buzz, were Derek "Dek"

was soon able to tell David Bowie and the Lower Third that their next single would be produced by Hatch for Pye Records. A recording session was scheduled for the end of November at the Pye studios on Great Cumberland Place, located just to the north of the famous Marble Arch in London. Two numbers were recorded: "Now You've Met the London Boys" and "You've Got It Made." Pye Records was not happy with the words of the first song where David described the protagonist, a young man just arrived from the suburbs, taking drugs: *"The first time that you tried a pill / You feel a little queasy, decidedly ill."* Tony Hatch was quick to point out that: "Some songwriters [...] are just commentators, but Bowie was a storyteller, and so he was going to go rummaging in all his experiences, to find things that he could write about. It was something new."[7] Not interested in the singer's realist

Fearnley on bass, John "Ego" Eager on drums, and Derek "Chow" Boyes on the Hammond B3 organ. David Bowie put aside his saxophone in favor of a more somber vocal style, and the group made their first appearance at the Leicester Mecca Ballroom on February 10, 1966, where they played the first half of a concert with the Graham Bond Organisation. (The drummer of the latter group was none other than Ginger Baker, soon to become a memer of the legendary trio Cream.) The audience reception was muted, but Horton remained convinced of Bowie's potential. Similarly convinced was a certain Shirley Wilson, who had also been at the concert. Helped by two friends, Sandra Gibling and Violet Neal, Wilson gave a boost to Bowie's career by setting up his first fan club.

On Thursday, March 3, 1966, David went to the Rediffusion TV Studios to record the instrumental part of "Can't Help Thinking About Me" that was to be aired on *Ready Steady Go!* The next day, the program—presented by Cathy McGowan—was filmed with David singing over the prerecorded backing. The program was used to promote Bowie's single, which had been released in January. Three days later, on March 7, 1966, the group was back in the studio to record a new single, once again produced by Tony Hatch for Pye Records. The single was "Do Anything You Say," with "Good Morning Girl" on the B-side. When the single came out on April 1, 1966, David Bowie's name appeared on the label with no mention of the backing group. Meanwhile, Ralph Horton was trying to convince Kenneth Pitt to agree to be joint manager with him. Too busy with promoting his increasingly successful protégé Crispian St. Peters—the singer of the hit song "You Were on My Mind," Pitt once again turned down the offer.

Arrival of a Rock Star

Every Sunday the Marquee put on an afternoon show from three to six called "The Bowie Showboat." It was basically a concert given by David Bowie and the Buzz. The title of the show was borrowed from the "Jerome Kern–Oscar Hammerstein II" musical *Show Boat*. David was probably thinking of the 1951 movie adaptation directed by George Sidney and featuring Ava Gardner and Kathryn Grayson. Starting on April 10, and for nine consecutive weeks, David and his group performed at this temple of rock music. John Hutchinson, the guitarist for the Buzz, recalls: "The Marquee

gig had several advantages. We could try out new material in relaxed surroundings, we had visits from musical celebrities like Long John Baldry who came to check us out, and we had free admission to the club on any evening of the week."[12]

During their second week at the Marquee, on April 17, Kenneth Pitt dropped in to hear Ralph Horton's protégé. Impressed by the singer's stage presence, particularly in the finale, he was finally persuaded by David's talent. As he writes in his 1983 book *David Bowie: The Pitt Report*: "His burgeoning charisma was undeniable, but I was particularly struck by the artistry with which he used his body, as if it were an accompanying instrument, essential to the singer and the song. At the close of his performance, he waited for the applause to die down then, after pausing a moment or two longer, he slowly walked a few paces forward, the group fell into darkness, a spot focused on David and with his head held high he sang 'When You Walk Through the Storm,' the Judy Garland classic. It was daring and delightful and then I began to think of Ralph's unyielding doors and the keys that could unlock them."[3]

After this memorable occasion, Kenneth Pitt accepted Horton's invitation to manage Bowie's burgeoning career. Liberated from paperwork, Horton could now concentrate on the group's engagements without having to worry about accounts, contracts, and the constant search for financial backers. All of those responsibilities now fell to Pitt. In June, financial difficulties and a desire to spend time with his wife, Denise, who was expecting their first child, led to the guitarist Hutch leaving the group. He was replaced by a sixteen-year-old Scottish guitarist named Billy Gray.

On July 5, David Bowie recorded his new single "I Dig Everything" with Pye Records, and once again produced by Tony Hatch. The single and it's B-side, "I'm Not Losing Sleep," were well received, but tensions had begun to emerge during the recording sessions. First of all, Pye found that Bowie's backing band was not good enough and decided to use its own musicians to accompany the singer. Then, relations with Hatch began to go downhill as the producer became increasingly insistent that David record his (Hatch's) compositions, presumably hoping to repeat the success he had had with "Downtown." The singer decided to leave Pye Records, and his contract came to an end on September 30, 1966.

DAVIE JONES WITH THE KING BEES
Liza Jane / Louie, Louie Go Home
UK Release on Vocalion Pop: June 5, 1964 (ref. V9221)
Best Chart Ranking: Did Not Chart

Side A

LIZA JANE
Leslie Conn / 2:14

Musicians
Davie Jones: lead vocals, saxophone
George Underwood: rhythm guitar, harmonica, backing vocals
Roger Bluck: lead guitar
Dave Howard: bass
Robert Allen: drums

Recorded
Decca Studios, London: May 1964

Technical Team
Producer: Leslie Conn
Sound Engineer: Glyn Johns

LIZA JANE
By LESLIE CONN

DAVIE JONES
Recorded by WITH THE KING-BEES
on DECCA VOCALIAN

DAVE   GEORGE   DAVIE   ROGER   BOB

DICK JAMES MUSIC LIMITED   2'6

Cover of the score of *Liza Jane*, by Davie Jones and the King Bees.

Genesis
While it is difficult to trace the exact origins of this traditional American song, its first official publication on a sheet of music dates back to 1916, when it was published by Sherman, Clay & Co. Entitled "Lil' Liza Jane," the song was signed by Ada de Lachau. The singer recorded this version for the musical *Come Out of the Kitchen*, starring Ruth Chatterton, which was a big hit on Broadway before being adapted into a film by John S. Robertson in 1919.

Countless versions of "Lil' Liza Jane" emerged throughout the twentieth century: in the jazz band style with Earl Fuller in 1917, performed on the banjo by Harry C. Browne and His Peerless Quartet in 1918, or divinely revisited by Nina Simone in 1960 under the title "Little Liza Jane." No matter what year it was created, one thing is certain: You can't rely on the credits listed on the disc for this single. In 2020, George Underwood, the King Bees' guitarist, still hadn't forgotten how Conn usurped authorship of the title he had written alongside his friend David Jones as an adaptation of the 1956 version that Huey Smith and His Rhythm Aces had written: "That was David and I, in my mum and dad's house, in the kitchen, sitting there with a guitar just fooling around. Leslie Conn put his name to that. He said, 'Oh, try this line.' He'd written some words; I don't think we even used them. He thought he wrote it."[13]

The single, released on June 5, 1964, was not a big hit with the public and would prove to be first in a long series of failures for the future David Bowie.

Production
While Conn also took on the role of producer on the track, it seems that Glyn Johns, the man behind Decca Studios' homemade console, was actually the one who took on the artistic direction of the recording. Although he was experienced, Johns's assignment couldn't have been a pleasant one since the equipment he had to work with left a great deal to be desired. Much-needed updates wouldn't be made at the studio until a few years later, in 1966. Sound engineer Jack Clegg, who worked there from 1960 until 1963, remembers: "There were ten channels, but if you wanted the bass on Track 1, you had to put the musician in a particular place in the studio. You actually had to physically move people around to get them on different tracks!"[14]

Side B

LOUIE, LOUIE GO HOME

Paul Revere, Mark Lindsay / 2:07

Musicians
Davie Jones: lead vocals, saxophone
George Underwood: rhythm guitar, harmonica, backing vocals
Roger Bluck: lead guitar, backing vocals
Dave Howard: bass
Robert Allen: drums

Recorded
Decca Studios, London: May 1964

Technical Team
Producer: Leslie Conn
Sound Engineer: Glyn Johns

Genesis

In 1963, two bands—Paul Revere and the Raiders, and the Kingsmen—each recorded a version of "Louie Louie," the rock 'n' roll anthem composed by Richard Berry in 1956. The Kingsmen's version became an international success and eclipsed Revere's, who developed a deep resentment over this perceived slight. In March 1964, Revere released "Louie Go Home." This somewhat parodic rock song took up the theme of "Louie Louie," which is about a man who has abandoned his wife only to endure feelings of loneliness and remorse as he thinks of the beautiful woman he has lost. Forsaking the good-natured humor that characterized the Raiders' style, David Jones and the King Bees offered this more muscular version of the track on the B-side of "Liza Jane," taking care to respect the blues rock style and doubling the first name of the title, as a nod to the original song.

Production

In "Louie, Louie Go Home," we clearly detect the influence that John Lennon, then a young guitarist-singer with the Beatles, would have on David Jones's fledgling career. When he angrily sings "My conscience is about to drive me wild," the singer's intonations, supported by the backing vocals of guitarists George Underwood and Roger Bluck, are reminiscent of those of the famous Liverpudlian star. If the production gives the song a furious energy, which was very much in the spirit of the times, it's because it was unofficially left in the hands of Glyn Johns. This unwitting magician gave birth to a number of rock anthems of the day, including "Jumpin' Jack Flash" by the Rolling Stones in 1968 and the prodigious "I'm One" by the Who, off of their masterpiece album *Quadrophenia* (1973).

A few years after the release of the record, while Conn was working in Mallorca, he received a call from his mother asking him what she should do with the hundreds of copies of the single she had packed in the family garage. Much to the chagrin of today's collectors, Leslie Conn told her to throw everything into the trash can.

Paul Revere and the Raiders performing their famous "Louie Louie," in Los Angeles, in September 1964.

THE MANISH BOYS
I Pity the Fool / Take My Tip
UK Release on Parlophone: March 5, 1965 (ref. R 5250)
Best Chart Ranking: Did Not Chart

Side A

I PITY THE FOOL

Deadric Malone / 2:10

Musicians
Davie Jones: lead vocals, alto saxophone
Johnny Flux: lead guitar
John Watson: bass
Mick White: drums
Bob Solly: organ
Paul Rodriguez: tenor saxophone, trumpet
Woolf Byrne: baritone saxophone
Jimmy Page: guitar

Recorded
IBC Studios, London: January 15, 1965

Technical Team
Producer: Shel Talmy
Sound Engineer: Glyn Johns

Bobby "the Lion of the Blues" Bland, the first singer of "I Pity the Fool," in 1961.

Genesis

Far more than just a reinterpretation of the original track by Bobby "the Lion of the Blues" Bland, which was composed for him by Deadric Malone, the founder of Duke Records, "I Pity the Fool" is a tribute to the soul championed by an immortal singer. Listening to the version that the Manish Boys recorded during a two-hour session in January 1965, you can also hear the influence that another classic, "Night Time Is the Right Time," might have had on Jones and his fellow musicians.

The blues was very much in vogue in 1965, and Davie Jones and his Manish Boys found themselves competing with Willie Dixon's "Red Rooster," which had been covered the previous year by the Rolling Stones (and renamed "Little Red Rooster" for the occasion). Endowed with vocal power borrowed from James Brown's "Please, Please, Please," the Manish Boys' cover of "I Pity the Fool" is an appropriate response, revealing the extent of Jones's musical influences.

Production

With the encouragement of Talmy, the Manish Boys called in a session guitarist who was then omnipresent in studios across London: a certain Jimmy Page. The young musician was always ready to put down some sharp riffs during recording sessions for EMI or Decca, and he had already left his mark on the hits "Baby, Please Don't Go" by Them and "As Tears Go By," which was sung by Marianne Faithfull and written by Mick Jagger and Keith Richards. Page quickly became the protégé of Shel Talmy, who got him involved in numerous recordings for the Kinks and the Who.

Delighted to introduce his new fuzz box pedal, which would become inseparable from the sound he developed with Led Zeppelin a few years later, Page played the abrasive solo on "I Pity the Fool" on January 15, 1965, imbuing the track with an added touch of soul. With Shel Talmy handling production, Glyn Johns at the controls behind the console (though not yet the hitmaker he would later become alongside the Stones, the Beatles, or Eric Clapton), and Jimmy Page on guitar, it's hard to imagine a better team to build around the Manish Boys. Sadly, however, the band's second single was not as successful as they'd hoped, just as Page had confidently predicted during the recording session: "Well, it's definitely not going to be a hit."[15]

Side B

TAKE MY TIP

Davie Jones / 2:15

Musicians
Davie Jones: lead vocals, saxophone
Johnny Flux: lead guitar
John Watson: bass
Mick White: drums
Bob Solly: organ
Paul Rodriguez: tenor saxophone
Woolf Byrne: baritone saxophone
Jimmy Page: guitar
Recorded
IBC Studios, London: January 15, 1965
Technical Team
Producer: Shel Talmy
Sound Engineer: Glyn Johns

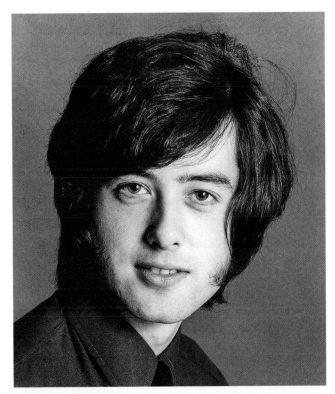

Jimmy Page, studio musician . . . before he became the famous composer of Led Zeppelin's "Stairway to Heaven."

Genesis
David "Davie" Jones's first recorded composition, "Take My Tip," sings the praises of someone who knows women well and offers advice to an inexperienced lover. In January 1965, Leslie Conn introduced David to the famous producer Shel Talmy, who was fresh off a success with the Kinks and their hit "You Really Got Me." The London-based American wasted no time in offering one of Jones's compositions to the actor and singer Kenny Miller, who was looking for a new success after several commercial failures. During a visit to London, Miller recorded the track "Take My Tip," which he placed on the B-side of his single "Restless." News of the single was announced in *Billboard* magazine's "This Week's Newsmakers Around the World" section, but Miller's single was not as successful as he had hoped. Talmy then suggested that David Jones and the Manish Boys record a version of "Take My Tip" on January 15, 1965. Two takes were all it took to record the track. A few years later, Kenny Miller asked Shel Talmy's former secretary what had become of Davie Jones, and was astonished at the amazement caused by his question: "I asked, 'Whatever happened to Davy Jones?' She looked at me like I just came from Mars. [...] I never knew David Bowie was Davy Jones."[16]

Production
Introduced by a walking bass and a jazzy ride cymbal, "Take My Tip" surprises the listener right from the start with its very popcentric chorus, on which Davie delivers a flood of lyrics. Talmy, who wanted to oust guitarist Johnny Flux in favor of Jimmy Page, had to resign himself to using his all-purpose guitar sparingly. Page had sprinkled "Take My Tip" with guitar rhythms that sadly didn't survive, unlike the majestic solo he delivered on "I Pity the Fool."

DAVY JONES
You've Got a Habit of Leaving / Baby Loves That Way
UK Release on Parlophone : August 20, 1965 (ref. R 5315)
Best Chart Ranking: Did Not Chart

Side A

YOU'VE GOT A HABIT OF LEAVING

Davy Jones / 2:30

Musicians

Davy Jones: lead vocals, harmonica
Denis Taylor: guitar, vocals
Graham Rivens: bass
Phil Lancaster: drums
Nicky Hopkins: piano
Shel Talmy: backing vocals
Leslie Conn: backing vocals
Glyn Johns: backing vocals

Recorded

IBC Studios, London: July 1965

Technical Team

Producer: Shel Talmy
Sound Engineer: Glyn Johns

FOR BOWIE ADDICTS

A second version of the song was released in 2017 on the compilation *Making Time—A Shel Talmy Production*, which brings together some of the producer's most legendary accomplishments. Named "You've Got a Habit of Leaving" (Alternate Outtake Version)," the track offers fans some nuances of interpretation, particularly in one psychedelic passage, which was significantly lightened for the occasion.

ON YOUR HEADPHONES

During the recording of "You've Got a Habit of Leaving," David dropped his harmonica, grabbed a bottle of beer, and slid it down the neck of Denis Taylor's guitar. That's what made the special sound that can be heard at 2:02 of the track.

Genesis

David Jones, now accompanied by the Lower Third and going by the name of Davy Jones, was about to record his second single for Parlophone in July 1965. While the chosen song had the light romantic characteristics of songs such as "Tired of Waiting for You" by the Kinks (produced by Talmy just a few months earlier), it was from the heart of quite a different track that the band drew its inspiration. Released in May 1965, the Who's rock hit "Anyway Anyhow Anywhere" included one of those psychedelic bridges that set Peter Townshend and Roger Daltrey's band apart. Recorded at the IBC Studios in April, the song was also produced by Shel Talmy, who acted as the producer of "You've Got a Habit of Leaving." This was enough to trigger, if not rage, then at least sarcasm on the part of Townshend, who persistently mocked the similarity between the two tracks, and particularly the break of "You've Got a Habit of Leaving," which begins at 0:55. Nevertheless, in Davy Jones and the Lower Third's song, neither the setup of the musicians nor the quality of execution give Townshend much to worry about. While the Who offered an incisive and original song for the time, the offering from the Lower Third fooled no one, and indeed Parlophone was under no illusions about the product they were selling; after all, not everyone can be Keith Moon. This would be the last single produced by the label, which quickly lost interest in Davy's music, pushing him in the direction of Pye Records. Indifferent to the mockery that his song provoked, Bowie would later cover "Anyway Anyhow Anywhere" on his album *Pin Ups*, in 1973.

Production

Another shared trait between "You've Got a Habit of Leaving" and the music of the Who was the presence of session pianist Nicky Hopkins. The virtuoso musician, who had been playing his instrument since the age of three, was one of Swinging London's most respected figures. Although he was soon to be found on some of the Rolling Stones' greatest hits (that's him on piano in "Sympathy for the Devil"), he was a faithful gig performer at the time, and he put a score on the song by Davy Jones and the Lower Third that was as discreet as it was vital, just as he had done on many songs for Townshend's band.

Side B

BABY LOVES THAT WAY

Davy Jones / 2:58

Musicians
Davy Jones: lead vocals, harmonica
Denis Taylor: guitar, vocals
Graham Rivens: bass
Phil Lancaster: drums
Nicky Hopkins: piano
Shel Talmy: backing vocals
Leslie Conn: backing vocals
Glyn Johns: backing vocals

Recorded
IBC Studios, London: July 1965

Technical Team
Producer: Shel Talmy
Sound Engineer: Glyn Johns

Pianist Nicky Hopkins, who recorded with the Rolling Stones, the Who, and Jefferson Airplane.

Genesis

Heavily influenced by "I'm into Something Good," the first big hit from the band Herman's Hermits, who were described as the "British Beach Boys" and led by the charismatic Peter Noone—"Baby Loves That Way" is an impressive B-side track, perhaps even overshadowing the A-side that it accompanies. The production is efficient and modern, and Shel Talmy claimed this was a result of recording methods discovered while he was still working in the United States. In particular, Talmy isolates the instruments on each track, rather than recording the band live, as was the tradition at the time. For the producer, these production techniques were tools used in the service of the artist, Davy Jones, in whom Talmy had only limited confidence, as he would later confide: "I honestly didn't think that what he was writing at the time had a snowball's chance in hell of making it. But I thought, 'He's so original and brash.'"[17]

Production

David wanted powerful and melodic backing vocals to be omnipresent on the track, so producer Shel Talmy, sound engineer Glyn Johns, and even manager Leslie Conn were all brought on board to contribute backing vocals. "Boy, were both Shel and Les out of tune!"[18] recalled Phil Lancaster, the band's drummer. But no matter, the effect worked well and was totally in keeping with the standards of the time.

DAVID BOWIE WITH THE LOWER THIRD
Can't Help Thinking About Me / And I Say to Myself
UK Release on Pye Records: January 14, 1966 (ref. Pye 7N 17020)
US Release on Warner Bros. Records: May 1966 (ref. 5815)
Best Chart Ranking: Did Not Chart

Side A

CAN'T HELP THINKING ABOUT ME

David Bowie / 2:43

Musicians
David Bowie: lead vocals, tambourine
Denis Taylor: electric guitar, twelve-string acoustic guitar, backing vocals
Graham Rivens: bass, backing vocals
Phil Lancaster: drums, backing vocals
Tony Hatch: piano

Recorded
Pye Recording Studios, London: November 1965

Technical Team
Producer: Tony Hatch

FOR BOWIE ADDICTS

On March 4, 1966, when David Bowie appeared on the BBC show *Ready Steady Go!* to promote his new single, only the singer performed live. John Hutchinson, the guitarist with the Buzz, mimed the sound of a twelve-string acoustic guitar on his Telecaster. This was in fact quite logical, since the instrumental part of the song had been recorded the day before with David's twelve-string acoustic guitar.

"Can't Help Thinking About Me" was Bowie's first single to be released in the United States, in May 1966. Warner Bros. Records, the licensee of Pye Records in the United States, was responsible for distributing the single.

Genesis
Although the single "You've Got a Habit of Leaving" received a disastrous reception, this painful step proved to be an important moment in the career of our singer, who, on the advice of the highly coveted manager to the stars, Ken Pitt, permanently changed his stage name to David Bowie. The newly christened Bowie then renewed his contract with Pye Records, and Ralph Horton, his new manager, organized a recording session for him. Horton pulled off a masterstroke by getting his hooks into Tony Hatch, the renowned producer behind Petula Clark's international hit "Downtown," a song he also wrote and composed. The first session went off without a hitch on November 25, 1965, but the track "Now You've Met the London Boys" was not at all to Pye's taste, who didn't appreciate the reference to drugs in the phrase *"You tried a pill"* and demanded new compositions from Bowie, thereby forcing him back into the studio. The song finally selected was "Can't Help Thinking About Me," which retraced the singer's youth in Bromley. The track was released as a single on January 14, 1966. Championed by Pye along with Sandie Shaw, the Kinks, and Donovan, the song appeared at the end of the year on the compilation *Hitmakers Vol. 4*, which was released by the record company in order to promote its younger artists in spite of the fact that David had already left the label. While it makes a nod to the Four Tops' "Reach Out (I'll Be There)" with its snare drum beat, the song nevertheless moves away from the soul music, often claimed as a major influence by David Jones during the Manish Boys era.

Production
During the recording, David, who forgot his notebook at home, had to improvise certain parts of the text, especially the third verse, which explains some awkward sentences that were written in a hurry: *"My girl calls my name 'Hi Dave! / Drop in, see around, come back / If you're this way again."* A good sport when it comes to memories of his early years, Bowie recalled these lines with humor: "[These are] two of the worst lines I've ever written."[19] While the musicians of the Lower Third play on the record, it was David's new backing band, the Buzz, that accompanied him on the single's promotion.

Side B

AND I SAY TO MYSELF

David Bowie / 2:25

Musicians
David Bowie: lead vocals, tambourine
Denis Taylor: electric guitar, twelve-string acoustic guitar, backing vocals
Graham Rivens: bass, backing vocals
Phil Lancaster: drums, backing vocals

Recorded
Pye Recording Studios, London: November 1965

Technical Team
Producer: Tony Hatch

Genesis

"And I Say to Myself" is undoubtedly one of the most underestimated songs of Bowie's early career, featuring lyrics that are imbued with the naiveté that characterized his early creations. The narrator is well aware that his girlfriend has him wrapped around her little finger: *"And I say to myself / I've got it wrong, wrong, wrong / She is a playgirl / She the wrong wrong girl for me / And I say to myself / You're a fool, fool, fool / She doesn't love you, / She doesn't need you."* David Bowie's lyrics would soon lose this adolescent candor and give way to deeper autobiographical themes like the rejection of suburban life, or the committal of his stepbrother, Terry Burns, to Cane Hill Hospital in Croydon. These darker subjects were more inspiring for the mature artist that David would quickly become.

Production

This song stands out from David's previous compositions thanks to surprising chord progressions that are sometimes difficult for the novice listener to grasp (this would become one of the specificities of superstar Bowie's repertoire). "And I Say to Myself" is nonetheless very catchy, and it's supported by effective choruses that remind the listener of the singer's great admiration for Berry Gordy's Motown label, and the voice arrangements perfected by Detroit's Holy Trinity of Brian Holland, Lamont Dozier, and Eddie Holland. From 0:22, when Phil Lancaster seems to have forgotten a snare drum stroke on the first bar, we discover a series of chords, which even transposed into *A / fam# / D / E* is still reminiscent of "Last Kiss," the hit song by Wayne Cochran that was released in 1961.

The rockabilly singer Wayne Cochran, whose hit "Last Kiss" inspired the chord sequence in "And I Say to Myself." He was known as much for the quality of his songs as for his extravagant coiffure.

DAVID BOWIE
Do Anything You Say / Good Morning Girl
UK Release on Pye Records: April 1, 1966 (ref. Pye 7N 17079)
Best Chart Ranking: Did Not Chart

David Bowie in 1966. The singer accompanied himself while composing on his Framus twelve-string guitar.

DO ANYTHING YOU SAY

David Bowie / 2:27

Musicians: David Bowie: lead vocals, tambourine / John "Hutch" Hutchinson: guitar, backing vocals / Derek "Dek" Fearnley: bass, backing vocals / John "Ego" Eager: drums, backing vocals / Derek "Chow" Boyes: backing vocals / Tony Hatch: piano / **Recorded:** Pye Recording Studios, London: March 7, 1966 / **Technical Team:** Producer: Tony Hatch

For his first single as David Bowie, the singer once again turned to the theme of his weakness for women. *"I'll do anything you say,"* he sings, resignedly, throughout the track. The omnipresent piano is no longer played by the brilliant Nicky Hopkins of the Shel Talmy era, but instead by the producer of the single, Tony Hatch. Once again, the Motown feel is assured by the drum pattern and its snare drum strokes (on all downbeats of the bar), which are reminiscent of the choruses of "Can't Help Thinking About Me." In 2014, John Hutchinson, the guitarist from Bowie's new backing band, the Buzz, recalled the coolness and discreet elegance of Tony Hatch during the recording sessions, but also the total lack of interest he showed in the star's backing musicians: "Tony seemed to be a pleasant enough chap, viewed through the control room glass, but he somehow managed the whole production job without a single word to the band, and he barely glanced in the direction of Chow, Dek, Ego and myself."[12]

GOOD MORNING GIRL

David Bowie / 2:12

Musicians: David Bowie: lead vocals / John "Hutch" Hutchinson: guitar / Derek "Dek" Fearnley: bass / John "Ego" Eager: drums / Derek "Chow" Boyes: Hammond organ / **Recorded:** Pye Recording Studios, London: March 7, 1966 / **Technical Team:** Producer: Tony Hatch

Despite Tony Hatch's insistence, there was no longer any question of David Bowie singing other people's songs, be they blues classics or lesser-known tracks. Liberating himself from the influences of his youth, the singer now began to lay claim to the status of singer-songwriter. "Good Morning Girl," on the B-side of this new single from Pye Records, is a light and innocent track, but with a rhythmic setting that lies somewhere between jazz and rock, and comes alongside a formidable efficiency from bassist Derek Fearnley and drummer John Eager, who played with the tip of his drumstick to give his ride cymbal a powerful and energetic swing. As if the jazz aspect of the track highlighted here wasn't enough, David Bowie marks the track with a note-to-note scat on Hutchinson's guitar during the solo at 0:52, reminiscent of the Spencer Davis Group's "Strong Love," which was released the year before.

DAVID BOWIE
I Dig Everything / I'm Not Losing Sleep

UK Release on Pye Records: August 1966 (ref. Pye 7N 17157)
Best Chart Ranking: Did Not Chart

David Bowie circa 1966, wearing the blue suit that he donned for many of the photo sessions arranged by his new manager, Kenneth Pitt.

I DIG EVERYTHING

David Bowie / 2:40

Musicians: David Bowie: lead vocals / **Unidentified musicians:** guitar, bass, drums, percussion, organ, backing vocals, transverse flute /
Recorded: Pye Recording Studios, London: July 5, 1966 /
Technical Team: Producer: Tony Hatch

On Monday June 6, 1966, David Bowie and the Buzz were about to take the stage at the California Pool Ballroom in Dunstable. The band was ready to battle it out with their audience, despite an emotional day. Just a few hours earlier, a recording session had been held at Pye Studios with the goal of giving birth to Bowie's new single. Backing vocalists Madeline Bell and Lesley Duncan were there, as well as Kiki Dee, who would appear a few years later with Elton John singing "Don't Go Breaking My Heart" as a duet. There was also a brass section, and hitmaker Tony Hatch was once again producing. Everything had been brought together to ensure that David's new song, "I Dig Everything," would be recorded under optimal conditions. But nothing happened as planned. The band was seriously unprepared, and Tony Hatch quickly put an end to the session. With the support of the record label, he decided to take things in hand, and one month later, on July 5, 1966, he summoned David Bowie to see him without the rest of his band. The list of musicians hired for that day remains unknown, but the single that was produced reveals a modern and colorful production—a far cry from the rock hits of the time, in which energy was king. The heady gimmick of the single, with its marked organ introduction (Is it a Vox Continental? A Farfisa Combo Compact?) was very much in tune with the times, and played to the rhythm of a güiro

like the one that would later find its place on Dusty Springfield's languid "The Look of Love" in 1967. Despite the presence of a high-level backing band, the song lacked the spirit of the singer, who until then had given all his songs that little extra touch of soul. What had been his trademark appears to have been set aside here in favor of a solid but dull production. Whether a curse, or simply the result of poor artistic direction, the track once again failed to make it onto the charts and led to the end of the collaboration between David Bowie and Pye Records.

I'M NOT LOSING SLEEP

David Bowie / 2:50

Musicians: David Bowie: lead vocals / **Unidentified musicians:** guitar, bass, drums, percussion, organ, backing vocals, transverse flute /
Recorded: Pye Recording Studios, London: July 5, 1966 /
Technical Team: Producer: Tony Hatch

The güiro made its big comeback in the introduction to "I'm Not Losing Sleep," this time accompanied by a transverse flute and arrangements that were too grandiose for David Bowie's intimate lyrics. Tony Hatch, who was not convinced by the artist's writing (although he did stress the originality of Bowie's compositions), nevertheless put all his energy into producing both sides of the single. He even came close to plagiarizing the hit he himself wrote and produced for Petula Clark in 1965, making the chorus of "I'm Not Losing Sleep" sound strangely reminiscent to "Downtown."

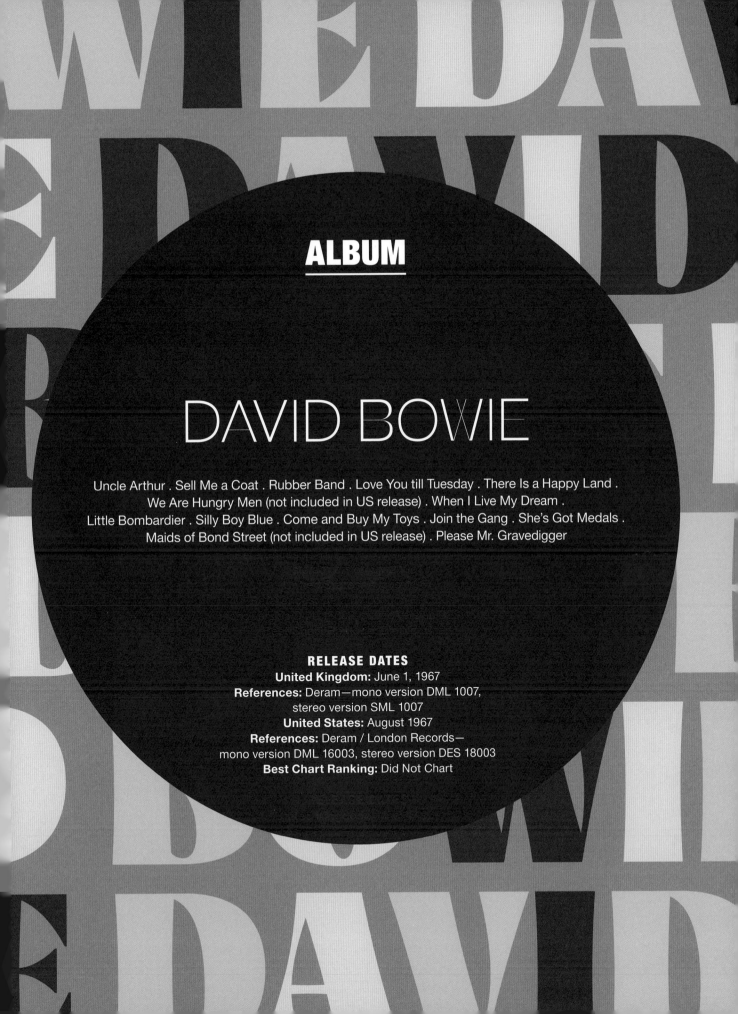

ALBUM

DAVID BOWIE

Uncle Arthur . Sell Me a Coat . Rubber Band . Love You till Tuesday . There Is a Happy Land .
We Are Hungry Men (not included in US release) . When I Live My Dream .
Little Bombardier . Silly Boy Blue . Come and Buy My Toys . Join the Gang . She's Got Medals .
Maids of Bond Street (not included in US release) . Please Mr. Gravedigger

RELEASE DATES
United Kingdom: June 1, 1967
References: Deram—mono version DML 1007,
stereo version SML 1007
United States: August 1967
References: Deram / London Records—
mono version DML 16003, stereo version DES 18003
Best Chart Ranking: Did Not Chart

AN ELEGANT AND GRACEFUL FIRST DISC

With the summer of 1966 nearing its end, the United Kingdom had the world at its feet: the famous 007, at that time played by Sean Connery, was recovering his strength in an interlude between two Ian Fleming adventures; the Beatles were riding the international success of the grandiose *Revolver* album, and above all, the whole country was in a state of joyful effervescence following the home turf victory of England over the Federal Republic of Germany on July 30, 1966, in the World Cup final.

Mime, Theater, and Music: Drivers of the Young Bowie

David Bowie, who was more interested in American football than British football, preferred to spend this period of national elation reflecting upon his future with his manager, Kenneth Pitt. Pitt was an erudite businessman, and his curiosity for the arts had a constant appeal for the young singer, who, through him, discovered *The Little Prince* (*Le Petit Prince*) by Antoine de Saint-Exupéry, *The Portrait of Dorian Gray* by Oscar Wilde, and *Nobody Knows My Name,* a collection of essays by James Baldwin. David, who was still living with his parents, Peggy and John, in Bromley, had the multifaceted spirit of an artist, with a fascination, among other things, for theater and mime. A few years before, the (musical) play *Stop the World–I Want to Get Off,* by Leslie Bricusse and Anthony Newley, had given him a taste for musical comedies and the burlesque nature of their comedic setups. He also took advantage of this period to extend his research into the religion of Buddhism, whose precepts and philosophy he adopted, as shown in an interview dated February 26, 1966, with *Melody Maker.* Despite this period of rich discovery, once 1966 was well underway, David Bowie had to accept reality: None of his three singles had found the public, and, despite the work of his successive managers, recognition and renown would have to wait. The artist parted ways with Pye Records on September 30, and then Kenneth Pitt had just one objective: finding partners who would be able to recognize the potential of his protégé.

"Rubber Band" and the Decca Adventure

On October 18, his manager organized and financed a recording session at the R. G. Jones Studios, in Morden, located to the southwest of London. David was joined once again by his loyal musicians who had been rescued from the Buzz and had come to lend a hand: Derek "Dek" Fearnley on bass, John "Ego" Eager on drums, and Derek "Chow" Boyes on keyboards. Two additional musicians were recruited, including the trumpet player Chick Norton. "Rubber Band," "The London Boys," and "The Gravedigger" (which would eventually be released as "Please Mr. Gravedigger") were recorded that day, with a view to being able to present the material very quickly to record production companies. It took his manager only a few days to attract the attention of the Decca brass. The label that had allowed the Beatles to slip through their fingers in January 1962 was open to young artists, notable via its new subsidiary, Deram Records. Despite their interest in signing new talent, Decca shut the door on Bowie in 1963 when he auditioned with the Kon-rads.

On October 20, Kenneth Pitt had Tony Hall, the label's production director, listen to "Rubber Band." Officially convinced of Bowie's potential, Hall organized a meeting on the twenty-fourth with Hugh Mendl, Decca's artistic director, and the producer Mike Vernon. The other two titles recorded the previous week were played at this meeting in the presence of the artist. "When Ken Pitt brought David Bowie to my office" recalled Mendl, "he brought a marvel. I thought David Bowie was incredible."[20] A contract with Deram was offered to the young man on the spot, and production of a single was

Bowie's patient manager, Ken Pitt, accompanying the young artist at a photo session in Paddington, in 1968.

quickly launched. This was "Rubber Band," accompanied by "The London Boys" on the B-side. The 45 rpm record was released on December 2 in the United Kingdom.

In November, Pitt took advantage of a business trip to the United States for a meeting at the American subsidiary of Decca, London Records, in New York. Walt A. Maguire, a World War II hero turned talent spotter for the American division of the London label, was seduced by the single and decided to distribute it stateside. However, only a promotional version of the number was sent to US radio stations in May 1967, and it was accompanied by "There Is a Happy Land" on the B-side because the label considered the lyrics of "The London Boys" and their references to drugs to be too subversive.

No matter, the ball had been set rolling for David Bowie, who went to Decca Studios on November 14, 1966, accompanied by his musicians, with the exception of keyboard player Derek Boyes, who was hospitalized with suspected appendicitis. The expanded team included Mike Vernon on production and Gus Dudgeon at the controls. This impressive duo was an asset for David Bowie, and while these two technicians were only at the beginnings of their respective careers, their two names would soon become associated with artists who went on to achieve timeless success. Vernon would go on to work with Fleetwood Mac and Eric Clapton, and Gus Dudgeon was the man behind one of Bowie's most famous songs, "Space Oddity."

Back to 1966. Following a successful second session, which led to the songs "Uncle Arthur" and "She's Got Medals," others were planned through to the end of December, which included the recording of the following tracks: "There Is a Happy Land," "We Are Hungry Men," "Join the Gang," "Sell Me a Coat," "Little Bombardier," "Silly Boy Blue," "Maids of Bond Street," "Come and Buy My Toys," and "Please Mr. Gravedigger."

A Priceless Gift

On his return to New York, Ken Pitt brought back a present for his protégé that was to change his life. During a visit to the Factory, his manager met the truculent Andy Warhol, who gave him a test pressing of the first album by a promising young group for whom he'd offered his services as producer: the Velvet Underground. In December 1966, David Bowie was thus the very first British adolescent to hear this now-legendary rock group, around whom floated a cloud of illegal substances. Bowie was transported by this music that he considered to be revolutionary, both in the refined production of the songs and in the subjects they addressed (mainly drugs and sex, recurrent themes in the New York music scene of the time). "To me, the Velvet Underground represented the wild side of existentialist America, the underbelly of American culture," Bowie would explain in 2019 in the BBC documentary *Finding Fame*. "That was everything that I thought we should have in England."[7]

While Kenneth Pitt became the young Bowie's mentor, Ralph Horton found himself confronting the debts accumulated by Horton during the rise of his young protégé. He therefore brought his collaboration with the singer and Pitt to an end.

On the set of *4-3-2-1 Hot and Sweet*, in Hamburg, Germany, on February 27, 1968.

When 1967 began, David Bowie's first album was finally complete. The artist did, however, go to Decca Studios on January 26 to lay down a new single that would enable his manager to continue seeking a range of partners, including the radio stations that had hitherto proved rather cautious in approaching the singular world of this singer. The 45 rpm "The Laughing Gnome" earned a degree of mockery for its creator, doubtless due to the speeded-up voice effects cobbled together with sound engineer Gus Dudgeon. Accompanied on the B-side by "The Gospel According to Tony Day," its release on April 14 was also unsuccessful, an unwelcome outcome with just six weeks to go before the release of the album.

On February 25 the team headed back to Decca Studios to record a new stereo version of "Rubber Band" and "Love You Till Tuesday." At that time, records were often sold in two versions, as the enthusiasts for mono had not yet capitulated in the face of the fashion for stereo, which enabled a separation of the instruments in the sound space. On this occasion, as with other sessions, several members of the London Philharmonic Orchestra were called upon to add substance to the production. The orchestral arrangements were by the Bowie-Fearnley duo, who, clearly, were novices at this kind of thing. "They only knew the basic facts of musical life [...]," Kenneth Pitt recalls with amusement in his memoirs. "Everything else about written music was a mystery to them so between them they invested in the *Observer's Book of Music*"—a reference work on musical theory intended for the general public, written by Freda Dinn in 1953—"from which they began to learn about such things as quavers and crotchets. They would sing a note then try to match it in the book."[3] Armed only with this work, which was intended for a public of neophytes, the apprentice arrangers were out of their depth, much to the dismay of the classical musicians assembled at Decca Studios. But, with the patience and goodwill of all those involved, the day eventually reached a successful conclusion.

Actor and singer Anthony Newley was a great inspiration for David Bowie and is shown here in 1961 miming a number during his show *Stop the World—I Want to Get Off.*

The Hiatus of the Riot Squad

Unable to wait for the release of his first album, in April, the insatiable David Bowie joined a group called the Riot Squad. The group had a growing reputation, notably for having welcomed into its number some high-caliber musicians, such as Mitch Mitchell, future drummer with the Jimi Hendrix Experience. It was Bob Evans—the group's saxophonist and a great admirer of Bowie since the Riot Squad had played at the Marquee on August 21, 1966—who called upon the services of the singer. The young musician agreed to take part in the project but discreetly, since his contract as a solo artist with Decca prohibited him from joining a new group. The musicians of the Riot Squad, who offered a less theatrical brand of rock than that of the singer, were pleased with this new working relationship. On April 5, when a slot became free at Decca Studios between 11:00 and midnight, some songs were recorded with the help of Dudgeon: "Silly Boy Blue," "Little Toy Soldier," a cover of "I'm Waiting for the Man" by the Velvet Underground, and a jam session based around the number "Silver Treetop School for Boys" were all immortalized in that single session. Twenty or so concerts were given in spring 1967, but then Bowie was to set off on some new adventures.

A Cautious Welcome for an Underestimated Album

David Bowie's first album was released on June 1, 1966. The jacket was illustrated with a photograph taken by Derek's older brother, Gerald Fearnley, in his apartment on Bryanston Street, where the two musician friends often rehearsed. The jacket for this eponymous disc contained a long text written by Kenneth Pitt that extolled the virtues of his little protégé: "Although he has rarely strayed far beyond his own suburban London, David Bowie, at 19, has seen more of the world than many people do in a far longer life-time," wrote Pitt. "[...] His line of vision is as straight and sharp as a laser beam."[21] The theatrical quality, inspired by Anthony Newley's shows, is omnipresent throughout the disc and was highlighted by the critics of the day, who mostly took a liking to the album: "Here is a new talent that deserves attention,"[22] said the June 10 edition of *Disc and Music Echo.* And *Melody Maker* went as far as to say: "Sounding like a young, good-looking Anthony Newley with the writing ability of Cat Stevens."[22] But despite these favorable opinions, Bowie's first album was a flop, as had been the case with all his previous singles. It should be noted that the competition during that spring of 1967 was stiff. In the United Kingdom, Pink Floyd

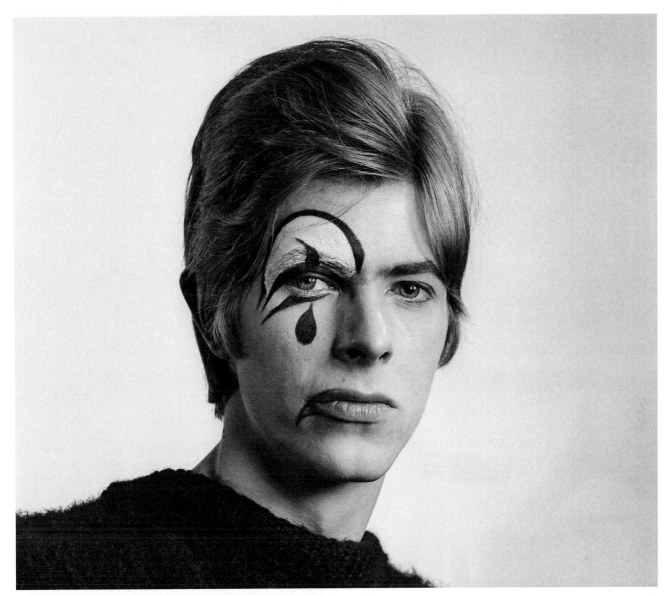

David Bowie as viewed through the lens of Gerald Fearnley in 1967. Singer, mime artist, comedian: the young artist had many different areas of interest.

pushed the youth into a new psychedelic era with *The Piper at the Gates of Dawn*, and they were closely followed by the Beatles' latest album, *Sgt. Pepper's Lonely Hearts Club Band*. On the other side of the Atlantic, the Doors had provided their first, eponymous album, with strong titles such as "Break on Through" and "The End," and they in turn were followed by Jimi Hendrix and his masterpiece *Are You Experienced* in May. Despite a favorable critical reception that praised the accomplished work of David Bowie and his musicians, the singer had to resign himself to another lackluster release. While Procol Harum dominated the *Melody Maker* Top 30 with "A Whiter Shade of Pale," Bowie's music seemed out of date and almost corny, and his references to children's stories and the visual spectacles he was fond of did not appeal to the public at this time of cultural revolution. Despite his disappointment and understandable feelings of frustration, the artist did not give up and continued to record new songs, which he submitted, unsuccessfully, to the Decca listening panel.

"Let Me Sleep Beside You," "Karma Man," "In the Heat of the Morning," "London Bye Ta-Ta"—the label rejected them all. Feeling abandoned by the team behind his first album, Bowie decided to leave Decca in April 1968. The following months were devoted to finding new professional partners, to multiple artistic adventures, and to the takeoff of Major Tom's rocket.

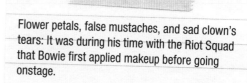

Flower petals, false mustaches, and sad clown's tears: It was during his time with the Riot Squad that Bowie first applied makeup before going onstage.

UNCLE ARTHUR

David Bowie / 2:07

Musicians

David Bowie: vocals, claps
John Renbourn: acoustic guitar
Derek "Dek" Fearnley: bass, backing vocals
John Eager: drums
Derek Boyes: Piano
London Philharmonic Orchestra: oboes, shawm

Recorded

Decca Studios, London: November 14, 1966

Technical Team

Producer: Mike Vernon
Sound Engineers: Gus Dudgeon
Arrangements: David Bowie, Derek "Dek" Fearnley

The English writer Alan Sillitoe, whose novels and stories inspired some of Bowie's first songs.

Genesis

The collaboration between David Bowie and the record label having been made official, the first recording sessions began at Decca Studios on November 14, 1966. "Uncle Arthur" was immortalized on that day. Through this ditty with its imitation of medieval airs and jigs (an effect supported by the use of the oboe and shawm), Bowie tells the story of the (mis)adventures of Uncle Arthur, who, having left the family home for the young Sally, finally returns to the arms of a somewhat jealous mother. Derek Fearnley explained on many occasions that he was the one who inspired the portrait of this hero, so much did the image of a thirty-year-old bachelor seem to have an affinity with him: "Uncle Arthur, still reads comics, follows Batman. It's only the seed of the idea he uses, I wasn't reading comics, but I recognised myself. 'Cos to him 29 was bloody old and I still wasn't married and I still didn't have my own place. That was a classic idea of the seeds David takes, and produces the song."[23]

Whatever Derek Fearnley said, Bowie probably found his inspiration elsewhere, most likely from reading Alan Sillitoe's collection of short stories called *The Loneliness of the Long Distance Runner*, which was published in 1959. This work (which also inspired the British group Iron Maiden for one of its greatest songs on the album *Somewhere in Time*, in 1986) includes a short story called "The Disgrace of Jim Scarfedale." In this story, the hero is torn between his possessive mother and his sweetheart, and he meets the same outcome as that of Uncle Arthur. Tired of married life, he resignedly returns to the maternal home: "Inside six months he was back [...], we saw him walking down the yard [...], looking as miserable as sin and wearing the good suit he'd got married in,"[24] wrote Sillitoe. We should mention another short story in the collection, "Uncle Ernest," whose title has an obvious similarity to the one used by the young musician. Often inspired by the art around him, every reading, every film he saw, and every show he went to would eventually form a piece in the David Bowie artistic puzzle.

Production

The rerelease of *David Bowie*, in 2018, which offers both versions of the album—the mono and stereo—enables us

Frequently alternating between wearing mod clothing and mime makeup, Bowie opts here for refinement while being photographed by Gerald Fearnley, brother of his friend Derek, himself the bassist with the Buzz.

to discover that only the stereo version of the track contains claps in the introduction that were performed by Bowie himself. It's no surprise to discover this kind of in-studio hijinks when we know that the man on the controls, Gus Dudgeon, was very keen on production effects. He had already been behind the sound concoctions on "The Laughing Gnome" and was continually offering his expertise and ideas to Bowie during the recording of this disc. The producer, Mike Vernon, gives insight into the qualities of the technician who was promoted in 1969 to producer on "Space Oddity": "I was helped enormously by Gus Dudgeon. I got him involved as he was a bit quirky and I thought he would get on well with Bowie, and in fact they did."[13]

"Uncle Arthur" was suggested to Peter, Paul and Mary for their disc *Album 1700*. The famous folk trio were not interested in the song and chose instead to include a cover of John Denver's "Leaving on a Jet Plane," which became one of the biggest successes of their career.

SELL ME A COAT

David Bowie / 2:07

Musicians
David Bowie: vocals
John Renbourn: acoustic guitar
Derek "Dek" Fearnley: bass, backing vocals
John Eager: drums
London Philharmonic Orchestra: French horn, cello

Recorded
Decca Studios, London: December 8 and 9, 1966

Technical Team
Producer: Mike Vernon
Sound Engineer: Gus Dudgeon
Arrangements: David Bowie, Derek "Dek" Fearnley

Genesis

Encouraged by his manager and his publisher, Essex Music, David Bowie had been offering some of his songs to artists that already had a reputation on the other side of the Atlantic. The Richmond Organisation (TRO to those in the know) was a branch of Essex Music, and they wanted to help the American public discover British material, particularly by placing their compositions with artists in their catalogue. This was how "Sell Me a Coat" was presented to the very traditional folk trio Peter, Paul and Mary, who were experiencing their last days of popularity in the face of the British Invasion and the revolutionary writings of Bob Dylan. It did not matter that the song was refused by the vocal harmony group; the song found its place on the first Bowie album and gave him one of his most beautiful melodies, with its effective and stirring refrains.

As is the case throughout this album, the lyrics for this track emphasize the childhood world of a young man. Bowie quotes Jack Frost in the first couplet; the legendary character from Anglo-Saxon culture is referred to in numerous books and stories as being responsible for the frost and cold that grips the land each winter. In this case, the narrator loses his sweetheart along the way.

Production

Despite some slightly awkward harmonizations in the introduction, the song is surprising for its very melancholic melody, which is a departure from the rock sonorities and urgency of the artist's first singles recorded before he signed with Decca. This very melodic piece showcases the acoustic guitar of John Renbourn, a specialist in American blues style, which he showcases in the chords on his Gibson J-50 throughout the album.

On January 25, 1969, while working with Feathers on a promotional film project *Love You Till Tuesday* at Trident Studios, the producer Jonathan Weston rerecorded the vocal tracks with Bowie, Hermione Farthingale, and John Hutchinson, providing the total number of vocal harmonies its author had hoped to hear with Peter, Paul and Mary.

The Feathers trio (John Hutchinson, Hermione Farthingale, and David Bowie) re-recorded "Sell Me a Coat" in 1969.

Single

RUBBER BAND

David Bowie / 2:17

ALBUM VERSION
Musicians
David Bowie: vocals
Derek "Dek" Fearnley: bass, backing vocals
John Eager: drums
Derek Boyes: organ
London Philharmonic Orchestra: tuba, oboe, trumpet
Recorded
Decca Studios, London: February 25, 1967
Technical Team
Producer: Mike Vernon
Sound Engineer: Gus Dudgeon
Arrangements: Arthur Greenslade, David Bowie

SINGLE VERSION
Musicians
David Bowie: vocals
Derek "Dek" Fearnley: bass
John Eager: drums
Derek Boyes: organ
Chick Norton: trumpet
Unidentified Musicians: tuba, oboe
Recorded
R. G. Jones Studios, London: October 18, 1966
Technical Team
Producers: David Bowie, Derek "Dek" Fearnley
Arrangements: David Bowie, Derek "Dek" Fearnley

SIDE A: *Rubber Band* / 2:17
SIDE B: *The London Boys* / 3:19
UK Release on Deram: December 2, 1966 (ref. DM 107)

The singer refers to Library Gardens, which are gardens of the Bromley library, in the town of his birth. This is where he made an appearance on September 13, 1969, in an acoustic set performed in front of a thousand lucky spectators.

Genesis

Destined to be a rabblerousing single, "Rubber Band" was recorded on October 18, 1966, at the R. G. Jones Studios, just as Ken Pitt was seeking to promote his artist. The song was rerecorded on February 25, 1967, for incorporation in the stereophonic version of the album. For the first time addressing the world of the military (as in "Little Bombardier" and "She's Got Medals"), Bowie enters the character of an infantryman, who, back from the front in 1918, discovers that his sweetheart has married someone else, in this case the leader of the municipal band. A mixture of lovesick complaint and humorous ode ("*I hope you break your baton,*" cries the narrator in a comical whimper at 2:06), the piece presents a Bowie who is out to amuse his public, in a register very close to "Your Mother Should Know" by the Beatles, which appeared the same year on the *Magical Mystery Tour* album. But for Bowie, there was no magic or success to be found here. Despite the quality of its writing, this single did not make an impression.

Production

Despite continual warnings by his producer Mike Vernon and his sound engineer Gus Dudgeon, the singer seemed to be incapable of separating himself from the influence of the singer and comedian Anthony Newley during this period in his life. The theatricality of "Rubber Band" clearly serves the depth of the text, and the performer even comes close to caricature when he bursts out laughing at the end of the song—which was exactly Newley's signature, since he also inserted laughter at the end of a piece to indicate to the listener that he did not take himself seriously, notwithstanding his madcap staging. "I never thought that I could sing very well and I used to kind of try on people's voices [...]," explained Bowie in 2002. "When I was a kid [...] I got into Anthony Newley like crazy. [...] He really did bizarre things. [...] I thought, 'I like what this guy's doing, where he's going, he's really interesting.' And so I started singing songs like him."[25]

Single

LOVE YOU TILL TUESDAY

David Bowie / 3:09

ALBUM VERSION

Musicians
David Bowie: vocals
John Renbourn: acoustic guitar
Derek "Dek" Fearnley: bass, backing vocals
John Eager: drums
Derek Boyes: piano
Unidentified Musicians: vibraphone, violins, cello, trumpet

Recorded
Decca Studios, London: February 25, 1967

Technical Team
Producer: Mike Vernon
Sound Engineer: Gus Dudgeon
Arrangements: Arthur Greenslade, David Bowie

SINGLE VERSION

Musicians
David Bowie: vocals
Unidentified Musicians: electric guitar, bass, drums, piano, flute, clarinet, oboe, bassoon, violins, cello

Recorded
Decca Studios, London: June 3, 1967

Technical Team
Producer: Mike Vernon
Sound Engineer: Bill Price
Assistant Sound Engineer: Dave Grinstead
Arrangements: Ivor Raymonde

SIDE A: *Love You Till Tuesday* / 2:59
SIDE B: *Did You Ever Have a Dream* / 2:05
UK Release on Deram: July 14, 1967 (ref. DM 135)
US Release on Deram / London Records: August 28, 1967 (ref. 45-DEM-85016)
Best Chart Ranking: Did Not Chart

Genesis

Light as a feather, and with the required level of innocence typical of radio broadcast, "Love You Till Tuesday" is uncontestably one of the most straightforward, pop-sounding songs on the entire album. In it, the narrator declares his love for his sweetheart, but this fire of love cannot last more than a few days...only "*till Tuesday.*" Also, the lucky, chosen one has to make a quick decision (even though the singer extravagantly offers her a possible extension: "*Well, I might stretch it till Wednesday*"). This is a lively and endearing song because of the naivety of its interpretation. Rerecorded as a single, it failed to find its public when it was released on July 14, 1967. "We all thought [it] was a potential hit single," as Mike Vernon put it "Nothing happened to Bowie for a couple of years after that. That was when he started to rethink things."[13]

Production

As with "Rubber Band," two versions of "Love You Till Tuesday" were recorded in 1967. The first, which appears on the album, is the product of the session on February 25, and benefits from the arrangements of Arthur Greenslade who, for unknown reasons, was not credited. Having been responsible for the mind-blowing orchestration of the title song in the 1964 film *Goldfinger*, which was the third cinematic outing of the British intelligence agent known as James Bond, Greenslade's work had won accolades for Shirley Bassey, and this time he created simmering arrangements in an easy listening, Tom Jones–like style for "Love You Till Tuesday" (reminiscent of "I've Got a Heart" or the "Skye Boat Song" on the first LP by the British crooner, released in 1965).

Wishing to offer the public a more polished version, in June 1967 Kenneth Pitt and Decca organized a new session under the direction of Ivor Raymonde, who was at that time famous for "I Only Want to Be with You," which he wrote for Dusty Springfield. Now provided with an orchestration rich with chords that overflowed from every corner of the mix, this single version offers nothing new for the listener, other than a demonstration of the arranger's skill. To crown it all, Raymonde concluded the piece with a pompous quotation from the famous song "Hearts and Flowers" by the Hungarian composer Alphons Czibulka. As for its interpretation, we should leave the last word to Bowie himself: "It's a strange little number. I sound like Tony Newley. I sound more like Tony Newley than Newley."[26]

THERE IS A HAPPY LAND

David Bowie / 3:11

Musicians
David Bowie: vocals
John Renbourn: acoustic guitar
Derek "Dek" Fearnley: bass, backing vocals
John Eager: drums
Derek Boyes: piano
London Philharmonic Orchestra: French horn, vibraphone

Recorded
Decca Studios, London: November 24, 1966

Technical Team
Producer: Mike Vernon
Sound Engineer: Gus Dudgeon
Arrangements: David Bowie, Derek "Dek" Fearnley

Cited in "There Is a Happy Land," this is Tiny Tim, musician, singer, and entertainer, in 1968.

Genesis

"There Is a Happy Land" was inspired by the eponymous book written by Keith Waterhouse and published in 1957. The idea of a place apart, far from adults, like the one depicted by Bowie in the song, seems to be one of a staggering naiveté, and yet the young singer was attached to it. Waterhouse's characters invent a language so that adults cannot understand them, adults also being unwelcome among the characters in the song, which are mostly derived from Charlie Brown and the *Peanuts* comic strip, or Tiny Tim, the famous singer known for his falsetto voice and who always accompanied himself with his ukulele. The child/narrator in "There Is a Happy Land" is surely addressing the listener/adult, saying: "*You've had your chance/And now the doors are closed sir, Mr. Grownup.*"

If there is somewhere that the young David Jones really wanted to ground himself in the 1960s, it was in this idealized depiction of youth. Like J. M. Barrie's Peter Pan, Bowie seems not yet ready to leave childhood for the cynical world of adults. With a passion for children's literature, he devoured the works of Randolph Caldecott, the famous illustrator celebrated for depicting the world of a bygone era with a carefree ethos. At that time, the singer also gave his manager Ken Pitt a copy of *The Farmer's Boy*, which was written by Caldecott and published in 1881.

Production

Accompanied by an effective use of the vibraphone, the song sparkles with lightness. The guitar of John Renbourn appears discreetly behind the French horn, whose anachronistic use in this period of psychedelic pop accentuates the song's childlike and baroque arrangement. Bowie's timid voice is well suited to the subject matter, sometimes almost to the point of caricature. Fortunately, the young artist set limits for himself and did not dare to assume the juvenile voice of the narrator. This song also provides a very pleasant pause before the curious "We Are Hungry Men," which is track six of Side 1 of the album. Our singer offers us a real roller-coaster ride with his first album.

WE ARE HUNGRY MEN

David Bowie / 2:58

Musicians
David Bowie: vocals, sound effects
John Renbourn: acoustic guitar
Derek "Dek" Fearnley: bass
John Eager: drums
Derek Boyes: organ
Gus Dudgeon: introduction voice
Mike Vernon: voice speaking in German
London Philharmonic Orchestra: trumpets

Recorded
Decca Studios, London: November 24, 1966

Technical Team
Producer: Mike Vernon
Sound Engineer: Gus Dudgeon
Arrangements: David Bowie, Derek "Dek" Fearnley

Gus Dudgeon, shown here, imitated presenter Kenneth Williams in the introduction to "We Are Hungry Men."

Genesis

With a passion for the dystopias of George Orwell (from whom he borrowed *1984* and "Big Brother" for two songs from *Diamond Dogs*, in 1974), Aldous Huxley, and H. G. Wells, Bowie often returned to his first loves: the science fiction works that dominated his childhood.

By delving into this world, which was also cherished by many of his contemporaries (Queen covered the subject matter in their video for "Calling All Girls" in 1982, and Iron Maiden's "To Tame a Land" was inspired by Frank Herbert's *Dune* trilogy), the artist prepares the listener for his future obsession: the discovery of other worlds, which was to become a frequent subject of his songs, such as in "Space Oddity," "Life on Mars?" and "Starman." Mixing caricature, humor, and a rock ambiance to push the limits of a type of punk rock that had yet to come into existence, "We Are Hungry Men" depicts a totalitarian state facing rampant overpopulation. The song would eventually be withdrawn from the American version of the album, as was "Maids of Bond Street." There are various references here and there to problems with copyright, but neither the artist nor his management would ever provide precise details surrounding the deletions of these tracks.

Production

As with "The Laughing Gnome," which the singer was soon to record with the involvement of Gus Dudgeon, "We Are Hungry Men" has a mark of theatricality in its interpretation, in which seriousness and the grotesque combine to muddy the waters. From the introduction, it is Gus Dudgeon who plays the role of a presenter appalled by the decline in our society, aping British actor Kenneth Williams, who was famous for his vocal imitations. At 1:27, producer Mike Vernon boldly provides the voice of a high-ranking Nazi that's full of rage and authoritarianism. Between the omnipresent brass, the strange joking manner of the participants, and the rhythmic, easy-listening vibe of the song, the final product is a strange and somewhat disturbing mix. This is a fairly dispensable track that tends to leave all but the most devoted listeners cold.

Single

WHEN I LIVE MY DREAM

David Bowie / 3:22

ALBUM VERSION

Musicians

David Bowie: vocals
John Renbourn: acoustic guitar
Derek "Dek" Fearnley: bass, backing vocals
John Eager: drums
Derek Boyes: organ
Unidentified Musicians: vibraphone, trumpet, violins, cello

Recorded

Decca Studios, London: February 25,1967

Technical Team

Producer: Mike Vernon
Sound Engineer: Gus Dudgeon
Arrangements: Arthur Greenslade, David Bowie

SINGLE VERSION

Musicians

David Bowie: vocals
Unidentified Musicians: electric guitar, bass, drums, piano, flute, clarinet, oboe, bassoon, violins, cello

Recorded

Decca Studios, London: June 3, 1967

Technical Team

Producer: Mike Vernon
Sound Engineer: Bill Price
Assistant Sound Engineer: Dave Grinstead
Arrangements: Ivor Raymonde

Genesis

The first love song by the artist, "When I Live My Dream" was, like "Love You Till Tuesday," rerecorded with strings, brass, and woodwind on June 3, 1967, with a view to winning over a public that remained hostile to Bowie's artistic world. Navigating between the froth of Broadway musical comedies and the ballads enjoyed by British teenagers, the single was once again rejected by Decca at a weekly listening panel, but it reappeared on the Deluxe Edition of *David Bowie* released in 2010. But returning to the album version, which is our concern here, the singer dares to provide a declaration to his sweetheart, who has become a fixture in his dreams. The phantasmagorical world Bowie loved so much once again dominates the proceedings, as he boasts of his courage to his love: "*Baby, I'll slay a dragon for you/Or banish wicked giants from the land.*" Lindsay Kemp, the famous British dancer with whom Bowie was soon to work, called this his favorite track, and the song was a real success, but unfortunately it suffers from a dated production by Mike Vernon. Invited to revisit various Bowie songs on classical guitar for the film *The Life Aquatic*, directed by Wes Anderson in 2004, the Brazilian musician Seu Jorge sang a delicious version of "When I Live My Dream" in his native language, which is available on the album *The Life Aquatic Studio Sessions Featuring Seu Jorge.*

Production

The bass of Derek Fearnley (co-arranger of the album with Bowie) is here deliberately discreet but still indispensable, imposing the harmonic changes between couplets and refrains.

The violins provide a heartfelt contribution to this number and emphasize the melancholic aspect of its catchy melody. This ballad was a real success, possibly due in part to where the tambourine struck on the fourth beat in the bar, which was reminiscent of the introduction to "Be My Baby" by the Ronettes. That song was produced in 1963 by the prolific producer, Phil Spector.

The Brazilian singer and guitarist Seu Jorge is shown here on the set of the 2004 Wes Anderson film *The Life Aquatic*, in which he performed "When I Live My Dream," along with a slew of other Bowie songs.

LITTLE BOMBARDIER

David Bowie / 3:24

Musicians
David Bowie: vocals
Derek "Dek" Fearnley: bass
John Eager: drums
Derek Boyes: honky-tonk (bastringue) piano
London Philharmonic Orchestra: tuba, violins
Unidentified Musician: accordion

Recorded
Decca Studios, London: December 8 and 9, 1966

Technical Team
Producer: Mike Vernon
Sound Engineer: Gus Dudgeon
Arrangements: David Bowie, Derek "Dek" Fearnley

Genesis

Determined to address the military world in multiple instances on this album (after "Rubber Band" and before "She's Got Medals"), here David Bowie sings a little waltz, which, although it appears rather abruptly, is still not lacking in charm, with its melodious refrain that supports a strong theme: the portrait of a veteran looking for a place in a society that has become hostile toward him. Alan Mair, bassist with the Beatstalkers and a friend of Bowie's, explains that the name Frankie Mair was given to the character in the song as an homage to his four-year-old son: "David really liked him as a person. [...] One day, David picked up an acoustic guitar and sang in a Scottish accent, 'The little character Frankie Mair, the little Bombardier.'"[27] The description by the singer, on the other hand, is more inspired by the same Uncle Ernest in the eponymous story by Alan Sillitoe (from his collection *The Loneliness of the Long Distance Runner*, a book whose spirit already hovered over "Uncle Arthur"), at the beginning of the album: "A middle-aged man wearing a dirty raincoat, who badly needed a shave and looked as though he hadn't washed for a month."[24] We are not far removed from Uncle Arthur in this new track.

Production

"Little Bombardier" was immortalized on December 8 and 9, at the same time as "Sell Me a Coat," "Silly Boy Blue," and "Maids of Bond Street," in Studio 2 at Decca Studios. Opinions vary among biographers as to the instrument played by Derek Boyes in this number, but it was definitely not a harpsichord. It was a honky-tonk piano, the same as the one he used in the recording of "Did You Ever Have a Dream," two weeks before "Little Bombardier." The instrument, which was sometimes deliberately detuned but was always equipped with drawing pins on its hammers, gives a very ragtime color to the recording with a sound that has particularly high frequencies. These basic-quality pianos were of the type often installed in the saloons of the American West, and in certain infamous little London bars, where the pianists did their best to keep up with the clientele.

SILLY BOY BLUE

David Bowie / 3:48

Musicians

David Bowie: vocals
Derek "Dek" Fearnley: bass, backing vocals
John Eager: drums, backing vocals
Derek Boyes: piano, backing vocals
Marion Constable: backing vocals
London Philharmonic Orchestra: cello, trumpet, violins, shawm

Recorded

Decca Studios, London: December 8 and 9, 1966

Technical Team

Producer: Mike Vernon
Sound Engineer: Gus Dudgeon
Arrangements: David Bowie, Derek "Dek" Fearnley

Billy Fury, a singer and pioneer of British rock, was one of the idols of the adolescent David Jones, and he produced a successful cover of "Silly Boy Blue," which was backed on the B-side with "One Minute Woman" for a single released on March 22, 1968.

FOR BOWIE ADDICTS

During the recording session on December 8 and 9, 1966, Marion Constable, who was with bassist Derek Fearnley, was invited to provide some backing vocals on the final part of "Silly Boy Blue." She was a star guest, since she was not only a distinguished singer, but also the great-great-granddaughter of the famous British painter John Constable.

Genesis

As an homage to Lhasa and Tibetan children, "Silly Boy Blue" was written by Bowie when he was still using his real name, David Jones, and it was played by the Buzz. The singer discovered the Buddhist religion through reading *The Rampa Story*, written in 1960 by T. Lobsang Rampa, the pseudonym of Cyril Henry Hoskin, a young writer who claimed to have been born in Tibet and that he had taken possession of the body of an Englishman, which was part of the process of transmigration that forms part of the Buddhist religion. This track encountered significant success among young people seeking spirituality and new age experiences. David became interested in these matters at the age of thirteen, and following frequent visits to the Buddhist center in London (the Buddhist Society) in 1967, he maintained a close link with this religion, putting it to the side from time to time but always finding his way back. "I was within a month of having my head shaved, taking my vows, and becoming a monk,"[28] he maintained. While many so-called hippies of the day seemed to adopt a somewhat superficial version of spirituality—and for whom Katmandu, the capital of Nepal, was their ultimate place of pilgrimage (Cat Stevens, a fellow Decca signee, wrote the city's official hymn in 1970 for his album *Mona Bone Jakon*)—Bowie himself opted for a more sincere approach to the religion, which he soon shared with the producer Tony Visconti.

Production

The finest song on the album, both because of its melody and its subject matter, which is profoundly anchored to its time, "Silly Boy Blue" has had many incarnations, unlike the other tracks on the disc. It was rerecorded with the Riot Squad in April 1967 and rearranged by Tony Visconti for BBC Radio 1's *Top Gear* in May 1968 with Alan Hawkshaw on keyboards, Herbie Flowers on bass, and John McLaughlin on guitar; it was again revisited with a modern approach for the album *Toy*. However, this album, with its focus on reworking early Bowie tracks, was to remain hidden at the bottom of a drawer at Virgin Records until its digital release in 2011.

The Englishman Cyril Henry Hoskin claimed to have been reincarnated as lama Lobsang Rampa.

COME AND BUY MY TOYS

David Bowie / 2:07

Musicians
David Bowie: vocals
John Renbourn: acoustic guitar
Derek "Dek" Fearnley: bass, backing vocals

Recorded
Decca Studios, London: December 12, 1966

Technical Team
Producer: Mike Vernon
Sound Engineer: Gus Dudgeon
Arrangements: David Bowie, Derek "Dek" Fearnley

FOR BOWIE ADDICTS

On December 12, 1966, another song was created at Decca Studios: "Bunny Thing" was basically a text read out against a musical background, and it was removed from the album to make way to the macabre "Please Mr. Gravedigger."

Genesis

After the lyrical flights and profound text of "Silly Boy Blue," listeners now find themselves back in the children's world that runs like a watermark through this album. In describing the days of a toy seller and what he sees through his shop window, Bowie is significantly inspired by the nursery rhyme *"Smiling Girls, Rosy Boys", from which he borrowed the first four verses: "Smiling girls, rosy boys/Come and buy my little toys/Monkeys made of gingerbread/And sugar horses painted red."* As a Peter Pan–like figure in a military jacket, the young singer seems to be hesitating between a lost childhood and the adult world of his half brother Terry Burns, who had signed up to join the British armed forces.

Production

Connoisseurs of the American folk musical style will recognize from the first arpeggios the finessed playing of John Renbourn. This guitarist, who is present throughout the album, was at that time one of the most famous exponents of fingerpicking, a technique perpetuated by Maybelle Carter, herself a giant of country and bluegrass music. This type of six-string playing was soon adopted by the great Norman Blake on his albums *Back Home in Sulphur Springs* (1972) and *Whiskey Before Breakfast* (1976). This Gibson J-50 scoring also bestows upon "Come and Buy My Toys" the award for the most American-sounding song on the disc!

JOIN THE GANG

David Bowie / 2:17

Musicians

David Bowie: vocals, sound effects
Derek "Dek" Fearnley: bass
John Eager: drums
Derek Boyes: piano, organ
Big Jim Sullivan: sitar, acoustic guitar

Recorded

Decca Studios, London: November 24, 1966

Technical Team

Producer: Mike Vernon
Sound Engineer: Gus Dudgeon
Arrangements: David Bowie, Derek "Dek" Fearnley

David Bowie during the writing of "Join the Gang," at a Clapham Common café on November 6, 1966.

Genesis

While the hippie youth of the world was getting used to living life set to the rhythm of the exotic Indian-inspired imaginings of the Beatles, David Bowie continued with the recording of his first album, which is sometimes burlesque, sometimes touching, sometimes quirky, but always fascinating. Hidden behind a forced naiveté and a polished image, which he indisputably used in order to convey some caustic messages, the young artist presented for the first time a scathing, almost mocking number that was directed squarely at the flower power generation. This "gang" whose adventures he narrates is formed out of a cluster of highly colorful characters such as Arthur the alcoholic, Molly the advertising model, and Johnny the once-famous sitar player. The song was written during a photo shoot session in a café on Clapham Common in London, on November 6, 1966. Sporting a serious air that belies the lightness of the text, we see Bowie in various views, writing long lines on his sheet of paper, elegantly dressed in very different attire from the fashionable set of the day. "We left him [to] compose it in peace," as a journalist present on that day described the scene. "Half an hour later when we got back, he was still there surrounded by a pile of cups and plates."[20]

Production

With two songs dating from the same period, it was probably by chance that the introduction to "Join the Gang" is similar to the classical soul number "Tramp," by Lowell Fulson, and immortalized in the version by Otis Redding and Carla Thomas from the album *King & Queen*. After a short drums interlude, the parody aspect of the song is sustained by the presence of the sitar, the characteristically Indian instrument—shortly after this, listeners would see George Harrison in the guise of a Western guru appearing on various TV channels with this instrument in tow. Played virtuosically by the talented Big Jim Sullivan, who also released an album in 1968 called *Sitar Beat*, the instrument fits in perfectly with this amusing track, which once again proves Bowie's penchant for creating songs that are sketches, rather than digging in to deeper subjects.

SHE'S GOT MEDALS

David Bowie / 2:23

Musicians
David Bowie: vocals
John Renbourn: acoustic guitar
Derek "Dek" Fearnley: bass, backing vocals
John Eager: drums
Derek Boyes: piano, organ
Unidentified Musician: shawm

Recorded
Decca Studios, London: November 14, 1966

Technical Team
Producer: Mike Vernon
Sound Engineer: Gus Dudgeon
Arrangements: David Bowie, Derek "Dek" Fearnley

The English journalist Dorothy Lawrence dressed in military uniform during World War I. Her adventures undoubtedly inspired the character of Mary in "She's Got Medals."

Genesis

"She's Got Medals" is launched to the sound of a shawm, invoking the military, which at this point on the album has become a common focus for Bowie. The title tells of the adventures of a young woman who has managed to pass all the stages necessary for her to join the army, an otherwise exclusively male preserve. It is with a touch of humor that Bowie provides certain details: *"She went and joined the army, passed the medical/Don't ask me how it's done."* There is no doubt that this Mary, having changed her name to Tommy, would have been inspired by the story of Dorothy Lawrence, the British journalist who disguised herself as a man in order to cover the conflict during the First World War. Only the outcome for the two women was different: While Mary rebuilt her life under the pseudonym of Eileen in London, Dorothy Lawrence's life ended in a mental hospital.

Production

It would be an understatement to say that the bassist Derek Fearnley was inspired by "Hey Joe" by the Leaves (released in 1965 on the Mira Records label) in the writing of his own bass line. In the couplets of "She's Got Medals" there is a harmonic descent to the song, popularized by Hendrix in 1967. It is fortunate for Bowie that this matter remained merely on the anecdotal level since the similarity is so striking. Once this "glimpse" at the other song has passed, there is a very Motown-like drums pattern, of the kind that Bowie was fond of in his early days. The effect of this pop number—with its psychedelic ambiance, which was very much in fashion at the end of the 1960s—is one of constant surprise.

Yves Saint Laurent's muse,
Betty Catroux, might have been
one of the "Maids of Bond
Street" encountered by Bowie.

MAIDS OF BOND STREET

David Bowie / 1:43

Musicians: David Bowie: vocals / John Renbourn: electric guitar / Derek "Dek" Fearnley: bass, backing vocals / John Eager: drums / Derek Boyes: piano / Unidentified Musicians: accordion, tuba, violins / **Recorded:** Decca Studios, London: December 8 and 9, 1966 / **Technical Team:** Producer: Mike Vernon / **Sound Engineer:** Gus Dudgeon / **Arrangements:** David Bowie, Derek "Dek" Fearnley

Many specialists, biographers, and rock historians have discussed the spelling of the title of this song. While the song is called "Maids of Bond Street" on the 1967 disc, it is subsequently referred to in the singular by most writers and scholars. The Deluxe Edition of the album, released on CD by Universal Music in 2010, ventured a modification of the title, but this outrage was corrected on the reissue of the vinyl in 2018. David Bowie, a great perfectionist, would probably never have allowed an error to appear in the title of one of his works. As such, this is the spelling that will be used in this publication, in accordance with the initial pressing of the album and as shown in the text of the song. In fact, it is very likely that the artist is addressing all the young women he came across in New Bond Street, the street where the Nevin D. Hirst advertising agency was located and where David Bowie worked in 1963. *"Maids of Bond Street drive round in chauffeured cars/Maids of Bond Street picture clothes, eyes of stars"* as he describes it at the end of the track. Bowie himself is explicitly the subject of the final couplet, recalling his dreams as a young man: *"This boy is made of envy / Jealousy / He doesn't have a limousine / Really wants to be a star himself."*

"Maids of Bond Street" is a little waltz composed in the traditional three beats to a bar. It's the only track on the album to use an electric guitar, although it is handled gently so as to avoid detracting from the work's period flavor, which is far removed from the rock sound of the guitars that were omnipresent on the airwaves at the time. All of which serves to enhance this effective song, enabling David Bowie to exorcise his frustrations through a text that, as in "The London Boys," depicts the English capital and its inhabitants in a less than flattering light.

PLEASE MR. GRAVEDIGGER

David Bowie / 2:35

Musicians: David Bowie: vocals, sound effects / Gus Dudgeon: sound effects / **Recorded:** Decca Studios, London: December 13, 1966 / **Technical Team:** Producer: Mike Vernon / **Sound Engineer:** Gus Dudgeon

While it is often said that this "unidentified sound object" is a piece of spoken word text set over a sound effects background, the reality is quite different. Here Bowie provides a cappella vocals, just as any regular person would be able to do when they are performing on their own. In "Please Mr. Gravedigger," the narrator explains to the village undertaker that he is digging a hole, intended to be his last resting place. This Mr. Gravedigger is in fact the only one who knows of the narrator's guilt, as the murderer of a ten-year-old girl. Gus Dudgeon, the artist's sound engineer and accomplice in this musical crime, exclaimed, when he heard the initials: *"Please Mr. G.D."* (for "Mr. Gravedigger") at 1:40: "They're my initials and it bugs me! Every time I hear it I think, "Oh no."[29]

Black humor and cynicism combine on this final track, which was the product of a burgeoning artistic complicity between Bowie and his sound engineer, who was subsequently responsible for the crazy track "The Laughing Gnome" but was also responsible for the success of "Space Oddity" three years later. Behind his console, the technician searched through the Decca music library to find all the sound effects he needed to re-create the lugubrious ambiance required for this number. But one vision stuck with him permanently, about which he later spoke to David Buckley, author of the biography *Strange Fascination: David Bowie: The Definitive Story*: "What I remember is Bowie standing there wearing a pair of cans with his collar turned up as [though] he was in the rain, hunched over, shuffling about in a box of gravel. And you thought Brian Wilson had lost it!"[29]

The Laughing Gnome / The Gospel According to Tony Day

First Release: UK Release on Deram: April 14, 1967 (ref. DM 123)
Best Chart Ranking: Did Not Chart
Second Release: UK Release on Deram: September 7, 1973 (ref. DM 123 / DR 39799)
Best Chart Ranking: 6

Side A

THE LAUGHING GNOME

David Bowie / 2:58

Musicians

David Bowie: vocals, voice of the gnome
Peter Hampshire: electric guitar
Derek "Dek" Fearnley: bass
John Eager: drums
Derek Boyes: organ
Gus Dudgeon: voice of the gnome
London Philharmonic Orchestra: bassoon, oboe

Recorded

Decca Studios, London: January 26, 1967; February 7 and 10, 1967; March 8, 1967

Technical Team

Producer: Mike Vernon
Sound Engineer: Gus Dudgeon
Arrangements: David Bowie, Derek "Dek" Fearnley

Coincidence or thought transference? The first Pink Floyd album, *The Piper at the Gates of Dawn*, which was released on August 5, 1967, contains a song called "The Gnome," written by Syd Barrett in the summer of 1966, when he was immersed in the world of J. R. R. Tolkien.

Genesis

David Bowie had to carry "The Laughing Gnome" with him throughout his career. Mocked, disowned, and then partially rehabilitated due to a second single release during the Ziggymania of 1973, this song marked a turning point as the last stage before the singer really emerged from his youthful artistic experimentation.

Finding the wait before the release of the album too long, Bowie decided to issue this surprising single, which tells of the misadventures of a narrator pursued by a gnome.

Nothing is held back in this 45 rpm, which combines grotesque plays on words (*metronome* becomes "metro-gnome") and studio concoctions, but these were 2:58 of temporarily skidding off the road for the artist, who would have difficulties taking control of his creature later in his career. "Aarrghh, God, that Anthony Newley stuff, how cringey. No, I haven't much to say about that in its favour,"[30] declared Bowie in 1990, probably forgetting that he had said to his producer Mike Vernon at the time of the recording: "I'm making this for kids. I love children, they'll love this."[13] The objective was not achieved, and the title was unranked on the 1967 British charts.

Production

Arising from a guitar line inspired by "I'm Waiting for the Man" by the Velvet Underground, "The Laughing Gnome" is the laboratory experiment of the duo of David Bowie and Gus Dudgeon. Accentuating the various sound effects and amusements that the technician enjoyed (as proof of this, listen again to the sound effects in "Please Mr. Gravedigger" or his imitation of British voice actor Kenneth Williams in the introduction to "We Are Hungry Men"), the number takes advantage of the fashion for songs containing high-pitched or altered voices, which gave the world hits such as "Petit Gonzales" by the Frenchman Danyel Gérard in 1962, or "Pepino the Italian Mouse" by Lou Monte in the United States, in the same year. As early as 1959, the effect was used to unrestrained effect in Alvin and the Chipmunks' successful "Ragtime Cowboy Joe." In the Bowie song, it is the voice of Dudgeon (mixed into the refrains with the singer's voice) that we hear when the gnome intervenes. Mike Vernon explains this technical pirouette: "You had to slow the tape down to pretty much the half speed and sing normal."[7] When played back at normal speed, the voices inevitably sound higher.

Side B

THE GOSPEL ACCORDING TO TONY DAY

David Bowie / 2:48

Musicians

David Bowie: vocals
Peter Hampshire: electric guitar
Derek "Dek" Fearnley: bass, backing vocals
John Eager: drums
Derek Boyes: piano
Bob Michaels: keyboards
Unidentified Musicians: bassoon, oboe

Recorded

Decca Studios, London: January 26, 1967

Technical Team

Producer: Mike Vernon
Sound Engineer: Gus Dudgeon
Arrangements: David Bowie, Derek "Dek" Fearnley

Producer Gus Dudgeon at the beginning of the 1970s, before collaborations with Elton John and David Bowie.

Genesis

Also inspired by the world of the Velvet Underground (this time more flagrantly so), "The Gospel According to Tony Day" is another curiosity in the discography of the young David Bowie. In this smoky number, where his Cockney accent seems to have returned (he had tried to lose it during some of the other recording sessions for the first album), the singer refers to various characters, all of whom spring from his imagination. Brendan O'Lear, Pat Hewitt, and Marianne Brent appear in succession without any apparent link between them. Whereas the single "The Laughing Gnome" was intended for a young audience, one might wonder about the choice of this kind of B-side track, which is closer to Andy Warhol's Factory than the children's world depicted in the engravings of Randolph Caldecott that Bowie loved so much. While such a lack of cohesion dug a hole between the singer and his label, it did also contribute to the creation of the character of a thousand faces that audiences would discover in later recordings.

Production

Inserted into the mixing in a way that is difficult for the human ear to tolerate, the oboes and the bassoon overwhelm "The Gospel According to Tony Day" with their clumsy lines for the full 2:48 duration of the track. The electric guitar marks the beat of a rhythmic soul provided by Peter Hampshire. Having been introduced to Bowie by Fearnley, this guitarist had been unsuccessful when auditioning for the Buzz in 1966. His tenacity was now rewarded, since he was able to put his mark, however discreetly, on a recording by one of the greatest artists of the twentieth century.

A promotional poster for "London Boys," the new T. Rex single, in 1976.

THE LONDON BOYS

David Bowie / 3:20

Musicians: David Bowie: vocals / Derek "Dek" Fearnley: bass / John Eager: drums / Derek Boyes: organ / Chick Norton: trumpet / **Unidentified Musicians:** tuba, oboe / **Recorded:** R. G. Jones Studios, London: October 18, 1966 / **Technical Team:** Producers: David Bowie, Derek "Dek" Fearnley / **Arrangements:** David Bowie, Derek "Dek" Fearnley

Bowie was an artist who liked to mix in his own experience with a vividly imagined, content-rich world filled with highly colorful characters and literary references. Here, he delivers one of his first autobiographical songs. It is indeed the young David Jones that we encounter in "The London Boys," and he's a seventeen-year-old boy setting out from his local suburbs to discover the pleasures (as well as the disillusionments) of the big city. "It's about a young boy who comes up to London, gets pilled out of his head, all those things. I used to do that—get dressed up, go up to town on Friday night, see what was going on, stay for the night."[31] Marvelously well-written and equipped with a very powerful finale, the song would have made an effective single if Decca had not deemed the text too subversive, as it makes reference here and there to various pill-induced highs. The song eventually appeared on the B-side of the single "Rubber Band" on December 2, 1966, and became one of the most highly appreciated songs by fans. Seemingly taking

a jab at Bowie, his number one rival in the glamosphere of the seventies, Marc Bolan also produced his own vision of the subject in 1976, issuing a single with his group T. Rex called "London Boys."

DID YOU EVER HAVE A DREAM

David Bowie / 2:05

Musicians: David Bowie: vocals / Derek "Dek" Fearnley: bass / John Eager: drums / Derek Boyes: honky-tonk (bastringue) piano / Big Jim Sullivan: banjo / **Unidentified Musician:** trumpet / **Recorded:** Decca Studios, London: November 24, 1966 / **Technical Team:** Producer: Mike Vernon / **Sound Engineer:** Gus Dudgeon / **Arrangements:** David Bowie, Derek "Dek" Fearnley

Released on the B-side of the 45 rpm "Love You Till Tuesday," "Did You Ever Have a Dream" would in itself have been a very good single. With its omnipresent honky-tonk piano line, the song is catchy, even danceable, like a ragtime number tossed off in an American saloon during the nineteenth-century gold rush. All that was missing was Big Jim Sullivan's banjo (also present on "Join the Gang"). Although effective, the song was removed from the album, making way for "When I Live My Dream." It ended up being pressed in acetate in

December 1966 so that Mike Vernon and David Bowie could listen to the takes during the end-of-year holidays. For collectors, obtaining this recording would be a very real gold rush! Only two copies were made.

KARMA MAN

David Bowie / 3:02

Musicians: David Bowie: vocals / John McLaughlin: acoustic guitar / Big Jim Sullivan: acoustic guitar / Tony Visconti: bass / Andy White: drums / Siegrid Visconti: backing vocals / Unidentified Musician: cello / **Recorded:** Advision Sound Studios, London: September 1, 1967 / **Technical Team:** Producer: Tony Visconti / **Sound Engineer:** Gerald Chevin

The fruit of the meeting between Bowie and his future associate, the producer Tony Visconti, "Karma Man" was recorded at the first working session at Advision Sound Studios in New Bond Street. The producer provided the bass on September 1, 1967, accompanied by his spouse, Siegrid, on backing vocals, and guitarist John McLaughlin on guitar. While Visconti's arrangements, which mixed backing vocals and chords streaming out from the stereo, did not really contribute too much to the song (the producer himself described the production as "horrible"), one does, however, appreciate the major shift achieved by our singer, who on this particular day seems to have given a new direction to his career, soon to be confirmed by the excellent "London Bye Ta-Ta." Once again, this song was rejected by the Decca listening panel.

LET ME SLEEP BESIDE YOU

David Bowie / 3:24

Musicians: David Bowie: vocals / John McLaughlin: electric guitar / Big Jim Sullivan: acoustic guitar / Tony Visconti: bass / Andy White: drums / Siegrid Visconti: backing vocals / Unidentified Musician: cello / **Recorded:** Advision Sound Studios, London: September 1, 1967 / **Technical Team:** Producer: Tony Visconti / **Sound Engineer:** Gerald Chevin

One evening when he was at Kenneth Pitt's place, Bowie announced: "I'm going to write some top ten rubbish." Inflexible in the face of this mad dog, the manager retorted: "I don't think you could ever knowingly write rubbish of any kind."[3]

As Pitt predicted, David instead wrote a song of real quality that day, and "Let Me Sleep Beside You" was born. The track was eventually produced by Tony Visconti at the Advision Sound Studios session on September 1, 1967.

IN THE HEAT OF THE MORNING

David Bowie / 2:54

Musicians: David Bowie: vocals / Mick Wayne: electric guitar / Tony Visconti: bass / Andy White: drums / Unidentified Musicians: organ, violins, tambourine, claps / **Recorded:** Decca Studios, London: March 12 and 29, April 10 and 18, 1968 / **Technical Team:** Producer: Tony Visconti / **Sound Engineer:** Gus Dudgeon / **Arrangements:** Tony Visconti

In the couplets of this pleasant song produced by Tony Visconti in spring 1968, one can see the makings of the future Ziggy Stardust. But the comparison stops at a few discreet similarities in the vocals because "In the Heat of the Morning" is an original and accomplished song, which has an introduction that mixes an electric guitar riff and an organ with a slightly saturated sound. Kenneth Pitt, who was present at the listening panel when the number was submitted, describes this sad episode: "I am still not sure that I believe what I saw and heard. Gentlemen of different ages but in similar suits sat informally around the room in what appeared to me to be varying degrees of somnolence. [...] Far too many were reading their morning papers and some hid behind them like ostriches burying their heads in the sand. The sight was depressing."[3] Naturally, the number was rejected by the Decca pundits at this particular meeting.

LONDON BYE TA-TA

David Bowie / 2:39

Musicians: David Bowie: vocals / Mick Wayne: electric guitar/ Tony Visconti: bass / Andy White: drums / Unidentified Musicians: piano, violins, cello / **Recorded:** Decca Studios, London: March 12 and 29, April 10 and 18, 1968 / **Technical Team:** Producer: Tony Visconti / **Sound Engineer:** Gus Dudgeon / **Arrangements:** Tony Visconti

"London Bye Ta-Ta" is really the song that would define David Bowie in the 1970s. The culmination of four studio sessions intended to give the artist a new direction, it has finely honed writing and lyrics that are easy to remember. The inspiration for its strange title came to the singer when he heard fellow Londoners of Indian origin saying goodbye at Victoria Station, which is one of London's biggest railway stations.

The listener discovers a rock singer whose voice, which is both powerful and rough, is allowing him to be enveloped in Visconti's impeccable arrangements. We have a feeling here of an artist finding his feet, his true colors, and his personal voice. David Jones is decidedly far away by this point. From this moment on, David Bowie was officially in the driver's seat. However, after listening to the song, Decca decided to abandon Bowie in favor of another promising new artist: Cat Stevens. "Cat won,"[26] Bowie commented later with some amusement, as a good loser if ever there was one.

The polymorphic group the Riot Squad welcomed David Bowie into their ranks in 1967, a period that included a handful of concerts and some recordings.

THE RIOT SQUAD

The Riot Squad emerged in December 1964 under the impetus of singer-guitarist Ronald Patrick "Ron" Ryan. He submitted a demo of the number "Anytime" to the famous producer Larry Page, whom he had encountered at various recording sessions while he was working as a guitarist. Page, who went on shortly afterward to produce hits for the Kinks and the Troggs, passed on some of his good fortune to the young artist, who had to form a group in haste in order to obtain a record company contract. In 1967, the Riot Squad was without a singer, and all it took was a meeting with the insatiable David Bowie for the collaboration to see the light of day. As Bowie's contract with Decca did not permit him to join a group officially, the artist performed a disappearing trick (the first of many) behind the back of his manager, Kenneth Pitt. Following a handful of concerts in the spring of 1967, when the musicians indulged in makeup and played at mixing things up a bit—audiences wondered if they were watching a mime show or a theatrical presentation, or if it was a real concert—Bowie left the group to focus on the release of his first album.

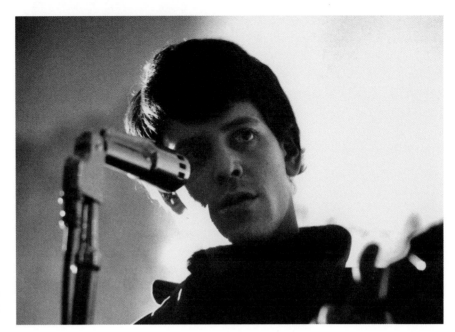

Lou Reed, charismatic singer and guitarist with the Velvet Underground and author of the legendary "I'm Waiting for my Man," onstage at the Delmonico Hotel, on January 13, 1966.

LITTLE TOY SOLDIER

David Bowie / 2:27

Musicians: David Bowie: vocals / **Rod Davies:** electric guitar / **Brian Prebble:** bass / **Derek Roll:** drums / **George Butcher:** organ Hammond / **Bob Evans:** saxophone, flute / **Gus Dudgeon:** sound effects / **Recorded:** Decca Studios, London: April 5, 1967 / **Technical Team:** Sound Engineer: Gus Dudgeon

Recorded by Gus Dudgeon on April 5, 1967, "Toy Soldier," like "The Laughing Gnome" (whose production had been completed a few weeks earlier), is a curious and cheeky number, pushing the boundaries of what most listeners would consider to be reasonable subject matter. It relates the strange relationship that the young Sadie has with one of her toys, a little soldier with a whip that he uses against the girl for her enjoyment. A strange idea, but in the end a coherent one when we understand Bowie's admiration for the Velvet Underground, who were keen on this kind of subversive subject matter. The British singer pushed the homage as far as borrowing some verses from "Venus in Furs," a track from the New York combo's first LP: *"Taste the whip, in love not given lightly / Taste the whip, now bleed for me"* was altered to become *"Taste the whip in love not given lightly / Taste the whip and bleed for me."* The song remained under lock and key and was not officially released or given any exposure other than being performed by the group in concert. In 2012, the label Sleazylistening All Stars released a Riot Squad compilation *The Last Chapter: Mods & Sods*, which presented the April 5, 1967, recordings to the fans: "Toy Soldier," the cover of "I'm Waiting for the Man" by the Velvet Underground (renamed "Waiting for My Man" by the Riot Squad), as well as two demos: "Silly Boy Blues" (revisited once again) and "Silver Tree Top School for Boys," which

Bowie had written for the Beatstalkers. The following year, the Acid Jazz label issued *The Toy Soldier EP* as a 45 rpm combining these four songs.

I'M WAITING FOR MY MAN

Lou Reed / 4:06

Musicians: David Bowie: vocals, harmonica / **Rod Davies:** electric guitar / **Brian Prebble:** bass / **Derek Roll:** drums / **George "Butch" Davis:** piano / **George Butcher:** Hammond organ / **Bob Evans:** saxophone, flute / **Gus Dudgeon:** sound effects, laughter / **Recorded:** Decca Studios, London: April 5, 1967 / **Technical Team:** Sound Engineer: Gus Dudgeon

A classic among classics, this hit by the Velvet Underground was discovered by Bowie in December 1966, when his manager Ken Pitt, just back from a trip to New York, gave him a copy of the group's first album. This recording session was an opportunity for the singer to pay homage to these artists from the other side of the pond, who represented all the irreverence that well-behaved Great Britain needed at the end of the decade. Not content with being inspired by this number for the writing of "The Laughing Gnome," here Bowie offers a cover of the future hit by Lou Reed, with whom he would collaborate on *Transformer*, the singer's 1972 solo album.

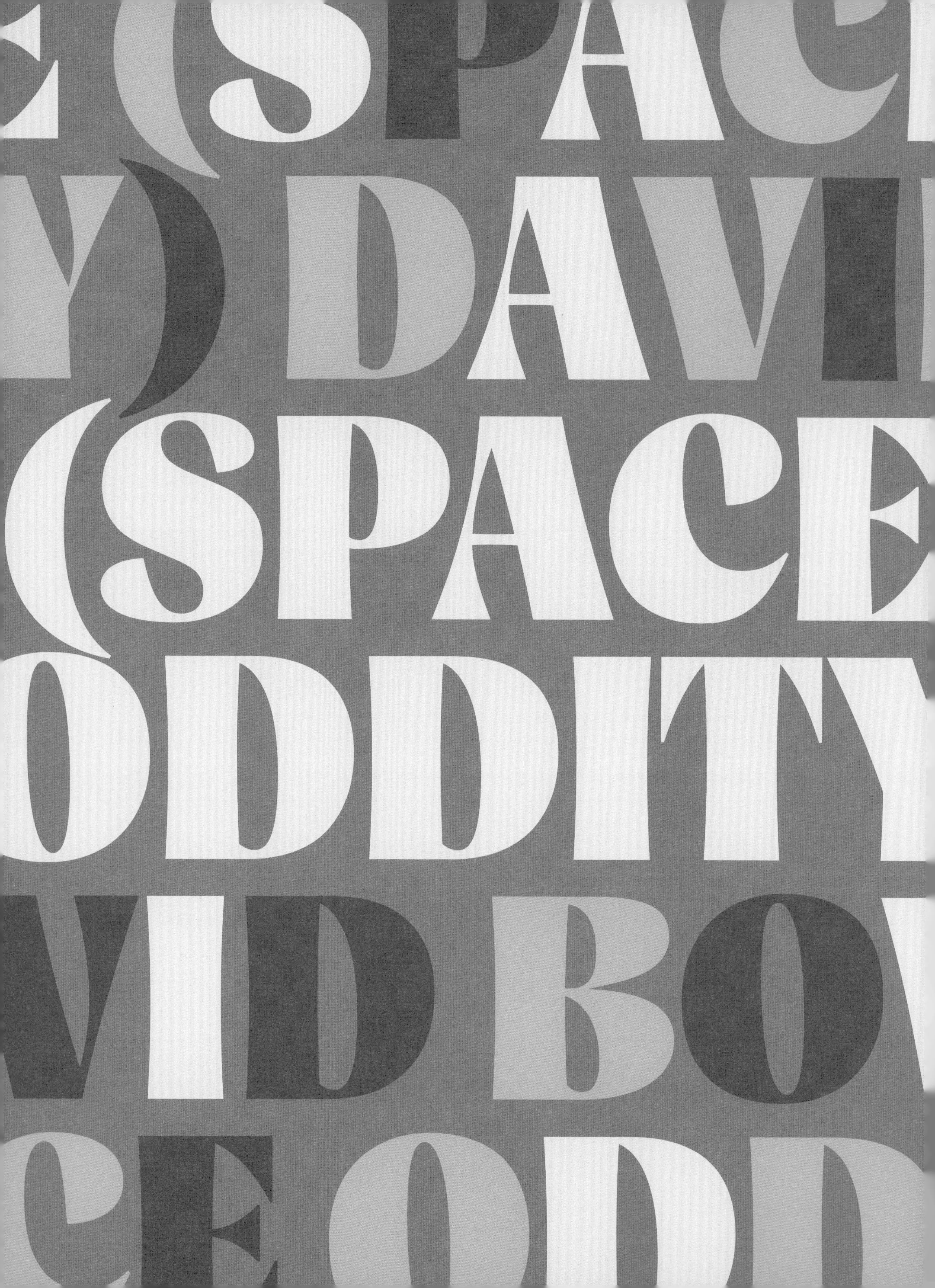
E(SPACE
Y) DAVI
(SPACE
ODDITY
VID BOW
CE ODD

ALBUM

DAVID BOWIE (SPACE ODDITY)

Space Oddity . Unwashed and Somewhat Slightly Dazed . Don't Sit Down .
Letter to Hermione . Cygnet Committee . Janine . An Occasional Dream .
Wild Eyed Boy from Freecloud . God Knows I'm Good . Memory of a Free Festival

RELEASE DATES

United Kingdom: November 14, 1969, with the title *David Bowie*
Reference: Philips—SBL 7912
United States: November 14, 1969, with the title *Man of Words / Man of Music*
Reference: Mercury—SR 61246
Best UK Chart Ranking: 5
Best US Chart Ranking: Did Not Chart

REISSUED IN 1972, WITH THE TITLE *SPACE ODDITY*

United Kingdom: November 10, 1972
Reference: RCA – LSP-4813
United States: November 10, 1972
Reference: RCA – LSP-4813
Best UK Chart Ranking: 17
Best US Chart Ranking: 16

THE FLIGHT OF MAJOR TOM

The negative reactions of Deram upon listening to "Let Me Sleep Beside You" and "London Bye Ta-Ta" led Bowie and his manager, Ken Pitt, to seek new creative partners. Although these very successful tracks did not win over their label, they were at the origin of an encounter that would change David Bowie's destiny forever.

Tony Visconti, the Man Behind the David Bowie "Sound"

It was David Platz, manager of the Essex Music publishing company, who introduced Bowie to Tony Visconti, a young American producer who had just arrived from New York. The rapport between the two men was immediate. But beyond the beginnings of a friendship, a real artistic reassessment was taking place for the artist. Visconti's mission was to refocus the singer on a new musical style in order to avoid repeating the disappointments of his first album. From the first recording sessions that took place in September 1967, the producer managed to ascertain what was previously dormant within the young musician: a talented *songwriter*, whose compositions could do with a few rich guitar riffs, as well as melodic and powerful orchestrations. But whatever Visconti might have thought, David Bowie was not yet the rocker that would one day be celebrated all around the world. He was attached to his twelve-string acoustic guitar like ivy to a tree, and his compositions were stamped with a late-1960s melancholy that would need to be showcased when the time was right.

An Insatiable Artist

Focused once more on writing and composition, the musician, supported by his manager, Ken Pitt, was now working in close collaboration with the publishing house responsible for his catalog (more than a hundred titles), in order to make his mark as a talented author among artists throughout the world. In 1967, a French singer named Claude François had a resounding success in his homeland with a piece called "Comme d'habitude," which he had written with Gilles Thibaut and Jacques Revaux. When Pitt found out that British publisher Geoffrey Heath wanted to have an English-language adaptation of the number, he suggested that his protégé should take this opportunity. Bowie wrote his own version of the text, called "Even a Fool Learns to Love," but it was not very convincing. The project was then entrusted to Paul Anka, who adapted the text for Frank Sinatra, and thus gave birth to the famous "My Way."

Always on the lookout for new experiences, Bowie continued on his own path. At the end of 1967, he sensed that a rupture with Deram was inevitable. But it also promised a freedom that he really needed in order to explore new horizons. He therefore entered unknown territory. When he learned that the mime artist Lindsay Kemp was playing songs from his first album during the breaks between his show *Clowns*, at the Little Theatre in Covent Garden, Bowie went to one of his performances to meet the man who would soon become his teacher. "I went to see him backstage. We were kind of pleased to meet each other, and he said would I write some more music for his things, and I said, 'If you teach me mime.'"[26] More than the beginning of a friendship (which transformed into an episodic romance), this was the establishment of a strong artistic collaboration. Bowie and Kemp lost no time in creating their own show, *Pierrot in Turquoise*, which enjoyed a large number of performances in the winter of 1968. Soon David began a relationship with the troupe's costume designer, Natasha Korniloff, and tensions among the team became inevitable. The adventure ended on March 30, following a final performance at the Intimate Theatre in Palmers Green, London.

David Bowie, Hermione Farthingale, and John Hutchinson formed the Feathers trio in 1968. The quality of their harmonies and melodies was at least on par with the American trio Peter, Paul, and Mary.

The Folk Experience

After the vaudevillian experimentations of his first album, which appeared in June 1967, Bowie seemed to be settling down. Accompanied by his faithful twelve-string guitar, he now explored the pathways of folk music and was heavily inspired by Simon and Garfunkel. In January 1968 their fourth studio album appeared, and it was the original soundtrack for *The Graduate*, directed by Mike Nichols, and very much driven by the hit "Mrs. Robinson." The poetical texts, threaded with the duo's oppositional stances to President Lyndon Johnson and America's involvement in the Vietnam War, stirred something inside of the young Bowie. Around the same time, he met Hermione Farthingale, a young classical dancer a few years older than him, and he fell head over heels in love with her. Within a short time, the couple added the services of a guitarist named Tony Hill to form the group Turquoise, which gave three concerts between September and November of 1968. Hill was soon replaced by John "Hutch" Hutchinson, Bowie's former bandmate and the guitarist on the tracks "Do Anything You Say" and "Good Morning Girl" from 1966. Renamed Feathers, the trio positioned itself as a British Peter, Paul and Mary, with vocal harmonies and a very gentle compositional style. They performed a number of concerts at the end of 1968, notably at Jim Haynes's Arts Lab, in London. At this point in history, Jim Haynes was a leading figure in the trend inspired by Andy Warhol's Factory, where artists, thinkers, and other emblematic figures of the time met each week to exchange ideas and perform during short sessions. The movement had a major influence on Bowie, who was in search of a community-oriented philosophy.

10, 9, 8, ... The Birth of Major Tom

Convinced that the success of his protégé would be image related, and therefore involve television appearances, Ken Pitt tried to secure partnerships with various European channels. The producer Malcolm J. Thomson was approached to make a promotional film that would publicize the various facets of David Bowie. In the manner of the Scopitones of the early 1960s, sketches illustrating the songs of the singer's first album were included in the project. The montage was intended to show the artist in all his various personae: solo singer, member of a trio, and even creative artist and actor in a mime show called *The Mask*. Feathers was involved in the filming, and an original piece called "Ching-A-Ling" was performed. Some of the numbers from Bowie's album were rerecorded with harmonizations sung by Hermione and Hutch. To win over audiences, Ken Pitt also commissioned a new piece that was recorded on February 2, 1969, by Bowie and Hutch at Morgan Studios— the musicians functioned as a duo at that time following a painful rupture between David and Hermione Farthingale.

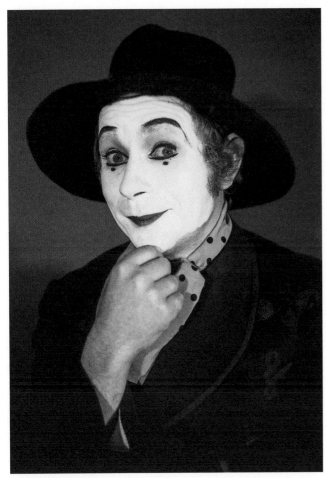

Bowie was a great admirer of comedian Lindsay Kemp, who taught him the rudiments of mime work in 1968.

David in mime makeup at a performance of the *Pierrot in Turquoise* show in 1968.

A few acoustic guitar chords were mixed with some discreet drumrolls on the tom, and a disquieting story in reverse and "Space Oddity" was born. The song soon intrigued the executives at Mercury Records, who saw an opportunity for success given that the Apollo 11 mission was due to make a round trip to the moon in just a few short months.

But, once completed, the film, called *Love You Till Tuesday*, was unable to find a broadcaster, and it remained unreleased until its issue on VHS in 1984 through PolyGram. Deram seized the opportunity to release an original soundtrack to go along with the VHS, which they also titled *Love You Till Tuesday*.

The Arts Lab in Beckenham

A few months after his split with Hermione—which inspired many songs on his next disc—Bowie met Mary Finnigan, a twenty-nine-year-old freelance journalist who lived with her two children in an apartment in Beckenham, in the London suburbs. Despite the loving relationship that was formed between them, the artist set up his residence in one of the empty rooms in the premises. With a passion for literature and music, Mary Finnigan became the singer's associate on his spiritual and artistic journeys, and she shared David's strong interest in Buddhism. The duo were very enthusiastic about the artistic experimentation workshops popularized by Jim Haynes, whom David met at a

Feathers concert. Assisted by their friends Barrie and Christina Jackson, Bowie and his companion created their own Arts Lab and facilitated encounters every Sunday at 6:00 in the evening in the back room of the Three Tuns pub in Beckenham. Starting on May 4, 1969, there were public concerts, mime shows, and talks on spirituality. The experience was such a success that it lasted a whole year.

While performing regularly at the Arts Lab—where, thanks to the release of his first album, he had a certain local reputation—David also occasionally went onstage with John Hutchinson, under the name "Bowie & Hutch." For his part, Kenneth Pitt continued working on the career of his protégé and won over the suits at Philips Records. But this should be viewed in a wider context. Pitt also made

approaches to Mercury Records. In the offices of this American subsidiary of Phonogram in London, Lou Reizner had the power of life and death over an artist's career. Given the highly topical subject matter, he was quickly won over by the "Space Oddity" demo. NASA's Apollo 11 mission planned to send men to the moon on July 16, 1969. Mercury Records—certainly an auspicious name!—was ready to launch itself into this adventure with Bowie, but only if the singer agreed to release "Space Oddity" on the same day as Apollo 11 launched itself into space. Pitt rushed to schedule a recording session on June 20! A contract covering the release of an LP and three singles was signed that same day with Mercury Records, who agreed to distribute the disc in North America, while Philips would be responsible for covering Europe, including the United Kingdom.

In the middle of the night on July 20 to 21, 1969, Neil Armstrong famously stepped onto the moon for the very first time. "Space Oddity" was simultaneously broadcast during the special program that the BBC devoted to the event, which they called "Man on the Moon" and which was watched by a television audience that numbered in the millions. Having been released five days earlier, the "Space Oddity" single had the benefit of the kind of promotion a performer could only dream of, which put it at the number five spot in the British charts as of September 5, 1969, and propelled its creator into the showbiz stratosphere.

A Success with a Bitter Taste

Tony Visconti, who, due to a lack of interest in the song, had left the production of "Space Oddity" in the hands of Gus Dudgeon, returned to his post for the recording of the other tracks on the album. The sessions took place at Trident Studios starting in mid-July, with a melancholic David Bowie at the helm—he was still devastated by his separation from Hermione Farthingale. Accompanied by his faithful twelve-string acoustic guitar, which is omnipresent on the disc, the artist settled in as a folk singer, almost hippie-like, and over-laying his productions with the same textural colors that

The Beckenham Arts Lab circa 1969.
This was a creative laboratory for
David Bowie and his artist friends,
who met every Sunday at the Three
Tuns pub in Beckenham.

During the filming of a sequence from *Love You Till Tuesday* on Hampstead Heath on January 26, 1969, David Bowie was wearing a wig, as he did not wish to adopt the military haircut imposed on him for his appearance in the film *The Virgin Soldiers*, directed by John Dexter between October 29 and November 4, 1968.

In 2012, the French author and illustrator Néjib provided a passionate and fascinating vision of the days at Haddon Hall in his graphic novel *Haddon Hall—Quand David Inventa Bowie* (Haddon Hall—When David Invented Bowie). "This was his slightly hippie moment, a long way from what we generally see of him,"[33] commented the talented writer.

made a name for his former colleague at Decca: Cat Stevens. The theatricality of Bowie's first disc was left behind, giving way to deeper subjects that were sometimes sad and often bitter. While all of this was happening, destiny took a moment to step in and tarnish Bowie's emerging success: on August 5, 1969, his father, John, suddenly died of pneumonia. The artist who saw the planets finally aligning in his professional favor was plunged into an existential crisis. First, he moved away from the practice of Buddhism, once a necessary aspect of his equilibrium. "I had this feeling that it wasn't right for me. [...] Though a lot of the basic ideas are still with me. But I don't believe it's suitable for the West in its Eastern format."[32] He then began to question the integrity of the artists around him. Organized by the members of the Arts Lab, the Beckenham Free Festival on August 16 of that same year was a success. Many artists took part in it, such as Sun or the Gas Works, and the audience of more than three thousand people who had made the trip were able to enjoy the good-natured atmosphere of the day and to savor the

hamburgers prepared in bulk by one of the event's organizers, a woman named Angela Barnett. The takings flowed into the refreshments stall, but the joy generated by this success was not to the singer's taste. He was in a foul mood. "He said 'You bunch of materialistic arseholes,' recalled Mary Finnigan. "David had been shitty to everyone all day."[3]

The First Days at Haddon Hall

The person who had the best outcome from this festive event was Angela Barnett. Bowie had met her at a King Crimson concert in April 1969; this straight-talking young American had completely captivated him with her sweet nature and gentle exuberance. That same August, Angela—who preferred to be called Angie— suggested that David should move into Haddon Hall, an immense Victorian dwelling in Southend Road, in Beckenham. The couple established themselves there with suitcases and guitars and were soon followed by Tony Visconti and his girlfriend, Liz Hartley. During the years that followed, everything that

David Bowie sports the vivid, futuristic colors of Major Tom, hero of the song "Space Oddity," in 1969.

Painter Victor Vasarely, a master of op art, shown here posing before his canvases in the late 1970s.

made up Bowie's world was concentrated in the ground floor of this old building, where other close associates also came to live. But the end of the decade sounded the death knell for the communal ideals that were bound up in this unconventional living situation. "In the beginning," explained Visconti, "David was all about the commune, the communal life: 'Let's live like hippies, let's share everything!' But then he had this money from 'Space Oddity,' which none of the rest of us had. [...] We barely had enough money to eat. So that's when it went sour. But to begin with it was a lot of fun."[34]

The Polymorphic Album Known as *Space Oddity*

David Bowie's second 33 rpm was released on November 14, 1969. In the United Kingdom it appeared under the name of *David Bowie*, with a jacket combining a portrait of the singer by Vernon Dewhurst and the artwork *CTA 25 BC*, created by the father of optical art, Victor Vasarely. On the back of the album was a psychedelic creation from George Underwood, Bowie's childhood friend, who specialized in album jacket designs. Notably, he had worked with Tyrannosaurus Rex on the visual for their first LP *My People Were Fair and Had Sky in Their Hair...But Now They're Content to Wear Stars on Their Brows* (1968). The drawing made on this occasion was the basis for the work on the back of the *Space Oddity* LP jacket.

In the United States, Mercury Records presented Bowie's album under the same name as the United Kingdom release, but it was accompanied by the subtitle *Man of Words/Man of Music*. As Kevin Cann indicated in his essential work *Any Day Now: The London Years, 1947–1974*, this was not actually the intended title for the American version of the album, but the album was given this title for the sake of greater simplicity. For technical reasons, Mercury Records also decided to replace the work by Vasarely with a blue background. The disc had to wait until 1972 to be rereleased by RCA under the new name *Space Oddity*.

However, for reasons of clarity, given the first album released with Deram in 1967, and as has been the case in most biographies of the artist, this second album by David Bowie will be referred to here as *Space Oddity*.

When it was released, the album did not meet with immediate success. Although it had the benefit of a singular style of writing, the record did not include any songs with the same power and originality of the lead single. Interestingly, and in spite of his increasing reputation and encouraging reviews, Bowie experienced a strange kind of successful failure. Holed up in Haddon Hall, the singer suffered from this paradox: He had become famous, but success had also eluded him...He would have to keep waiting, and experimenting many different formulae before his work finally paid off and gave him the glory he had so long hoped to achieve.

TONY VISCONTI: A "VERY BRITISH" AMERICAN PRODUCER

Tony Visconti was born on April 24, 1944, in Dyker Heights, Brooklyn, located in the heart of New York City's Italian-American community. With a father who was a carpenter by profession but a musician by passion, little Tony grew up in a house filled with the sound of the harmonica and the accordion, where Italian songs were belted out at full volume. His destiny was mapped out from an early age: He would become a musician.

The Brooklyn Boy's First Notes

As was common at the time, the young Tony cut his teeth on a plastic ukulele, decorated with characters from Popeye cartoons. Using a manual that came with his purchase, Tony discovered the pleasure of playing simple songs on his uku-lele, such as "Goodnight, Ladies" by Edwin Pearce Christy, or "Ain't She Sweet" by Milton Ager and Jack Yellen, which can be played using chords that do not require much left-hand dexterity. "The coloured strings corresponded to the coloured strings in the book," explained the producer in his autobiography. "I taught myself every chord in the book; it only took an hour. I realize now that even as a five-year-old I had good powers of concentration."[35]

Soon he learned to play the mandolin with his grand-father, with whom the Visconti family had now moved in. The young man then bought himself his first guitar and started dreaming of becoming a pop star, like the musicians he loved most: Buddy Holly and Elvis Presley. But his six-string guitar teacher, Leon Block, had a different musical approach. Block was aware of the latent capabilities of his student, and so he chose to teach Visconti music theory and how to play classical guitar, both disciplines that were far removed from basic pop songs with their *I-IV-V* chords. Bach's *Two-Part Inventions* opened Tony's eyes and ears to a completely new and unexpected world of sound, a world that was made up of dotted crotchets and clefs with sharps, and he soon acquired a precise and impressively technical

ability to play, as well as a thorough knowledge of sight reading and musical scores. But rock 'n' roll—that terror of classical music teachers everywhere—was a demon sitting in silent wait on the young guitarist's shoulder. Plugging your electric guitar into a Fender valve amp is worth all the symphonies in the world to an adolescent, and when he was thirteen, Tony joined his first group, which was called Mike D and the Dukes. Shortly after joining, Tony played a wed-ding for his first concert and was paid a fee of five dollars. In the years that followed, this music lover sang with the White Bucks, played double bass in the school orchestra, played tuba in the brass band, and then learned the cello. "I just couldn't wait to get out into the world and be a full-time musician,"[35] he said many years later.

A Decisive Meeting by the Thames

Newly arrived from New York, Tony Visconti was twenty-three when David Platz, manager of Essex Music and Bowie's publisher, called upon him as a reinforcement to refocus the artist on a musical style and to give a cohesion to his repertoire that was seriously lacking. The singer's first album had encountered a critical success only among an enthusiastic musical press. As for the general public, they did not know what to do with this music, which was sometimes burlesque and sometimes moving, and turned away from this first opus that was, to say the least, elusive. The artist's manager, Ken Pitt, desperately tried to convince the Decca label that the new Bowie songs had definite potential. The understanding between the young producer and the artist was immediate and led to the production of several tracks in 1967 and 1968: "Karma Man," "Let Me Sleep Beside You," "In the Heat of the Morning," and "London Bye Ta-Ta."

A Producer with a Worldwide Reputation

Despite a successful collaboration on two albums, Visconti left the adventure in May 1970 due to a disagreement with

Tony Visconti and David Bowie at Trident Studios in May 1970.

Bowie's legal adviser, Tony Defries. The low level of commitment by the young musician during the recording sessions for "The Man Who Sold the World" had already adversely affected the friendship between the singer and his producer, who preferred to offer his services to an artist whose motivation was not in doubt: Marc Bolan. Bowie shunned Visconti for this disloyalty, and it was not until 1974 that the two men were reconciled and made the groovy *Young Americans* album, then the famous Berlin Trilogy alongside Brian Eno. Visconti and Bowie worked together again intermittently until the singer's premature death in 2016, when the associates had just finished their final record, the somber *Blackstar*.

Tony Visconti's discography shines with other prestigious collaborations with artists such as Iggy Pop and Morrissey, and groups such as Sparks and Thin Lizzy. Now, with numerous accolades from the music industry for his work with Bowie, the producer has also been behind the success of rock monuments represented by the albums *Electric Warrior* and *The Slider* by T. Rex. He is also the man to whom we owe the success of the three albums by Les Rita Mitsouko: *The No Comprendo* in 1986, *Marc et Robert* in 1988, and *Re* in 1990. Still highly sought after, Tony Visconti is now working on new Bowie-related projects. "I can't tell you. If I did, I'd be killed and you'd find me floating in a canal," he declared in 2019.[34]

Single

SPACE ODDITY

David Bowie / 5:16

FOR BOWIE ADDICTS

In 1970, David Bowie recorded the song in Italian, under the name "Ragazzo Solo, Ragazza Sola" (Boy Alone, Girl Alone) with the adapted lyrics authored by Ivan Mogol.

Musicians
David Bowie: vocals, twelve-string acoustic guitar, Dubreq Stylophone, backing vocals, claps
Mick Wayne: electric guitar
Herbie Flowers: bass
Terry Cox: drums
Rick Wakeman: Mellotron
Paul Buckmaster: cello
Unidentified Musicians: violins, cello, double bass, organ

Recorded
Trident Studios, London: late June 1969

Technical Team
Producer: Gus Dudgeon
Sound Engineer: Barry Sheffield
Arrangements: Paul Buckmaster, David Bowie

SIDE A: *Space Oddity*
SIDE B: *Wild Eyed Boy from Freecloud*
UK Release on Philips: July 11, 1969 (ref. BF 1801)
US Release on Mercury: July 11, 1969 (ref. DJ-133, 72949)
Best UK Chart Ranking: 5
Best US Chart Ranking: Did Not Chart

Rerelease in 1972
SIDE A: *Space Oddity*
SIDE B: *The Man Who Sold the World*
US Release on RCA: December 13, 1972 (ref. 74-0876)
Best US Chart Ranking: 16

Rerelease in 1975
SIDE A: *Space Oddity*
SIDE B: *Changes* / Velvet Goldmine
UK Release on RCA: September 26, 1975 (RCA 2593)
Best UK Chart Ranking: 1

1969

Genesis

Sung by the Bowie & Hutch duo in their concerts at the beginning of 1969, "Space Oddity" was not yet the hit we know today. Bowie had written the piece for two voices—himself in the role of Major Tom and Hutch as Ground Control—at the request of his manager, who wanted an effective number to feature in the promotional film *Love You Till Tuesday*. Rerecorded at the Trident Studios on June 20, 1969, the new version of "Space Oddity" was perfectly coordinated with the moon landing, which took place at roughly four o'clock in the morning (Greenwich Mean Time) on July 21, 1969, with the landing of the lunar module carrying Buzz Aldrin and Neil Armstrong. However, the lyrics were not specifically written in order to illustrate the momentous event. The movie *2001: A Space Odyssey*, released the previous year, was the real catalyst for this epic track. Bowie was inspired by the solitude of the main character and the imagination of the dreamlike masterpiece directed by Stanley Kubrick. "I was very stoned when I went to see it, several times, and it was really a revelation to me. It got the song flowing."[36]

On December 27, 1968, a few months before Bowie recorded "Space Oddity," the Apollo 8 mission returned from its orbit around the moon. The world held its breath. There was something in the air, and everyone could feel it: Man would soon step foot on the moon. The astronauts James Lovell, Frank Borman, and William Anders returned as heroes, and in its edition dated Monday January 6, 1969, the London *Times* published a photograph taken by Anders from the spacecraft under the title "The Colour of Space," which showed the incredible "earthrise" over the moon's surface. This image deeply moved David Bowie.

This all relates to the main theme of the album, but what of the misadventures of Major Tom, floating alone above Earth after a technical incident that occurred on his space module? Bowie gives us some indications concerning this mysterious text: "I related it to myself a lot more than anything I'd written until then. There's something about [...] my fears, about my own insecurity socially and maybe emotionally, this feeling of isolation I had ever since I was a kid, which was really starting to manifest itself."[7] The only thing still connecting Major Tom with life was this cable hanging in space, a metaphor for the umbilical cord that still connects the child to the mother for a short period. Having been

A promotional poster created by illustrator Robert McCall for the Stanley Kubrick film *2001: A Space Odyssey*.

Earth immortalized by William Anders during the Apollo 8 mission in December 1968.

fascinated by science fiction since childhood (although terrified by the program, he never missed *The Quatermass Experiment* on the BBC), here David Bowie immerses the listener into a world about which he was continually writing.

Having provided the artist with a welcome dose of fame when it was released in the summer of 1969—eventually reaching fifth place on the British charts on September 5— "Space Oddity," then disappeared from the radar. In December 1979, a newly refined version of the song, produced by Visconti and Bowie, was rerecorded for broadcast on a television show called *Will Kenny Everett Make It to 1980?* which was aired on December 31, 1979. It was released by RCA as the B-side of the single "Alabama Song," on February 15, 1980.

Production

As with numbers such as "The London Boys" or "Silly Boy Blue," "Space Oddity" had several incarnations. Its first professional recording was on February 2, 1969, at the

Morgan Studios in the Willesden neighborhood of London with Dave Clague on bass, Tat Meager on drums, John Hutchinson and David Bowie on guitars, Colin Wood on keyboards and flute. When the contract with Mercury Records was about to be signed, the decision was taken to rerecord the song under the direction of Visconti. However, Visconti refused to produce the single, on the grounds that he was not interested in the piece. Gus Dudgeon, sound engineer on the first album (and also Bowie's associate on "The Laughing Gnome"), seized the opportunity. Meanwhile, Hutch, who had definitively given up in the face of the hard reality of the artist's life, had quit the adventure. "David lived from day to day, [...] without earning very much money. [...] I had to live like a grown-up and so [I] returned to Yorkshire,"[12] he commented, with regret, in his biography *Bowie & Hutch*, published in 2014.

During this June in 1969, while Dudgeon was playing out his career behind the knobs of the console at Trident Studios, there was a festive ambiance. Angela Barnett, Bowie's new

1969

Following the success of the "Space Oddity" single in 1969, David Bowie became the ambassador for the Dubreq brand and their famous Stylophone.

girlfriend, was there, and as usual, she was unfailingly supportive of the hero of the day. Mary Finnigan, the friend from the Arts Lab in Beckenham, was also present: "Everybody was incredibly excited,"[34] she recalled in 2019. The musician Paul Buckmaster wrote the string arrangements for the number, which earned him the position of being much in demand later on, eventually working on two of the biggest hits of the seventies: "Your Song," by Elton John in 1970, and the cover of Badfinger's "Without You" by Harry Nilsson in 1971. For his part, David strummed his Harptone six-string guitar.

For the session, Dudgeon had hired a Mellotron but was unable to tame the beast, as the fine tuning of the instrument was so temperamental. On the advice of Visconti, the keyboard player Rick Wakeman, aged twenty at that time, came to the rescue: "David wanted it because he wanted it to sound not like strings, but like strings. And I knew exactly what it meant,"[7] he commented. A keyboard instrument that is omnipresent in the Beatles hit "Strawberry Fields Forever," the operation of the Mellotron is as follows: Each key press triggers a raft of chords prerecorded on a magnetic tape, which runs on demand. The precursor of the sampler! But each of these recordings only lasts eight seconds, so the musician needs to be very awake to ensure that the chords last for the time required by the bar lengths of the music. So David asked Dudgeon to wash the instrument

in reverb so the notes would last longer. "It was a very simple part that I played, but David was really happy with it. That was the start of us working together."[34] This virtuoso, soon to be working with the prog band Yes, immortalized his delicate piano playing in 1971 on "Life on Mars?"

Another important instrument in "Space Oddity" appears from 0:29—the Stylophone. Marketed by Dubreq in 1967 (with more than three million of them sold since then), this pocket organ, which was played using a stylus, was, as legend has it, given to Bowie by Marc Bolan. By popularizing this little instrument, Bowie became its ambassador in the advertising of the time.

UNWASHED AND SOMEWHAT SLIGHTLY DAZED

David Bowie / 6:12

Musicians: David Bowie: vocals, twelve-string acoustic guitar / **Mick Wayne:** electric guitar / **Tim Renwick:** electric guitar / **John Lodge:** bass / **John Cambridge:** drums / **Benny Marshall:** harmonica / **Unidentified Musicians:** strings, brass / **Recorded:** Trident Studios, London: August–September 1969 / **Technical Team:** Producer: Tony Visconti / **Sound Engineer:** Ken Scott

Feeling vulnerable following the split with Hermione Farthingale, David Bowie wrote this song in 1969, in the words of the author, "about a boy whose girlfriend thinks he is socially inferior."[37] Was he referring to the woman who had just left him to join the production of the film *Song of Norway*, or was it a reference to his associate John Hutchinson's girlfriend, for whom he wrote the corrosive "Janine"? We shall never know, but one thing is certain: Bowie was determined to get back at his detractors, those who found his Anthony Newley aspects amusing, which, furthermore, were fully embraced. From the second track of the album, Bowie unleashes a number that is both rock and folk at the same time, with a gently psychedelic ambiance reinforced by the harmonica of Benny Marshall. The harmonica player, introduced to Bowie by his drummer, John Cambridge, made the trip from Hull, 190 miles north of London, where he sang in a group called the Rats. Another member of this band, the guitarist Mick "Ronno" Ronson, would soon be joining the Bowie adventure.

DON'T SIT DOWN

David Bowie / 0:40

Musicians: David Bowie: vocals, twelve-string acoustic guitar / **Mick Wayne:** electric guitar / **Tim Renwick:** electric guitar / **John Lodge:** bass / **John Cambridge:** drums / **Recorded:** Trident Studios, London: August–September 1969 / **Technical Team:** Producer: Tony Visconti / **Sound Engineer:** Ken Scott

Running on from the finale of "Unwashed and Somewhat Slightly Dazed" on the American version of the album, "Don't Sit Down" is an extract from a jam session rather than a separate song per se. In the British version of the disc, Bowie did however decide to give this forty-second interlude the status of a stand-alone track. Its title is derived from improvisations by the singer, who hums—probably directed at one of his musicians—"*Don't sit down, don't sit down.*" This illustrates the relaxed atmosphere of the recording sessions. The piece is also a track in its own right on 1990's Rykodisc rerelease, thereby making it consistent with the initial track listing.

LETTER TO HERMIONE

David Bowie / 2:30

Musicians: David Bowie: vocals, twelve-string acoustic guitar / **Keith Christmas:** acoustic guitar / **Recorded:** Trident Studios, London: July 16 and 17, 1969 / **Technical Team:** Producer: Tony Visconti / **Sound Engineer:** Ken Scott, Malcolm Toft

The split with Hermione Farthingale is at the heart of this melodic folk ballad, performed on twelve-string guitar by an audibly taxed Bowie. "I once wrote a letter I never sent to Hermione," he explained. "I'd thought I'd record it instead and send her the record."[37] The only song in his repertoire that is explicitly written for one of his girlfriends, "Letter to Hermione" is moving in its sincerity and presents a sensitive and touching look at the artist. In the evocation of this lost love that would leave a permanent mark on Bowie, we are very far from the burlesques of "The Laughing Gnome" or "We Are Hungry Men." "I think that's the one and only time in his life that he *did* have his heart broken," confided his friend Visconti. "I think he just went into every relationship after that with caution."[34]

CYGNET COMMITTEE

David Bowie / 9:36

Musicians: David Bowie: vocals, twelve-string acoustic guitar / **Mick Wayne:** electric guitar / **Tim Renwick:** electric guitar / **John Lodge:** bass / **John Cambridge:** drums / **Unidentified Musician:** organ / **Recorded:** Trident Studios, London: August–September 1969 / **Technical Team:** Producer: Tony Visconti / **Sound Engineer:** Ken Scott

A veritable manifesto against hippie ideals, "Cygnet Committee" is in every way an indictment against the Arts Lab in Beckenham that Bowie himself created. "It started to deteriorate, because we found that the mass percentage of the people that came just came to be entertained," explained the singer. "The participation element was gone—the wave of enthusiasm that the whole thing captured in the beginning. It gradually became just another place to go. In fact the only place to go in Beckenham."[26] Also disillusioned by the euphoria generated from the team's substantial takings at the Beckenham Free Festival in August 1969, the singer decided, during the ten minutes or so of the song, to settle the accounts concerning a philosophy that seemed to escape his own followers: "It's me looking at the hippie movement, saying how it started off so well but went wrong when the hippies became just like everyone else, materialistic and selfish."[38] Despite some resentments, at the end of the album David Bowie buried the ax with his friends at the Arts Lab, joyfully singing the hymn to the end of the hippie golden age: "Memory of a Free Festival."

David Bowie and Hermione Farthingale in 1968, in the midst of another Feathers adventure.

JANINE

David Bowie / 3:22

Musicians: David Bowie: vocals, twelve-string acoustic guitar, sanza / Mick Wayne: electric guitar / Tim Renwick: electric guitar / Keith Christmas: acoustic guitar / John Lodge: bass / John Cambridge: drums, tambourine / **Recorded:** Trident Studios, London: July 16 and 17, 1969 / **Technical Team:** Producer: Tony Visconti / **Sound Engineers:** Ken Scott, Malcolm Toft

When in the winter of 1969 the Bowie & Hutch duo sang this cheerful two-part folk number, John Hutchinson was immediately suspicious that the song was about George Underwood's girlfriend. Bowie admitted that he was trying to convey a message to Underwood about the true nature of his girlfriend. Whether a case of clairvoyance or fraternal jealousy, we will never know exactly what it was that the artist had against this girl, referred to as Janine for the purposes of this song. "I couldn't figure out what David was trying to say with the song," explained Underwood. "[…] I think he was trying to tell me something but I still don't know what. He never came out and said he didn't like my girlfriend or anything, he was always nice to her and she never upset him as far as I knew."[6]

AN OCCASIONAL DREAM

David Bowie / 2:55

Musicians: David Bowie: vocals, twelve-string acoustic guitar, backing vocals / Mick Wayne: acoustic guitar / Tim Renwick: acoustic guitar, recorder, clarinet / Keith Christmas: acoustic guitar / John Lodge: bass / John Cambridge: drums / Tony Visconti: flute, recorder / **Recorded:** Trident Studios, London: July 16 and 17, 1969 / **Technical Team:** Producer: Tony Visconti / **Sound Engineers:** Ken Scott, Malcolm Toft

The second piece in the folk diptych dedicated to Hermione Farthingale (after "Letter to Hermione"), "An Occasional Dream" closes the chapter concerning this painful split. However, in the middle of this ballad (to which, it should be admitted, the flutes played by Visconti and Renwick add a slightly mannered effect), Hermione, when asked by biographer Paul Trynka, denied that she was their inspiration. "They weren't written and handed to me," she declared concerning these two songs. "[…] Obviously they strike into the heart. They're wonderful, wonderful love songs, whoever they're for."[39]

WILD EYED BOY FROM FREECLOUD

David Bowie / 4:49

Musicians

David Bowie: vocals, twelve-string acoustic guitar, claps
John Lodge: bass
Paul Buckmaster: cello
Mick Ronson: claps
Unidentified Musicians: orchestra

Recorded

Trident Studios, London: June–September 1969

Technical Team

Producer: Tony Visconti
Sound Engineers: Ken Scott, Barry Sheffield
Arrangements: Tony Visconti

Genesis

When Gus Dudgeon produced the recording session that was to change his life on June 20, 1969, two numbers were scheduled. "Space Oddity" was immortalized in a few hours (although other sessions were required for the overdubs and mixing), and all that was left to do was record the single's B-side, "Wild Eyed Boy from Freecloud." Paul Buckmaster was on cello, and David Bowie accompanied himself on the twelve-string guitar. As planned, the number appeared on the B-side of the single when it was released on July 11, 1969, but Tony Visconti, now at the controls for the album's production, decided to rerecord the song.

Concerning the text, the analogy between this wild child living in the Freecloud mountain, and the discovery, in 1797, of a child abandoned in the heart of the Caune forest, in the Tarn region of France, is emphasized by the biographers and was confirmed by Bowie. The artist was fascinated by the writings of Dr. Jean Itard, to whom the child was entrusted and who spent a good part of his life trying to understand him; Dr. Itard gave him the name of Victor, as the sound of "O" was the only one he could utter. His *Mémoires et rapport sur Victor de l'Aveyron* was published in Great Britain under the title *The Wild Boy of Aveyron*. The musician took to heart this incredible story, which he combined with his passion for the phantasmagorical stories of Tolkien and fantastical literature. "It was about the disassociated, the ones who feel as though they're left outside, which was how I felt about me," Bowie later admitted. "I always felt I was on the edge of events, the fringe of things, and left out."[40]

Production

"I didn't like the throwaway B-side version that Dudgeon recorded," the producer later explained. "[...] I heard a Wagnerian orchestra in my head. I convinced Mercury to allow me to use a fifty-piece orchestra for just this song and I spent five days writing an arrangement."[35] On the day of the recording, the producer plunged Bowie into the heart of the song, asking him to play his guitar part alongside the musicians. His voice was recorded subsequently. But there was a problem with the console at the Trident Studios, and the end

The young actor Jean-Pierre Cargol in the role of Victor de l'Aveyron, in François Truffaut's 1970 film, *L'Enfant sauvage*.

of the day was fast approaching. An hour before handing back the keys to the studio, everything was fixed and everyone in their place, and one take was enough to wrap up "Wild Eyed Boy from Freecloud." Later, during the mixing, there was a guest in the studio: Mick Ronson, who was there with the drummer John Cambridge. The blond rocker was recruited to contribute hand claps at the end. "We needed an extra pair of hands," the producer later explained. "[...] This was his first appearance on a David Bowie record. He was never credited, but that's where it began."[13] While we can enjoy this anecdote, confident in the accuracy of the producer's memory, it remains the case that the real encounter between Ronson and Bowie only happened in February of the following year.

GOD KNOWS I'M GOOD

David Bowie / 3:19

Musicians: David Bowie: vocals, twelve-string acoustic guitar / Tim Renwick: acoustic guitar / Keith Christmas: acoustic guitar / **Recorded:** Trident Studios, London: September 16, 1969 / **Technical Team:** Producer: Tony Visconti / Sound Engineers: Ken Scott, Malcolm Toft

Recorded for the first time at Pye Studios in London on September 11, 1969, "God Knows I'm Good" had a second session at Trident Studios on September 16, because Bowie really did not like the first takes. The song, performed by a trio of acoustic guitars, tells of the misfortunes of an old lady who is obliged to steal some meat in a shop. Constantly repeating *God knows I'm good*, the shoplifter commits her theft and is caught, then feigns a fainting spell, all while continually repeating the titular phrase, as though it were somehow capable of changing her destiny.

MEMORY OF A FREE FESTIVAL

David Bowie / 7:07

Musicians: David Bowie: vocals, twelve-string acoustic guitar, Rosedale organ, backing vocals / **Mick Wayne:** electric guitar / **Tim Renwick:** electric guitar / **Keith Christmas:** acoustic guitar / **John Lodge:** bass / **John Cambridge:** drums / **Marc Bolan:** backing vocals / **Bob Harris:** backing vocals / **Sue Harris:** backing vocals / **Tony Woollcott:** backing vocals / **Girl:** backing vocals / **Recorded:** Trident Studios, London: September 8 and 9, 1969 / **Technical Team:** Producer: Tony Visconti / **Sound Engineers:** Ken Scott, Malcolm Toft

Despite doubts and self-questioning, David Bowie was convinced: In a world dominated by consumerism and self-interest, one could not possibly stoop any lower, and things could only get better. The Free Festival mentioned in the last song on the album was an event that David and his friends at the Arts Lab organized on August 16, 1969, at Croydon Road Recreation Ground, in Beckenham. Although "Memory of a Free Festival" conveys a positive impression of the day—"*I kissed a lot of people that day*," sings Bowie—it is run through with nostalgia for an era that was coming to a close. In fact, confronted by a series of tragic episodes, the hippie movement was already gradually fading out of fashion. Six months later, the disastrous Rolling Stones concert at Altamont, in California—where a spectator was killed by one of the Hells Angels who was supposed to be managing security—precipitated the fall of flower power. Syd Barrett's departure from Pink Floyd also forced young people to confront the consequences of the excess consumption of hard drugs. The Beatles were soon to break up for obscure reasons, all of which were far removed from the Peace and Love doctrine they previously upheld. Hippies would later mourn their fallen idols: Jimi Hendrix, Janis Joplin, and Jim Morrison, who would all eventually die from overdoses. One had to grow up and face the world, and David Bowie was fully aware of this fact. But for the time being, he and his friends joined hands for a memorable finale set to the sounds of "Hey Jude," and they sang in unison "*The sun machine is coming down and we're gonna have a party*."

Confident of its commercial potential, David Bowie and Tony Visconti rerecorded the song the following year, dividing it into two parts for the two sides of a 45 rpm released on June 26, 1970.

David Bowie photographed by David Bebbington onstage
at the Beckenham Art Festival in August 1969.

THE MAN WHO SOLD THE WORLD

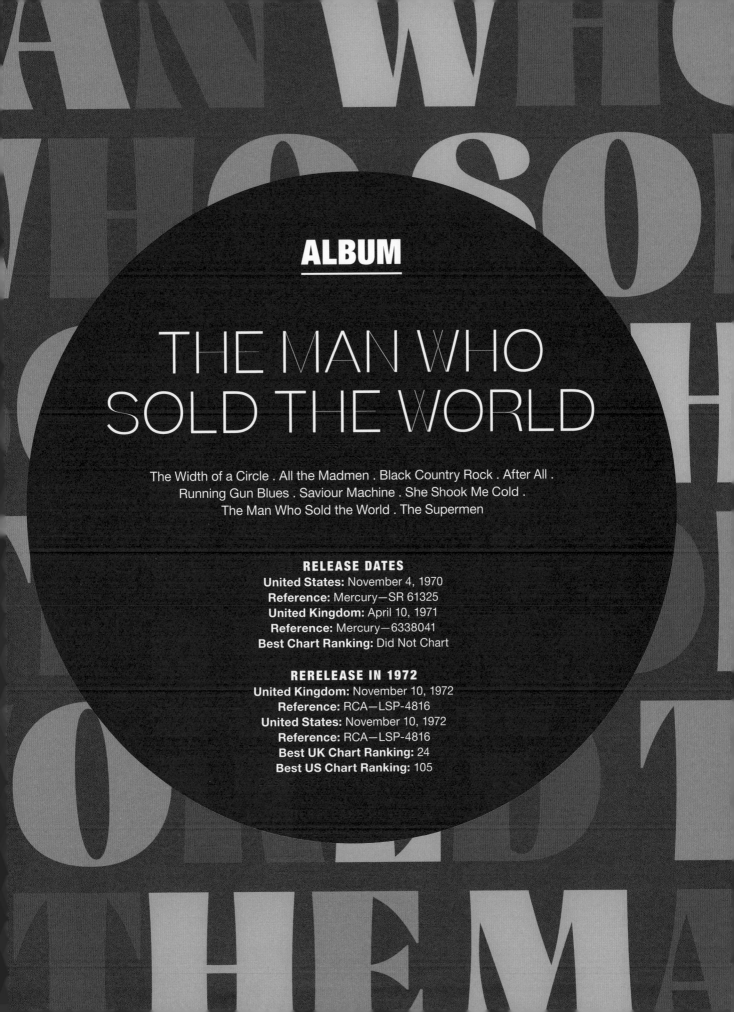

ALBUM

THE MAN WHO SOLD THE WORLD

The Width of a Circle . All the Madmen . Black Country Rock . After All .
Running Gun Blues . Saviour Machine . She Shook Me Cold .
The Man Who Sold the World . The Supermen

RELEASE DATES
United States: November 4, 1970
Reference: Mercury—SR 61325
United Kingdom: April 10, 1971
Reference: Mercury—6338041
Best Chart Ranking: Did Not Chart

RERELEASE IN 1972
United Kingdom: November 10, 1972
Reference: RCA—LSP-4816
United States: November 10, 1972
Reference: RCA—LSP-4816
Best UK Chart Ranking: 24
Best US Chart Ranking: 105

TONY VISCONTI'S HEAVY ROCK AMBITIONS

At the beginning of 1970, David Bowie had withdrawn to Haddon Hall, his sumptuous residence located in Beckenham, England. He occupied the ground floor with Angie and some friends for £7 a month, and he spent this time working to understand and accept the failure of his second album. One floor down, in the cellar, Tony Visconti had set up a rehearsal studio. Angie dealt with the decoration, scouring antique shops to furnish the residence, and she also frequently cooked for a large number of guests.

Haddon Hall, the Beckenham "Factory"

Haddon Hall was the perfect place to host meetings and friendly get-togethers, as it readily lent itself to the free-flowing exchange of ideas. "It was kind of like the London equivalent of Andy Warhol's the Factory if you want to sort of put it like that," recalled TV host Bob Harris, friend of the singer. "Kind of that's what David might have had in his mind, that it could become."[41]

Haddon Hall was also a place for new sexual experiences for the singer, and he and his companion, Angie, engaged in endless intimate adventures. "I have no idea what went on in their bedroom," declared Visconti, who lived there with his girlfriend, Liz Hartley, "except we used to be wide awake in ours hearing all the laughter and screams emanating from theirs. When their guests tried to enter our bedroom in the early hours of the morning, we knew we had to move."[29] The producer moved out in February, making way for a new arrival: the guitarist Mick Ronson.

It is difficult to determine the exact date on which Bowie and Ronson first met, but we do know that the meeting came about at the behest of John Cambridge. Some say it was on February 3, 1970, at the Marquee in London, during a Junior's Eyes concert—a group whose members were sometimes David's backup musicians—but Tony Visconti has on several occasions confirmed the presence of the guitarist at the mixing sessions for "Wild Eyed Boy from Freecloud" at Trident Studios in the summer 1969. Regardless of the exact moment when the spark

of friendship was struck, it would kindle the flame of a newly formed creative team in search of a new direction. Mick Ronson, with his wide array of musical influences and technical knowledge, would help redefine Bowie's artistic direction. "We were scratching our heads, thinking, 'How do we get a big "rock" sound for David?'" Visconti later said. "David felt very awkward up to that point. He hadn't worked with serious rock musicians. Mick was the first person we met who had dedicated his life to being a 'rock' guitarist and specializing in this genre."[42]

Rainbow Man, or the Birth of Glam Rock

While Ziggy Stardust was soon to be the most famous ambassador of the glam-rock movement, Marc Bolan was incontestably Ziggy's precursor. A touch of femininity in a testosterone-charged world of rockers was really something that turned heads in a business so focused on constant artistic renewal...and on finding new acts that would sell millions of records! Gary Glitter, Mud, Slade, Mott the Hoople, and Roxy Music can all stake their claim as early exhibitors of this musical style, which was eventually brought to the general public during an appearance of T. Rex on the popular show UK television show *Top of the Pops* in July 1971. When Bolan, the band's lead singer, performed their hit "Bang a Gong (Get It On)" with silver makeup under his eyes, England swooned and welcomed this movement with open arms. The glam-rock fad would fade away by the mid-1970s with the advent of punk. Suffice it to say, Bowie did not invent glam rock, but the trend did give him the final push he needed to achieve megastardom.

On February 22, 1970, the singer took the stage at a London nightclub called the Roundhouse, and he was accompanied by his new backing band, Hype, which consisted of Mick Ronson on guitar, Tony Visconti on bass, and John Cambridge on drums. Angie, who was often the driving force behind the team from Haddon Hall, had a few tricks up her sleeve for the event. Assisted by Liz Hartley, she designed and created costumes for the musicians who

all appeared under the pseudonyms of Gangster Man (Ronson), Hype Man (Visconti), and Cowboy Man (Cambridge). Bowie was Rainbow Man, a silver-coated character that harkened back to Major Tom from "Space Oddity." The public was not won over by the concert, and the atmosphere within the group was not good, but these disguises became their trademark as the group started to gain momentum. And so, on that fateful evening, and ever so unobtrusively, David Bowie insinuated himself into a culture that he would eventually make his own.

Angie Bowie: The Artist's Muse and Greatest Supporter

On March 20, 1970, David married Angie Barnett in Beckenham in a quick, no-nonsense ceremony that was followed by a party at Haddon Hall. Fifteen days before the

event, on March 6, the singer's new single, "The Prettiest Star," was released to the general indifference of the music-buying public. It had been written for his fiancée and recorded two months earlier. Despite the assured guitar riffs provided by Marc Bolan, the track was not successful. Visconti and Bowie remained undaunted, and on March 23 they followed up on the recording with a new version of "Memory of a Free Festival," whose commercial potential seemed uncertain. The session was marked by growing tensions between Ronson and Cambridge over the latter's drumming style, which eventually led to his replacement by another musician from the flourishing musical scene in the small town of Kingston upon Hull, England—a drummer named Mick "Woody" Woodmansey.

Bowie spent the money he made from the success of *Space Oddity* fairly liberally, doing the rounds at the

Dressed in his famous "man's dress" from Mr. Fish, Bowie poses in front of his Beckenham home, Haddon Hall.

David and his wife Angie at Haddon Hall on April 20, 1971.

London clothes and antiques shops. His musicians, on the other hand, were very far removed from this opulent lifestyle. It is true that David did give them a roof over their heads, but the end of each month was difficult. Once again, it was Angie who called upon her connections to come to the aid of her friends. The model made overtures to her friend Olav Wyper, the manager of Philips, in order to secure the musicians' financial situation. The members of Hype thus signed a contract with the label on April 7, 1970. This timely influx of funds also meant that they could buy some equipment. Work on the new David Bowie album proceeded forthwith.

Tony Defries: A New Ally for Bowie

Olav Wyper was to play an important role in David Bowie's career, particularly at the beginning of 1970.

Bowie did not hesitate to clear the decks when his career was involved, and after Ralph Horton, Leslie Conn, and John Cambridge, Ken Pitt's time had come. Without Pitt, David would certainly never have left the sphere of amateur groups from the London suburbs...but lately the artist had not been happy with the direction his career was taking. He confided in Angie, who arranged a meeting with Olav Wyper. The manager of Philips offered him a list of three legal advisers. Bowie made a selection at random, and the name he chose was Tony Defries. This lawyer, who worked with the firm Godfrey, Davis, and Batt, had walked the corridors of record companies for years, resolving various disputes between managers and record labels whenever the opportunity arose. When he met David Bowie—who had grown disillusioned over the lack of success of his various singles—the opportunity to

shine was too good to pass up. Defries orchestrated the rupture between the artist and his manager and, on May 7, 1970, he became David Bowie's legal adviser.

A New Album with a Raw and Powerful Sound

The recording sessions for the new album began at Advision Sound Studios on the night of April 17, 1970. Bowie's detachment and visible lack of interest in the creation of his new opus was flagrant, and Visconti and Ronson took up the reins of the project. While the singer loitered in the foyer of the studios with his new wife, the members of Hype were committed to the recording process. Throughout the five

weeks it took to record the album, they put in some serious work at both Trident and Advision Sound Studios. "Bowie wrote all the songs, but we three musicians [...] arranged most of them," Woodmansey wrote in 2016. "Some of the songs were just chord sequences when Bowie brought them to us. He'd say, 'This is the verse' and 'Here's the chorus' and 'Maybe we'll do this for the middle eight' and so on, so we would take what Bowie had written on a twelve-string acoustic guitar and adapt it for a rock band."[43]

The production of the album was adventurous, to say the least. Distancing himself from the very Simon and Garfunkel–esque folk stylings of *Space Oddity*, *The Man*

The singer at Haddon Hall, the day when the album sleeve photo for *The Man Who Sold the World* was shot.

Charles Berberian tells the story of Bowie's 1971 tip to America in his book *Jukebox*, published by Fluide Glacial in 2011. This talented cartoonist offers a unique perspective on the story behind the emergent Ziggy Stardust.

refrigerators, lined up by side by side,"[42] recalls the producer. This instrument is noted for its ability to produce a range of acoustic tones and sounds, which can be modified by filters, and it had a particular importance for this album, plunging David Bowie into a hitherto unknown sonic plane that was far outside his normal acoustic bearings.

From an artistic perspective, the experience was an enriching one for Visconti and Ronson, but the distance it placed between the producer and Bowie cost them their friendship. As the singer seemed to be placing his destiny in the hands of Tony Defries, Visconti (who did not warm to the lawyer) decided to abandon ship. The lack of interest that his friend had shown in the recording of his own album was in stark contrast with the commitment Marc Bolan had to T. Rex, and Visconti had already been working with the band for many years. While Bowie seemed to be on a search for stardom, Bolan took his victories from creating impactful rock anthems that were the fruits of a lot of hard work. The die was cast, and Visconti was to become the man for just one project: T. Rex. Sometime later, Bowie, Ronson (who temporarily assumed the role of bass player), and Wood-mansey went to Birmingham to do a three-handed concert. But tired of the lack of consideration they were being shown by the singer, his two musicians changed their itinerary at the last minute and went back to Hull. On that day, David Bowie played the concert on his own, without a producer, a manager, or any musicians.

As the summer neared its end, only Angie was there to help keep David on the straight and narrow for the purposes of promoting his next album. Tony Defries was notable only through his absence, as he'd suddenly become very busy trying to sign Stevie Wonder. But, despite her best intentions, Angie was barely able to secure any concert dates that would be worth playing.

In September, back at Haddon Hall, Bowie organized one of his most famous photo shoots with Keith McMillan. Wearing a man's dress that Angie had managed to find for him at Mr. Fish, the shop run by the couturier Michael Fish on Clifford Street, the artist assumed a seductive approach to the camera, adopting a pose inspired by the paintings of the Pre-Raphaelite master Dante Gabriel Rossetti. As all of this was happening, Bowie's contract with Essex

Who Sold the World toys with the hard-rock tones of Led Zeppelin on "Black Country Rock" and "Running Gun Blues," as well as the smoky atmospheres of Pink Floyd on "After All" and the blues rock sizzle of Jimi Hendrix on "She Shook Me Cold." "The album is my favourite album I've ever produced," confided Tony Visconti in 2017. "It's adventurous, we broke all the rules; we just threw caution to the wind."[1] The incisive playing of Ronson, Visconti's overmixed bass, and the brutal beat of Woodmansey were supported on the keyboards by Ralph Mace, who had overlaid Bowie's music with a new, revolutionary instrument: "We had one of those 200-lb. Moog synthesizers. It looked like four black

Publishing was coming to an end, and the singer decided to join Chrysalis, a promising young music company.

The Split with Mercury

No release date was announced in the United Kingdom, but David Bowie's new album came out in the United States on November 4, 1970. The artist was furious, however, because no one on the Mercury Records management team followed the instructions he had given for the American jacket design of his magnum opus. In consultation with the musician, Mike Weller, a friend from the Beckenham Arts Lab, the singer had created an illustration representing a John Wayne–like figure from the 1950s parading around with a gun under his arm in front of Cane Hill Hospital, where Terry, Bowie's half brother, was living at the time. A word balloon containing the text *"Roll up your sleeves take a look at your arms"* emanated from the character's mouth, and the name of the album was *Metrobolist*, a reference to the film *Metropolis* directed by Fritz Lang (1927). The instructions were clear: Weller's design was to appear on the reverse and a photo by Keith McMillan that showed the singer posing lasciviously and lying on a sofa with playing cards in his hand was to be shown on the inside of the gatefold. The reverse was meant to show a montage of various photographs and a drawing by Mike Weller. When Bowie discovered that none of his requirements had been adhered to, he was apoplectic. While the jacket did show Weller's drawing, his signature and the text that was meant to be included in the speech bubble had both been dropped, and most egregiously, the name of the album had been changed without the singer's consent! The suits at Mercury Records had renamed David Bowie's third album *The Man Who Sold the World*. The label's UK branch was also unable to provide a release date, and this ultimately led to the end of the collaboration between Bowie and Mercury Records.

The Trip to the United States

In the midst of all this chaos, Tony Defries decided to break the contract between the singer and his label in January of 1971. In order to demonstrate his abilities in managing his client's career, the lawyer arranged for the two of them to take a trip to America. As he did not have the necessary work visa required for giving concerts, Bowie took advantage of this outing, which lasted several weeks, as a chance to promote his third album. While he was abroad, he met Tom Ayres, a producer with RCA. Quickly seduced by his new environment, Bowie recorded a number of demos with Ayres. A friendly relationship was established between the two men, which was later cemented into a strong collaboration. In defiance of the law, the singer gave his first, unofficial transatlantic concert during his trip with Defries. At a party arranged by the lawyer Paul Feigen on

Bowie's fancy footwork was immortalized on the album sleeve of *The Man Who Sold the World,* which was reissued by RCA in 1972.

The reissue of the album by RCA in November 1972 presented a David Bowie in a vigorous action pose, with his left leg high in the air and a guitar slung over his shoulder. This was a nod to his couturier friend Freddie Burretti, who had assumed a similar pose for his brochure in July 1972.

February 14, 1971, David Bowie perched on a mattress wearing a suit and performed some of his songs, including "Space Oddity" and "Amsterdam" by the Belgian singer Jacques Brel, whom Bowie had long admired. Some of the guests who were present that evening did not know that they were attending a significant event, and they did not pay attention to the artist. One of the guests, however, was the radio presenter Rodney Bingenheimer, and he fell under the artist's spell: "I'd never seen anyone look like that, and at the same time he was friendly, real funny, very positive. He was talking a lot about this creation he was thinking of writing songs for, an alter ego, Ziggy Stardust."[1]

His time in America inspired Bowie in the creation of his most famous alter ego. It also gave him a certain confidence in his art and in his status as a rising star, which was something that his native country still seemed to be denying him. "I became disillusioned after 'Space Oddity,'" he commented later. "The album was released at the same time and did absolutely nothing. No-one even bothered to review it and I'm convinced that some of the tracks were really good. [...] The only thing that gave me faith again was being asked to go across to America. [...] In America, although you might not believe it, I'm regarded as an underground artist."[22]

On his return to England, David Bowie and his wife Angie prepared for the arrival of their first child, expected in May. Meanwhile, *The Man Who Sold the World* finally appeared in the United Kingdom on April 10, 1971.

The Prettiest Star / Conversation Piece

UK Release on Mercury: March 6, 1970 (ref. MF 1135)
Best Chart Ranking: Did Not Chart

With hits like "Get It On," "Hot Love," or "20th Century Boy," Marc Bolan, creator of the glam movement, left his mark on the history of rock.

FOR BOWIE ADDICTS

"The Prettiest Star" is the only studio collaboration between Bowie and Bolan. The duo was reunited on the set of the TV music series *Marc*, during which Bolan invited his musician friends, including Bowie, to create some new collaborations in 1977. The T. Rex singer was killed in a road accident just a few days before the broadcast aired on September 28, 1977.

THE PRETTIEST STAR

David Bowie / 3:13

Musicians: David Bowie: vocals, acoustic guitar / Marc Bolan: electric guitar / Tony Visconti: bass / Godfrey McLean: drums, percussion / Derek Easton: organ / Unidentified Musicians: orchestra / **Recorded:** Trident Studios, London: January 8, 13, and 15, 1970 / **Technical Team:** Producer: Tony Visconti / **Sound Engineers:** Ken Scott, Barry Sheffield / **Arrangements:** Tony Visconti

Before appearing on *Aladdin Sane* in 1973 with rockabilly arrangements, "The Prettiest Star" was released as a single in March 1970. On January 8 of the same year, a recording session was booked at Trident Studios to give the public a new David Bowie single, after his album, *Space Oddity*, had appeared a few months before to an overwhelmingly indifferent reception. Two numbers were immortalized during the January 8 recording session: "The Prettiest Star," a ballad with a repetitive but addictive guitar riff, and a new version of "London Bye Ta-Ta," which the singer had previously recorded in the spring of 1968. This was not used for the single's B-side, but was replaced, in extremis, by "Conversation Piece." It did appear several years later on various different reissues and compilations.

The recording session was marked by the involvement of Marc Bolan, the singer behind the famous group Tyrannosaurus Rex (soon to be renamed T. Rex). Equipped with a Fender Stratocaster with an astonishing bite to its sound, he recorded a light and catchy riff for the song, but his contribution was limited, and he left the studio once his guitar parts had been recorded. The song was not a success when it was released. This was another disappointment for Bowie; not only was the public unimpressed by this rather timeless ballad, but the media was also completely indifferent. "I think a lot of people are expecting another 'Space Oddity,'" the singer said regretfully, in the columns of *Melody Maker*, "and 'Prettiest Star' is nothing like it. I'm sure this is why the BBC aren't plugging it. Everyone wanted another song with the same feel as 'Space Oddity' but as I'd done it, I didn't see the point of doing it again."[44]

CONVERSATION PIECE

David Bowie / 3:06

Musicians: David Bowie: vocals, twelve-string acoustic guitar / Mick Wayne: electric guitar / John Cambridge: drums / John Lodge: bass / Unidentified Musicians: orchestra / **Recorded:** Trident Studios, London: August–September 1969 / **Technical Team:** Producer: Tony Visconti / **Arrangements:** Tony Visconti

Dropped from the second album, "Conversation Piece" is a curiosity with a country sound, supported by the guitar of Mick Wayne and played with a bottleneck. This is a charming and effective number, and could rightfully have had a place on the disc. It was selected for the B-side of "The Prettiest Star" at the expense of the new version of "London Bye Ta-Ta."

LONDON BYE TA-TA

David Bowie / 2:35

Musicians: David Bowie: vocals, twelve-string acoustic guitar /
Mick Wayne: electric guitar / **Delisle Harper:** bass / **Godfrey McLean:**
drums, percussion / **Derek Easton:** organ / **Rick Wakeman:** piano /
Susan Glover: backing vocals / **Heather Wheatman:** backing vocals /
Lesley Duncan: backing vocals / **Unidentified Musicians:** orchestra /
Recorded: Trident Studios, London: January 8, 13, and 15, 1970 /
Technical Team: Producer: Tony Visconti / **Sound Engineers:**
Ken Scott, Barry Sheffield / **Arrangements:** Tony Visconti

The first version of "London Bye Ta-Ta" was recorded in
spring 1968, while Bowie and his manager were desperately trying to convince Decca of the commercial potential of the artist's new songs. This was a fruitless attempt,
but Tony Visconti felt that this very effective piece of rock
music deserved a more fully developed production. This
number, which had been seriously considered for the
B-side of the single "The Prettiest Star," was finally
replaced by a by-product of the *Space Oddity* sessions:
"Conversation Piece." "London Bye Ta-Ta" would reappear in 1989 on the box set *Sound + Vision*, which offers
quite a few rarities for the enjoyment of the fans. Although
recorded on the same day as "The Prettiest Star" at London's Trident Studios, this new version of "London Bye
Ta-Ta" has no guitar line by Marc Bolan. Encouraged by
his fiancée, June Child, who did not trust Bowie, Bolan
had left the premises well before the team started on the
takes for this second number.

THE WIDTH OF A CIRCLE

David Bowie / 8:04

ON YOUR HEADPHONES

At 5:36, observant listeners will recognize a bluesy riff in Ronson's playing, which would eventually be remodeled and used again in "The Jean Genie," on the album *Aladdin Sane*, in 1973.

Musicians

David Bowie: vocals, twelve-string acoustic guitar
Mick Ronson: electric guitar, backing vocals
Tony Visconti: bass
Mick "Woody" Woodmansey: drums, timbales

Recorded

Trident Studios and Advision Sound Studios, London: April 17, 1970–May 22, 1970

Technical Team

Producer: Tony Visconti
Sound Engineer, Trident Studios: Ken Scott
Sound Engineers, Advision Sound Studios: Gerald Chevin, Eddie Offord

Genesis

The title "The Width of a Circle" takes its name from the drawing that George Underwood, David Bowie's childhood friend, made in 1969 to illustrate the reverse side of the album *Space Oddity*. Psychedelia and spirituality are at the heart of the song, which in its middle section quotes the successful writer Kahlil Gibran, whose famous collection of poetic essays, *The Prophet*, was much liked by Bowie: "*So we asked a simple black bird, who was happy as can be/And he laughed insane and quipped 'Kahlil Gibran.'*" "I went to the depths of myself in that,"[26] Bowie confided. But it is difficult to fathom the soul of the author through this mysterious and elusive text.

Production

When he joined the Bowie stable, Mick Ronson did not disguise his admiration for Cream. The precise playing of Eric Clapton, the brutal beat of Ginger Baker, and omnipresent bass of Jack Bruce were all influences that Ronno had absorbed and used to maximum effect on *The Man Who Sold the World*, while he was acting as its unofficial coproducer alongside Visconti. The album jacket may have Bowie in a traditionally feminine pose, but the first notes of the disc, in all their aggressive power, were at complete odds with this image. Therein lies the paradox of this opus, which both the critics and the public found difficult to pin down upon its release. As Bowie was only partly involved in its production, the duo at the controls gave expression to a bluesy rock sound that was reminiscent of Jeff Beck and sometimes even verged on the hard rock intonations of Led Zeppelin or Deep Purple. They also added a spontaneity to the music that Cream would not have been unhappy with. "We had been playing 'A [*sic*] Width of a Circle' live, but we felt like it needed another section," Visconti said later. "[...] We listened to a playback of the boogie jam for a laugh, and we decided to make this as a permanent part of the song."[35] The producer left in a few "la la las" in the track's middle section, at 5:11, pending rewrites from Bowie that never appeared.

Writer and poet Khalil Gibran, whose book *The Prophet* made such an impression on David Bowie.

1970

Single

ALL THE MADMEN

David Bowie / 5:36

Musicians

David Bowie: vocals, twelve-string acoustic guitar, backing vocals, spoken word
Mick Ronson: electric guitar, backing vocals, recorder (?)
Tony Visconti: bass, recorder
Mick "Woody" Woodmansey: drums
Ralph Mace: Moog synthesizer

Recorded

Trident Studios and Advision Sound Studios, London: April 17, 1970—May 22, 1970

Technical Team

Producer: Tony Visconti
Flutes Arrangements: Mike Ronson
Sound Engineer, Trident Studios: Ken Scott
Sound Engineers, Advision Sound Studios: Gerald Chevin, Eddie Offord

SIDE A: *All the Madmen*
SIDE B: *Janine*
US Release on Mercury: December 1, 1970 (ref. 73173)
Best Chart Ranking: Did Not Chart

Cane Hill Hospital, where Terry Burns, David Bowie's half brother, was a patient.

Genesis

In 1970, Terry Burns, David's half brother, was admitted as an inpatient to Cane Hill Hospital, a psychiatric institution located thirty minutes to the south of Beckenham. In "All the Madmen," the singer, speaking on behalf of Terry, gives a new interpretation of the bipolar problems from which Terry suffered. With his lyrics, Bowie suggests that perhaps the sanest people in a society are those who are willing to confront their own madness. "'All the Madmen' was written for my brother and it's about my brother," Bowie indicated in 1971. "He's the man inside, and he doesn't want to leave. He's perfectly happy there—perfectly happy: Doesn't have to work, just lies there on the lawn all day, looking at the sky. He's very happy."[26] But beyond the homage to Terry, David Bowie opens up here about one of his own personal, recurring struggles: feeling too closely linked with insanity, which had been a blight on his own family. He confided to the BBC in 1993 that his status as an artist preserved him from a state of alienation into which he feared he could fall at any moment: "As long as I could put those psychological excesses into my music and into my work I could always be throwing it off."[29] His brother Terry escaped from Cane Hill in 1985 and jumped onto the tracks at Coulsdon train station. He was forty-seven.

Much ink has also been spilled on another subject, one fueled by exchanges between fans and the pens of biographers: the repetition of the phrase "Zane, zane, zane, ouvre le chien" at the end of the song. Nicholas Pegg suggests in his work *The Complete David Bowie* that this is a reference to *Thus Spake Zarathustra* by Friedrich Nietzsche, in which the German philosopher writes: "Thy wild dogs want liberty; they bark for joy in their cellar when thy spirit endeavoureth to open all prison doors."[45] Knowing the interest that Bowie had at that time in the work of Nietzsche, it is certain that he would not have been able to remain indifferent to such an image when he decided to write for Terry. The phrase is used again at the end of "Buddha of Suburbia" in 1993, and it was projected on the stage during the *Outside* tour in 1995, this time using the imperative, as though to better convey the injunction to the thousands of spectators: "Ouvrez le chien!"

Robert Moog poses in front of his invention: the Moog synthesizer, which revolutionized the music world in the 1970s.

Production

While the production of "All the Madmen" included some surprises in the use of some sound devices, including the voice of a child at 2:40—here Bowie revisits the gag used in the single "The Laughing Gnome"—the great novelty in this song was the heavy use of the Moog synthesizer. "The synth was a passion of mine at the time,"[29] confided Tony Visconti. Presented to the public by its inventor, Robert Moog, in 1968, this revolutionary electronic instrument aroused unprecedented interest on the international musical scene, following the release of the disc *Switched-on Bach*, on which the pianist Wendy Carlos used the instrument to reinterpret the repertoire of Johann Sebastian Bach. But this was not a docile beast, and taming it was not a straightforward matter. Ralph Mace, a production manager at Philips with whom Bowie and Visconti had got on well during the promotion of *Space Oddity*, was the one who saved the day for the group, proving unable to use the multiple functions of the Moog they had hired for the sessions. "And that's how I became a Spider From Mars,"[46] Mace commented with amusement in 2013, referring to the group that was about to join the singer onstage.

ON YOUR HEADPHONES

If you listen carefully: The riff played by Mick Ronson at 4:15 will be used again by Tony Visconti in the string arrangements for "Five Years," at 1:58, on the album *The Rise and Fall of Ziggy Stardust and the Spiders from Mars*. Jimmy Page, for his part, adapted this artifice to an Asian-inspired sound at 1:20 of Led Zeppelin's masterpiece "Kashmir" in 1975.

BLACK COUNTRY ROCK

David Bowie / 3:33

Musicians: David Bowie: vocals, twelve-string acoustic guitar / Mick Ronson: electric guitar, backing vocals / Tony Visconti: bass, piano / Mick "Woody" Woodmansey: drums, tambourine / **Recorded:** Trident Studios and Advision Studios, London: April 17, 1970–May 22, 1970 / **Technical Team:** Producer: Tony Visconti / Sound Engineer, Trident Studios: Ken Scott / Sound Engineers, Advision Sound Studios: Gerald Chevin, Eddie Offord

The spirit of Jimi Hendrix floats over this blues-rock number, marked by the trenchant riffs of Mick Ronson. Tony Visconti, producer of the opus and bassist during the recording sessions, used this as justification of his belief that his instrument was overmixed throughout the LP: "Mick's idols were Cream. He coached Woody to play like Ginger Baker and me to play like Jack Bruce. David was loving the sound of his new band."[47] He detailed his thoughts on this in another interview: "If you have complaints that the bass is too high in the mix, blame Ronno."[35] While the instrumental tapes were recorded quickly, they had to wait for the lyrics, which annoyed Visconti greatly. Bowie had to resolve to write a text at the last minute, and based on a working title, which was "Black Country Rock." But he had neither the time nor the inclination to complete his work, which is why the couplets and refrains repeat throughout the song.

The cover of the score for the song "Oh By Jingo!" (1919), which was quoted in "After All." The song was a big Tin Pan Alley hit in the period after WWI, but its othering of distant cultures means it has not aged well.

AFTER ALL

David Bowie / 3:50

Musicians: David Bowie: vocals, twelve-string acoustic guitar, Stylophone / Mick Ronson: electric guitar, backing vocals / Tony Visconti: bass, recorder / Mick "Woody" Woodmansey: drums / Ralph Mace: Moog synthesizer / **Recorded:** Trident Studios and Advision Studios, London: April 17, 1970–May 22, 1970 / **Technical Team:** Producer: Tony Visconti / Sound Engineer, Trident Studios: Ken Scott / Sound Engineers, Advision Sound Studios: Gerald Chevin, Eddie Offord

Reminiscent of the folk ballads on *Space Oddity*, "After All" borrows as much from the world of Pink Floyd (one thinks of the somber psychedelia of "If" or "Fat Old Sun," which appeared in the same year on the album *Atom Heart Mother*) as from *Sgt. Pepper's Lonely Hearts Club Band* by the Beatles, which buried David Bowie's first album on the charts in June 1967. How can one not see in the fairground musical interlude at 1:56 an homage—or borrowing, whichever one chooses—from "Being for the Benefit of Mr. Kite" by the Liverpool four? Other hat tips are lurking in this melancholic track, which seem to be jibes at the past experiences of the singer. Is he referring to the adventure of the Riot Squad when he sings *"We're painting our faces and dressing in thoughts from the skies"*? Is he questioning the

hippie values that pervaded at the Beckenham Arts Lab with *"Some people are marching together and some on their own / Quite alone / Others are running, the smaller ones crawl"*? Repeated like a mantra at the end of each phrase, the formula *"Oh by Jingo"* is a reference to a song written in 1919 by Albert von Tilzer and Lew Brown for the musical comedy *Linger Longer Letty*, whose main subject is a young woman courted by all the men in the town of Santo Domingo, in the Dominican Republic. The actress Debbie Reynolds and two men are shown singing this phrase in the Mike Weller illustration that appears on the back of the American version of *The Man Who Sold the World*.

RUNNING GUN BLUES

David Bowie / 3:11

Musicians: David Bowie: vocals, twelve-string acoustic guitar, harmonica / Mick Ronson: electric guitar, backing vocals / Tony Visconti: bass / Mick "Woody" Woodmansey: drums, tambourine, timbales / Ralph Mace: Moog synthesizer / **Recorded:** Trident Studios and Advision Sound Studios, London: May 4–22, 1970 / **Technical Team:** Producer: Tony Visconti / Sound Engineer, Trident Studios: Ken Scott / Sound Engineers, Advision Sound Studios: Gerald Chevin, Eddie Offord

Lieutenant William Calley at his initial hearing for the murder of hundreds of Vietnamese civilians during the My Lai massacre in 1968.

Allusions to the military world are recurrent in the early compositions of David Bowie, who was born only two years after the end of World War II. But compared to the antimilitary manifesto of "Running Gun Blues," his previous songs like "Little Bombardier," "She's Got Medals," or "Rubber Band" were just nice little stories. The assassination of sixteen people by Charles Whitman, a former marine, at the University of Texas on August 1, 1966, is doubtless the event that inspired this song about the murderous folly of men. But the artist was also haunted by another massacre perpetuated by the regiment of Lieutenant William Calley in the village of My Lai, in Vietnam, on March 16, 1968. On this day, nearly five hundred people were executed in cold blood, including nine at the hands of Calley. His trial, which received international coverage, had significant consequences for public opinion, which was already hostile to the Vietnam War. The narrator in "Running Gun Blues" is styled in the same mold as the perpetrator of this massacre: He is nostalgic for the years spent spreading terror at the front. *"It seems the peacefuls stopped the war / Left generals squashed and stifled,"* he complains, determined to kill some civilians with a weapon not handed in after the war ended.

SAVIOUR MACHINE

David Bowie / 4:25

Musicians: David Bowie: vocals, twelve-string acoustic guitar / **Mick Ronson:** electric guitar, backing vocals / **Tony Visconti:** bass / **Mick "Woody" Woodmansey:** drums / **Ralph Mace:** Moog synthesizer / **Recorded:** Trident Studios and Advision Sound Studios, London: May 4–22, 1970 / **Technical Team: Producer:** Tony Visconti / **Sound Engineer, Trident Studios:** Ken Scott / **Sound Engineers, Advision Sound Studios:** Gerald Chevin, Eddie Offord

"Saviour Machine" plunges us back into a dystopic world, overwhelmed by the totalitarian power of an imaginary leader, an obsession of Bowie's, who sometimes liked to play with fire in the declarations he made to journalists. In 1976, he went so far as to announce: "As I see it I am the only alternative for the premier in England."[48] But when he wrote "Saviour Machine" in 1970, the singer had not yet made these provocative outbursts that made him a celebrity during his American exile in the mid-1970s. For the time being, his words were those of an artist nervous about the world that surrounded him and who had taken refuge in his Beckenham palace, among his disciples, who were all committed to doing what he expected of them. The malaise generated by the singer in this number is reinforced by the presence of an omnipresent Moog, which unfurls rapid arpeggios, precursors of the sound experiments of Wendy Carlos for the original soundtrack of the film *A Clockwork Orange* (1972), directed by Stanley Kubrick.

SHE SHOOK ME COLD

David Bowie / 4:12

Musicians: David Bowie: vocals / **Mick Ronson:** electric guitar / **Tony Visconti:** bass / **Mick "Woody" Woodmansey:** drums / **Recorded:** Trident Studios and Advision Sound Studios, London: April 17, 1970–May 22, 1970 / **Technical Team: Producer:** Tony Visconti / **Sound Engineer, Trident Studios:** Ken Scott / **Sound Engineers, Advision Sound Studios:** Gerald Chevin, Eddie Offord

The use of the Cry Baby wah-wah pedal by Mike Ronson turns "She Shook Me Cold" into a seeming homage to "Voodoo Child (Slight Return)" by Jimi Hendrix. The effect is emphasized from the introduction by Bowie's vocals, covered with drum rolls from Woodmansey. The listener is then treated to a deluge of riffs, which also created a certain amount of enthusiasm among the team: "The two guys I was working with [...] are semi-pro musicians from the North," the singer explained shortly afterward with amusement. "They had a lot of trouble with my stuff 'cause they're blues freaks, ah, and it's all very hard and ultra-masculine stuff, so I thought I'd write one for them. And they loved it; they played their guts out on it!"[49] Woodmansey confirmed this: "For me, this album was Bowie jumping into rock 'n' roll with both feet."[43]

Convinced of Lulu's talent,
David Bowie was determined
to make her a pop star.

THE MAN WHO
SOLD THE WORLD

David Bowie / 3:55

Musicians
David Bowie: vocals, twelve-string acoustic guitar, backing vocals
Mick Ronson: electric guitar, backing vocals
Tony Visconti: bass
Mick "Woody" Woodmansey: drums, güiro, percussion
Ralph Mace: Moog synthesizer

Recorded
Trident Studios and Advision Sound Studios, London: April 17,
1970–May 22, 1970

Technical Team
Producer: Tony Visconti
Sound Engineer, Trident Studios: Ken Scott
Sound Engineers, Advision Sound Studios: Gerald Chevin,
Eddie Offord

The American writer Robert A. Heinlein, one of the fathers of science
fiction, and from whom David Bowie borrowed the title for his song.

Genesis

Although this haunting midtempo ballad is now considered
to be one of the singer's most important compositions, it
could have had a very different outcome. There was nothing
to suggest that "The Man Who Sold the World" would be
used as the album title because David Bowie had previously
stipulated that the disc should be called *Metrobolist*. The
decision by the Mercury label to make this the title track of
Bowie's third album focused the spotlight on this song with
its irresistible melody and arrangements. These same
arrangements were popularized by Nirvana on their live
acoustic album *MTV Unplugged in New York* in November
1994, where they became a grunge anthem.

But at the time of its original recording, this song was
not Bowie's top priority. Tony Visconti had to repeatedly
chase the singer for his lyrics while he was busy loitering
in the corridors of Trident Studios with his young wife,
Angie, instead of getting on with the task at hand. When
the last day of mixing arrived, on May 22, 1970, Bowie was
being hounded by Visconti, who was tired of having to
wait for him to get to work. Even before knowing what the
song was really about, Bowie decided on a title inspired by
the novella *The Man Who Sold the Moon* (1950) by Robert
A. Heinlein. The novella tells the story of the colonization
of the moon by humans. The rest came to Bowie naturally,
and in a continuous flow he unfolded the text of his masterpiece. The subject matter was debated for a long time,
but Bowie is doubtless singing about his encounter with a
double, in a near future, and is thus initiating his first personality duplication. *"We passed upon the stair / We spoke
of was and when / Although I wasn't there / He said I was
his friend."* In January 1971, in answer to the journalist
John Swanson who asked him: "What is David Bowie?" the
singer, whose taste for the unexpected was becoming well-
known by this time (and which he worked hard to cultivate
over the following decade), replied: "What is David Bowie?
David Bowie is the image, David Jones is me."[49]

Production

Behind the timeless riff of "The Man Who Sold the World" is
Mick Ronson, the guitarist of Hype, Bowie's new backing
band. Recorded during the last working session at Advision

Sound Studios, the voice is covered with a phaser effect more often used by the producers on Charleston drum tracks, or guitar riffs. This effect adds a mysterious aspect to the track that is perfectly suited to the text. With the percussion, the real curiosity lies in the instruments used by Mick Woodmansey. "I remember the day Tony brought me a güiro," as the drummer confided. "[...] He obviously assumed that I knew about percussion, but I looked at this hollow cylinder, with ridges down one side and a hole at the end, and thought, 'What the fuck do I do with this?' 'Do I blow across the hole?' I asked. He said 'No, you prat!' and gave me a stick to rub across the ridges, producing a ratchet sound."**43**

FOR BOWIE ADDICTS

In 1973, David Bowie offered Lulu, the famous Scottish actress, singer, and television presenter a disco version of "The Man Who Sold the World," which was as surprising as it was convincing. "I want to record you. I'm gonna make a big hit record with you,"**50** he assured her. The promise was kept: The track reached third place on the British charts in January 1974.

THE SUPERMEN

David Bowie / 3:37

Musicians

David Bowie: vocals, twelve-string acoustic guitar
Mick Ronson: electric guitar, backing vocals
Tony Visconti: bass
Mick "Woody" Woodmansey: drums, timbales

Recorded

Trident Studios and Advision Sound Studios, London: March 23, 1970; April 17, 1970–May 22, 1970

Technical Team

Producer: Tony Visconti
Sound Engineer, Trident Studios: Ken Scott
Sound Engineers, Advision Sound Studios: Gerald Chevin, Eddie Offord

FOR BOWIE ADDICTS

Bowie decided to rerecord the song on November 12, 1971, in order to give it a new clarity. The new version, with a more folksy feel, has the sound of the Spiders from Mars, and appeared on the compilation *Revelations: A Musical Anthology for Glastonbury Fayre*, intended to promote the British festival where the singer performed on June 24, 1972.

Genesis

With a fascination for the writings of the philosopher Friedrich Nietzsche and his concept of the "superman" ("*Übermensch*"), the singer provides a song that picks up on this idea, but with a more fantastical rather than a philosophical approach. When asked to explain his own ideas surrounding the writing of this album, Bowie alluded to an excessive consumption of cannabis: "*The Man Who Sold the World* is actually the most drug-oriented album I've made. That was when I was the most fucked up. [...] *The Man* was when I was holding on to some kind of flag for hashish. As soon as I stopped using that drug, I realized it dampened my imagination. End of slow drugs."[51]

Production

With a heavy impact like an army banging the drums to instill courage in its combatants, "The Supermen" is driven by Mick Woodmansey striking drums and timbales with power and precision. The guitar riff is a gift from Jimmy Page, who in 1965 was a young session guitarist at the recording sessions for "I Pity the Fool" at the IBC Studios, on January 15, 1965. While David and his group the Manish Boys were recording their new single, a young session guitarist called Jimmy Page had been recruited to provide the number with a solo for which he had the secret. Between two takes, the virtuoso said to the singer: "Look, I've got this riff but I'm not using it for anything so why don't you learn it and see if you can do anything with it?"[47] Like a good student, David did it. He reused this gimmick on "The Supermen," then on "Dead Man Walking," on the album *Earthling*, in 1997.

The writings of the German philosopher and poet Friedrich Nietzsche (1844–1900) were an influence in some of Bowie's songwriting.

Memory of a Free Festival Part 1 / Memory of a Free Festival Part 2
UK release on Mercury: June 26, 1970 (ref. 6052 026) / Best Chart Ranking: Did Not Chart

Side A

MEMORY OF A FREE FESTIVAL

David Bowie / 4:02

Musicians
David Bowie: vocals, twelve-string acoustic guitar, Rosedale organ, backing vocals
Mick Ronson: electric guitar, backing vocals
Tony Visconti: bass
John Cambridge: drums
Ralph Mace: Moog synthesizer
Marc Bolan: backing vocals
Bob Harris: backing vocals
Sue Harris: backing vocals
Tony Woollcott: backing vocals
Girl: backing vocals

Recorded
Trident Studios, London: March 21 and 23; April 4, 1970
Advision Sound Studios, London: April 3, 14, 15, 1970

Technical Team
Producer: Tony Visconti

SIDE A: *Memory of a Free Festival Part 1*
SIDE B: *Memory of a Free Festival Part 2*

A young music fan dances in front of the emblematic pyramid stage at famous Glastonbury Festival, in June 1971.

Genesis

The recording of this new version of "Memory of a Free Festival" is divided into two parts with a view to a single format and was marked by tensions that would bring to an end the collaboration between David Bowie and his drummer John Cambridge. Once the single had been recorded, the musicians launched into the writing of a new number, "The Supermen," but the rhythmic pattern caused Cambridge difficulties. Mick Ronson, who was already thinking of suggesting Mike "Woody" Woodmansey to replace him, blames the drummer for time lost in this session. Taking the advice of his new guitarist friend, Bowie split with Cambridge and welcomed Woodmansey with open arms into Hype. Since then, Cambridge constantly had to remind people of his role on this recording: "When it came out, it was like, 'This is Woody's first thing,' but he didn't do it. That's me playing, not Woody. But he's credited with playing on it."[13] The song did not appeal to the public on its release as a single on June 26, 1970, in Great Britain, and only a promotional record was issued in the United States.

Production

During these recording sessions, the Moog synthesizer made its appearance in David Bowie's musical world. The artist, who was doing his best to sing while playing some chords on his Rosedale organ—which had a blower as loud as a hair dryer—was incapable of handling the multiple functionalities of the Moog. Ralph Mace, one of the Philips staff with whom Visconti got on well, was enlisted to help. "The Moog part for 'Memory of a Free Festival' was a little tricky," recalled Mace. "It needed pianistic fingers and none of the group made a very good job of it. I suggested to David [...] to let me have a stab at it. David smiled and nodded and I sat down in front of a Moog for the first time. My fingers were in pretty good shape and after a couple of trial runs we had the part in the can. Then the parts from several other tracks appeared and I put those tracks down too."[46]

Holy Holy / Black Country Rock

UK release on Mercury: January 15, 1971 (ref. 6052 049) / Best Chart Ranking: Did Not Chart

Side A

HOLY HOLY

David Bowie / 3:10

Musicians
David Bowie: vocals, guitar
Alan Parker: electric guitar
Herbie Flowers: bass
Barry Morgan: drums

Recorded
Island Studios, London: November 9, 13, and 16, 1970

Technical Team
Producer: Herbie Flowers

SIDE A: *Holy Holy*
SIDE B: *Black Country Rock*

Chris Blackwell, founder of Island Records, whose studios hosted Bowie for a number of sessions in November 1970.

Genesis

In autumn 1970, the contract between David Bowie and his publisher Essex was coming to an end. Laurence Myers—whose artist support structure, GEM Management, was associated from that point with Tony Defries and the development of the singer's career—presented him with an ally of some stature: Bob Grace, newly recruited by the music publishing company Chrysalis. Grace was won over by Bowie's new songs and added him to his catalogue of successful writers on October 23, 1970. It was "Holy Holy," a rock curiosity, that the team decided to record straightaway and that would be distributed by Mercury on January 15 the following year. Except for a television airing on *Six-O-One: Newsday*, where the singer accompanied himself alone on the guitar, the single was given very little promotion. On January 23, 1971, the artist flew off to the United States, where he was involved with promoting his third album.

Production

The recording session took place at Island Studios in London. This complex, created by Chris Blackwell in the building that housed the offices of his Island Records label, was renamed Basing Street in 1976. The biggest stars of the 1970s would immortalize their songs here (Bob Marley and the Wailers, the Rolling Stones, and Led Zeppelin). This was a first for David Bowie, who was accustomed to working in his usual way at Trident Studios. Herbie Flowers, who played bass on *Space Oddity*, was tasked with producing this number, following the departure of Visconti for new adventures with T. Rex. Flowers suggested that the musicians of his group, Blue Mink, should accompany Bowie: Barry Morgan was on drums and Alan Parker on guitar. This was not the famous producer of *The Wall* or *Midnight Express*, but the no less talented session musician who accompanied Serge Gainsbourg on his concept album *L'Homme à tête de chou* in 1976. The production, which was rather shaky and lacking in real artistic direction, struggled to please, even though the song was not without merit and had the stamp of a Bowie at a stage of rapid transformation, definitively leaving folk style behind for the glam rock look and sound that would make his name. As usual, the singer recorded a second (much more convincing) version in the autumn of 1971, after the working sessions on the album *The Rise and Fall of Ziggy Stardust and the Spiders from Mars* had already started.

MICK RONSON: THE MAN BEHIND THE SPIDERS FROM MARS

Everything suggested that it was little Michael Ronson's destiny to reach great heights. Born May 26, 1946, in Hull, nearly two hundred miles north of London, Mick grew up in the ruins of a port town destroyed by the Axis forces during World War II. His father, George, although affectionate, ruled the house with a rod of iron. Minnie, his mother, was receptive to the little blond kid who already showed leanings toward playing music from an early age. When he was five, Mick had his first piano lessons on the family instrument.

From Violin to Six-String Guitar

While attending the Maybury primary school, the young music lover learned the violin, with which he parted company after a few years due to the jeering he suffered walking down the street with the instrument under his arm. When he was fourteen, Ronson left school to work on a mobile grocery van so that he could provide his family with some welcome financial support.

When he was seventeen, Ronson bought his first guitar for £14, a Rosetti Solid 7, made by the Dutch company Egmond, who specialized in value instruments (Paul McCartney sported the same instrument in 1960 at the first Beatles concert in Germany, which added some kudos to the brand). This basic instrument gave him some problems. But a new world was revealed when he tried to play the fashionable rocker songs. "The first thing I ever played on the guitar was a Duane Eddy number 'Shazam,'" he later confided. "I was playing around with melodies, single notes. I kind of developed from there. I never used books because I was too lazy."[52] His assumed laziness made him an exception in the world of guitar heroes: "I don't see any reason for practicing. I can only play if I'm playing with somebody else. I can't sit at home and just play for myself. I can't see the point."[52]

From 1963, Mick Ronson joined various bands and discovered the pleasure of performing onstage in the groups like the Mariners, the Voice, the Wanted, and the Crestas. After he met singer Benny Marshall, he became the guitarist for the Rats, leaving his mark on the group's first single, "The Rise and Fall of Bernie Gripplestone." In 1969, he

bought his first Les Paul Custom at the Cornell's shop in Hull, and so it was that the Mick Ronson legend was born.

From Hype to the Spiders from Mars

In summer 1969 John Cambridge, also a native of Hull, spoke to Mick about a vacancy in David Bowie's group. Bowie, a young artist, had released his first album in 1968. Although legend has it that the meeting took place in February 1970 at a concert at the Marquee, Tony Visconti later clarified that the guitarist was already present in the studios at the time of the recording of *Space Oddity*, even contributing some claps to "Wild Eyed Boy from Freecloud." Whichever it was, Mick's baptism by fire took place on February 5, 1970, at the recording of BBC Sessions, for which the blond guitarist barely had time to rehearse. "After Mick had played five notes I knew he was the one," said Tony Visconti, at that time Bowie's bassist and producer. "David and I looked at each other and we couldn't stop smiling. Mick at the time was like Jeff Beck, Eric Clapton, and Jimi Hendrix all rolled up in one person. [...] He knew the right note to play, the right way to play a song."[1] Quicker than one could get the words out, Mick Ronson became "Ronno," the guitarist with Hype, David Bowie's backing band.

The Man Behind the Icon

The years spent alongside Bowie brought him credit and recognition in the rock world, but Ronson also excelled in his qualities as an arranger, which he developed on "Life on Mars?" then worked in tandem with the singer on Lou Reed's *Transformer* album. His involvement in the production of "All the Young Dudes," a megahit written by Bowie for Mott the Hoople, confirmed his talent and contributed to his legend.

Revealed when Ziggy Stardust and his Spiders from Mars appeared on *Top of the Pops* on July 6, 1972, the guitarist shared the microphone on this occasion with his glam leader, who did not hesitate to put his arm round his shoulders for a duet on the refrain of "Starman." This historic image anchored Ronson in the history of rock, while also linking him eternally with David Bowie. Ronno

remained the man behind the icon, the one who brought rock to David Bowie on a silver plate, navigating between the different musical styles. The author of two solo albums, *Slaughter on 10th Avenue* in 1974 and *Play Don't Worry* in 1975, Ronson struggled to get his own career as a singer off the ground. His final outing was his involvement in the Freddie Mercury Tribute Concert at Wembley Stadium on April 20, 1992, where he performed "All the Young Dudes" and "Heroes" alongside David Bowie, in front of an audience of seventy thousand. He died a year later of liver cancer, on April 29, 1993, aged only forty-six.

FOR BOWIE ADDICTS

At the *Turn and Face the Strange* exhibition (taken from the refrain in "Changes" on *Hunky Dory*), the famous Les Paul guitar that Ronson originally purchased at Cornell's in 1969 was returned to the place where it all started. Eventually, Mick donated the guitar to the Hard Rock Cafe in Sydney, and it is now owned by the collector Rick Tedesco.

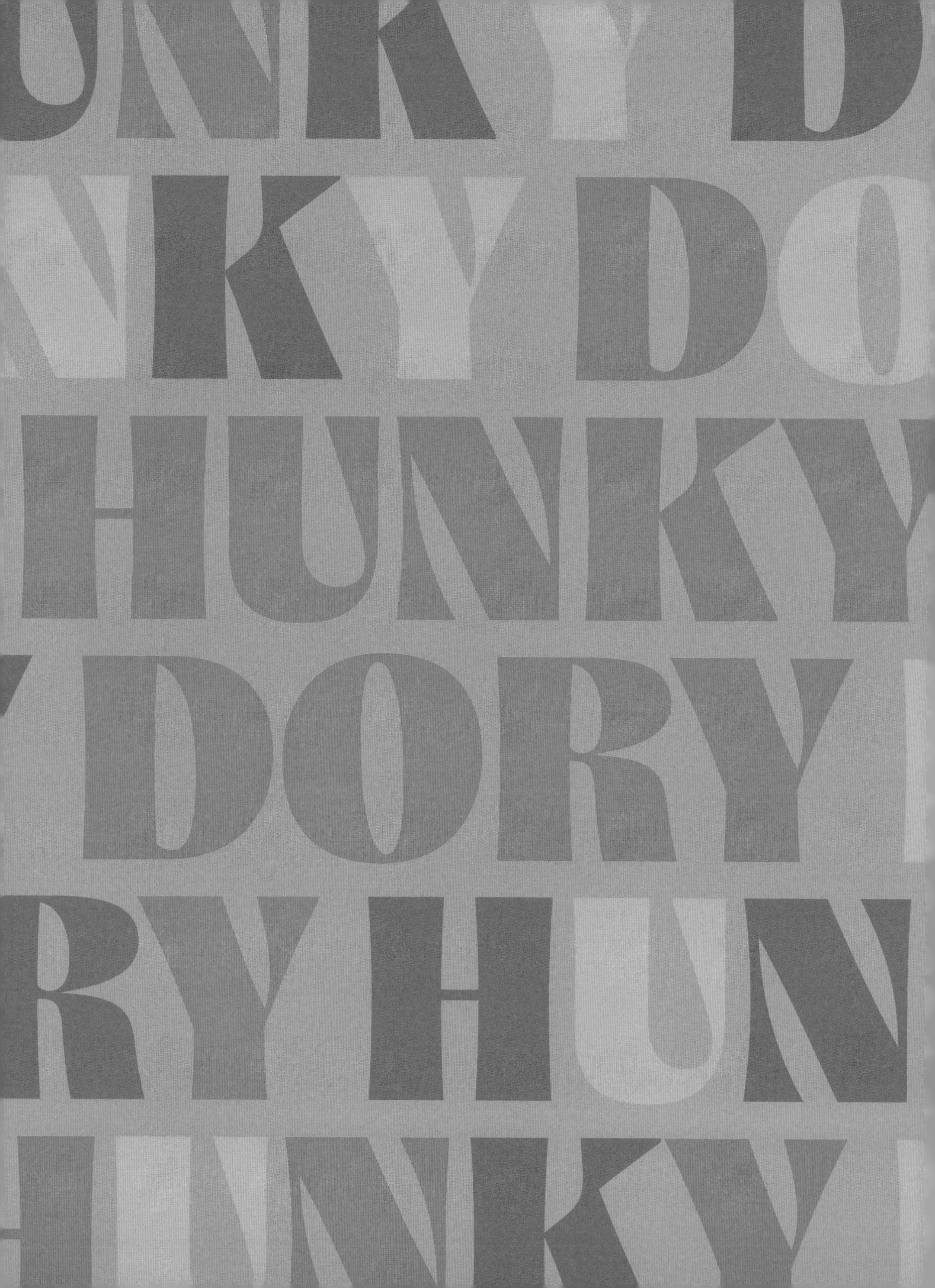
UNKY D
NKY DO
HUNKY
Y DORY
RY HUN
HUNKY

ALBUM

HUNKY DORY

Changes . Oh! You Pretty Things . Eight Line Poem . Life on Mars? .
Kooks . Quicksand . Fill Your Heart . Andy Warhol . Song for Bob Dylan .
Queen Bitch . The Bewlay Brothers

RELEASE DATES

United States: December 4, 1971
Reference: RCA—LSP-4623
United Kingdom: December 17, 1971
Reference: RCA—SF 8244
Best UK Chart Ranking: 3
Best US Chart Ranking: 57

THE MOVE TO POP

As the year 1970 drew to a close, the departure of Tony Visconti and the breakup of his group Hype led David Bowie to reinvent himself. On his return from the United States, he set in motion the production of the first single by the Arnold Corns, a group to which he added his friend Freddie Burretti as the apparent—but not the actual—lead singer. Burretti was a talented fashion designer whom Bowie had met some time before at the El Sombrero club. Attracted to this charismatic young man and wishing to see the spotlight fall on him, Bowie predicted a dazzling future in British rock for the young Burretti. On February 25, 1971, two numbers—"Moonage Daydream" and "Hang On to Yourself"—were recorded in the London studio of Radio Luxembourg. But Burretti was not as good at singing as he was at designing, so it was Bowie who provided the lead vocals. Despite this, the single was a resounding flop. The deception was, of course, supposed to remain a secret known only to the studio. Nobody—apart from some fans—asked questions about Burretti's supposed performance. The two songs reappeared in 1972 on the album *The Rise and Fall of Ziggy Stardust and the Spiders from Mars.*

"Oh! You Pretty Thing," or the Return to Center Stage

It was also early in 1971 that Bowie composed one of his most famous numbers, "Oh! You Pretty Thing," written in a moment of inspiration in the middle of the night. As he described it: "I woke up at four o'clock, had this song going in my head and I had to get out of bed, work it out on the piano and get it out of my head so I could go back to sleep."[53] Liking it on first hearing, Bob Grace, publisher at Chrysalis, saved an initial version and hastened to bring it to the attention of Mickie Most, producer and superstar. Most, whose intransigence was only matched by his influence in

the world of British show business, was won over. He wanted to use "Oh! You Pretty Thing" to launch the career of his new protégé Peter Noone, who had just left Herman's Hermits to embark on a solo career. In no time at all, a session was organized at Kingsway Studios. Bowie played the piano while Noone acted as lead singer, both performers bringing out the melody and energy of the piece.

When it came out on April 30, 1971, the single (with the title given as singular "Thing"; the plural "Things" was used for the rerecording made a few months later) drew the critics' attention to the figure of Bowie, who was by now making frequent appearances in the British rock scene. It was at this propitious moment that *The Man Who Sold the World* finally came out in the UK. But this third album, unsupported by any singles, offered a glimpse of a Bowie that no longer existed. It had been recorded a year earlier, and those who had been present at its inception had by now jumped ship. No sooner had the album been released than it disappeared off the radar, not least because Tony Defries was on the other side of the Atlantic and more interested in signing up Stevie Wonder—just then coming to the end of his contract with Motown—than in promoting Bowie's album. His attempts to lure Stevie Wonder ended in a crushing failure, and Defries returned to London and his protégé, whom he found attracting attention with the success of Noone's recording of his song. It was enough to remotivate Bowie, who now began to work day and night on his new compositions in his "Beckenham palace," Haddon Hall.

Installed in the room left vacant by Tony Visconti and his girlfriend, Bowie composed on the grand piano, moving it around so he could see into the extensively landscaped garden, which served as an inspiration to creation. Angie, now far along in her pregnancy, kept an eye on things. She prepared breakfast, made sure there were cigarettes, and

1971

The singer poses in front of a large billboard promoting the hit he had just written for Peter Noone.

maintained contacts with the outside world while her husband was composing. In May 1971, Bowie was ready. He called Mick Ronson and asked him to come back. The guitarist recalls, "David called me up and he said, 'I met a new manager; Tony Defries. You've got to come tomorrow!'"[41] At the end of the month, the group re-formed around Bowie, who was preparing his contribution to John Peel's television program *In Concert*, which was due to be recorded on June 3 and broadcast on the June 20. David Bowie was supported by his new backing band, consisting of Mick Ronson on guitar, Mick "Woody" Woodmansey on bass, and a new recruit, Trevor Bolder, on brass.

From both a personal and a professional standpoint, the spring of 1971 was to be a decisive period for David Bowie. As Peter Noone's "Oh! You Pretty Thing" reached twelfth place in the British charts, Angie gave birth to a baby, Duncan Zowie Haywood Jones, on May 30, 1971, in the Bromley hospital. The happy father did not allow this event to upset his bookings, as his fourth album had been produced over the course of the previous weeks.

A Team Gathered Round Ken Scott

The absence of Visconti acted as motivation for Bowie. He was determined to create a major, unified album with an unusually powerful lyricism, something that developed during his long months of solitary work at Haddon Hall. The team was at his service, and the Ronson-Woodmansey-Bolder trio was ready. Virtuoso musician Rick Wakeman, who had played the Mellotron on *Space Oddity* in 1969, was invited to perfect the album with his incomparable piano playing, and the powerful guitar riffs of "The Man Who Sold the World" were temporarily set aside. On the production front, Bowie enlisted the services of Ken Scott, one of the sound engineers who had worked on two of his previous albums. Having learned the trade at Abbey Road Studios working with George Martin on the Beatles' *White Album* and *Magical Mystery Tour*, Scott was the right man at the right time. Scott describes how this working relationship came about in his 2012 autobiography: "During a tea break I happened to mention to him that I wanted to start moving into the producing side of things. Much to my surprise he replied, 'Well, I've just got a new management deal, and I'm about to start a new album. I was going to produce it myself but I don't know if I can. Will you produce it with me?' […] Just like that, I was a producer."[54]

On June 8, 1971, recording on the new album began at Trident Studios. Every session saw the birth of a new gem, captured after only one or two takes. Everyone there knew

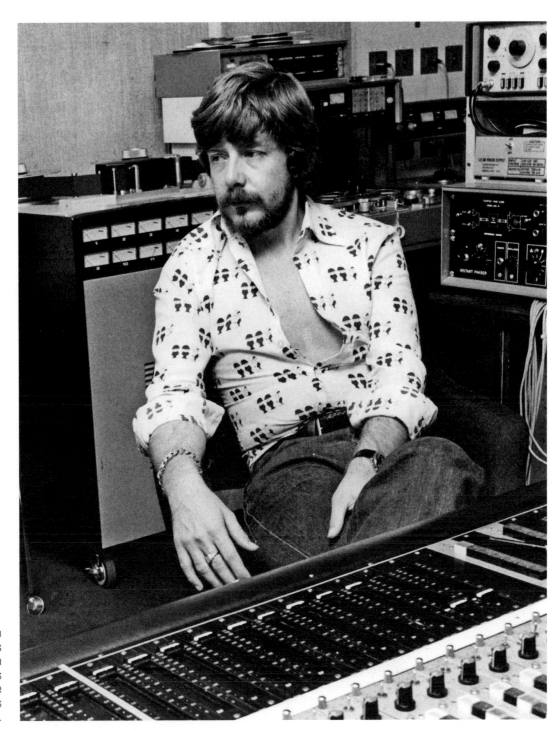

Although one often thinks of Bowie's collaborations with Eno or Visconti, it was Ken Scott who gave the singer some of his finest productions.

what was expected of them and they also knew that David Bowie hated being in the studio, generally declaring himself satisfied with his first attempt at a vocal line. Woodmansey recalls: "We'd play a song together twice, and he'd say, 'OK, that's done. Next song!' and we'd say 'What?' I'd say, 'We've only played it twice, and only once correctly, so if we do it again, we can probably get a better one'—but he'd say, 'No, it's perfect.' [...] I started to realize that while Bowie wanted the parts played correctly, more importantly he wanted them to sound fresh. If you record multiple takes of a song, you automatically end up playing from memory of what worked on a previous take and so the recording loses that freshness and spontaneity."[43]

With the recording and mixing were safe in Scott's hands, the indefatigable David Bowie was on a roll, carried away by the multiplicity of artistic ideas swarming in his head. On June 17, unhappy that the single resulting from the Arnold Corns project had been a complete flop, Bowie began production on two new numbers at Trident Studios: "Man in the Middle" and "Looking for a Friend." On June 23, he gave a very early morning concert at Glastonbury Festival, and the audience was appreciative though somewhat hazy-eyed due to lack of sleep. When Bowie, accompanied by Mick Ronson, sang "Memory of a Free Festival," with its famous chorus *The sun machine is coming down and we're gonna have a party*," the sun rose (rather than

set) over the horizon as if to greet the singer's magnificent performance. The event was a catalyst for Bowie, who was now becoming more confident and ready to confront his public again. Shortly afterward, in August, everyone was talking about Andy Warhol's play *Pork*, which had just opened. All the irreverence of Warhol's New York Factory, nudity, and immorality descended on the British capital to the great delight of one David Bowie, who soon became friendly with the play's cast. Actor Tony Zanetta was later to become one of his closest collaborators.

Taking on the United States

When Bowie, accompanied by Ronson and Angie, went to New York to sign his contract with RCA on September 9, a new world opened up before him. He visited the Factory, where Tony Zanetta introduced him to Andy Warhol. The great man did not pay much attention to the singer and was even rather disparaging when he heard the tribute paid him by David in the form of a song composed for the forthcoming album. Later meetings proved more constructive. David was also finally able to meet two of his American idols. The first was Lou Reed, who had recently left the Velvet Underground and who was looking for a reliable artistic partnership for the recording of his first solo album. Then Bowie became friendly with Iggy Pop who, having left the Stooges, came to stay at David's hotel, the Warwick Hotel, in an attempt to deal with his alcohol and drug dependency. In recovery, Iggy soon signed up with GEM Management, the company run by Laurence Myers. Despite these important contacts, which proved to be hugely influential in the metamorphosis Bowie

The cast of *Pork*, the irreverent Andy Warhol show, during its London tour in 1971.

The photographer Edward Steichen took this picture of Greta Garbo in 1928, which inspired Bowie for the album cover of *Hunky Dory*.

was to undergo in the following years, there was something left unfinished about this trip to America. He would have to return when he had become something else...an extraterrestrial with universal success and adored by all the world. The likelihood was that Andy Warhol himself would not be so high-handed with superstar Ziggy Stardust...

Hunky Dory: The First Masterpiece

Back in London, Bowie started preparing for his fourth album. On the jacket, the singer was immortalized by Brian Ward in a pose inspired by a photo of Greta Garbo that had appeared on the cover of *Life* magazine's January 10, 1955, issue. George Underwood and Terry Pastor then airbrushed color onto the black-and-white image, giving it a pointillist effect. This first disc distributed by RCA was a

revelation. Produced in record time—two weeks for recording and two weeks for mixing—the album finally revealed the extent of Bowie's genius. All outstanding, the songs also had undeniable commercial potential ("Oh! You Pretty Things," "Changes," "Life on Mars?") or a pop/folk minimalism guaranteed to please his fans ("Quicksand," "Andy Warhol," "The Bewlay Brothers"). Every number speaks of urgency and spontaneity; there is no calculation. History was being made, and there was no doubting that the disc was a masterpiece. And yet, once again, the album was met with general indifference when it was released on December 17, 1971. But nothing could stop David Bowie and his followers now. Since November, they had been back in the studio preparing a successor to *Hunky Dory*. The duke would soon be crowned.

Single

CHANGES

David Bowie / 3:34

Musicians

David Bowie: lead vocals, saxophone, backing vocals
Mick Ronson: electric guitar, backing vocals
Trevor Bolder: bass
Mick "Woody" Woodmansey: drums
Rick Wakeman: piano
BBC Symphony Orchestra: orchestra

Recorded

Trident Studios, London: July 9, 1971–August 6, 1971

Technical Team

Producers: Ken Scott, David Bowie
String Arrangements: Mick Ronson

SIDE A: *Changes*
SIDE B: *Andy Warhol*
UK Release on RCA: January 7, 1972 (ref. RCA 2160)
US Release on RCA: December 1971 (ref. 74-0605)
Best UK Chart Ranking: 49
Best US Chart Ranking: 41

In 2004, the Australian singer Butterfly Boucher was asked to contribute to the soundtrack of the animated film *Shrek 2*. She suggested a particularly successful version of "Changes," duetting with David Bowie during an extraordinarily long gap in his career. He was not to record a new album until 2013.

Genesis

Sometimes it is only with hindsight that we appreciate good things. Like a good wine that will reach perfection only after many years, a good single sometimes struggles initially to find its public. Such was the case with "Changes," a song that, when it came out in January 1972 in Great Britain, was another disappointing addition to David Bowie's discography. And yet this recently composed piece, performed for the first time on the stage at the Glastonbury Festival on June 23, 1971, was outstanding. Turning away from the folk hippie style of "Space Oddity" and the powerful guitar riffs of "The Man Who Sold the World," here the singer finds a unique sound balance, a rare alchemy heralding good things for the lucky purchasers of *Hunky Dory*, making them eager to discover the rest of the album. All is velvety delicacy in this perfect number: Rick Wakeman's piano and Bowie's voice and saxophone are at the service of the unforgettable refrains that make "Changes" one of Bowie's most timeless classics. But for the time being, apart from Tony Blackburn, host of BBC Radio 1's *Breakfast Show*, who made the song his "single of the week," no one was interested. Despite this chilly reception, the disc made it onto the American *Billboard* charts, reaching number 66 on May 13, 1972. This was to be the first time one of David's songs appeared in this famous American listing.

Production

When Bowie and his musicians recorded *Hunky Dory*, each of them had his own role. The piano is ubiquitous on the main tracks of the album while Mick Ronson's guitar remains in the background. Ronson had instead concentrated on the string arrangements that he had written for some of the songs, including "Changes." This new role was one he valued, and he had taken advantage of a few months in Hull to reacquaint himself with his music theory lessons. As for Mick Woodmansey, the drummer, he sought to make his contribution something honest and not showy, lending itself to the music. Herein lies the mark of the true musician as enunciated by that master of refinement, Miles Davis, who asked, "Why play so many notes when it's enough to play the best ones?" Or, as Woodmansey put it: "My job was to find the drum part that integrated with the song's meaning, and that made me concentrate more on what I was doing and what Bowie needed."[43]

Drummer Mick "Woody" Woodmansey dyed his hair blond to fit in with the glam rock image of the Spiders from Mars.

OH! YOU PRETTY THINGS

David Bowie / 3:12

Musicians: David Bowie: lead vocals, piano, claps / **Mick Ronson:** electric guitar, backing vocals, claps / **Trevor Bolder:** bass / **Mick "Woody" Woodmansey:** drums / **Unidentified Musician:** cello / **Recorded:** Trident Studios, London: July 9, 1971–August 6, 1971 / **Technical Team:** Producers: Ken Scott, David Bowie

Genesis

Having helped launch the solo career of ex–Herman's Hermit Peter Noone, David Bowie was quick to reclaim his song "Oh! You Pretty Things" so that he could include it on his fourth album. The controversial theme of the existence of a superior race is reflected in such lyrics as "*You gotta make way for the Homo Superior.*" Bowie had already referred explicitly to this subject in his song "The Supermen." This time, it seems the theme arose from a meeting on January 18, 1971, with the television producer Roger Damon Price, when David Bowie went to record an acoustic version of "Holy Holy" for *Six-O-One: Newsday* in Manchester. Price discussed some of his own work with Bowie, including a science fiction series for children he was writing featuring examples of the *Homo superior*. Called *The Tomorrow People*, the series came out in 1973, and Price later claimed that he was the inspiration for the song.

Production

Abandoning the rather disconcerting offbeat rhythm of Noone's version, Bowie rerecorded the piano parts of "Oh! You Pretty Things" himself on the famous Bechstein piano at Trident Studios, the same one that can be heard in the Beatles' 1968 song "Hey Jude." The song would have been a successful single if it had not already been made popular by Noone. Radio producers and programmers loved its delightful and instantly memorable melody and the hook of its refrain. But it didn't matter—David could be patient. Ken Scott did a magnificent job in refining the sound, using the state-of-the-art facilities at Trident Studios. Trevor Bolder's Gibson EB-3 bass, recorded in DI (a direct injection device allowing recording without the use of an amplifier, connecting the instrument directly to the console), set the tempo in perfect sync with Woodmansey's bass drum. The singer's voice, recorded for the most part in a first take, is warm and powerful.

In 2012 Producer Ken Scott revealed to fans some of his secrets: "What I quite often did while recording David's vocals was use an AKG C 12A and a U 67 and place them at a 90° angle to each other so he was singing in-between them. I came up with this method so I could instantly switch between the two to see which mic sounded better. [...] We didn't have many tracks at that time, so even if both mics were used, they were mixed together to a single track. Unlike many other recordings of the time, we never recorded the effects because David only did one take, so there was never any time to set them up."[54]

Peter Noone, a singer with Herman's Hermits, launched his solo career thanks to the hit "Oh! You Pretty Things" by David Bowie.

EIGHT LINE POEM

David Bowie / 2:53

Musicians: David Bowie: lead vocals, piano / **Mick Ronson:** electric guitar / **Recorded:** Trident Studios, London: July 9, 1971–August 6, 1971 / **Technical Team:** Producers: Ken Scott, David Bowie

The third track on the album, this number is like a short interlude. The poem describes a room in the early morning in New York, at the hour when shops on the West Side are opening up. In a famous conversation between William Burroughs (one of the fathers of the Beat Generation, along with Jack Kerouac and Allen Ginsberg) and David Bowie published in *Rolling Stone*'s February 28, 1974, issue Burroughs asks the singer about his relationship with literature. Commenting on the links between the text of this song and *The Waste Land*, the long poem by T. S. Eliot, Burroughs received an enigmatic and laconic answer.

Burroughs: What is your inspiration for writing, is it literary?
Bowie: I don't think so.
Burroughs: Well, I read this eight-line poem of yours and it is very reminiscent of T. S. Eliot.
Bowie: Never read him.[55]

Single

LIFE ON MARS?

David Bowie / 3:54

Musicians
David Bowie: lead vocals
Mick Ronson: electric guitar, Mellotron
Trevor Bolder: bass
Mick "Woody" Woodmansey: drums
Rick Wakeman: piano
BBC Symphony Orchestra: orchestra

Recorded
Trident Studios, London: August 6, 1971

Technical Team
Producers: Ken Scott, David Bowie
String Arrangements: Mick Ronson

SIDE A: *Life on Mars?*
SIDE B: *The Man Who Sold the World*
UK Release on RCA: June 22, 1973 (ref. RCA 2316)
Best Chart Ranking: 3

FOR BOWIE ADDICTS

In September 1976, Bowie was interviewed by journalist (and future film director) Cameron Crowe, who asked him about the cover version of "Life on Mars?" that Barbra Streisand had just recorded. He replied: "Bloody awful. Sorry, Barb, but it was atrocious."[51] It seems likely that he would have preferred the poignant interpretation offered by Jessica Lange in *American Horror Story: Freak Show*, where she sings in a circus setting reminiscent of Tod Browning's 1932 movie *Freaks*.

Genesis

In February 1968, the still unknown David Bowie suffered a decisive rejection when he put forward an English version of Claude François's hit "Comme d'habitude." His adaptation, "Even a Fool Learns to Love," was not successful. It was to be Paul Anka's version—"My Way," written for Frank Sinatra—that won out. Frustrated by this setback, in 1971 Bowie decided to reuse the descending chords for the verses of his new composition, "Life on Mars?" He would later describe how the melody of the chorus came to him while out walking in London at a time when he was immersed in composing his fourth album: "A really beautiful day in the park [...], I took a walk to Beckenham High Street to catch a bus to Lewisham to buy shoes and shirts but couldn't get the riff out of my head. Jumped off two stops into the ride and more or less loped back to the house up on Southend Road. I started working it out on the piano and had the whole lyric and melody finished by late afternoon."[56]

Drummer Mick Woodmansey was able to offer some insight on the hidden meaning of the words: "[David] said it was about a young girl's view of the modern world and how confusing it was. In the song she's watching a film and unable to relate to either reality or the film. The film tells her there's a better life somewhere else—but she doesn't have access to it."[43]

Rick Wakeman: A Virtuoso Guest

In addition to Bowie's talent in writing a masterpiece while out on a shopping expedition, it was also thanks to the quality of the production that "Life on Mars?" acquired its status among the greatest pop songs of the twentieth century. The piano part plays an essential role, bringing a feeling of melancholy and gentleness to the song. Rick Wakeman, who had played the Mellotron on "Space Oddity" for the modest fee of £9 sterling, once again answered Bowie's invitation to contribute to the *Hunky Dory* album. David played him the piano line as a simple series of chords on the accented beats. Using the studio's Bechstein piano, Wakeman's nimble fingers transformed the part. As he recalled: "I remember leaving St. Anne's Court, Trident Studios, and coming home saying to a couple of friends I met that evening in the local pub, that I'd just played on what I considered to be the best song I'd ever had the privilege to work on."[1]

Pianist Rick Wakeman gave Bowie some of his finest work for "Life on Mars?"

Mick Ronson, Apprentice Conductor

A second element gives "Life on Mars?" further emotional power: the string arrangements made by Mick Ronson. Ronson's guitar features very little in this song (although he was allowed a wonderful guitar solo played on a powerful but velvety Gibson Les Paul), but he was responsible for the orchestral parts. On the day of recording, Ronson conducted the strings. Concealed beneath his cool rock 'n' roll manner, the guitarist was petrified. Anxious by nature, he took this job very seriously and knew he must face up to the BBC Symphony Orchestra, whose members were consummate musicians with high standards. "Mick knew that he was going to have to deal with them. [...] On the day, the string players came to Trident and took their seats, ready for the session. Bowie and I were looking through the large glass window in the control room at the scene below. [...] Mick then stood in front of them and carefully rolled a cigarette."[43] The musicians played their parts, led by this novice conductor. After two takes approved by Bowie, one of the players said to Ronson: "We love the arrangement, but we'd like to do another one. I think we can do it better."[43] The third take was the one that features on the album.

A Ringing Phone Immortalized

Why on earth do we hear a phone ringing at the end of "Life on Mars?" The answer is simple and, like all studio anecdotes, is worth its weight in gold. Trident Studios had a small bathroom that had a telephone available for musicians wishing to call out between takes. According to Ken Scott, this phone had never rung before, mainly because no one knew the number. As Wakeman was coming to the end of his best take on August 6, the cursed machine began ringing, and the sound was inevitably captured by the microphones. The team decided to rerecord over the interruption, but Scott wound back the tape a bit too far and began recording a few seconds earlier on the tape. As a result, some of the notes from the first version can be heard on the second one. When Bowie, Scott, and the other musicians listened carefully to the rerecorded version in the control room, they were able to hear not only the ringing phone at the end of the piece but also the musicians' reactions. Amused by this accidental addition, they decided to keep it as it was, but when it came to the mixing, Scott was careful to cut out Mick Ronson's angry exclamation: *"For fuck's sake."*

David, Angie, and Duncan
"Zowie" Bowie in the garden
at Haddon Hall in 1971.

KOOKS

David Bowie / 2:51

Musicians: David Bowie: lead vocals, twelve-string acoustic guitar /
Mick Ronson: electric guitar, backing vocals / **Trevor Bolder:** bass,
trumpet / **Mick "Woody" Woodmansey:** drums / **Rick Wakeman:**
piano / **BBC Symphony Orchestra:** orchestra / **Recorded:** Trident
Studios, London: July 9, 1971–August 6, 1971 / **Technical Team:**
Producers: Ken Scott, David Bowie / **String Arrangements:**
Mick Ronson

When David's son Zowie Bowie (who later preferred to be
known by one of his other given names, Duncan) was born
on May 30, 1971, David was at Haddon Hall. When the hospital in Bromley called him, the elder Bowie was in the middle of listening to a Neil Young album, *After the Gold Rush*.
Thus the joy of being a father was not the only thing to
inspire him in the writing of "Kooks," a little folk-style ballad
in which he presents himself as a reassuring protector of his
child. You can hear the bluesy lament of the Loner, and
there are multiple nods to *After the Gold Rush*: the ragtime
piano, the drum rhythm, and even the trumpet (played here
by Trevor Bolder) taking up the melody of the singer's line,
exactly as in "Till the Morning Comes." But in Bowie's song,
the happy mood is tinged with fear. He wonders if a couple
of "kooks" are capable of taking care of a fragile baby. With
humor and self-mockery, the new father warns: "If you're
gonna stay with us you're gonna grow up bannanas [sic]!"[57]

QUICKSAND

David Bowie / 5:06

Musicians: David Bowie: lead vocals, twelve-string acoustic guitar,
backing vocals / **Mick Ronson:** acoustic guitar, backing vocals / **Trevor
Bolder:** bass / **Mick "Woody" Woodmansey:** drums / **Rick Wakeman:**
piano / **BBC Symphony Orchestra:** orchestra / **Recorded:** Trident
Studios, London: July 14, 1971 / **Technical Team:** Producers:
Ken Scott, David Bowie / **String Arrangements:** Mick Ronson

Composed during Bowie's first trip to the United States in
January 1971, "Quicksand" is a wonderful acoustic number
looking back to the singer's early folk style and reminiscent
of some of his most tuneful ballads such as "Silly Boy Blue,"
"Letter to Hermione," "Wild Eyed Boy from Freecloud," or
"After All." But he had been working on and refining this
composition during the time spent at Haddon Hall, and
"Quicksand" is technically head and shoulders above those
earlier works. This monument to acoustic performance, of a
depth unparalleled in his repertoire, is further enhanced by
the contribution of producer Ken Scott, fresh from recording
sessions for George Harrison's *All Things Must Pass*. To give
Bowie's song all the power it deserved, Scott used his own
secret method: He asked David to record each of his guitar
passages as many as four times. During mixing, Scott introduced the tracks one by one into the line of the song, the
effect being one of ever-increasing power. "I think it
worked,"[54] Scott was to say in 2012. Not one of the 3.6 million people who bought *Hunky Dory* would be likely to
contradict him!

FILL YOUR HEART

Biff Rose, Paul Williams / 3:07

Musicians: David Bowie: lead vocals, saxophone / **Trevor Bolder:**
bass / **Mick "Woody" Woodmansey:** drums / **Rick Wakeman:** piano /
BBC Symphony Orchestra: orchestra / **Recorded:** Trident Studios,
London: July 9, 1971–August 6, 1971 / **Technical Team:** Producers:
Ken Scott, David Bowie / **String Arrangements:** Mick Ronson

At the beginning of February 1971, Bowie attended a concert in Los Angeles featuring Biff Rose. Bowie admired
Rose's music and had covered some of his songs in his live
appearances. One of the numbers on the album *The Thorn
in Mrs. Rose's Side* particularly appealed to him. Written
with composer Paul Williams (who was soon to produce the
much praised movie score for Brian De Palma's *Phantom of
the Paradise*), "Fill Your Heart" has much of the honky-tonk
sound that Williams was to use in his score for Alan Parker's
Bugsy Malone, for which he received an Oscar nomination
for best music and musical adaptation in 1977.

On the back of the *Hunky Dory* jacket, Bowie acknowl-
edges the work of the arranger of the original version of
the number: "Mick and I agree that the 'Fill Your Heart'
arrangement owes one hell of a lot to Arthur G. Wright and
his proto-type."[58]

1971

ANDY WARHOL

David Bowie / 3:54

Musicians: David Bowie: lead vocals, twelve-string acoustic guitar, laughing, claps / **Mick Ronson:** acoustic guitar, backing vocals, claps, percussion / **Ken Scott:** spoken voice, ARP 2500 synthesizer / **Recorded:** Trident Studios, London: July 9, 1971–August 6, 1971 / **Technical Team:** Producers: Ken Scott, David Bowie / **String Arrangements:** Mick Ronson

From his side of the Atlantic, David Bowie was already a devotee of the Factory and the artists connected with it. Since 1968, its ambassadors, the Velvet Underground, had been spreading the message of peace and love (and sex and drugs) throughout the world. When Bowie eventually met the founder of the Factory in September 1971, he brought him a song written especially for him, entitled "Andy Warhol." The high priest of op art came into the room where Bowie and Ronson were waiting, put the tape in the cassette player and walked out, murmuring quite audibly that he couldn't stand the tribute paid to him by the English singer. Bowie had no hard feelings and was to relate a touching memory of the meeting: "I tried to make small talk with him, and it wasn't getting anywhere. But then he saw my shoes. I was wearing a pair of gold-and-yellow shoes, and he says, 'I adore those shoes, tell me where you got those shoes.' [...] My yellow shoes broke the ice with Andy Warhol."[55]

Before appearing on Bowie's fourth album, "Andy Warhol"—with its Middle Eastern–sounding riff borrowed from Ron Davies's "Silent Song Through the Land"—had been recorded on June 6, 1971, by Dana Gillespie, a singer friend of David's who had been taken under Tony Defries's wing. The song appeared on a promotional disc he had made when looking for a label for the two artists, giving them one side each. The rare copies of this disc, called *BOWPROMO*, are among the most sought-after items for collectors.

SONG FOR BOB DYLAN

David Bowie / 4:12

Musicians: David Bowie: lead vocals, twelve-string acoustic guitar /
Mick Ronson: acoustic guitar, backing vocals / Trevor Bolder: bass /
Mick "Woody" Woodmansey: drums / Rick Wakeman: piano /
Recorded: Trident Studios, London: August 6, 1971 /
Technical Team: Producers: Ken Scott, David Bowie

Never judge by appearances: This song is in no way a tribute to the king of American folk, Bob Dylan. It is more of a
settling of scores, backing Dylan's fans who felt that Dylan
had betrayed them as, with Telecaster in hand and the
amplifiers turned up to maximum, he turned his back on
his folk guitar in favor of modern pop rock. Bowie never
liked Dylan very much and, when compared to him in
1970, said: "His songs are boring and he has a bad voice."[59]
This hostility increased over time, and in 1976 Bowie said
on his return from the United States: "I saw Dylan in New
York seven, eight months ago. We don't have a lot to talk
about. We're not great friends. Actually, I think he hates
me."[51] The title of Bowie's "Song for Bob Dylan" is a parody
of Dylan's 1962 "Song to Woody," the singer's tribute to his
idol Woody Guthrie, pioneer of political folk music,
embodiment of the hobo singer, and the influence behind
the slightly unpolished style affected by the early Dylan.

QUEEN BITCH

David Bowie / 3:15

Musicians: David Bowie: lead vocals, twelve-string acoustic guitar /
Mick Ronson: electric guitar, backing vocals / Trevor Bolder: bass /
Mick "Woody" Woodmansey: drums / **Recorded:** Trident Studios,
London: July 9, 1971–August 6, 1971 / **Technical Team: Producers:**
Ken Scott, David Bowie

A true tribute to the Velvet Underground, "Queen Bitch" is
a response to their 1968 album *White Light / White Heat*.
The reference is explicit; a notice on the back of the *Hunky
Dory* jacket reads: "Some V.U. White Light returned with

thanks."[58] With its vocal line inspired by Lou Reed's phrasing and a guitar gimmick borrowed from Eddie Cochran's
"Three Steps to Heaven," the song is rhythmical and effective, and it achieves its aim of emphasizing the British singer's connections with the Velvet Underground's unique
universe. A little later, David Bowie, together with Mick
Ronson, produced Lou Reed's second album, *Transformer*,
and shared in the singer's first solo success: "Walk on the
Wild Side."

THE BEWLAY BROTHERS

David Bowie / 5:21

Musicians: David Bowie: lead vocals, twelve-string acoustic guitar,
piano / Mick Ronson: guitar, backing vocals / **Recorded:** Trident
Studios, London: July 30, 1971 / **Technical Team: Producers:**
Ken Scott, David Bowie

"The Bewlay Brothers" gave rise to much discussion
among Bowie's fans and gave observers the opportunity to
offer interpretations of its text. It seems to refer to the relationship between David and his brother Terry, some commentators writing—perhaps correctly—that the song
should have been called "The Bowie Brothers." The singer
never tried to conceal his original intentions. Everyone,
from producer Ken Scott to the musicians, confirm it: The
text has no hidden meaning; he wrote it with the simple
aim of making American critics tie themselves in knots trying to find one. Ken Scott remembers Bowie saying: "We've
got to do this song and it's specifically for the American
market. [...] Well the lyrics make absolutely no sense, but
the Americans always like to read things into things, so let
them read into it what they will."[29] On July 30, 1971, when
all the other musicians had gone off to eat, Bowie recorded
this breathtakingly melancholy song by himself. When
they got back, he presented them with the piece completed, ready for mixing by Ken Scott. A wonderful piece
with which to conclude an outstanding album!

THE ARNOLD CORNS
Moonage Daydream / Hang On to Yourself
UK Release on B&C Records: May 7, 1971 (ref. CB 149)
Best Chart Ranking: Did Not Chart

FOR BOWIE ADDICTS

Bowie took the name of his group, the Arnold Corns, from the very first Pink Floyd single, "Arnold Layne."

Freddie Burretti was not the only one to change his name for this occasion. Mark Pritchett became Mark Carr-Pritchard, and Tim Broadbent became Timothy James Ralph St. Laurent Broadbent. De Somogyi opted for Polak De Somogyi.

MOONAGE DAYDREAM

David Bowie / 3:49

Musicians: David Bowie: lead vocals, twelve-string acoustic guitar, piano / Mark Pritchett: electric guitar / Peter de Somogyi: bass / Tim Broadbent: drums, tambourine / **Recorded:** Radio Luxembourg Studio, London: February 25, 1971 / **Technical Team:** Producer: David Bowie / **Sound Engineer:** Ken Scott

When Bowie returned from his first trip to the United States, he pulled two discs from the Stooges out of his suitcase: their first and second albums, *The Stooges* and *Fun House.* Iggy Pop and his pals had introduced Bowie to their wild, uninhibited prepunk rock (today called *protopunk*). This discovery, along with his encounter with the psychedelic blues of Kim Fowley's *The Day the Earth Stood Still,* gave him the idea of setting up a rock group, the Arnold Corns. He recruited the members of the Rungk trio: lead singer and bass player Mark Pritchett—a friend from Beckenham—bass player Pete de Somogyi, and drummer Tim Broadbent. The front man was already found: Freddie Burretti, a stylist and fashion designer whom Bowie had met at the El Sombrero club. Burretti, taking the name Rudi Valentino for the project, was to become a valuable collaborator, designing most of Bowie's costumes for the *Ziggy Stardust* tour, but unfortunately he was not much of a singer. Bowie had to cover the vocals for all the takes of the single "Moonage Daydream" and its B-side, "Hang On to Yourself," recorded on February 25 at the London studio of Radio Luxembourg. He reused the two songs later on *The Rise and Fall of Ziggy Stardust and the Spiders from Mars* album, but the Arnold Corns single was to be a flop. Nevertheless, Bowie repeated the experience a few months later with a second recording session for "Man in the Middle" and "Looking for a Friend."

HANG ON TO YOURSELF

David Bowie / 2:50

Musicians: David Bowie: lead vocals, guitar / Mark Pritchett: acoustic guitar, electric guitar / Pete de Somogyi: bass / Tim Broadbent: drums, tambourine / **Recorded:** Radio Luxembourg Studio, London: February 25, 1971 / **Technical Team:** Producer: David Bowie / **Sound Engineer:** Ken Scott

"Hang On to Yourself" and its open-chord guitar rhythm was used again in "Queen Bitch" for the *Hunky Dory* album and reveals the important influence on Bowie of the Velvet Underground in the early 1970s. During his time in America, Bowie had recorded a demo of this number with the intention of giving it to one of his idols, Gene Vincent. The meeting never came about; the composer of "Be-Bop-a-Lula," an alcoholic for many years, died of a perforated stomach ulcer on October 12, 1971.

Before adapting it as a rockabilly number on *The Rise and Fall of Ziggy Stardust and the Spiders from Mars,* Bowie suggested it for the B-side of the debut single by his short-lived group the Arnold Corns.

The artistic collaboration between Freddie Burretti and David Bowie continued after the Arnold Corns adventure. The couturier designed costumes for the singer during his "Ziggy Stardust" and "Aladdin Sane" periods.

MAN IN THE MIDDLE
(THE ARNOLD CORNS)

David Bowie / 4:08

Musicians: David Bowie: lead vocals / Freddie Burretti: lead vocals / Mark Pritchett: electric guitar, lead vocals / Mick Ronson: electric guitar / Trevor Bolder: bass / Mick "Woody" Woodmansey: drums / **Recorded:** Trident Studios, London: June 17, 1971 / **Technical Team:** Producer: David Bowie / Sound Engineer: Roy Thomas Baker

The lack of success of the first Arnold Corns single did not discourage David Bowie, who decided, in the spring of 1971, to continue the project. This time it was the musicians of the new version of the Ronno group (Ronson, Woodmansey, and Bolder)—aka Bowie's backing group—who were drafted into the recording session. Two titles were produced at Trident Studios: "Man in the Middle" and "Looking for a Friend." Some of Burretti's vocal lines were retained in the mixing but are hidden by Bowie's voice. Woodmansey wrote later: "That was when we realized that although Freddie looked like the ultimate rock frontman, he couldn't sing a note. The guy had no voice whatsoever. He tried to sing while Bowie sang along with him, but the recordings were terrible."[43] No single resulted from this recording session, and it was not until *The Rise and Fall of Ziggy Stardust and the Spiders from Mars* became successful that a 45 rpm was issued by the B&C label in August 1972. With this failure to create an idealized rock star, in the following months David Bowie decided to salvage the original concept and use it to create the figure of Ziggy Stardust.

LOOKING FOR A FRIEND
(THE ARNOLD CORNS)

David Bowie / 3:19

Musicians: David Bowie: lead vocals / Mark Pritchett: acoustic guitar, lead vocals / Mick Ronson: electric guitar / Trevor Bolder: bass / Mick "Woody" Woodmansey: drums, tambourine / **Recorded:** Trident Studios, London: June 17, 1971 / **Technical Team:** Producer: David Bowie / Sound Engineer: Roy Thomas Baker

Intended for the B-side of "Man in the Middle," the hippie-style "Looking for a Friend" is a fine piece. It was to be rerecorded in 1971 during the making of *The Rise and Fall of Ziggy Stardust and the Spiders from Mars*. As Ken Scott was not available for this second Arnold Corns recording session, another sound engineer from Trident Studios, Roy Thomas Baker, filled in for him. Baker went on to be co-producer of several Queen albums: *Queen* (1973), *Queen II* (1974), *Sheer Heart Attack* (1974), *A Night at the Opera* (1975), and *Jazz* (1978).

LIGHTNING FRIGHTENING

David Bowie / 3:35

Musicians: David Bowie: lead vocals, saxophone, harmonica / Mark Pritchett: electric guitar / Herbie Flowers: bass / Barry Morgan: drums / **Recorded:** Trident Studio, London: April 23, 1971 / **Technical Team:** Producer: Ken Scott

On April 23, 1971, David Bowie arrived at Trident Studios to record "Rupert the Riley," a number he had written for his friend Micky King. This was the first occasion that Ken Scott was offered the sought-after role of producer, earned thanks to his work as sound engineer on *Space Oddity*. The collaboration was a success, and once recording was completed, the musicians launched into a well-chosen blues-rock piece strongly influenced by "Dirty Dirty," a song by Crazy Horse, Neil Young's backing band. Although more of a jam session than a properly produced number, "Lightning Frightening" (with the original working title of "The Man") is not without interest, not least for Mark Pritchett's use of slide guitar and Bowie's confident saxophone playing. With this session, Ken Scott introduced the modern sound that was to be so important to Bowie's success. Rarely receiving the recognition he was due, Ken Scott had a hand in several of Bowie's masterpieces—*Hunky Dory, Aladdin Sane,* and *The Rise and Fall of Ziggy Stardust and the Spiders from Mars*—but his role has been too often eclipsed by Bowie's collaborations with Tony Visconti and Brian Eno. It should be remembered, however, that without Ken Scott the world might never have become interested in David Bowie and his music.

BOMBERS

David Bowie / 2:40

Musicians: David Bowie: lead vocals, backing vocals / Mick Ronson: electric guitar, backing vocals / Trevor Bolder: bass / Mick "Woody" Woodmansey: drums / Rick Wakeman: piano / **Recorded:** Trident Studios, London: July 9, 1971 / **Technical Team:** Producers: Ken Scott, David Bowie

While Bowie and colleagues were recording *BOWPROMO*, the promotional disc made by Tony Defries in an attempt both to find a new label for his protégé, a session took place at Trident Studios on July 9, during which "Bombers" was recorded. The song owes a debt to Anthony Newley, the British singer in whom Bowie had taken a great interest in the early years of his career. Newley's influence can be detected particularly in the phrasing at the end of each refrain, where David exaggerates some of the syllables. The end of the piece when only the voice and piano remain continues the same style, so reminiscent of "Love You Till Tuesday."

The majestic Spiders from Mars playing with David Bowie in 1972. Left to right: Mick Ronson, Trevor Bolder, David Bowie, and Mick "Woody" Woodmansey.

THE RISE

AND FAL

F ZIGGY S

STARDUS

SPIDERS

S FROM M

MARS T

ALBUM

THE RISE AND FALL OF ZIGGY STARDUST AND THE SPIDERS FROM MARS

Five Years . Soul Love . Moonage Daydream . Starman . It Ain't Easy .
Lady Stardust . Star . Hang On to Yourself . Ziggy Stardust .
Suffragette City . Rock 'n' Roll Suicide

RELEASE DATES
United Kingdom: June 6, 1972
Reference: RCA—RCA SF 8287
United States: June 6, 1972
Reference: RCA—LSP-4702
Best UK Chart Ranking: 5
Best US Chart Ranking: 77

One of the first photo sessions
with Mick Rock and David
Bowie at Haddon Hall in 1972.

ZIGGY STARDUST: BOWIE'S ALTER EGO

When "Changes," the only single from *Hunky Dory*, was released on January 7, 1972, work on a new album had already been underway at Trident Studios since November, and Ken Scott would soon be mixing the first tracks. The production of this fifth opus, which would earn David Bowie international recognition, effectively buried an album that, for want of promotion, was released to general indifference in December 1971.

To the great displeasure of his distributor, RCA, Bowie already had an idea firmly in his mind, which he had been developing since his first trip to the United States. The creation of an ultimate rock star had failed with Rudi Valentino and the Arnold Corns, so now Bowie would embody it himself. Disregarding everything he had invented in the past, he would give birth to this new avatar in the blink of an eye. He would be a real star, a star broken by his own fame, transported to the heavens by his audience. He already knew what his first name would be. The singer borrowed the name of a tailor whose sign had caught his eye: "Ziggy." "It had that Iggy [Pop] connotation but it was a tailor's shop, and I thought, 'Well, this whole thing is gonna be about clothes,' so it was my own little joke calling him Ziggy."[30] The name "Stardust" he borrowed from the Legendary Stardust Cowboy, an American rocker whose music and eccentricity he admired. For his character's attitude, on the other hand, Bowie was inspired by the lifestyle of Vince Taylor, a British musician plagued by drugs and alcohol who left behind a string of hits, notably including "Brand New Cadillac," covered by the Clash in 1979. "At his last performance with his band in France," Bowie recalls, "he dismissed the band, then went on stage dressed in white robes as Jesus Christ and said, I am the Resurrection, I am Jesus Christ, this whole thing. They nearly lynched him there and then. It was his last performance. [...] He used to hang out on

Tottenham Court Road and I got to know him then. [....] And so he re-emerged in this Ziggy Stardust character."[30]

The Spiders Take the Stage

During the same period, Bowie, Woodmansey, Ronson, and Bolder discovered *A Clockwork Orange*, the new movie from American movie director Stanley Kubrick, which tells the story of a sociopath, Alex DeLarge, played by Malcolm McDowell, and his gang of "droogies." The film, which mixes ultraviolence and unbridled sexuality, is driven by an anxiety-provoking soundtrack by Wendy Carlos, in which great classical melodies are played on a Moog synthesizer. The idea of a clan strongly appealed to Bowie, and as soon as the screening was over, he realized that he no longer wanted a backing band to accompany him onstage, but a gang to support his central character Ziggy Stardust. It was Mick Woodmansey who suggested the name for the band, during one of their rehearsals: "Bass drum skins had to have the name of the band on them back then. I had a blank one [...] so I took it off and wrote 'The Spiders' on it. Bowie came in and looked at it for two minutes. [...] No expression. And then went, 'OK, what's the first number we're doing?' So it passed the audition. It was Ziggy and the Spiders from then on."[1]

It was time to fine-tune the team's image, and this was Angie Barnett's domain. Trevor Bolder was the first victim of Mrs. Bowie's eccentricities. The bass player shaved off his imposing beard, and on her advice left enormous sideburns, which were immediately dyed in a silver color, perfectly matching the outfits designed by Freddie Burretti: blue for him, gold for Mick Ronson, pink for Woodmansey, and multicolored for Bowie. They all wore chiné boots from Russell & Bromley, a famous shoemaker on Beckenham High Street. The singer had his hair cut and dyed, first red, and then bright red—by Suzi Fussey,

1972

Vince Taylor, whose rock posture and stage movements were used as inspiration for the character of Ziggy Stardust.

The American musician known as the Legendary Stardust Cowboy, in the early 1970s.

the Beckenham hairdresser already responsible for taking care of Angie's hairstyle whims.

The "Ziggy" Concept

Ever since the 1972 release of *The Rise and Fall of Ziggy Stardust and the Spiders from Mars*, everyone has come up with their own theory concerning the genesis of the greatest concept album in the history of rock. Like *Tommy* or *Quadrophenia* by the Who, or *Dark Side of the Moon* by Pink Floyd, this album seems to have been written in one go, following Ziggy Stardust on the way to his unavoidable destiny. The reality was very different. While David Bowie's idea was to create a stage character who would mark the history of rock, the album itself was conceived in a totally disjointed way. The songs, first of all, were composed and recorded in a disordered manner. "Starman" was recorded at the very end of the process and at the request of the president of RCA, who wanted an effective single that was as close as possible to the theme of Bowie's last big hit, "Space Oddity." "It Ain't Easy," the Ron Davies cover, was immortalized in July 1971 while Bowie and his manager, Tony Defries, were working on the promotional record of the artist and his friend Dana Gillespie. And what about the

album's title, borrowed from "The Rise and Fall of Bernie Gripplestone," the one and only single by the Rats, the band from Hull in which both Ronson and Woodmansey played?

It was only after its release that Bowie, with the recurrent idea of creating a pop star figure, would turn his album into a concept album by establishing a post hoc link between the songs on the record. Producer Ken Scott would later comment, "There's always been this whole thing about 'Ziggy' being a concept album, but it really wasn't. [...] 'Ziggy' is just a patchwork of songs. [...] All this about Ziggy being Starman is bullshit. [...] So while it's true that there were a few songs that fitted the 'concept,' the rest were just songs that all worked well together as they would in any good album. Even David didn't take the Ziggy concept too seriously at first (that would come later)."[54] The Spiders' drummer confirmed this version of events: "We never talked about it having a concept. Bowie never mentioned one."[43]

Glam Rock's Flagship Album

When David Bowie was interviewed by *Melody Maker* for its January 22, 1972, issue, he innocently told them, "I'm gay, and always have been, even when I was David Jones."[60] Just as the *Ziggy* tour was beginning, this statement was a

Actor Malcolm McDowell and his "droogs," the antiheroes of
Stanley Kubrick's 1971 classic, *A Clockwork Orange*.

spectacular advertisement for the band, which played with sexual ambiguity onstage (despite the fact that the members were very much heterosexual). On June 17, the iconic photograph by Mick Rock taken at Oxford Town Hall and showing Bowie simulating oral sex on Ronson, with his hands on the blond man's buttocks and his guitar strings between his teeth, also set tongues furiously wagging.

When the single "Starman" was released on April 28, 1972, it received excellent critical acclaim and was quickly broadcast on the radio. The public, delighted to reconnect with the space adventures of Bowie's characters, was ready and willing. Everything seemed to be going well for Bowie, who had also just written a song for Mott the Hoople, one of his favorite bands, that would become the anthem of the glam-rock generation: "All the Young Dudes." While the band was on the verge of splitting up, Bowie offered them an unexpected success, simultaneously highlighting his own songwriting talents to the public. This succession of events served to boost the singer's popularity, and from May onward, the lines in front of the concert halls grew longer and the concerts were frequently sold out. So when *The Rise and Fall of Ziggy Stardust and the Spiders from Mars* hit the record stores on June 6, 1972, it was an immediate success. Eight thousand copies were sold in the United Kingdom in the first week, while Bowie and Ronson flew to the United States to promote the album. The record's cover is the work of graphic designer Terry Pastor, George Underwood's partner at Main Artery, who used the same airbrush coloring technique used on *Hunky Dory* to add yellow to various areas of Brian Ward's shots, particularly to Bowie's hair. The artist was dressed in a quilted outfit made by Burretti, and a pair of platform

Angie Bowie couldn't bear to see David and his musicians walking around in jeans and T-shirts offstage. She asked Freddie Burretti to design a line of streetwear, "using only mohairs, silks and cashmeres."[61]

FOR BOWIE ADDICTS

During the production of Lou Reed's *Transformer* at Trident Studios, Bowie and Ronson became friends with a young band recording their debut album when the venue was unoccupied: Queen. While David and his guitarist had already crossed paths with Brian May and Roger Taylor, they now got the chance to meet the band's charismatic singer, Freddie Mercury.

David Bowie was never satisfied with the mix of *The Rise and Fall of Ziggy Stardust and the Spiders from Mars*, convinced that the sound wasn't raw enough.

boots by Kansai Yamamoto. The Gibson Les Paul that he wore across his shoulder belonged to his friend Marc Pritchett, an occasional guitarist in the backing band. Ward immortalized Bowie in front of furrier K. West at 21 Heddon Street, while the Spiders refused to leave the studio and brave the cold and rain.

The album's production announced a new turnaround for the chameleon David Bowie. Abandoning the hippie folk of *Space Oddity*, the heavy metal riffs of *The Man Who Sold the World*, and the polished pop of *Hunky Dory*, the singer offers a genuine rock album, in which the combination of instruments was carefully mastered by Ken Scott, always at the service of songs whose commercial potential are now beyond dispute. Following the success of "Starman," Bowie and the Spiders landed a slot on the BBC's July 6 broadcast of *Top of the Pops*. Accompanied onstage by pianist Robin Lumley, they delivered a performance that marked the very apex of the glam-rock movement, at the same time dethroning friend and competitor Marc Bolan. The song itself was strong and Bowie was at the top of his artform, as were his musicians, who reflected the spotlight like no one had before. When Mick Ronson approached the singer's microphone and sang the chorus beside him, the viewers were convinced: Bowie had become the star he had been claiming to be for years.

Ziggy Stardust Takes On the World

In early August, Bowie moved to the Rainbow Theatre to work with Lindsay Kemp, in preparation for the concerts scheduled for August 19, 20, and 30. At the same time, he and his associate Mick Ronson began production of Lou

Reed's second album at Trident Studios. Ken Scott was at the controls as sound engineer but was never credited on the album, and this incident was to mark the beginning of a troubled period between Bowie and his producer. Ronson and Bowie offered the former Velvet Underground singer some exceptional arrangements, particularly on the song that would become his greatest hit: "Walk on the Wild Side." For the final part of the song, David Bowie called upon his former saxophone teacher, Ronnie Ross, whose smooth, gentle sax contribution on the track has passed into rock 'n' roll legend. Back at the Rainbow, the artist found his team, with the addition of keyboardist Matthew Fisher, responsible for the mythical Hammond organ introduction of "A Whiter Shade of Pale" (1967) by Procol Harum. As Bowie's band changed keyboardists many times during this tour, it was Nicky Graham's name that was mistakenly put on the concert posters. Kemp's dance troupe, renamed the Astronettes, rehearsed their choreography on a stage covered with silver scaffolding while the backdrop screen was readied for the projection of Luis Buñuel's mythical film *Un chien andalou* between Roxy Music's opening act and the concert.

These concerts marked a turning point in Bowie's career, leaving his audience thoroughly under his spell. It merely remained for him to seduce America, the promised land for all self-respecting rockers. In September, a twenty-two-date tour was launched, and a new keyboardist, Mike Garson, joined the Spiders. In spite of poor organization, the tour was a success, and Bowie took advantage of this trip to write the songs that would build the second and last album of his character Ziggy Stardust: *Aladdin Sane*.

1972

FIVE YEARS

David Bowie / 4:43

Musicians: David Bowie: lead vocals, twelve-string acoustic guitar / Mick Ronson: electric guitar, piano, autoharp, backing vocals / Trevor Bolder: bass / Mick "Woody" Woodmansey: drums / Unidentified Musicians: orchestra / **Recorded:** Trident Studios, London: November 15, 1971 / **Technical Team:** Producers: Ken Scott, David Bowie / **Sound Engineer:** Dennis MacKay / **Arrangements:** David Bowie, Mick Ronson

Still angry with Ken Scott after the *Hunky Dory* sessions, Mick Woodmansey warned the producer that his drums must never again sound like "boxes of corn flakes." Although this muffled sound had been in fashion in the early 1970s, the Spiders' drummer wanted a more percussive sound, which we can savor from the first bars of "Five Years," unfolding like a red carpet before Bowie takes the stage. The song, redolent with despair, paints a picture of humanity condemned to disappear in the next five years. The artist explained that the lyrics were inspired by a dream in which he was told by his father that he had only five years left to live. Bowie gave his all during the recording of the song, screaming the finale into the Trident Studios microphone as tears streamed down his face. After the extraordinary public reception of the album, the artist played the concept game right to the end, coming up with a story that probably didn't exist at the conception of *The Rise and Fall of Ziggy Stardust and the Spiders from Mars*: "Ziggy was in a rock & roll band and the kids no longer want rock & roll. There's no electricity to play it. Ziggy's adviser tells him to collect news and sing it, 'cause there is no news. So Ziggy does this and there is terrible news. 'All the Young Dudes' is a song about this news."[55]

SOUL LOVE

David Bowie / 3:34

Musicians: David Bowie: lead vocals, twelve-string acoustic guitar, saxophone, backing vocals, claps / Mick Ronson: electric guitar, backing vocals / Trevor Bolder: bass / Mick "Woody" Woodmansey: drums, percussion / **Recorded:** Trident Studios, London: November 12, 1971 / **Technical Team:** Producers: Ken Scott, David Bowie / **Sound Engineer:** Dennis MacKay / **Arrangements:** David Bowie, Mick Ronson

The Rise and Fall of Ziggy Stardust and the Spiders from Mars is far more complex than a classic rock album from the '70s. And this is precisely where the composer's magic lies, blending his soul, blues, and heavy metal influences with his 1972 goal of producing the ultimate pop-rock record. "Soul Love," which portrays a mother mourning the loss of her son in battle, is peppered with a gentle line of percussion, accompanied by a saxophone solo performed by the singer himself. This beautiful song, which is all too often underestimated, was interpreted in a funk version during the "Stage Tour" of 1978, the singer's velvety sax being replaced for the occasion by a majestic synthesizer solo by Roger Powell. In 1976, Mick Ronson also recorded the song in an astonishing country-blues version, which remained in his record company's drawers until the rerelease of his second LP, *Play Don't Worry*, in 1997.

MOONAGE DAYDREAM

David Bowie / 4:40

Musicians: David Bowie: lead vocals, twelve-string acoustic guitar, recorder, saxophone, backing vocals / Mick Ronson: electric guitar, piano, backing vocals / Trevor Bolder: bass / Mick "Woody" Woodmansey: drums / Unidentified Musicians: orchestra / **Recorded:** Trident Studios, London: November 12, 1971 / **Technical Team:** Producers: Ken Scott, David Bowie / **Sound Engineer:** Dennis MacKay / **Arrangements:** David Bowie, Mick Ronson

Recorded for the first time with the Arnold Corns, "Moonage Daydream" came out of Bowie's bag to become one of the pillars of his fifth album, and one of the Spiders' favorite songs. The track proved to be something of a challenge for Ken Scott and the musicians, however, who were used to doing only one or two takes on each song. For this track, no less than ten takes were required, since the frequency of breaks at the beginning of each verse caused a number of false starts by one or the other artist during the recording. The solo is played by Bowie on the saxophone and, unusually, on the recorder, which was an instrument he rarely used. The influence of "Sho' Know a Lot About Love" from the Hollywood Argyles is palpable when you listen to the mix, which blends the two instruments. This title, released as the B-side of "Alley-Oop" in 1960, might have inspired David Bowie to write "Life on Mars?"

1972

STARMAN

David Bowie / 4:12

Musicians
David Bowie: lead vocals, twelve-string acoustic guitar, claps
Mick Ronson: acoustic guitar, electric guitar, piano, backing vocals
Trevor Bolder: bass
Mick "Woody" Woodmansey: drums
Unidentified Musicians: orchestra

Recording
Trident Studios, London: February 4, 1972

Technical Team
Producers: Ken Scott, David Bowie
Sound Engineer: Dennis MacKay
Arrangements: David Bowie, Mick Ronson

SIDE A: *Starman*
SIDE B: *Suffragette City*
UK Release on RCA: April 28, 1972 (ref. RCA 2199)
US Release on RCA: May 1972 (ref. 74-0719)
Best UK Chart Ranking: 10
Best US Chart Ranking: 65

1972

FOR BOWIE ADDICTS

When the Spanish branch of RCA published the artist's new single, subtitles were added to the songs. "Starman" literally became "El Hombre Estrella," and "John, I'm Only Dancing" was translated by "John, Sólo Estoy Bailando."

Genesis

As the production of the album came to an end in February 1972, Dennis Katz, the artistic director at RCA, wanted to repeat the achievement of "Space Oddity" with a single whose theme was similar to the singer's space anthem. "They [the label's big shots] liked the album, but they didn't feel that it had a song that would grab people instantly,"[43] explained drummer Mick Woodmansey in 2016. In response, Bowie wrote "Starman," which immediately replaced the cover of "Around and Around" by Chuck Berry, which the band had recorded for the album in November. Although David always had a passion for science fiction, his attachment to a singer known as the Legendary Stardust Cowboy (from whom he borrowed the name "Stardust") is undoubtedly at the origin of the song's theme. In 1968, with the release of his single "I Took a Trip on a Gemini Spaceship" (which Bowie subsequently covered on *Heathen* in 2002), the American rocker talked about his childhood, declaring: "At this age I used to look at the moon and told myself that someday man will go to the moon. I would like to go to Mars instead of the moon."[29] As Mick Woodmansey would later recall, "It was an obvious single! I think Mick [Ronson] and I went out in the car after David played it for us the first time, and we were already singing it, having only heard it only once. [...] It's not a fluke to be able to write all those amazing tunes."[62] Promoted by a successful performance on *Top of the Pops* on July 6, 1972, and rendered unforgettable by the sexually ambiguous image reflected by Bowie and Ronson side by side in front of the microphone, the song would become one of the biggest hits of 1972.

Production

In 1972, Marc Bolan, the lead singer with T. Rex, then at the height of his fame after the success of his album *Electric Warrior*, became Bowie's obsession...and vice versa. An outstanding performance on *Top of the Pops* in February 1971, in which the singer with the brown curls wore silver makeup under each eye, made him the undisputed creator of the glam-rock movement, but he was closely followed by David Bowie. Everything in "Starman" seems to be inspired by Tony Visconti's polished production of *Electric Warrior*:

David Bowie and his Spiders from Mars performing "Starman" on the set of Lift Off with Ayshea on June 15, 1972.

muffled drums, discreet strings that support Bowie's soaring vocals, claps on the post-refrains that accompany Ronson's riffs, as biting as T. Rex's rhythms. Bowie even adds a wink to Bolan's hit "Hot Love" at 3:17 with his "na-na-na." As if to satisfy Dennis Katz, the song's introduction with its delicate chords on the acoustic twelve-string is reminiscent of the first measures of "Space Oddity." The main melody revisits Judy Garland's hit song "Over the Rainbow," taken from *The Wizard of Oz* (1939). For the "Morse code," as the musicians call it, that appears before each chorus of the song, Ken Scott first recorded the note A on the piano, then the double with two guitars, both played in octaves, all treated with a phaser effect that was very fashionable at the time.

In 1973, Mick Ronson presented his friend Kevin Richardson with a tape featuring some of the tracks recorded by Bowie and the Spiders during rehearsals. The idea was that he could learn to play the songs of his favorite band. In 2019, Richardson stumbled upon the tape, which contained demo versions of "Starman," "Moonage Daydream," and "Hang On to Yourself." The tape was auctioned by Omega Auctions on March 12, 2019, and sold for €47,963.

David Bowie and his friend, singer Dana Gillespie, whose vocals were immortalized in "It Ain't Easy."

IT AIN'T EASY

Ron Davies / 2:54

Musicians: David Bowie: lead vocals, twelve-string acoustic guitar / Mick Ronson: electric guitar, backing vocals / Trevor Bolder: bass / Mick "Woody" Woodmansey: drums / Rick Wakeman: harpsichord / Dana Gillespie: backing vocals / **Recorded:** Trident Studios, London: July 9, 1971 / **Technical Team:** Producers: David Bowie, Ken Scott / **Arrangements:** David Bowie, Mick Ronson

This song by the American singer Ron Davies, from whom Bowie had previously borrowed the riff of "Silent Song Through the Land" for "Andy Warhol," had already been covered in 1970 by the American band Three Dog Night, then by the British bluesman John Baldry in 1971, with Ron Wood on guitar and Scottish singer Maggie Bell on backing vocals (all produced by Rod Stewart).

Recorded in July 1971, this new version had been eliminated from the track-listing of *Hunky Dory* at the last minute. If Dana Gillespie, David Bowie's longtime friend, provides some discreet backing vocals on the track, it is because at that time the two singers were preparing *BOWPROMO*, a promotional disc that Tony Defries was planning to use to find them a contract. The singer would have to wait for EMI's rerelease of *The Rise and Fall of Ziggy Stardust and the Spiders from Mars* in 1999 to finally appear in the credits. Another musician, whose harpsichord line provides the tempo, also appears on the track. This is David's friend Rick Wakeman, who was already at work on "Life on Mars?" "Kooks," and "Changes," and at that time was a member of the famous prog rock group Yes.

LADY STARDUST

David Bowie / 3:19

Musicians: David Bowie: lead vocals, twelve-string acoustic guitar, backing vocals / Mick Ronson: piano, backing vocals / Trevor Bolder: bass / Mick "Woody" Woodmansey: drums, tambourine / **Recorded:** Trident Studios, London: November 12, 1971 / **Technical Team:** Producers: Ken Scott, David Bowie / Sound Engineer: Dennis MacKay / Arrangements: David Bowie, Mick Ronson

When the lights went out in the Rainbow Theatre on August 19, 1972, the theme tune "March from a *Clockwork Orange*," a reinterpretation of Ludwig van Beethoven's Ninth Symphony done by Wendy Carlos for the film *Clockwork Orange*, rang out. After the score concluded, Bowie came onstage to the sounds of the introduction to "Lady Stardust," which was played on the piano by Matthew Fisher, the former keyboardist with Procol Harum, who joined the Spiders for the evening and for a concert the following day. While Bowie began the first verse, "*People stared at the makeup on his face / Laughed at his long black hair, his animal grace*," a photo of Marc Bolan, the lead singer from T. Rex, appeared on a giant screen in the background. Here Bowie paid tribute to his fellow singer and archrival who, since stealing his friend and producer Tony Visconti, had gone on to reach the top of the charts with his hits "Hot Love" and "Bang a Gong (Get It On)."

A first demo of "Lady Stardust" was recorded at the London studio of Radio Luxembourg on March 9 and 10, 1971, at the same time as another song, "Right On Mother," which Bowie offered to Peter Noone, in addition to the future hit "Oh! You Pretty Thing." Performed on the piano by its composer, this original version would later reappear as a bonus track on Rykodisc's 1990 reissue of *The Rise and Fall of Ziggy Stardust and the Spiders from Mars*. The track was rerecorded at Trident Studios on November 12, 1971, along with "Moonage Daydream," "Soul Love," and a new version of "The Supermen," which would be released in 1972 on the compilation album *Revelations: A Musical Anthology for Glastonbury Fayre*. The Brazilian Seu Jorge's adaptation of the song for the soundtrack of Wes Anderson's movie *The Life Aquatic* in 2003 underlines the timeless melody of this song, which remains, definitively, one of the true grace moments of David Bowie's most famous album.

FOR BOWIE ADDICTS

As the working title of the song, "Song for Marc," would have been a little too explicit in the eyes of the general public, Bowie decided that "Lady Stardust" (Ziggy's female alter ego) would be appropriate for Marc Bolan, king of the glam-rock style, who was on the precipice of losing his crown.

STAR

David Bowie / 2:45

Musicians: David Bowie: lead vocals, backing vocals / Mick Ronson: electric guitar, piano, backing vocals / Trevor Bolder: bass / Mick "Woody" Woodmansey: drums / **Recorded:** Trident Studios, London: November 11, 1971 / **Technical Team:** Producers: Ken Scott, David Bowie / Sound Engineer: Dennis MacKay / Arrangements: David Bowie, Mick Ronson

On July 18, 1971, Bob Grace, David Bowie's publisher at Chrysalis, introduced him to a young rock band called Chameleon. The artist offered them the song "Star," of which they recorded a very successful pop version thanks to the voice of the charismatic Les Payne. Unfortunately for Chameleon, "Star" never made it beyond the demo stage. Bowie reclaimed the track and gave it a very rockabilly flavor, with a piano line worthy of Jerry Lee Lewis at his best. For his part, Mick Woodmansey acknowledged having borrowed Mitch Mitchell's drum pattern from the Jimi Hendrix song "I Don't Live Today," on the 1967 album *Are You Experienced*.

HANG ON TO YOURSELF

David Bowie / 2:38

Musicians: David Bowie: lead vocals, twelve-string acoustic guitar, claps, backing vocals / Mick Ronson: electric guitar, claps, backing vocals / Trevor Bolder: bass / Mick "Woody" Woodmansey: drums / **Recorded:** Trident Studios, London: November 11, 1971 / **Technical Team:** Producers: Ken Scott, David Bowie / Sound Engineer: Dennis MacKay / **Arrangements:** David Bowie, Mick Ronson

Glen Matlock, the first bassist with the Sex Pistols before the arrival of the sulfurous Sid Vicious, confessed that the riff of their punk anthem "God Save the Queen" was borrowed from Bowie's "Hang On to Yourself." No hard feelings, since before composing this song, Bowie himself had undoubtedly listened many times to Eddie Cochran's "Summertime Blues" (1958) or Tammy Wynette's country hit "Your Good Girl's Gonna Go Bad" (1967). The riff that launches the verses of "Hang On to Yourself" is a classic gimmick of the rockabilly style and was not uncommon in songs of this period. Once again, Bowie offers a new version of a previous song. In this case the B-side of the single from the Arnold Corns, the project that Freddie Burretti had created from scratch, and the A-side, "Moonage Daydream," had also been reused for this album. Two sessions were necessary for the production of the track. A first version was recorded at Trident Studios on November 8, 1971, with sound engineer Mike Stone at the controls. This was then rejected in favor of a new take, recorded three days later by Ken Scott and Dennis MacKay.

ZIGGY STARDUST

David Bowie / 3:14

Musicians

David Bowie: lead vocals, twelve-string acoustic guitar, backing vocals
Mick Ronson: electric guitar, backing vocals
Trevor Bolder: bass
Mick "Woody" Woodmansey: drums, shaker

Recording

Trident Studios, London: November 1971

Technical Team

Producers: Ken Scott, David Bowie
Sound Engineer: Dennis MacKay
Arrangements: David Bowie, Mick Ronson

1972

Genesis

A pillar of the concept that fans love to develop around the album and the Ziggy character, "Ziggy Stardust" is an emblematic song of the glam-rock movement, and one of the most eagerly awaited by fans at concerts. "People would be waiting and waiting for that song," recalled Mick Woodmansey in 2017. "Like when we were in Japan and he would sing that line 'like some cat from Japan' and the place would just go berserk!"[62] Not merely a pop song with irresistible verses, "Ziggy Stardust" announces the event that will soon rock the glamosphere. The prediction comes in the last verse, when Bowie sings about his superstar character, killed by his own fans: *"When the kids had killed the man / I had to break up the band."* On July 3, 1973, he did the same by destroying the fruit of several years of hard work on the stage of the Hammersmith Odeon, where he announced the dissolution of his band, the Spiders, shortly before ending his set with the aptly named "Rock 'n' Roll Suicide." Although it didn't enjoy the privilege of appearing as a single at the time of the release of the album (RCA having a clear preference for the hit "Starman"), "Ziggy Stardust," with its famous introduction in *G-R-D* adored by all budding guitarists, did have the honor of being the B-side of the hit "The Jean Genie" when it was released on November 24, 1972.

Production

On February 12, 1972, when the album was finished, Bowie performed at Imperial College in London. This venue, beyond the excellence of its teaching staff, is famous for having seen the birth within its walls of the band Smile, the first iteration of Queen. The founding members, Brian May and Roger Taylor, were in the audience that night. At the end of the concert, they came up to the stage and asked the roadies about certain technical aspects of the show, including how Mick Ronson obtained that special guitar sound with its accentuated midrange. It wasn't until later that the guitarist revealed the trick: He used a wah-wah pedal, originally designed to change frequencies in real time. But unlike Jimi Hendrix, who made his guitar sing while playing his riffs—listen to the intro of "Voodoo Child (Slight Return)"—Ronson blocked the pedal's movement in the

David Bowie performing for an audience at Imperial College on February 12, 1972. In the audience that evening were two members of Queen: drummer Roger Taylor and guitarist Brian May.

high-mids, didn't touch it anymore, and thus obtained this sound, the same sound that we hear in Brian May's playing throughout his career. The *single notes* that Ronson plays throughout the verses of "Ziggy Stardust" (especially at 0:28) were to have a lasting influence on the smooth play of Queen's exceptional guitarist.

The drum pattern was inspired in Woodmansey by the drum rolls on "21st Century Schizoid Man," which appeared on King Crimson's 1969 album *In the Court of the Crimson King*. Indeed, the musician categorically rejected the muffled and very discreet sound that Ken Scott had refined on *Hunky Dory* (and that can also be found on other albums, including Elton John's *Madman Across the Water*, on which Scott served as sound engineer alongside producer Gus Dudgeon). "I knew instinctively that the drum sounds that we used previously [...] wouldn't work for this record,"[54] the producer explained. Using gaffer tape—the black tape used by technicians for all kinds of tasks—and pieces of sponge he stuck on the drumheads, Scott effectively eliminated all kinds of disturbing harmonics, allowing Woodmansey to produce a powerful drum sound, which was brought to the forefront during mixing. You can hear

the rock 'n' roll sound of the drummer right from the introduction of "Ziggy Stardust," and then his numerous snare drum rolls on each chorus. "It was a subtle difference from the *Hunky* drum sound, but enough to make them fit with the harder rock 'n' roll sound of what would soon become *Ziggy*,"[54] they would later confirm. Bowie's voice was recorded twice, and then spaced out in the stereo on the choruses, giving it a strange sound when responding to guitarist Mick Ronson's powerful and incisive chords.

FOR BOWIE ADDICTS

For the character of Gilly, quoted in the first verse of the song, David was inspired by Brian Gill, the leader of a motorcycle gang who became a local celebrity when he was expelled from Bromley Grammar School after insulting the principal, who had asked him to shave his sideburns.

Single

SUFFRAGETTE CITY

David Bowie / 3:25

Musicians
David Bowie: lead vocals, twelve-string acoustic guitar, backing vocals
Mick Ronson: electric guitar, piano, ARP synthesizer, backing vocals
Trevor Bolder: bass
Mick "Woody" Woodmansey: drums

Recording
Trident Studios, London: February 4, 1972

Technical Team
Producers: Ken Scott, David Bowie
Sound Engineer: Dennis MacKay
Arrangements: David Bowie, Mick Ronson

SIDE A: *Suffragette City* / 3:25
SIDE B: *Stay* / 6:08
UK Release on RCA: July 9, 1976 (ref. RCA 2726)
Best Chart Ranking: Did Not Chart

1972

FOR BOWIE ADDICTS

George Underwood, Bowie's childhood friend, maintains that he was behind the famous gimmick of the title. "I remember being at Haddon Hall when he first played 'Suffragette City.' And at the end of the performance [...] I shouted out, 'Wham bam, thank you ma'am!' [...] And it obviously ended up on the record."[1]

Genesis

Introduced by its famous line "Wham Bam Thank You Ma'am," which was borrowed from the pianist Charles Mingus and often used to describe a sexual encounter performed in haste and without any tenderness, the finale of "Suffragette City" is a monument of rock 'n' roll. While its title refers to the young women who fought for their right to vote at the beginning of the twentieth century, the narrator seems to be returning from a place populated by pretty girls with loose morals. Before being included in the album's track listing, the song was offered to Mott the Hoople, who elegantly refused it due to its lack of commercial potential. Bowie took "Suffragette City" back for his own album, and the track appeared on the B-side of the single "Starman" on April 28, 1972. It was once again released as a single in July 1976 to promote the *ChangesOneBowie* compilation produced by RCA.

Production

When the young David Jones discovered Little Richard and his synchronized moving brass section in 1957, he swore that one day he would be one of those saxophonists with irresistible charisma. The idea came back to him like a boomerang in 1972, at the time of producing the highly rock-sounding "Suffragette City." But technology had evolved, and the saxophones had been replaced by Trident Studios' brand-new ARP 2500 synthesizer. Ken Scott, tasked with testing the new beast by the studio's bosses, the Sheffield brothers, programmed the machine with a sound close to the saxophone. Bowie offered a melody, Mick Ronson performed it, and Scott and sound engineer Dennis MacKay recorded it. So there was in fact no real saxophone played on the track. That wouldn't stop its author from claiming the opposite in an interview on *In the Studio with Redbeard*. Ken Scott would comment much later: "Then again, lest we forget, we're talking about Mr. Bowie. One can never tell if he didn't remember or he was just telling the interviewer what he wanted to hear."[54]

ROCK'N' ROLL SUICIDE

David Bowie / 2:55

Musicians

David Bowie: lead vocals
Mick Ronson: acoustic guitar, electric guitar, backing vocals
Trevor Bolder: bass
Mick "Woody" Woodmansey: drums
Unidentified Musicians: orchestra

Recording

Trident Studios, London: February 4, 1972

Technical Team

Producers: Ken Scott, David Bowie
Sound Engineer: Dennis MacKay
Arrangements: David Bowie, Mick Ronson

SIDE A: *Rock 'n' Roll Suicide*
SIDE B: *Quicksand*
UK Release on RCA: April 11, 1974 (ref. LPBO 5021)
US Release on RCA: April 11, 1974 (ref. LPBO 5021)
Best UK Chart Ranking: 22
Best US Chart Ranking: Did Not Chart

The writing of "Rock 'n' Roll Suicide" was inspired by Otis Redding's poetic sensibility.

Genesis

The final track of the album is the ideal song to close the concerts of the *Ziggy Stardust* tour. Extremely melancholic for the repertoire of a glam-rock artist, "Rock 'n' Roll Suicide" invokes the spirit of the soul singers that Bowie held up as idols since his time with the Manish Boys. James Brown leads the way, falling to his knees on the stage of the T.A.M.I. Show as his Famous Flames play "Please, Please, Please." In his lyrics, Bowie also pays tribute to Jacques Brel. Since 1966, a musical show by Eric Blau, presented initially in New York and then in the rest of the world, offered English translations of the Belgian singer's repertoire: *Jacques Brel Is Alive and Well and Living in Paris*. The American Mort Shuman translated Brel's masterpieces with Eric Blau, including the classic "Jef," with its refrain "*Non Jef, t'es pas tout seul*," translated for the show as "No love, you're not alone." This last line will be the climax of "Rock 'n' Roll Suicide," and more broadly of *The Rise and Fall of Ziggy Stardust and the Spiders from Mars*.

Production

While "Rock 'n' Roll Suicide" inescapably calls to mind the work of James Brown, it is another artist who is quoted at the end of the track. To give his already melancholic song a dark ending, Bowie borrowed one of Otis Redding's most famous conclusions. Following the example of the coda of "I've Been Loving You Too Long (to Stop Now)" by the African-American singer, the melody of "Rock 'n' Roll Suicide" breaks in its finale, at 2:15, when the score rises a semitone, going from *C-A* to *C#-A#*. This little trick enabled Redding to share his overwhelming feeling with his audience, and it worked equally well in Bowie's song. The brass section added by Mick Ronson accentuates the soul-hit feeling where pain and despair are blended together.

Exceptionally, Ken Scott didn't record the vocals in a single take, as he was prevented from doing so by a technical aspect of production. Because vocal power varied throughout the track, from quiet singing to a cry of desperation, the producer had to record two separate parts, changing the preamp settings between takes to avoid signal saturation. There was only one take for each part, however!

A festive atmosphere at
Speakeasy, near Oxford
Circus in 1967 London.

Side A

JOHN, I'M ONLY DANCING

David Bowie / 2:51

Musicians
David Bowie: lead vocals, twelve-string acoustic guitar, claps
Mick Ronson: electric guitar, backing vocals, claps
Trevor Bolder: bass, claps
Mick "Woody" Woodmansey: drums, claps
Lindsay Scott: violin
The Faces: claps

Recording
Olympic Studios, London: June 26, 1972

Technical Team
Producer: David Bowie
Sound Engineer: Keith Harwood

SIDE A: *John, I'm Only Dancing*
SIDE B: *Hang On to Yourself*

Genesis
But who is this John that's so upset to see David dancing with a man? The origin of this glam-rock anthem, which openly echoes Bowie's declaration of his homosexuality in the pages of *Melody Maker* in January 1972, was finally revealed by journalist Paul Trynka in his 2011 biography, *Starman*. During a party at the Speakeasy, a club on Margaret Street in London, John Cambridge, the first drummer of the Hype (before his replacement by Mick "Woody" Woodmansey), was shocked to see David dancing with a man, leaving his wife, Angie, on the sidelines where she didn't seem at all bothered by the situation. Amused, Bowie transformed the situation into the title and theme of his song "John, I'm Only Dancing."

The song was released as a single in September 1972 in the United Kingdom only, as the American market was not considered ready for a song with such explicit sexual connotations. Mick Rock, the famous photographer of the 1970s, took advantage of the band's rehearsals at the Rainbow Theatre to film a short video to accompany the release of the single. It shows a Bowie all dressed in leather, proud to show off a small temporary tattoo in the shape of an anchor on the top of his cheek.

Production
There are several versions of "John, I'm Only Dancing." The first was recorded on June 24, 1972, at Trident Studios, with Ken Scott at the controls, but for some unknown reason, the band met again two days later at Olympic Studios on Church Road for new takes. This time, it was sound engineer Keith Harwood at the controls, under the orders of producer Bowie. This version was released as a single, without Scott's knowledge, with the members of the Faces as prestigious guests, clapping in the entrance lobby alongside the Spiders. The natural reverb of the venue is perceptible when listening to the track. The song would be rerecorded twice: the first time accompanied by saxophone, on January 20, 1973, to feature on *Aladdin Sane*, and then a second time during the sessions for *Young Americans*, with this last version being released as a single in 1979.

VELVET GOLDMINE

David Bowie / 3:08

Musicians: David Bowie: lead vocals, twelve-string acoustic guitar / Mick Ronson: electric guitar, backing vocals / Trevor Bolder: bass / Mick "Woody" Woodmansey: drums, percussion / **Recorded:** Trident Studios, London: November 11, 1971 / **Technical Team:** Producers: Ken Scott, David Bowie / **Sound Engineer:** Dennis MacKay

"Velvet Goldmine," which would give its title to Todd Haynes's fictional film recounting the glory years of glam rock and the iconic Ziggy Stardust, was recorded on the same day as other precious outtakes, including "Sweet Head" and "Looking for a Friend." The song, which benefitted from an extremely high level of writing and production (including a majestic finale of whispers, laughter, and whistles) has, surprisingly, disappeared from the track listing of *The Rise and Fall of Ziggy Stardust and the Spiders from Mars.* In September 1975, "Velvet Goldmine" was the perfect choice of B-side for the rerelease of "Space Oddity" by RCA.

SWEET HEAD

David Bowie / 4:14

Musicians: David Bowie: lead vocals, twelve-string acoustic guitar / Mick Ronson: electric guitar, backing vocals / Trevor Bolder: bass / Mick "Woody" Woodmansey: drums, percussion / **Recorded:** Trident Studios, London: November 11, 1971 / **Technical Team:** Producers: Ken Scott, David Bowie / **Sound Engineer:** Dennis MacKay

"Sweet Head" and its lyrics, perceived as irreverent due to their reference to fellatio, were removed from the album's track listing so as not to compromise its release in America. In spite of its catchy rhythm, reminiscent of good old "Hound Dog" by Elvis Presley, in terms of quality the track doesn't live up to the songs that were selected for *The Rise and Fall of Ziggy Stardust and the Spiders from Mars.* It did nevertheless appear as a bonus track on the rerelease of the opus by Rykodisc in 1990, alongside "Velvet Goldmine."

LOOKING FOR A FRIEND

David Bowie / 2:11

Musicians: David Bowie: lead vocals, twelve-string acoustic guitar / Mick Ronson: electric guitar, backing vocals / Trevor Bolder: bass / Mick "Woody" Woodmansey: drums, percussion / **Recorded:** Trident Studios, London: November 11, 1971 / **Technical Team:** Producers: Ken Scott, David Bowie / **Sound Engineer:** Dennis MacKay

Accustomed to recording multiple versions of his songs, Bowie couldn't resist the temptation to once again set in stone this blues track offered to Freddie Burretti for the Arnold Corns. There were no major differences in this third recording (the first having been made during the BBC Session of June 3, 1971, and the second for Burretti on June 17), except perhaps for the quality of the setup, fruit of the cohesion of the Spiders: Mick Ronson, Trevor Bolder, and Mick Woodmansey.

THE SUPERMEN

David Bowie / 2:41

Musicians: David Bowie: lead vocals, twelve-string acoustic guitar / Mick Ronson: electric guitar, backing vocals / Trevor Bolder: bass / Mick "Woody" Woodmansey: drums, percussion / **Recorded:** Trident Studios, London: November 12, 1971 / **Technical Team:** Producers: Ken Scott, David Bowie / **Sound Engineer:** Dennis MacKay

Recorded for the first time during the sessions for *The Man Who Sold the World,* "The Supermen" was the subject of a second recording session on November 12, 1971. The Spiders decided to get rid of Visconti's bass in favor of Bowie's folk guitar, letting Ronson's powerful and effective riffs come in on the choruses. Admittedly, revisiting his repertoire had by then become a custom for the British singer, but the new version of this mysterious track had a precise goal here: to be included in a compilation devoted to the Glastonbury Fayre Festival of June 1971, where Bowie was headliner. This compilation, *Revelations: A Musical Anthology for Glastonbury Fayre,* was released in July 1972.

ROUND AND ROUND

Chuck Berry / 2:39

Musicians: David Bowie: lead vocals, tambourine, claps / Mick Ronson: electric guitar, claps, backing vocals / Trevor Bolder: bass / Mick "Woody" Woodmansey: drums / **Recorded:** Trident Studios, London: November 1971 / **Technical Team:** Producers: Ken Scott, David Bowie / **Sound Engineer:** Dennis MacKay

Ever since childhood, David Bowie had been inspired by the energy of rockers such as Little Richard and Chuck Berry. Recorded at Trident Studios in London during the sessions for *The Rise and Fall of Ziggy Stardust and the Spiders from Mars,* this cover of Chuck Berry, originally titled "Around and Around," was eventually dropped from the album's track list in favor of "Starman," which was recorded at the last minute at the request of RCA, who wanted a single. One year later, when Bowie wrote "Aladdin Sane" on the road in America, mixed the single "The Jean Genie" in Nashville and performed in St. Louis on October 11, 1972, the hometown of the author of "Johnny B. Goode," he once again immersed himself in this rock culture. "Round and Round" thus finds its place on the B-side of "Drive-In Saturday," another tribute to the idealized America of the 1950s.

Although Bowie covered Jacques Brel's "La Mort" onstage, it was Brel's version of "Amsterdam" that appeared on the B-side of "Sorrow" in 1973.

AMSTERDAM

Jacques Brel / 3:20
(English adaptation: Mort Shuman, Eric Blau)

Musicians: David Bowie: lead vocals, twelve-string acoustic guitar /
Recorded: Trident Studios, London: November 1971 /
Technical Team: Producers: Ken Scott, David Bowie / **Sound Engineer:** Dennis MacKay

Bowie was introduced to the work of Jacques Brel by the first eponymous album of American Scott Walker, who, in 1967, was already revisiting some of the singer's songs in English. The young David was completely won over by the artist's repertoire when, in July 1968, at the Buchess Theatre, he attended the musical *Jacques Brel Is Alive and Well and Living in Paris*, in which Mort Shuman, Elly Stone, Shawn Elliot, and Alice Whitfield presented English adaptations of the great Jacques. Bowie especially enjoyed "My Death (La Mort)," which he would later cover a number of times onstage, as well as "The Middle Class (Les Bourgeois)" and "You're Not Alone (Jef)," which later inspired him for the finale of "Rock 'n' Roll Suicide." "Amsterdam," the last song of the first act of the show, is about the sailors who come to the busy Dutch port. A song with immense lyrical power, known to French speakers for Brel's unforgettable performance of it at the Olympia in 1964, it had never been recorded in the studio. This was finally achieved with David Bowie's cover, recorded in November 1971 at Trident Studios, which was even considered for inclusion on the album *The Rise and Fall of Ziggy Stardust and the Spiders from Mars*. It was finally selected as the B-side of "Sorrow," released on October 12, 1973. While the Belgian artist magnified his composition with an omnipresent accordion, appropriate to the theme of the song, Bowie offered a more refined version, with a discreet acoustic guitar, which harmonizes with his interpretation. Legend has it that despite the insistence of his British admirer, Brel would never agree to meet with Bowie.

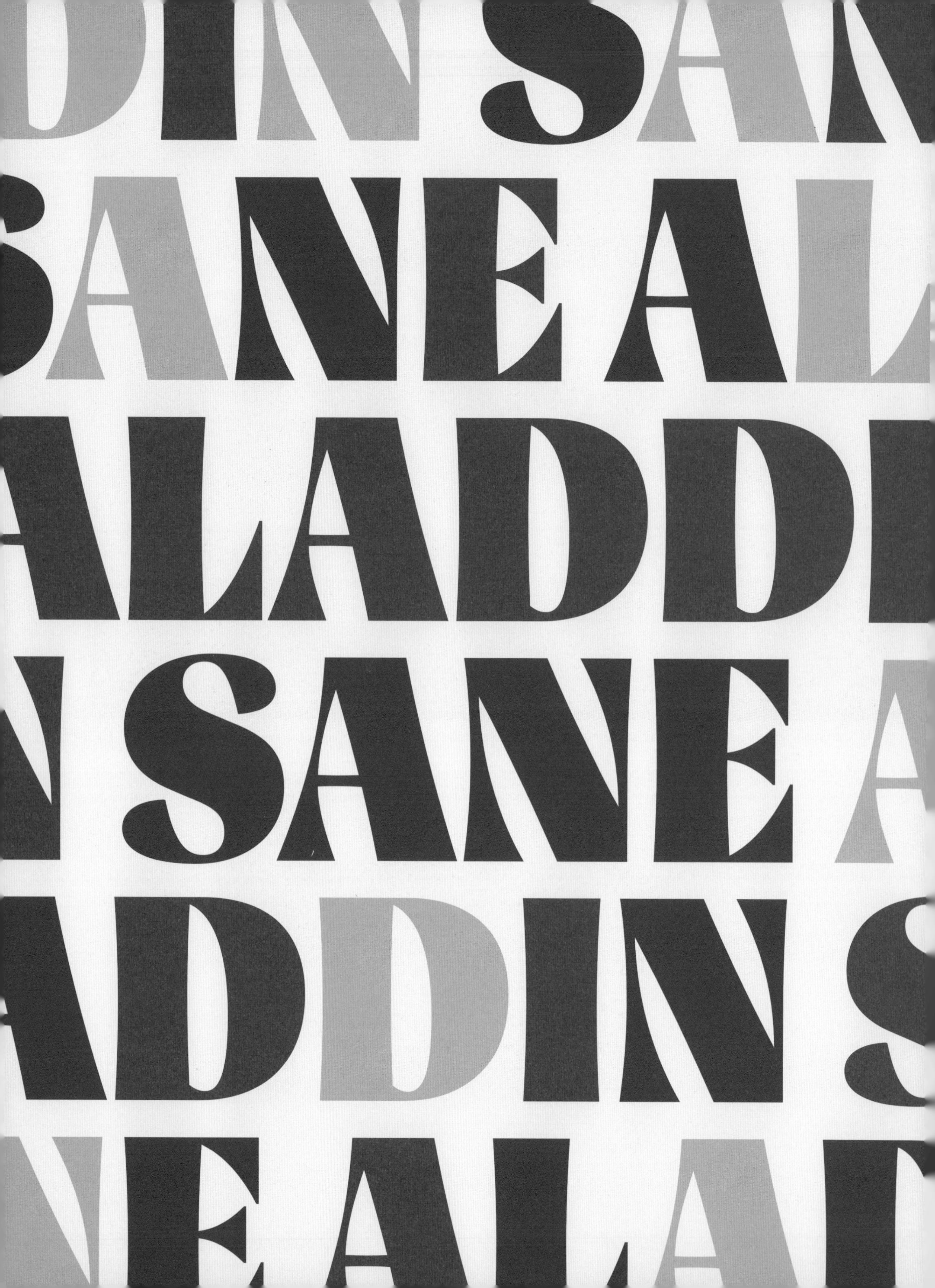

DIN SA
ANE A
LADD
SANE
ADIN
EAL

ALBUM

ALADDIN SANE

Watch That Man . Aladdin Sane (1913-1938-197?) . Drive-In Saturday .
Panic in Detroit . Cracked Actor . Time . The Prettiest Star . Let's Spend the Night Together .
The Jean Genie . Lady Grinning Soul

RELEASE DATES

United Kingdom: April 19, 1973
Reference: RCA—RS 1001 / LSP-4852
United States: April 13, 1973
Reference: RCA—LSP-4852
Best UK Chart Ranking: 1
Best US Chart Ranking: 17

David Bowie between two
concerts at Radio City Music Hall,
in New York circa February 1973.

On the first UK version of *Aladdin Sane*, Bowie
added a note in brackets to each track with the
name of the city in which it had been written:
New York for "Watch That Man," Los Angeles for
"Cracked Actor," and RHMS *Ellinis* for "Aladdin
Sane (1913-1938-197?)," the last being the
name of the ship they traveled home on.

ZIGGY STARDUST IN AMERICA

1973

On September 12, 1972, David Bowie, accompanied by
Angie, George Underwood, and Underwood's wife, Birgit,
embarked on the *Queen Elizabeth II*, sailing from
Southampton, England, to New York. Terrified of airplanes,
for years the singer refused to fly even for long journeys.
After a five-day crossing, the group met up with the rest of
their team: the Spiders, hairdresser Suzi Fussey, body-
guards Stuey George and Tony Frost, several members of
MainMan—Tony Defries's production company—and the
photographer Mick Rock, who from now on was to go
everywhere with David. Organized by Tony Zanetta, this
North American tour was to prove to be quite an adventure. Although they were to crisscross the United States for
three months, only twenty-two concert dates had been
arranged. Sometimes, as in Phoenix, the group stayed shut
up in their hotel for days, expecting to set off again shortly
for concerts in Texas, only to then find them canceled. The
team indulged in every kind of excess. Bowie sought out
new experiences, experimenting particularly with cocaine,
something that was to become a habit for much of the
1970s. Tony Defries, faithful to his motto—"To be a star,
you had to act like a star"[41]—spent RCA's money like water,
booking Bowie and his entourage into the Plaza rather
than a cheap motel. Zanetta was to remember: "We spent
about four hundred and some thousand dollars, we
grossed a hundred thousand dollars. But by December,
David was on the cover of *Rolling Stone* magazine."[41]

"The Jean Genie," the First American Recording

Taking advantage of a stop-off in New York, the team went
to the RCA Studios on October 6 to record a blues-rock
number written in the back of the tour bus during a jam
session. Coming out as a single the following month, on
November 24, "The Jean Genie" was to lead to a series of
notably rock 'n' roll compositions. Based on a classic R&B
riff, it is a glam-rock manifesto with an insistent guitar
rhythm, heralding the direction Bowie's character Ziggy
Stardust was taking on his way to conquering the world.
More faithful than ever to his early influences, Bowie's songs
were now based on the three chords of Black American
blues that were taken up by rock 'n' roll in the 1950s.

This American odyssey was marked by an unusual collaboration. Iggy Pop, whom Bowie had first met in
September 1971, was attempting to resurrect his group, the
Stooges, with the help of his new manager, Tony Defries.
To seal this reunion, an album had just been recorded at
the CBS Studios in London. Presented with compositions
he judged to be too aggressive, Defries urgently asked
Bowie to carry out a new mixing before the album was put
on the market. Despite this divine intervention, Iggy and
the Stooges broke up a few months later. Nevertheless, for
Iggy it marked a return to grace in the world of rock 'n' roll
and the beginning of a long artistic collaboration between
him and Bowie.

Encouraged by the success of his new single, Bowie
embarked on the composition of a new album. The virtuoso
jazz pianist, Mike Garson, had joined the Spiders for the
duration of the tour, contributing his brilliant technique to
the recording sessions. "One night I got a series of phone
calls...the third was from Bowie. I didn't know who he
was. [...] I played four chords for him and Mick Ronson...
I was hired for eight weeks."[63] While able to hammer the
piano in the style of Jerry Lee Lewis or Little Richard, Garson
was also able to accompany the singer's most intimate compositions with great sensitivity, as Rick Wakeman had done
with "The Man Who Sold the World." Written mostly while

Fans sport the colors of *Aladdin Sane* in front of the Earls Court Exhibition Centre in London, where Bowie performed on May 12, 1973.

Following double page
David Bowie and his Spiders from Mars onstage at Earls Court, London, on May 12, 1973.

Bowie once again dressed by couturier Kansai Yamamoto, during his Japanese tour in April 1973.

on tour in the United states, *Aladdin Sane* is Bowie's most American-sounding album, imbued as it is with the spirit of '50s rock.

Aladdin Sane: Last Chapter of the Ziggy Stardust Story

Partly recorded in December 1972 at RCA Studios in New York during the first part of Bowie's American tour, and partly recorded during the following January at the Trident Studios in London, *Aladdin Sane* (a pun on "A lad insane") was released on April 13, 1973, in the United States and April 19 in the UK, where it was acclaimed as a triumph. RCA worked hard to organize presales and the disc went straight to the top of the charts, with more than one hundred thousand copies sold in one week. While it chiefly featured tracks inspired by the blues rock in the style of the Rolling Stones ("Watch That Man," "The Jean Genie," "Cracked Actor") and the American music of the 1950s ("The Prettiest Star," "Drive-In Saturday"), a new and much darker universe emerges between the lines of "Aladdin Sane (1913-1938-197?)" and "Lady Grinning Soul."

David asked the photographer Brian Duffy to do the jacket, and a session was set up in Duffy's studio in Camden. Also present was makeup artist Pierre La Roche, inventor of the famous lightning flash on Ziggy Stardust's face.

Once the recording of the album was complete, the second half of the American tour began, followed by a series of concerts in Japan. For these dates, the group was reinforced by old friends: Geoffrey MacCormack backing vocals and John Hutchinson on acoustic guitar. The guitarist was to recall: "My role really was to play 12-string because David [...] wanted more freedom to move around the stage. And the idea was that he'd get someone to play guitar who could also do backing vocals. I think there was a bit of a budget cut so we didn't get backing vocalists. So Geoff MacCormack and I practiced our falsettos and we did the girly vocals instead."[8]

When Bowie got back to the UK at the beginning of May 1973 to continue the *Ziggy Stardust* world tour, he was faced with discontent from his backing group, the Spiders. Trevor Bolder and Mick Woodmansey had discovered that Mike Garson was being paid much more than them ($800 a

week for Garson, while Woodmansey and Bolder were only getting $80 each) and, on their return from Japan, had become angry about this lack of consideration. Tony Defries, a subtle strategist, seemed to be on their side but at the same time was telling Mick Ronson that he had a future as a solo artist and that the other Spiders were perhaps not needed for Bowie's future projects. As Trevor Bolder described it: "We only saw him [Bowie] as he walked on stage. He separated himself from us toward the end, he was like a solo artist that didn't need us, while in the beginning, he definitely needed us."[29] Many years later, he added: "The bigger he got, the bigger his head got. [...] While he needed you, he was very friendly towards you, but as soon as he'd used you for what he wanted, then he wouldn't go around your door, never to be seen or talked to again."[64]

The high point of the *Ziggy Stardust* tour came on July 3, 1973. The concert at the Hammersmith Odeon in London was designed to celebrate the glory of this figure invented by a Bowie that was still relatively unknown but carried away by the international success of his albums *The Rise and Fall of Ziggy Stardust and the Spiders from Mars* and *Aladdin Sane*. But a few minutes before the end of the concert, just as the group were about to play the appropriately named "Rock 'n' Roll Suicide," and to the great surprise of the musicians, Bowie turned to the audience and announced the end of his group: "Of all the shows on this tour, this particular show will remain with us the longest because not only is it the last show of the tour, but it's the last show that we'll ever do."[65]

FOR BOWIE ADDICTS

In November 1972, Tony Defries approached Phil Spector about producing David Bowie's next album. The notorious producer, who had just produced John Lennon's first solo album, *John Lennon / Plastic Ono Band*, was then at the peak of his fame. Defries's idea was, unfortunately, to come to nothing.

The influence of "Brown Sugar" (1971), by the Rolling Stones, can be heard in "Watch That Man."

WATCH THAT MAN

David Bowie / 4:24

Musicians: David Bowie: lead vocals / **Mick Ronson:** electric guitar, backing vocals / **Trevor Bolder:** bass / **Mick "Woody" Woodmansey:** drums / **Mike Garson:** piano / **Ken Fordham, Brian Wilshaw:** saxophones / **Juanita Franklin, Linda Lewis, Geoffrey MacCormack:** backing vocals / **Recorded:** Trident Studios, London: January 1973 / **Technical Team:** Producers: David Bowie, Ken Scott / Sound Engineer: Ken Scott / **Mixing:** Ken Scott, Mick Ronson / Arrangements: David Bowie, Mick Ronson

Heavily influenced by the Rolling Stones album *Exile on Main St.*, released in May 1972, David Bowie launched his fifth album with "Watch That Man," a number composed in a blues rock style that suits Bowie perfectly. The piano accompaniment, hammering out quavers, lends something of the feel of one of young David's idols, Little Richard and his "Good Golly Miss Molly." RCA thought Bowie's voice was too faint in the initial recording, so they had it remixed several times before eventually being persuaded by Ken Scott to keep the original version. For this first explosive track, Bowie used an expanded team with backing vocals by Juanita Franklin, Linda Lewis, and Geoffrey MacCormack—a childhood friend who would soon to change his name to Warren Peace.

Bowie, a frequent user of quotations from other songs, here uses a slightly altered line from John Lennon's song "I Found Out" (1970): "*The freaks on the phone won't leave me alone*" becoming "*The girl on the phone wouldn't leave me alone.*" Commenting on this bad habit in 1973, he said: "I've always found that I collect. I'm a collector. And I've always just seemed to collect personalities, ideas."[66]

FOR BOWIE ADDICTS

On July 16, 1973, at the Château d'Hérouville, Bowie produced a disco version of "The Man Who Sold the World" for the pop star Lulu. An occasional lead singer, she was also to perform "Watch That Man," using it for the B-side of this single, released January 11, 1974.

While it's not exactly plagiarism, listening to "Givin' Up" from the Darkness' excellent first album (produced in 2003) reveals the extent to which the group must have listened to David Bowie's "Watch That Man"!

After Rick Wakeman, Mike Garson was one of the many talented pianists who appeared on a Bowie album.

ALADDIN SANE (1913–1938–197?)

David Bowie / 5:08

Musicians: David Bowie: lead vocals, twelve-string acoustic guitar / **Mick Ronson:** electric guitar, backing vocals / **Trevor Bolder:** bass / **Mick "Woody" Woodmansey:** drums / **Mike Garson:** piano / **David Bowie (?), Ken Fordham (?), or Brian Wilshaw (?):** saxophone / **Recorded: RCA Studios, New York:** December 1972 / **Trident Studios, London:** January 1973 / **Technical Team: Producers:** David Bowie, Ken Scott / **Sound Engineers:** Mike Moran (RCA Studios), Ken Scott (Trident), Dennis MacKay (Trident) / **Mixing:** Ken Scott, Mick Ronson / **Arrangements:** David Bowie, Mick Ronson

Moving on from the overwhelming rock 'n' roll sound of "Watch That Man," David Bowie next plunges us into a dark and mysterious world inhabited by almost dissonant sounds. Written in December 1972 on board the RHMS *Ellinis* on the way back from the American tour, the song is inspired by the dystopia created in 1930 by the writer Evelyn Waugh in his book *Vile Bodies*, in which the aristocratic youth of Britain are ridiculed for their relaxed morals and thoughtless behavior. There is a reference to the fear of international armed conflict in the song's title, which contains the dates 1913 and 1938, both a year before the outbreak of the two World Wars. The third and incomplete date, with its question mark, implies that peace is fragile

and that this unstable equilibrium is always under threat. Along with the intimate writing and the recurring lament with its punning meaning *"Who'll love Aladdin Sane"* ("Who'll love a lad insane"), the song is enhanced by a wonderful piano solo—lasting over two minutes—by Mike Garson. Bowie had asked him for an improvisation in the avant-garde style of the interwar period, in which musical experimentation took precedence over traditional piano playing. A specialty of Garson's, and characteristic of the "cabaret" spirit Bowie was exploring at this time, this way of playing gave the song an interesting sonority and backing for the lead singer. The sound of piano, saxophone (we don't know who played this—Bowie, Ken Fordham, or Brian Wilshaw?), and the insistent bass of Trevor Bolder intricately interweave to produce a long musical experiment that is both troubling and intoxicating.

The atmosphere of the Berlin cabarets of the interwar period was to inspire many artists. American singer Marilyn Manson—who has always acknowledged his debt to Bowie—was to make it the theme of his 2003 song "The Golden Age of Grotesque." He would use the same title for his fifth album.

1973

DRIVE-IN SATURDAY

David Bowie / 4:28

Musicians: David Bowie: lead vocals, twelve-string acoustic guitar, Moog synthesizer, saxophone, claps / **Mick Ronson:** electric guitar, claps, backing vocals / **Trevor Bolder:** bass / **Mick "Woody" Woodmansey:** drums / **Mike Garson:** piano / **Recorded:** RCA Studios, New York: December 1972 / **Technical Team:** Producers: David Bowie, Ken Scott / **Sound Engineer:** Mike Moran / **Mixing:** Ken Scott, Mick Ronson / Arrangements: David Bowie, Mick Ronson / **Single:** Side A: *Drive-In Saturday* / Side B: *Round and Round* / UK Release on RCA: April 6, 1973 (ref. RCA 2352) / **Best Chart Ranking:** Did Not Chart

Like the new version of "The Prettiest Star" featured on the album or other rock numbers of the period such as Elton John's "Crocodile Rock" (1973) or Alvin Stardust's "My Coo Ca Choo" (1974), nostalgia for the America of the 1950s is very apparent in this song, written on a train between Seattle and Phoenix. Before its inclusion on the *Aladdin Sane* album, this second single, "Drive-In Saturday," was offered to Mott the Hoople, for whom Bowie had just written the hit number "All the Young Dudes." Ian Hunter, lead singer of the group, was annoyed by this suggestion. In his view his group had no need of this kind of outside help and so he turned the song down. He might not have been entirely wrong; Mott the Hoople had a hit with "Honaloochie Boogie" in July 1973, which made it to twelfth place in the UK charts. Bowie's "Drive-In Saturday," by contrast, didn't even get listed when it came out...

The saxophone plays an essential role in this ballad while the use of compound time and backing vocals take us back to the golden days of American doo-wop and hits like "(I'll Remember) in the Still of the Night" by the Five Satins or "The Great Pretender" by the Platters. This effect is emphasized by Mike Garson playing quavers on the piano just as arranger and musician Buck Ram had done on "Only You," one of the greatest doo-wop hits in the United States.

PANIC IN DETROIT

David Bowie / 4:26

Musicians: David Bowie: lead vocals / **Mick Ronson:** electric guitar, backing vocals / **Trevor Bolder:** bass / **Mick "Woody" Woodmansey:** drums / **Juanita Franklin, Linda Lewis:** backing vocals / **Geoffrey MacCormack:** congas, maracas, claps, backing vocals / **Recorded:** Trident Studios, London: January 1973 / **Technical Team:** Producers: David Bowie, Ken Scott / **Sound Engineers:** Ken Scott, Dennis MacKay / **Mixing:** Ken Scott, Mick Ronson / **Arrangements:** David Bowie, Mick Ronson

"Panic in Detroit" was the result of a discussion one night between David Bowie and Iggy Pop, during the remixing of Iggy and the Stooges' *Raw Power* in Los Angeles. Iggy told his English friend about the exploits of the activist John Sinclair, leader of the White Panthers and, incidentally, future manager of the group MC5. Militant pacifist and anti-racist, Sinclair had spent three years in prison after offering an undercover police officer a couple of joints. Many artists campaigned for his release, including John Lennon, Stevie Wonder, and Allen Ginsberg. Iggy Pop also told David about the riots that had taken place in Detroit on July 23, 1967, leading to numerous cases of police brutality and causing lasting damage to the city. Thousands of buildings and shops were

destroyed between July 23 and 27, and forty-three people, of whom thirty-three were black, lost their lives. Quite apart from the seriousness of the subject, "Panic in Detroit" marks a notable turning point in Bowie's artistic development. With a part for conga drums added to the rhythm section, the song gives an important role to the powerful backing vocals provided by Juanita Franklin and Linda Lewis, paving the way for the soul music that was to come.

CRACKED ACTOR

David Bowie / 2:59

Musicians: David Bowie: lead vocals, harmonica / Mick Ronson: electric guitar, backing vocals / Trevor Bolder: bass / Mick "Woody" Woodmansey: drums, tambourine / **Recorded:** Trident Studios, London: January 1973 / **Technical Team:** Producers: David Bowie, Ken Scott / **Sound Engineers:** Ken Scott, Dennis MacKay / **Mixing:** Ken Scott, Mick Ronson / **Arrangements:** David Bowie, Mick Ronson

In the early 1970s, David Bowie, who seemed to be obsessed with both the rise and the fall of stars, was surprised by the outward respectability of Hollywood when he visited California in October 1972. In this song he depicts the seedy, tacky, and damaging end of the reign of an actor, still able to impose his pathetic power on young actors, male and female, hoping to become famous: *"Suck, baby, suck / Give me your head / Before you start professing / That you're knocking me dead."* This first contact with Hollywood did nothing, however, to dent his dreams of being an actor, a hope he would entertain in the coming years. While waiting for his break into acting, he was able to please his fans with a harmonica part that runs right through the number. When first recorded, it was too quiet, buried beneath a wall of guitar sound from Mick Ronson. To get a fuller sound, Ken Scott plugged the harmonica's microphone into the guitarist's Marshall amplifier, using the natural distortion of the amplifier when recording.

TIME

David Bowie / 5:11

Musicians
David Bowie: lead vocals, twelve-string acoustic guitar
Mick Ronson: electric guitar, backing vocals
Trevor Bolder: bass
Mick "Woody" Woodmansey: drums
Mike Garson: piano
Ken Fordham: saxophone
Ben Wilshaw: transverse flute

Recorded
Trident Studios, London: January 1973

Technical Team
Producers: David Bowie, Ken Scott
Sound Engineers: Ken Scott, Dennis MacKay
Mixing: Ken Scott, Mick Ronson
Arrangements: David Bowie, Mick Ronson

SIDE A: *Time*
SIDE B: *The Prettiest Star*
US Release on RCA: June 1, 1973 (ref. RCA APBO-0001)
Best Chart Ranking: Did Not Chart

ON YOUR HEADPHONES
At 1:11, in a nod to his beloved rock 'n' roll, Bowie borrows a phrase from Chuck Berry's "Reelin' and Rockin'": "*Well, I looked at my watch / It was nine twenty-one,*" changing it to "*Well, I look at my watch / It says nine twenty-five.*"

Genesis
While fans and rock music critics of the time might have been watching as David Bowie rose to fame after years of all kinds of different artistic experiments, nothing could have prepared them for this moment of grace. It is true that Bowie had included a fair number of gems on his previous album and perhaps even more on *Hunky Dory*, but nothing to rival "Time," a monument to rock celebrating the rise of '70s glam, worthy to stand alongside Elton John's "Tiny Dancer" (1971) or Queen's "Bohemian Rhapsody" (1975). When Bowie got his friend George Underwood to make a demo of the song to offer to the famous producer Mickie Most, the title was still "We Should Be On by Now." It was to be included on *Aladdin Sane* in 1973 as "Time," the words suggesting a singer plunged into a new mood of nostalgia, trying desperately to slow down the passing of time. Was it prompted by a presentiment of the devastating effects that drugs, the excesses of life as a rock star, and then AIDS were to have on his entourage in the coming fifteen years? Certainly, in this song, he refers to Billy Murcia, original drummer with the New York Dolls, who not long before, at a party given by his girlfriend Marilyn Woolhead, had died of an overdose of methaqualone (not helped by the consumption of large amounts of champagne, black coffee, and an ice bath administered by panicking guests at the party): "*Time, in Quaaludes and red wine / Demanding Billy Dolls / And other friends of mine.*" Paradoxically, when it came out as a single, the song was partly censured for the US market not for the words "*Time, he flexes like a whore / Falls wanking to the floor*" but for its reference to drugs.

Production
Like the solo in "Aladdin Sane (1913-1938-197?)," the piano introduction in "Time" evokes the European cabarets in the interwar period. Talking in 2020, Mike Garson remembered: "[David] told me he wanted it to sound like one of those old pianos from the early 1900s. So I did that style, but he wanted a twist on it, so I played some of those runs a little wacky."[13] The result is unforgettable, the pianist leaving his indelible mark on Bowie's discography, just as

Four-handed guitar playing with Bowie and Mick Ronson,
as captured by the photographer Debi Doss.

Rick Wakeman had done before him on "Life on Mars?" Notable, too, is the omnipresent guitar played by Ronson who, here and there, slips in brief but perfectly structured solos on his Les Paul. Bowie was to describe the unusual method used by his guitarist to enliven solos like that in "Time," at 2:15 and 3:20: "He was actually brilliant at divining what I meant when I would describe in words what I wanted as the shape of the solo in certain songs. The one on 'Time' is a perfect example. [...] One thing he adored

doing while recording was building up layered tracks, so that there would be a great wedge of sound in certain areas of songs, and from there he could fly off into his sinewy lines and riffs in a heartbeat."[41]

Included in the set list of the 1987 "Glass Spider Tour," "Time" sat comfortably among the powerful and modern arrangements typical of the concerts given in the 1980s. Guitarist Carlos Alomar included a brief quotation from *All the Young Dudes* in his classic guitar solo.

THE PRETTIEST STAR

David Bowie / 3:25

Musicians: David Bowie: lead vocals, twelve-string acoustic guitar, claps / Mick Ronson: electric guitar, backing vocals / Trevor Bolder: bass / Mick "Woody" Woodmansey: drums / Mike Garson: piano / Ken Fordham, Brian Wilshaw: saxophones / **Recorded:** RCA Studios, New York: December 1972 / **Technical Team:** Producers: David Bowie, Ken Scott / **Sound Engineer:** Mike Moran / **Mixing:** Ken Scott, Mick Ronson / **Arrangements:** David Bowie, Mick Ronson

Although Bowie had already recorded a memorable version of this song in 1970 with Marc Bolan on guitar, "The Prettiest Star," a little blues number written for Angie at the time they first met, makes its reappearance here.

It differs very little from the original version. Mick Ronson follows Bolan's part note for note, although—as in the album as a whole—there is a more pronounced '50s-style rock feel, heightened by claps, "wap-doo-wap"'s from the backing singers, and some rather superfluous saxophones.

LET'S SPEND THE NIGHT TOGETHER

Keith Richards, Mick Jagger / 3:10

Musicians: David Bowie: lead vocals, twelve-string acoustic guitar, Moog synthesizer, saxophone / Mick Ronson: electric guitar, backing vocals / Trevor Bolder: bass / Mick "Woody" Woodmansey: drums / Mike Garson: piano / **Recorded:** Trident Studios, London: January 1973 / **Technical Team:** Producers: David Bowie, Ken Scott / **Sound Engineers:** Ken Scott, Dennis MacKay / **Mixing:** Ken Scott, Mick Ronson / **Arrangements:** David Bowie, Mick Ronson / **Single:** Side A: *Let's Spend the Night Together* / Side B: *Lady Grinning Soul* / US Release on RCA: July 1973 (ref. APBO-0028) / **Best Chart Ranking:** Did Not Chart

This version of the Rolling Stones single, released in the UK on January 13, 1967, was a godsend for David Bowie. Boycotted when released in the United States on January 14, 1967, this song had all the irreverence required by the provocative Ziggy, but Bowie gives it a more modern feel, singing in the elastic style of Iggy Pop that he both admired and imitated. Here and there, he adds a touch of Minimoog, the revolutionary synthesizer popularized by Wendy Carlos, particularly in the soundtrack of the movie *A Clockwork Orange*, which was an important influence on him. Although it had scandalized prudish America in 1967, "Let's Spend the Night Together" this time was able to come out as a single there in July 1973. It disappeared almost immediately, sinking without a trace.

THE JEAN GENIE

David Bowie / 4:03

Musicians: David Bowie: lead vocals, twelve-string acoustic guitar, harmonica / Mick Ronson: electric guitar, backing vocals / Trevor Bolder: bass / Mick "Woody" Woodmansey: drums / **Recorded:** RCA Studios, New York: October 6–7, 1972 / RCA Studios, Nashville: October 12–13, 1972 (mixing and overdubs of the single version) / **Technical Team:** Producers: David Bowie / **Sound Engineer:** Mike Moran / **Mixing:** David Bowie, Mick Ronson (single version); Ken Scott, Mick Ronson (album version) / **Arrangements:** David Bowie, Mick Ronson / **Single:** Side A: *The Jean Genie* / Side B: *Ziggy Stardust* (UK version) / *Hang On to Yourself* (US version) / **UK Release on RCA:** November 24, 1972 (ref. RCA 2302) / **US Release on RCA:** October 28, 1972 (ref. 74-0838) / **Best UK Chart Ranking:** 2 / **Best US Chart Ranking:** 71

Genesis

Composed at the back of the tour bus at the very beginning of the American tour, "The Jean Genie" was the first song to be recorded by Bowie in the United States, during the time he was staying in New York at the beginning of October 1973. His producer, Ken Scott, had not even packed his bags for departure when Bowie produced this blues rock on his own, including a riff borrowed from the Yardbirds' version of Bo Diddley's "I'm the Man" (1964). This piece also appeared in 1966 as "La Fille du Père-Noël," sung by Jacques Dutronc, and again in 1973 as performed by Sweet in "Blockbuster." It consists essentially of a classic blues sequence, used by all self-respecting guitarists.

In a tribute to Iggy Pop, lead singer of the Stooges, the singer makes an indirect reference to his nickname, "the Iguana": *"Sits like a man but smiles like a reptile."* In 1975, writer Tina Brown explained, "[It's] a portrait satire of Iggy Pop [...], so 'tired' at a recent concert that two heavies had to hurl him on stage. He overshot and landed in the audience, his face connecting with a bag of peanuts."[67] Mick Woodmansey also remembers: "He was rapping about the weird scenes we were hanging out in in New York at the time. [...] There was weirdness in there, things you couldn't understand, sex, drugs and rock & roll are all in that song."[62] Other sources of inspiration can be found, including Cyrinda Foxe, muse of the New York Dolls and publicity agent for MainMan, who had an affair with Bowie during his American tour. As for the title, some say that he is referring to Jean Genet, whose first novel, *Notre-Dame-des-Fleurs*, had recently been adapted for the stage by Lindsay Kemp. Or was he was thinking of Eddie Cochran's 1958 rock hit "Jeanie, Jeanie, Jeanie"? As always, Bowie covers his tracks, leaving his fans to form their own opinions.

FOR BOWIE ADDICTS

David Bowie made Mick Ronson's dream come true when he invited the guitarist's idol, Jeff Beck, to come up and join the Spiders on the stage of the Hammersmith Odeon on July 3, 1973, for an unforgettable version of "The Jean Genie."

Production

Mixed in Nashville in October 1972 by Ronson and Bowie, the single version of "The Jean Genie" was remixed in January 1973 by Ken Scott for inclusion in the album. Whenever the group played this piece, it seemed to be cursed; Trevor Bolder always played the same wrong note. In fact, fate had no hand in it—there is another explanation. In the studio, the first take was correct but, nevertheless, a second was also recorded with a glaringly wrong note by the bass player at 3:07. This was the take chosen for the album. Later, an unrepentant Bolder was to confess: "It fits, so we keep it, and [...] today, if I play that song, I still play that mistake because you gotta play that mistake."[68] Bolder persisted and left his mark when Bowie appeared on *Top of the Pops* on January 3, 1973. Very unusually for this program, the group performed "The Jean Genie" live. Bolder was able to gratify the viewers with a wrong note at 2:58: a cult moment in the history of rock 'n' roll!

For a mixing session in Nashville, the unflappable guitarist Mick Ronson had to record the song's driving rhythm with a small traveling amplifier. His 200-watt Marshall stack had been left on the tour bus that was headed toward Kansas City, where the Spiders were to have their next concert. In June 1973, Ronson revealed some of the secrets of his trade to the readers of *Melody Maker*: To get a sound that was both powerful and compressed, he was from that time on to use a Sola Sound Tone Bender MK1 fuzz pedal coupled to his famous wah-wah pedal kept in a fixed position. The history of this little metal device is interesting. Originally belonging to Pete Townshend, guitarist for the Who, the pedal was sold to a friend of Ronson's who passed it on to Ronson for £5 (about $7). Nowadays, a guitarist wanting one of these little treasures would have to part with well over $1,000, since only a thousand were manufactured.

LADY GRINNING SOUL

David Bowie / 3:50

Musicians: David Bowie: lead vocals, twelve-string acoustic guitar / **Mick Ronson:** electric guitar, classical guitar, backing vocals / **Trevor Bolder:** bass / **Mick "Woody" Woodmansey:** drums / **Mike Garson:** piano / **Ken Fordham, Brian Wilshaw:** saxophones / **Juanita Franklin:** backing vocals / **Recorded: Trident Studios, London:** January 1973 / **Technical Team: Producers:** David Bowie, Ken Scott / **Sound Engineers:** Ken Scott, Dennis MacKay / **Mixing:** Ken Scott, Mick Ronson, David Bowie

David Bowie never disclosed who this Spanish-influenced delicate declaration of love was intended for. Amanda Lear, at that time the muse of Brian Ferry and his group Roxy Music, is often mentioned, but it is more likely to have been Claudia Lennear. The American singer had already inspired the Rolling Stones to write their famous "Brown Sugar," and she was someone Bowie seemed to have been fond of. In 2008, he gave a mysterious but touching hint: "This was written for a wonderful young girl whom I've not seen for well over thirty years. When I hear this song she's still in her twenties, of course. A song will put you tantalizingly close to the past, so close that you can almost reach out and touch it. The sound of ghosts again."[56] Particularly attached to this song, Bowie insisted, for the first time, on taking part in the mixing to make sure it came out as he wanted it.

Ian Hunter, the charismatic singer of Mott the Hoople, took advantage of the success of "All the Young Dudes" to get his group back on track.

ALL THE YOUNG DUDES

David Bowie / 4:10

Musicians: David Bowie: lead vocals, twelve-string acoustic guitar, saxophone / **Mick Ronson:** electric guitar, backing vocals / **Trevor Bolder:** bass / **Mick "Woody" Woodmansey:** drums / **Mike Garson:** piano / **Geoffrey MacCormack:** backing vocals / **Recorded:** RCA Studios, New York: December 9, 1972 / **Technical Team:** Producers: David Bowie, Ken Scott / **Sound Engineer:** Mike Moran / **Mixing:** Ken Scott, Mick Ronson / **Arrangements:** David Bowie, Mick Ronson

"All the Young Dudes" was originally offered to Mott the Hoople, and the success of their single saved the group from an imminent breakup. Hoping to produce a better version, Bowie couldn't resist recording his own version of the song a few months later. Although it was to become one of the stock numbers in his concerts, the studio version was not popular with the public, particularly after Ian Hunter, lead singer of Mott the Hoople, stated that it was not as good as his group's version. Guided by his instinct—and by the reviews—Bowie put away this version. It did not reappear until 1997, in the compilation *The Best of David Bowie 1969/1974*, along with another rarity: "Velvet Goldmine."

JOHN, I'M ONLY DANCING

David Bowie / 2:45

Musicians: David Bowie: lead vocals, twelve-string acoustic guitar / **Mick Ronson:** electric guitar, backing vocals / **Trevor Bolder:** bass / **Mick "Woody" Woodmansey:** drums, tambourine / **Ken Fordham:** saxophone / **Brian Wilshaw:** saxophone / **Recorded:** Trident Studios, London: January 20, 1973 / **Technical Team:** Producers: Ken Scott, David Bowie / **Sound Engineers:** Ken Scott, Dennis MacKay

Although a very successful first version of this song had come out as a single in the UK in September 1972, the indefatigable Bowie hoped that a more aggressive version, involving Ken Fordham and Ben Wilshaw on saxophones, could be included on *Aladdin Sane*. While it is true that its rockabilly style fits the general tone of the album, the best is the enemy of the good, and Bowie was to shelve this (third!) version of "John, I'm Only Dancing." Not content with that, he recorded an unrecognizable disco/funk version during the recording sessions for *Young Americans* in 1974, issuing it as a single in 1979.

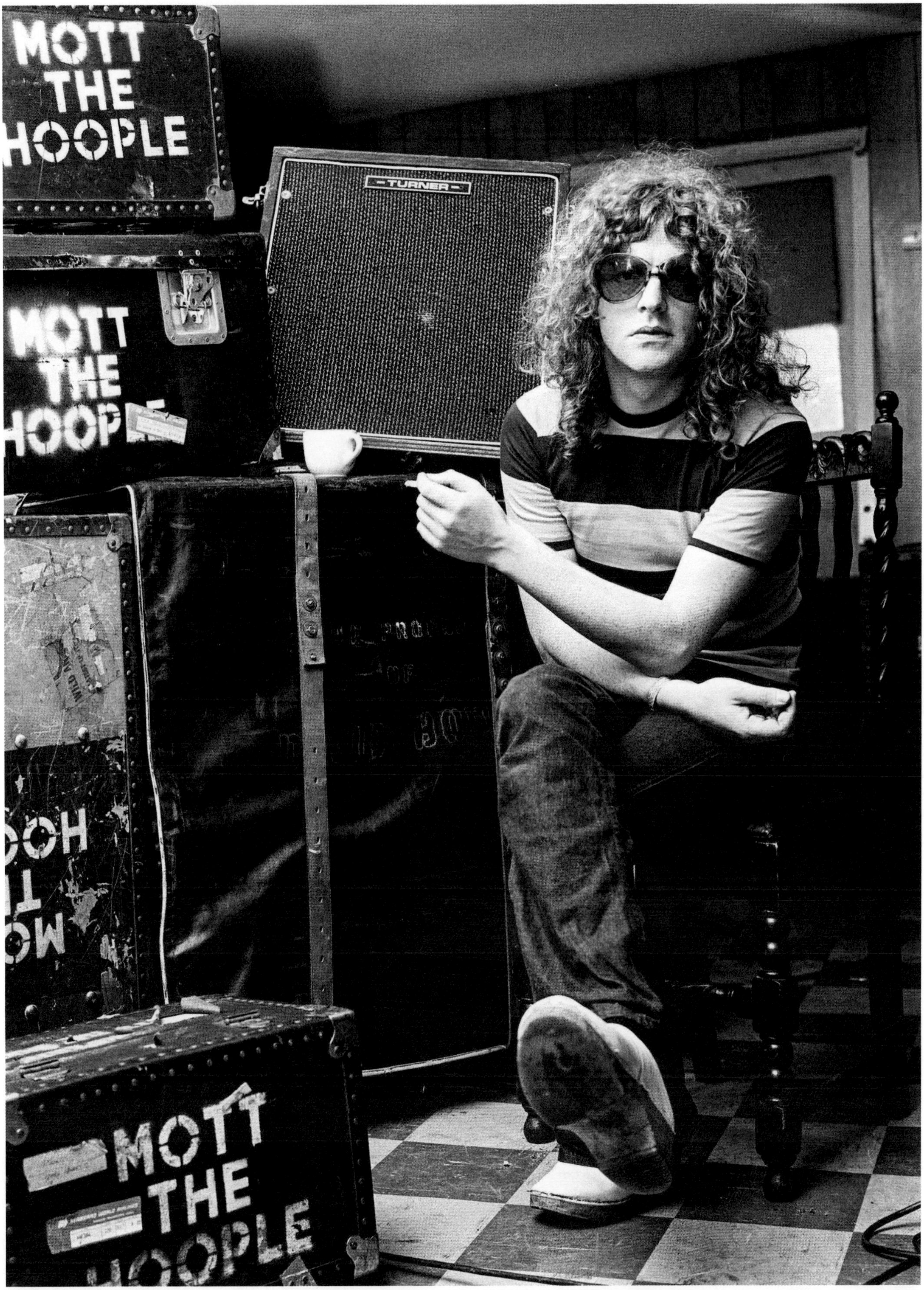
MOTT
THE
HOOPLE
TURNER
MOTT
THE
MOTT
THE
HOOPLE

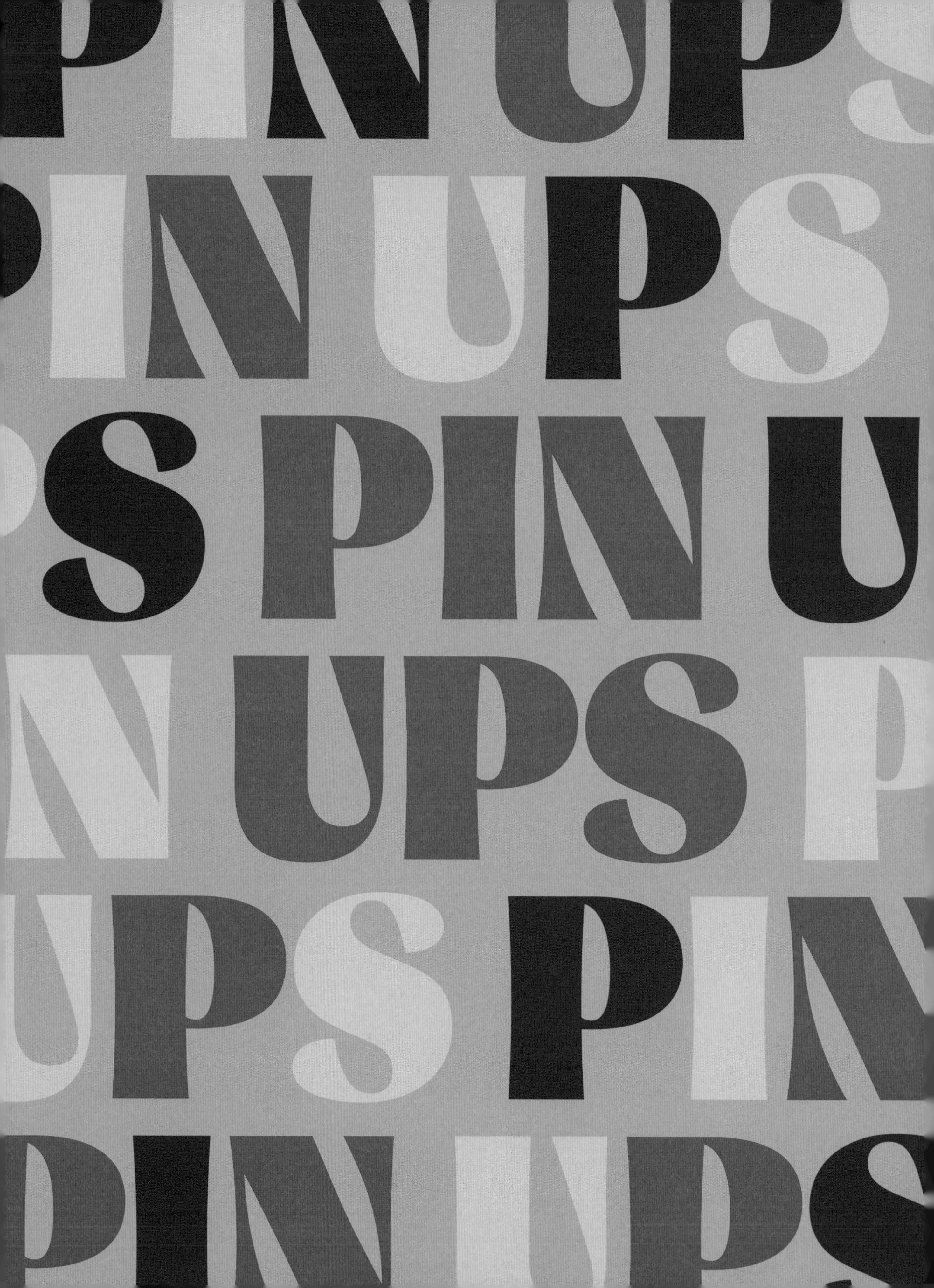
PIN UPS

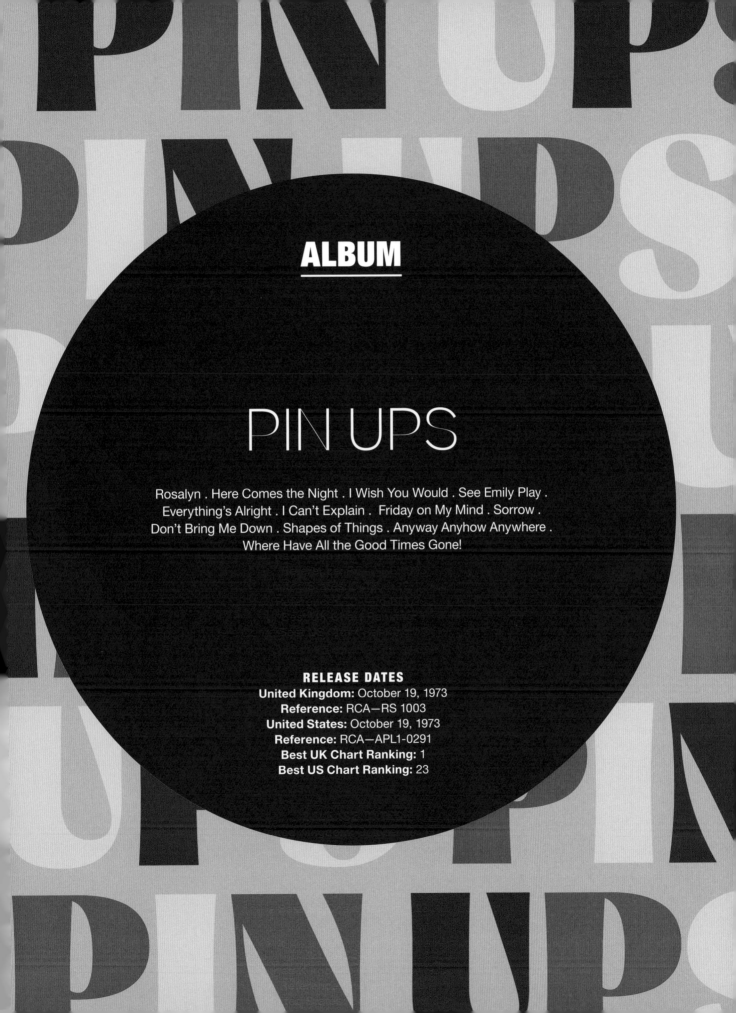

ALBUM

PIN UPS

Rosalyn . Here Comes the Night . I Wish You Would . See Emily Play .
Everything's Alright . I Can't Explain . Friday on My Mind . Sorrow .
Don't Bring Me Down . Shapes of Things . Anyway Anyhow Anywhere .
Where Have All the Good Times Gone!

RELEASE DATES
United Kingdom: October 19, 1973
Reference: RCA—RS 1003
United States: October 19, 1973
Reference: RCA—APL1-0291
Best UK Chart Ranking: 1
Best US Chart Ranking: 23

EARLY DAYS AT THE CHÂTEAU D'HÉROUVILLE

1973

On July 3, 1973, in words that became legendary, David Bowie committed the unthinkable onstage at the Hammersmith Odeon in London by killing off Ziggy Stardust and his Spiders from Mars. In so doing, he destroyed in a few seconds the fruit of several years' work. Far from being a sudden, self-destructive whim, this decision had been arrived at secretly with Tony Defries and Mick Ronson after the Japan tour of April 1973. A few days later, on his wedding day, the group's drummer, Mick Woodmansey, was to be politely dismissed. Bowie, sitting near his group, declined to speak directly to his drummer, leaving Tony Defries to bring an official end to their collaboration.

Bowie instantly threw himself a new project: recording a disc of cover versions. A playlist was quickly drawn up that was a patchwork of mainly British rock numbers from the late 1960s. On July 9, he crossed the English Channel to France, settling in at the Château d'Hérouville, fifty kilometers north of Paris, in the Val-d'Oise. Owned by the composer Michel Magne, since the beginning of the decade the chateau, built in 1740, had been a refuge for British musicians fleeing the United Kingdom to avoid the taxman. During this period, discs recorded abroad were not subject to tax. The Rolling Stones chose the Côte d'Azur, and Queen chose Switzerland and Germany.

Michel Magne's setup was not the usual kind of recording studio. The Strawberry Studio stood in the middle of nearly five acres of land with a tennis court, a swimming pool, and ten bedrooms. Although not operating officially, its existence was well-known by word of mouth, particularly because of the recordings made there not long before of two of Elton John's greatest albums: the appropriately named *Honky Château* and *Don't Shoot Me I'm Only the*

Piano Player, the latter notable for the magnificent singles "Daniel" and "Crocodile Rock." An attractive recommendation, particularly since Ken Scott, co-producer of David Bowie's recent recordings, had worked alongside Gus Dudgeon as sound engineer on Elton John's two discs. It did not take much to convince Bowie that this was the place he was looking for.

From Ziggy Stardust to *Pin Ups*

After the breakup of the Spiders and departure of Mick Woodmansey, a new backing band had to be found. Aynsley Dunbar, formerly drummer with the Mojos and then with the Jeff Beck Group, met Bowie in London while he was playing the drum parts for *Berlin*, Lou Reed's third solo album. He agreed to join Bowie and was to feature on two albums. Jack Bruce, the bass player with Cream, declined the invitation to join, forcing Bowie to call on Trevor Bolder again. This was to be the last time they worked together. Ken Scott was invited to co-produce the disc—the last time for him, too—assisted by his faithful sound engineer Dennis MacKay, now calling himself "Blackeye." The team spent three weeks at Hérouville, in an atmosphere that felt like the end of an era, with the accent on serious work. "It didn't have the same camaraderie as when we're at Trident doing *Aladdin Sane*, but it was certainly very special,"[13] Scott was to say. David Bowie was more positive: "The *Pin Ups* album was a pleasure. And I knew the band (the Spiders) was over. It was a last farewell to them in a way."[69]

The new album consisted of twelve songs. When it came out on October 19, 1973, it was even more successful than *Aladdin Sane*. Nothing could stop the singer now. The album's jacket shows Bowie alongside the famous British

Composer Michel Magne in his studio in Hérouville in 1970.

model Twiggy, his pale skin contrasted with her tanned body. Originally intended for the Christmas issue of British *Vogue*, this photo by Justin De Villeneuve, manager and Twiggy's ex-boyfriend, had been turned down by the magazine. Photographer and model were delighted to allow Bowie—who mentions Twiggy in "Drive-In Saturday"—to use the picture for his seventh album.

"The 1980 Floor Show"

After *Pin Ups*, Bowie planned to compose a musical version of George Orwell's novel *1984*. The copyright owners refused permission, however, so he turned to writing new songs. In October 1973, recording sessions were booked at the Olympic Studios with the intention of making a new album. Meantime, the singer was busy with another project. Seeking to capitalize on Bowie's increasing fame in the United States, Tony Defries had done a deal with the American TV channel NBC, selling them a music show, *The 1980 Floor Show*, filmed at the Marquee club in London between October 18 and 20, 1973, before an audience chosen in a draw. The performers included the Troggs, Marianne Faithfull (who had recently duetted in a rather inferior version of Sonny and Cher's "I Got You Babe" and was the muse of Roxy Music), and Amanda Lear, rebaptized "Dooshenka" for this occasion. "David decided I should introduce the show. We wanted to do something about the Russian comic strip

hero from the book *Octobriana and the Russian Underground* by Petr Sadecký. Octobriana represented freedom and David was fascinated by the character so he invented the name Dooshenka for me for the show because it sounded Russian."[70] Broadcast on November 16 as part of NBC's *Midnight Special* series, the program was to be a turning point in David Bowie's career; besides gaining acceptance for his androgynous image among a somewhat prudish American public, it also marked the end of his collaboration with his closest allies, Ken Scott and Mick Ronson.

Bowie probably got the idea of releasing an album of cover versions from Brian Ferry in July 1973. The lead singer of Roxy Music, who had performed with his group in the first half of the Bowie concert at the Rainbow Theatre in August 1972, had recorded his first solo album, *These Foolish Things*, not long before, featuring cover versions of English and American hits.

1973

ROSALYN

Jimmy Duncan, Bill Farley / 2:20

Musicians: David Bowie: lead vocals / Mick Ronson: electric guitar, backing vocals / Trevor Bolder: bass / Aynsley Dunbar: drums, shaker / **Recorded:** Strawberry Studio, Château d'Hérouville, France: July 9–31, 1973 / **Technical Team:** Producers: David Bowie, Ken Scott / **Sound Engineer:** Dennis "Blackeye" MacKay / **Assistant Sound Engineer:** Andy Scott / **Mixing:** Ken Scott, David Bowie / **Arrangements:** David Bowie, Mick Ronson

This title is the first of two tributes to the legendary group of the mod scene of the 1960s, the Pretty Things, a group for whom David Bowie had genuine admiration and affection. "Rosalyn" was composed in 1964 by the group's manager, Jimmy Duncan, with words by Bill Farley, owner of the studios where the Pretty Things recorded for the Fontana label the song that was to be their first hit. The name of the group was cited several times in David Bowie's songs throughout his career: "Oh! You Pretty Things" on *Hunky Dory* (1971), "Pretty Thing" on *Tin Machine* (1989), and once again in "The Pretty Things Are Going to Hell" on the *Hours...* album of 1999. As performed here, "Rosalyn" is almost identical to the original with its guitar slide and rhythm that was later to influence the Australian group Jet in their 2003 hit number "Are You Gonna Be My Girl."

HERE COMES THE NIGHT

Bert Berns / 3:08

Musicians: David Bowie: lead vocals, saxophone / Mick Ronson: electric guitar, backing vocals / Trevor Bolder: bass / Aynsley Dunbar: drums / Mike Garson: piano / Ken Fordham: saxophone / Geoffrey MacCormack: backing vocals / Michel Ripoche: violin / **Recorded:** Strawberry Studio, Château d'Hérouville, France: July 9–31, 1973 / **Technical Team:** Producers: David Bowie, Ken Scott / **Sound Engineer:** Dennis "Blackeye" MacKay / **Assistant Sound Engineer:** Andy Scott / **Mixing:** Ken Scott, David Bowie / **Arrangements:** David Bowie, Mick Ronson

Bert Berns, the highly talented American composer and producer, was responsible for numbers like "Piece of My Heart" by Erma Franklin (elder sister of Aretha), "Twist and Shout" by the Beatles, and the timeless "Under the Boardwalk" by the Drifters. In 1964 he wrote the hit "Here Comes the Night" for Them, the song featuring session guitarist Jimmy Page, who went on to found Led Zeppelin. Berns, who had moved to London to do the recording, used the occasion to produce a second version of the hit, performed this time by Lulu, the young British singer who was very popular at that time. The version by Them reached number two in the British charts when it came out in 1965,

doing better than Lulu's version, which rose no higher than number fifty. David Bowie, here paying tribute to Van Morrison and Them, also offered a helping hand to Lulu, who was to come for two days to Hérouville to record her next single, a disco version of "The Man Who Sold the World," which would reach number three in the charts on January 26, 1974. Bowie's "Here Comes the Night" is almost identical to the Them version, changing none of the interpretation and old-fashioned charm, confining himself to the addition of a saxophone line that gives a touch of rhythm 'n' blues to an otherwise typically rock 'n' roll piece.

I WISH YOU WOULD

Billy Boy Arnold / 2:48

Musicians: David Bowie: lead vocals, harmonica, Moog synthesizer / Mick Ronson: electric guitar, backing vocals / Trevor Bolder: bass / Aynsley Dunbar: drums / Michel Ripoche: violin / **Recorded:** Strawberry Studio, Château d'Hérouville, France: July 9–31, 1973 / **Technical Team:** Producers: David Bowie, Ken Scott / **Sound Engineer:** Dennis "Blackeye" MacKay / **Assistant Sound Engineer:** Andy Scott / **Mixing:** Ken Scott, David Bowie / **Arrangements:** David Bowie, Mick Ronson

Composed by Billy Boy Arnold in 1955, the Yardbirds revived this number in 1964. Bowie, in turn, imbues it with a more modern sound. The Moog synthesizer, used here and there in some of the songs on his previous album ("Drive-In Saturday," "Let's Spend the Night Together"), is used here to provide some welcome new sonorities. The harmonica played by Yardbird Keith Relf is here replaced by Mick Ronson's guitar riff at the end of each verse. Another notable innovation is the involvement of onetime member of Zoo and colleague of Léo Ferré, French violinist Michel Ripoche. In the middle of the track, he doubles Ronson's guitar note for note. In 2016, Ripoche was to say of Bowie: "He was a strange guy in all senses of the word. He was watching all the time, speaking very little. When he did speak, it was in a way that was polite and measured but authoritative. He was interested in everything. If I had handed my violin over to him, he would have learned how to play it. He asked me to play him some Mozart. He was always wanting to discover, try out and learn new things."[71] Dominique Blanc-Francard, a famous sound engineer at Strawberry Studio between 1970 and 1973 who worked in particular on T. Rex and Elton John albums, also recalled meeting Bowie: "I wasn't working directly with him but I saw him every day. [...] He looked very extraordinary—like he looked on the disc sleeves of the time. For two weeks I saw him having his breakfast looking as if he had just come off stage—androgenous, with makeup and glamorous clothes. He would play foosball in his stage getup. [...] The first time he looked directly at me, I really felt as if I were being pierced by lasers."[72]

Nick Mason, Rick Wright, Roger Waters, and Syd Barrett, of Pink Floyd. Their first recordings impressed a young David Bowie.

SEE EMILY PLAY

Syd Barrett / 4:12

Musicians: David Bowie: lead and backing vocals, Moog synthesizer / Mick Ronson: electric guitar, piano, backing vocals / Trevor Bolder: bass / Aynsley Dunbar: drums / Mike Garson: piano, harpsichord / Geoffrey MacCormack: backing vocals / Unidentified Musicians: violin, cello / **Recorded:** Strawberry Studio, Château d'Hérouville, France: July 9–31, 1973 / **Technical Team:** Producers: David Bowie, Ken Scott / **Sound Engineer:** Dennis "Blackeye" MacKay / **Assistant Sound Engineer:** Andy Scott / **Mixing:** Ken Scott, David Bowie / **Arrangements:** David Bowie, Mick Ronson

Only David Bowie would dare take on a version of this second single by Pink Floyd, composed by the tragic Syd Barrett and released by Columbia Records on June 16, 1967. The two musicians had a deep respect for each other. "The few times I saw him perform in London at UFO and the Marquee clubs during the 60s will forever be etched in my mind. He was so charismatic and such a startlingly original songwriter. [...] His impact on my thinking was enormous. A major regret is that I never got to know him."[73] Faithful to the original version, Bowie's tribute is effective, emphasizing both the melancholy of the verses and the burlesque tones of the choruses. There are many layers of vocal backing, including a contribution from Geoffrey MacCormack, Bowie's childhood friend, soon to change his name to Warren Peace.

ON YOUR HEADPHONES

At 2:43, Mike Garson quotes from 2001: A Space Odyssey, Stanley Kubrick's revolutionary movie and the inspiration behind David Bowie's "Space Oddity." The pianist plays the opening theme from Richard Strauss's symphonic poem Thus Spoke Zarathustra, which is featured at the beginning of the movie.

EVERYTHING'S ALRIGHT

Nicky Crouch, John Conrad, Stu James, Keith Karlson, Simon Stavely / 2:27

Musicians: David Bowie: lead and backing vocals / Mick Ronson: electric guitar, backing vocals / Trevor Bolder: bass / Aynsley Dunbar: drums / Mike Garson: piano / Geoffrey MacCormack: backing vocals / Ken Fordham: saxophone / **Recorded:** Strawberry Studio, Château d'Hérouville, France: July 9–31, 1973 / **Technical Team:** Producers: David Bowie, Ken Scott / Sound Engineer: Dennis "Blackeye" MacKay / Assistant Sound Engineer: Andy Scott / **Mixing:** Ken Scott, David Bowie / **Arrangements:** David Bowie, Mick Ronson

The Mojos' "Everything's Alright," with its blues riff (the inspiration in 1977 for AC/DC's earsplitting "Whole Lotta Rosie"), did well in Great Britain when it came out in April 1964, reaching number nine in the charts, alongside the Beatles' "Can't Buy Me Love" (number four) and Peter and Gordon's "A World Without Love" (number one). As in the original version, Bowie's is peppered with very American-style arrangements and punctuated by a Little Richard–style rockabilly piano part. Bowie and Fordham underscore the effect on saxophone, departing from the British beat feel in a nostalgic leaning toward 1950s US rock. The singer

feels free to try some vocal experiments, similar to those in "Let's Spend the Night Together" on *Aladdin Sane.* Other innovations making this version notably different from that of the Mojos include the multiplication of the vocal backing tracks in the refrains and the bridge at 1:41.

I CAN'T EXPLAIN

Pete Townshend / 2:11

Musicians: David Bowie: lead vocals, saxophone / Mick Ronson: electric guitar, backing vocals / Trevor Bolder: bass / Aynsley Dunbar: drums / Mike Garson: piano / Ken Fordham: saxophone / Geoffrey MacCormack: backing vocals / **Recorded:** Strawberry Studio, Château d'Hérouville, France: July 9–31, 1973 / Trident Studios, London: August 1973 / **Technical Team:** Producers: David Bowie, Ken Scott / Sound Engineer: Dennis "Blackeye" MacKay / Assistant Sound Engineer: Andy Scott (Strawberry Studio) / **Mixing:** Ken Scott, David Bowie / **Arrangements:** David Bowie, Mick Ronson

When still young David Jones, Bowie had already recorded a version of this hit by the Who that was produced by Shel Talmy, who had also overseen his singles "I Pity the Fool" and "You've Got a Habit of Leaving." Recorded on June 24, 1972, at Trident Studios during a first session dedicated to the single "John, I'm Only Dancing," this early Ziggy

The Who, shown here in 1965, were the authors of the hit "*I Can't Explain.*"

The Easybeats were an Australian rock band and also the composers of the 1966 hit song "Friday on My Mind," which was covered by Bowie. Guitarist George Young (foreground) also produced the first albums for AC/DC.

Stardust version of "I Can't Explain" was shelved. It was never released because Bowie refused to let it appear as a bonus addition to the 1990 rerelease of *Pin Ups* on the Rykodisc label, preferring to offer his fans cover versions of "Growin' Up" and "Amsterdam."

This second version of "I Can't Explain" was originally recorded at the Château d'Hérouville but was reworked at Trident when the mixing took place. Ken Scott and Bowie decided to slow down the drum track, making the overall tempo of the piece slower. The inevitable consequence of this change was that all the musicians had to rerecord their parts to fit with the new speed. This new version—the third recorded by Bowie—was to be the one included on *Pin Ups*.

FOR BOWIE ADDICTS

Typical of the patchwork feel of the album, at 1:38 of "I Can't Explain" Mick Ronson quotes the introductory riff from "Shakin' All Over," the hit taken to number one by Johnny Kidd and the Pirates in June 1960.

FRIDAY ON MY MIND

George Young, Harry Vanda / 2:56

Musicians: David Bowie: lead and backing vocals, saxophone / Mick Ronson: electric guitar, backing vocals / Trevor Bolder: bass / Aynsley Dunbar: drums / Ken Fordham: saxophone / Geoffrey MacCormack: backing vocals / Mike Garson: piano / **Recorded:** Strawberry Studio, Château d'Hérouville, France: July 9–31, 1973 / **Technical Team:** Producers: David Bowie, Ken Scott / **Sound Engineer:** Dennis "Blackeye" MacKay / **Assistant Sound Engineer:** Andy Scott / **Mixing:** Ken Scott, David Bowie / **Arrangements:** David Bowie, Mick Ronson

For once, Bowie paid tribute to a group that was not British, the Easybeats. The rock music of this group, heavily influenced by the British Invasion, took all the prizes in November 1966 with the worldwide hit "Friday on My Mind." George Young, composer of this six-chord number with his friend Harry Vanda, happened to be the elder brother of Malcolm and Angus Young, one the rhythm guitar and the other the solo guitar of AC/DC. In revisiting this number, David Bowie must have remembered his early years when he was just a London Boy slumming it in the streets of the capital and when "Friday on My Mind" stood at number six in the charts. In this version we can admire a supercharged performance by Trevor Bolder, last survivor of the Spiders, on his Gibson EB-3.

David Bowie with Amanda Lear,
muse of Roxy Music, on the set of
The 1980 Floor Show, broadcast on
November 16, 1973, on NBC.

SORROW

*Bob Feldman, Jerry Goldstein,
Richard Gottehrer / 2:48*

1973

Musicians
David Bowie: lead vocals, twelve-string acoustic guitar, saxophone
Mick Ronson: electric guitar, backing vocals
Trevor Bolder: bass
Aynsley Dunbar: drums
Mike Garson: piano
Geoffrey MacCormack: backing vocals
Ken Fordham: saxophone
Unidentified Musicians: violin, cello

Recorded
Strawberry Studio, Château d'Hérouville, France: July 9–31, 1973

Technical Team
Producers: David Bowie, Ken Scott
Sound Engineer: Dennis "Blackeye" MacKay
Assistant Sound Engineer: Andy Scott
Mixing: Ken Scott, David Bowie
Arrangements: David Bowie, Mick Ronson

SIDE A: *Sorrow*
SIDE B: *Amsterdam*
UK Release on RCA: October 12, 1973 (ref. RCA 2424)
US Release on RCA: October 12, 1973 (ref. APBO-0160)
Best UK Chart Ranking: 3
Best US Chart Ranking: Did Not Chart

Genesis
The Merseys had already taken their cover version of the McCoys number to number four in the charts on May 4, 1966. Bowie chose it in October 1973 as the only single to come out of *Pin Ups*. The Beatles, too, had cited this song with a passage at 4:13 of "It's All Too Much" from the album *Yellow Submarine* (1969) identical to one in "Sorrow," twice including the phrase *"With your long blond hair and your eyes of blue."* When RCA brought out Bowie's "Sorrow" as a single on October 12, 1973, the spotlight fell on the 45 rpm reissued by Decca of "The Laughing Gnome." Decca was trying desperately to jump onto the Bowie bandwagon, much to the singer's chagrin. He was embarrassed to see the reappearance of this number, which he had never liked. Nevertheless, it made it to number six in the charts while *Sorrow* made it to number three. The song was performed live for *The 1980 Floor Show* in October 1973, in a romantic sequence where Bowie, in an immaculate white suit designed by Freddie Burretti, sings to a feline Amanda Lear dressed by Natasha Korniloff—designer of the costumes for David and Lindsay Kemp in the show *Pierrot in Turquoise*.

Production
The chord sequences were composed by the talented Mick Ronson, while the sound of the piano at the end of the piece has an unusual sonority. Sounding more like an electric piano of the Fender Rhodes Suitcase type with its "stereo vibrato" effect full on, it is in fact Strawberry Studio's Steinway piano played by Garson. The microphones were plugged into a socket in a Leslie speaker, an impressive piece of carpentry containing a rotating drum initially combined with a Hammond organ. Garson, always ready to experiment, was delighted with Ken Scott's re-creation here of the oscillating effect used in the introduction to Deep Purple's "Lazy" (1972). "We were experimenting even then with limited technology. [...] We didn't have access to the synths we have today and samplers and all that stuff, but we still found something."[13]

DON'T BRING ME DOWN

Johnny Dee / 2:05

Musicians: David Bowie: lead vocals, harmonica, claps / Mick Ronson: electric guitar, backing vocals, claps / **Trevor Bolder:** bass / Aynsley Dunbar: drums, tambourine / **Recorded:** Strawberry Studio, Château d'Hérouville, France: July 9–31, 1973 / **Technical Team:** Producers: David Bowie, Ken Scott / **Sound Engineer:** Dennis "Blackeye" MacKay / **Assistant Sound Engineer:** Andy Scott / **Mixing:** Ken Scott, David Bowie / **Arrangements:** David Bowie, Mick Ronson

The second number taken from the Pretty Things to appear on this album, "Don't Bring Me Down" was their biggest ever hit, reaching number ten in the UK charts in October 1964. Written by Johnny Dee, also manager of the short-lived group the Fairies, the song is inspired by American blues with its three-chord structure, so frequently used by groups in that period. Bowie's version is almost identical, featuring a harmonica as if to remind people in case they haven't noticed that *Pin Ups* is imbued with the spirit of the Rolling Stones and *Exile on Main St.*

SHAPES OF THINGS

Jim McCarty, Keith Relf, Paul Samwell-Smith / 2:53

Musicians: David Bowie: lead vocals, saxophone, Moog synthesizer / Mick Ronson: electric guitar, backing vocals / **Trevor Bolder:** bass / Aynsley Dunbar: drums / Ken Fordham: saxophone / Geoffrey MacCormack: backing vocals / **Unidentified Musicians:** violin, cello / **Recorded:** Strawberry Studio, Château d'Hérouville, France: July 9–31, 1973 / **Technical Team:** Producers: David Bowie, Ken Scott / **Sound Engineer:** Dennis "Blackeye" MacKay / **Assistant Sound Engineer:** Andy Scott / **Mixing:** Ken Scott, David Bowie / **Arrangements:** David Bowie, Mick Ronson / **String Arrangements:** Mick Ronson

A huge hit for the Yardbirds, "Shapes of Things," composed by their new guitarist Jeff Beck, stood at No. 3 in the charts in March 1966. Beck, already a legend for his six-chord style so admired by Mick Ronson, had replaced Eric Clapton—and was succeeded by Jimmy Page—in a group made famous because of the number of its guitarists who went on to have brilliant careers. Bowie retains the initial structure of the song. He takes advantage of the military-sounding pattern of the drums at the end of each verse, to return—once the introduction is over—to an earlier style in his career, as in his "Rubber Band" of 1967. His fans from those early days must have enjoyed his return to his Anthony Newley–ish singing style, highlighted by the slightly old-fashioned layers of violin in the verses. By contrast, the refrains, with their dissonant saxophones and vocal backings manipulated with a *reverse* effect still rarely used at that time, offer a modern reinterpretation of the song.

ANYWAY ANYHOW ANYWHERE

Pete Townshend, Roger Daltrey / 3:06

Musicians: David Bowie: lead and backing vocals, saxophone / **Mick Ronson:** electric guitar, backing vocals / **Trevor Bolder:** bass / Aynsley Dunbar: drums / Mike Garson: piano / **Recorded:** Strawberry Studio, Château d'Hérouville, France: July 9–31, 1973 / **Technical Team:** Producers: David Bowie, Ken Scott / **Sound Engineer:** Dennis "Blackeye" MacKay / **Assistant Sound Engineer:** Andy Scott / **Mixing:** Ken Scott, David Bowie / **Arrangements:** David Bowie, Mick Ronson

Following "I Can't Explain," here is another cover version taken from Pete Townshend and Roger Daltrey's group the Who, a tribute to a title that reached number ten in the charts in 1965. The mixing here creates a particularly powerful sound, thanks in part to the stereophonic-sounding drum part, exploding at every cymbal crash. Ken Scott applied a phaser effect to these, detectable at 1:39 and 1:44 of the track. A small but important detail: While the Who's version of the title appeared without commas, RCA added one between each word on the *Pin Ups* album, putting an exclamation mark at the end. The words on the back of the album are written by Bowie himself—in his "best" handwriting—and here the song title appears in its original form.

WHERE HAVE ALL THE GOOD TIMES GONE!

Ray Davies / 2:39

Musicians: David Bowie: lead vocals, saxophone / Mick Ronson: electric guitar, backing vocals / **Trevor Bolder:** bass / Aynsley Dunbar: drums / Mike Garson: piano / Ken Fordham: saxophone / Geoffrey MacCormack: backing vocals / **Recorded:** Strawberry Studio, Château d'Hérouville, France: July 9–31, 1973 / **Technical Team:** Producers: David Bowie, Ken Scott / **Sound Engineer:** Dennis "Blackeye" MacKay / **Assistant Sound Engineer:** Andy Scott / **Mixing:** Ken Scott, David Bowie / **Arrangements:** David Bowie, Mick Ronson

This song, written in 1965 by Ray Davies, leader of the Kinks, at the age of twenty-one, was inspired by a conversation overheard in a pub. It is a comment on aging, something that happens much sooner than you imagine, with all its regrets and disillusionment. Although he was twenty-six when he recorded his version of the song, David Bowie was already a kind of phoenix, forever being reborn from the ashes of his old self. And the story goes that the midwife who was present when Margaret, David's mother, gave birth, exclaimed as soon as she saw the newborn baby: "This child has been on earth before!"[29] Although Bowie was able to look toward future horizons, he was nostalgic by temperament, often returning to childhood memories, endlessly incorporating references to his past.

Bowie worked with Bruce Springsteen on "Growin' Up" and "It's Hard to Be a Saint in the City."

GROWIN' UP

Bruce Springsteen / 3:23

Musicians: David Bowie: lead vocals / Herbie Flowers: bass / Aynsley Dunbar (?), Tony Newman (?): drums, bells / Mike Garson: piano / Geoffrey MacCormack: backing vocals / Ron Wood: guitar / **Recorded:** Olympic Studios, London: October 1973 / **Technical Team:** Producer: David Bowie / **Sound Engineer:** Keith Harwood /

Shortly after landing in the United States for the *Aladdin Sane* tour, Bowie went to a Biff Rose concert in New York on February 5, 1973, where Bruce Springsteen was the opening performer. He was amazed to hear the singer mix folk and rock 'n' roll in front of a packed audience, gaining huge publicity for his first album *Greetings from Asbury Park, N.J.* Bowie was bowled over by the young American's stage presence and his willingness to punctuate his performance with political comments. A few

months later, once the *Pin Ups* album was finished, the British singer recorded his own version of "Growin' Up." It was not to be released until Rykodisc brought out the reissue of *Pin Ups* in 1990. Apart from the presence of Ron Wood of the Faces, not much is known about the recording of this title except that it was made at the Olympic Studios in London when recording sessions for *Diamond Dogs* were getting underway. The credits on the back of the promotional disc released by Rykodisc in 1990 are incorrect (Ken Scott and Trevor Bolder were no longer working for Bowie at this time and there is no saxophone on the track), so mystery still hangs over this important outtake that pays tribute to the man who would be named "the Boss." Trevor Bolder having been definitively dismissed when *Pin Ups* had been completed, it now fell to Herbie Flowers, creator of the famous contrabass glissando (harmonized on the bass) of Lou Reed's "Walk on the Wild Side," to take up the four-stringed bass for this song.

DOGS D
MONDD
DIAMON
DOGS
AMOND
GS DIA

ALBUM

DIAMOND DOGS

Future Legend . Diamond Dogs . Sweet Thing . Candidate . Sweet Thing (Reprise) .
Rebel Rebel . Rock 'n' Roll with Me . We Are the Dead . 1984 . Big Brother .
Chant of the Ever Circling Skeletal Family

RELEASE DATES
United Kingdom: May 24, 1974
Reference: RCA—APL1-0576
United States: May 24, 1974
Reference: RCA—CPL1-0576
Best UK Chart Ranking: 1
Best US Chart Ranking: 5

David Bowie with Zowie and
Angie and his Halloween
eyepatch in 1974.

A CONCEPT ALBUM
INSPIRED BY *1984*

In the autumn of 1973, having failed to obtain the adaptation rights, David Bowie had to resign himself to abandoning the plan for a musical spectacle inspired by George Orwell's *1984*. He also put to one side a show based around the character of Ziggy Stardust. The adaptation of *1984* was not possible, but nothing prevented the singer from appropriating the dystopic world of Orwell, in which the inhabitants of Oceania, permanently under the surveillance of Big Brother, the incarnation of a totalitarian party, are subjugated and deprived of their fundamental liberties. For this album, Bowie invented his own city, Hunger City, in which the Diamond Dogs wander, young people without future or hope, who instill terror in the city. This was the first disc that was really envisaged as a concept album by the artist, who was also inspired by the unhealthy world of William Burroughs in *The Wild Boys*, and horror or science-fiction films of the interwar years, such as *The Cabinet of Dr. Caligari* by Robert Wiene (1920), *Metropolis* by Fritz Lang (1927), or *Freaks* by Tod Browning (1932).

David Bowie began the production of his eighth album at the Olympic Studios in Barnes, near London. Now assuming the role of producer and arranger, he was able to develop his concept through some bold compositions such as "Sweet Thing" or "1984," in which a new, more soul-funk style is revealed, which he was to embrace wholeheartedly on his next album. Moving away from the deluge of hits provided on *Hunky Dory* or *The Rise and Fall of Ziggy Stardust and the Spiders from Mars*, he set off on the paths of a more experimental type of rock, sounding the death knell on the Ziggy era.

The major absence from this adventure was the guitarist Mick Ronson, who was fully occupied by the recording of his first album, *Slaughter on 10th Avenue*, for which Bowie wrote the number "Growin' Up and I'm Fine."

Released on March 1, 1974, the guitarist's first LP was a critical success, but without his alter ego Bowie, Ronson had difficulty passing the test of stage performances and did not win over critics or audiences. "Mick was slung out there before he was ready," said his wife, the hairdresser Suzi Fussey. "Mick has always worked better with somebody else. I think he missed having that other key person."[74] "Mick was the perfect foil for the Ziggy character," added Bowie. "He was very much a salt-of-the-earth type, the blunt northerner with a defiantly masculine personality, so that what you got was the old-fashioned yin and yang thing. As a rock duo, I thought we were every bit as good as Mick and Keith."[75]

Farewell to Glam Rock

A few months earlier, on February 7, 1973, when he went to the Genesis club in New York for a party organized after the Stevie Wonder concert at Carnegie Hall, David Bowie met the singer Ava Cherry. The confrontation of his pop-rock world with the soul classics of this young woman plunged him back into this kind of music that he had always enjoyed but for a while had put aside for the guitar riffs and rock rhythms of the Spiders. Like a long-lost friend, he rediscovered the inspired—and inspiring—music of Motown, the famous Berry Gordy label, with its catalog of a thousand hits, sung by Marvin Gaye, the Supremes, and Smokey Robinson. Already familiar with the Detroit African-American culture due to Iggy Pop, Bowie began a transition toward soul and rhythm 'n' blues. Still discreet on his new album—although audible on songs such as "1984" or "We Are the Dead"—this metamorphosis became obvious on *Young Americans*, which the singer recorded a few months later.

While he was busy with the production of *Diamond Dogs* at Olympic Studios in autumn 1973, David Bowie

The singer in a listening session for *Diamond Dogs*, recorded between Barnes, London, and the Netherlands in the winter of 1974.

An impressive Great Dane getting into the spirit of the photo shoot while the singer, unflustered, focuses on Terry O'Neill's lens.

found the time to compose the first opus for the group he had created especially for Ava Cherry, with whom he fell deeply in love. Consisting of the singer, the New Yorker Jason Guess, and Geoffrey MacCormack, the Ava Cherry and the Astronettes trio recorded a large number of covers intended for a future album. But the project did not come to fruition. We had to wait until 1995 for the Golden Years label to release the recordings under the title *People from Bad Homes*. It was a trace of this brief encounter that was, however, responsible for transforming David Bowie.

A Cult Album Jacket by Guy Peellaert

When *Diamond Dogs* came out on May 24, 1974, the massive promotion that Tony Defries had put in place ensured an immediate success, especially in the United Kingdom, where the disc was at the top of the charts for four consecutive weeks. In the United States, despite a promotional budget of $400,000, he had to "put up with" fifth place in July, beaten by Elton John and his *Caribou* album, at the top of the *Billboard* charts with the formidable single "Don't Let the Sun Go Down on Me." Despite a direction that was less oriented toward the general public and the disquieting

concept of the work, the fans were behind it from the start, and Bowie was convincing once again.

The album jacket was the work of the Belgian artist Guy Peellaert, who had just designed the cover for *It's Only Rock 'n' Roll* for the Rolling Stones, recorded at Olympic Studios at the same time as *Diamond Dogs*. The photographer Terry O'Neill, who covered *The 1980 Floor Show* at the Marquee, six months earlier, was called upon for the shoot, from which two of the most famous portraits of the singer were produced. The image used for the disc's jacket was inspired by a photograph of Joséphine Baker taken by Paul Colin, a French painter and poster artist famous for his art déco image of the singer with "two loves." Like Terry Pastor for the jacket of *Hunky Dory*, Peellaert used an airbrush to transform Bowie into a disturbing man-dog. His canine sexual organs disturbed the American representatives of RCA, who had them painted over for American publicity. The second portrait of Bowie taken that day was marked by the presence of a German mastiff, who, despite being quite agitated, seemed not to bother our singer, who remained calm. Terry O'Neill provides some details of this famous photo shoot. "The idea was that they'd bring a Great Dane

The ultimate privilege: a fan receives a kiss from their idol on September 5, 1974, at the Gibson Amphitheatre located at Universal Studios in Los Angeles.

Fancy footwork during the *Diamond Dogs* tour.

to the studio, along with Bowie, and then I'd shoot the dog, and David would copy them. I showed all the Polaroids to David, then he posed like the dog, and I shot him like the dog. [...] When we'd finished I just said, 'Let's do a couple of shots with the dog,' and David's sitting there and suddenly this dog leaps up in the air, trying to bite the strobe light. Every time the strobe went off, the dog jumped up. [...] Thank God I had a wide-angle lens on. As for David, he didn't move at all. He was completely focused."[1] The Bowie album was released before the Rolling Stones album, whose jacket passed as a copy of the one for *Diamond Dogs*... "Mick was silly," Bowie testified. "I mean, he should never [have] shown me anything

new. [...] Mick's learned now, as I've said. He will never do that again. You've got to be a bastard in this business."[51]

Diamond Dogs Tour: Between Audacity and Extravagance

On March 29, 1974, when the album had yet to be released, David Bowie left the United Kingdom for the United States, where the first dates for the *Diamond Dogs* tour had been arranged. He should have said his farewells to his homeland, as he would never live there again, except on a temporary basis. Once he reached the New York waterfront, a new life offered itself to the singer, who launched himself body and soul into the preparation for the tour that was to begin in

June. The décors of Hunger City were created by the designers Chris Lanhart and Mark Ravitz, in close collaboration with lighting designer Jules Fisher. Toni Basil, the well-known actress and choreographer, was responsible for the—overloaded—staging of the concerts, and new musicians joined the group. Joining Mike Garson, Herbie Flowers, and the drummer Tony Newman, a former member of the Jeff Beck Group, were newcomers recommended by the tour's artistic director, Michael Kamen. He also wrote the arrangements for the show and played oboe and Minimoog synthesizer onstage. Alongside him, the saxophonists David Sanborn and Richard Grando, percussionist Pablo Rosario, and Warren Peace (alias Geoffrey MacCormack) supported by Gui Andrisano on backing vocals. It was at this time that a new guitarist made his appearance among Bowie's entourage: Earl Slick.

The triumphant tour was exhausting. Its exorbitant cost prevented it from transferring to the United Kingdom, and the debts accumulated by Defries started to worry the singer. Bowie was always convinced that he was associated on an equal footing in MainMan, the management and production structure that the manager created to support him. In reality, Defries was the only person in charge, and the artist soon understood that the only revenues he could expect to receive were devoured by a show of which he was rapidly

beginning to tire. He was in fact just one of the artists in the MainMan table, on the same footing as Mick Ronson or Dana Gillespie. The tensions with Defries became inevitable, exacerbated by the singer's paranoia, which was in turn fueled by a heavy consumption of cocaine. After two months of the tour, and the recording of a live album at the Tower Theater in Philadelphia in July 1974, Bowie split from Kamen, distanced himself from rock 'n' roll, and prepared to give birth to the successor to the tormented *Diamond Dogs*.

FOR BOWIE ADDICTS

While the composers Michel Berger and Luc Plamondon have always claimed certain sources of inspiration for *Starmania*—a rock opera whose subject is the wanderings of populations left to their own devices in a city of the future, dominated by television screens—it is highly probable that the world of *Diamond Dogs* had a major influence on them. After all, one of the heroes of *Starmania* is called…Ziggy?

One of the posters for Fritz Lang's *Metropolis* (1927), which was an inspiration for many musicians in the seventies.

FUTURE LEGEND

David Bowie / 1:00

Musicians: David Bowie: vocals, electric guitar, spoken word, Moog synthesizer / **Recorded:** Olympic Studios, Barnes: January 1974 / **Island Studios, London:** January 1974 (overdubs) / **L Ludolf Studio, Hilversum, Netherlands:** February 14, 1974 (overdubs) / **Technical Team:** Producer: David Bowie / **Sound Engineer:** Keith Harwood (Olympic Studios) / **Assistant Sound Engineer:** Andy Morris (Olympic Studios) / **Mixing:** David Bowie, Tony Visconti / **Arrangements:** David Bowie

Conceived as the introduction to a show that never saw the light of day, "Future Legend" is a short and somber presentation of the Orwellian world that David Bowie develops throughout the disc. Alone, and without his most precious associates, Ken Scott and Mick Ronson, the singer is the captain of a ship deprived of its crew. His solitude is reflected in that of the inhabitants of Hunger City, at the mercy of the Diamond Dogs wandering in the city.

The Minimoog is a simplified (and, above all transportable) version of the Moog synthesizer Modular System 55 used at Trident Studios on Bowie's previous albums. It has pride of place in "Future Legend," and with its futuristic sonorities contributes to the disquieting content of the text declaimed by the singer. The guitar melody that appears at 0:29 is the one from the refrain of "Bewitched, Bothered and Bewildered," a jazz standard by Richard Rodgers and Lorenz Hart, written in 1940 for the musical comedy *Pal Joey* and covered by artists such as Julie London and Ella Fitzgerald. On the UK version of the album in 8-track cassette format (a format that has now disappeared from use), the track listing separates "Future Legend" into two parts; the second part, called "Bewitched" for the occasion, is credited to "Rogers and Hart," depriving the composer of the letter *D* from the middle of his surname.

Sex symbol and leader of the Faces, Rod Stewart was also a reluctant guest star on Bowie's album.

Single

DIAMOND DOGS

David Bowie / 6:02

Musicians: David Bowie: vocals, electric guitar, saxophone, backing vocals / **Herbie Flowers:** bass / **Tony Newman:** drums / **Mike Garson:** piano / **Recorded:** Olympic Studios, Barnes: January 15 and 18, 1974 / Island Studios, London: January 1974 (overdubs) / L Ludolf Studio, Hilversum, Netherlands: February 14, 1974 (overdubs) / **Technical Team: Producer:** David Bowie / **Sound Engineer:** Keith Harwood (Olympic Studios) / **Assistant Sound Engineer:** Andy Morris (Olympic Studios) / **Mixing:** David Bowie, Tony Visconti / **Arrangements:** David Bowie / **Single: Side A:** *Diamond Dogs* / 6:02 / **Side B:** *Holy Holy* / 2:22 / **UK Release on RCA:** June 14, 1974 (ref. APBO 0293) / **Best Chart Ranking:** 21

While "Future Legend" provided a description of the sinister Hunger City, this second track presents its inhabitants, including the Diamond Dogs. This gang of adolescents comes straight out of Bowie's imagination, calling upon his childhood memories, when his father talked to him about poor children living on the roofs of London. Halloween Jack also makes his appearance, a character that the singer portrayed in a promotional video in the Netherlands: *"The Halloween Jack is a real cool cat / And he lives on top of Manhattan Chase / The elevator's broke, so he slides down a rope."* Again, as always showing his love for the music of the Rolling Stones, who were also using the other studio at Olympic for their production of *It's Only Rock 'n' Roll*, David Bowie on his own provides the guitar parts in "Diamond Dogs," which are not dissimilar to the edgy rhythms of his colleague Keith

Richards. And although the assistant sound engineer Andy Morris affirms that Bruce Springsteen inspired Bowie in the creation of his disc—"'Spirit in the Night.' We listened to that record for days and days in the studio"[76]—the singer claims instead his attachment to the rock 'n' roll of his childhood: "Little Richard. If it hadn't have been for him, I probably wouldn't have gone into music."[36] Released as a single in June 1974, the number did not repeat the success of "The Jean Genie," a hit sharing the same characteristics that drove the audiences wild eighteen months earlier. For the B-side, Bowie opted for a version of "Holy Holy" revisited by the Spiders in November 1971, while everyone was immersed in the glam-rock world of Ziggy Stardust.

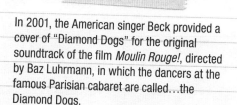

In 2001, the American singer Beck provided a cover of "Diamond Dogs" for the original soundtrack of the film *Moulin Rouge!*, directed by Baz Luhrmann, in which the dancers at the famous Parisian cabaret are called…the Diamond Dogs.

A key meeting in February 1974 between rocker David Bowie and the writer William Burroughs, featured in the pages of *Rolling Stone* magazine.

SWEET THING

David Bowie / 3:38

Musicians: David Bowie: vocals, electric guitar, saxophone, backing vocals / **Herbie Flowers:** bass / **Tony Newman:** drums / **Mike Garson:** piano / **Recorded:** Olympic Studios, Barnes: January 1974 / **Island Studios, London:** January 1974 (overdubs) / **L Ludolf Studio, Hilversum, Netherlands:** February 14, 1974 (overdubs) / **Technical Team:** Producer: David Bowie / **Sound Engineer:** Keith Harwood (Olympic Studios) / **Assistant Sound Engineer:** Jon Astley (Olympic Studios) / **Mixing:** David Bowie, Tony Visconti / **Arrangements:** David Bowie

Genesis

The first strand of a triptych conceived as the culmination of this concept album, "Sweet Thing" plunges the listener into the darkness of Hunger City, and also into the torments David Bowie was experiencing in his struggles with cocaine. Behind the heavy cadence and erotic languor of this title are the latent violence and despair of the city's inhabitants. The author here cites Charles Manson and Cassius Clay, and immerses himself in his trilogy, following the "cut up" literary technique with which William Burroughs experimented. "You write down a paragraph or two describing several different subjects," explained Bowie, "creating a kind of story ingredients-list, I suppose, and then cut the sentences into four- or five-word sections; mix 'em up and reconnect them."[56] Brian Eno, the keyboard player with Roxy Music, who was soon to become Bowie's producer, specified: "It's not 'cause you're short of ideas necessarily. It's because it puts you into territories that you wouldn't otherwise get into."[2] This was an innovative, even revolutionary experiment, but the meaning of the text escaped the listeners...and with good reason! Bowie used this procedure on several of his albums, until *1. Outside* in 1995. In 2003, he explained, not without humor, the evolution of the technique over the years: "I'm amazed these days at the amount of cut-up sites that are now on the Internet. [...] I've used them, too—I've put a bunch of pieces of text into the thing, then hit the 'cut-up button,' and it slices it up for me!"[36]

A new version of the song was recorded by Ava Cherry and the Astronettes at the Sigma Sound Studios in Philadelphia, in the summer of 1974, while Bowie was working on *Young Americans*, but was not released. Two other songs, "Give It Away" and "Everything That Touches You," were immortalized on July 9, 1974, by the trio, under the direction of the singer.

Production

Herbie Flowers explained the composition method that the singer made his specialty. The working sessions were quick and effective. Accompanied by his acoustic guitar and some lines of text on a sheet of paper, Bowie always started by presenting the piece to the drummer and bass player. The song then started to come to life with the impetus of the musicians and was recorded with only a few takes. The singer then added the arrangements, including piano, interpreted by the loyal Mike Garson.

Andy Morris, assistant sound engineer at Olympic Studios, who worked on some of the album numbers, recalled how motivating it was to work with a creative force like Bowie: "David was like Orson Welles! He was a visionary, highly intelligent."[76]

The young assistant sound engineer at the Olympic Studios, Jon Astley, was given two sheets containing draft material for the lyrics of "Sweet Thing," "Candidate," and "Sweet Thing (Reprise)." In exchange, he undertook to stay longer in the studio while Bowie and Ronson finished the production of the disco version of "The Man Who Sold the World" for Lulu. At an auction sale at Christie's on June 14, 2011, this collection of documents found a buyer at £8,750!

CANDIDATE

David Bowie / 2:39

Musicians: David Bowie: vocals, electric guitar, saxophone, backing vocals / Herbie Flowers: bass / Tony Newman: drums / Mike Garson: piano / **Recorded:** Olympic Studios, Barnes: January 1974 / Island Studios, London: January 1974 (overdubs) / L Ludolf Studio, Hilversum, Netherlands: February 14, 1974 (overdubs) / **Technical Team:** Producer: David Bowie / Sound Engineer: Keith Harwood (Olympic Studios) / Assistant Sound Engineer: Jon Astley (Olympic Studios) / Mixing: David Bowie, Tony Visconti / Arrangements: David Bowie

Structured around the line of chords of "Sweet Thing," "Candidate" follows on from the previous track with a very pop rhythm. Immersed in the creation of his concept album, David Bowie asked his musicians, during the recording, to assume the role of certain characters. "He

asked me to imagine myself as a young, French drummer who was witnessing his first execution,"[13] recalled the drummer Tony Newman. It should be said that the singer is referring here to the Tricoteuses, a term designating the young women who, during the French revolution, took part in the sessions of the Convention, the popular assemblies, and the revolutionary court; it was said they attended the executions while knitting. Another song recorded at the same time, often called "Alternative Candidate" by the fans, appeared on the reissue of *Diamond Dogs* by Rykodisc in 1990.

SWEET THING (REPRISE)

David Bowie / 2:31

Musicians: David Bowie: lead and backing vocals, acoustic guitar, electric guitar, saxophone / Herbie Flowers: bass / Tony Newman: drums / Mike Garson: piano / Unidentified Musician: flute / **Recorded:** Olympic Studios, Barnes: January 1974 / Island Studios, London: January 1974 (overdubs) / L Ludolf Studio, Hilversum, Netherlands: February 14, 1974 (overdubs) / **Technical Team:** Producer: David Bowie / Sound Engineer: Keith Harwood (Olympic Studios) / Assistant Sound Engineer: Jon Astley (Olympic Studios) / Mixing: David Bowie, Tony Visconti / Arrangements: David Bowie

For the conclusion of his trilogy, David Bowie returned one last time to the theme of "Sweet Thing" and at the end of the number developed his first krautrock influences. Krautrock was a minimalist musical style born in West Germany at the end of the 1960s, and the singer would explore it more intensively from 1977, during his so-called Berlin period. The riff at the end, from 1:30, mechanical and persistent, seems to have had its inspiration in the introduction to "Negativland" (at 0:39), which appears on the first album of the German group Neu!, released in 1973. Because everything always transforms in the world of rock 'n' roll, other artists adapted this classic two-chord feature, such as Skin (the singer of the British group Skunk Anansie) in "Listen to Yourself" (2003) or the American Marilyn Manson for his Dantesque "Rock Is Dead," in 1998.

ON YOUR HEADPHONES
A master of subtle allusions, the pianist Mike Garson at 1:31 in "Sweet Thing (Reprise)" cites the piano contrivance from "Changes" (at 0:11), on *Hunky Dory*.

Single

REBEL REBEL

David Bowie / 4:27

Musicians
David Bowie: vocals, electric guitar, tambourine, backing vocals
Alan Parker: electric guitar
Herbie Flowers: bass
Aynsley Dunbar: drums
Mike Garson: piano
Warren Peace: castanets, congas, güiro, backing vocals (US single version)

Recorded
Trident Studios, London: December 27, 1973
Olympic Studios, Barnes: January 14–16, 1974 (mixing and overdubs)
RCA Studios, New York: April 1974 (remixing and overdubs, US single version)

Technical Team
Producer: David Bowie
Sound Engineer: Keith Harwood (Olympic Studios)
Assistant Sound Engineer: Andy Morris (Olympic Studios)
Mixing: David Bowie, Keith Harwood
Arrangements: David Bowie

Original Single Mix
SIDE A: *Rebel Rebel* / 4:31
SIDE B: *Queen Bitch* / 3:15
UK Release on RCA: February 15, 1974 (ref. LPB05009)
Best UK Chart Ranking: 5

US Single Version
SIDE A: *Rebel Rebel* / 3:01
SIDE B: *Lady Grinning Soul* / 3:50
USA release by RCA: May 1974 (ref. APB0-0287)
Best US Chart Ranking: 64

Genesis

Extremely disappointed by his performance and the final result of the show *The 1980 Floor Show*, recorded at the Marquee in London for future broadcast on the American television network NBC, in October 1973 Bowie immersed himself in two new projects: an adaptation of *1984* by George Orwell and a new staged version of Ziggy Stardust, whose contours remained to be planned out. As it was not possible for these two ideas to come to fruition, the songs that had already been written found their way into *Diamond Dogs*. This was the case with "Rebel Rebel," with an irresistible Stones-like riff, which became one of the artist's biggest hits in the United Kingdom. The first song recorded for this album was also the very last that Bowie recorded at Trident Studios, where so many of his hits had seen the light of day.

Bowie had understood very well that in order to please his adolescent public and, more particularly, his fans who saw something of themselves in the androgynous image he adopted, there was nothing better than a song praising a rebellious, misunderstood youth. *"You've got your mother in a whirl 'cause she's / Not sure if you're a boy or a girl,"* he sang in this ode to emancipation, having himself had the courage to assert his sexual orientation in a Great Britain that was still very chaste during the 1970s—although the country was about to be shaken up by the irreverence of the disco, punk, and new wave movements. Multiple versions of this song would be produced. This version, from the album, appeared as a single in the United Kingdom and initially in the United States. It was withdrawn in the US in May 1974 and replaced by a new one. Rearranged by Bowie in New York in April, the second American version was given stodgy phaser effects on guitar, Hispanic-sounding backing vocals, and grotesque castanets played by Warren Peace. This terrible US single version, which reached only sixty-fourth place on the *Billboard* chart, eventually ran aground in 2004 in the reissue of the album by EMI/Virgin.

The Bruce Springsteen homage version is much preferable. On January 16, 2016, a few days after Bowie's death, Springsteen introduced the encores at his concert at the PPG Paints Arena in Pittsburgh with these words: "I want to take a moment and just note the passing of my good friend David Bowie. David—not that many people know, but he supported our music way, way, way back at the very, very

1974

FOR BOWIE ADDICTS

One evening, while trying to get to sleep in a London hotel room, David Bowie was disturbed by an amateur guitarist who was painfully attempting the riff in "Rebel Rebel." He decided to go up and give the unfortunate some lessons on the six-string guitar. When the door opened, he found himself face-to-face with the tennis player John McEnroe, an electric guitar around his neck...

beginning—1973. [...] He covered some of my music, [...] and he was a big supporter of ours. [...] Anyway, we're thinking of him."[77] That evening the Boss enchanted his public with a moving and electrifying rendition of "Rebel Rebel."

An Unmistakably Recognizable Guitar Riff

While winding up the last cables after a session at Olympic Studios that had dragged on until four in the morning, the assistant sound engineer Andy Morris witnessed the birth of this mythical riff. Bowie asked him to record on the only microphone still connected, a contrivance that he was continually strumming while waiting for his driver, Tony Mascia.

A session was then organized at Trident Studios, which had the equipment needed in order to carry out rapid mastering on the final mixing. That day, December 27, 1973, it was Alan Parker who came to the artist's assistance. The guitarist, who had been involved in the recording of the single "Holy Holy" in November 1970, when Ronson, Woodmansey, and Visconti had left the Bowie ship, was credited on the album for "1984," but a big gap remained in this cult song. "On 'Rebel Rebel,' he had the riff about 75% sorted out," Parker recalled. "He wanted it a bit like a Stones riff, and he played it to me as such, and I then tinkered around with it. I said, 'Well, what if we did this and that and made it sound more clangy and put some bends in it?' and he said, 'Yeah, I love that, that's fine.'"[78] Unlike Mick Ronson, who, as a real guitar hero, played on Marshall amps and made his fuzz pedal roar, Parker was content with the warmth of the valves in his Fender Twin Reverb, a benchmark amp for all self-respecting blues players, which was equipped at that time with a single Wharfedale speaker. Using his black Les Paul Standard, he delivered a short but unforgettable performance, also adding the famous bend that concluded each refrain (at 1:24 especially). Being uncredited, one has to take his word for it, when he said in 2011: "I can tell my own playing, and my own sound, and I know it's me."[53]

Another character, Peter Hince, who is rarely referred to by the biographers, but whose story is intimately linked with the advent of seventies rock, was witness at that time to the sound experimentations of Bowie. At that time the very young roadie for the star was present at most of the sessions for *Diamond Dogs*. As a future technical manager,

confidant, and photographer of Queen, Hince was in the early days of his career when he was working for David Bowie. He provides an important detail on the tambourine that is present throughout this song: "I was there in case anything was needed, and he wanted a tambourine, so I was sent out to get one. Instead of playing the tambourine with his hand, David was banging it on the front of an acoustic guitar to get a different type of sound. [...] He always wanted to push the boundaries."[79]

A Cult Video with an Ephemeral Character

When he was in the Netherlands to receive the prestigious Edison Award, Bowie took advantage of the occasion to promote his new single. On the stage of the Dutch program *Top Pop*, on February 13, 1974, he did a playback of "Rebel Rebel"—which was due to be released two days later—equipped with a Japanese Kent PB-24-G guitar, which he nearly dropped several times. He was wearing a Freddie Burretti suit but without the jacket, which had been taken off him during a previous press conference by Elly De Waard, a journalist who had been refused an interview. To cap it all, the singer was suffering from conjunctivitis, which he disguised with a pirate's eye patch. This unexpectedly successful video assumed mythical status, notably due to the way Bowie was dressed, with some identifying him subsequently with Halloween Jack, one of the characters from *Diamond Dogs*. But after the video was broadcast, and the conjunctivitis had disappeared, the singer adopted more orthodox attire on the tour.

One person's misfortune can sometimes be the good fortune of another. On February 21, 1974, the team of *Top of the Pops*, the cult BBC program, was desperately awaiting the tape of "Rebel Rebel" for Bowie's appearance. As it failed to arrive, they had to resign themselves to canceling his appearance. Queen, an as-yet-unknown group, was then invited to perform their single "Seven Seas of Rhye." This was the start of a glorious era for Freddie Mercury's band.

David Bowie was inspired by George Orwell's totalitarian dystopia during the writing of *Diamond Dogs*.

ROCK'N'ROLL WITH ME

David Bowie, Warren Peace / 3:59

Musicians: David Bowie: vocals, acoustic guitar, electric guitar, saxophone, backing vocals / **Herbie Flowers:** bass / **Aynsley Dunbar:** drums / **Mike Garson:** piano, Hammond organ / **Recorded:** Olympic Studios, Barnes: January 14–15, 1974 / **Island Studios, London:** January 1974 (overdubs) / **L Ludolf Studio, Hilversum, Netherlands:** February 14, 1974 (overdubs) / **Technical Team:** Producer: David Bowie / **Sound Engineer:** Keith Harwood (Olympic Studios) / **Assistant Sound Engineer:** Andy Morris (Olympic Studios) / **Mixing:** David Bowie, Keith Harwood / **Arrangements:** David Bowie

Genesis

David Bowie had already worked on a draft version for this piece, which he wanted to use for his future musical show *Ziggy Stardust*—which was ultimately abandoned—when he received a visit from his friend Geoffrey MacCormack, alias Warren Peace. "One evening [...] I went to visit David," recalled Peace in 2008. "I sat down at the piano and began to play a couple of chords that had been spinning in my head for some time. And then he said: 'Wait a minute,' and pushed me aside. Then he played 'Rock 'n' Roll with Me.'"[80] Written for four parts, "Rock 'n' Roll with Me" is a song that Bowie

dedicated to his fans, whose loyalty and devotion have given him international success. Peace commented, not without an element of humor: "After all these years, it's nice to brag that I was a co-author of a song from the *Diamond Dogs* album."[80]

Production

Following an introduction that is reminiscent of the famous descending chords of "Lean on Me" (1972) by Bill Withers, the song explores quite an unusual register for Bowie: The piano is used with a pop sound, as with his compatriot Elton John, and moves away from the lyrical flights of Rick Wakeman in "Life on Mars?" The presence of other guitarists on the number fueled all sorts of rumors among the fans. It was claimed that Alan Parker, who worked on "Rebel Rebel" and "1984," was the one providing the six-string acoustic guitar rhythms. But the musician himself denied this. We also read elsewhere that Earl Slick was the one who set the number on fire with his surly riffs, but this was not the case. Slick had not yet met with Bowie at the time of the recording. He does, however, appear on the live version of the number, which appeared on the American market in September 1974, hence the doubts in some people's mind. David Bowie is the only person playing on this piece, probably with his new acquisition: a gleaming Dan Armstrong 341 in Honduras mahogany, whose Kent Armstrong microphones can easily be changed using a revolutionary rail system.

WE ARE THE DEAD

David Bowie / 4:52

Musicians: David Bowie: vocals, electric guitar, saxophone, backing vocals / **Herbie Flowers:** bass / **Aynsley Dunbar:** drums / **Mike Garson:** Rhodes guitar / **Recorded:** Olympic Studios, Barnes: January 16, 1974 / **Island Studios, London:** January 1974 (overdubs) / **L Ludolf Studio, Hilversum, Netherlands:** February 14, 1974 (overdubs) / **Technical Team:** Producer: David Bowie / **Sound Engineer:** Keith Harwood (Olympic Studios) / **Assistant Sound Engineer:** Andy Morris (Olympic Studios) / **Mixing:** David Bowie, Keith Harwood / **Arrangements:** David Bowie

In the novel *1984* by George Orwell, a major source of inspiration for the writing of *Diamond Dogs*, Winston and Julia try to escape from the thought police, which was the terror of Oceania, where they tried to survive. Shortly before the enforcement agency comes to arrest them, Winston utters the desperate words: *"We are the dead."* Bowie picks up this phrase, which recurs as a leit-motiv in the novel, and uses it as the title of his piece. With a delicate melody, accompanied by the warm and enveloping sound of the Rhodes guitar, this electronic piano with its inimitable sound, played here by Mike Garson, the singer makes us experience the turmoil of the heroes. On listening to this powerful number, one can image the dramatic impact such a song might have had, if the artist had been able to make his dream of staging a musical comedy adapted from this major prescient work into a reality.

1984

David Bowie / 3:27

Musicians
David Bowie: vocals, electric guitar, saxophone, backing vocals
Alan Parker: electric guitar
Herbie Flowers: bass
Aynsley Dunbar: drums
Mike Garson: piano, Rhodes
Unidentified Musicians: strings

Recorded
Olympic Studios, Barnes: January 1974
Island Studios, London: January 1974 (overdubs)
L Ludolf Studio, Hilversum, Netherlands: February 14, 1974
(overdubs)

Technical Team
Producer: David Bowie
Sound Engineer: Keith Harwood (Olympic Studios)
Assistant Sound Engineer: Andy Morris (Olympic Studios)
Mixing: David Bowie, Tony Visconti
Arrangements: David Bowie
String Arrangements: Tony Visconti

First Release
SIDE A: *1984* / 3:27
SIDE B: *Queen Bitch* / 3:15
US Release on RCA: July 1974 (ref. PB-10026)
Best US Chart Ranking: Did Not Chart

Second Release
SIDE A: *1984* / 3:27
SIDE B: *TVC 15* / 5:29
US Release on RCA: 1984 (ref. PB-13769)
Best US Chart Ranking: Did Not Chart

ON YOUR HEADPHONES
In the introduction and conclusion of "1984," Mike Garson has fun quoting the theme of *The Twilight Zone* by Marius Constant, whose catchy melody sent shivers down the spine of many generations of television viewers.

Genesis
An initial demo of "1984" was recorded at Trident Studios with the Spiders on January 19, 1973, but the version that really had made an impression was the one that Bowie reworked for *The 1980 Floor Show* and was recorded at the Marquee club in October 1973. Among the pieces recorded for this NBC broadcast was a medley combining two compositions: "1984/Dodo." This potpourri was part of the set of pieces prepared for the adaptation of Orwell's book, but after the project was abandoned, "1984" ended up on *Diamond Dogs*.

Production
With this major number, the artist took a 180-degree turn, sweeping aside pop, glam rock, and all the styles he'd explored in the past. With encouragement from his girlfriend at the time, the soul singer Ava Cherry, he became an advocate for a frenzied form of funk, borrowing from the "Theme from Shaft" by Isaac Hayes its charleston roll, flirting with a wah-wah guitar executed with metronomic precision. It was Alan Parker who took on the performance of this exceptional six-string guitar passage. "David wanted the '60s funk style guitar on it," he explained in 2020, "which I was obviously doing a hell of a lot of at the time for everybody. We put it down in 20 minutes and then we were done, that's what it's all about."[13] Andy Morris, assistant sound engineer, stressed the pugnacity of a Bowie determined to give birth to a monumental work: "'1984' was the song we spent the most time on because David wanted to get it perfect, and it turned out perfect, it's a masterpiece. Bowie was a workhorse. [...] He would come in at one o'clock in the afternoon and some days we wouldn't leave until five in the morning."[76] The other major influence is very clearly "Papa Was a Rolling Stone" by the Temptations, on which the arranger Visconti drew freely in the writing of his blistering string score. The result was a key piece by the new Bowie, who would soon embrace African-American culture to the extent of recording in the prestigious Sigma Sound Studios in Philadelphia, temple of soul and R&B.

BIG BROTHER

David Bowie / 3:19

Musicians: David Bowie: lead and backing vocals, twelve-string acoustic guitar, electric guitar, Moog synthesizer, Mellotron, saxophone, claps, tambourine / **Herbie Flowers:** bass / **Aynsley Dunbar:** drums / **Recorded:** Olympic Studios, Barnes: January 14–15, 1974 / Island Studios, London: January 1974 (overdubs) / L Ludolf Studio, Hilversum, Netherlands: February 14, 1974 (overdubs) / **Technical Team: Producer:** David Bowie / **Sound Engineer:** Keith Harwood (Olympic Studios) / **Assistant Sound Engineer:** Andy Morris (Olympic Studios) / **Mixing:** David Bowie, Tony Visconti / **Arrangements:** David Bowie

Launched by a Moog melody with a sonority similar to that soon to be heard on the introduction to "Shine On You Crazy Diamond" by Pink Floyd, "Big Brother" formed part of the series of numbers that Bowie recycled following the cancellation of his *1984* project. This is an effective number, whose appearance as a single would certainly have been a big success, but RCA and Bowie preferred to bank on the potential of "Diamond Dogs" as the album's second single. Here the singer delivers an ode to Big Brother, the key character in *1984*, the authoritarian leader of the Party governing Oceania, one of the three great totalitarian powers in the novel. "*We want you, Big Brother,*" cries the narrator, enslaved by the charisma and propaganda of the undisputed leader. The Mellotron, the instrument whose rafts of prerecorded chords were immortalized in "Space Oddity," assumes an important position, especially in the somber introduction, combining all types of futuristic sounds. Bowie plays a series M400 model. Since it was first made available in 1970, this keyboard offered new sound registers, including the famous "8 Voice Choir," which offered a sample of an eight-part choir (four male voices, and four female voices) used more than once in studios by the prog-rock groups Genesis and Yes.

CHANT OF THE EVER CIRCLING SKELETAL FAMILY

David Bowie / 2:02

Musicians: David Bowie: vocals, electric guitar, tambourine, backing vocals / **Herbie Flowers:** bass / **Aynsley Dunbar:** drums, güiro / **Recorded:** Olympic Studios, Barnes: January 1974 / Island Studios, London: January 1974 (overdubs) / L Ludolf Studio, Hilversum, Netherlands: February 14, 1974 (overdubs) / **Technical Team: Producer:** David Bowie / **Sound Engineer:** Keith Harwood (Olympic Studios) / **Assistant Sound Engineer:** Andy Morris (Olympic Studios) / **Mixing:** David Bowie, Tony Visconti / **Arrangements:** David Bowie

As short as it is surprising, "Chant of the Ever Circling Skeletal Family" is the perfect finale for the audacious *Diamond Dogs*, where Bowie indulged in all types of musical experimentation. It should be said that in 1973, technology was advancing at a great pace, and it offered artists a multitude of new ways of having fun with sound frequencies, including the new rack effects of the American brand Eventide. Visconti, at that time responsible for the mixing on part of this opus, recorded some very short sequences of sound effects, with which he played as he saw fit. "David asked if I could capture the word 'brother' at the end of the last track, [...] and repeat it ad infinitum. Of course I could, but lo and behold, that short word was too long for the puny memory banks in the machine," he explained later. "[...] So I managed to capture just 'bro' with a snare drum hit and that actually sounded amazing, like a robot with AI that was not working very well singing it."[81]

It was during the preparation for *The 1980 Floor Show*, at the London Marquee Club, that the very funky "1984" first emerged.

1984/DODO

David Bowie / 5:27

Musicians: David Bowie: lead and backing vocals, saxophone / **Mick Ronson:** electric guitar / **Marc Pritchett:** electric guitar / **Trevor Bolder:** bass / **Aynsley Dunbar:** drums / **Mike Garson:** piano, electronic piano / **Geoffrey MacCormack:** backing vocals, congas / **Ava Cherry:** backing vocals / **Unidentified Musicians:** orchestra / **Recorded:** Trident Studios, London: September 29, October 1973 / **Technical Team:** Producer: David Bowie, Ken Scott / **Sound Engineer:** Ken Scott

Written for the musical comedy *1984* that David Bowie wanted to stage, "1984/Dodo" is a medley of two numbers recorded at Trident Studios, for a stage set performance on *The 1980 Floor Show*, from October 18 to 20, 1973. With Ava Cherry and Geoffrey MacCormack by his side, the singer revealed the very soul-oriented musical direction he would be taking in 1974 and 1975. After he abandoned the *1984* project, the song was divided into two parts: The first became one of the highlights of the album *Diamond Dogs*, and the second was offered to Lulu, for whom Bowie and Ronson produced the disco single "The Man Who Sold the World" at the Château d'Hérouville a few months earlier. This number also marked the end of the collaboration between the singer and the producer Ken Scott, the man behind the success of *Hunky Dory, The Rise and Fall of Ziggy Stardust and the Spiders from Mars*, and *Aladdin Sane*.

DODO

David Bowie / 2:52

Musicians: David Bowie: lead and backing vocals, electric guitar, saxophone / **Lulu:** vocals / **Alan Parker:** electric guitar / **Herbie Flowers:** bass / **Tony Newman (?)** or **Aynsley Dunbar (?):** drums / **Mike Garson:** piano, electronic piano / **Unidentified Musicians:** trumpet, saxophone / **Recorded:** Trident Studios, London: September 1973, December 1973 / **Technical Team:** Producer: David Bowie

"Lulu's got this terrific voice, and it's been misdirected all this time, all these years,"[82] said David Bowie to the *Sounds* journalist Martin Kirkup in 1974. "People laugh now, but they won't in two years time, you see! [...] She's got a real soul voice, she can get the feel of Aretha."[82] If the artist was going perhaps a bit far in comparing the famous multifaceted singer with the American diva, it was that he was very pleased with the success of the disco version of "The Man Who Sold the World" that he had produced for her with Mick Ronson. While the medley "1984/Dodo" was carved up in the autumn, a demo of "Dodo" was recorded with Lulu and temporarily renamed "You Didn't Hear It from Me." This number, which was to remain at the demo stage, emphasizes the weaknesses of the singer, who struggled to blend her voice with Bowie's. This is a rarity to be discovered on YouTube.

ALTERNATIVE CANDIDATE

David Bowie / 5:07

Musicians: David Bowie: lead and backing vocals, twelve-string acoustic guitar / **Herbie Flowers:** bass / **Tony Newman:** drums / **Mike Garson:** piano / **Recorded:** Olympic Studios, Barnes: January 1974 / **Technical Team:** Producer: David Bowie / **Sound Engineer:** Keith Harwood (Olympic Studios) / **Assistant Sound Engineer:** Andy Morris (Olympic Studios)

Commonly referred to as "Alternative Candidate," "Candidate" (Alternate Version), or "Candidate 1," this song, which remained at the demo stage, bears no similarities with the fourth track of *Diamond Dogs*, other than the phrase "*[I'll] pretend [I'm] walking home.*" Recorded during the album sessions, it has a pleasing and rather catchy melody, which would not have gone amiss with the fans. They would have to wait, however, until the rerelease of the disc by Rykodisc in 1990 to discover the piece among the bonus items. In this number we find the appeal for David of the delay effect, which enabled hm to repeat the ends of phrases. "The digital delay fascinated David," explained Tony Visconti, recruited at the last minute to remix some of the album's tracks. "We were applying it to backing vocals, guitar solos, drum fills and several other elements. With David anything goes."[81]

Rock 'n' Roll with Me / Panic in Detroit

US Release on RCA: September 1974 (ref. PB-10105) / Best Chart Ranking: Did Not Chart

Bowie onstage at the Tower Theater in Upper Darby, Pennsylvania, where his live album *David Live* was recorded.

Side A

ROCK'N'ROLL WITH ME

David Bowie, Warren Peace / 4:17

Musicians: David Bowie: vocals / Earl Slick: electric guitar / Herbie Flowers: bass / Tony Newman: drums / Pablo Rosario: percussion / Richard Grando: baritone saxophone / David Sanborn: alto saxophone / Warren Peace, Gui Andrisano: backing vocals / Mike Garson: piano / Michael Kamen: electronic piano, Moog synthesizer / **Recorded:** Tower Theater, Philadelphia: July 12 or 13, 1974 / **Mixing:** Electric Lady Studios, New York: August–September 1974 / **Technical Team:** Producer: Tony Visconti / **Recorded:** Keith Harwood / **Mixing:** Tony Visconti, Edwin H. Kramer / **Arrangements:** Michael Kamen / **Single:** Side A: Rock 'n' Roll with Me (Live) / 4:17 / **Side B:** Panic in Detroit (Live) / 5:43

On completion of a triumphal but exhausting tour, on October 29, 1974, Bowie issued *David Live*, a double disc demonstrating how monumental the *Diamond Dogs* tour was, in particular the concerts played at the Tower Theater in Philadelphia on July 12–13, 1973. The dates of the recording are the subject of some debate for the fans, as the artist performed in the Pennsylvania city between July 8 and 13. But only the last two concerts were recorded, as stated on the reissue of the live performance, in a single-disc (nine-song) version for the Netherlands in 1982.

In September 1974, RCA launched an extract of this concert as a single in America: "Rock 'n' Roll with Me," mixed by Tony Visconti at the Electric Lady Studios in New York, accompanied by the manager of the premises, Edwin H. Kramer, a sound engineer renowned for his work on numerous live Jimi Hendrix albums. The rapport was not the most cordial between the two technicians, but the album from which this single was derived is of undeniable quality and provides a record of this period when David Bowie decided to make the African-American musical culture his own. Herbie Flowers, the bassist on the tour, was a witness to the birth of this album, which is as brilliant as it is controversial: "A lot of people think [it] is his worst. But aficionados think it's his greatest."[13]

Knock on Wood / Panic in Detroit
UK Release on RCA: September 13, 1974 (ref. RCA 2466) / Best Chart Ranking: 10

While in Detroit with the Stax label, Eddie Floyd, author of "Knock on Wood," also wrote hits for Carla Thomas and Wilson Pickett.

Side A

KNOCK ON WOOD

Steve Cropper, Eddie Floyd / 3:24

Musicians: David Bowie: vocals / **Earl Slick:** electric guitar / **Herbie Flowers:** bass / **Tony Newman:** drums / **Pablo Rosario:** percussion / **Richard Grando:** baritone saxophone / **David Sanborn:** alto saxophone / **Gui Andrisano, Warren Peace:** backing vocals / **Mike Garson:** piano / **Michael Kamen:** electronic piano, Moog synthesizer / **Recorded:** Tower Theater, Philadelphia: July 12 or 13, 1974 / **Mixing:** Electric Lady Studios, New York: August–September 1974 / **Technical Team:** Producer: Tony Visconti / **Recorded:** Keith Harwood / **Mixing:** Tony Visconti, Edwin H. Kramer / **Arrangements:** Michael Kamen / Side A: *Knock on Wood (Live)* / 3:08 / Side B: *Panic in Detroit (Live)* / 5:43

While the American market was offered "Rock 'n' Roll with Me" as a single, derived from the double album *David Live*, the British inherited another extract, issued as a 45 rpm: a frenetic interpretation of the hit by Eddie Floyd, "Knock on Wood" (1966). In borrowing this hit from the Stax label—which was to be even more widely popularized by the disco diva Amii Stewart in 1979—Bowie took a very soul-oriented, even funk direction. Mixed by Visconti and Kramer in New York, the song was accompanied on the B-side by another piece recorded at the Tower Theater in Philadelphia but not included on the live album: "Panic in Detroit," from the *Aladdin Sane* album. As stated on the disc jacket notes, the recording is faithful to the musicians' performance. Only the backing vocals of Gui Andrisano and Warren Peace, which were impeded during the concert by feedback problems, were rerecorded, as the tracks were unusable.

YOUNG

YOUNG YOU

YOUNG

AMERIC

RICANS

GAMER

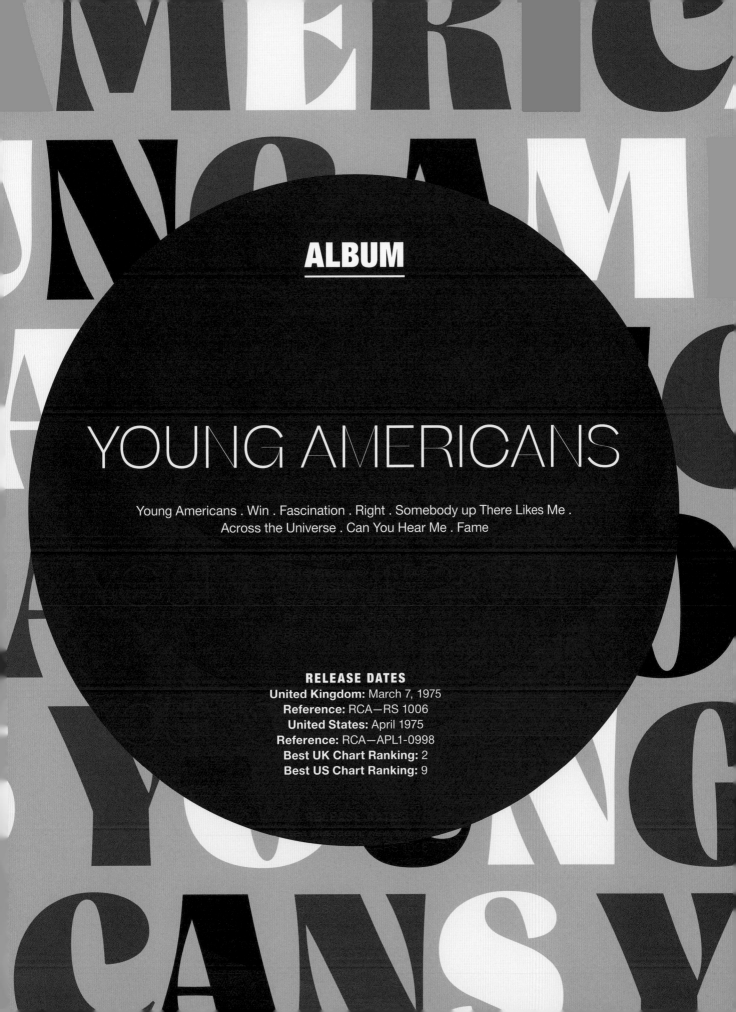

ALBUM

YOUNG AMERICANS

Young Americans . Win . Fascination . Right . Somebody up There Likes Me .
Across the Universe . Can You Hear Me . Fame

RELEASE DATES

United Kingdom: March 7, 1975
Reference: RCA—RS 1006
United States: April 1975
Reference: RCA—APL1-0998
Best UK Chart Ranking: 2
Best US Chart Ranking: 9

David Bowie under the influence of
soul and funk, and ready to produce
one of his greatest albums.

1975

THE SOUL YEARS

October 29, 1974, saw the launch of *David Live*, the first recording to demonstrate the magic wrought during Bowie's concerts. This double album had a message for those still clinging to the past: Ziggy Stardust is dead; make way for the Bowie of 1974, sensual, elegant...but exhausted. Worn out by a demanding tour, he was tired, suffering from paranoia and the effects of drugs—a dangerous cocktail in the land of rock 'n' roll, where he had now ended up. London and the port of Southampton seemed very far away. It was time for David Bowie to embrace America, travel its highways and bewitch its journalists, fulfilling the dream of so many British artists.

Immersion in the "Philly Sound"

First of all, he needed to do away with the excesses of the *Diamond Dogs* tour, the only souvenir of which he had preserved in the tracks of *David Live*. "There's nothing more boring than a stylized show, because there was no spontaneity and no freedom of movement. Everything was totally choreographed and it was very stiff."[83] He was to find the freedom he sought by immersing himself in the culture of African American soul music.

A few months earlier, in July 1974, Bowie had been appearing at the Tower Theater in Philadelphia, and it was here that the live recordings for the disc were made. It was also in Philadelphia that, through the recording of an album by Ava Cherry and the Astronettes, Bowie heard about Sigma Sound Studios. Overseen by Michael Kamen, the artistic director of the *Diamond Dogs* tour, three numbers by this soul singer had been recorded on July 9: "Everything That Touches You," "Give It Away," and a new version of "Sweet Thing" from *Diamond Dogs*. They were destined to languish in a drawer at MainMan, Tony

Defries's company. Bowie, however, was won over by the place and its history. Set up by sound engineer Joseph Tarsia in 1968, the studio owed its international fame to two composer-producers, Kenny Gamble and Leon Huff, who established their label, Philadelphia International Records, here. The three men formed an impressive team. Gamble and Huff provided their artists with a magnificent array of highly skilled session musicians, known collectively as the MFSB (Mother Father Sister Brother) group. Bowie had been struck by the quality of their second single, "TSOP (The Sound of Philadelphia)," from 1973. This number was also used to introduce *Soul Train*, the popular TV program featuring all the big names in funk, soul, and R&B that was faithfully followed by Bowie. As Ava Cherry was to recall: "David Bowie was fascinated by soul music. I took David one night at [*sic*] the Apollo because he wanted to hear soul groups. He got out of the limo with his electric blue dress and red hair. Inside, Carlos Alomar and Luther Vandross were playing on stage. It is this night that David found his companions for the *Young Americans* album."[84]

Carlos Alomar described that fateful day, when he met a musical companion who would soon become a close friend: "We started talking and he was very curious about my group The Main Ingredient, my work with James Brown, and all the R'n'B acts I'd played with. [...] This guy knew his black people, more than most Americans, as regrettable as that might be. And I really found him so interesting. I didn't know anything about the Spiders from Mars or any of that stuff."[79]

Encouraged by Alomar and Ava Cherry, Bowie haunted the New York concert halls, discovering not only the star qualities but also the emotional power of performances by

During production, the album had the provisional title *The Gouster*. This African American slang word refers to a hip teen in 1960s Chicago.

Leon Huff (left) and Kenny Gamble (right), owners of Philadelphia International Records and masters of the Philly Sound, circa 1970.

artists such as Marvin Gaye, the Temptations, and the Jackson Five. When he booked the Sigma Sound Studios for the month of August 1974, it was with the intention of leaving his mark on the city where soul music reigned supreme.

A Made-to-Measure Group

Eager to take advantage of the studio know-how, Bowie asked to have MFSB for his backing group. They said they were busy with other projects, and the only member to step up was the percussionist Larry Washington. The rumor that reached Bowie's ears suggested something very different; the truth was that none of these talented musicians, all much involved in the American rhythm 'n' blues movement, was prepared to play for a young white singer setting himself up as a *funkateer*. Bowie had to call on his usual musicians: Mike Garson on keyboards, David Sanborn on saxophone, Pablo Rosario for percussion, and Ava Cherry doing the backing vocals. Tony Newman and Herbie Flowers had both been dismissed after a rebellion in July—they had threatened to not go onstage if they were not featured on the album's live recording. To replace them, Alomar recommended two legendary musicians: bass player Willie Weeks and drummer Andy Newmark,

Anthony Hinton, Diane Sumler, and Luther Vandross: three famous singers who gave *Young Americans* a high-class soul sound.

the latter having made an impressive appearance on Sly and the Family Stone's 1973 album *Fresh*. He also suggested his wife, Robin Clark, and their friend Luther Vandross to assist Warren Peace on backing vocals. Two other backing singers soon joined the team: Anthony Hinton and Diane Sumler.

Rehearsals and writing began on August 8, 1974, at Sigma Sound Studios with the studio's sound engineer, Carl Paruolo. Everyone contributed their different skills, Bowie providing a framework of chords but allowing the musicians to play together until a composition emerged. Alomar described Bowie's state of mind, saying: "I think that at [this moment], theatrics were not necessary; what he needed was heart and soul."[13]

Over three days, as the musicians put together the skeleton of the forthcoming album, the walls of the studio reverberated with the groove. Although he had wanted to get the MFSB to produce the incomparable Philly Sound, Bowie was prepared to give free rein to his New York team on several of the tracks, including "Right," "Can You Hear Me," and the one that provided the name for the album, "Young Americans." With recording due to start the following day, Bowie was not happy with the current state of the demos, and he decided to summon Tony Visconti to the rescue. The producer jumped on the first available plane; scarcely had he arrived on the evening of August 11 before immediately getting to work. He didn't even check in at his hotel! He was struck by the spontaneity, creativity, and

Always ready to skewer his own behavior, Bowie was very aware that he was only a novice and that he was essentially stealing soul music. He himself described his album as "plastic soul," a pale synthetic derivative of authentic soul music.

crazy atmosphere of Sigma Sound Studios, saying later: "Nothing was organized, and it turned out to be one enormous jam session."[85]

Young Americans: Conquering America!

The result of that first summer session, with its peaceful and collaborative atmosphere, was a vigorously rhythmical work characterized by its freshness. As Tony Visconti put it: "The goal was to make a kick-ass R&B record."[13]

Bowie returned to Sigma Sound Studios in November, before moving to the New York Record Plant studios in December. American TV introduced the public to Bowie's new hit "Young Americans," with its memorable refrain and irresistible groove. The artistic revolution the singer was undergoing was clearly apparent. The track did not come out as a single until the following year, on February 21. Appearing on *The Dick Cavett Show* on December 5, 1974, David Bowie and his fellow musicians gave a successful performance, and Bowie was convincing

The singer Ava Cherry and Bowie childhood friend Geoffrey MacCormack, who was later known as Warren Peace: two loyal colleagues from the singer's "Plastic Soul" period.

in his role of soul singer. Unfortunately, the interview he gave afterward was a disaster. Betraying his serious cocaine habit with his constant sniffing, he gave confused replies, brandishing his newly adopted dandified cane. "It was horrendous. I had no idea where I was, I couldn't hear the questions. To this day, I don't know if I bothered answering them, I was so out of my gourd."[59]

Corinne "Coco" Schwab, Guardian Angel

The "Soul Tour" (also called the "Philly Tour"), a new version of the *Diamond Dogs* tour, expanded to include some of the numbers from the future album. Stripped of the elaborate effects of the preceding concerts, it soon got underway under the direction of Mike Garson—Michael Kamen having been let go by this point. It was in this context that Bowie was featured in a documentary that would immortalize his time in America. Directed by Alan Yentob, *Cracked Actor* shows a pale and emaciated man, obsessed with the search for the authenticity of soul music and suffering from a cocaine-fueled paranoia that,

day by day, became increasingly pronounced. All at sea, the singer's whole universe was falling to pieces. He had become very close to Ava Cherry, but his marriage to Angie seemed to be in its death throes. "I heard she showed up one night, trashed his hotel room and left,"[29] Tony Visconti was to recall. Angie was less dramatic in her description of their relationship: "Our marriage was a partnership to accomplish making David a worldwide star. In the meantime, we also had a love affair which was very nice, and a child, which was even better."[1]

On the business side, the collaboration with Tony Defries was becoming unsatisfactory. Already cautious about his position in relation to MainMan, Bowie sought to distance himself from his manager. Corinne Schwab, someone he had met a few months earlier, became his personal assistant. Nicknamed "Coco" by Warren Peace, she was to be Bowie's confidante, friend, and guardian angel until his death in 2016. Following the advice of John Lennon, with whom he had struck up a friendship in December 1974 (a relationship that led to the making of two recordings that

Viewers in the United States were treated to a funkier version of Bowie (who was also under the influence of various substances) on the stage of *The Dick Cavett Show*, on February 5, 1974.

This photo of Toni Basil, shot by Eric Stephen Jacobs for the cover of *After Dark* magazine, inspired the look of *Young Americans*.

were to complete the album's track listing), he severed his relationship with MainMan and Tony Defries. Corinne Schwab placed the affair in the hands of the famous Californian lawyer Michael Lippman. Bowie was now free to concentrate on the launch of his ninth album, its appearance in early April in the United States officially cementing his status as a star. Although now internationally famous, he did not rest on his laurels. Instead, he agreed to take on the role of Thomas Jerome Newton in the science fiction movie *The Man Who Fell to Earth,* from the English director Nicolas Roeg. Filming took place in New Mexico, not far from California where Bowie was soon to settle. There, he would sink into a hell from which only Coco Schwab would be able to rescue him.

FOR BOWIE ADDICTS

The sleeve photo of *Young Americans* was taken by the photographer Eric Stephen Jacobs. He took his inspiration from a portrait of the choreographer Toni Basil photographed by Jacobs on the cover of the magazine *After Dark* (September 1974). Bowie recalled that "I really wanted Norman Rockwell to do an album cover for me [but] his wife said [...] 'I'm sorry, but Norman needs at least six months for his portraits.' So I had to pass."[51]

Single

YOUNG AMERICANS

David Bowie / 5:10

Musicians

David Bowie: lead vocals, acoustic guitar
Carlos Alomar: electric guitar
Willy Weeks: bass
Andy Newmark: drums
Mike Garson: piano
David Sanborn: saxophone
Pablo Rosario: percussion
Larry Washington: conga drums
Ava Cherry, Robin Clark, Luther Vandross, Warren Peace:
backing vocals

Recorded

Sigma Sound Studios, Philadelphia: August 13–14, 1974, and
November 20–22, 1974

Technical Team

Producer: Tony Visconti
Sound Engineer: Carl Paruolo
Assistant Sound Engineer: Mike Hutchinson
Mixing: Tony Visconti

SIDE A: *Young Americans* / 3:11
SIDE B: *Suffragette City (Live)* / 3:46 (UK); *Knock on Wood (Live)* /
2:59 (USA)
UK Release on RCA: February 21, 1975 (ref. RCA 2523)
US Release on RCA: February 21, 1975 (ref. PB-10152)
Best UK Chart Ranking: 18
Best US Chart Ranking: 28

ON YOUR HEADPHONES
Despite his impeccable skill, drummer Andy
Newmark misses a snare drum beat at the
beginning of the first refrain (0:49)!

Genesis

David Bowie's appearance on *The Dick Cavett Show* on December 5, 1974, set the tone for his new personae. Abandoning his rhinestones and sequins, he now presented himself with sensual elegance, driven by the musical experience of his new team. Anticipating the furor caused by the album when it was released in the spring, *Young Americans* draws its energy both from its dancing rhythm, swaying and passionate, and its irresistible melody forged during the sessions at the Sigma Sound Studios between August 8 and 10, 1974. The chorus already in place, two of the invited musicians, discreetly installed in the control room next to Visconti, were to become—to their surprise—part of a legend: Robin Clark and Luther Vandross. Carlos Alomar, who had introduced Bowie to the majority of the musicians on this album, invited his wife and their friend Luther to take part in the sessions. The two stowaways could not resist joining in, improvising a backing to what was to become a famous refrain: "Young American, young American, she wants the young American." Alomar remembered how "Bowie heard it and said, "Weyhey ! You go into the studio and do just that." They weren't hired initially, they just came to be my friends and be with me on the session."[29] This was typical of the mood of these sessions where spontaneity ruled. For Luther Vandross, "it was my first experience of recording and it cemented my desire to pursue a career in music,"[47] a career that earned him a Grammy Award in 1991 for the album *Power of Love*.

The instrumental section of "Young Americans" was the result of a jam session lasting several hours. Carlos Alomar remembered how "it started off just as little fragments, ideas and riffs that he'd bang out on the piano or on his acoustic guitar. I would work with those ideas, supplying him with signature guitar lines. [...] It was only about four hours into the first session. We got to the guitar breakdown, and we knew we had something."[86] It was more than merely "something"; "Young Americans," while not hitting the top of the charts, did bring Bowie international recognition and the respect of musicians he had admired since he was young.

Milk and cocaine: Bowie's less-than-ideal diet during the mid-1970s.

Production

When Visconti arrived at Sigma Sound Studios on August 11, 1974, he found that Bowie was unhappy with the demo versions produced by Carl Paruolo—a bit rich, considering that this sound engineer had already worked with the likes of Muddy Waters, Charles Mann, and Billy Paul! Paruolo, who had hoped to leave a more individual mark on the album, was sidelined while Visconti took over, applying his usual methods to the disc's production. It was his habit to apply the necessary effects for the sound of the voice from the beginning, unlike other American producers who tended to insert them at the mixing stage in case they changed their minds about the artistic style required.

Immersed in the power of the moment, Bowie recorded the vocal line live. Tony Visconti recalled how "his vocals were so perfectly sung and so heartfelt that we hardly had to replace any lines. I would say that eighty per cent of the vocals are live takes, with the band playing at the same time. That's the time-honored way most earlier soul records were made."[29]

ON YOUR HEADPHONES
As the song reaches its peak during the last verse at 3:54, the backing singers pay tribute to the Beatles' "A Day in the Life," singing in unison: "*I heard the news today, oh boy.*"

WIN

David Bowie / 4:44

Musicians: David Bowie: lead vocals / **Carlos Alomar:** electric guitar/ **Emir Ksasan :** bass / **Dennis Davis:** drums / **David Sanborn:** saxophone / **Robin Clark, Luther Vandross, Ava Cherry:** backing vocals / **Unidentified Musicians:** strings / **Recorded:** Sigma Sound Studios, Philadelphia: November 20–22, 1974 / The Record Plant, New York: December 1974 / AIR Studios, London (strings): January 1975 / **Technical Team: Producer:** Tony Visconti / **Sound Engineers:** Carl Paruolo (Sigma Sound Studios), Harry Maslin (Record Plant) / **Assistant Sound Engineers:** Mike Hutchinson (Sigma Sound Studios), Kevin Herron (Record Plant), David Thoener (Record Plant) / **Mixing 1:** Tony Visconti / **Mixing 2:** David Bowie, Harry Maslin / **String arrangements:** Tony Visconti

The sweet tone of Bowie's voice in this languid and sensual number invites the listener to confront life's difficulties. "All you've got to do is win," he sings, continuing: "That's all you got to do," a phrase borrowed from Otis Redding, who murmurs it at 1:22 on his hit song "Try a Little Tenderness." A number of discreet similarities with "Win" can be heard at the beginning and in the verses of Prince's "Diamonds and Pearls" from 1991; the introduction is also used by Beck in his song "Debra" on the *Midnite Vultures* album, released in 1999.

David Sanborn provides a saxophone line with strange sonorities, something that met with David Bowie's approval, as we know from the 2008 notes accompanying the compilation disc *iSelect*: "He [Sanborn] was experimenting with sound effects at the time and I'd rather hoped he would push further into that area, but he chose to become rich and famous instead. So he did win really, didn't he?"[87]

FASCINATION

David Bowie, Luther Vandross / 4:44

Musicians: David Bowie: lead vocals / **Carlos Alomar:** electric guitar / **Emir Ksasan :** bass / **Dennis Davis:** drums / **Pablo Rosario:** percussion / **Mike Garson:** electric piano/ **David Sanborn:** saxophone / **Robin Clark, Luther Vandross, Ava Cherry:** backing vocals / **Recorded:** Sigma Sound Studios, Philadelphia: November 20–22, 1974 / The Record Plant, New York: December 1974 / **Technical Team: Producer:** Tony Visconti / **Sound Engineers:** Carl Paruolo (Sigma Sound Studios), Harry Maslin (Record Plant) / **Assistant Sound Engineers:** Mike Hutchinson (Sigma Sound Studios), Kevin Herron (Record Plant), David Thoener (Record Plant) / **Mixing 1:** Tony Visconti / **Mixing 2:** David Bowie, Harry Maslin

Now things were really grooving! As his friendship with his magnificent backing vocalists, including Luther Vandross, became ever closer, David Bowie continued to find his inspiration through discussions with his musicians for whom he had the greatest respect. Robin Clark recalled, "David asked Luther if he had any songs. Luther had a song called 'Funky Music.' He played it on the piano for David and David asked him if he could change the lyrics to 'Fascination.'"[88] Vandross commented: "He said he didn't want to be so presumptuous as to say 'funky music,' since he was a rock artist. [...] I said 'You're David Bowie, I live at home with my mother, you can do what you like.'"[1] The original version of the song, "Funky Music (Is a Part of Me)," appeared in 1976 on Luther's own album bearing his name. As for the production, Carlos Alomar plays his Gibson ES-355 using a wah-wah pedal with well-judged restraint while David Bowie takes on the tones of Curtis Mayfield on his tracks "Superfly" and "Little Child Runnin' Wild" from the 1972 album *Super Fly*. This is a funky title not to be missed!

Bassist Willie Weeks, notably present on "Right," "Somebody Up There Likes Me," and "Can You Hear Me," was one of the key musical elements on the album.

RIGHT

David Bowie / 4:13

Musicians: David Bowie: lead vocals / Carlos Alomar: electric guitar / Willy Weeks: bass / Andy Newmark: drums / Mike Garson: clavinet / David Sanborn: saxophone / Pablo Rosario: percussion / Larry Washington: conga drums / Ava Cherry, Robin Clark, Luther Vandross, Anthony Hinton, Diane Sumler, Warren Peace: backing vocals / **Recorded:** Sigma Sound Studios, Philadelphia: August 11–22, 1974 / The Record Plant, New York: December 1974 / **Technical Team:** Producer: Tony Visconti, Harry Maslin / **Sound Engineers:** Carl Paruolo (Sigma Sound Studios), Harry Maslin (Record Plant) / **Assistant Sound Engineers:** Mike Hutchinson (Sigma Sound Studios), Kevin Herron (Record Plant), David Thoener (Record Plant) / **Mixing 1:** Tony Visconti / **Mixing 2:** David Bowie, Harry Maslin

You can feel Isaac Hayes's Memphis Sound in this superb funk song, as Garson—on the Hohner Clavinet—pays tribute to Ray Jackson's famous introduction to the 1972 Bill Withers's track, "Use Me." The careful attention to vocals is also notable. From 1:09, Bowie initiates a call-and-response sequence with his six backing singers, the result being unusually effective. Backing singer Robin Clark described Bowie's way of working: "At that point in my career I had done a lot, but I had never worked in that way. [...] David knew where he wanted things to go. He came in and worked on those parts with us. [...] David wrote a chart for us. [...] It's a bunch of words, dots, and dashes! David would coach us with: 'You're singing here, you're out there, you're back in here, you're out over there.' He had this all in his head. I had never seen anything like that, but I got it and so did Luther. It was David's language."[88]

Paul Newman was unforgettable as boxer Rocky Graziano in the film *Somebody Up There Likes Me*, directed by Robert Wise in 1956.

SOMEBODY UP THERE LIKES ME

David Bowie / 6:30

Musicians: David Bowie: lead vocals, synthesizer / **Carlos Alomar:** electric guitar / **Willy Weeks:** bass / **Andy Newmark:** drums / **Mike Garson:** piano / **David Sanborn:** saxophone / **Pablo Rosario:** percussion / **Larry Washington:** conga drums / **Ava Cherry, Robin Clark, Luther Vandross, Anthony Hinton, Diane Sumler:** backing vocals, claps / **Recorded: Sigma Sound Studios, Philadelphia:** August 11–22, 1974 / **The Record Plant, New York:** December 1974 / **Technical Team: Producers:** Tony Visconti, Harry Maslin / **Sound Engineers:** Carl Paruolo (Sigma Sound Studios), Harry Maslin (Record Plant) / **Assistant Sound Engineers:** Mike Hutchinson (Sigma Sound Studios), Kevin Herron (Record Plant), David Thoener (Record Plant) / **Mixing 1:** Tony Visconti / **Mixing 2:** David Bowie, Harry Maslin /

Legend has it that Bowie took his inspiration for this song from "I Am Divine," which he had written for Ava Cherry and the Astronettes. In fact, only a descending chord motif—such as is commonly found in the classic soul-funk numbers—is similar. The title of the song was taken from the 1956 movie directed by Robert Wise based on the colorful life of boxer Rocky Graziano, a petty criminal who became World Middleweight Champion in 1947. Bowie departs from the theme of the movie but nevertheless paints a portrait of an ordinary man who becomes a kind of messiah. He stresses the downside of this kind of hero worship, returning once again to the subject of the terrible effects that heaping so much praise and power on one leader can have on the masses. In a 1974 interview with Robert Hilburn of *Melody Maker,* he said: "What I've said for years under various guises is that 'Watch Out, the West is going to have a Hitler!' I've said it in a thousand different ways. That song is yet another way. [...][69]

Once again, this track produced by Visconti gives marked prominence to the saxophone. Bowie had alerted David Sanborn to this: "Bowie said to me, 'We're not going to have a lead guitar on this record, you're going to fill the role of lead guitar.'"[89] A gamble that paid off—the saxophone is an integral part of "Young Americans," making its entry in every gap left by the singer along with a solid rhythmic backing provided by Andy Newmark and Willy Weeks.

ACROSS THE UNIVERSE

John Lennon, Paul McCartney / 4:30

Musicians: David Bowie: lead vocals / John Lennon: twelve-string acoustic guitar, backing vocals / Carlos Alomar, Earl Slick: electric guitars / Emir Ksasan: bass / Dennis Davis: drums / Jean Fineberg, Jean Millington: backing vocals / **Recorded:** Electric Lady Studios, New York: January 12–15, 1975 / **Technical Team:** Producers: David Bowie, Harry Maslin / Sound Engineer: Edwin H. Kramer / Assistant Sound Engineer: David Thoener / Mixing: David Bowie, Harry Maslin

The first of two numbers that were recorded by Bowie and Lennon during the sessions in New York in January 1975, this cover of a famous Beatles song was something of a gamble for David Bowie. Despite criticism from some quarters, David Bowie tackles this song with ease, transforming the pervasive melancholy of the Lennon-McCartney original—in fact composed by Lennon only—into a rock ballad. It's a lively track, although it is true that it does not entirely fit in with the rest of the album. Visconti was already doing the mixing for the album in London when Bowie added two new songs, "Across the Universe" and "Fame," to the album's track list. Harry Maslin, obliged to take over as producer for this pair of tracks, remembered this episode well: "It was rather bizarre for me, as I came into a scene I wasn't used to and I had [...] John Lennon in the control room, looking at what I was doing. It was a little disconcerting for the first week or so. [...] David [...] said, 'You have to do me a favour [...] you have to produce the rest of *Young Americans.*' [...] A favour? I said, 'Well, David, I think I can do you this favour.'"[1] In the end, even if this cover version of "Across the Universe" was not as successful as "Fame," it once again demonstrated the respect Bowie felt for the musicians who influenced him, and whom he regularly acknowledged on his albums.

CAN YOU HEAR ME

David Bowie / 5:04

Musicians: David Bowie: lead vocals / Carlos Alomar: electric guitar / Willy Weeks: bass / Andy Newmark: drums / Mike Garson: piano / David Sanborn: saxophone / Pablo Rosario: percussion / Larry Washington: conga drums / Ava Cherry, Robin Clark, Luther Vandross, Anthony Hinton, Diane Sumler: backing vocals / Unidentified Musicians: strings / **Recorded:** Sigma Sound Studios, Philadelphia: August 11–22, 1974, and November 20–22, 1974 / AIR Studios, London (strings): January 1975 / **Technical Team:** Producer: Tony Visconti / Sound Engineer: Carl Paruolo / Assistant Sound Engineer: Mike Hutchinson / Mixing 1: Tony Visconti / Mixing 2: David Bowie, Harry Maslin / String Arrangements: Tony Visconti

An earlier version of "Can You Hear Me" was recorded in January 1974 at the Olympic Studios in London, during the *Diamond Dogs* sessions. Originally called "Take It in Right," the song's name was changed when David Bowie offered it to Lulu after her success with a disco interpretation of "The Man Who Sold the World." The future single, with Carlos Alomar on guitar, was recorded a second time at Olympic Studios in March 1974, and then the following month at RCA Studios in New York. For some unknown reason, the project was abandoned, and Bowie returned to the song for *Young Americans.* Once the album was completed in December 1974, Tony Visconti returned to the UK for the recording of the string sections of "Can You Hear Me," "Win," and "It's Gonna Be Me" at AIR Studios in London. Thanks to the addition of this dreamy orchestration, Bowie's singing takes on the sensuality he so much admired in the songs of Barry White and the Love Unlimited Orchestra. Some people assert that this song was written for Ava Cherry, with Bowie commenting in the *New Musical Express* in August 1975: "'Can You Hear Me' was written for somebody but I'm not telling you who it is. That is a real love song. I kid you not."[90]

Single

FAME

David Bowie, Carlos Alomar, John Lennon / 4:12

1975

Musicians
David Bowie: lead and backing vocals, piano
John Lennon: lead and backing vocals, acoustic guitar, piano
Carlos Alomar: electric guitar
Earl Slick: electric guitar
Emir Ksasan: bass
Dennis Davis: drums
Pablo Rosario: percussion
Ralph MacDonald: percussion
Jean Fineberg, Jean Millington: backing vocals

Recorded
Electric Lady Studios, New York: January 12–15, 1975

Technical Team
Producers: David Bowie, Harry Maslin
Sound Engineers: Edwin H. Kramer
Assistant Sound Engineers: David Thoener
Mixing: David Bowie, Harry Maslin

SIDE A: *Fame* / 3:30
SIDE B: *Right* / 4:13
UK Release on RCA: July 25, 1975 (ref. PB-2579)
US Release on RCA: July 25, 1975 (ref. PB-10320)
Best UK Chart Ranking: 17
Best US Chart Ranking: 1

FOR BOWIE ADDICTS

Carlos Alomar had already used the *cocotte* guitar technique that we hear in "Fame" in his work with James Brown in the late 1960s. The Godfather of Soul recovered the sound, which he felt was his by right, when he copied all the guitar lines of Bowie's hit to use in his "Hot (I Need to Be Loved)" of 1975. Apparently flattered, Bowie decided he would not object unless Brown's song entered the charts (which it never did).

Genesis

David Bowie met John Lennon in December 1974 at the Record Plant in New York, where the former Beatle was completing the production of his disc of cover songs, *Rock 'n' Roll*. Although David was very much in awe of his idol, the two soon became firm friends. During the long winter nights, the two exiled Englishmen whiled away the time in endless conversation, often joined by May Pang, Lennon's new girlfriend (Lennon being at the time temporarily separated from Yoko Ono). Bowie remembered: "I spent quite a lot of time getting to know Lennon, and I do remember we went to a lot of bars together. We spent hours and hours discussing fame, and what you had to do to get it, to get there. If I'm honest it was his fame we were discussing, because he was so much more famous than anyone who had been before."[1]

The idea of getting together in the studio came up almost at once. In January, when Visconti was busy mixing *Young Americans* in London, several days were reserved at Electric Lady Studios in New York. It was here that the famous encounter took place. Sound engineer Harry Maslin, who had worked with Bowie in December at the Record Plant, was brought on as co-producer. Excluded from the event, Visconti was to say ruefully: "I would've happily paid to fly over on the Concorde just to be at that session."[35] Two tracks were recorded: a cover version of the Beatles' "Across the Universe" and a new number resulting from the collaboration between the two men and guitarist Carlos Alomar. Called "Fame," the song is about the problems of success and was highly topical. Lennon had caused his friend to have doubts about his relationship with his manager Tony Defries. While Defries exercised considerable influence over Bowie, it was not entirely clear how he managed the singer's finances. In 2003, Bowie was to say: "John was the guy who opened me up to the idea that all management is crap. That [...] you should try to do without it. It was at John's instigation that I really did without managers, and started getting people in to do specific jobs for me, rather than signing myself away to one guy forever."[36] Ironically, this manifesto denouncing fame—something that Bowie had always striven for—and its downside was to give him his first number one in the United States.

Once production of the two songs was completed, Bowie asked Tony Visconti to change the album's track list. Visconti, who had already finished the mixing, had to cut out "Who Can I Be Now?" "It's Gonna Be Me," and "After Today," replacing them with the two new pieces that were mixed by Bowie and Harry Maslin.

Production

After completing "Across the Universe," Bowie turned his attention to "Foot Stomping Part 1," a standard doo-wop number produced by the Flares in 1961, which David performed on *The Dick Cavett Show* on December 5, 1974. In the end, he abandoned this project, retaining only the guitar riff that had been added to the cover version by Carlos Alomar. Starting with this guitar sound, he developed an entirely new song. In the heady atmosphere of the studio, ideas flowed thick and fast. David Thoener, assistant sound engineer, suggested beginning the song with the piano part inverted. Bowie approved, and Maslin was given the job of doing the impossible. "I asked John if he would be so kind as to go out to the piano and just hit one chord when given the appropriate cue,"[1] Maslin recalled. He then applied his mixing know-how to the task of reversing the order of the piano notes. Alomar took the lead on the guitar, accompanied by Earl Slick, the rock guitarist used for the *Diamond Dogs* tour and who appears on the album. "I was there, but that's a complete blank. The only thing that convinced me I was there was John."[89]

The rhythm section consisted of drummer Dennis Davis and bass player Emir Ksasan, both of whom had joined the group for the November sessions. Pablo Rosario and Ralph MacDonald's parts on percussion, normally very audible, here seem to be relegated to the background. The backing vocals here are provided by Jean Millington, a friend of Bowie's who had just popped in to say hello on the day of recording along with her friend Jean Fineberg. In addition, we find no less a vocalist than John Lennon himself, whose high-register voice is responsible for the second "Fame" at the beginning of each phrase! Jean Fineberg recalled that "We were listening to the tracks and my friend told him I played sax and the flute. David [...] said, 'Why don't you go there and put something down?' So I went in and put down a wild flute solo on 'Fame.' Which [...] did not make it on the record."[13] She added, in another interview in 2015: "The album comes out, and there's no flute solo on it, but I'm listed under vocals, which was very nice of him. I still get the cheques—I got one this week!"[89]

The song is credited to Bowie and Alomar, but also to Lennon who, in point of fact, had not contributed to the writing of the piece. Bowie explained this decision: "The riff came from Carlos and the melody and most of the lyrics came from me. But it wouldn't have happened if John hadn't been there. He was the energy, and that's why he got a credit for writing it. He was the inspiration."[47]

David Bowie performed "Fame" on November 4, 1975, on an episode of *Soul Train*. He was the second white artist (after Elton John) to sing on this legendary program, which featured other major stars of the day, including Tina Turner and the Jackson Five.

Aretha Franklin in 1969. Franklin was one of David Bowie's major influences during the writing of *Young Americans*.

WHO CAN I BE NOW?

David Bowie / 4:35

Musicians: David Bowie: lead vocals / Carlos Alomar: electric guitar / Willy Weeks: bass / Andy Newmark: drums / Mike Garson: piano / David Sanborn: saxophone / Pablo Rosario: percussion / Larry Washington: conga drums / Ava Cherry, Robin Clark, Luther Vandross, Anthony Hinton, Diane Sumler: backing vocals / **Recorded:** Sigma Sound Studios, Philadelphia: August 11–22, 1974 / **Technical Team:** Producer: Tony Visconti / **Sound Engineer:** Carl Paruolo / **Assistant Sound Engineer:** Mike Hutchinson / **Mixing:** Tony Visconti

Once the mixing of "Fame" and "Across the Universe" was completed, David Bowie informed Tony Visconti, who had returned to London to put the finishing touches to *Young Americans*, that room would have to be found on the album for his new collaboration with John Lennon. The producer had to sacrifice three tracks that he particularly liked: "Who Can I Be Now?" "After Today," and "It's Gonna Be Me." "He [David] was very apologetic and nice about it. He said he hoped I wouldn't mind if we took a few tracks off and included these. The first time I heard of 'Fame' and 'Across The Universe' was when the record was released."[91] While the inclusion of "Fame" on the tracklisting of *Young Americans* was a good idea, ensuring Bowie's superstar status in the United States, it is also a shame that "Who Can I Be Now?" was dropped. This powerfully emotional ballad is a gem that can now be found in the box sets *Sound + Vision* and *Who Can I Be Now? (1974–1976)*, released in 1989 and 2016, respectively.

IT'S GONNA BE ME

David Bowie / 6:23

Musicians: David Bowie: lead vocals / Carlos Alomar: electric guitar / Willy Weeks: bass / Andy Newmark: drums / Mike Garson: piano / David Sanborn: saxophone / Pablo Rosario: percussion / Larry Washington: conga drums / Ava Cherry, Robin Clark, Luther Vandross, Anthony Hinton, Diane Sumler: backing vocals / Unidentified Musicians: strings / **Recorded:** Sigma Sound Studios, Philadelphia: August 13, 1974 / AIR Studios, London: January 1975 (strings) / **Technical Team:** Producer: Tony Visconti / **Sound Engineer:** Carl Paruolo / **Assistant Sound Engineer:** Mike Hutchinson / **Mixing:** Tony Visconti / **String Arrangements:** Tony Visconti

"It's Gonna Be Me," whose original working was "Come Back My Baby," suffered the same fate as "Who Can I Be Now?" when it was removed from the album to make room for the Bowie-Lennon duos. For Visconti, Bowie's request was difficult to accommodate because he had already written and supervised the recording of some lavish string arrangements. "It's Gonna Be Me" reminds us how much Bowie admired the celebrated singer. In Alan Yentob's 1975 documentary *Cracked Actor*, we see David Bowie and his personal assistant, Coco Schwab, driving thru the California desert and singing along to the diva's classic song "(You Make Me Feel Like) A Natural Woman." The influence of this song on Bowie when he was writing "It's Gonna Be Me" is very clear. In the late 1980s, the Thin White Duke agreed to a reissue of his back catalog with the Rykodisc label, to which would be added a number of rare songs, but the version of "It's Gonna Be Me" with the string arrangements was nowhere to be found. Visconti instead produced a remix of the track without strings. He found the original tracks eventually in his archives, and the 1975 version of "It's Gonna Be Me" could at last be heard on the 2007 reissue of *Young Americans*.

AFTER TODAY

David Bowie / 3:47

Musicians: David Bowie: lead vocals / Carlos Alomar: electric guitar / Willy Weeks: bass / Andy Newmark: drums / Mike Garson: piano / David Sanborn: saxophone / Pablo Rosario: percussion / Larry Washington: conga drums / Ava Cherry, Robin Clark, Luther Vandross, Anthony Hinton, Diane Sumler, Warren Peace: backing vocals / **Recorded:** Sigma Sound Studios, Philadelphia: August 13, 1974 / **Technical Team:** Producer: Tony Visconti / Sound Engineer: Carl Paruolo / Assistant Sound Engineer: Mike Hutchinson / Mixing: Tony Visconti

Conceived during the working sessions of 1974, both Bowie's singing and the arrangements of "After Today" sound more like a rehearsal trial run than a finished product. Available in the box set *Sound + Vision* put out by Rykodisc in 1989, the song was a roaring success with Bowie's insatiable fans. A second version, with a faster tempo, known as "After Today (Fast Version)," has been circulating on streaming sites since its 2009 discovery on a demo tape dated August 13, 1974.

Single

JOHN, I'M ONLY DANCING (AGAIN)

David Bowie / 6:57

Musicians: David Bowie: lead vocals / Carlos Alomar: electric guitar / Willy Weeks: bass / Andy Newmark: drums / Mike Garson: piano / David Sanborn: saxophone / Pablo Rosario: percussion / Larry Washington: conga drums / Ava Cherry, Robin Clark, Luther Vandross: backing vocals / **Recorded:** Sigma Sound Studios, Philadelphia: August 11–22, 1974, and November 20–22, 1974 / **Technical Team:** Producer: Tony Visconti / Sound Engineer: Carl Paruolo / Assistant Sound Engineer: Mike Hutchinson / Mixing: Tony Visconti / Side A: *John, I'm Only Dancing (Again)* / Side B: *John, I'm Only Dancing* / UK Release on RCA: December 7, 1979 (ref. BOW 4; PB 9482) / Best UK Chart Ranking: 12

Leaving aside the curiosity aroused by the discovery of this new version of the glam rock classic "John I'm Only Dancing," what is notable here is the skill with which David Bowie borrows the newly arrived disco style. There is no hint here of his debt to the Philly Sound nor to the opulent funk of Bobby Womack, or Sly and the Family Stone. Here we have a number that is pure American disco, energetic and very sexy, and reminiscent of the Jackson Five's "Dancing Machine" or MFSB's "Love Is the Message." The result of endless jam sessions on August 8, 9, and 10, 1974, at Sigma Sound Studios, this bold offering calls up the ghost of Ziggy Stardust and sets it dancing alongside Donna Summer. The song was forgotten about until RCA issued it as a single in December 1979, just as disco was on the way out.

IT'S HARD TO BE A SAINT IN THE CITY

Bruce Springsteen / 3:46

Musicians: David Bowie: lead vocals, twelve-string acoustic guitar / Unidentified Musicians: electric guitar, bass, drums, piano, strings / **Recorded:** Sigma Sound Studios, Philadelphia: November 21, 1974 (?) / **Technical Team:** Producer: Tony Visconti

David Bowie discovered the music of Bruce Springsteen one February evening in 1973. He was greatly impressed by Springsteen's passion and political commitment and decided to record his own version of the energetic "It's Hard to Be a Saint in the City." Included in the box set *Sound + Vision* put out by Rykodisc in 1989, this very convincing cover version is shrouded in mystery. Fans and biographers have failed to come up with precise dates for this recording, or the names of the musicians involved. If the title was the result of a first studio session in 1973, it must have been completed while work was in progress on *Young Americans*. Springsteen was to come specially by Greyhound bus to meet Bowie, who said of him: "He was very shy. [...] He didn't like what we were doing, I remember that. At least, he didn't express much enthusiasm."[63] Tony Visconti was to say regretfully: "David and I never worked on 'Saint' after that."[92] For historians of rock, this fine outtake is thought by some to date from the period of *Station to Station*, but Tony Visconti confirmed in his *The Autobiography: Bowie, Bolan and the Brooklyn Boy* that the song was completed in Philadelphia in November 1974.

ALBUM

STATION TO STATION

Station to Station . Golden Years . Word on a Wing . TVC 15 . Stay . Wild Is the Wind

RELEASE DATES
United Kingdom: January 23, 1976
Reference: RCA—APL1 1327
United States: January 23, 1976
Reference: RCA—APL1 1327
Best UK Chart Ranking: 5
Best US Chart Ranking: 3

MUSICAL EXPERIMENTATIONS IN THE LOS ANGELES SUN

With no tour planned to promote the album, the *Young Americans* chapter of Bowie's recording career closed at the beginning of summer 1976. Newly installed in Los Angeles, the singer seemed to have distanced himself from the stage and locked himself in a gilded cage, where he lived off just milk and vegetables and devoted himself to his passion for painting. He sank into a significant cocaine dependence that progressively isolated him. Only his involvement in the Nicolas Roeg film *The Man Who Fell to Earth* during the summer of 1976 would be able to bring him out of this condition, as the filmmaker required that Bowie could not touch any drugs for eleven weeks prior to shooting the film in New Mexico. The singer took advantage of the downtime between takes on the set of the film to start writing a collection of short stories, *The Return of the Thin White Duke*. In Nicolas Roeg's film, Bowie played the part of Thomas Jerome Newton, an extraterrestrial on a mission to Earth to find a solution to the drought on his home planet. The artist identified with this strange being who had been sent on an impossible quest, and was now lost under the leaden sun of an alien place. Bowie even adopted the character's elegant, orange-tinted blond hair style. Much like his character, Bowie seems to have felt similarly at sea during his time in California, and he quickly quit the state and returned to England.

An Album Under the Influence

Having broken things off with Ava Cherry, and distanced himself from his wife, Angie, and his manager, Tony Defries, the singer now had only his assistant, Coco Schwab, and his bodyguard and driver, Tony Mascia, for company. To complete his self-imposed exile, Bowie started to take a keen interest in a new musical subgenre referred to as "krautrock," which served as a perfect metaphor for his currently languid mental state. Represented by the West German groups Neu!, Tangerine Dream, Kraftwerk, and Can, this was a musical style that transcended the frontiers of progressive rock and pushed the envelope of what electronic music could do. The darker flavors of krautrock were soon to be mixed among what was left of "Bowie funk" and together they would drive the birth of a surprising album that mixes disco, blues, pop, and funk.

In a creative awakening, the Englishman launched himself precipitously into the recording of his new album at Cherokee Studios in Los Angeles, in October, with Harry Maslin in charge of production.

"Cherokee was a very new studio at the time," explained Maslin. "[...] I chose it because it was quiet and because it was new. I felt we would get less paparazzi and less glamour from the media and I think I was right."[1] Tony Visconti was absent from the disc's creative process, but Bowie surrounded himself with a solid if somewhat reduced team. Carlos Alomar was there with his six-string guitar, along with Earl Slick, the guitarist from the *Diamond Dogs* tour. Dennis Davis, who took part in the previous opus, was on drums, and the vocalist Warren Peace, henceforth a frequent contributor to his friend David's albums, was behind the microphone. On bass, Bowie brought in George Murray. Roy Bittan, Bruce Springsteen's E Street Band pianist, replaced Mike Garson. "I was staying at the Sunset Marquis in Los Angeles when we were on the [Springsteen] *Born to Run* tour in 1975," recalled Bittan. "David's guitar player, Earl Slick, was a friend of mine. I bumped into him at the hotel and he said, 'I can't believe you're here. We were just talking about you.' David knew we were coming

The singer carrying some precious tapes while leaving Los Angeles's Cherokee Studios in 1975.

Following double page:
Bowie received a warm welcome upon his arrival at London's Victoria Station on May 2, 1976.

to town and he wanted a keyboard player. [...] I wound up playing on every song besides 'Wild Is the Wind.' It must have only been about three days. It's one of my favorite projects I've ever worked on."[93]

Six Numbers Somewhere Between Funk and Pop

Unlike the slightly anarchic jam sessions that took place during the recording of *Young Americans*, the working sessions on this new opus were quite structured: The songs were constructed via a small committee that consisted of Alomar, Murray, and Davis, who worked from outlines of pieces provided by Bowie. Once the backing tracks were recorded, the other musicians added their parts, then David contributed his vocal lines. The album consisted of only six pieces and took its title from the first track, "Station to Station." Following the krautrock style, Bowie lengthened the introductions, and stretched out the instrumental passages—offering Earl Slick many minutes of edgy guitar solos—and then inserted all kinds of sound effects into the songs. Despite some flamboyant rhythmic surges provided by Alomar and others, *Station to Station* left behind the finely crafted writing of the Bowie songs of the old days. But numbers such as "Word on a Wing" and "Golden Years" provide the assurance that although the artist is a chameleon who loathes the idea of replicating his previous works, he is still a talented composer capable of producing some heartfelt melodies. We should note, however, that Bowie had only a scant recollection of these recordings, such was the extent of his drug use at the time. "I can't

George Murray, David Bowie, and Stacey Heydon onstage at the Forest National in Brussels, on May 11, 1976.

even remember the studio," he declared in 1998. "I know it was in LA because I've read it was in LA."[94] "There is a feeling of despair and loneliness in this album," confided Warren Peace. "[...] The fact that we then used drugs left its mark. It would be wrong to say that the album arose as a result of a 'happy event,' but it is still surprising that everything came together. You just remember these songs—they are very unusual. Sometimes David [...] said: 'I don't want to do anything today.' It was a kind of decadence, but there was a lot of creativity in it."[80]

Bowie Presents...the Thin White Duke

Once the recording of the disc was completed, Bowie began work on the original soundtrack of *The Man Who Fell to Earth* with Paul Buckmaster, the musician and arranger who had previously recorded some cello parts featured on "Space Oddity" and "Wild Eyed Boy from Freecloud" in 1969. Nicolas Roeg wasn't satisfied with the tracks that Bowie and Buckmaster produced, and the working sessions came to an end. Bowie would eventually reuse some of this material to create songs on other albums that would often give way to long, soaring instrumental passages.

Station to Station appeared on January 23, 1976. The public was disconcerted by the audacious structures of its songs, and it took some time for this tenth album to find its audience. But David Bowie was a groundbreaking musician, a mad scientist of sorts who cared little for opinions and criticism.

The "Isolar Tour" (sometimes referred to as the *Station to Station* tour) was launched on February 2, 1976, in Vancouver, and then traveled through the United States before transferring to Europe, culminating at the Pavillon de Paris on May 18. With Carlos Alomar on guitar, George Murray on bass, and Dennis Davis on drums, the group was complemented by Stacey Heydon, replacing Earl Slick, and Tony Kaye, from the group Yes, on keyboards. The whitish stage lighting revealed a minimalist spectacle, led by an elegant David Bowie, dressed in black trousers, a white shirt, and a jacket in whose pocket could be seen a packet of Gitanes. The darkness of the new arrangements took precedence over the hits of the past, and David Bowie presented his new avatar: the Thin White Duke.

STATION TO STATION
David Bowie / 10:10

Musicians
David Bowie: lead and backing vocals, melodica, claps
Carlos Alomar: electric guitar
Earl Slick: electric guitar
Dennis Davis: drums, percussions
George Murray: bass
Roy Bittan: piano, organ
Warren Peace: backing vocals

Recorded
Cherokee Studios, Los Angeles: October and November 1975
The Record Plant, Los Angeles: October and November 1975

Technical Team
Producers: David Bowie, Harry Maslin
Sound Engineer: Harry Maslin

Genesis

David Bowie was already fascinated by the writings of Aleister Crowley, the famous member of the Hermetic Order of the Golden Dawn, a British secret society dedicated to the practice of the occult. In fact, Bowie had already referred to Crowley in "Quiksand" in 1971: *"I'm closer to the Golden Dawn / Immersed in Crowley's uniform."* During his stay in California in the summer of 1976, the singer immersed himself once more in these readings that combined esoterism and spirituality. He was interested in the writings of the Kabbala, a mystical and allegorical interpretation of the Bible from the Jewish tradition. Kether (Keter) and Malkuth, two of the ten Sephiroth (powers at the origins of the creation of the world), are thus evoked in the lyrics of this song. The title itself, "Station to Station," is a reference to Christ's fourteen stations of the cross. This profound and mysterious text contrasts with the disco direction that the piece takes from 6:06. Bowie specifically states at 6:02: *"It's not the side effect of the cocaine."* However, the white powder doing the rounds at Cherokee Studios certainly had a role to play in the experimental writing of this song, which features no couplets or refrains, departing from the classical pop structure and more closely resembling the work of Pink Floyd or Yes.

Production

The influence of the West German krautrock style is palpable right from the introduction, which lasts nearly two minutes and starts up with locomotive noises—in the manner of Kraftwerk, which electronically simulated the sound of klaxons in the album *Autobahn,* from 1974.

This introduction is also marked by the Larsen feedback effects on the guitars of Earl Slick, the fruits of a curious recording session that Bowie described in 1998: "I remember working with Earl on the guitar sounds out in the studio itself and screaming the feedback sound that I wanted at him!"[94] He also required the guitarist to stay in the same range during his solo! "I remember telling him to take a Chuck Berry riff and just play it all the way through the solo: 'Don't deviate, just play that whole riff over and over

Guitarist Earl Slick contributed to multiple Bowie albums through *The Next Day* in 2013.

again, even though the chords are changing underneath, just keep it going.' He said, 'What, man?' I said, 'It'll work! It'll work!'"[94] But the singer's memory must have been playing tricks on him, becuase this repetitive guitar part is actually in the song's introduction, from 1:28. "That album's a little fuzzy—for the obvious reasons," confirmed Earl Slick. "We were in the studio and it was nuts—a lot of hours, a lot of late nights. We didn't start a lot of times till one or two in the morning. I like the album very much, but the recording process was very vague. I don't remember a lot about it."[29]

Flattered by the krautrock influence on Bowie, the group Kraftwerk returned the compliment, referring to him in their song, "Trans-Europe Express" in 1977: *"Von Bahnhof zu Bahnhof / Zurück nach Düsseldorf / Treffe Iggy Pop und David Bowie"* ("I go from station to station / And back to Düsseldorf / I meet Iggy Pop and David Bowie").

Single

GOLDEN YEARS

David Bowie / 3:58

Musicians

David Bowie: lead and backing vocals, melodica, claps, whistling
Carlos Alomar: electric guitar, acoustic guitar
Earl Slick: electric guitar
Dennis Davis: drums, percussion
George Murray: bass
Warren Peace: backing vocals, congas

Recorded

Cherokee Studios, Los Angeles: October and November 1975
The Record Plant, Los Angeles: October and November 1975

Technical Team

Producers: David Bowie, Harry Maslin
Sound Engineer: Harry Maslin

SIDE A: *Golden Years* / 3:27
SIDE B: *Can You Hear Me* / 5:04
UK Release on RCA: November 21, 1975 (ref. RCA 2640)
US Release on RCA: November 21, 1975 (ref. PB-10441)
Best UK Chart Ranking: 8
Best US Chart Ranking: 10

ON YOUR HEADPHONES

At exactly 0:04 into the introduction, David Bowie himself plays the three notes heard on the melodica. He had to play them in unison with the electric guitar but did not manage to achieve this. Following a number of unsuccessful attempts, he asked Harry Maslin if he needed to play the line once more, but the producer decided to keep the take, exclaiming: "No. It's perfectly out of time!"[1]

Angie Bowie in 1975, when she was trying to create a career for herself as an actress.

FOR BOWIE ADDICTS

In June 2011, David Bowie offered his fans an iPhone app that enabled budding producers to remix "Golden Years" and then share their version. Sadly, this app is no longer available.

Genesis

On September 26, 1975, Angie Bowie was the special guest on *The Mike Douglas Show*, recorded in Philadelphia. She performed "I've Got a Crush on You," a standard from the musical comedies of Ira and George Gershwin. "David was pleased with the way I came across and dedicated another song to me, 'Golden Years.' I think it was coincidence, because he had just finished recording the track about two hours before he saw the California airing of *The Mike Douglas Show* and he told me the song was for me."[61] In any case, "Golden Years" was the first song recorded by Bowie and his musicians at Cherokee Studios in the autumn of 1975. It was released as a single in November, while the recording work for the album was still ongoing. Carlos Alomar decided to give the song a new guitar riff, which was otherwise far too similar to "On Broadway" by the Drifters.

Production

Other than the standard set by the Drifters, two other songs seem to have inspired the writing of the very disco-tinged "Golden Years": "Funky Broadway" by Dyke and the Blazers (1967), with its repetitive structure that focused on a single chord; and "Happy Years" by the Diamonds (1958), from which Bowie borrowed its famous backing vocals, reworking them with Warren Peace. "I could not sleep," explained the backing singer, "and I went downstairs, and there David worked on the arrangements. It must have cleared up in my head because I said, 'Let's try this,' and added such a yodel ('Golden years, wah, wah, wah'), something like that was jazz, and he liked it."[80]

For the main vocals, David opted for an unorthodox approach. He locked himself in the studio toilets and wrote the lyrics in record time, just before he went behind the microphone for a lightning-fast recording session, as producer Harry Maslin attested: "[He] did the song in one take. I was blown away. He told me that he didn't consider himself to be a vocalist, but I told him that that was one of the most amazing performances I had ever seen."[1]

WORD ON A WING

David Bowie / 6:00

Musicians: David Bowie: lead and backing vocals, acoustic guitar, Mellotron, organ, synthesizer / Carlos Alomar: acoustic guitar / Earl Slick: electric guitar / Dennis Davis: drums, shaker / George Murray: bass / Roy Bittan: piano, electric piano / Warren Peace: backing vocals, congas / **Recorded:** Cherokee Studios, Los Angeles: October and November 1975 / The Record Plant, Los Angeles: October and November 1975 / **Technical Team:** Producers: David Bowie, Harry Maslin / Sound Engineer: Harry Maslin

On listening to this touching piece, with its gospel feel, in which Bowie addresses God—"*Oh Lord, Lord, Lord, my prayer flies / Like a word on a wing*"—we find a singer at peace with himself. "There's a song—'Word on a Wing' [...] that I wrote," said Bowie in 1976, "when I felt very much at peace with the world. I had established my own environment with my own people for the first time. I wrote the whole thing as a hymn. What better way can a man give thanks for achieving something that he had dreamed of achieving, than doing it with a hymn?"[95] Like Mike Garson before him, pianist Roy Bittan took Bowie's interpretation to the heights of melancholy. On the six-string, Carlos Alomar adorns the piece with some very delicate acoustic guitar while Earl Slick produces his famous incessant feedback, which Bowie had requested on the introduction to "Station to Station."

Always influenced by the work of other musicians, in the introduction to "TVC 15," Bowie cites the "oh oh oh oh ohs" from the Yardbirds' classic "Good Morning Little School Girl."

Single

TVC 15

David Bowie / 5:29

Musicians: David Bowie: lead and backing vocals, tenor saxophone / Carlos Alomar: electric guitar / Earl Slick: electric guitar / Dennis Davis: drums / George Murray: bass / Roy Bittan: piano / Warren Peace: backing vocals / Harry Maslin: saxophone, baryton / **Recorded:** Cherokee Studios, Los Angeles: October and November 1975 / The Record Plant, Los Angeles: October and November 1975 / **Technical Team:** Producers: David Bowie, Harry Maslin / Sound Engineer: Harry Maslin / **Side A:** *TVC 15* / 3:29 / **Side B:** *We Are the Dead* / 4:53 / **UK Release on RCA:** April 30, 1976 (ref. RCA 2682) / **US Release on RCA:** April 30, 1976 (ref. PB-10664) / **Best UK Chart Ranking:** 33 / **Best US Chart Ranking:** 64

When David Bowie recruited Roy Bittan, the pianist from Bruce Springsteen's E Street Band, for the recording of *Station to Station*, he acquired the support of an exceptional musician, with a decidedly classical approach but with a fine facility for adaptation, the mark of great session musicians. "I always did studio work, even before I joined Bruce," explained Bittan. "Working with other artists was intellectually stimulating and challenging. [...] The band was always my first priority, but it was important for me to break out and do whatever I could elsewhere—I always felt like it helped me bring something fresh back to the band."[96] For "TVC 15," the first number recorded during these three days of collaboration, Bowie asked the musician to play like Professor Longhair, the famous singer and pianist from New Orleans who had an inimitable playing style that combined honky-tonk, blues, and swing sonorities. By a stroke of luck, Bittan had attended a Professor Longhair concert at a club in Houston just three weeks earlier, a coincidence that sealed his musical relationship with Bowie. This type of playing—at the crossroads between blues and jazz—appears alongside a humoristic element, inspired by Iggy Pop (henceforth the inseparable friend of the Thin White Duke), who told Bowie about the apathy of one of his female friends who had been hypnotized by her television screen. Also worthy of note is the appearance of the saxophone, which was played by Bowie and the producer Harry Maslin, on this occasion forming an elite brass section!

STAY

David Bowie / 6:10

Musicians: David Bowie: lead and backing vocals / Carlos Alomar: electric guitar / Earl Slick: electric guitar / Dennis Davis: drums, percussion / Roy Bittan: synthesizer / George Murray: bass / Warren Peace: backing vocals, congas, tambourine / **Recorded:** Cherokee Studios, Los Angeles: October and November 1975 / The Record Plant, Los Angeles: October and November 1975 / **Technical Team:** Producers: David Bowie, Harry Maslin / Sound Engineer: Harry Maslin / Side A: *Stay* / 3:21 / Side B: *Word on a Wing* / 3:10 / US Release on RCA: July 1976 (ref. PB-10736) / Best Chart Ranking: Did Not Chart

From the introduction of "Stay," with the meeting of Alomar's funk guitar and the rock riffs of Slick, we find influences of the famous Blaxploitation movement in the cinema of the 1970s, where Black heroes such as Shaft, Priest, or Foxy Brown appeared in films featuring music with a strong beat that was created by the likes of Isaac Hayes, Curtis Mayfield, and Willie Hutch. Originating during the working sessions for "John I'm Only Dancing (Again)" in the summer of 1974, this song was reworked at Cherokee Studios during a night spent under the influence of various substances. A perfect synthesis of the two guitarists, to whom Bowie had given free rein, the song includes a solo by Earl Slick that lasts more than two minutes. "It wasn't worked out in advance," said Slick. "I think I was feeling right that night too. [...] I was very spaced out that night. It was done about five in the morning. I'd been waiting around four hours, drinking a lot of beer...Right, that was a beer song."[97] "'Stay' was fabulous!" confirmed Carlos Alomar. "We had a field day with that one. That was recorded very much in our cocaine frenzy."[29] A song made for stage performance, "Stay" was given a single release in the United States and was also released on the B-side of "Suffragette City" in July 1976, when RCA decided to promote the compilation *ChangesOneBowie* in the United Kingdom.

WILD IS THE WIND

Dimitri Tiomkin, Ned Washington / 5:58

Musicians: David Bowie: vocals / Carlos Alomar: electric guitar, acoustic guitar / Earl Slick: electric guitar / Dennis Davis: drums / George Murray: bass / **Recorded:** Cherokee Studios, Los Angeles: October and November 1975 / **Technical Team:** Producers: David Bowie, Harry Maslin / Sound Engineer: Harry Maslin / Side A: *Wild Is the Wind* / 3:34 / Side B: *Golden Years* / 4:03 / UK Release on RCA: November 13, 1981 (ref. BOW 10; PB 9815) / **Best Chart Ranking:** 24

As the only song cover included on the album, this American standard performed by the crooner Johnny Mathis was written by Ned Washington, with music by Dimitri Tiomkin, for the film *Wild Is the Wind*, directed by George Cukor in 1957. The song was covered in 1966 by Nina Simone, in a refined, pared-down variation without the sonorous symphonic arrangements of the original. Without seeking to add any personal touch to the track, Bowie wanted to come close to Simone's more recent interpretation, which gave this magnificent composition a new heft of emotional power.

David Bowie and Nina Simone met in a New York club called the Hippopotamus in July 1974, a few days after Simone had attended Bowie's concert at Madison Square Garden. The singer, who was suffering from chronic depression at the time, was touched by the Englishman, who invited her to join him at his table and supported her in the face of criticism from the press: "You're not crazy—don't let anybody tell you you're crazy, because where you're coming from, there are very few of us out there."[98]

The conclusion of an album that treats the listener to the full gamut of disco meanderings, this musical homage has the benefit of a relatively restrained production that allows Bowie's powerful vocals to shine through. This final track would eventually be featured on the compilation album *ChangesTwoBowie* in 1981, appearing as a single in a version that was shortened to 3:34. A video was created by David Mallet, who staged an imagined jazz group consisting of Tony Visconti on double bass, Andy Hamilton on saxophone, Mel Gaynor on drums, and Coco Schwab on acoustic guitar. This newly formed "group" plays the song in playback alongside the singer.

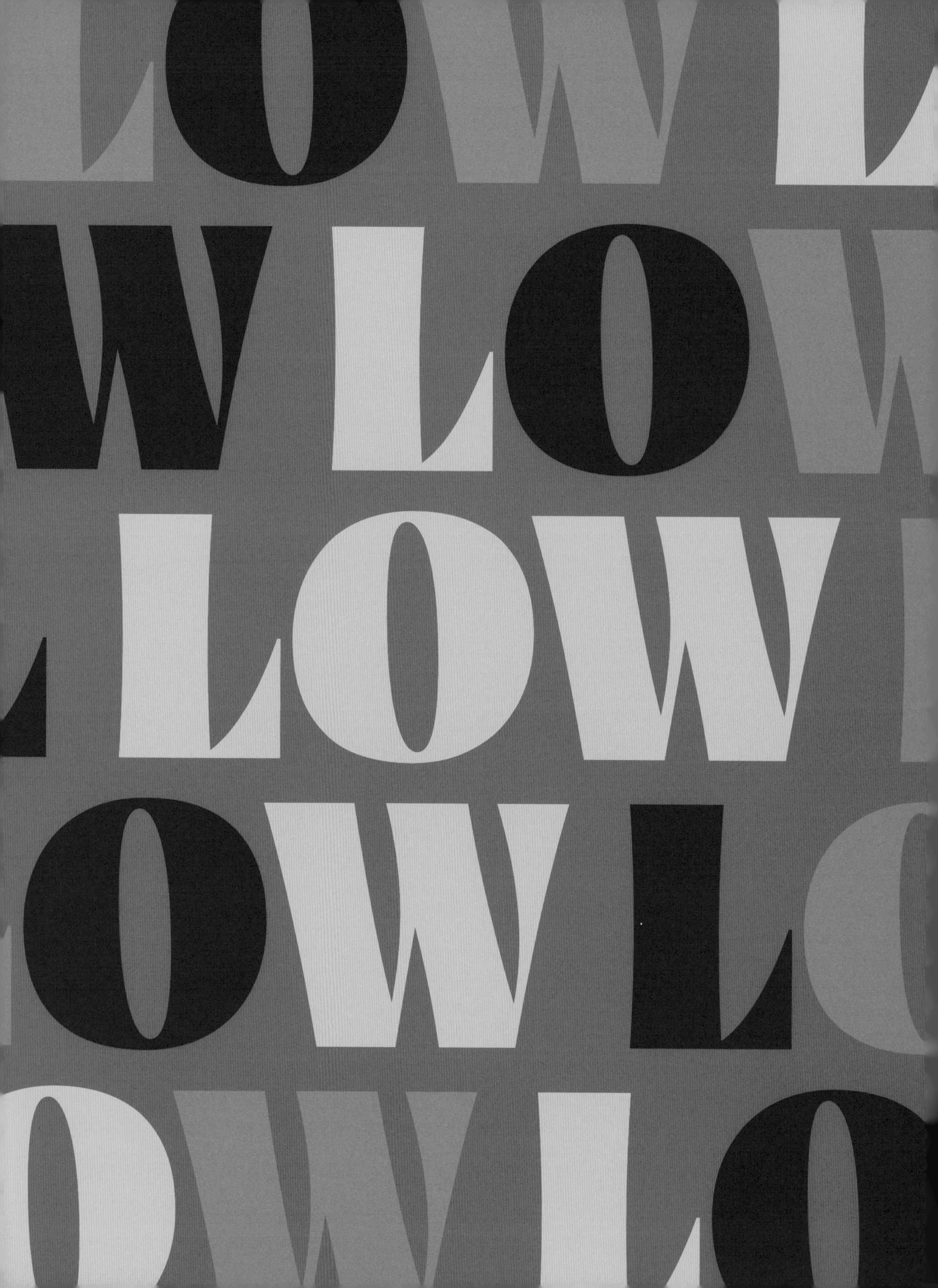
LOW

ALBUM

Speed of Life . Breaking Glass . What in the World . Sound and Vision .
Always Crashing in the Same Car . Be My Wife . A New Career in a New Town .
Warszawa . Art Decade . Weeping Wall . Subterraneans

RELEASE DATES
UK Release on RCA: January 14, 1977 (ref. RCA—PL 12030)
US Release on RCA: January 14, 1977 (ref. RCA—CPL1-2030)
Best UK Chart Ranking: 2
Best US Chart Ranking: 11

ENTER BRIAN ENO

David Bowie's return to Europe in the spring of 1976 was a huge success thanks to the "Isolar Tour." Now he was able to renew his relationship with a public that had been neglected during his time exploring Philadelphia soul music and then sunny Los Angeles. Not even rumors relating to his supposed tolerance of Nazism eclipsed his fame. In addition to ambiguous remarks about Hitler that Bowie had made in the past, he had also been detained at the Soviet-Polish border in April 1976 while in possession of memorabilia from the Third Reich. Back in London, a photo of David in the *New Musical Express* showed him at Victoria Station on May 2, 1976, standing in an open-topped Mercedes with his right arm raised in salute, which added fuel to the scandal as some felt he was giving a Nazi salute. It is now generally accepted that he was merely waving to his fans, but given his ideological equivocations on the subject, the attraction he felt for the cool and minimalist anti-Nazi German kraut-rock was reassuring for his fans.

So his return to the Old World was indeed a triumph, but, exhausted by the many tours and weakened by the excesses of the California scene, he was now in a protracted dispute with his lawyer and manager, Michael Lippman, whom he was hoping to get rid of. Angie, meanwhile, was trying to save what was left of their marriage while organizing their move to Switzerland, where she had recently bought a house. Bowie, always searching for something new, was not interested in the quiet life Angie was suggesting at the house they called Le Clos des Mésanges, which was located in Blonay, near Montreux. No sooner had the family settled into the new home than David left again to meet up with James Osterberg, aka Iggy Pop, who was about to record his first solo album, *The Idiot*, at the Château d'Hérouville where, three years earlier, *Pin Ups* had been produced.

The Idiot: The Beginning of Bowie's Experimental Phase

As co-producer of the album alongside Tony Visconti, David Bowie was as chameleonlike as always, throwing himself into this new musical adventure. The experiments of *Station to Station* were now to be pushed to a new extreme, creating the basis for his future discography. The album was recorded in June and July of 1976 in a feverish atmosphere of artistic creativity and spontaneity. In this stimulating environment, Bowie wrote several songs for his friend. Also present at the château was the guitarist Carlos Alomar, who went along with this new compositional direction, strongly influenced by the German groups with which Bowie was now associating himself: Kraftwerk, Can, Neu!, and Tangerine Dream. David Bowie was to say: "Poor Jim [Iggy], in a way, became a guinea pig for what I wanted to do with sound. I didn't have the material at the time, and I didn't feel like writing it all. I felt much more like laying back and getting behind someone else's work, so that album was opportune, creatively."[99]

The Arrival of a Versatile "Nonmusician"

Despite the crushing heat of the summer of 1976, this was a happy time for the musicians living at the Château d'Hérouville. Far from the distractions of America, the creative atmosphere seemed to suit Bowie, who was soon to reestablish contact with an old friend: Brian Eno. A former keyboard player with Roxy Music and the inventor of ambient music, Eno was an unusual artist, experimental, and expert in sound textures rather than musical composition; he described himself as a "nonmusician." He turned up in David Bowie's life at the moment when the singer was trying to get his life together again and determined to give up his cocaine habit.

The First of the Berlin Trilogy

After a few days spent together at Blonay, each congratulating the other on their respective albums—Eno loved *Station to Station*, Bowie loved Eno's *Discreet Music,* which had been released in December 1975—the two artists decided to work together at the first opportunity. At the time he had just finished mixing *The Idiot*, and Visconti recalled how Bowie had phoned him: "Tony, Brian is on the extension phone listening in and I have to tell you we've been experimenting with some ideas. We're thinking of going into a studio in September for a month. We don't have any actual songs yet but we're trying to combine Brian's ambient music techniques into writing rock songs. What do you think you would bring to the table?"[35]

In the first week of September, Bowie and Visconti met at the Château d'Hérouville, managed since 1974 by sound engineer Laurent Thibault, who had worked on *The Idiot* during that summer. David chose to use the same players he'd worked with on *Station to Station*: Dennis Davis on drums and George Murray on bass. Carlos Alomar was naturally part of the group on guitar, along with Ricky Gardiner; the latter was introduced to Bowie by Visconti when Michael Rother of Neu! had declined an invitation to take part in the recording. Roy Young, formerly keyboard player with the British rock group the Rebel Rousers, was taken on to play piano and Farfisa organ.

Three albums make up what has been called the Berlin trilogy: *Low* (1977), *"Heroes"* (1977), and *Lodger* (1979). The title "Bowie/Eno Trilogy" might be more appropriate, since Brian Eno was responsible for the sound textures used by Bowie. In fact, the only album to be entirely recorded in Berlin was *"Heroes."* Most of *Low* was created at Hérouville, and *Lodger* was made in Montreux and New York. The use of the name "Berlin" is more a reference to the influence the German city had on David Bowie than an indication of the studios where he recorded his work.

At Hérouville, in the first three weeks of September, the atmosphere was relaxed, despite Eno's relatively strange methods. He had not come empty-handed; in fact, Eno brought his EMS Synthi AKS synthesizer, which was housed in a small portable case. Some biographies suggest he used an AKS VCS3, a much larger nonportable model encased in wood, but this was contradicted by Bowie in an interview on June 16, 2002, with the online music magazine *ConcertLivewire*. Eno also brought his *Oblique Strategies*, a device that, like his music, played an important role in his fame. He had invented this game of 113 cards with the Berlin painter Peter Schmidt a year earlier. A prompt to creativity, the cards bear instructions to be followed during recording, being drawn at random by the

David Bowie, Tony Visconti, and Eduard Meyer at the console at Hansa Studios in Berlin.

The singer out for a walk in the streets of West Berlin.

musicians. "Remove specifics and convert to ambiguities"; "You don't have to be ashamed of using your own ideas"; "Use filters"; "Use an old idea": These are just some of the suggestions designed to help a creator lacking inspiration at moments of stress. The game proved effective in the case of Bowie and his fellow musicians; ideas came thick and fast and were immediately recorded. Visconti related how "David called them 'demos' but I recorded them carefully, knowing full well that these could end up as masters, and they did."[35]

Discovering Berlin

After several weeks in Hérouville, where tracks like "Speed of Life," "Breaking Glass," and "Sound and Vision" first saw the light of day, Bowie, Eno, and Visconti moved

to Hansa Studios in West Berlin. David, together with Coco Schwab and Iggy Pop, lived in a small apartment on the Hauptstrasse, and it was not long before the group of friends learned to love the very special atmosphere of the city during the time of the Cold War. In Visconti's words, "David just liked living in Berlin. There was so much of it, in those days, that was fantastic, fantasy-like, that didn't exist anywhere else in the world. The impending danger of the divided military zones, the bizarre nightlife, the extremely traditional restaurants with aproned servers, reminders of Hitler's not-too-distant presence, a recording studio five hundred yards from the Wall."[1] Everything about this divided city fascinated Bowie, his view echoed in the novels he read by British writer Christopher Isherwood, *Mr. Norris Changes Trains,*

published in 1935, and *Goodbye to Berlin* from 1939. These works re-create the wild nightlife of Berlin in the interwar period. Bowie had also been intrigued by Lou Reed's 1973 album *Berlin*, and now he became an enthusiastic fan of German krautrock groups. And it wasn't only music that he explored; as soon as he arrived in Berlin in October 1976, Bowie became a frequent visitor to museums and exhibitions. In 2001, he said this: "Since my teenage years I had obsessed on the angst-ridden, emotional work of the Expressionists, both artists and filmmakers, and Berlin had been their spiritual home. This was the nub of Die Brücke movement, Max Reinhardt, Brecht and where Metropolis and Caligari had originated. [...] My attention had been swung back to Europe with the release of Kraftwerk's *Autobahn* in 1974. The preponderance of electronic instruments convinced

me that this was an area that I had to investigate a little further."[100] With Iggy Pop, Bowie flung himself into Berlin nightlife, frequenting clubs in unlikely places. Guitarist Ricky Gardiner said of this period: "Together David and Iggy were a pair of naughty boys really. They explored Berlin and the clubs and quite frankly they were dreadful. People talk about Berlin as if it were marvellous, but frankly it was just weird."[1]

An Instrumental Moment

Begun during the sessions in Hérouville, the experimental phase of the future album, which was given the working title *New Music: Night & Day*, was only intensified once the singer reached Berlin. Working closely together, Eno and Bowie created several instrumental pieces using synthesizers like the Solina String Ensemble and the Minimoogou as

Ralf Hütter, Karl Bartos, Wolfgang Flür, and Florian Schneider from the group Kraftwerk, which heavily inspired *Low*. Here they're shown appearing in Rotterdam on March 21, 1976.

FOR BOWIE ADDICTS

When David Bowie decided at the last minute to change the album's title, RCA Canada had already released the album on cassette tape. Fans who bought this version found themselves the owners of a valuable collector's piece, as its cover showed the album's original name: *New Music: Night and Day*. The disc sleeve bore the final title, *Low*.

well as the ever-present EMS Synthi AKS. While Side 1 of the disc consists of pop songs that are accessible even with the synthetic textures created by Brian Eno, Side 2 features four compositions as enigmatic as they are surprising. Some of them came out of the sessions working on the soundtrack for the movie *The Man Who Fell to Earth*, which was eventually scrapped.

Once finished, the album was sent to RCA, who had a rude awakening. The directors of the label hated the disc and wanted Bowie to make a return to hits like "Fame." According to the terms of his contract, however, Bowie had complete control over his work and was able to state that the album should come out unchanged, and under the title *Low*. The disc sleeve, illustrated with an image from *The Man Who Fell to Earth*, shows how much the singer had distanced himself from the glamour of the Ziggy

Stardust era. Given the new minimalist line his career was taking, even the idea of a photo session seemed absurd. The only thing that mattered was the music, which had now been stripped of sequins and glitz.

Tony Visconti was supportive: "We started *Low* on the premise that we might simply waste a month—that it might be a load of rubbish that, in the end, we would just throw away. But halfway through the making of the album, we knew we were on to something incredibly exciting. We couldn't wait to release it to the public. Fortunately, the public and the critics reacted beautifully. They really felt the album was remarkable. It was the record company that hated it. They wanted 'Young Americans Part 2,' and they said as much. But no, David doesn't really care, and I don't really care. It's nice to have a hit record, but we want to have a hit record on our own terms."[42]

BRIAN ENO: COLLABORATION AND INSPIRATION

Brian Peter Eno was born in 1948 in Woodbridge, England. He studied at various universities in the United Kingdom before finally earning his diploma in fine arts in 1969. In 1971, with singer Brian Ferry and bass player Graham Simpson, Eno was involved in the creation of Roxy Music. He became the keyboard player for the group, with whom he recorded two fabled albums, *Roxy Music* in 1972 and *For Your Pleasure* in 1973. Skilled in the manipulation of his synthesizers, an EMS VCS3 and a Minimoog, he provided avant-garde and experimental sounds for Roxy Music's albums, presenting himself onstage as an androgenous figure very much in tune with the glam-rock style of the period. It was at this time that he met David Bowie, who invited Roxy Music to appear with him at a series of concerts given at the Rainbow Theatre in London, in August 1972.

Brian Eno left Roxy Music in 1973. Fascinated by the minimalist works of John Cage and compositions by Terry Riley and Steve Reich, he put out two albums: *Here Come the Warm Jets* (1973) and *Taking Tiger Mountain (By Strategy)* in 1974. He also worked on two albums with King Crimson guitarist Robert Fripp: *(No Pussyfooting)* in 1973 and *Evening Star* in 1976. He became his own producer and, rejecting formal musical training, declared himself a "nonmusician," describing himself instead as a professional composer.

The Inventor of Ambient Music

In January 1975, during his convalescence after a car accident, Brian was relaxing by listening to harp music. He discovered that the speakers on his sound system were faulty and the music could not drown out the sound of the rain outside. Far from upsetting him, this mixture of natural and fabricated musical sounds enriched his experience. This event marked the beginning of ambient music. As Eno described it: "An ambience is defined as an atmosphere, or a surrounding influence: a tint."[106] Like John Cage before

him, Brian developed the use of music as an integral element of a person's complete environment. The instrumental aspect of his compositions came to the fore in *Another Green World*, which was released in 1975, and particularly in *Discreet Music*, his much celebrated album that was also released in 1975 and is regarded as the cornerstone of ambient music. David Bowie greatly admired Eno's work and, always on the lookout for new collaborators, he proposed that they work together.

From Bowie to Coldplay by Way of U2

When he collaborated with Bowie on *Low*, "*Heroes*," and *Lodger*, Brian Eno introduced many of the elements used in his own recordings: fading in at the beginning and fading out at the end, mechanical rhythms, floating sounds, tracks that are entirely instrumental or with only the occasional voice added, and voices that are sometimes distorted and even sometimes speaking in imaginary languages. Whatever the case, in Eno's world, narrative was secondary to invention. With his 1978 disc *Ambient 1: Music for Airports*, he went on to develop the theory of "the studio as a compositional tool," which was also the title of an essay he published in 1983. For Eno, the work carried out in the recording studio was an integral part of artistic creation and should not be separated from the final product itself—that is, the album.

By 1980, Eno had acquired a reputation as an exceptionally versatile and talented composer. In 1987, together with Daniel Lanois, he produced U2's critically acclaimed album *The Joshua Tree* and, a few years later, the famous *Achtung Baby*, which was recorded partly at Hansa Studios in Berlin. Eno participated in another internationally successful collaboration with the British group Coldplay, co-producing their album *Viva la Vida or Death and All His Friends*. The single version of "Viva La Vida" topped the *Billboard* charts in 2008.

Angie Bowie and her new companion, drummer Roy Martin. This relationship inspired Bowie to write the lyrics for "Breaking Glass."

On his 1978 album *Jesus of Cool*, the British singer Nick Lowe had a hit with "I Love the Sound of Breaking Glass." Was it a tribute to David Bowie? All signs point to yes. The title refers to Bowie's "Breaking Glass," and the song itself borrows the very recognizable chord sequence from "Sound and Vision."

SPEED OF LIFE

David Bowie / 2:46

Musicians: David Bowie: synthesizers / Carlos Alomar: electric guitar / Dennis Davis: drums / George Murray: bass / Roy Young: piano / **Recorded:** Château d'Hérouville, France: September 1976 / **Technical Team:** Producers: David Bowie, Tony Visconti / **Sound Engineers:** Tony Visconti, Laurent Thibault

"Speed of Life" is a kind of instrumental prelude that, in almost three minutes, prepares the ground for the new Bowie-Eno-Visconti sound and an album characterized by new, distorted sonorities created with modern instruments and apparently infinite possibilities. When David Bowie called his producer to ask what he would contribute to such a disc, Visconti was able to respond that he had just acquired a new version of the Eventide effects harmonizer. The famous H910 was to revolutionize the work of producers everywhere, making it possible to change the pitch of a recording—raising or lowering it—without changing its duration. Bowie had, of course, used a similar effect for "The Laughing Gnome" and "All the Madmen" to alter the pitch of the voice. This required the sound engineers to record the voice parts at a slower speed before adding them in during the mixing process at normal speed. The new device made the technicians' job much easier. In point of fact, as he says in his memoirs published in 2007, Visconti had already used the Harmonizer H910 during the *Diamond Dogs* recording sessions, but he used this wondrous machine, only recently made available, more for the strange effects it could produce rather than for its main function, which he had not yet come to grips with. Surprisingly, Visconti used the device to alter the timbre of Dennis Davis's drumming, giving it a synthetic sound. At the first session, Visconti prepared the various percussion elements, including the snare drum, which he lowered by a semitone, adding feedback that created an avant-garde sound. Visconti reports: "Everyone was amazed."[35]

BREAKING GLASS

David Bowie, Dennis Davis, George Murray / 1:51

Musicians: David Bowie: lead vocals / Carlos Alomar, Ricky Gardiner: electric guitar / Dennis Davis: drums / George Murray: bass / Brian Eno: synthesizers / **Recorded:** Château d'Hérouville, France: September 1976 / Hansa Studios, West Berlin: September and October 1976 / **Technical Team:** Producers: David Bowie, Tony Visconti / **Sound Engineers:** Tony Visconti, Laurent Thibault (Château d'Hérouville), Eduard Meyer (Hansa Studios)

By the spring of 1976, relations between David Bowie and his wife were not good. Despite her attempts to keep him with her at their house in Switzerland, Angie was unable to connect with her husband. David threw himself into work on Iggy Pop's first LP in June and then went to work on *Low* in September. While little Duncan was at Hérouville with his father during the recording sessions, Angie visited the château accompanied by her new lover,

the musician and singer Roy Martin. In fact, Angie wrote the words for his single, "Soul House." The arrival of the couple so enraged David that a fight broke out between the two men, who were quickly separated by the recording team. This episode inspired David Bowie's heavily rhythmical "Breaking Glass," a number that influenced many musicians, including the band Franz Ferdinand in their 2009 album *Tonight*. The words of the song, short but explicit, can have done little to calm the tensions between David and Angie: "*Baby, I've been / Breaking glass in your room again / Listen, don't look at the carpet / I drew something awful on it.*" The couple eventually divorced in 1980.

Guitarist Carlos Alomar recalls: "The music of the song needed to represent the way people argue. [...] I really thought out the arrangement. [...] David loved it, Angie hated it."[101] Alomar wanted to have a kind of buzzing drone, similar to the sound of a mouth harp, underpinning the song. He uses his guitar to create the same insistent chord throughout the verse, just after the reggae introduction to the track. The bass, with its short "bang" typical of traditional Jamaican music, appears at the beginning before moving into the disco rhythm of the verses. It closely follows Dennis Davis's drumming, which was recorded at the same time as the song's backing tracks, and quite a while before the arrival of Ricky Gardiner and Roy Young. "That was just done with three members of the band,"[29] as the down-to-earth Alomar was to comment.

WHAT IN THE WORLD

David Bowie / 2:21

Musicians: David Bowie: lead vocals / Carlos Alomar, Ricky Gardiner: electric guitars / Dennis Davis: drums / George Murray: bass / Roy Young: Farfisa organ / Brian Eno: synthesizers / Iggy Pop: backing vocals / **Recorded:** Château d'Hérouville, France: September 1976 / Hansa Studios, West Berlin: September and October 1976 / **Technical Team:** Producers: David Bowie, Tony Visconti / **Sound Engineers:** Tony Visconti, Laurent Thibault (Château d'Hérouville), Eduard Meyer (Hansa Studios)

"What in the World," originally called "Isolation," had been worked up with Iggy Pop during the recording sessions for *The Idiot* but was dropped from the track list. David's friend Iggy was always there, welcome not least for his hilarious stories, which delighted the assembled team. Here, Iggy provides backing vocals, while Roy Young moves from piano to provide an accompaniment of chords on the Farfisa organ. In the 1970s, this Italian instrument, a much cheaper version of the top-of-the-range Vox Continental, was commonly found in the homes of families with a view to learn to play keyboards and enjoy popular tunes of the time. It seems probable that one of these (perhaps a Farfisa Matador?) was lying about at the Château d'Hérouville. Brian Eno fooled around in the studio on his EMS Synthi AKS, portable in its little case and operated with a small joystick, the sounds he produced sounding like something from a 1980s Atari video game. The effect today seems somewhat old-fashioned, but it was revolutionary in its time.

Tony Visconti with his wife,
Mary Hopkin, in 1973.

Single

SOUND AND VISION
David Bowie / 3:02

Musicians
David Bowie: lead vocals, saxophone, synthesizers
Carlos Alomar: electric guitar
Ricky Gardiner: electric guitar
Dennis Davis: drums
George Murray: bass
Roy Young: piano
Brian Eno: backing vocals
Mary Hopkin: backing vocals

Recorded
Château d'Hérouville, France: September 1976
Hansa Studios, West Berlin: September and October 1976

Technical Team
Producers: David Bowie, Tony Visconti
Sound Engineers: Tony Visconti, Laurent Thibault (Château d'Hérouville), Eduard Meyer (Hansa Studios)

SIDE A: *Sound and Vision* / 3:02 (UK); 3:00 (US)
SIDE B: *A New Career in a New Town* / 2:51 (UK); 2:50 (US)
UK Release on RCA: February 11, 1977 (ref. PB-0905; APL1 2030)
US Release on RCA: February 11, 1977 (ref. PB-10905)
Best UK Chart Ranking: 3
Best US Chart Ranking: 69

In 2013, Sonjay Prabhakar made a remix of "Sound and Vision" for the advertising campaign for the new Sony Smartphone Xperia Z. The producer used only the voices of Mary Hopkin and David Bowie, accompanied by Roy Young on the piano, the sound of which had originally been drowned out in the album version's arrangements. Interest from Bowie fans led Parlophone to make the song available for download.

Genesis
Listening to this joyful track, it is hard to believe the extent to which David Bowie was struggling with his own personal demons when it was recorded in September 1976. Withdrawal from cocaine and the loss of his bearings in a professional world that no longer seemed his own led to an ever-increasing malaise and even depression. Carlos Alomar described this period: "It was a very sad period for David. I don't want to put it in some glamorous place. He was fighting for his marriage, his son; his business was horrible, the touring [was] exhausting and taking every bit of money that he had."[102] The elusive and mysterious words of "Sound and Vision" reflect his state of mind: *"And I will sing / Waiting for the gift of sound and vision / Drifting into my solitude / Over my head."* And yet, more generally, the atmosphere at Hérouville was a happy one. But Bowie was already elsewhere, ready to bury himself in the dark streets of Berlin to discover both the city's seamy side and its lively cultural life. He was to say later: "At that time, I was vacillating badly between euphoria and incredible depression. Berlin was at that time not the most beautiful city of the world, and my mental condition certainly matched it. I was abusing myself so badly. My subtext to the whole thing is that I'm so desperately unhappy, but I've got to pull through because I can't keep living like this. There's actually a real optimism about the music. In its poignancy there is, shining through under there somewhere, the feeling that it will be all right."[103]

Production
Mary Hopkin, Tony Visconti's wife, was staying at the château when the team was working on "Sound and Vision." The first female singer to be signed up to the Beatles' label, Apple, in the 1960s, she was taking a break in her career. She recalled later how her stay in the Val-d'Oise region of France was commemorated, nevertheless, in the introduction to "Sound and Vision": "One evening, Brian called me into the studio to sing a quick backing vocal with him on 'Sound and Vision.' We sang his cute little 'doo doo' riff in unison. It was meant to be a distant echo but, when David heard it, he pushed up the fader until it became a prominent vocal—much to my embarrassment, as I thought it very twee."[47] The song's elegance and memorable melody earned it a place in the British charts, reaching number three on March 26, 1977.

To mark the fortieth anniversary of the single "Be My Wife," Parlophone and Rhino jointly brought out a vinyl picture-disc of the song on June 16, 2017, and it was eagerly bought up by fans.

Single

ALWAYS CRASHING IN THE SAME CAR

David Bowie / 3:28

Musicians: David Bowie: lead vocals, Chamberlin / **Carlos Alomar, Ricky Gardiner:** electric guitars / **Dennis Davis:** drums / **George Murray:** bass / **Roy Young:** piano, organ / **Brian Eno:** synthesizers / **Recorded:** Château d'Hérouville, France: September 1976 / Hansa Studios, West Berlin: September and October 1976 / **Technical Team:** Producers: David Bowie, Tony Visconti / **Sound Engineers:** Tony Visconti, Laurent Thibault (Château d'Hérouville), Eduard Meyer (Hansa Studios)

Written after a minor incident in an underground garage in Berlin, the song's lyrics contain a clear metaphor. It appears that David Bowie was indeed "always crashing in the same car," but in a more general sense he was also constantly repeating the same mistakes in his life. Is the car a rather unkind reference to his wife, Angie, with whom he finally and permanently separated during the summer of 1976? We'll never know...

During the recording of the song (which incidentally contains all the elements found in the future British group Pulp and their charismatic singer, Jarvis Cocker: sotto voce singing, languor, elegance, and a touch of sensuality), David hummed the notes to Ricky Gardiner to show him what he wanted to hear on the guitar at the beginning of the six-string guitar solo. About developing his part from this snatch of melody, Gardiner was to say, "I took it from there. These things don't evolve as such. They happen spontaneously and the engineer has to catch them."[104]

In rehearsing the third verse, David Bowie amused himself by sarcastically imitating Bob Dylan's nasal voice. The verse was dropped, as Tony Visconti recounted, because the folk singer was at the time recovering from a motorbike accident, and to make fun of him in a song with such a title would have been in very bad taste. "David asked me to erase it and I did."[100]

BE MY WIFE

David Bowie / 2:56

Musicians: David Bowie: lead vocals, electric guitar, synthesizers / **Carlos Alomar, Ricky Gardiner:** electric guitars / **Dennis Davis:** drums / **George Murray:** bass / **Roy Young:** piano, Farfisa organ / **Recorded:** Château d'Hérouville, France: September 1976 / Hansa Studios, West Berlin: September and October 1976 / **Technical Team:** Producers: David Bowie, Tony Visconti / **Sound Engineers:** Tony Visconti, Laurent Thibault (Château d'Hérouville), Eduard Meyer (Hansa Studios) / **Side A:** *Be My Wife* / 2:56 (UK); 2:51 (US) / **Side B:** *Speed of Life* / 2:46 (UK); 2:45 (US) / **UK Release on RCA:** June 17, 1977 (ref. PB 1017) / **US Release on RCA:** June 17, 1977 (ref. PB-11017) / **Best Chart Ranking:** Did Not Chart

The title of the sixth track on *Low* contains an implicit reference to Nina Simone, a singer for whom Bowie had the deepest admiration and who had previously recorded the moving gospel number "Be My Husband" in 1965. The diva's version, where she implores her lover to marry her and not to hurt her—*"Stick the promise man you made me / That you stay away from Rosalie / [...] Please don't treat me so now doggone mean / You're the meanest man I ever see"*—finds an echo in Bowie's version. Even as his own relationship was crumbling, Bowie uses this upbeat song to make a marriage proposal to a mysterious, unknown lover. Despite its disco backing, this was the last single to be released from *Low*, in June 1977, and it proved to be a resounding flop. Nevertheless, the members of Blur, standard bearers for Britpop in the 1990s, must have listened to it a few times in their youth because its influence can be heard on such wonderful songs as "For Tomorrow" and "Clover over Dover."

Nina Simone in 1967. The suffering and torment experienced by the gifted performer inspired Bowie during the 1970s.

A NEW CAREER IN A NEW TOWN

David Bowie / 2:50

Musicians: David Bowie: harmonica, synthesizer, piano / **Carlos Alomar, Ricky Gardiner:** electric guitars / **Dennis Davis:** drums, percussion / **George Murray:** bass / **Roy Young:** piano / **Brian Eno:** synthesizers, programming / **Recorded:** Château d'Hérouville, France: September 1976 / **Technical Team:** Producers: David Bowie, Tony Visconti / **Sound Engineers:** Tony Visconti, Laurent Thibault

Unbelievably avant-garde in its sound, with a minimalist melody and dance-floor tempo, "A New Career in a New Town" (the title an obvious reference to the composer's own life) is a key track on *Low*, the keystone of new wave and cold wave music that overturned punk and disco—styles that were now, at the end of the 1970s, in their dying days. Just one hearing of this revolutionary song is enough to justifiably claim that, in 1976, David Bowie invented two new musical movements—cold wave and new wave—which would join the mainstream only several years later, when taken up by groups like New Order, Orchestral Manoeuvres in the Dark, and Depeche Mode.

The introduction to this piece, which was the closing number on the pop side of *Low*, features an electronic drum kit of unknown make. We do know, however, that Brian Eno's programming was greatly influenced by the Kraftwerk sound. Guitarist Carlos Alomar recalled: "David introduced us to Kraftwerk, all that crazy electronic stuff. We loved it. It wasn't verse/chorus/bridge like American music. He wanted our funk rhythm section to be the electronic component of that kind of music."[102]

WARSZAWA

Musicians: David Bowie: lead vocals / **Brian Eno:** synthesizer, piano, Chamberlin / **Delaney Visconti:** piano / **Recorded:** Château d'Hérouville, France: September 1976 / Hansa Studios, West Berlin: September and October 1976 / **Technical Team: Producers:** David Bowie, Tony Visconti / **Sound Engineers:** Tony Visconti, Eduard Meyer (Hansa Studios)

In September 1976, Bowie, accompanied by Visconti, went to Paris to sort out the dispute between himself and his former lawyer and manager, Michael Lippman. Brian Eno was left to his own devices at Hérouville, a place full of mystery—he found himself thinking that the ghosts of George Sand and Frédéric Chopin had come back to haunt the scene of their famous love affair. He took advantage of this break in recording for the album to record a piece that was to become the first of the four (almost) instrumental tracks on Side 2 of *Low*. Eno recalled, "I decided to start on a piece on my own, with the understanding that if he didn't like it I would use it myself."[101] He used all the studio instruments—Minimoog, EMS Synthi AKS, Chamberlin—to create the light and synthetic sound that he so favored. Tony Visconti's little boy, Delaney (now known as Morgan Visconti), also took part, playing three notes on the piano, which Brian then duplicated, modified, and manipulated. The influence of

Wendy Carlos and the title theme to *A Clockwork Orange* (adapted from *Music for the Funeral of Queen Mary* by Henry Purcell) is clearly evident from the start of this soaring, multilayered track over which David Bowie was to add his vocal line.

Before recording the voice portion, Eno added some additional arrangements inspired by a children's choir he had heard in Warsaw—*Warszawa* in Polish—in April 1976. He created layered voices, coming in at 4:00, where he sings words of his own invention. As he explained: "It was a phonetic language, it doesn't exist—just sounds. But it seemed to capture the feeling between East and West, West Germany and Poland."[105] To modify the pitch of the voice and give it the timbre of an eleven-year-old child, Visconti used the tried-and-true technique of recording three semitones lower on a slowed-down tape, and then speeding it up during mixing.

ART DECADE

David Bowie / 3:43

Musicians: David Bowie: Chamberlin, programming, piano, electric guitar, synthesizers / **Brian Eno:** piano, synthesizers, Chamberlin / **Eduard Meyer:** cello / **Recorded:** Château d'Hérouville, France: September 1976 / **Hansa Studios, West Berlin:** September and October 1976 / **Technical Team:** Producers: David Bowie, Tony Visconti / **Sound Engineers:** Tony Visconti, Eduard Meyer (Hansa Studios) / **Cello Arrangements:** Tony Visconti

Bowie fell under the spell of the country as soon as he arrived in Berlin. The East was divided from the West, and the effects of World War II were still all too evident. Filled with mixed emotions of admiration and empathy, he was attracted by the darkness of the city, saying: "'Art Decade' is West Berlin—a city cut off from its world, art and culture, dying with no hope of retribution."[105] While Bowie and Visconti were putting the final touches to this instrumental number at Hansa Studios, they discovered that the sound engineer, Eduard Meyer, played the cello. They invited him to play along with Visconti's arrangements and, just this one time, an acoustic instrument replaces the layers of synthesizers found everywhere else on this album. The retro-sounding electronic rhythm at the beginning of the piece is created by a rhythm box integrated into one of the studio keyboards and programmed by Bowie himself.

WEEPING WALL

David Bowie / 3:25

Musician: David Bowie: lead vocals, xylophone, vibraphone, synthesizers, piano, electric guitar / **Recorded: Hansa Studios, West Berlin:** September and October 1976 / **Technical Team: Producers:** David Bowie, Tony Visconti / **Sound Engineers:** Tony Visconti, Eduard Meyer

Although intended for use on the soundtrack of *The Man Who Fell to Earth*, "Weeping Wall" was, like "Art Decade," composed as a homage to Berlin. On October 8, 1976, David Bowie was at one of the first performances of Steve Reich's *Music for 18 Musicians*, given as part of the Berlin Metamusik Fest. This fourteen-section work, an important example of the American composer's minimalist style, made an immediate impression on Bowie. He took inspiration particularly from the first of Reich's sections, "Pulses," with

its heavy use of xylophones and vibraphones. Following Reich's lead, in "Weeping Wall" Bowie—the only person to perform on this track—uses the two instruments to create repetitive and obsessive melodies, adding the sound of distant voices here and there throughout. It is significant that Hansa Studios was only five hundred and fifty yards from the Berlin Wall, hence the words "Hansa by the wall" in the disc's credits. Bowie, like Brian Eno and Visconti, felt strongly the atmosphere of latent conflict between the two countries. Visconti recalled: "From the control room we could see the Wall and we could also see over the Wall and over the barbed wire to the red guards in their gun turrets. They had enormous binoculars and they would look into the control room and watch us work. [...] We asked the engineer one day whether he felt a bit uncomfortable with the guards staring at him all day. They could easily have shot us from the East, it was that close. [...] He said you get used to it after a while and then he turned, took an overhead light and pointed it at the guards, sticking his tongue out. [...] David and I just dived right under the recording desk. [...] We were scared to death!"[99]

SUBTERRANEANS

David Bowie / 5:38

Musicians: David Bowie: lead vocals, piano, electric guitar, saxophone / **Carlos Alomar:** electric guitar / **George Murray:** bass / **J. Peter Robinson, Paul Buckmaster:** piano, ARP Odyssey synthesizer / **Recorded:** Hansa Studios, West Berlin: September and October 1976 / **Technical Team:** Producers: David Bowie, Tony Visconti / **Sound Engineers:** Tony Visconti, Eduard Meyer

David Bowie grew up reading the books of Jack Kerouac. He knew not only the famous *On the Road*, but also *The Subterraneans*, a thinly disguised autobiography dating from 1958. It relates the New York adventures of Kerouac, the idol of the Beat Generation, and his love affair with an Alene Lee, a Black woman living in Greenwich Village. When, in the summer of 1976, Bowie returned to this piece that he had originally worked on with Paul Buckmaster for the soundtrack of *The Man Who Fell to Earth*, he was still affected by the end of his relationship with the singer Ava Cherry, whom he had met in New York. It is easy to see the parallels between Bowie's own life and Kerouac's novel. The "Peter and Paul" credited on the disc are musicians Paul Buckmaster and John Peter Robinson, who played piano and ARP Odyssey synthesizer. They were not present at the recording sessions at Hérouville and Hansa Studios, so Bowie and Visconti worked using the original tapes, adding in different sound textures that they felt were appropriate for what was to be the last track on Side 2 of *Low*.

SOME ARE

David Bowie, Brian Eno / 3:14

Musicians: David Bowie: lead vocals, synthesizers / Brian Eno: piano (?), synthesizers (?) / David Richards: synthesizers (?) / **Recorded:** Château d'Hérouville, France (?): September 1976 / Hansa Studios, West Berlin (?): September and October 1976 / Mountain Studios, Montreux (overdubs and mixing): 1991 / **Technical Team:** Producer: David Bowie / Mixing: David Bowie, David Richards (Mountain Studios)

Like "All Saints," "Some Are" is a track that was added in for fans when *Low* was reissued by Rykodisc in 1991. Mystery surrounds these two pieces. Very similar to "Warszawa" and "Subterraneans," it seems likely that they were recorded during the sessions spent preparing the album in September and October 1976. In 1991, "Some Are" and "All Saints," never previously mixed, were worked on in detail by David Bowie and David Richards, the sound engineer at Mountain Studios in Montreux. Richards had formerly been assistant sound engineer when *"Heroes"* was being mixed in Switzerland in 1977. Everything points to the voice part being recorded by Bowie during the mixing sessions in 1991, because the register of his voice seems much closer to that of the Tin Machine period. The synthesizers, probably added by the experienced Richards, have a very modern, cold sound that's quite different from that of the Hérouville Minimoog. But these are only guesses because no one knows exactly how these two titles came into being. "Some Are" was included in the 2008 *iSelect* compilation, for which Bowie personally chose the track list. At the time, the song was listed as "Recorded between 1976 and 1979." As if to shroud the piece in even more mystery, Bowie writes in the accompanying booklet for the album that this was "a quiet little piece Brian Eno and I wrote in the seventies. The cries of wolves in the background are sounds that you might not pick up on immediately. Unless you're a wolf."[56]

ALL SAINTS

David Bowie, Brian Eno / 3:34

Musicians: David Bowie: lead vocals, synthesizers / Brian Eno: piano (?), synthesizers (?) / David Richards: synthesizers (?) / **Recorded:** Château d'Hérouville, France (?): September 1976 / Hansa Studios, West Berlin (?): September and October 1976 / Mountain Studios, Montreux (overdubs and mixing): 1991 / **Technical Team:** Producer: David Bowie / Mixing: David Bowie, David Richards (Mountain Studios)

Another item rescued from David Bowie's archives for the 1991 reissue of *Low*, "All Saints" was the object of the same nineties-era mixing as "Some Are." The same sense of mystery regarding the recording of "Some Are" also surrounds this instrumental piece of only minor quality. Tony Visconti could not remember it at all, making its dating problematic for Bowie enthusiasts. "I have no idea where it came from. I never worked on it. The electronic loops are more eighties—we didn't have anything like that for *Low* or '*Heroes*.'"[47] The title of the piece was also used for a two-CD compilation issued in 1993. Only 150 copies were made, and Bowie gave these to his closest collaborators as a Christmas present. They are now highly sought after by collectors around the world.

ABDULMAJID

David Bowie, Brian Eno / 3:36

Musicians: David Bowie: lead vocals, synthesizers / Brian Eno: piano (?), synthesizers (?) / David Richards: synthesizers (?) / **Recorded:** Hansa Studios, West Berlin (?): July–August 1977 (?) / Mountain Studios, Montreux (overdubs and mixing): 1991 / **Technical Team:** Producer: David Bowie / Mixing: David Bowie, David Richards (Mountain Studios)

Like "All Saints" and "Some Are," "Abdulmajid" was written somewhere between 1976 and 1979. Once again mixed by Bowie and Richards in 1991, for some reason the song was included in the reissue of *"Heroes"* rather than that of *Low* (probably in order to have something extra to offer people buying the new version of the album). There is nothing very authentic about this track with its modern sound except perhaps the title, a reference to Iman Mohamed Abdulmajid, whom Bowie married in 1992.

Bowie met Iman Abdulmajid in 1990, and he gave her name to a previously recorded song that appeared on the rerelease of *"Heroes"* in 1991.

ALBUM

"HEROES"

Beauty and the Beast . Joe the Lion . "Heroes" . Sons of the Silent Age .
Blackout . V-2 Schneider . Sense of Doubt . Moss Garden . Neuköln .
The Secret Life of Arabia

RELEASE DATES

United Kingdom: October 14, 1977
Reference: RCA—PL1 2522
United States: October 14, 1977
Reference: RCA—AFL1 2522
Best UK Chart Ranking: 3
Best US Chart Ranking: 35

Bowie at the keyboards
during Iggy Pop's *Idiot* tour.

Following double page
The duo onstage during the
Iguana's tour in 1977.

FOLLOWING ON FROM *LOW*

At the beginning of 1977, David Bowie decided to ease up on his frenetic working pace, and so he did not give the *Low* album a tour, which it would have merited. A close friend of Iggy Pop, whose first solo effort he produced in the summer of 1976, Bowie opted instead to join the Iguana's international tour in the capacity of keyboard player, quietly established behind his upright piano. The brothers Tony and Hunt Sales were positioned on bass and drums, and Ricky Gardiner was on guitar, thereby completing the band's lineup. Throughout the thirty or so dates of the *Idiot* tour, these merry men offered Iggy Pop a return to fame on the international rock scene. Inseparable following weeks spent haunting the Berlin clubs at the end of the previous summer, the duo affirmed their friendly bonds with a return to Hansa Studios in West Berlin at the end of their tour. Together, they began work on a new opus by the elastic singer from Detroit, *Lust for Life*. Bowie put aside his latest penchant for krautrock-inspired minimalism to work with his friend on a disc full of tight rock nuggets, including the timeless title track as well as "Some Weird Sin" and "Success." Spontaneity was king during these recording sessions, and all the tracks were completed in record time, as Iggy Pop confirmed: "We did it quick, this record. The entire thing was done in just two weeks, including the mixing. The best of the stuff was written in about two and a half days."[107] This dynamic had a regenerating force for David Bowie, who decided to take back control of his life after his California decline. "We both—Iggy and I—felt it might be time to clean up,"[108] he confided in 1997.

The Logical Next Step After *Low*

In August 1977, as soon as Iggy's album was completed, Bowie moved to Hansa Studio 2—a large hall that had once held balls organized by the Gestapo, to begin work on his own new album. This was a place with an atmosphere that was, to say the least, rather a strange one, and only the thick curtains concealed the musicians from the view of the East German guards on duty in their watchtowers. It was, despite everything, a relaxed atmosphere in which the recording sessions began, once the band—which was identical to the one for *Low*—was complete. Alomar was once again on guitar, Murray on bass, Davis on drums, Eno on synthesizers, and the Bowie-Visconti duo managed production. The only external contributors were Robert Fripp, guitarist of King Crimson, and the German backing vocalist Antonia Maass, whom the players met in a club in the city. Like Earl Slick and Ricky Gardiner before him, Fripp provided an aggressive guitar sound that complemented the subtle and more funky playing of Carlos Alomar. On this album David Bowie seems to have taken control of his life once again, even though giving up cocaine was "compensated" for via a major increase in the intake of spirits of all kinds. "I became an alcoholic," the singer confessed. "[...] What the body does is it lets itself open for any other kind of addiction. You replace one with another and in my case I went straight to whisky and brandy."[47] The creation of *"Heroes"* followed the same working method that had been used on *Low*, which makes these two albums something of a pair. Both follow the same basic format—one side filled with rock songs, and one side filled with experimental compositions—and the extensive use of synthesizers and minimalist soundscapes that filled in for the more narrative-forward leanings of Bowie's earlier works. Brian Eno was present this time from the first day of work, and he pushed Bowie even further in the direction of electronic experimentation. "I think

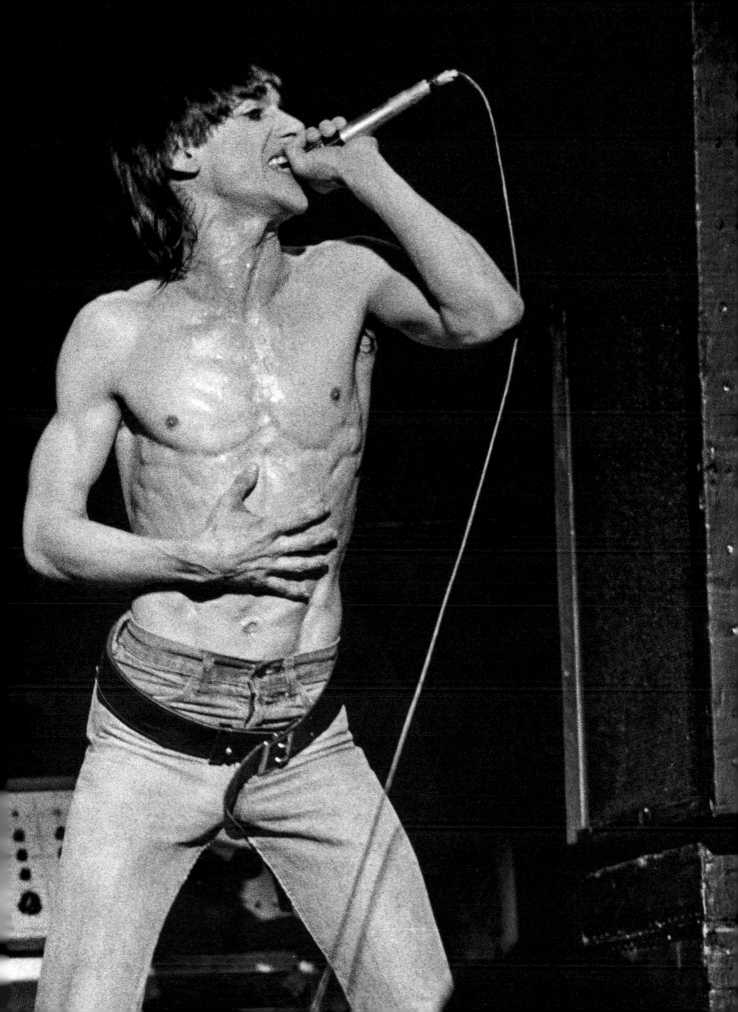

Eno opened up new doors of perception," confided the singer. "In terms of the use of the studio, I'd never used a studio in quite the way that Brian was using it."[109] The backing tracks on the first songs were recorded in a few days. While the musicians would sometimes record four of five takes in quick succession, it was often the first recording that was kept and used, since Bowie preferred the accidents that occurred in early takes because of their spontaneity. As with *Low*, Eno and Bowie added overdubs that were, for the most part, the fruits of electronic experiments on keyboards. The straightforward rock effectiveness of the title track, "Heroes," along with the audacious pop-disco leanings of "Beauty and the Beast" and "Blackout," and the ambient tracks "Sense of Doubt" and

"Moss Garden" came together in a perfect cohesion that provided the perfect follow-up to *Low*.

Farewell to Marc Bolan

When the recording was finished, Tony Visconti left Berlin for Switzerland, where he mixed the album with David Richards at Mountain Studios in Montreaux. On September 7, 1977, Bowie went to Granada Studios in Manchester for the filming of the sixth episode of the television series *Marc*, in which Marc Bolan was master of ceremonies. As was standard practice during the broadcast, the former glam-rock star invited his star guests to perform songs either by themselves or with Bolan as a duet partner. Bowie performed "Heroes," which was scheduled for release as a single

Left to right: Robert Fripp, Tony Visconti, David Bowie, and Brian Eno at Hansa Studios, during the production of "Heroes."

The final meeting between Bowie and his old friend Marc Bolan, on the stage of *Marc*, September 7, 1977.

sixteen days later. Then, for a great piece of television, he joined Bolan on "Sitting Next to You," a song they had worked on prior to the show's taping. After a few chords, the T. Rex singer slipped and hit the microphone, still with a smile on his face. There was a close-up of Bowie looking amused by this, followed by the final applause and credits. A week later, on September 16, 1977, Marc Bolan and his girlfriend, Gloria Jones, crashed their car into a tree in South London. The young woman had a broken jaw, legs, and arms, and the musician died instantly, two weeks before his thirtieth birthday. David Bowie's episode of *Marc* was still broadcast, however, on September 28, 1977, and did indeed end with the footage of Bolan falling over, and Bowie's sardonic glance.

It is difficult for Bowie and Bolan fans to agree on the title of the song that the duo performed onstage for the *Marc* broadcast on September 28, 1977. Some think it is called "Sleeping Next to You," and others believe it is called "Standing Next to You." The T. Rex singer fell over before he had time to sing the refrain, but on listening to the rehearsal recordings, one can clearly hear the duo harmonizing "*sitting next to you*."

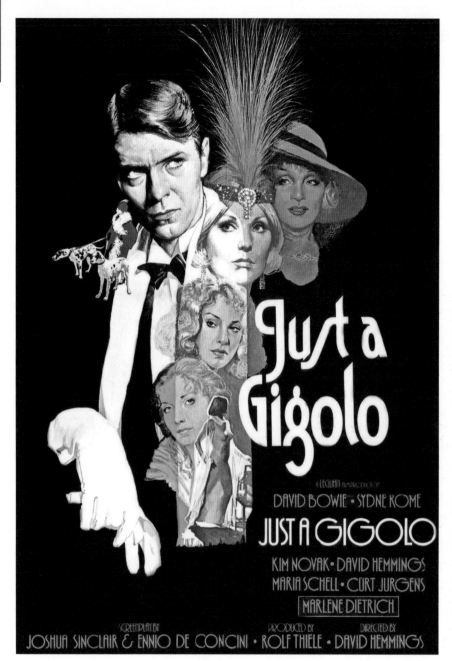

In *Just a Gigolo*, Bowie played a young Prussian officer forced to sell his favors in the decadent Berlin of the 1920s.

Erich Heckel, *Roquairol*, 1917.

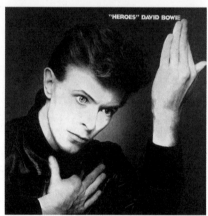

A few days earlier, on September 11, 1977, David launched himself into an adventure that came as something of a surprise to his fans. Having been invited to take part in the filming of the Christmas broadcast of *Bing Crosby's Merrie Olde Christmas,* the singer agreed and sang two songs with the famous crooner: "Peace on Earth" and "Little Drummer Boy." Once again, singing in the company of David seems to have been an ill-fated omen, because Crosby died of a heart attack just over a month later, on October 14. RCA, who owned the songs recorded that day, released them on a 45 rpm in December 1983.

As a curious coincidence, October 14, 1977, was also the release date for *"Heroes,"* David Bowie's twelfth album. The album sleeve was illustrated with a photograph taken by Masayoshi Sukita at the Harajuku Studios in Tokyo, in April 1977, when the Thin White Duke was accompanying Iggy Pop during his promotion of *The Idiot.* Sukita photographed the Iguana for an hour, and then allocated the same amount of time to Bowie. Bowie reproduced a pose from the painting *Roquairol*, made by the celerated German artist Erich Heckel. Bowie had seen the painting previously on a visit to the Brücke Museum in Berlin.

The "Isolar II Tour"

Boosted by the creative energy conjured on *Low* and *"Heroes,"* and by the warm reception for his new album, David Bowie prepared for an international tour. Taking advantage of the few months of respite before setting off, he provided the voice of the narrator in *Peter and the Wolf*

Simon House, Sean Mayes, David Bowie, and Carlos Alomar onstage at the Earls Court
Exhibition Centre in London, during the "Isolar II Tour" in July 1978.

by Sergei Prokofiev as a gift for his son. The music was played by the Philadelphia Orchestra, and Bowie recorded his voice track at RCA Studios in New York in the autumn of 1977. Then, in January 1978, he played the part of Paul Ambrosius von Przygodski in the David Hemmings feature film *Just a Gigolo*, for which he co-wrote "The Revolutionary Song" with the composer Jack Fishman. The song was performed by the group the Rebels.

On March 28, 1978, Bowie launched the "Isolar II Tour" (or "Stage Tour") at the San Diego Sports Arena. With him for the journey were Carlos Alomar, George Murray, and Dennis Davis, along with guitarist Adrian Belew (a former member of Frank Zappa's group), violinist Simon House, and keyboard players Sean Mayes and Roger Powell. The concerts were structured in two distinct sections. The first half consisted of the songs from the singer's last two discs, and the second half contained pieces from Bowie's earlier albums. To the surprise of his fans, Bowie said farewell to the emaciated Thin White Duke, appearing in good shape, and dressed in modern, relaxed suits designed by Natasha Korniloff. This world tour had multiple dates in the United States, Europe, Japan, and Australia, and also had the effect of reconciling the singer with air travel. When the journalist

Anthony O'Grady asked him about his phobia in June 1977, Bowie answered: "Fear of flying...fear of elevators...fear is not a word in my vocabulary anymore. I am a man of great inner strength and courage these days."[59] The tour was immortalized in the recording of Bowie's second live album, *Stage*, produced by Tony Visconti between April and May 1978. When it was released on September 25, 1978, it marked the public's recognition of the singer's artistic renaissance after years of excess and unsavory living.

FOR BOWIE ADDICTS

"The D.A.M. Trio" is the name given to David Bowie's rhythm section on *Station to Station*. *D.A.M.* stands for Davis, Alomar, and Murray.

Robert Fripp and his famous Les Paul Gibson, shown here in 1973, were already inseparable during the King Crimson years.

BEAUTY AND THE BEAST

David Bowie / 3:35

Musicians: David Bowie: lead and backing vocals, synthesizers, piano / **Carlos Alomar:** electric guitar / **Dennis Davis:** drums / **George Murray:** bass / **Robert Fripp:** electric guitar / **Antonia Maass, Tony Visconti:** background vocals / **Brian Eno:** synthesizers / **Recorded:** Hansa Studios, West Berlin: July–August 1977 / Mountain Studios, Montreux (mixing): late August 1977 / **Technical Team: Producers:** David Bowie, Tony Visconti / **Sound Engineers:** Tony Visconti, Colin Thurston (Hansa Studios) / **Assistant Sound Engineers:** Eduard Meyer (Hansa Studios), Michael Zimmerling (Hansa Studios), Peter Burgon (Hansa Studios), David Richards (Mountain Studios), Eugene Chaplin (Mountain Studios) / **Side A:** *Beauty and the Beast* / 3:29 / **Side B:** *Sense of Doubt* / 3:57 / **UK Release on RCA:** January 6, 1978 (ref. PB 1190) / **US Release on RCA:** January 6, 1978 (ref. PB-11190) / **Best UK Chart Ranking:** 39 / **Best US Chart Ranking:** Did Not Chart

As with "Station to Station," "Golden Years," and "A New Career in a New Town" before it, "Beauty and the Beast" is a gem of a song with a disco feel to it, and closely hewing to the conventions of the disco style, which was at the time very much in fashion—kick drum on all the beats, sixteenth-note Charleston, and a groovy bass rhythm. While taking advantage of Berlin to restore his health—in a relative

sense—the singer provided an explosive opening number for his twelfth opus. Proclaiming his remission to whoever wanted to hear it ("*Nothing will corrupt us / Nothing will compete / Thank God heaven left us / Standing on our feet*"), Bowie takes the beast by the horns.

Having met Bowie in a Berlin club a few days previously, the German singer Antonia Maass was invited to provide some background vocals to add a welcome touch of femininity to this dance number, which combines the rhythm of Alomar and rich playing of Robert Fripp. The eminent guitarist of the prog-rock band King Crimson, exiled to the United States, was recruited by Brian Eno to add his trenchant riffs to the album. In 2017, he described his epic arrival at the studio in detail to the biographer Dylan Jones. "[I] went to Hansa Studios By The Wall for about quarter to six in the evening, jet-lagged, pretty sleepless, and [...] Eno said, 'Why don't you plug in?' [...] What you hear on the record, the first track of '*Heroes*,' is the first note I played on the session."[1] The next morning, having used his Gibson Les Paul on five of the album's songs, Fripp took the plane back to New York.

Chris Burden during his *Trans-Fixed* performance on April 23, 1974, in Los Angeles.

JOE THE LION

David Bowie / 3:07

Musicians: David Bowie: lead and backing vocals, synthesizers / Carlos Alomar: electric guitar / Dennis Davis: drums / George Murray: bass / Robert Fripp: electric guitar / Brian Eno: synthesizers / **Recorded:** Hansa Studios, West Berlin: July–August 1977 / Mountain Studios, Montreux (mixing): late August 1977 / **Technical Team:** Producers: David Bowie, Tony Visconti / **Sound Engineers:** Tony Visconti, Colin Thurston (Hansa Studios) / **Assistant Sound Engineers:** Eduard Meyer (Hansa Studios), Michael Zimmerling (Hansa Studios), Peter Burgon (Hansa Studios), David Richards (Mountain Studios), Eugene Chaplin (Mountain Studios)

Impressed by the television appearances of Chris Burden, David Bowie here pays homage to the artist who specialized in giving provocative performances in which he cheated death, having become particularly famous for having an assistant shoot him during a performance called *Shoot*, in 1971. In a 1974 performance, Burden was "crucified" on the hood of a revving Volkswagen, and this caught Bowie's attention. "Chris Burden, he was an extraordinary guy," recalled Bowie in 1995. In "Joe the Lion," Burden is

"the guy [singing] 'Nail me to my car, tell you who you are.' He also made a film where he had himself sewn into a mailbag and thrown in the middle of a highway, where he lay for 5 hours in heavy traffic and emerged unscathed."[110] The lyrics for this homage to the performer came to him in an almost instantaneous way: "Most of my vocals were first takes, some written as I sang. Most famously 'Joe the Lion' I suppose. I would put the headphones on, stand at the mike, listen to a verse, jot down some key words that came into mind then take. Then I would repeat the same process for the next section, etc."[100] To give this piece more bite, Bowie asked Robert Fripp to play his riff like the blues guitarist and singer Albert King, on a groove at 120 bpm, a tempo often associated with the big disco hits of the era. Brian Eno plugged Fripp's six-string guitar into his EMS Synthi AKS synthesizer and played the alchemist of sound, processing the signal during the recording to obtain some futuristic textures.

On June 6, 1987, more than sixty thousand people were present at Bowie's performance in front of the Reichstag during the Concert for Berlin.

Bowie provided some surprising adaptations of "Heroes" for the fans. For Germany first of all, where the refrain, thanks to the words of Antonia Maass, becomes: "*Werden wir helden / Für Einen Tag*"; and then for France, where the singer cries: "On peut être héros / Juste une journée" ("We can be heroes / Just for one day").

Single

"HEROES"

David Bowie, Brian Eno / 6:10

Musicians

David Bowie: lead and backing vocals, synthesizers, piano, Chamberlin, percussions
Carlos Alomar: electric guitar
Dennis Davis: drums
George Murray: bass
Robert Fripp: electric guitar
Brian Eno: synthesizer
Tony Visconti: percussion, background vocals

Recorded

Hansa Studios, West Berlin: July–August 1977
Mountain Studios, Montreux (mixing): late August 1977

Technical Team

Producers: David Bowie, Tony Visconti
Sound Engineers: Tony Visconti, Colin Thurston (Hansa Studios)
Assistant Sound Engineers: Eduard Meyer (Hansa Studios), Michael Zimmerling (Hansa Studios), Peter Burgon (Hansa Studios), David Richards (Mountain Studios), Eugene Chaplin (Mountain Studios)

SIDE A: *"Heroes"* / 3:29
SIDE B: *V-2 Schneider* / 3:10
UK Release on RCA: September 23, 1977 (ref. PB 1121)
US Release on RCA: September 23, 1977 (ref. PB-11121)
Best UK Chart Ranking: 12
Best US Chart Ranking: Did Not Chart

ON YOUR HEADPHONES

Bowie wanted to end the instrumental part of "Heroes" with the sound of a bell, something that was impossible to find in the studio. Making do with the resources at hand, the singer and his producer took up a tambourine and a metal plate, which they struck in front of the microphone starting at 2:56.

Genesis

While married to the singer Mary Hopkin, Tony Visconti had a brief fling in Berlin with the album's backing singer, Antonia Maass. This was kept a secret, and the romance was only revealed by Visconti many years later. For his part, Bowie was immersed in the cultural life of Berlin, and he fell under the spell of the painting *Liebespaar zwischen Gartenmauern* (*Lovers between the Garden Walls*), by the expressionist painter Otto Mueller, and discovered by Bowie in the Brücke Museum. Inspired by the romanticism of this intertwined couple, he felt that he could create a song out of it. The wall enclosing the couple was reminiscent of the *Schandmauer* ("wall of shame") that divided Berlin. The work also echoed a book the singer had recently read: *A Grave for a Dolphin*, written by Alberto Denti Di Pirajno and published in 1956, which tells the story of an impossible love between an Italian soldier and a young Somalian woman during World War II.

One day, when they were busy with the production of the song that would become "Heroes," Bowie asked Visconti to leave him alone in the studio so that he could write the lyrics. As always with the singer, everything happened in a hurry: musical production, writing lyrics, recording vocals, then on to the next song! Visconti complied, and left Bowie to get on with his work. Later, the singer surprised Visconti in the middle of a kiss with Antonia Maass, which was taking place with the Berlin Wall as a backdrop. This was all he needed to complete the lyrics for "Heroes" in just a few minutes, as he explained in 2003. "I'm allowed to talk about it now. I wasn't at the time. I think possibly the marriage was in the last few months, and it was very touching because I could see that Tony was very much in love with this girl, and it was that relationship which sort of motivated the song."[36] "I can't tell you where he pulled the other images in his song," testified Visconti, "but we were the couple that inspired 'I can remember / Standing by the wall / And the guns / Shot above our heads / And we kissed / As though nothing could fall.'"[35]

More than an ode to impossible love, "Heroes" is also a cry of hope for the East Germans, cut off from the western world. In 1987, David Bowie sang this song during the highly publicized Concert for Berlin, where the stage was

placed opposite the Reichstag and right next to the wall. Powerful speakers were directed toward the Brandenburg Gate and sent the sound out to the East. "I was in tears," recalled the singer. "[...] We kind of heard that a few of the East Berliners might actually get the chance to hear the thing. [...] There were thousands on the other side that had come close to the wall. [...] We would hear them cheering and singing along from the other side. [...] It was breaking my heart. I'd never done anything like that in my life. And I guess I never will again."[36]

Production

As usual, Visconti recorded the backing tracks quickly before leaving Eno and Bowie free to experiment during the overdub sessions. Alomar on guitar, Murray on bass, Davis on drums, and Bowie on the piano—they all initially established the structure of the piece. Eno then colored this basic framework with synthetic tapestries, using his EMS Synthi AKS, before handing the track over to Bowie, who added a touch of the Solina String Ensemble, and then some Chamberlin synthesizer. Robert Fripp later recorded three guitar takes, including some Larsen feedback, which became the subject of much discussion among the six-string fans. Contrary to what people said, the King Crimson guitarist was not using an Ebow—a little electronic "bow" that uses an electromagnet to generate an electromagnetic field, which causes the required string on the guitar to vibrate, thereby creating an infinite resonance of sound

(a sustain, in technical language). Fifteen years later, at the Freddie Mercury Tribute Concert in 1992, Mick Ronson did use this marvelous tool on the introduction to "Heroes," although the method used at Hansa in 1977 was much more rudimentary. Reproducing what he had experimented with for the Marc Bolan solo on "Ballrooms of Mars" by T. Rex in 1972, Visconti recorded three similar guitar takes, which, when superimposed with a slight lag between them, created Larsen feedback just as Earl Slick had done to such great effect on the introduction to *Station to Station* in 1975. "Fripp didn't realize we were going to use all three takes," recalls the producer. "That's why that line isn't exactly in sync. It's wavy and floaty, and very similar to 'Ballrooms of Mars,' in that way."[42] Finally, when it was time to record Bowie's voice, there was only one free track left on the console. The producer then connected three microphones in the spacious Hansa Studio 2. The first "proximity" mic was positioned right in front of the singer; the second, five yards away; and the third, sixteen yards away, almost at the back of the room. The last two microphones were equipped with a gate, an electronic system that enabled sound to be captured only at a given volume level. As the song progressed, and as Bowie sang with more and more energy, the cells on each microphone opened up one by one, and all three microphones began working at the same time during the finale of the song. This increased the power of the voice and added in some of the room's natural reverb.

The Manhattan skyline was plunged into darkness during the July 1977 blackout.

The famous American jazz musician Lionel Hampton also released an album in 1977 called *Blackout*, also in memory of the events of July 1977. On the album cover, Hampton can be seen playing his vibraphone in a New York apartment lit only with candles.

SONS OF THE SILENT AGE

David Bowie / 3:19

Musicians: David Bowie: lead and backing vocals, synthesizers, saxophone / Carlos Alomar: electric guitar / Dennis Davis: drums / George Murray: bass / Robert Fripp: electric guitar / Brian Eno: synthesizers / Tony Visconti: background vocals / **Recorded:** Hansa Studios, West Berlin: July–August 1977 / Mountain Studios, Montreux (mixing): late August 1977 / **Technical Team:** Producers: David Bowie, Tony Visconti / **Sound Engineers:** Tony Visconti, Colin Thurston (Hansa Studios) / **Assistant Sound Engineers:** Eduard Meyer (Hansa Studios), Michael Zimmerling (Hansa Studios), Peter Burgon (Hansa Studios), David Richards (Mountain Studios), Eugene Chaplin (Mountain Studios)

The only song written by David Bowie before the sessions for *"Heroes,"* "Sons of the Silent Age" reverts to the harmonic structures used on the album *The Man Who Sold the World*, whose original chord progressions captured listeners' imaginations in the early 1970s. There is another reference here to Jacques Brel, whom David Bowie discovered in 1968 with the show *Jacques Brel Is Alive and Well and Living in Paris*, on which he performed the song "Old Folks."

For the creation of this number, Eno once again suggested to the musicians that they use his *Oblique Strategies* and draw cards at random. Alomar, who had previously been reticent about this, agreed to give it a try. "Once I was blocked on what to play […]," he explained. "I picked up a card that read 'Do We Need Holes?' It was perfect. I then proceeded to play a continuous line without stopping!"[101]

BLACKOUT

David Bowie / 3:49

Musicians: David Bowie: lead and backing vocals, synthesizers, piano / Carlos Alomar: electric guitar / Dennis Davis: drums, congas, percussion / George Murray: bass / Robert Fripp: electric guitar / Brian Eno: synthesizers / **Recorded:** Hansa Studios, West Berlin: July–August 1977 / Mountain Studios, Montreux (mixing): late August 1977 / **Technical Team:** Producers: David Bowie, Tony Visconti / **Sound Engineers:** Tony Visconti, Colin Thurston (Hansa Studios) / **Assistant Sound Engineers:** Eduard Meyer (Hansa Studios), Michael Zimmerling (Hansa Studios), Peter Burgon (Hansa Studios), David Richards (Mountain Studios), Eugene Chaplin (Mountain Studios)

On July 13 and 14, 1977, after some violent storms, New York was plunged into darkness when the city's power went out for nearly forty-eight hours (with the exception of Queens, which had a separate source of electricity). The city was vulnerable to looters, and there were several riots, clustered mostly in Manhattan. Many thousands of people were involved, and the event, which inspired the song's lyrics for Bowie, lingered in people's memories simply as the *blackout*. This piece also makes reference to Japan (*"I'm under Japanese influence"*), a reference that would pop up again in "Moss Garden."

Dennis Davis, the drummer on this dynamic cut, decided during recording to enhance his part using a variety of different percussion instruments, including congas, which he positioned next to the drums and struck at the same time as his kick drum. This can be heard at 2:10 in the song.

Bowie paid homage to Kraftwerk and its singer, Florian Schneider (far left), in "V-2 Schneider."

V-2 SCHNEIDER

David Bowie / 3:11

Musicians: David Bowie: lead and backing vocals, synthesizers, piano, saxophone / Carlos Alomar: electric guitar / Dennis Davis: drums / George Murray: bass / Brian Eno: synthesizers / **Recorded:** Hansa Studios, West Berlin: July–August 1977 / Mountain Studios, Montreux (mixing): late August 1977 / **Technical Team:** Producers: David Bowie, Tony Visconti / Sound Engineers: Tony Visconti, Colin Thurston (Hansa Studios) / Assistant Sound Engineers: Eduard Meyer (Hansa Studios), Michael Zimmerling (Hansa Studios), Peter Burgon (Hansa Studios), David Richards (Mountain Studios), Eugene Chaplin (Mountain Studios)

"V-2 Schneider" was in fact a nice tribute by Bowie, who was a great admirer of the German band Kraftwerk, and he used this song as a hat tip to one of the band's founders, Florian Schneider, after the group referenced "Station to Station" in their own song "Trans-Europe Express." The singer was also inspired by the sound-processing expertise of the members of the krautrock band, so he covered his voice with a vocoder effect that was close to the one that that German group created for itself. A V-2 was a missile commonly used by the Germans during World War II, and it is represented in this song by a major flanger, a filter whose swirling effect seems to reproduce the sound of a jet plane. This is the filter that can be heard at 0:07 and that guitarists (such as Chris Gentry of Menswear, on the 1995 track "Daydreamer") and drummers (like Travis Barker on Blink-182's 2003 song "Feeling This") liked to use as a way to add atmospheric effects to their instruments.

SENSE OF DOUBT

David Bowie / 3:58

Musicians: David Bowie: synthesizers, piano, Chamberlin, vocal effects / Brian Eno: synthesizers / **Recorded:** Hansa Studios, West Berlin: July–August 1977 / Mountain Studios, Montreux (mixing): late August 1977 / **Technical Team:** Producers: David Bowie, Tony Visconti / Sound Engineers: Tony Visconti, Colin Thurston (Hansa Studios) / Assistant Sound Engineers: Eduard Meyer (Hansa Studios), Michael Zimmerling (Hansa Studios), Peter Burgon (Hansa Studios), David Richards (Mountain Studios), Eugene Chaplin (Mountain Studios)

Reproducing the Side 2 format from *Low*, the Bowie-Eno combination here delivers a four-handed instrumental score constructed from four piano notes covered with reverb. Each musician used the *Oblique Strategies* very rigorously for the creation of this number (and for the following one, "Moss Garden"); they advanced in accordance with the randomly drawn cards, and without knowing what rules were being imposed on their colleagues. In the end, the cards' demands resulted in their mixing the darkness of the piano with the gentleness of the Chamberlin, the melancholy of its melody with the unsettling sonorities of the famous portable EMS Synthi AKS. All of these are sustained by Bowie's guttural voice, which can be heard at 1:05.

MOSS GARDEN

David Bowie, Brian Eno / 5:05

Musicians: David Bowie: synthesizers, koto / Brian Eno: synthesizers / Tony Visconti: synthesizers / **Recorded:** Hansa Studios, West Berlin: July–August 1977 / Mountain Studios, Montreux (mixing): late August 1977 / **Technical Team:** Producers: David Bowie, Tony Visconti / **Sound Engineers:** Tony Visconti, Colin Thurston (Hansa Studios) / **Assistant Sound Engineers:** Eduard Meyer (Hansa Studios), Michael Zimmerling (Hansa Studios), Peter Burgon (Hansa Studios), David Richards (Mountain Studios), Eugene Chaplin (Mountain Studios)

Taken from the memory of his visit to Japan's Hakone Moss Garden in April 1973, during the *Ziggy Stardust* tour, David Bowie was inspired by the lush landscape to create this instrumental track. In order to pay tribute to the place, the enchantment of nature, and the richness of Japanese dress style, the singer even decided to play the koto. This traditional Japanese instrument is played by plucking at strings and is somewhat like playing a harp. The instrument lends the piece its full character and a gentle voluptuousness. According to Brian Eno, a new synthesizer also appears on this piece: the Yamaha CS-80, a polyphonic keyboard with multiple sonorities, which was used on a good number of songs created in the 1980s, including the famous soundtrack composed by Vangelis for Ridley Scott's 1982 classic film, *Blade Runner*.

NEUKÖLN

David Bowie, Brian Eno / 4:34

Musicians: David Bowie: saxophone, synthesizers, Chamberlin, electric guitar / Brian Eno: synthesizers / **Recorded:** Hansa Studios, West Berlin: July–August 1977 / Mountain Studios, Montreux (mixing): late August 1977 / **Technical Team:** Producers: David Bowie, Tony Visconti / **Sound Engineers:** Tony Visconti, Colin Thurston (Hansa Studios) / **Assistant Sound Engineers:** Eduard Meyer (Hansa Studios), Michael Zimmerling (Hansa Studios), Peter Burgon (Hansa Studios), David Richards (Mountain Studios), Eugene Chaplin (Mountain Studios)

Neukölln (the song title has only one *l*) was one of David Bowie's favorite Berlin districts—he lived in the neighboring district of Schöneberg, to the west of the Tempelhof airport (which is now a gigantic park in the center of this German city). The cosmopolitan character of Neukölln, whose Turkish community made up a large part of the population, inspired a saxophone score of great virtuosity, in which Bowie's playing imitates the sound of the ney, a flute made of cane with a unique sound that is characteristic of much Middle Eastern music. This is a contribution of quality from Bowie, who provides one of his finest saxophone performances on this track. The saxophone was Bowie's favorite instrument, but unfortunately it remained all too often in its case during recording sessions.

THE SECRET LIFE OF ARABIA

David Bowie, Brian Eno, Carlos Alomar / 3:45

Musicians: David Bowie: lead and backing vocals, synthesizers, piano, tambourine, claps / Carlos Alomar: electric guitar / Dennis Davis: drums, congas / George Murray: bass / Brian Eno: synthesizers / Antonia Maass: background vocals / **Recorded:** Hansa Studios, West Berlin: July–August 1977 / Mountain Studios, Montreux (mixing): late August 1977 / **Technical Team:** Producers: David Bowie, Tony Visconti / **Sound Engineers:** Tony Visconti, Colin Thurston (Hansa Studios) / **Assistant Sound Engineers:** Eduard Meyer (Hansa Studios), Michael Zimmerling (Hansa Studios), Peter Burgon (Hansa Studios), David Richards (Mountain Studios), Eugene Chaplin (Mountain Studios)

Determined to conclude his album on a disco note, David Bowie here delivers an unbeatable ritornello—in which the whole team contributes a recurring musical passage, with the exception of guitarist Robert Fripp. Carlos Alomar's funk rhythm is supported by the virtuoso playing of bassist George Murray, and for the number's grand finale, from 1:50, there is all the darkness of the streets of Berlin. Something that is present throughout the Berlin Trilogy, this darkness made many of Bowie's songs perfect for the dance floors of the day. The following year, Bowie would collaborate with Brian Eno for the final time on his thirteenth studio album, *Lodger*. Who knows what might have been if the pair had continued to work and create together? Soon, Bowie would move in a decidedly more commercial artistic direction with the albums *Scary Monsters (And Super Creeps)* and *Let's Dance*.

David Bowie enjoyed walking in the cosmopolitan district of Neukölln during his Berlin years.

Single

David Bowie and Bing Crosby

PEACE ON EARTH / LITTLE DRUMMER BOY

Ian Fraser, Larry Grossman, Alan Kohan
Katherine Kennicott Davis, Harry Simeone, Harry Onorati, traditional

Musicians
David Bowie: vocals
Bing Crosby: vocals
Studio Orchestra on Recorded Tape

Recorded
Elstree Studios, Borehamwood: September 11, 1977 (vocals)

Technical Team
Producer: Frank Konigsberg
Sound Engineer: Ted Scott

SIDE A: *Peace on Earth / Little Drummer Boy* / 2:37
SIDE B: *Fantastic Voyage* / 2:52
UK Release on RCA: November 27, 1982 (ref. BOW 12, PB 13400)
US Release on RCA: November 27, 1982 (ref. BOW 12, PB 13400)
Best UK Chart Ranking: 3
Best US Chart Ranking: Did Not Chart

The strange collaboration between Bowie and the American crooner Bing Crosby took place on the stage of *Bing Crosby's Merrie Olde Christmas* in September 1977.

Bowie's "Crooner" Digression

For the promotion of "Heroes," his new single that was going to be released on September 23, 1977, David Bowie agreed, quite astonishingly, to take part in a Christmas special with famous crooner Bing Crosby. Bowie knew what pleasure his participation would give his mother, Peggy Jones, who was a great admirer of the singer of "White Christmas." The program was as follows: after singing a Christmas duet with Crosby, Bowie would sing "Heroes" in playback. The *Bing Crosby's Merrie Olde Christmas* broadcast was filmed on September 11, 1977, at Elstree Studios Borehamwood, near London. Everything went off without a hitch, despite some reticence on the part of Bowie; when faced with the prospect of singing the classic "Little Drummer Boy," he called out: "I hate this song. Is there something else I could sing?"[111] The production team was understandably nervous, and everyone was worried. Alan Kohan, the broadcast's scriptwriter, worked to meet Bowie's request of a song change with composers Ian Fraser and Larry Grossman. In just over an hour, the three men wrote "Peace on Earth," which Bowie could sing over the chord sequences of "Little Drummer Boy," as performed by Crosby. The duo worked brilliantly, due in large part to the professionalism of both artists. Despite the crooner's talent, Bowie had a bemused memory of his singing partner: "I was wondering if he was still alive. He was just...not there. He was not there at all. He had the words in front of him. [...] And he looked like a little old orange sitting on a stool. 'Cos he'd been made up very heavily. [...] It was the most bizarre experience. I didn't know anything about him. I just knew my mother liked him."[112]

A Late Release as a Single

Once the program was broadcast, RCA asked for a recording of the song. Unfortunately, as Ted Scott—the sound engineer on the day—explained, everything was recorded on videotape, and the two voices were mixed together on the film itself: "The master tape that [RCA] wanted to use for a pre-Christmas [release had] been erased and as a result, the record company decided to use my on-line mix. So where's my gold disc [...]?"[113] The song finally appeared as a single in December 1982, giving Bing Crosby, who had died from a heart attack on October 14, 1977, a posthumous number three hit.

Single

DAVID BOWIE NARRATES PROKOFIEV'S PETER AND THE WOLF

Sergei Prokofiev / 14:40

Musicians
David Bowie: spoken word
Philadelphia Orchestra: orchestra
Eugene Ormandy: conductor

Recorded
Scottish Rite Cathedral, Philadelphia: October 8, 1975
(music, Side A), March 27 and 29, 1974 (music, Side B)
RCA Studios, New York: November 17 and 19, 1977
(narration, Side A)

Technical Team
Producer: Jay David Saks
Sound Engineer: Paul Goodman

SIDE A: *Peter and the Wolf, Op. 67 (Sergei Prokofiev) / 14:40*
SIDE B: *Young Person's Guide to the Orchestra, Op. 34
(Benjamin Britten) / 40:52*
UK Release on RCA Red Seal: May 2, 1978 (ref. RL 12743;
ARL1 2742)
US Release on RCA Red Seal: May 2, 1978 (ref. RL 12743)
Best Chart Ranking: Did Not Chart

While the relationship between David Bowie and his wife, Angie, was deteriorating, the links that bound the singer to his son, Duncan, seemed to be growing ever stronger. Although immersed in his work, Bowie became inseparable from his little boy, taking temporary custody of Duncan after Angie attempted suicide in 1978, then taking full custody once their divorce was finalized in March 1980. It was with a view of creating something that his toddler could listen to that David agreed to provide the narration for *Peter and the Wolf*, which little Duncan adored. This musical children's story was composed by Sergei Prokofiev in 1936, and RCA had recorded the music two years earlier in Philadelphia under the direction of the American conductor Eugene Ormandy. The actors Peter Ustinov and Alec Guinness had previously declined to provide their voices for this new version of the classic tale, and so RCA turned to David Bowie and asked if he'd like to participate. Following his improbable collaboration with Bing Crosby in September 1977, Bowie surprised his fans once again by crossing over from his usual experimental music to a children's production. But the artist had always affirmed his interest in children's songs. His first album in 1967 includes references to the illustrations of Randolph Caldecott, which were made for young children.

"I'm getting older now," the singer confided to *Rolling Stone* in 1978. "I have a son. I don't want to throw my sanity into art and end up forsaking the people around me. I'd rather stay alive until I'm fifty. [...] At nineteen, I thought I had something important to say. Now, I find it important to communicate with myself. I haven't met David Jones for such a long time that I have to get to know him all over again." [114] In 1987, when Zowie was sixteen, the singer declared: "In the middle seventies, when it really occurred to me that what my son needed more than anything else in the world was a good father. I think that changed everything in my outlook, and it's been a question of me learning to grow up, and probably it's been the best thing that's happened to me, to undertake that kind of responsibility. I have no idea what I would be like if I didn't have a son. I think I'd be a very different person, but stupid." [115]

Bowie recorded his own version of *Peter and the Wolf* specifically for his son.

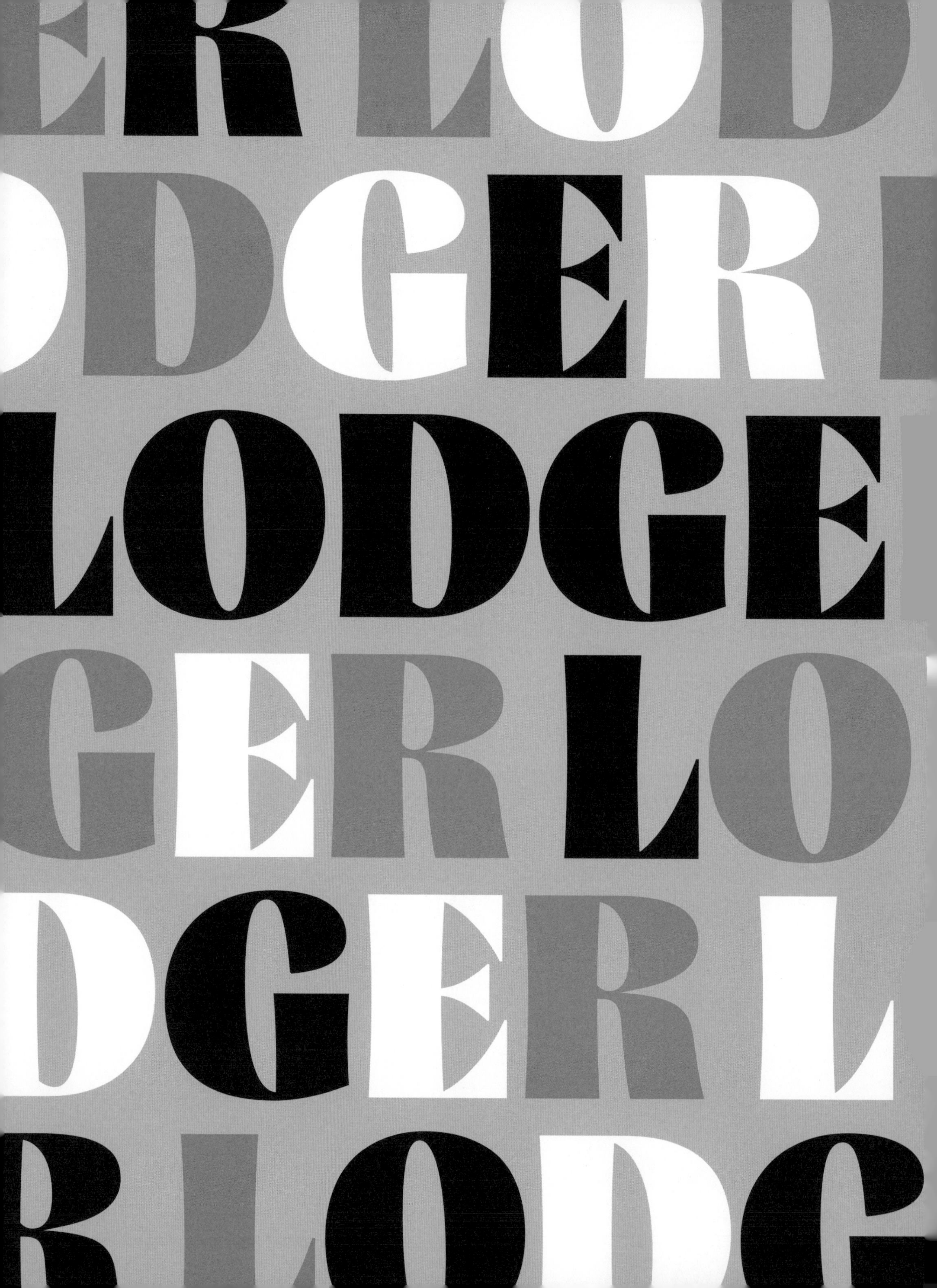
ER LOD
DGER L
LODGE
GER LO
DGER L
R LODG

ALBUM

LODGER

Fantastic Voyage . African Night Flight . Move On . Yassassin . Red Sails . D.J. .
Look Back in Anger . Boys Keep Swinging . Repetition . Red Money

RELEASE DATES
United Kingdom: May 18, 1979
Reference: RCA—BOW LP1; PL 13254
United States: May 18, 1979
Reference: RCA—AQL1-3254
Best UK Chart Ranking: 4
Best US Chart Ranking: 20

David Bowie in front of the
entrance to Studio 54 in New
York on May 24, 1979.

THE END OF THE ENO-BOWIE TRILOGY

Feeling energized by the new backing group that had been accompanying him since March 1978 on his "Isolar II Tour," David Bowie wanted to get back into the studio immediately following concerts given in North America and Europe. Four months on the road had not gotten the better of the singer, who, in September 1978, took his band to Mountain Studios in Montreux, where Tony Visconti had mixed *"Heroes"* in the autumn of 1977. Far from the dark and lugubrious atmosphere of Berlin and its vibrant nightlife, Montreux was a haven of peace where Bowie found solace and serenity. He often stayed at his Swiss residence in Blonay in the company of his son, Duncan.

Mountain Studios is located on the ground floor of the Casino de Montreux, just opposite from Lake Geneva. The casino was ravaged by a fire that occurred during a Frank Zappa concert on December 4, 1971, but the building was reconstructed in 1975 and a small recording facility had been added. During the summer of 1978, Queen recorded the greater part of their *Jazz* album in the new studios. In order to achieve a powerful sound, Freddie Mercury's group had managed to lease the Casino's grand salon, which regularly hosted concerts during the Montreux Jazz Festival. Linked to the control panel on the ground floor, this hall offered the space and depth of sound that Bowie had enjoyed previously at the Hansa Studios in Berlin. Unfortunately, Bowie was unable to benefit from this facility and had to resign himself to using the complex's smaller recording booth. "The studio [...] had such a dead sound," recalled Visconti. "The floor was carpeted, the walls were carpeted and there were acoustic tiles in the ceiling! [...] We tried to get the hall, but we couldn't get it, so we had to record everything in this little, stuffy, hot room. I have so many pictures of Brian Eno topless!"[116] "Once we got a

take," he also said, "everyone scrambled for the doors. They didn't even wanna hear the playback."[102]

From the first sessions, which took place at the beginning of September, the rhythm section—George Murray, Carlos Alomar, and Dennis Davis—worked diligently on laying down the backing tracks. This working method was identical to the one used on Bowie's two previous albums, but Brian Eno now assumed a position of even greater importance within the creative process. It may be that Eno's presence loomed a little too large, as this would be his final collaboration with Bowie.

An Album Recorded Between Two Tours

The structure of the albums *Low* and *"Heroes"*—wherein one side was devoted to relatively straightforward rock 'n' roll songs, while the other side was given over to instrumental experimentation—was abandoned for a more classical track-listing format, where the synthetic textures that Eno was so fond of were coupled with a classic pop-rock writing style. It is no coincidence, then, that the working title of the album was *Planned Accidents*. Once the backing tracks had been recorded, Eno and Bowie decided to collect all the tracks together and to prioritize the serendipitous magic that occurred on the tracks where mistakes had been made, rather than focusing on the songs that had been recorded perfectly and without incident.

The musicians from the "Isolar II Tour"—Sean Mayes on piano, Simon House on violin, and Adrian Belew on guitar—soon joined the team and added their own personal touches to the production. Only keyboard player Roger Powell was not called upon for the new album. Instead, Brian Eno handled most of the synthesizers, and Mayes handled the piano. "Two synthesizers were not

needed," confirmed Mayes. "But I missed him. It felt strange for the band to be incomplete."[117]

Only the instrumental part was recorded in September. In October, the whole team separated so they could take some downtime before getting back on the road. In November and December 1978, they set off on the second phase of the "Isolar II Tour." This phase took them to Australia, New Zealand, and Japan.

Bowie worked on the album's lyrics for several months, and they were finally recorded at the Record Plant in New York City in March 1979. For the first time, the artist did not simply jot down lyrics on paper whenever the mood struck, as usually a matter of urgency and/or spontaneity. For Side 1

of the new album, David was able to take a step back, structure his thoughts, and draw upon the many trips he made in 1978, which included stops in Japan, Australia, and New Zealand, but also Kenya, which he visited with Duncan. The songs on Side 2 of the album focus heavily on critiquing the state of the world. Globalization, the nuclear arms race, the loss of moral values in the music industry—everything seemed to inspire a songwriter who was clearly working at top form. These disparate influences meshed together to form an eclectic album that laid the foundations for the concept of "world music," which would soon be developed by Peter Gabriel in his third eponymous album, in 1980, and by Paul Simon on *Graceland*, in 1986.

Bowie and his musicians at Charles-de-Gaulle airport in 1979. Left to right: Dennis Davis, Sean Mayes, Adrian Belew, Roger Powell, Carlos Alomar, and George Murray.

FOR BOWIE ADDICTS

Visconti and Bowie were visited by Mick Jagger during the mixing of *Lodger* at the Record Plant in New York City, and they gave him an exclusive preview of one of the songs on the album. Not mincing words, the Rolling Stones singer gave frank assessment of what he'd heard before getting up and walking out with the parting words: "OK, I'm leaving. I'm going to Joni Mitchell's session and see if I can sabotage that."[35]

In 2015, when they were working on "★" (*Blackstar*), Visconti surprised Bowie by having him listen to new versions of "Yassassin" and "Red Sails." Once *Blackstar* was complete, the producer was given the green light to remix the other numbers on *Lodger*. Bowie's death the following January prevented Visconti from completing this project.

A Taste for the Unfinished

In order to complete the album, Visconti had to make do with Studio D at the Record Plant in New York. Although they were very disappointed by the sound of the disc, Bowie and Visconti had to stop work on the album in order to meet the deadlines imposed by RCA. "I think Tony and I would both agree that we didn't take enough care mixing," Bowie confessed in 2001. "This had a lot to do with my being distracted by personal events and I think Tony lost heart a little as it never came together as easily as *Low* and '*Heroes*' had."[100]

David Bowie's thirteenth album was released on May 18, 1979. The album sleeve was illustrated with a photograph taken by Brian Duffy and showing the singer on his back, with his nose broken. Here Bowie is reproducing the pose assumed by Austrian painter Egon Schiele in his 1914 *Selbstbildnis als St. Sebastian* (*Self-Portrait as St. Sebastian*), sans arrows. The session took place at Duffy's house in Switzerland, with the makeup artist Antony Clavet, whom Bowie had met on the film set of *Just a Gigolo*, in attendance. The photographer took several pictures, but the singer opted for a blurred Polaroid of relatively poor quality, once again affirming his preference for songs and images that were not studio perfect, but rather a little rough around the edges.

FANTASTIC VOYAGE

David Bowie, Brian Eno / 2:53

Musicians: David Bowie: lead and backing vocals, piano / Carlos Alomar: electric guitar / George Murray: bass / Dennis Davis: drums / Adrian Belew: mandolin / Sean Mayes: piano / Simon House: mandolin / Brian Eno: synthesizers / Tony Visconti: mandolin, backing vocals / **Recorded:** Mountain Studios, Montreux: September 1978 / The Record Plant, New York: March 1979 / **Technical Team:** Producers: David Bowie, Tony Visconti / **Sound Engineers:** Tony Visconti, David Richards (Mountain Studios), Rod O'Brien (Record Plant) / **Assistant Sound Engineers:** Eugene Chaplin (Mountain Studios), Gregg Caruso (Record Plant)

The "fantastic voyage" in the title of this song (initially called "Portrait of an Artist") is a reference to the history of humanity and to the challenges faced by the great leaders of the day—ready to set the world on fire and spill blood in order to defend their self-interests: *Dignity is valuable / But our lives are valuable too.* The songwriters particularly single out Leonid Brezhnev, leader of the USSR, and Jimmy Carter, president of the United States, who they felt were taking the world hostage in an interminable Cold War that was compounded by a merciless nuclear arms race. The world felt on the brink of disaster, and many held their breath to see what would happen next.

Some of the elements of this ballad, including the chord sequences, structure, and tonality, appear again at the end of the disc on the single "Boys Keep Swinging." "Just the tempo and instrumentation are different,"[59] acknowledged Tony Visconti. Behind Sean Mayes's piano, the listener can make out the subtle sounds of the mandolin, played by Tony Visconti, Simon House, and Adrian Belew. The trio had hired three instruments for the occasion from a music shop in Montreux.

"Fantastic Voyage" is one of three songs (with "Wild Is the Wind" and "Changes") that David Bowie performed during his very last appearance onstage. Bowie appeared at the Hammerstein Ballroom in New York City as part of a charity gala raising money for the children of Africa on November 9, 2006.

AFRICAN NIGHT FLIGHT

David Bowie, Brian Eno / 2:55

Musicians: David Bowie: lead and backing vocals / Carlos Alomar: electric guitar / George Murray: bass / Dennis Davis: percussion / Sean Mayes: prepared piano / Brian Eno: programming, backing vocals / **Recorded:** Mountain Studios, Montreux: September 1978 / The Record Plant, New York: March 1979 / **Technical Team:** Producers: David Bowie, Tony Visconti / **Sound Engineers:** Tony Visconti, David Richards (Mountain Studios), Rod O'Brien (Record Plant) / **Assistant Sound Engineers:** Eugene Chaplin (Mountain Studios), Gregg Caruso (Record Plant)

As he explained later in the pages of *Melody Maker*, Bowie was struck by the large number of German fighter pilots that he met during his trip to Kenya. Most of these men, whose careers were now well behind them, spent their days propping up the bars in Kenya's local watering holes. "They are always saying they have been there for seventeen years," said the singer, "and really must go back to Germany. You've got a good idea why they are there in the first place, but they live strange lives flying about in their little Cessnas over the bushland, doing all kinds of strange things."[118] "African Night Flight" is surprising on more than one count. Bowie, who became a great collector of African art in the 1990s, allows himself to experiment stylistically. His lyrics, which includes words in Swahili at 1:01, run at the speed of a Maasai incantation. In order to produce these sounds taken from faraway lands, everyone in the little studio in Montreux had to work creatively. Dennis Davis played percussion; Brian Eno provided some backing vocals and attached some pairs of scissors and other metal objects to Sean Mayes's piano. He also played some complex experimental sounds on David's brand-new Roland CR-78 CompuRhythm, a drum machine that was also heard on the Blondie hit "Heart of Glass" a few months later. To provide this sound of "enraged crickets,"[119] as it was called on the track sheet for the recording, Eno used one of the rhythmical patterns on the machine, which it generated at great speed. A real curiosity in Bowie's larger discography, and a precursor of the *jungle* experimentations that he developed in the 1990s, this track combines saturated guitars, frenzied rhythms, and electronic sound effects to produce a sound that was unlike anything Bowie had done before.

MOVE ON

David Bowie / 3:17

Musicians: David Bowie: lead and backing vocals / Carlos Alomar, Adrian Belew: electric guitar / Tony Visconti: electric guitar, backing vocals / George Murray: bass / Dennis Davis: drums, percussion / Sean Mayes: piano / **Recorded:** Mountain Studios, Montreux: September 1978 / The Record Plant, New York: March 1979 / **Technical Team:** Producers: David Bowie, Tony Visconti / **Sound Engineers:** Tony Visconti, David Richards (Mountain Studios), Rod O'Brien (Record Plant) / **Assistant Sound Engineers:** Eugene Chaplin (Mountain Studios), Gregg Caruso (Record Plant)

Travel was again at the heart of "Move On," whose arrangements seem to reproduce the noise of a train moving at speed, and echoing the lyrics of the song: *Sometimes I feel / The need to move on / So I pack a bag / And move on / Move on / Well I might take a train / Or sail at dawn.*

For the piano section, Bowie asked Sean Mayes to compose a score worthy of Antonín Dvořák—something really grandiose. The keyboard player complied, and hastily recorded his part. "Every number was dispatched quickly and by the end of the day I was left with no clear impression of anything I had played,"[117] he explained. Another important event marked the production of this number. When he wanted to listen to an old recording of "All the Young Dudes," David Bowie played the tape backward by mistake. This effect appealed to him and his producer, and they decided, with the help of Alomar, to write the chord grid as they heard the music on this tape played backward. Then the group played this new sequence of chords. Once recorded, Visconti played it backward; he and Bowie then recorded the backing vocals on top. Finally, the producer played everything backward yet again, and this (complicated) feat was now complete.

YASSASSIN

David Bowie / 4:10

Musicians: David Bowie: lead and backing vocals, synthesizer / Carlos Alomar, Tony Visconti: electric guitar, backing vocals / George Murray: bass, backing vocals / Dennis Davis: drums, backing vocals / Simon House: violin, backing vocals / **Recorded:** Mountain Studios, Montreux: September 1978 / The Record Plant, New York: March 1979 / **Technical Team:** Producers: David Bowie, Tony Visconti / **Sound Engineers:** Tony Visconti, David Richards (Mountain Studios), Rod O'Brien (Record Plant) / **Assistant Sound Engineers:** Eugene Chaplin (Mountain Studios), Gregg Caruso (Record Plant)

In this number, David Bowie pays homage to the Turkish people, who he spent time with during his walks in the Berlin district of Neukölln. "Yassassin" is a song whose arrangements invite the listener on a journey, supported by the virtuoso playing of the violinist Simon House, who executes a masterful solo with a reggae rhythm, a new sound that Bowie and his musicians had begun dabbling in. Six months before recording "Yassassin"—the word means "long life" in Turkish—the singer declared to a *Melody Maker* journalist that reggae was not a genre close to his heart: "I don't like [reggae] very much. I got rather biased against it...I heard an awful lot of it when I was a kid, and I heard even more of it when I was a teenager of the ska and bluebeat variety, and it rather unfortunately—I know it's terribly bigoted—but I find it very hard to come back into liking it again. It still doesn't move me."[120] One must conclude that the singer, seeking to explore new territories once more, and encouraged by Tony Visconti, changed his mind with regard to reggae and achieved a success with this new track. Based on a riff by Carlos Alomar that was very close to the one used in "Fame," the song was officially launched. Visconti had to show the New York musicians how to play on the back beat. "As the Rhythm section was American they were none too familiar with reggae. David and I coached Davis in the art of putting the kick drum on the back beat, where the snare usually goes, and I played a Jamaican 'up-chop' rhythm guitar live with the band."[35] Surprising but exhilarating, this very successful number was not released as a single anywhere except in the Netherlands...and in Turkey. In 1984, David Bowie returned to the reggae style in a very effective duo with Tina Turner on the single "Tonight."

RED SAILS

David Bowie, Brian Eno / 3:43

Musicians: David Bowie: lead and backing vocals / Carlos Alomar, Adrian Belew: electric guitar / George Murray: bass / Dennis Davis: drums / Sean Mayes: piano / Simon House: violin / Brian Eno: synthesizers, backing vocals / Tony Visconti: backing vocals / Stan Harrison: saxophone / **Recorded:** Mountain Studios, Montreux: September 1978 / The Record Plant, New York: March 1979 / **Technical Team:** Producers: David Bowie, Tony Visconti / **Sound Engineers:** Tony Visconti, David Richards (Mountain Studios), Rod O'Brien (Record Plant) / **Assistant Sound Engineers:** Eugene Chaplin (Mountain Studios), Gregg Caruso (Record Plant)

Bowie has never hidden the fact that the opening of "Red Sails" was inspired by the introduction of "Hero" by the band Neu!, which appeared in 1975. However, Bowie later specified that he was more influenced by Harmonia, the side-project of Michael Rother, the group's guitarist, whose song "Monza" does indeed have some similarities with this piece in both its structure and harmonic line. "[With 'Red Sails'], "here we took a German new-music feel," explained David Bowie, "and put against it the idea of a contemporary English [...] Errol Flynn, and put him in the China Sea. We have a lovely cross-reference of cultures. I honestly don't know what it's about.""[118] What is certain is that Adrian Belew, recruited to add an aggressive touch to Bowie's backing ensemble, did not have time to refine his guitar playing before recording the track! "When they brought me in," he recalled, "they already had a lot of songs recorded. [...] They said this to me: 'We want you to [...] put on the headphones, get ready. You'll hear a count-off and we want you to start playing.'"[119] Emphasizing their "planned accidents" strategy, Bowie and Eno refused to let him hear any of the tracks before launching into the recording, or to let him know in advance what key the piece was in: "We just want to get your accidental responses." [119] Once the riffs and other guitar gimmicks had been recorded, Visconti, Eno, and Bowie cut them up for inclusion in the piece, composing this surprising six-string guitar line in an anarchic way, which we hear at 0:59 or 2:37 in the number. "I lucked out on [...] 'Red Sails,' 'cos I started the guitar feeding back and it was right in key,"[47] said the guitarist, not without a touch of humor.

D.J.

David Bowie, Brian Eno, Carlos Alomar / 3:59

Musicians: David Bowie: lead and backing vocals, piano, Chamberlin / Carlos Alomar, Adrian Belew: electric guitar / George Murray: bass / Dennis Davis: drums / **Recorded:** Mountain Studios, Montreux: September 1978 / The Record Plant, New York: March 1979 / **Technical Team:** Producers: David Bowie, Tony Visconti / **Sound Engineers:** Tony Visconti, David Richards (Mountain Studios), Rod O'Brien (Record Plant) / **Assistant Sound Engineers:** Eugene Chaplin (Mountain Studios), Gregg Caruso (Record Plant) / **Side A:** *D.J.* / 3:20 / **Side B:** *Repetition* / 2:59 (UK); *Fantastic Voyage* / 2:53 (US) / **UK Release on RCA:** June 29, 1979 (ref. BOW 3; PB 9412) / **US Release on RCA:** July 2, 1979 (ref. PB-11661) / **Best UK Chart Ranking:** 29 / **Best US Chart Ranking:** Did Not Chart

"D.J." was written to call out radio disc jockeys, who could make or break an artist's career on nothing more than a whim. Most radio DJs had never particularly objected to broadcasting David Bowie's music, and in fact many had always supported him, at least since the days of *Hunky Dory*. But, by 1978, the DJ's power grew as the world suddenly had the urge to dance in places like Studio 54 in New York and Annabel's in London. In this effective song, which forecast the FM hits to come in the 1980s via its straightforward rhythm and catchy refrains, the singer mocks DJs who believe themselves to be all-powerful: "*I am a D.J. / I am what I play / I've got believers / Believing me.*" He was also emphasizing the superficiality of this star status. "This is somewhat cynical, but it's my natural response to disco," Bowie said in 1979. "The DJ is the one who is having ulcers now, not the executives, because if you do the unthinkable thing of putting a record on in a disco not in time, that's it. If you have thirty seconds' silence, your whole career is over."[118] Issued as a single in the summer of 1979, the song also had the advantage of being accompanied by a video from producer David Mallet, which featured David Bowie as a disc jockey. In the video, Bowie's character destroyed his studio and wandered the streets of London receiving spontaneous accolades from passersby (unaware at the time that a film was being shot). This video was a precursor to the video age and thus paved the way for the all-powerful television music channels that took hold of the popular culture in the decades that followed. In many ways, the video for "D.J." served as a metaphorical passing of the baton from nightclubs to MTV.

LOOK BACK IN ANGER

David Bowie, Brian Eno / 3:08

Musicians

David Bowie: lead and backing vocals
Carlos Alomar: electric guitar
George Murray: bass
Dennis Davis: drums, congas
Sean Mayes: piano
Brian Eno: synthesizers
Tony Visconti: backing vocals

Recorded

Mountain Studios, Montreux: September 1978
The Record Plant, New York: March 1979

Technical Team

Producers: David Bowie, Tony Visconti
Sound Engineers: Tony Visconti, David Richards (Mountain Studios), Rod O'Brien (Record Plant)
Assistant Sound Engineers: Eugene Chaplin (Mountain Studios), Gregg Caruso (Record Plant)

SIDE A: *Look Back in Anger* / 3:08
SIDE B: *Repetition* / 2:59
US Release on RCA: August 20, 1979 (ref. PB-11724)
Best Chart Ranking: Did Not Chart

As the music video became increasingly important in promoting a musician's new album, Bowie called upon the producer David Mallet to help bring his song to life. Taking his inspiration from *The Picture of Dorian Gray* by Oscar Wilde, the video shows a Bowie physically transformed by a portrait he is painting.

Genesis

When the British division of RCA released "Boys Keep Swinging" in April 1979, the American branch of the company rejected the single, which they considered to be indecent—like "John, I'm Only Dancing" in 1972, the label's objection had to do with Bowie's metaphorical lyrics, which were far too sexual for their tastes, and which they felt would not appeal to the American public. "Look Back in Anger" was the single they preferred, and in August 1979, radio stations everywhere broadcast this song, with its incredible rhythm driven by the drumbeat of Dennis Davis in top form. This song adopts the title of a 1956 play by John Osborne, which focused on the dysfunctional relationship of a traditional British couple.

Production

During the working sessions, Brian Eno imposed a mode of working that the musicians had grown used to after their experiences on *Low*. He wrote a list of chords on a chart, which he showed to Alomar and Murray whenever he saw fit to do so. They were then required to play the chords, regardless of what bar they were at. Alomar, who had solid academic training in music theory, was strongly opposed to this way of working. "This is bullshit, this sucks, this sounds stupid!"[99] he exclaimed. But he softened his view a few years later: "I mean, some of it worked, some of it didn't, but quite honestly it did take me out of my comfort zone, and it did make me leave my frustration at what I was doing and totally look at it from another different point of view."[109] The guitarist, who was more flexible in approach than he appeared, and was always receptive to whatever Bowie had to say, was also asked to write a solo, which appears on the track at 1:16. But the six-string prodigy wanted to distance himself from the overly flamboyant guitar solos of the time, where musicians became technicians and were expected to constantly top themselves in order to please the crowds. "If I'm going to take a solo, I'm going to take a rhythm-guitar solo," he explained. "In this, John Lennon influenced me. I really appreciated what he did with rhythm guitar."[29] As he had done in the bridge passage in "Young Americans," Alomar once again provided an instant funk number that was very far from the deluge of notes provided by Earl Slick on "Stay," for example.

Single

BOYS KEEP SWINGING

David Bowie, Brian Eno / 3:16

Musicians
David Bowie: lead and backing vocals, electric guitar
Adrian Belew: electric guitar
Tony Visconti: bass, backing vocals
Carlos Alomar: drums
Brian Eno: piano
Simon House: violin

Recorded
Mountain Studios, Montreux: September 1978
The Record Plant, New York: March 1979

Technical Team
Producers: David Bowie, Tony Visconti
Sound Engineers: Tony Visconti, David Richards (Mountain Studios), Rod O'Brien (Record Plant)
Assistant Sound Engineers: Eugene Chaplin (Mountain Studios), Gregg Caruso (Record Plant)

SIDE A: *Boys Keep Swinging* / 3:16
SIDE B: *Fantastic Voyage* / 2:53
UK Release on RCA: April 27, 1979 (ref. BOW 2; PB 1585)
Best Chart Ranking: 7

Genesis

While "Boys Keep Swinging," with its very Motown-inspired intro, was offered as a single to the British public in April 1979, the United States division of RCA preferred to release "Look Back in Anger" as its single. This was essential in order for the Americans to endorse a music video in which David Bowie, who plays the part of three backing singers, appears in drag.

During the recording of this song's lyrics in New York during March 1979, Bowie received a visit from Adrian Belew, who came to lay down some guitar overdubs. Bowie confided to Belew that the lyrics, which emphasize the advantages of being a young man in the 1970s, had been written in his honor. "I think he saw me as a naïve person who just enjoyed life," explained Belew. "I was thrilled with that."[104]

Production

If the faultless precision of drummer Dennis Davis seems to be a big gap in this effective single, this is because Bowie wanted the song to have a spontaneous, loose feel, which the professionals surrounding him were not really capable of producing. "Our methodology was perfection. That was the problem," explained Carlos Alomar. "I couldn't get that lack of syncopation from George and Dennis because they were so locked. They couldn't play like fourteen-year-old kids playing in a garage would. And that's what David wanted."[102] To satisfy his desire for musical youthfulness, David Bowie asked each of the band members to swap their instruments with the person next to them. Alomar went behind the drums (during the song one can hear the musician's involuntary changes in rhythmic patterns), Eno took the piano, Bowie played the guitar, and Dennis Davis played the bass, which was deleted in the final mixing when Visconti decided to re-record the track himself. The result was a success, particularly due to the enthusiasm of the musicians, who were won over by this joyful idea of Bowie's, and thus gave the single an amateurish, friendly aspect that makes it all the more enjoyable.

Adrian Belew, the indispensable guitarist on the *Lodger* album and the "Isolar II Tour," shown here onstage at the Convention Center in Fresno, April 2, 1978.

REPETITION

David Bowie / 2:59

Musicians: David Bowie: lead and backing vocals / Carlos Alomar, Adrian Belew: electric guitar / Dennis Davis: drums / George Murray: bass / Simon House: violin / Roger Powell : synthesizers / **Recorded:** Mountain Studios, Montreux: September 1978 / The Record Plant, New York: March 1979 / **Technical Team:** Producers: David Bowie, Tony Visconti / **Sound Engineers:** Tony Visconti, David Richards (Mountain Studios), Rod O'Brien (Record Plant) / **Assistant Sound Engineers:** Eugene Chaplin (Mountain Studios), Gregg Caruso (Record Plant)

In addressing the theme of domestic violence, David Bowie paints a picture of a man whose life has passed him by and who makes his wife pay for this, although she is loving and devoted: *"Johnny is a man / And he's bigger than her / I guess the bruises won't show / If she wears long sleeves."*

Still keen on the idea of achieving spontaneity in his music, the singer decided to superimpose Adrian Belew's less perfected guitar tracks as a way to create a chaotic carpet of sound. Then, during the overdub sessions in March 1979, Bowie and Visconti asked Roger Powell to add some synthesizer tracks. The singer was very particular about what he wanted for this: "Can you make a sound like bodies falling behind doors?"[117] The keyboard player did what was required, and using layers and effects of all kinds, he supported the violin of Simon House and added some anguished textures to the song, which are particularly noticeable at the end of the track. In 1996, during the recording of the broadcast *ChangesNowBowie* for the BBC, Bowie delivered a convincing acoustic version of this song, accompanied by bassist Gail Ann Dorsey, guitarist Reeves Gabrels, and Mark Plati on keyboards.

RED MONEY

David Bowie, Carlos Alomar / 4:16

Musicians: David Bowie: lead and backing vocals, electric guitar / Carlos Alomar, Phil Palmer: electric guitar / Dennis Davis: drums / George Murray: bass / **Recorded:** Château d'Hérouville, France: July 1976 / Mountain Studios, Montreux: September 1978 / The Record Plant, New York: March 1979 / **Technical Team:** Producers: David Bowie, Tony Visconti / **Sound Engineers:** Tony Visconti, David Richards (Mountain Studios), Rod O'Brien (Record Plant), Laurent Thibault (Château d'Hérouville) / **Assistant Sound Engineers:** Eugene Chaplin (Mountain Studios), Gregg Caruso (Record Plant)

What could be better to conclude this third section of the misnamed Berlin Trilogy than paying homage to Bowie's friend Iggy Pop, from whom he had become inseparable? "Red Money" appears at the end of the album and is therefore the song that serves as the unofficial end of this trilogy. In September 1978, Tony Visconti, who was also responsible for the mixing on *The Idiot*, retrieved the recording of "Sister Midnight," which was written by Alomar and Bowie and recorded for Iggy Pop at Château d'Hérouville during the summer of 1976. He slightly slowed down the tape on which the song had been recorded, and then he revived Alomar's syncopated rhythm. We also find the sonorous guitar of Phil Palmer, whose fuzzy sound remains mysteriously mesmerizing, even to the other musicians who were there on the day of recording. A young session guitarist at the time, Palmer simply followed the instructions of producer Bowie and sound engineer Laurent Thibault. "I remember they got me plugging in to all kinds of weird and wonderful stuff,"[121] he later testified. In March 1979, David Bowie recorded a new vocal line and gave the song a second life, repeating the curious line "Project cancelled." So ends *Lodger*, and so ends a golden decade for David Bowie.

SINGLE

Alabama Song / Space Oddity (1979 Version)
UK Release on RCA: February 15, 1980 (ref. BOW 5; PB 9510) / Best Chart Ranking: 23

ALABAMA SONG

Kurt Weill, Bertolt Brecht / 3:51

Musicians: David Bowie: lead and backing vocals / Carlos Alomar: electric guitar / Dennis Davis: drums / George Murray: bass / Sean Mayes: piano / Roger Powell: synthesizer / **Recorded:** Good Earth Studios, London: July 2, 1978 / **Technical Team:** Producers: David Bowie, Tony Visconti / **Sound Engineer:** Tony Visconti

On July 1, 1978, the European part of the "Isolar II Tour" came to an end in front of nearly twenty thousand spectators at the Earls Court Exhibition Centre in London. Before closing the concert with "Station to Station," "TCV 15," and "Stay," as he had done many times during the tour, Bowie performed a version of "Alabama Song," written by Kurt Weill and Bertolt Brecht in 1927 for their musical spectacle *Mahagonny Songspiel*. The singer decided to produce his own version of the number that had been popularized by the Doors in 1967 on their first eponymous album. On Sunday July 2, 1978, he went with his musicians to Tony Visconti's studio on Dean Street, and together they quickly recorded the song. "David had some new ideas for the drumming," recalled Sean Mayes. "He wanted Dennis to play very freely against the rhythm to give an unstable, insane atmosphere to the track."[117] But the musicians proved incapable of settling into Davis's unsettling rhythm and ended up recording without him; he then added his syncopated drums part later to provide the desired effect. The number appeared as a single on February 15, 1980, in the United Kingdom, just as Bowie was deep into the production of his fourteenth album, *Scary Monsters (And Super Creeps)*. Despite an audacious production, the destabilizing arrangements proposed by Bowie did not help this 45 rpm get off the ground, and it stagnated at twenty-third place on the British charts.

SPACE ODDITY (1979 VERSION)

David Bowie / 4:47

Musicians: David Bowie: vocals, twelve-string acoustic guitar / Zaine Griff: bass / Andy Duncan: drums / Andy Clark: piano / **Recorded:** Good Earth Studios, London: September 1979 / **Technical Team:** Producers: David Bowie, Tony Visconti / **Sound Engineer:** Tony Visconti

To close the 1970s, British radio presenter Kenny Everett was entrusted with a television program that would be broadcast on December 31, 1979. The *Will Kenny Everett Make It to 1980?* show was produced by David Mallet, who had already been responsible for Bowie's music videos "D.J.," "Boys Keep Swinging," and "Look Back in Anger." The producer asked the singer to perform a new version of one his most famous hits. "He wanted 'Space Oddity,'" the artist explained. "I agreed as long as I could do it again without all its trappings and do it strictly with three instruments. Having played it with just an acoustic guitar onstage early on, I was always surprised as how powerful it was just as a song, without all the strings and synthesizers."[122] When production of the broadcast began in September 1979, Tony Visconti introduced Bowie to the singer and bassist Zaine Griff, a talented artist whose album *Ashes and Diamonds* Visconti had just produced. Bowie liked this young man and suggested recording a few songs with him. Griff agreed and suggested getting some of his own musicians involved, including the drummer Andy Duncan, and one of his keyboard players. There are various opinions concerning the name of this musician. Rumor often has it that this was Hans Zimmer, who was indeed Griff's pianist at the time, and who would go on to compose some of the most famous film scores of all time, including the scores for everything from *True Romance* to *Inception*. Zaine Griff said that it was actually Andy Clark who was present on the day, and that on this occasion it was Bowie who stole his keyboard player for his next opus: "And then he stole my keyboard player."[101] Either way, the team met at the beginning of September at Visconti's Good Earth Studios and reinterpreted three Bowie songs: "Space Oddity," "Rebel Rebel," and "Panic in Detroit." It was this refined version of the Major Tom classic that was broadcast as part of the Everett program, and "Panic in Detroit" appeared on the bonus tracks of the reissue for *Scary Monsters (And Super Creeps)* that came out from Rykodisc in 1992. The new version of "Rebel Rebel" remains unreleased to this day.

Singer Zaine Griff was a temporary bassist who played on "Panic in Detroit" in 1979.

I PRAY, OLE

? / 3:54

Musicians: David Bowie: vocals / Unidentified Musicians: electric guitar, synthesizer, drums, bass / **Recorded:** Mountain Studios, Montreux: 1979 (recorded) and 1991 (overdubs and mixing) / **Technical Team:** Producer: David Bowie / **Sound Engineer:** David Richards

While "I Pray, Olé" was a relic from the *Lodger* period, its conception was shrouded in mystery, as were "All Saints," "Some Are," and "Abdulmajid." The only certainty was the presence of David Richards, the sound engineer of Mountain Studios in Montreux, who was there for the mixing of the song in 1991. Offered as a bonus on the re-release of *Lodger* that same year, "I Pray, Olé" has all the features of Bowie's Tin Machine period. Mixed between the two albums, it has the machinelike sound of drums that were ever-present on the rock albums of the early 1990s, represented by the masters of this genre, Nine Inch Nails, whose Bowie-esque influences have repeatedly been emphasized. Once again, with this track now completely anchored in a new decade, Bowie was reborn from his own ashes, embracing a whole new range of musical styles: industrial rock, electro, techno, and more.

PANIC IN DETROIT (1979 VERSION)

David Bowie / 2:58

Musicians: David Bowie: vocals, twelve-string acoustic guitar / Steve Bolton: electric guitar / Zaine Griff: bass / Andy Duncan: drums / Andy Clark: piano / Tony Visconti: robotic voice / **Recorded:** Good Earth Studios, London: September 1979 / **Technical Team:** Producers: David Bowie, Tony Visconti / **Sound Engineer:** Tony Visconti

In September 1979, David Bowie brought together a powerful team inside Tony Visconti's small Dean Street studio, and together they recorded a new version of "Space Oddity" that was intended for the December 31 Kenny Everett program. During this session, Bowie decided to immortalize two other numbers with the singer Zaine Griff (on bass) and the rest of his musicians. "Rebel Rebel" and "Panic in Detroit" were recorded during the same session. The first recording remains un-issued, but the second was offered up to fans as a bonus on the re-release of *Scary Monsters (And Super Creeps)* in 1992. Without the vocal harmonies of the original 1973 version, which had been provided by Juanita Franklin and Linda Lewis, the song lost its appeal. The rather lackluster production also did not serve this piece well.

SCARY MONSTERS (AND SUPER CREEPS)

ALBUM

SCARY MONSTERS (AND SUPER CREEPS)

It's No Game (No. 1) . Up the Hill Backwards . Scary Monsters (And Super Creeps) .
Ashes to Ashes . Fashion . Teenage Wildlife . Scream Like a Baby . Kingdom Come .
Because You're Young . It's No Game (No. 2)

RELEASE DATES
United Kingdom: September 12, 1980
Reference: RCA—BOW LP 2; PL 13647
United States: September 12, 1980
Reference: RCA—AQL1-3647
Best UK Chart Ranking: 1
Best US Chart Ranking: 12

A POP ALBUM CRAFTED FOR THE MEDIA

The *Lodger* album was not followed by a world tour, and the only real effective promotion for the album was the band's high-profile performance on *Saturday Night Live* alongside the flamboyant Klaus Nomi and Joey Arias on December 15, 1979. In general, *Lodger* was frequently misunderstood and even disliked by the general public. Eventually deciding to turn his back on the album, which he believed had been produced too quickly, Bowie returned to the studio in February 1980, determined to attack the new decade and to produce an album that would meet his exacting standards. He summoned the D.A.M. Trio (Dennis Davis, Carlos Alomar, and George Murray) to Power Station Studios in New York to work on the backing tracks for the nascent album. Several dozen tracks were presented to the musicians, in a more polished mode of working than the relative free-form structure used on the previous three albums. While Alomar and his colleagues undeniably brought their own personal touch to these tracks, Bowie had taken the time to think about the structure of his songs and the more commercial artistic direction he wanted to take with his work. Bowie's goal was clear: He wanted to launch an all-out musical attack on TV and radio stations around the world.

Back to Basics

Now distancing himself from Brian Eno in favor of appeasing his own artistic temperament, David Bowie returned to what he considered to be the fundamentals of musical composition. Abandoning experimentation and overintellectualization of his musical production in favor of spontaneity and creative flow, David created what was to become one of his most popular albums. For three weeks, he locked himself up with Tony Visconti at Power Station Studios, where he benefited from the technical support of in-house sound engineer Larry Alexander, who was unrivaled in his mastery of the state-of-the-art equipment at this internationally renowned studio. In the studio next door, Bruce Springsteen was recording his double album *The River*. "It was a wonderful, wonderful time," recalled Carlos Alomar. "Everybody was happy. On a family level it was very rich, and on an artistic level too. You'd have John Lennon coming over, you'd have Art Garfunkel coming over, artists, so many other people. We were having a great time."[102] As usual, once the backing tracks had been recorded, Bowie invited various musicians to add their own personal contributions to the recordings. Roy Bittan, the pianist working with Bruce Springsteen, was featured on three tracks (he previously appeared on *Station to Station*), as was Lou Reed's guitarist Chuck Hammer, a master of guitar experimentation who played a Roland GR-300 Guitar Synthesizer—an electric guitar with a sensor that converts notes into MIDI signals. This instrument enabled the musician to produce all types of sounds, which would eventually find their way onto "Ashes to Ashes" and "Teenage Wildlife." Adrian Belew was dropped from the recording sessions in spite of the fact that he had already been paid an advance for Bowie's next album. Learning about the album while on tour with Talking Heads, the guitarist remained philosophical. "It's not surprising for artists like David to do that," he later explained, "someone who's ever changing and moving forward. [...] I respect that, of course, but at the time it was a big disappointment."[29]

Distinguished Guests

In May 1980, David Bowie joined Visconti at his Good Earth Studios on Dean Street, in London, to continue recording *Scary Monsters (And Super Creeps)*. According to legend, the title was inspired by a Kellogg's advertising

While Bowie and his team were working on *Scary Monsters* at Power Station Studios in New York, Bruce Springsteen was recording *The River* at the same venue. The musicians would often get together at lunch, and on one occasion while he was tucking into his pork ribs alongside the Boss, Dennis Davis, Bowie's drummer, actually turned to Springsteen and asked, "What band are you in?"[59]

campaign that had appeared on cereal boxes everywhere: Scary Monsters and Super Heroes. Once again, various guests were invited to contribute. Constantly experimenting with the sounds delivered by his Gibson Les Paul, guitarist Robert Fripp delivered thunderous riffs on six tracks featured on the album. Pete Townshend, of the Who, provided his famous windmill arm movements on "Because You're Young," adding his powerful and inimitable playing style to the album. The vocal tracks were added last, and the disc was finally ready for release.

A Single to Step into the 1980s

In August 1980, the single "Ashes to Ashes" preceded the release of David Bowie's fourteenth album. The album itself was released on September 12, 1980, and it was greeted by an enthusiastic press and by fans who were already declaring it a masterpiece. The artist pushed himself fearlessly into the 1980s with tracks featuring innovative and stylish music videos, including "Fashion" and "Ashes to Ashes." These songs were tailor-made for MTV, which was now *the* pop culture trendsetter. The cover of *Scary Monsters (And Super Creeps)* features a strange clown that is reminiscent of Bowie's *Pierrot in Turquoise* era, when the singer honed his mime skills alongside Lindsay Kemp. Costume designer Natasha Korniloff, who was also Bowie's ex-girlfriend, designed the clown costume David wore during the photo shoot organized by Brian Duffy. The portrait, immortalized in black and white, was then colored by artist Edward Bell. On the back of the album, relics from the covers of the previous three albums clearly establish that those records are a thing of the past. Bowie is a new man, determined to seize a new crown as the conqueror of the airwaves.

The *Elephant Man* Adventure

In spite of the success of the album, which took the number one spot on the British charts on September 27, 1980 (and stayed on the charts for a full thirty-two weeks!), the singer decided not to promote his album with a tour, which the fans had been waiting for impatiently. Preferring to focus on his acting career, Bowie soon set his sights on an ambitious new project. In February, he attended a performance of the play *The Elephant Man* in New York City. Adapted from the memoirs of Dr. Frederick Treves and directed by Jack Hofsiss, the play's leading actor, Philip Anglim, had to leave the production in July 1980. Bowie quickly found himself

with an unexpected and attractive proposal. "He [Hofsiss] asked if I would take over the role," Bowie would later explain. "I had never met him and I didn't know he knew anything about me, but he had apparently seen a few of my concerts and felt I'd be able to undertake the role successfully. I said, 'If you want to take the risk, I'd love to take the plunge.'"[123] "I was familiar with his music [...]," the director explained. "But the piece of work he did that was most helpful in making the decision was *The Man Who Fell to Earth*, in which I thought he was wonderful, and in which the character he played had an isolation similar to the Elephant Man's. His perceptions about the part and his interest were all so good that we decided to investigate the possibility of doing it."[124] Always ready to take a risk for his art, the singer, who had only twenty-four hours to give his answer, said yes and joined the cast of the play in San Francisco for several weeks of rehearsals in July 1980. The play's premiere took place at the Center of the Performing Arts in Denver on July 29, 1980. A huge success, the play then moved to the Blackstone Theatre in Chicago, where it ran from August 5 to August 31, and then it played at the Booth Theatre on Broadway from September 23 to January 3, 1981. It was yet another success for Bowie, who would soon appear again on the silver screen, playing himself in the movie *Christiane F. (Christiane F.—Wir Kinder vom Bahnhof Zoo)*.

The End of an Era

At the end of the *Elephant Man* tour, a dramatic event upset the balance that David Bowie had struck between recording albums and developing his acting career. On December 8, 1980, at around 11 p.m., John Lennon was murdered by a fan in front of the Dakota, the apartment building where he lived with Yoko Ono. The day after the murder, Bowie performed in front of three empty seats facing the stage: that of his dead friend, his widow, and his would-be murderer. The event was a huge blow for the artist, who left the United States shortly afterward and isolated himself in Montreux, far from a world that was becoming increasingly violent. Bowie later confided, "It was awful, just awful. A whole piece of my life seemed to have been taken away; a whole reason for being a singer and a songwriter seemed to be removed from me. It was almost like a warning."[53] It would take time for his wounds to heal and for Bowie to find the inspiration to write and to eventually return to the stage. Nevertheless, his eventual return was nothing short of spectacular.

1980

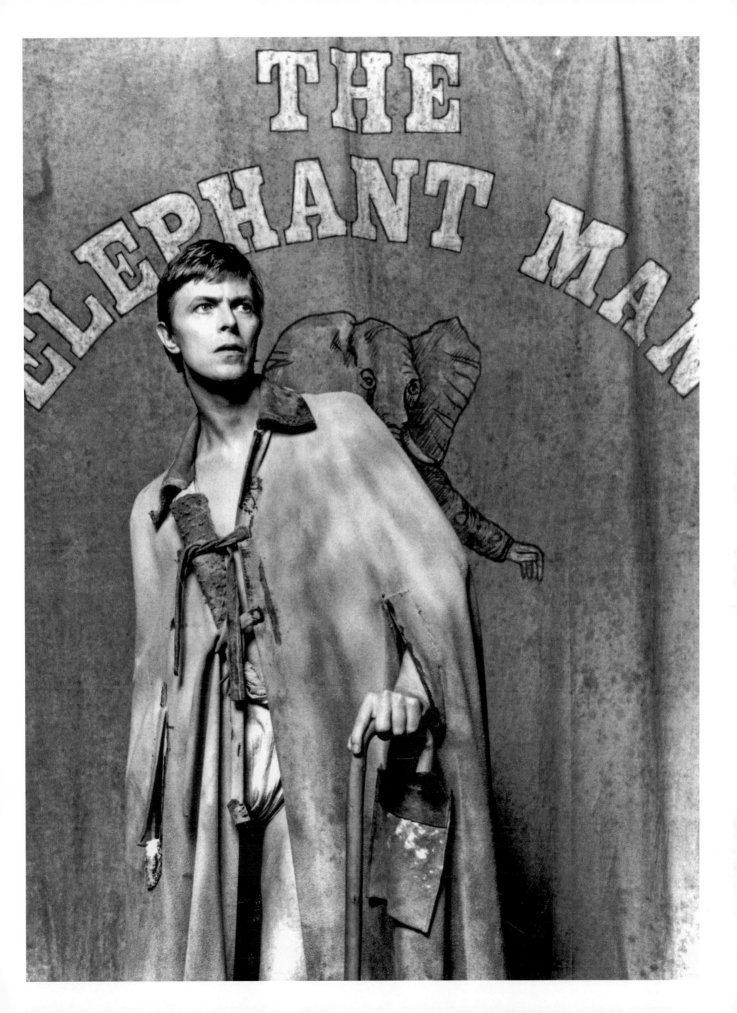

IT'S NO GAME (NO. 1)

David Bowie / 4:16

Musicians: David Bowie: lead and backing vocals, yells, synthesizer / Carlos Alomar, Robert Fripp: electric guitar / George Murray: bass / Dennis Davis: drums / Tony Visconti: backing vocals / Michi Hirota: spoken voice / **Recorded:** Power Station Studios, New York: February 15 1980–early March 1980 / **Good Earth Studios, London:** April–June 1980 / **Technical Team:** Producers: David Bowie, Tony Visconti / **Sound Engineers:** Tony Visconti, Larry Alexander (Power Station Studios) / **Assistant Sound Engineers:** Chris Porter (Good Earth Studios)

In May 1970, as he was about to record the vocal portion of *The Man Who Sold the World*, Bowie recorded a demo of a song he called "Tired of My Life," with his partner in crime at the time, Mick Ronson, on backing vocals. The song remained at the demo stage before finally reappearing in 1980 in the form of a new track called "It's No Game," which features twice on *Scary Monsters (And Super Creeps)*. The song first appears as an introduction to the album, and then appears again at the album's conclusion. "It's No Game (No. 1)" introduces us to Bowie's new girlfriend: Michi Hirota, the Japanese actress playing in Oscar Hammerstein II and Richard Rodgers's hit musical *The King and I* at the London Palladium. Bowie had the text of his song translated by a bilingual friend, Hisashi Miura, and his initial idea was for Michi Hirota to sing the lyrics in Japanese, alternating with his own lyrics in English. During the recording session at Good Earth Studios in May 1980, the actress felt that the literal translation was not tuneful enough, nor was it poetic enough. The singer then asked her to recite her text, without taking into account the melody, and he added a few yells that turn this first title of the record into something extremely distinctive and memorable. At 2:52, Robert Fripp lets rip with a flamboyant guitar solo, for which Bowie asked him to imagine having a guitar duel with legendary bluesman B. B. King. The result is an imposing and powerful solo, as disconcerting as the track itself.

UP THE HILL BACKWARDS

David Bowie / 3:14

Musicians: David Bowie: lead and backing vocals / Carlos Alomar, Robert Fripp: electric guitar / Tony Visconti: acoustic guitar, backing vocals / George Murray: bass / Dennis Davis: drums / Roy Bittan: piano / Lynn Maitland: backing vocals / **Recorded:** Power Station Studios, New York: February 15 1980–early March 1980 / **Good Earth Studios, London:** April–June 1980 / **Technical Team:** Producers: David Bowie, Tony Visconti / **Sound Engineers:** Tony Visconti, Larry Alexander (Power Station Studios) / **Assistant Sound Engineers:** Chris Porter (Good Earth Studios) / **Side A:** *Up the Hill Backwards* / 3:14 / **Side B:** *Crystal Japan* / 3:26 / **UK Release on RCA:** March 1981 (ref. BOW 9; PB 9671) / **Best Chart Ranking:** 32

The fourth single off the album, "Up the Hill Backwards" (whose working title was "Cameras in Brooklyn") benefitted from meticulous writing and melodious verses, which could have given Bowie another number one hit in the United Kingdom alongside "Ashes to Ashes." The lyrics of this single include some borrowings from an essay on Dadaism by German painter Hans Richter, which was originally published in 1964 and titled "Dada: Art and Anti-Art." The phrase *The vacuum created by the arrival of freedom / and the possibilities it seems to offer*, in particular, was singled out. Recently divorced, Bowie was coming to terms with his newly acquired freedom—he was free from the hassles of his conflict with Angie, but nevertheless marked by the failure of his marriage.

The song begins with a Bo Diddley–style rhythm, played on acoustic guitar by Tony Visconti in 7/4. The producer-guitarist himself had difficulty keeping up with this unnatural rhythm. "I [was] clenching my teeth during the performance," he explained, "consciously counting all the time."[35] Robert Fripp's dissonant guitar rapidly finds its place, and then the song takes a new turn when the verse begins, sung in unison by Tony Visconti, Bowie, and one of Bowie's friends, Lynn Maitland. This was a first for the singer, who shared the spotlight with his backing singers, offering an effective and catchy choral track.

David and Angie's divorce was finalized in 1980.

SCARY MONSTERS (AND SUPER CREEPS)

David Bowie / 5:11

Musicians: David Bowie: lead and backing vocals, synthesizer / Carlos Alomar, Robert Fripp: electric guitar / Tony Visconti: acoustic guitar / George Murray: bass / Dennis Davis: drums / Chris Porter: backing vocals / Tony Visconti: programming / **Recorded:** Power Station Studios, New York: February 15 1980–early March 1980 / Good Earth Studios, London: April–June 1980 / **Technical Team:** Producers: David Bowie, Tony Visconti / Sound Engineers: Tony Visconti, Larry Alexander (Power Station Studios) / Assistant Sound Engineers: Chris Porter (Good Earth Studios) / Side A: *Scary Monsters (And Super Creeps)* / 3:29 / Side B: *Because You're Young* / 4:52 / UK Release on RCA: January 2, 1981 (ref. BOW 8; PB 9654) / Best Chart Ranking: 20

And now we come to the album's title track, whose introduction, played on acoustic guitar by Visconti, along with its aerial tones, would go on to have an influence on the Smiths' "Bigmouth Strikes Again" in 1986. The lyrics, once again elusive, portray a jealous and mysterious young woman whose attributes seem close to those of Angie:

"When I looked in her eyes they were blue but nobody home / She could've been a killer if she didn't walk the way she do, and she do / She opened strange doors that we'd never close again." To match these enigmatic lyrics, the song offers an equally enigmatic production: What is that bark you hear at the beginning of the song and then again during Robert Fripp's breathtaking solo? It's an amusing use of a small synthesizer called the Wasp, designed by the British company Electronic Dream Plant in 1978. After recording a bark-like descending bass line on the keyboard, Tony Visconti placed a microphone on the snare drum, which he then plugged into the WASP trigger, an element that allows a signal to be triggered from audio information (in this case the snare drum). Dennis Davis could then launch the bass line with each beat. What Visconti hadn't foreseen was that the sensor would pick up a wide range of information at the same time, and that each element of the drum kit would then trigger the bark randomly!

Single

ASHES TO ASHES
David Bowie / 4:22

Musicians
David Bowie: lead and backing vocals
Carlos Alomar: electric guitar
Chuck Hammer: Roland GR-300 Guitar Synthesizer
George Murray: bass
Dennis Davis: drums
Roy Bittan: piano
Andy Clark: synthesizers
Tony Visconti: percussion

Recorded
Power Station Studios, New York: February 15, 1980–early March 1980
Good Earth Studios, London: April–June 1980

Technical Team
Producers: David Bowie, Tony Visconti
Sound Engineers: Tony Visconti, Larry Alexander (Power Station Studios)
Assistant Sound Engineers: Chris Porter (Good Earth Studios)

SIDE A: *Ashes to Ashes* / 3:35
SIDE B: *Move On* / 3:17 (UK); *It's No Game (Part 1)* / 4:16 (US)
UK Release on RCA: August 1, 1980 (ref. BOW 6; PB 9575)
US Release on RCA: August 1, 1980 (ref. PB-12078)
Best UK Chart Ranking: 1
Best US Chart Ranking: Did Not Chart

In 1991, Erasure, one of the leading British techno-pop bands, shot the video for their single "Chorus" on Hastings Beach, in homage to Bowie's "Ashes to Ashes." They used the same early computer graphics palette provided by Quantel Paintbox, which, among other things, allowed for colorization of the videos.

Genesis
Even if the comparison is probably limited to a shared rhythmic pattern and some harmonic similarities, David Bowie confessed that he was inspired by a song he enjoyed as a child: "Inchworm," which was originally composed by Frank Loesser and performed by Danny Kaye in 1952 as part of the musical *Hans Christian Andersen*. "I was [a child] when that came out," he later revealed. "The chords were some of the first I learned on a guitar. They're remarkable chords, very melancholic. 'Ashes to Ashes' is influenced by that. It's childlike and melancholic in that children's story way."[47] His song "is an ode to childhood, if you like, a popular nursery rhyme," the singer explained, before adding, with a burst of laughter, "It's about space men becoming junkies."[122] One of these astronauts is, of course, Major Tom from "Space Oddity," whose adventures Bowie takes up again here, recounting his decline due to excessive drug use. *"Do you remember a guy that's been / In such an early song? / I've heard a rumor from Ground Control,"* he asks the listener, before informing us of the state of our hero: *"I ain't got no money and I ain't got no hair,"* and then concluding with *"We know Major Tom's a junkie."* Bowie identifies with the loneliness of the astronaut from 1969, and it is a good bet that through "Ashes to Ashes" (which would become one of the fans' favorite songs), David Bowie is evoking the time when his addiction to cocaine caused him to lose his footing, both personally and professionally.

A special mention must be made of the video, which was filmed by David Mallet on the beach at Hastings, in the south of England. The images, which have an old-fashioned charm today, were hailed at the time for their modernity and the ingenuity of the director, who used the latest colorization techniques to produce a visual spectacle that would influence an entire wave of so-called New Romantics. This movement, championed by groups such as Spandau Ballet, Visage, and Duran Duran, was characterized by elegant clothing and makeup that underlined the mysterious aspect of its most famous ambassadors. It has been said that "Ashes to Ashes" is the song that gave birth to this entire movement.

An iconic image by Brian Duffy showing Bowie in his clown costume designed by Natasha Korniloff.

Production

This track, whose working title was "People Are Turning to Gold," offers many surprises. First of all, the introductory piano riff that carries the song is played by Roy Bittan, the Bruce Springsteen keyboardist who was recording Springsteen's *The River* at the same time that Bowie was recording his own album at Power Station Studios. Bowie was eager for Bittan to play a Wurlitzer—an electric piano equipped with a tremolo function that, as its name suggests, makes the notes vibrate by varying their volume at a speed predefined by the user. But the instrument that was delivered to the studios didn't work, and it was too late to find another one. So Visconti decided to have Bittan play on an acoustic piano, to which he simply added an Eventide Instant Flanger effect. The bass playing is also surprising, with George Murray offering the listener a *slap* that's a pleasure to hear on a Bowie track and that underlines once again the artists's soul-funk influences.

Robert Fripp, absent from this track, was replaced by Chuck Hammer, a guitarist who had already proved himself on *Growing up in Public*, the album that Lou Reed

had just recorded at George Martin's AIR Studios on the Caribbean island of Montserrat. The creator of "Guitar-chitecture," a term designating the use of six-strings to deliver sound textures close to those of synthesizers, Chuck Hammer used a truly revolutionary instrument: the GR-300 Guitar Synthesizer, from the Japanese brand Roland. One of the pickups on this guitar picks up the sound, transforms it into a MIDI signal, and sends it into a pedalboard that generates all kinds of sounds, which the musician chooses. The effect is a powerful one, especially when combined with Andy Clark's Minimoog and Yamaha CS-80 tracks. To intensify this guitar sound, Tony Visconti asked sound engineer Larry Alexander to place Hammer's amplifier close to the control room door on the second floor of the building so that the sound could escape to the stairs. Two microphones were installed in the stairwell, the first on the second floor and the second on the third floor, capturing all the resonance of the building and providing a spectacular sound at the end of the title, from 3:36.

FASHION

David Bowie / 4:47

Musicians

David Bowie: lead and backing vocals
Carlos Alomar: electric guitar
Robert Fripp: electric guitar
George Murray: bass
Dennis Davis: drums
Andy Clark: synthesizers
Chris Porter: backing vocals, claps
Tony Visconti: programming

Recorded

Power Station Studios, New York: February 15 1980–early
March 1980
Good Earth Studios, London: April–June 1980

Technical Team

Producers: David Bowie, Tony Visconti
Sound Engineers: Tony Visconti, Larry Alexander (Power Station
Studios)
Assistant Sound Engineers: Chris Porter (Good Earth Studios)

SIDE A: *Fashion* / 3:23
SIDE B: *Scream Like a Baby* / 3:33
UK Release on RCA: October 24, 1980 (ref. BOW 7; PB 9622)
US Release on RCA: October 24, 1980 (ref. PB-12134)
Best UK Chart Ranking: 5
Best US Chart Ranking: 70

Genesis

"Fashion," which began life during a jam session of the previous year, was originally given the working title "Jamaica." Seriously uninspired with regard to lyrics, Bowie had so far only come up with the gimmick of the chorus "Wo-Oh, Ja-mai-ca." Tony Visconti wanted to keep the title in the album's track listing but feared that his friend, true to his usual way of working, would abandon the song if the lyrics didn't come to him. But as the sessions came to an end in the spring of 1980, Bowie had a poetic burst of inspiration and notably transformed the chorus into the irresistible "Wo-Oh, Fashion."

Indeed, who better than Bowie to talk about fashion and its peculiarities? While many pop superstars of the '90s tried their hand at the theme (examples include "The Latest Fashion" by Prince and the Time, as well as "Vogue" by Madonna in 1990, and George Michael's "Too Funky" video in 1992), Bowie turned the theme into an irresistible disco song with two unforgettably catchy gimmicks: the "Beep-Beep" of the chorus and the "Fa-Fa-Fa-Fashion" of the finale. Right from the beginning of the song, Bowie announces that a new dance (which he demonstrates in the accompanying video) is on the rise, an idea that was taken up throughout the '80s by Prince on tracks such as "The Bird" or on an outtake of "The Line" with Sheila E. and Boni Boyer, in which he proclaims *"People, I've got a brand-new dance."* David Bowie also makes a nod to Ava Cherry and the Astronettes, quoting one of the songs recorded by the singer during the unfinished sessions of her 1973 album *People from Bad Homes.*

Production

Although the principle of "planned accidents" used during the production of *Lodger* was no longer in use during the recording sessions for this new album, Bowie and Visconti nevertheless strove to capture those precious moments of grace in the studio. Thus, the "whoop-whoop" that can be heard in the introduction of the track is actually a capture of the *click* (internal metronome used in software and digital instruments) that keyboardist Andy Clark was adjusting on his Yamaha CS-80. New York band the Strokes did the same thing in 2013, keeping the Pro Tools software click as the outro on their hit "One Way Trigger."

1980

On the percussion side of things, in order to give the extremely tight rhythmic pattern used in the song a more mechanical aspect, Tony Visconti asked drummer Dennis Davis to play over a digital pattern. "The original plan was to leave the machine out of the mix," explained the producer, "playing Dennis's drums only, but he was so tight with it we left it in for parts of the song. I treated it with digital effects to make it more techno."[35]

On August 17, 1980, "Ashes to Ashes" beat ABBA and their hit "The Winner Takes It All" on the British charts, but the Swedish band would get their revenge a few months later with "Super Trouper," which shot to the top position on the charts on November 23, ahead of Bowie's "Fashion."

TEENAGE WILDLIFE

David Bowie / 6:53

Musicians: David Bowie: lead and backing vocals / Carlos Alomar, Robert Fripp: electric guitar / Chuck Hammer: Roland GR-300 Guitar Synthesizer / George Murray: bass / Dennis Davis: drums / Roy Bittan: piano / Lynn Maitland: backing vocals / **Recorded:** Power Station Studios, New York: February 15 1980–early March 1980 / Good Earth Studios, London: April–June 1980 / **Technical Team:** Producers: David Bowie, Tony Visconti / **Sound Engineers:** Tony Visconti, Larry Alexander (Power Station Studios) / **Assistant Sound Engineers:** Chris Porter (Good Earth Studios)

When he wrote the lyrics for "Teenage Wildlife," David Bowie had just celebrated his thirty-third birthday. The singer appears to be preaching to the younger generation—the one he encountered at the Blitz Club in Covent Garden and of which Rusty Egan and Steve Strange, of the band Visage, were the ambassadors—ready to transform their admiration for their idol Bowie into the new trends that would be labeled new wave, cold wave, new romantics, or techno-pop. But as Bowie would later reveal, this track, originally called "It Happens Every Day," was originally intended more for the teenager that he once was: "If I had my kind of mythical younger brother, I think it might have been addressed to him. It's for somebody who's not mentally armed. [...] I guess the younger brother is my adolescent self."[122]

Three guitarists compete for the top spot in this pop-sounding midtempo track: The faithful Carlos Alomar brings the rhythm, Robert Fripp brings driving riffs, and Chuck Hammer handles the guitar synthesizer. Encouraged by Lou Reed to develop the use of this revolutionary instrument, Hammer became one of its chief ambassadors, along with Andy Summers from the Police.

SCREAM LIKE A BABY

David Bowie / 3:34

Musicians: David Bowie: lead and backing vocals / Carlos Alomar: electric guitar / George Murray: bass / Dennis Davis: drums / Andy Clark: synthesizers / **Recorded:** Power Station Studios, New York: February 15, 1980–early March 1980 / Good Earth Studios, London: April–June 1980 / **Technical Team:** Producers: David Bowie, Tony Visconti / **Sound Engineers:** Tony Visconti, Larry Alexander (Power Station Studios) / **Assistant Sound Engineers:** Chris Porter (Good Earth Studios)

Openly taking up the melody of the verse and chorus of "I Am a Laser," which was written for Ava Cherry and the

Astronettes in 1973 and then set aside, David Bowie kept the name as a working title until he decided, for the voice-recording sessions at Good Earth Studios in May 1981, to rewrite the lyrics. For the bridge of the song, Visconti modified his friend's voice, and Bowie recorded the same line of the song twice. The producer slowed down the recorder during the recording of the first take and then accelerated it for the second, giving the bridge of "Scream Like a Baby" a pitched voice effect that would later inspire Prince for his female avatar Camille, in 1986.

"Scream Like a Baby" appeared on the B-side of the single "Fashion," released on October 24, 1980, both in Great Britain and in the United States—an apt way to pay tribute to this quality track. Ava Cherry's version was released in 1995, when a collection of the songs she recorded for her album in 1973 and 1974 was released.

KINGDOM COME

Tom Verlaine / 3:43

Musicians: David Bowie: lead and backing vocals, synthesizer / Carlos Alomar, Robert Fripp: electric guitar / George Murray: bass / Dennis Davis: drums, tambourine / Chris Porter, Lynn Maitland, Tony Visconti: backing vocals / **Recorded:** Power Station Studios, New York: February 15 1980–early March 1980 / Good Earth Studios, London: April–June 1980 / **Technical Team:** Producers: David Bowie, Tony Visconti / **Sound Engineers:** Tony Visconti, Larry Alexander (Power Station Studios) / **Assistant Sound Engineers:** Chris Porter (Good Earth Studios)

A big fan of the American band Television, David Bowie had already planned to work with their singer, Tom Verlaine, who had released his first eponymous disc in 1979. Carlos Alomar offered to try his hand at a cover of one of the songs from the album, "Kingdom Come." With the backing tracks completed, Bowie and Visconti invited Verlaine to come and record some guitar lines at Power Station Studios. The musician asked if he could rent a few guitar amps for the occasion, and the request was willingly granted. The producer later described the surprising result: "The next day David and I were met with the sight of Tom Verlaine auditioning every amp in New York City. No exaggeration—there were about 30 guitar amps in the studio. He would play the same phrase in one, unplug his guitar and move to the next amp. We talked to him about the part and he said he had some ideas, but was searching for a good sound."[35] Whatever score Tom Verlaine finally recorded that day, it was omitted from the album's mix in favor of Robert Fripp's Gibson Les Paul.

The day after Bowie's death, Pete Townshend offered a poignant tribute to his friend by declaring on the Who website: "David Bowie was my Salvador Dalí."[125]

BECAUSE YOU'RE YOUNG

David Bowie / 4:52

Musicians: David Bowie: lead and backing vocals / Carlos Alomar, Pete Townshend: electric guitar / George Murray: bass / Dennis Davis: drums / Andy Clark: synthesizers / **Recorded:** Power Station Studios, New York: February 15 1980–early March 1980 / Good Earth Studios, London: April–June 1980 / **Technical Team:** Producers: David Bowie, Tony Visconti / Sound Engineers: Tony Visconti, Larry Alexander (Power Station Studios) / **Assistant Sound Engineers:** Chris Porter (Good Earth Studios)

What rock fan could ever have imagined the famous Who guitarist Pete Townshend taking part in the recording of a disco track? None other than David Bowie could have persuaded the rocker to come and add his powerful chords to this dance track, whose lyrics are addressed to Bowie's son, Duncan: *"Because you're young / You'll meet a stranger some night / Because you're young / What could be nicer for you? / And it makes me sad."* As Bowie later explained, "I think repeatedly that having got a nine-year-old son that's an area where I can try and talk to an age group that I've been through."[122] Despite some concerns from Bowie and Visconti, who were worried about Townshend's mood on the day he came to record at Good Earth Studios, everything went well. The guitarist (and his bottle of red wine) proved to be a perfectly mild-mannered combo, and he performed his famous six-string set with the powerful arm movements for which he was justly famous. "[He] did a perfect windmill on his guitar [...]," as Visconti would later recall. "Within 30 minutes the chords were laid on the tracks, the bottle of red wine was drained and Townshend exited onto Dean Street."[35]

IT'S NO GAME (NO. 2)

David Bowie / 4:22

Musicians: David Bowie: lead and backing vocals / Carlos Alomar, Robert Fripp: electric guitar / George Murray: bass / Dennis Davis: drums / Tony Visconti: backing vocals / **Recorded:** Power Station Studios, New York: February 15 1980–early March 1980 / **Technical Team:** Producers: David Bowie, Tony Visconti / Sound Engineers: Tony Visconti, Larry Alexander

Visconti and Bowie made no secret of the fact that with *Scary Monsters (And Super Creeps)* they wanted to create their own version of *Sgt. Pepper's Lonely Hearts Club Band.* Following their idea through to the end, they decided, as the Beatles did in 1967, to close the album with a reprise of the first track. Using the same backing tracks, this time slightly slowed down, the song is the only one for which the voices were entirely recorded in New York, and for which no overdub at Good Earth Studios was necessary. Tony Visconti later explained the sound effects that can be heard at the end of the track: For "It's No Game (No. 1)," after placing a microphone in front of his twenty-four-track Lyrec tape recorder, the producer recorded himself rewinding the tape and then pressing the Play button. At 3:46 on the last track of the album, he did the same by immortalizing the sound of the tape, which, once it reached its end, was ejected from the tape deck.

Single

CRYSTAL JAPAN
David Bowie / 3:26

Musicians
David Bowie: synthesizers
Tony Visconti: backing vocals

Recorded
Power Station Studios, New York: February 15, 1980–early March 1980

Technical Team
Producers: David Bowie, Tony Visconti
Arrangements: Tony Visconti
Sound Engineers: Tony Visconti, Larry Alexander (Power Station Studios)

SIDE A: *Crystal Japan* / 3:26
SIDE B: *Alabama Song* / 3:50
Japanese Release on RCA: 1980 (ref. SS-3270)

David Bowie in a 1980 advertisement for Crystal Jun Rock sake.

Genesis
With the recording of *Scary Monsters (And Super Creeps)* completed, David Bowie agreed to take part in two commercials promoting a sake liqueur called Crystal Jun Rock and produced by the Japanese spirits brand Takaru Shuzo Co. Limited, on one condition: Bowie would create all the music. The first thirty-second promo showed the artist sitting quietly in the garden of a Kyoto temple and delivering the slogan "Crystal Jun Rock, Japan" in voice-over. The second promo, lasting 3:09, featured an enigmatic David Bowie raising his glass at the end of the commercial. "Cheers!" he seemed to be saying to the audience. He would later be quite candid in explaining his reasons for this collaboration: "There are three reasons [why I agreed], the first one being that no one has ever asked me to do it before. And the money is a very useful thing. And the third, I think it's very effective that my music is on television 20 times a day."[59] The track, which was released as a single in Japan in 1980, proved to be extremely popular with Japanese fans.

Production
For this project, Bowie began by working on a track originally planned for the end of *Scary Monsters (And Super Creeps)*. Then he changed his mind and created the track solely from layers of synthesizers that seemed to come straight from the mellotron used on the track "Big Brother" from his earlier album *Diamond Dogs*. To this, Tony Visconti added some high-pitched backing vocals. As worthy successors of Bowie, the members of Nine Inch Nails offered a tribute to "Crystal Japan" with their track "A Warm Place," from their album *The Downward Spiral* in 1994.

UNDER PRESSURE

Freddie Mercury, Brian May, John Deacon, Roger Taylor, David Bowie / 4:03

Musicians
David Bowie: lead vocals, synthesizer, claps
Freddie Mercury: lead vocals, backing vocals, synthesizer, claps
Brian May: electric guitar, claps
John Deacon: bass, electric guitar, claps
Roger Taylor: drums, backing vocals, claps
David Richards: synthesizer

Recorded
Mountain Studios, Montreux: July–August 1981
Power Station Studios, New York: September 11, 1981

Technical Team
Producers: Queen, David Bowie
Sound Engineer: Reinhold Mack
Assistant Sound Engineer: David Richards

SIDE A: *Under Pressure* / 4:03
SIDE B: *Soul Brother* / 3:40
UK Release on EMI: October 26, 1981 (ref. EMI 5250)
US Release on Elektra: October 27, 1981 (ref. E-47235)
Best UK Chart Ranking: 1
Best US Chart Ranking: 29

During a session at Mountain Studios, David Bowie recorded some backing vocals on another track from Queen's new album: "Cool Cat." But feeling, rightly, that his performance wasn't up to his reputation, he demanded that the album be released without his vocal contribution, forcing EMI to delay the release of the album.

Genesis
In the summer of 1981, David Bowie was enjoying the calm of Switzerland at his home in Blonay. Just a few miles away, the members of Queen were busy recording their tenth album, *Hot Space*, at Mountain Studios in Montreux, which they had bought in 1979. The paths of these five talented musicians had crossed on many occasions in the bustling London of the 1970s, and many were the recording nights spent at Trident Studios when Bowie and Mercury exchanged opinions on this or that artist currently in vogue in the glamosphere. But the most notable link between the two singers was undoubtedly the photographer Mick Rock, who took the most famous photographs of both men. The atmosphere in the studio was excellent in July 1981, when David Bowie was invited to a jam session with Roger Taylor, Brian May, John Deacon, and Freddie Mercury.

Production
Back at the studio, the musicians tried out different ideas, one of which came from John Deacon, the band's bassist, and grabbed their attention. This unstoppable bass riff, memorable from the very first listen, would form the basis of this legendary collaboration, for which the two singers worked separately on their lyrics and recorded fragments of phrases in turn. In the end, between Mercury's scats and Bowie's nonsensical lyrics, the song made very little sense. The result of this exceptional collaboration between the two British stars is a song of rare emotional power, which shot to the top of the charts upon its release in October.

"Under Pressure" would go on to become an integral part of Bowie's repertoire. In 1995, he performed it on the *Outside* tour, accompanied by bassist Gail Ann Dorsey, who had no choice but to sing and play at the same time. "I was just horrified," the musician would later confess, "because I thought 'This is it, I'm going to get fired.' [...] I went away and started figuring out how to play it. He gave me a cassette of that version and I listened to it and just started figuring it out. I drilled it, I learned it section by section, really, really slow. And then I got a metronome and slowly brought it up to speed. By two weeks' time, I could do it at the right tempo and hoped it was going to come together. We started trying it, and it worked."[127]

David Bowie in Bertolt Brecht's Baal

UK Release on RCA: February 13, 1982 (ref. BOW 11) / US Release on RCA: February 13, 1982 (ref. CPL1 4346).
Best UK Chart Ranking: 29 / Best US Chart Ranking: Did Not Chart

Bertolt Brecht at the piano in his Berlin apartment in 1927.

DAVID BOWIE IN BERTOLT BRECHT'S BAAL

Musicians: / David Bowie: lead vocals / Eckehard Scholl: piano / Bernd Machus: bandoneon / Ingo Cramer: guitar / Michael Bucher: tuba / Thomas Hoffmann: drums / Erwin Milzkott: flute / Joachim Welz: clarinet / David Kreitner: alto saxophone / Axel-Glenn Müller: tenor saxophone / René Waintz: trumpet / Ralf Armbruster: trombone / Hans-Joachim Glas: conductor / Uwe Weniger: viola / Rolf Becker: cello / Ulrich Berggold: double bass / **Recorded:** Hansa Studios, West Berlin: September 1981 / **Technical Team:** Producers: David Bowie, Tony Visconti / **Sound Engineer:** Eduard Meyer / **Assistant Sound Engineer:** Michael Zimmerling / **Arrangements:** Dominic Muldowney

The first works of the German playwright Bertolt Brecht for *Baal* date back to 1918. His first play, a seminal work of his career, and the lines from which he would modify throughout his life, recounts the story of the misadventures of a young poet. In 1981, the British director Alan Clarke—censored in 1979 for his film *Scum*, whose violent images denounced the repressive methods of public institutions toward the youth of the United Kingdom in the 1970s—offered the BBC an adaptation of *Baal* for the small screen. Produced by Louis Marks, adapted by John Willett, and accompanied by musical arrangements from Dominic Muldowney, the play clearly required an all-star cast. Impressed by David Bowie's performance in *The Elephant Man*, Willett and Clarke offered him a role. Who better than Bowie, with his hedonistic reputation and a tumultuous past, to embody this poet lacking all morals and values, and whose only goal is to enjoy the pleasures

of life? A longstanding fan of the works of Brecht (whose "Alabama Song" he recorded in 1978), Bowie immediately agreed to join the cast, which was also composed of actors Robert Austin, Russell Wootton, and Juliette Hammond-Hill, among others. Four weeks of rehearsals in Acton, West London, were followed by an uneventful shoot. In order to extend the experience, David Bowie decided to record a few titles from the play's libretto at Hansa Studios in West Berlin. He asked Muldowney to work on the arrangements and Tony Visconti to produce the disc. Broadcast on March 2, 1982, on BBC1, the musical drama proved a great success. The EP *David Bowie in Bertolt Brecht's Baal* is certainly worth (re)discovering, especially since it underscores Bowie's rich vocal power and his love for the theater.

BAAL'S HYMN

Bertolt Brecht, Dominic Muldowney / 4:02

Having missed his plane to Berlin, Bowie arrived at the tail end of the recording sessions at Hansa Studios. As usual, he was satisfied with his work after just a few takes, which were recorded by Tony Visconti. The producer, who took advantage of Bowie's delay to clean the tracks and work on a quality premix, offered a sound of enormous emotional power, carried by the play of the musicians, some of whom, such as the bandoneonist Bernd Machus, had actually worked for Brecht during the interwar period.

REMEMBERING MARY A.

Bertolt Brecht, Dominic Muldowney / 2:04

Brecht wrote the poem "Erinnerung an die Marie A." (Memories of Marie A.) on February 21, 1920, during a train journey to Berlin. It tells the story of a lost love and the memory of a fleeting kiss. The song, arranged by Dominic Muldowney, benefits from all the devices and artifice one expects of a light love story: discreet chord lines on the piano, effective layers of strings, and some well-chosen flutes. A loving interlude as touching as it is ephemeral, the song is perfectly interpreted by Bowie, who uses his smoothest voice for the occasion.

BALLAD OF THE ADVENTURERS

Bertolt Brecht, Dominic Muldowney / 1:54

To give the singer's voice a natural resonance, Visconti took advantage (as he did during the recording of *"Heroes"*) of Hansa's vast Studio 2. At the request of the producer, the in-house sound engineer placed a microphone in front of Bowie's mouth, then a second mic a few meters away from him. Two further microphones, known as "atmosphere" microphones, were also placed in the large room to capture the reverb. Right from the beginning of "Ballad of the Adventurers," when the singer is accompanied by only a few guitar chords, we immediately get a sense of the vastness of the space.

THE DROWNED GIRL

Bertolt Brecht, Kurt Weill / 2:24

What extraordinary emotional power David Bowie offers here, making use of his deepest voice to mark the title with unstoppable melancholy! As Muldowney later recalled, "The stand-out was 'The Drowned Girl.' [...] He's singing about 'Her slow descent' below the water, right down in the bass baritone. Then halfway through he jumps up the octave."[53] *"Wreck and duck weed slowly increased her weight / By clasping her in their slimy grip / Through her limbs, the cold blooded fishes played / Creatures and plant life kept on, thus obstructing her last trip."*

Brecht, who was inspired by Arthur Rimbaud for the character of Baal, paid a final homage to the cursed poet by adapting his poem "Ophelia," itself inspired by the famous painting of the same name from Pre-Raphaelite painter John Everett Millais and representing the inert body of the heroine of Shakespeare's *Hamlet*. "The wind kisses her breasts and arranges her great veils / cradled softly by the waves, in a halo around her / the shivering willows weep on her shoulder, / the reeds bend above her wide dreaming forehead."

The video for the song was the work of David Mallet, and it was shot on the same day and under the same conditions as the single "Wild Is the Wind," released on the *ChangesTwoBowie* compilation, in which a fake band, including Tony Visconti and Coco Schwab, accompanies the singer.

THE DIRTY SONG

Bertolt Brecht, Dominic Muldowney / 0:37

A short track whose text reveals all the debauchery of Baal's character, "The Dirty Song" is as fleeting as it is bawdy. A real "drinking song," as they're known in the German *Bierpalast*, the vast beer halls where musicians and singers set the rhythm for thirsty beer drinkers.

Single

CAT PEOPLE
(PUTTING OUT FIRE)

David Bowie, Giorgio Moroder / 4:08

Giorgio Moroder, godfather of the Munich disco scene, probably in the process of producing one of his numerous hits.

Musicians

David Bowie: lead vocals
Michael Landau: electric guitar
Tim May: electric guitar
Leland Sklar: bass
Keith Forsey: drums, percussion
Giorgio Moroder: synthesizers, electric guitar, bass
Brian Banks: synthesizers
Charles Judge: synthesizers
Sylvester Levai: keyboards
Alex Brown: backing vocals
Paulette McWilliams: backing vocals
Stephanie Spruill: backing vocals

Recorded

Carla Ridge Camp, Beverly Hills: 1981 (music)
Mountain Studios, Montreux: July 1981 (vocals)

Technical Team

Producer: Giorgio Moroder
Sound Engineers: David Richards, Brian Reeves

SIDE A: *Cat People (Putting out Fire)* / 4:08
SIDE B: *Paul's Theme (Jogging Chase)* / 3:52
UK Release on MCA Records: March 12, 1982 (ref. MCA 770)
US Release on MCA Records / Backstreet: March 12, 1982 (ref. BSR-52024)
Best UK Chart Ranking: 26
Best US Chart Ranking: 67

Genesis

In 1982, the American director Paul Schrader decided to adapt Jacques Tourneur's movie *La Féline*, which was originally released in 1942. For the soundtrack of his remake, entitled *Cat People*, he called on the "godfather" of Munich disco, Giorgio Moroder. As early as 1969, the producer had given Munich its status as a musical city by developing the cutting-edge Musicland Studios, which had already played host to innumerable stars, including the Rolling Stones, Led Zeppelin, Electric Light Orchestra, and Queen. Their fame made him the undisputed master of disco, with hits such as the main theme of Alan Parker's "Midnight Express" in 1979, or "Call Me," sung by Blondie for the movie *American Gigolo* in 1980. For *Cat People*, Giorgio Moroder wanted to work with David Bowie. He met up with Bowie in Montreux to record the vocal tracks of this high-caliber track, which would be re-recorded later for the album *Let's Dance*.

Production

On the day of recording the vocals, director Paul Schrader was present in the small control room at Mountain Studios. As usual, Bowie had the session successfully in the can after two takes. Perfectly satisfied, he was getting ready to end the day's work when Schrader, who was used to the multiple takes needed on movie sets, asked him to continue. The British singer replied that everything seemed perfect to him, and the director had no choice but to resign himself. "We recorded it in less than an hour," Moroder would later confirm. "[...] It was one of my easiest, fastest and greatest recordings ever."[1]

The track's success owes a great deal to its finale, featuring three exceptional backing vocalists: Alex Brown, discovered alongside Ray Charles fifteen years earlier; Paulette McWilliams, heard singing on "Don't Stop Til You Get Enough" by Michael Jackson in 1979; and Stephanie Spruill, in charge of backing vocals on several recordings by the Jacksons, such as "Can You Feel It" (1980). Add to that one of the most famous choruses of the eighties—*"And I've been putting out fire...with gasoline!"*—and you get a rich, powerful, and compelling track that establishes a new artistic direction for the singer.

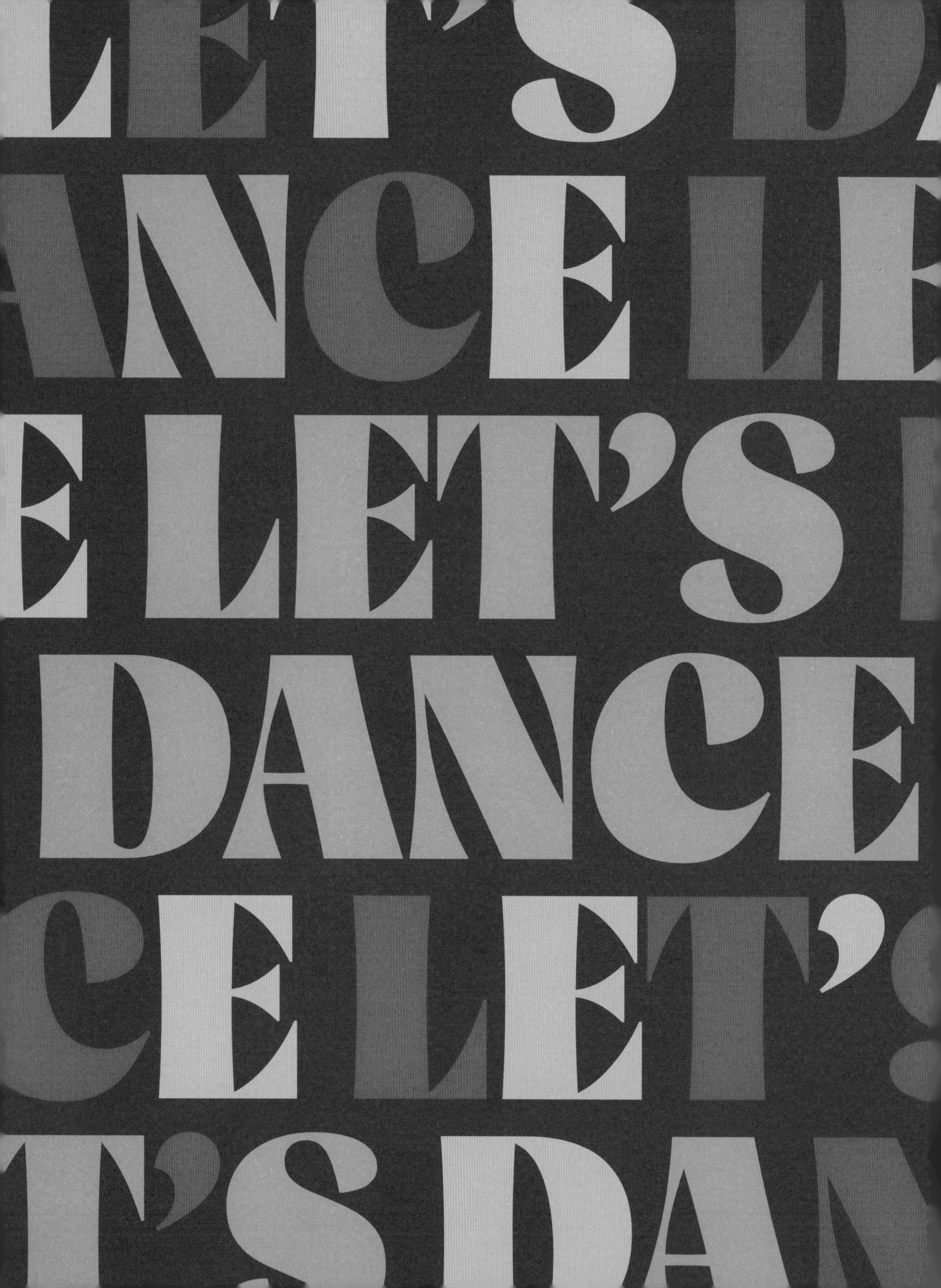
LET'S
DANCE

ALBUM

LET'S DANCE

Modern Love . China Girl . Let's Dance . Without You . Ricochet .
Criminal World . Cat People (Putting Out Fire) . Shake It

RELEASE DATES
United Kingdom: April 14, 1983
Reference: EMI America—AML 3029
United States: April 14, 1983
Reference: EMI America: SO-517093
Best UK Chart Ranking: 1
Best US Chart Ranking: 4

TACKLING THE DANCE FLOORS

After the public and critical success of the play *The Elephant Man* and the movie *Christiane F.*, Bowie made the most of 1982 by working tirelessly to expand his filmography. He appeared in Tony Scott's *The Hunger*, alongside Catherine Deneuve and Susan Sarandon, and *Merry Christmas, Mr. Lawrence*, from Japanese director Nagisa Ōshima, famous for directing *In the Realm of the Senses* in 1976. On the South Pacific set of *Merry Christmas, Mr. Lawrence*, the singer dove back into listening to the singers and musicians who had been his early musical influences. He rediscovered the records of James Brown, Buddy Guy, Albert King, and Johnny Otis, going back and forth from blues to rock to soul; Bowie wondered why he hadn't brought any records to listen to that had been recorded in the past fifteen years. His answer was simple: "It [the music of the 1950s and '60s] was very non-uptight music, and it comes from a sense of pleasure and happiness. There is enthusiasm and optimism on those recordings."[127]

His recent collaborations had also prompted him to rethink his conception of musical writing and production after the success of the singles "Under Pressure," with Queen, and "Cat People (Putting Out Fire)," which was made in collaboration with the European godfather of disco, Giorgio Moroder. These singles proved to Bowie, if he still had any doubt, that he was quite capable of appealing to a wide listening audience. Freed from his contract with RCA, with whom his professional relationship had been continually deteriorating, Bowie was now the captain of his own ship. With no record label to answer to, the singer was eager to continue his conquest of the airwaves that had begun with *Scary Monsters (And Super Creeps)*. At the end of 1982, Bowie wrote a handful of tracks built around simple chord lines, in heavy contrast to the tortuous melodies of *Lodger*, which had been released three years earlier.

Satisfied with EMI's efforts to promote "Under Pressure," Bowie chose EMI America to distribute his next album, which he produced—in the financial sense—all on his own.

A Miraculous Encounter

To create the sequel to *Scary Monsters (And Super Creeps)*, Bowie initially approached Tony Visconti, who set aside three months for him in his calendar. But in the fall of 1982, after a chance meeting at a New York club called the Continental, the singer changed his mind. That evening, dressed in an elegant suit, Bowie was sipping a sensible orange juice at the bar when out of the blue he was approached by the famous American composer, guitarist, and producer Nile Rodgers, who had just managed to shake off his drunken friend, the rocker Billy Idol. His musical exploits in the band Chic made Rodgers the King Midas of modern funk—not disco, a term he considers too simplistic to describe his playing, even though he believes himself to be one of the founders of the genre. Despite the success of the album he produced for Diana Ross two years earlier, Rodgers's career had come to a standstill, and the recent "disco sucks" campaign, which encouraged vinyl disco owners to burn their records, had certainly not worked in his favor. In short, the musician was going through a difficult patch when he bumped into Bowie. "All of my friends had been in the *Young Americans* band," he would later reveal. "Luther Vandross, Carlos Alomar, Dennis Davis. We all went to school together. So I thought we already had a connection."[1] From their first meeting, the two artists immediately felt a mutual sense of trust, and during their second meeting at the Bemelmans Bar inside the Carlyle Hotel, Bowie asked Rodgers: "I'm wondering what it would be like to do a record together."[128] The two musicians then got together to listen to records and discuss their musical tastes.

David Bowie performing
with guitarist Carlos Alomar
at the Arènes de Fréjus in
May 1983.

Following double page:
Bowie performing for an
immense crowd at the
National Bowl in July 1983.

Bowie with Catherine
Deneuve in Tony Scott's
1983 film *The Hunger.*

Rodgers, who had just completed his first solo album, *Adventures in the Land of the Good Groove*, was very much aware that there were no hit singles on his album and that his career was on the wane. But Bowie, who listened to a test pressing of the album, was reassuring: "Nile, darling, if you make a record for me half as good as that I'll be the happiest man in the world."[129] With that, the collaboration between the two artists was officially sealed, and the result was one of the most popular albums of the 1980s.

A Sparkling Collaboration

With Tony Visconti now out of the way, preproduction on Bowie's next record could begin. A few informal working sessions initially took place at Rodgers's apartment (ironically, Rodgers was Visconti's next-door neighbor at New York's Lincoln Plaza Towers), and then at Bowie's new Swiss home, the Château du Signal, located near the Sauvabelin forest in the heights of Lausanne, where he lived with his son, Zowie, and Coco Schwab. With the help of David Richards from Mountain Studios, Bowie requisitioned various local musicians to assist on the album. Multi-instrumentalist Erdal Kizilçay, who would take part on *Tonight* in 1984, programmed the rhythm boxes and played synthesizers and bass. For guitar, Bowie brought in an amateur musician close to Richards named André Tésaury, who also took part in the sessions where the first demos of "Let's Dance" and "Ricochet" were recorded. Thanks to the confidence that the singer had placed in him, Rodgers was able to book Power Station Studios in

New York in December, which was the same location where he had already created a number of hits, including "Everybody Dance," "Le Freak," and "Good Times" with Chic, as well as Sister Sledge's "We Are Family," in 1978. "David's directive was clear, and he was not interested in doing *Scary Monsters 2* (no offense to Tony Visconti)," Nile Rodgers would later explain. "He wanted to make hits. The professional producer in me was like the Terminator. I would not stop until my mission was completed."[128]

Two weeks were all that were needed to record the entire album, the track listing of which consisted of five new songs ("Modern Love," "Let's Dance," "Without You," "Ricochet," and "Shake It") and two covers ("China Girl" by Iggy Pop and "Criminal World" by Metro), as well as a new, more rock-flavored version of "Cat People (Putting Out Fire)." Nile Rodgers recounted this lightning-fast recording with his legendary good humor: "Believe it or not, it took 17 days from start to mix, done. After the 18th day there was a bunch of people sitting in the recording studio listening to it like this. The 19th day, Nile was out getting drunk, the 20th day, Nile was out getting drunk, the 21st day...We never touched this record again. It was done in 17 days, mixed, delivered."[129]

Chosen by Nile Rodgers, each musician brought a touch of virtuosity that added the finishing touch to the compositions. Chic's drummer, Tony Thompson, nicknamed the "human metronome," added his drumsticks to the recording. He shared the sessions with another virtuoso: Omar Hakim, the new rhythmic linchpin of the band Weather Report. It's impossible to gauge the level of participation of

either musician on the record, as Rodgers and Bowie left the answer to who contributed what relatively unclear. Bernard Edwards, Rodgers's Chic bandmate, had been a favorite but was eventually dropped in favor of bassist Carmine Rojas. Robert Sabino, Chic's keyboard player, and percussionist Sammy Figueroa were added to the lineup along with backing singers George and Frank Simms and David Spinner. Last, trumpeter Mac Gollehon and saxophonists Robert Aaron, Stanley Harrison, and Steve Elson formed a high-flying brass section that appeared on several tracks on the album. A last musician, discovered by Bowie during the Montreux Jazz Festival, completed the lineup. This was Texan guitarist Stevie Ray Vaughan, who added a highly rock 'n' roll flavoring to this album, where pop-funk hits flow in quick succession.

International Recognition

It has been said that *Let's Dance*, which the fans love to hate, marked the end of David Bowie, or the beginning of a vertiginous descent into the insipid pop music of the 1980s. But whatever the purists may claim, this album is another masterpiece in Bowie's discography. Thanks to this album, Bowie made a majestic entrance into a decade that could easily have sounded his professional death knell. He changed tack completely, turning his back on what had worked so well for him in the past. It was a risky bet for a musical artist without a record company. He could have sunk into the maelstrom of the 1980s, leaving nothing today but a footnote in the memory of rock historians, like so many artists who weren't able to move forward with the times. Instead, after his short retirement in 1981, the singer returned to the forefront with eager fans snapping up more than ten million copies of *Let's Dance*.

By all accounts the "Serious Moonlight Tour," which followed the release of the record in April 1983, was spectacular. Bowie, who was now selling out hundred-thousand-seat stadiums, joined the ranks of the top ten English-speaking pop superstars of the day, alongside such illustrious names as Michael Jackson, Madonna, and Prince. According to Carlos Alomar, who was in charge of the artistic direction of the concerts, "*Let's Dance* was way bigger than he [David] expected it to be. And there's this sort of success remorse that goes on when you are accustomed to being eclectic and cool and underground. But *Let's Dance* is still a cool record. It's just *big*. It's a *big cool record*."[130]

Bernard Edwards, Norma Jean Wright, Nile Rodgers, and Tony Thompson formed the band Chic in 1977. Their sound was emblematic of high-quality American disco/funk.

NILE RODGERS: THE MASTER OF AMERICAN DISCO-FUNK

The man who would become the greatest guitarist of the disco era was born on September 19, 1952, on the Lower East Side of Manhattan. His mother, Beverly Goodman, was just fourteen years old. His father, Nile Gregory Rodgers, was a percussionist who specialized in Afro-Cuban music and was constantly away on tour. Initially given up for adoption, the toddler, nicknamed Baby Boy Goodman, was finally recognized by his mother, who gave him the name of his biological father. Nile Gregory Rodgers Jr. grew up in Greenwich Village, alongside Beverly and her future husband, Bobby Glanzrock. The family's apartment often welcomed a rotating cast of celebrities, including comedians Richard Pryor and Lenny Bruce and jazz pianist Thelonious Monk, who were regular dinner guests. Growing up surrounded by such illustrious influences, little Nile began learning music from a very early age. He first played the flute and the clarinet, then took up the guitar at the age of sixteen. He eventually joined various different bands and made New York his playground, hanging out in concert halls, clubs, and rehearsal studios all around the city.

The Birth of Chic

Hired as a guitarist for the *Sesame Street* band, Nile Rodgers was eighteen years old when he met bassist Bernard Edwards, who was also a band member. They soon formed a backing band called the Big Apple Band, playing for, among others, the successful vocal group New York City, which, despite its name, had a remarkable Philly-centric sound. The 1973 release of the highly acclaimed single "I'm Doing Fine Now" enabled Rodgers and his friends to open for the Jackson Five, the O'Jays, and the funk combo Parliament-Funkadelic. That same year, the guitarist fell under the spell of Roxy Music, not because of the steamy album covers Brian Ferry's band had a penchant for, but because of the rich arrangements featured on *Stranded* and *For Your Pleasure*, which were released just a few months

apart. Rodgers and Edwards, by then accompanied by drummer Tony Thompson, began thinking about starting their own band: This would eventually become Chic. Revolutionizing the emerging disco sound by moving away from its machine-like rhythm and emphasizing its funk roots, Nile Rodgers set about blurring the lines between two popular musical genres. The band, with its exceptional musicians—now including keyboard player Robert Sabino and singer Norma Jean Wright—quickly emerged as a new force on the vibrant and fashionable disco scene. Virtuoso guitar playing and agile and graceful bass lines were the founding elements of the Chic musical style, to which must be added the metronomic precision of drummer Thompson. The hits just kept coming: "Dance, Dance, Dance (Yowsah, Yowsah, Yowsah)" and "Everybody Dance" (1978), "Le Freak" (1978), and the ultrasampled "Good Times" (1979) all left a lasting impression. The group's meteoric rise was finally halted by the "disco sucks" movement, started by people who felt that the genre was corrupting the record industry and wanted Americans to burn their Chic albums alongside records from Donna Summer and ABBA. By the early eighties, disco disappeared from the airwaves, and its leading lights disappeared with it.

A Major Producer

Nile Rodgers then became a producer to the stars. After helping Diana Ross to achieve immense success with her album *Diana* in 1980, he produced, among others, such mythical recordings as *Let's Dance* for David Bowie, *Like a Virgin* for Madonna (1984), and *Notorious* for Duran Duran (1986). In 2013, he was (re)discovered by a whole new generation thanks to his contribution to the Daft Punk album, *Random Access Memories*. Alongside Giorgio Moroder and Paul Williams, Rodgers gained access to a new generation of fans, co-writing the worldwide hit "Get Lucky," which safely enshrined him in the hall of greats after a phenomenal career spanning more than forty years.

Single

MODERN LOVE
David Bowie / 4:46

Musicians
David Bowie: lead and backing vocals
Nile Rodgers: electric guitar
Stevie Ray Vaughan: electric guitar
Carmine Rojas: bass
Tony Thompson (?) or Omar Hakim (?): drums
Robert Sabino: synthesizers
Mac Gollehon: trumpet
Stan Harrison: tenor saxophone
Robert Aaron: tenor saxophone
Steve Elson: baritone saxophone
Frank Simms: backing vocals
George Simms: backing vocals
David Spinner: backing vocals

Recorded
Power Station Studios, New York: December 3–20, 1982

Technical Team
Producers: David Bowie, Nile Rodgers
Sound Engineer: Bob Clearmountain
Assistant Sound Engineer: Dave Greenberg

SIDE A: *Modern Love* / 3:56
SIDE B: *Modern Love (Live)* / 3:43
UK Release on EMI America: September 12, 1983 (ref. EA 158)
US Release on EMI America: September 12, 1983 (ref. B-8177)
Best UK Chart Ranking: 2
Best US Chart Ranking: 14

Nile Rodgers nicknamed Bowie the "Picasso of rock" "[...] because of his prodigious creativity," he explained, "but also because he looks sort of like Picasso drew him."[128]

Genesis

With its irresistibly danceable drum intro (the following year's "Footloose" by Kenny Loggins included a very similar sound), "Modern Love" unmistakably warned the listener that *Let's Dance* was going to set the dance floor alight in 1983. The song would become one of David Bowie's most famous tracks, and it had several moments of glory. His line *"I never wave bye bye"* was used as his exit line during concerts on the "Serious Moonlight Tour." Bowie also performed the song at Live Aid on July 13, 1985, alongside a new roster of musicians, including guitarist Kevin Armstrong, bassist Matthew Seligman, and drummer Neil Conti.

Leaving aside the song's many covers (the most memorably offbeat of which was undoubtedly the Sunshiners' reggae version in 2006), let's look at how "Modern Love" featured in a commercial for Pepsi in 1987. Lasting 1:07, the long version of the commercial, entitled "Creation," was inspired by the movie *A Dream Creature*, which was directed by John Hughes and released in 1985. In it we find David Bowie in the role of a mad scientist who works in his laboratory to give life to the ideal woman, who arises from magazine pages that Bowie throws into a machine. A spilled bottle of Pepsi thwarts the singer's plans and brings out an unexpected partner in the person of Tina Turner, with whom Bowie begins a frantic dance under an impressive display of fireworks. All the corporate magic of the 1980s was encapsulated in a single commercial! The two stars re-recorded "Modern Love" for the occasion, changing the chorus to "The choice is mine," in reference to the Pepsi slogan: "The choice of a new generation." "Modern Love" will thus be forever anchored in the collective popular consciousness as being one of the most spectacular, mainstream pop explorations of the singer's entire discography.

Production

Led by a piano-sounding synthesizer played by Rob Sabino, this first track on the album is a tribute to some of the more upbeat songs of David Bowie's idol, Little Richard. The question-and-answer game on the chorus is a reference to this rock 'n' roll pioneer, and more broadly to the too-often-underestimated role played by backing singers in soul, rock 'n' roll, and rhythm 'n' blues music.

Bowie during the colossal "Serious Moonlight Tour," which included nearly one hundred shows between May and December 1983.

The ultramodern production by Nile Rodgers, who, for the first time on a David Bowie album, replaced the piano with a keyboard that mimicked its sounds, plunged the album right into the heart of the 1980s, when synthesizers were king. While others made use of the many drum machines that were flooding the market at the time, Bowie and Rodgers wanted to keep an acoustic sound, notable thanks to the presence of drummers Omar Hakim and Tony Thompson. No one can say for sure which one of the drummers actually played on "Modern Love," but based on what Nile Rodgers remembers, it's a safe bet that it was Thompson, who was on fire that day, and whose powerful drum strikes can be felt throughout the track. "After we were solidly into the recording process," explained the producer, "I finally brought in Tony Thompson, who struck the drums so hard that the sound pressure levels dimmed the studio lights with each backbeat. It was like 'Yeah, motherfuckers, *take that!*'"[128] The brass instruments also have a special importance, as they support the rockabilly side of the track. Stan Harrison, who had already brought his tenor saxophone playing to "Red Sails" on *Lodger,* decided to complete the album's brass section with a baritone saxophone. He got in touch with a colleague, Steve Elson, who would later recount: "I was smart enough to say, '[...] I'm the best baritone sax player you've ever heard in your life.' I showed him my baritone sax and it went really well and I did that solo on 'Modern Love' that very first day."[131]

CHINA GIRL
David Bowie, Iggy Pop / 5:32

Musicians
David Bowie: lead and backing vocals
Nile Rodgers: electric guitar
Stevie Ray Vaughan: electric guitar
Carmine Rojas: bass
Tony Thompson (?) or Omar Hakim (?): drums
Robert Sabino: synthesizers
Frank Simms: backing vocals
George Simms: backing vocals
David Spinner: backing vocals

Recorded
Power Station Studios, New York: December 3–20, 1982

Technical Team
Producers: David Bowie, Nile Rodgers
Sound Engineer: Bob Clearmountain
Assistant Sound Engineer: Dave Greenberg

SIDE A: *China Girl* / 4:14
SIDE B: *Shake It* / 3:49
UK release on EMI America: May 31, 1983 (ref. EA 157)
US release on EMI America: May 31, 1983 (ref. B-8165)
Best UK Chart Ranking: 2
Best US Chart Ranking: 10

Genesis

In 1976, while Bowie and Iggy Pop were recording the Iguana's first solo album at the Château d'Hérouville in France, the two musicians met Kuêlan Nguyen, who was staying nearby. "It was such a different time," she recalled in 2016. "The end of the war in Vietnam wasn't the end of the Cold War, we were still carrying the wounds inside us, I, the little Vietnamese girl, Iggy the American and David the Englishman. Like all artists, we were witnesses and wounded by the time, raw in our personal histories and worried about the future of the world. [...] [David] fell in love at first sight, and so did I. But I listened to the voice of reason. [...] The most civilized way was to become a perfect neighbor, and I resolved to spend almost every night, from then on, with them both, Iggy and David, setting the world to rights. That was how, with Iggy and David, the three of us forged a passionate loving friendship."[132] As a tribute to this fleeting time spent together, a song that was currently being written—tentatively named "Borderline"—was renamed "China Girl." Bowie was probably inspired to choose this name by another song of the same name; in 1967 this other song opened *The Sophisticated Beggar*, the first album from singer Roy Harper—a regular at Haddon Hall in the early 1970s.

"China Girl" first appeared on Iggy Pop's debut solo album, *The Idiot*, in 1977. However, in 1982, while he was recording *Let's Dance*, David Bowie decided to give the track a second lease on life, since it went relatively unnoticed in 1977.

Production

Nile Rodgers was deeply skeptical upon first listening to Iggy Pop's original track. He even wondered if Bowie was playing a joke on him. How could the hit-seeking artist believe for a second that "China Girl" would be a success with audiences? "The original [version] was way overproduced to my tight, minimalist ears, but David insisted that the song was a hit."[128] The producer then decided to work on the harmonic line, changing some of the chords. He wrote the introductory guitar line, which he borrowed from Rufus and Chaka Khan's "Sweet Thing," released in 1975, and then added the famous riff that would help make the song such a success. After putting together new

1983

arrangements, Rodgers was on the verge of showing his work to Bowie: "I told the band, 'This is so pop, so corny, he really might fire me.' I played it for David, expecting to get fired, or at least expecting to have an argument. He looked at me and went, 'That's fucking fantastic.'"[133] Carmine Rojas added a bass line influenced by the Rolling Stones' hit track "Under My Thumb," which he had heard on the radio that morning, and whose famous marimba line was played by Brian Jones. In the hands of the magician Nile Rodgers, the dark rock track from Iggy Pop's *The Idiot* became a tangy pop anthem with a melody that was expertly underlined by Bowie's smooth vocals. Much to the chagrin of some fans who hated the song, "China Girl" was a huge success in both the UK and the United States, and it provided a much-welcome boost to the coffers of one Iggy Pop.

LET'S DANCE
David Bowie / 7:38

Musicians
David Bowie: lead and backing vocals
Nile Rodgers: electric guitar
Stevie Ray Vaughan: electric guitar
Carmine Rojas: bass
Omar Hakim: drums
Robert Sabino: synthesizers, B3 Hammond organ
Mac Gollehon: trumpet
Stan Harrison: tenor saxophone
Robert Aaron: tenor saxophone
Steve Elson: baritone saxophone
Sammy Figueroa: percussion
Frank Simms: backing vocals
George Simms: backing vocals
David Spinner: backing vocals

Recorded
Power Station Studios, New York: December 3–20, 1982

Technical Team
Producers: David Bowie, Nile Rodgers
Sound Engineer: Bob Clearmountain
Assistant Sound Engineer: Dave Greenberg

SIDE A: *Let's Dance* / 4:08
SIDE B: *Cat People (Putting Out Fire)* / 5:09
UK Release on EMI America: March 14, 1983 (ref. EA 152)
US Release on EMI America: March 14, 1983 (ref. B-8158)
Best UK Chart Ranking: 1
Best US Chart Ranking: 1

1983

FOR BOWIE ADDICTS
In an interview with Talia Schlanger for NPR.org's *World Cafe* on August 29, 2019, Nile Rodgers played one of the "Let's Dance" demos recorded at Mountain Studios on December 19, 1982. It features an enthusiastic David Bowie, who at 22:30 exclaims: "That's it! You got it!"[136]

When he joined the Kon-rads in 1962, the young David Jones regularly played one of the hits of the year, sung by Chris Montez and entitled…"Let's Dance"!

Genesis
In the fall of 1982, Nile Rodgers crossed the Atlantic to spend a few days at the Château du Signal, David Bowie's new home in Lausanne, Switzerland. After their meeting in New York, the two musicians had decided to begin an ongoing collaboration. No songs had been created, and Rodgers didn't know quite what to expect. But sometimes all it takes is one small creative spark to create a track with universal appeal. One morning, Bowie came knocking on his guest's door to inform him that he had something, a diamond in the rough, that the producer would have to help shape into a quality song. Accompanied by an old twelve-string guitar (of which six strings were lost…), the singer played a two-chord folk tune, hummed a few words, and then assured the producer that this was to be his future number one hit. After some hesitation—Rodgers was actually convinced that his host was making fun of him—Nile began working on the track alone. He first changed the chord grid, abandoning the *C-F* turn, which was too close to that of the Velvet Underground's classic song "I'm Waiting for the Man." Instead, he opted for an *A-F-A* transposition, accompanied by a funk rhythm. On December 19, 1982, Bowie recruited some local musicians to begin preproduction at Mountain Studios in Montreux, and they started working on the arrangements for "Let's Dance." Immediately won over by the song, Bowie recorded it as soon as he arrived at Power Station Studios in New York later in December 1982. "My instinct to start with 'Let's Dance' paid off," Rodgers later revealed. "We cut the song in one or two takes and it set the tone for the rest of the project. This song was going to be a major hit, and we all knew it. David relaxed into my team's capable, wickedly creative, loving hands."[128]

Production
Nile Rodgers, who had never revealed whether Tony Thompson or Omar Hakim played on each song of the album, finally revealed the information on his Twitter account on February 1, 2016: It was indeed Omar Hakim who beat the measure on the title track of David Bowie's fifteenth studio album. The groove he delivered with bass player Carmine Rojas was absolute perfection, leaving ample room for the brass, synthesizers, and the singer's voice. Nile Rodgers himself provided the guitar rhythm,

Virtuoso Omar Hakim on drums for "Let's Dance." Hakim was a key contributor to the groove of *Random Access Memories*, the 2013 Daft Punk album that also featured an appearance by…Nile Rodgers!

trying to move away from the traditional funk, which had helped to forge his success but which by then had fallen very much from favor. To achieve this, the producer used an extremely ingenious strategy: He struck the main chord, which was then repeated in a precise manner thanks to the programming of a delay effect. "I just played straight," explained the guitarist. "I just played all up strokes, and you let the delay make the groove."[134] This new groove was adopted by a number of artists who followed in Bowie's footsteps; for example, Elly Jackson, aka La Roux, in the introduction to "Uptight Downtown" in 2014.

To further polish production of "Let's Dance," Rodgers used the famous vocal cannon that we hear at 1:31 of the Isley Brothers' "Twist and Shout" (1962) as an introduction, thus creating the kind of hook that artists use to capture the attention of their audience. Then, after each phrase of the verses, he inserted a short brass section inspired by Henry Mancini's "Peter Gunn." Last, he called upon guitarist Stevie Ray Vaughan, who worked on the entire album, to conclude the recording with a majestic solo. Vaughan himself—as Chris Layton, the drummer with his band

Double Trouble, would later recount—was furious to see Bowie mime his solo in the video for "Let's Dance": "Stevie was about to become world famous as the guy who played that solo, but the video really bothered him. [...] Stevie said, 'That motherfucker shouldn't be pretending to be playing shit he wasn't playing!' He couldn't understand why Bowie would do that."[135]

ON YOUR HEADPHONES
Preferring the synthesizer sounds of the time, Bowie had banned Nile Rodgers from using analog organs on the album. Without informing him, the producer and sound engineer Bob Clearmountain nevertheless added a Hammond B3 organ track to "Let's Dance," which can be heard at 0:59. It wasn't until 2011 that Rodgers finally revealed this secret to fans...and to David Bowie!

Without bassist Bernard Edwards (left) and guitarist Nile Rodgers (right), tracks like "Everybody Dance," "Freak," and "Good Times" would never have been possible.

WITHOUT YOU

David Bowie / 3:08

Side A: *Without You* / 3:08 / **Side B:** *Criminal World* / 4:25 /
US Release on EMI America: November 1983 (ref. B-8190) /
Best US Chart Ranking: 73

Musicians: David Bowie: lead and backing vocals / Nile Rodgers, Stevie Ray Vaughan: electric guitar / Bernard Edwards: bass / Tony Thompson (?) or Omar Hakim (?): drums / Robert Sabino: synthesizers / Sammy Figueroa: percussion / Frank Simms, George Simms, David Spinner: backing vocals / **Recorded:** Power Station Studios, New York: December 3–20, 1982 / **Technical Team:** Producers: David Bowie, Nile Rodgers / Sound Engineer: Bob Clearmountain / Assistant Sound Engineer: Dave Greenberg

Although several Chic musicians played on *Let's Dance*, one of its founding members was missing from the lineup: prominent bassist Bernard Edwards, Rodgers's partner in the Chic Organization Ltd., the production company created to produce Diana Ross's 1980 album *Diana*. Having left his mark on tracks such as "Good Times" (1979) and the unmistakable solo on "Everybody Dance" (1978), Edwards was acknowledged as one of the greatest bassists of the disco era. But after several commercial failures, as well as his addiction to drugs, Nile Rodgers decided that he could do without this exceptional musician. "I was sad not to have [him] involved," he later admitted, "but I had a job to do."[128] Faithful in friendship, he nevertheless invited him to participate in a single session to lay down a bass line on the track "Without You," the only midtempo ballad on the record. This seemed to create some difficulties for Carmine Rojas, the official bass player on the record. On the day of recording, Edwards needed only one take to place his delicate

and inimitable touch on the track, as Nile Rodgers later revealed: "I had bet David that Nard would finish the song in fifteen minutes. He did it in thirteen."[128]

RICOCHET

David Bowie / 5:14

Musicians: David Bowie: lead and backing vocals / Nile Rodgers, Stevie Ray Vaughan: electric guitar / Carmine Rojas: bass / Tony Thompson (?) or Omar Hakim (?): drums / Robert Sabino: synthesizers / Mac Gollehon: trumpet / Stan Harrison, Robert Aaron: tenor saxophone / Steve Elson: baritone saxophone / Sammy Figueroa: percussion / Frank Simms, George Simms, David Spinner: backing vocals / **Recorded:** Power Station Studios, New York: December 3–20, 1982 / **Technical Team:** Producers: David Bowie, Nile Rodgers / Sound Engineer: Bob Clearmountain / Assistant Sound Engineer: Dave Greenberg

The fifth track on the album, "Ricochet" was recorded at Mountain Studios with Nile Rodgers and sound engineer David Richards, and is unquestionably one of the songs on the album that most directly recalls the boldness of *Aladdin Sane* and *Diamond Dogs*. The song is led by a bold drum pattern, which the singer was never really happy with. "The beat wasn't quite right," he declared in 1987. "It didn't roll the way it should have, the syncopation was wrong. It had an ungainly gait; it should have flowed... Nile did his own thing on it, but it wasn't quite what I'd had in mind when I wrote the thing."[47] The result is nevertheless brilliant and gives a much-needed boost to the track, supported by a detonating set of brass and backing vocals that hit the listener with a reassuring line: *"It's not the end of the world."*

CRIMINAL WORLD

Peter Godwin, Duncan Browne, Sean Lyons / 4:25

Musicians: David Bowie: lead and backing vocals / Nile Rodgers, Stevie Ray Vaughan: electric guitar / Carmine Rojas: bass / Tony Thompson (?) or Omar Hakim (?): drums / Robert Sabino: synthesizers / Stan Harrison (?), Robert Aaron (?), Steve Elson (?): flute / Frank Simms, George Simms, David Spinner: backing vocals / **Recorded:** Power Station Studios, New York: December 3–20, 1982 / **Technical Team: Producers:** David Bowie, Nile Rodgers / **Sound Engineer:** Bob Clearmountain / **Assistant Sound Engineer:** Dave Greenberg /

When British band Metro released their first eponymous album in 1977, they had no idea that their first single would be banned from the BBC. "Criminal World," which highlighted the androgynous appearance of some young Britons, was not to the taste of the managers of the famous London radio station. *"The boys are like baby-faced girls,"* sang lead singer Peter Godwin, eight years before French band Indochine would take up the theme with their song "3e Sexe," proclaiming: *"Des garçons au féminin / Des filles au masculin"* (Boys in the feminine / Girls in the masculine). The anecdote inevitably caught the attention of David Bowie, who decided to record his own version of the song in December 1983. But times had changed, and faced with the arrival of the elegant New Romantics—hard rockers with androgynous looks and new wave stars—the song had lost its scandalous edge. It must be remembered that one of the biggest British hits in 1983 was the single "Karma Chameleon" by Culture Club, whose charismatic lead singer, Boy George, sported some of the most ambiguous outfits and attitudes of the day.

CAT PEOPLE (PUTTING OUT FIRE)

David Bowie, Giorgio Moroder / 5:09

Musicians: David Bowie: lead and backing vocals / Nile Rodgers, Stevie Ray Vaughan: electric guitar / Carmine Rojas: bass / Tony Thompson (?) or Omar Hakim (?): drums / Robert Sabino: synthesizers / Sammy Figueroa: percussion / Frank Simms, George Simms, David Spinner: backing vocals / **Recorded:** Power Station Studios, New York: December 3–20, 1982 / **Technical Team: Producers:** David Bowie, Nile Rodgers / **Sound Engineer:** Bob Clearmountain / **Assistant Sound Engineer:** Dave Greenberg

Accompanied by Bowie on vocals, producer Giorgio Moroder created a deep track with a slightly anguished atmosphere, which was used for the soundtrack of Paul Schrader's movie *Cat People* in 1982. Finding that this version "lacked a bit of guts,"[137] as he would later declare during a press conference given at Claridge's Hotel in London on March 17, 1983, to launch the "Serious Moonlight Tour," David Bowie decided to reclaim the title for his new album. Considered a sacrilege by some and a bold attempt by others, the track offers a quite-convincing rewrite for fans of saturated guitars, especially thanks to the raging six-string of Stevie Ray Vaughan. Even without the original backing vocals, now provided by the Simms brothers and David Spinner, the finale was still a great success. David Bowie delivers a song worthy of the greatest FM rock standards of the early 1980s, but the quality of the original version of "Cat People (Putting Out Fire)," which was highly appreciated by the fans, was destined to disappear into the limbo of his discography, filed away alongside other second versions that have been relatively forgotten, such as "All the Young Dudes" (1972), "Space Oddity (1979 Version)," or "John I'm Only Dancing (Again)," recorded in 1974 during the sessions of *Young Americans.*

SHAKE IT

David Bowie / 3:49

Musicians: David Bowie: lead and backing vocals / Nile Rodgers: electric guitar / Stevie Ray Vaughan: electric guitar / Carmine Rojas: bass / Tony Thompson (?) or Omar Hakim (?): drums / Robert Sabino: synthesizers / Mac Gollehon: trumpet / Stan Harrison: tenor saxophone / Robert Aaron: tenor saxophone / Steve Elson: baritone saxophone / Sammy Figueroa: percussion / Frank Simms: backing vocals / George Simms: backing vocals / David Spinner: backing vocals / **Recorded:** Power Station Studios, New York: December 3–20, 1982 / **Technical Team: Producers:** David Bowie, Nile Rodgers / **Sound Engineer:** Bob Clearmountain / **Assistant Sound Engineer:** Dave Greenberg

Bowie seems to be reconnecting here with his adopted city, New York, which he had left in a hurry in December 1980, after the assassination of his friend John Lennon. He would soon return to the city to live permanently: *"I could take you to heaven / I could spin you to hell / But I'll take you to New York / It's the place that I know well."*

It is a track with a truly danceable and swaying groove, which serves as the perfect close to *Let's Dance.* As for the bass, this was well and truly the work of Carmine Rojas, who, to the delight of four-string fans everywhere, would later detail the equipment he used during the album's recording: "The bass used on the session was my 1974 Fender jazz body combined with my 1968 Tele neck and the pick-ups were two different ones. One was an EMG Jazz pick-up and one was a DiMarzio."[138] The result is a warm and round sound, tailor-made for this funk-infused track whose rhythm has just one goal: to get fans dancing on the floor of Studio 54 in New York City, hopefully until the early hours of the morning.

TONIGHT

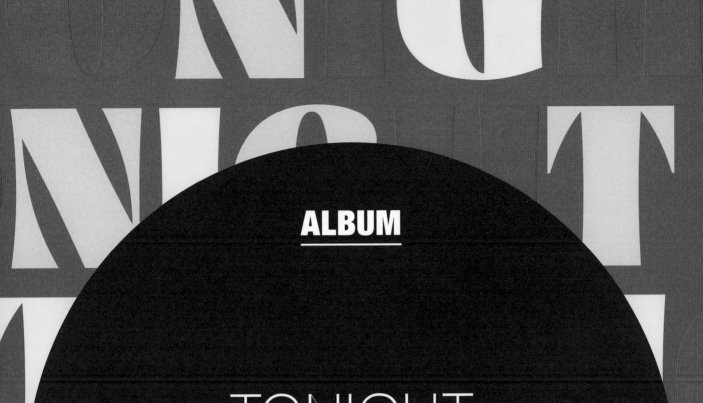

ALBUM

TONIGHT

Loving the Alien . Don't Look Down . God Only Knows . Tonight . Neighborhood Threat .
Blue Jean . Tumble and Twirl . I Keep Forgettin' . Dancing with the Big Boys

RELEASE DATES

United Kingdom: September 24, 1984
Reference: EMI America—EL 2402271
United States: September 24, 1984
Reference: EMI America—SJ-17138
Best UK Chart Ranking: 1
Best US Chart Ranking: 11

A TIME OF DOUBTS

From May to December 1983, the "Serious Moonlight Tour" was carried by David Bowie in triumph, from London to Toronto, and from Tokyo to Sydney. Following this marathon tour, the artist was taking advantage of some well-earned respite on the islands of Bali and Java, in the company of Coco Schwab, Iggy Pop, and Iggy's fiancée, Suchi Asano. EMI America, hoping to ride the wave of the success after *Let's Dance*—whose sales ran into the millions—pressured Bowie to get back to work. The singer then considered a collaboration with the Iguana, which would enable his friend to find a way out of a difficult financial situation, due in part to the failures of his latest albums, *New Values* (1979), *Soldier* (1980), *Party* (1981), and *Zombie Birdhouse* (1982). While the option of a joint album was initially considered, it was soon put aside in favor of two discs. Before focusing on *Blah-Blah-Blah,* which would provide a return to favor for the rocker from Detroit in 1986, Bowie decided to work on his own new opus, hoping to repeat the success of the previous album. Iggy Pop would nonetheless be omnipresent and co-write several of the numbers on the new record.

Derek Bramble: A New Producer

Suffering from an unprecedented level of writer's block—a break would probably have been beneficial—David Bowie struggled to reinvent himself and found only a few new paths to explore. He decided to dispense with the services of Nile Rodgers, whom he carefully avoided citing during the promotion of *Let's Dance* in order to appear as the sole producer on the successful disc. In any case, he considered that he owed nothing to this ex-icon of disco, whose career he felt he had saved.

Once again, the artist assumed the role of "discoverer" of talents. Acting on the advice of Bernard Doherty, his PR manager with the Rogers & Cowan agency in London,

Bowie called upon the young Derek Bramble, the ex-vocalist of the band Lynx, who had just co-written and produced David Grant's single "Love Will Find a Way." This collaboration made him one of the rising stars of the synth-funk sound, a new musical wave launched by the album *Dirty Mind* from Prince in 1980, and followed by the single "Friends" (1982) by Shalamar and various productions from Rick James and other performers of the day. Bramble thus took charge of the production of Bowie's next opus, accompanied by sound engineer Hugh Padgham, who had been recommended by Bob Clearmountain, the man behind the console on *Let's Dance.*

Following in the Footsteps of the Police

From the first days of May 1984, Bowie and his team unpacked their bags in Canada, and quickly set themselves up at Le Studio, a complex located at the center of Morin-Heights, a village about an hour and a half north of Montreal. This residential structure was suggested to them by Hugh Padgham, who had recorded a large part of *Synchronicity* there the previous year, the final opus by the Police that was carried by the hit "Every Breath You Take." Located far away from urban temptations, the studio was ideal for the singer, who had lately rekindled his cocaine addiction. Unfortunately, he did not find the inspiration he needed, nor did he rekindle the magic of the *Let's Dance* sessions.

Following in the footsteps of Sting's group, Bowie decided to try producing some rock with a reggae touch. The guitarist Carlos Alomar, bassist Carmine Rojas, drummer Omar Hakim, and percussionist Sammy Figueroa were part of the process from the beginning. George Simms, Curtis King, and Robin Clark provided backing vocals. The brass section was made up of the Borneo Horns, comprised of Stanley Harrison, Steve Elson, and Lenny Pickett, who supported the pieces with their

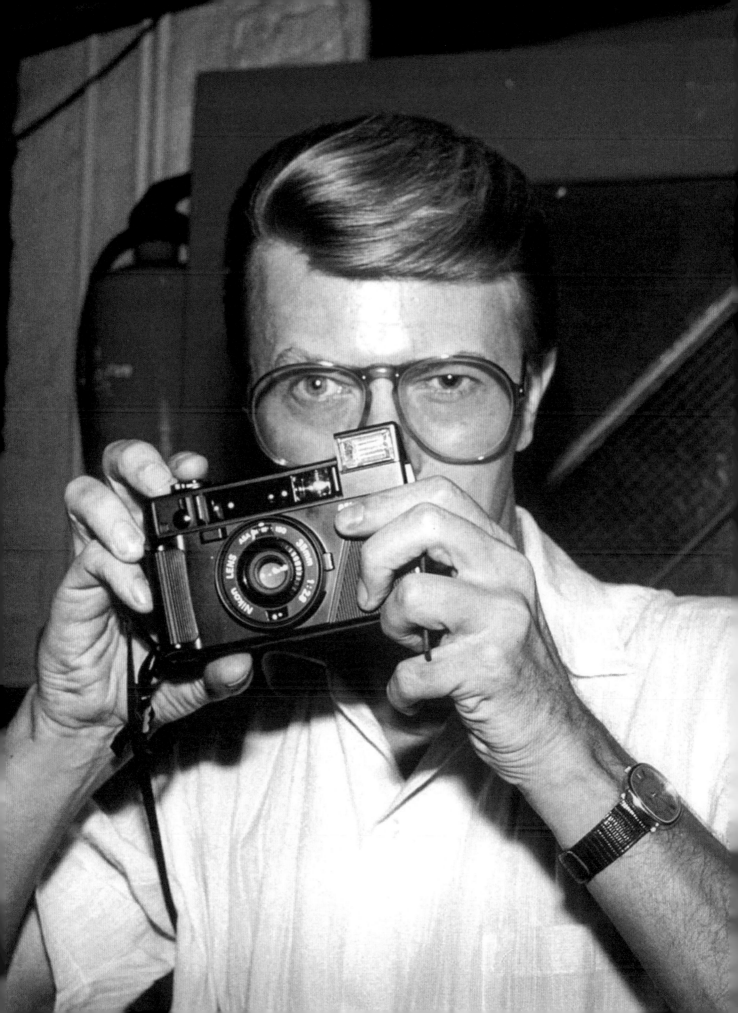

On November 21, 1984, *Tonight* was David Bowie's first album to be released in CD format, but only in Japan. Subsequent albums appeared in this format throughout the world.

Bowie in the music video for "Loving the Alien."

powerful playing. Special guests, such as Tina Turner, Iggy Pop, and Mark King, the singer-bassist from Level 42, also contributed to the album. But the production of the disc proved difficult, especially due to the growing discord between Derek Bramble and Bowie; the former insisted on multiple takes in spite of Bowie's preference for the spontaneity of single takes. After taking a break for a few days, Derek Bramble never returned, and Hugh Padgham was promoted to producer. Padgham tried to salvage the situation, but the songs were cruelly short on writing work, and many of the numbers were simply lacking in ambition. Besides all of this, there were only two new songs by Bowie on the disc: "Loving the Alien" and "Blue Jean." The rest of the LP consisted of covers as well as old and new tracks written jointly with Iggy Pop.

A Partial Welcome

Thanks to the advantage of Bowie's immense celebrity, *Tonight* went to the top of the British charts when it was released on September 24, 1984. But this was a short-lived success. The disc was weak and lacking in cohesion, most likely due to a lack of a decisive artistic direction, and therefore the album teetered dangerously on the cusp of easy listening. Even with the single "Tonight," sung as a duo with Tina Turner, this album is often considered to be David Bowie's worst. *Tonight* was virtually unpromoted by its author, who gave only very few interviews and no concerts upon its release. Conscious of having missed the mark, the artist quickly moved on to new collaborations, in particular with the Pat Metheny Group and Mick Jagger.

Two masked extras posing with
the artist on the set of the
"Loving the Alien" music video.

LOVING THE ALIEN

David Bowie / 7:11

Musicians

David Bowie: lead and backing vocals
Carlos Alomar: electric guitar
Derek Bramble: bass, electric guitar, synthesizer
Carmine Rojas (?): bass
Omar Hakim: drums
Guy St-Onge: marimba
Rob Yale: Fairlight CMI synthesizer
Robin Clark: backing vocals
George Simms: backing vocals
Curtis King: backing vocals
Unidentified Musicians: strings

Recorded

Le Studio, Morin-Heights, Quebec, Canada: May 1984

Technical Team

Producers: David Bowie, Derek Bramble, Hugh Padgham
Sound Engineer: Hugh Padgham
String Arrangements: Arif Mardin

SINGLE VERSION

Technical Team

Additional Production: Steve Thompson
Mixing: Steve Thompson, Michael Barbiero
Assistant Sound Engineer: Alex Haas
Consultant: Carlos Alomar

SIDE A: *Loving the Alien (Re-Mixed Version)* / 4:43
SIDE B: *Don't Look Down (Re-Mixed Version)* / 4:04
UK Release on EMI America: June 1985 (ref. EA 195)
US Release on EMI America: June 1985 (ref. BG-8271)
Best UK Chart Ranking: 19
Best US Chart Ranking: Did Not Chart

FOR BOWIE ADDICTS

The "ah-ah-ahs" mumbled by David Bowie in the introduction to "Loving the Alien" were inspired by the Philip Glass opera *Einstein on the Beach*, written in 1976 and staged by Robert Wilson for the Philip Glass Ensemble.

Genesis

Heavily influenced by reading Donovan Joyce's best-selling book, *The Jesus Scroll,* which appeared in 1972, this first number features David Bowie launching into an acerbic critique of violence perpetuated over the centuries in the name of religion. In an interview given to Charles Shaar Murray for *New Musical Express* in September 1984, the singer confided that the lyrics did not mesh with the light-hearted and relaxed spirit of the disc: "It really doesn't fit in there very much, does it? That was the most personalised bit of writing on the album for me; not to say that the others were written from a distance, but they're a lot lighter in tone. That one was me in there dwelling on the idea of the awful shit that we've had to put up with because of the Church. That's how it started out: for some reason I was very angry."[139]

Subtitled "Re-Mixed Version," "Loving the Alien" appeared as a single in a version remixed by Steve Thompson and Michael Barbiero in June 1985 and only just made it to nineteenth place on the British charts.

Production

It is sometimes difficult to step back and reflect on a disc whose songs are not up to our expectations, and some, like biographer Nicholas Pegg, have been very critical: "The opening track of *Tonight* perfectly summarizes the album's malaise: it's a terrific piece of songwriting, but what should be a flight of operatic grandeur is dragged from the heights by insipid, over-elaborate production, spangly synth flourishes, dated echo-laden drumbeats and a ridiculously polite guitar break."[47] Bowie himself disowned the track: "When I listen to those demos it's, 'How did it turn out like that?' You should hear 'Loving the Alien' on demo. It's wonderful on demo. I promise you! But on the album, it's...not as wonderful. What am I meant to say?"[140] It must be admitted that the song breaks with the extremist experimentations of Bowie on *Low, "Heroes,"* and even *Let's Dance*, and the singer in this case has just handed over the keys to Derek Bramble, who many believe to be responsible for the cold treatment applied to the album overall.

Somewhere between rock and reggae: two different readings of Iggy Pop's "Don't Look Down."

DON'T LOOK DOWN

Iggy Pop, James Williamson / 4:08

Musicians: David Bowie: lead and backing vocals / Carlos Alomar: electric guitar / Derek Bramble: bass, electric guitar, synthesizer, programming / Omar Hakim: drums / Stan Harrison: tenor saxophone, alto saxophone / Lenny Pickett: tenor saxophone / Steve Elson: baritone saxophone / Marc Pender: trumpet / Robin Clark: backing vocals / George Simms: backing vocals / Curtis King: backing vocals / **Recorded:** Le Studio, Morin-Heights, Quebec, Canada: May 1984 / **Technical Team:** Producers: David Bowie, Derek Bramble, Hugh Padgham / **Sound Engineer:** Hugh Padgham / **Brass Arrangements:** The Borneo Horns (Stan Harrison, Lenny Pickett, Steve Elson)

While the members of the Police managed to successfully mix reggae with rock and pop on their album *Reggatta de Blanc* in 1979 (a title that could be translated as "White Reggae"—whose self-mocking tone should be stressed), the same exercise remained perilous for musicians who had neglected to immerse themselves in Jamaican culture and music before attempting to pay homage to the reggae tradition.

Although the rhythmic basis of 1978's "Yassassin" was already reggae, David Bowie now adopted the sound again in this cover of "Don't Look Down" by Iggy Pop, a delicious rock nugget unearthed from *New Values* (1979). Set to the soaring sonorities borrowed from the guitar of Andy Summers (the Police), Bowie added some (rather too clean) brass and an offbeat piano rhythm that feels closer to the synthesizers of UB40 than the blistering chords of Peter Tosh armed with his guitar in the shape of a M16 machine gun—a reminder that reggae is a weapon against oppression, rather than a languorous form of music. Bowie modified Iggy Pop's original number to the extent that it became almost unrecognizable. "I think it was the drum machine [used in the demos]!" he explained. "I was trying to rearrange 'Don't Look Down' and it wouldn't work. I tried it every-which-a-way. I tried it jazz-rock, I tried it as a march, and then I just hit on an old ska-sounding beat, and it picked up life. Taking energy away from the musical side of things reinforced the lyrics and gave them their own energy. I think working with Derek Bramble really helped a lot, because he played proper reggae bass lines..."[139]

GOD ONLY KNOWS

Brian Wilson, Tony Asher / 3:06

Musicians: David Bowie: lead and backing vocals / Carlos Alomar: acoustic guitar / Derek Bramble: synthesizer / Carmine Rojas: bass / Omar Hakim: drums / Rob Yale: Fairlight CMI synthesizer / Stan Harrison: tenor saxophone, alto saxophone / Lenny Pickett: tenor saxophone / Steve Elson: baritone saxophone / Marc Pender: trumpet / Robin Clark, George Simms, Curtis King: backing vocals / Unidenitifed Musicians: strings / **Recorded:** Le Studio, Morin-Heights, Quebec, Canada: May 1984 / **Technical Team:** Producers: David Bowie, Derek Bramble, Hugh Padgham / **Sound Engineer:** Hugh Padgham / **String and Synthesizer Arrangements:** Arif Mardin / **Brass Arrangements:** The Borneo Horns (Stan Harrison, Lenny Pickett, Steve Elson)

As soon as the album was released, critics unanimously condemned this cover of one of the finest songs ever produced by the Beach Boys, which was composed by Brian Wilson and written by the famous lyricist Tony Asher, for the album *Pet Sounds* in 1966. Who would dare to modify "Stairway to Heaven" by Led Zeppelin, "Little Wing" by Jimi Hendrix, or "Hotel California" by the Eagles without inciting the fury of fans around the world? This was the challenge picked up by Bowie on "God Only Knows," which the singer had previously considered covering in the days of *Pin Ups*. Even emptied of the lyrical power and amorous passion that Brian Wilson had brought to life, the piece still shines with its (rather pompous) string arrangements by Arif Mardin, who was famous for his collaboration on "Respect" by Aretha Franklin in 1967. Bowie brings out his very best crooner voice for this version produced by Hugh Padgham, who unhesitatingly commented: "'God Only Knows' was a bit of a dodgy song to cover. I've never thought it was a good idea to cover a classic unless you have a fairly strong chance of improving it, which is unlikely, or subverting it in some way."[1]

TONIGHT

David Bowie, Iggy Pop / 3:50

Side A: *Tonight* / 3:42 / **Side B:** *Tumble and Twirl* / 4:56 / **UK Release on EMI America:** November 1984 (ref. EA 187) / **US Release on EMI America:** November 1984 (ref. B-8246) / **Best UK Chart Ranking:** 53 / **Best US Chart Ranking:** 53

Musicians: David Bowie: lead and backing vocals / Tina Turner: vocals / Carlos Alomar: electric guitar / Derek Bramble: bass, electric guitar, synthesizer / Carmine Rojas (?): bass / Omar Hakim: drums / Rob Yale: Fairlight CMI synthesizer / Guy St-Onge: marimba / Stan Harrison: tenor saxophone, alto saxophone / Lenny Pickett: tenor saxophone / Steve Elson: baritone saxophone / Robin Clark, George Simms, Curtis King: backing vocals / **Recorded:** Le Studio, Morin-Heights, Quebec, Canada: May 1984 / **Technical Team:** Producers: David Bowie, Derek Bramble, Hugh Padgham / **Sound Engineer:** Hugh Padgham / **Arrangements:** Arif Mardin / **Brass Arrangements:** The Borneo Horns (Stan Harrison, Lenny Pickett, Steve Elson)

Despite an evident lightness and naiveté that could entice a listener into sipping a cocktail by the sea, "Tonight" was originally a serious and profound song, composed in 1977 by Bowie and Iggy Pop for the American rocker's album *Lust for Life*. When the idea occurred to David Bowie to cover this number, which contains the last words of a man to his companion dying of an overdose, he thought of a duet with Tina Turner, whose charisma, voice, and music had fascinated him since his childhood. A meeting between the singers took place at the Morin-Heights studio in May 1984. According to him, it would have been

impossible to ask Tina Turner to sing the song as it was. He therefore chose to cut out its introduction, and in so doing removed all allusions to drugs, thereby also removing the entire substance of the song. The following phrases were also removed: "*I saw my baby / She was turning blue / I knew that soon, her / Young life was through / And so I got down on my knees / Down by her bed / And these are the words / To her I said.*" "I didn't want to inflict it on her either," explained Bowie. "It's not necessarily something that she would particularly agree to sing or be part of. I guess we changed the whole sentiment around. It still has that same barren feeling, though, but it's out of that specific area that I'm not at home in. I can't say that it's Iggy's world, but it's far more of Iggy's observation than mine."[139] Without this introduction and accompanied by its new arrangements, the piece assumed a completely different direction, passing from a dark punk-rock anthem to this little reggae number designed for FM radio. With no promotional video put out upon its release, the song was not a success, managing to hit only fifty-third place on the British and North American charts.

In reality, nothing somber remains in this new version of "Tonight." Quite unlike the rage expressed by Iggy Pop, Bowie performs this love song with an assumed languor, supported by an ensemble of musicians newly introduced to the concept of playing reggae. Whether one loves or hates this new attempt at reggae music, this is an effective number, and the brass arrangements of the Borneo Horns are there to prove it. There is nonetheless a little downside when the indigestible marimba solo enters at 2:15 (with a 1980s Club Med feel to it!), a total steal from the very Caribbean-inspired "Unconditional Love" by Donna Summer and Musical Youth, which was released in September 1983. A question remains when listening to this light-as-a-feather number: Why does Tina Turner's voice, which is of impeccable precision, seem to be lost in the background in the final mix? It seems that the vocal power of the singer did not suit Bowie, who preferred to submix it rather than take on the celebrated singer's inimitable vocal timbre.

When Tina Turner issued her *Tina Live in Europe* album in March 1988, it included a version of "Tonight" recorded with David Bowie at the Birmingham, England, National Exhibition Center on March 23, 1985.

NEIGHBORHOOD THREAT

David Bowie, Iggy Pop / 3:12

Musicians: David Bowie: lead and backing vocals / Carlos Alomar: electric guitar / Derek Bramble: bass, electric guitar, synthesizer / Carmine Rojas (?): bass / Omar Hakim: drums / Robin Clark: backing vocals / George Simms: backing vocals / Curtis King: backing vocals / **Recorded:** Le Studio, Morin-Heights, Quebec, Canada: May 1984 / **Technical Team:** Producers: David Bowie, Derek Bramble, Hugh Padgham / **Sound Engineer:** Hugh Padgham

Bowie's first number leaning toward the kind of hard FM sounds performed by American groups such as Van Halen and Quiet Riot, "Neighborhood Threat" is not the most remarkable piece on *Tonight*, with reverb to the max, oozing synthesizers, and a guitar solo played with the tapping style used by Eddie Van Halen all heavily featured. These effects support this four-hander number written with Iggy Pop at the Morin-Heights studio. Bowie himself disowned this song, declaring in 1987: "It went totally wrong. It sounded so tight and compromised. [...] It was the wrong band to do it with—wonderful band, but it wasn't right for that song."[47]

BLUE JEAN

David Bowie / 3:08

Side A: *Blue Jean* / 3:08 / **Side B:** *Dancing with the Big Boys* / 3:32 / **UK Release on EMI America:** September 1, 1984 (ref. EA 181) / **US Release on EMI America:** September 1, 1984 (ref. B-8231) / **Best UK Chart Ranking:** 6 / **Best US Chart Ranking:** 8

Musicians: David Bowie: lead and backing vocals / Carlos Alomar: electric guitar / Derek Bramble: electric guitar, synthesizer / Carmine Rojas: bass / Omar Hakim: drums / Guy St-Onge: marimba / Stan Harrison: tenor saxophone, alto saxophone / Lenny Pickett: tenor saxophone / Steve Elson: baritone saxophone / Robin Clark, George Simms, Curtis King: backing vocals / **Recorded:** Le Studio, Morin-Heights, Quebec, Canada: May 1984 / **Technical Team:** Producers: David Bowie, Derek Bramble, Hugh Padgham / **Sound Engineer:** Hugh Padgham / **Brass Arrangements:** The Borneo Horns (Stan Harrison, Lenny Pickett, Steve Elson)

Barely reaching sixth place on the British charts, "Blue Jean" serves up a tired brand of rock, inspired by some of the author's idols. "'Blue Jean' reminds me of Eddie Cochran," he confided. "It was inspired from that Eddie Cochran feeling, but that of course is very Troggs as well. I dunno...it's quite eclectic, I suppose. What of mine isn't?"[139] Promoted with a twenty-minute video created by Julien Temple with the title *Jazzin' for Blue Jean*, the single

surfed the fashion for minifilms launched by Michael Jackson and his scary "Thriller," which was filmed by John Landis in 1983. Steve Elson, one of the Borneo Horns saxophonists, recalled long afterward: "We spent about ten days together and at night we watched videos. This was early in MTV and Bowie was real interested in videos at that point."[131]

TUMBLE AND TWIRL

David Bowie, Iggy Pop / 5:00

Musicians: David Bowie: lead and backing vocals / Carlos Alomar: electric guitar / Derek Bramble: synthesizer, programming / Mark King: bass / Omar Hakim: drums / Stan Harrison: tenor saxophone, alto saxophone / Lenny Pickett: tenor saxophone / Steve Elson: baritone saxophone / Marc Pender: trumpet, bugle / Robin Clark, George Simms, Curtis King: backing vocals / **Recorded:** Le Studio, Morin-Heights, Quebec, Canada: May 1984 / **Technical Team:** Producers: David Bowie, Derek Bramble, Hugh Padgham / **Sound Engineer:** Hugh Padgham / **Brass Arrangements:** The Borneo Horns (Stan Harrison, Lenny Pickett, Steve Elson)

Even though David Bowie and Iggy Pop did not go to Borneo during their stay in the Indonesian islands after the "Serious Moonlight Tour," this track evokes memories of holidays on the island: T-shirts featuring images of Bob Marley or *Playboy* logos, dancing on the sand...Although the attempt at reviving the spirit of "African Night Flight" falls flat here, one could applaud the enthusiasm with which the team performs this joyful number. Once we get past the very "Boogie Wonderland"–sounding brass introduction, a guest artist—not credited on the disc—brings a smile to the listener's face with his inimitable technique. Mark King, Level 42 singer and bassist, famous for his famous "machine gun" slap triplets that are characteristic of his playing, lends his support to a brass section that really keeps this number going.

I KEEP FORGETTIN'

Jerry Leiber, Mike Stoller, Gil Garfield / 2:34

Musicians: David Bowie: lead and backing vocals / Carlos Alomar: electric guitar / Derek Bramble: bass, synthesizer / Carmine Rojas (?): bass / Omar Hakim: drums / Guy St-Onge: marimba / Stan Harrison: tenor saxophone, alto saxophone / Lenny Pickett: tenor saxophone / Steve Elson: baritone saxophone / Marc Pender: trumpet / Robin Clark, George Simms, Curtis King: backing vocals / **Recorded:** Le Studio, Morin-Heights, Quebec, Canada: May 1984 / **Technical Team:** Producers: David Bowie, Derek Bramble, Hugh Padgham / **Sound Engineer:** Hugh Padgham / **Brass Arrangements:** The Borneo Horns (Stan Harrison, Lenny Pickett, Steve Elson)

Pioneer of the rhythm 'n' blues style, Chuck Jackson worked at the Motown label between 1967 and 1970.

Once again, David Bowie covers a song that was part of the soundtrack of his youth: "I Keep Forgettin'" by Chuck Jackson. "I've always wanted to do that song...," said Bowie. "I think that this album gave me a chance, like *Pin Ups* did a few years ago, to do some covers that I always wanted to do."[139] Although the symbiosis between the musicians works throughout this strongly delivered homage, the number is of limited interest and creates part of the album's lack of a coherent theme, which runs the significant risk of losing the listener along the way.

DANCING WITH THE BIG BOYS

David Bowie, Iggy Pop, Carlos Alomar / 3:52

Musicians: David Bowie: lead and backing vocals / Iggy Pop: vocals / Carlos Alomar: electric guitar / Derek Bramble: bass (?), electric guitar, synthesizer, programming / Carmine Rojas (?): bass / Omar Hakim: drums / Stan Harrison: tenor saxophone, alto saxophone / Lenny Pickett: tenor saxophone /

Steve Elson: baritone saxophone / **Marc Pender:** trumpet / Robin Clark, George Simms, Curtis King: backing vocals / **Recorded:** Le Studio, Morin-Heights, Quebec, Canada: May 1984 / **Technical Team:** Producers: David Bowie, Derek Bramble, Hugh Padgham / Sound Engineer: Hugh Padgham / Brass Arrangements: The Borneo Horns (Stan Harrison, Lenny Pickett, Steve Elson)

Co-written with Iggy Pop and Carlos Alomar, "Dancing with the Big Boys" concludes *Tonight* with a touch of rock that sits better with the Iguana than it does with his British counterpart. Before the *Tin Machine* adventure, which added two raucous, even aggressive works to Bowie's discography, this last song gave pride of place to the searing guitars of Carlos Alomar. Looking for a new sound identity, Bowie loses himself here in rock FM radio experimentations that he would later refine on his subsequent albums. "There's a particular sound I'm after that I haven't really got yet and I probably won't drop this search until I get it," he confided at the time. "[...] I think I got quite close to it on 'Dancing with the Big Boys.' [...] I think I should be a bit more adventurous."[139]

This Is Not America / This Is Not America (Instrumental)

UK Release on EMI America: February 1985 (ref. EA 190) / Best UK Chart Ranking: 14
US Release on EMI America: February 1985 (ref. B-8251) / Best US Chart Ranking: 32

David Bowie and Pat Metheny Group

THIS IS NOT AMERICA

David Bowie, Pat Metheny, Lyle Mays / 3:51

Musicians

David Bowie: lead and backing vocals
Pat Metheny: electric guitar, synthesizers, Synclavier, Roland GR-300 Guitar Synthesizer, programming
Lyle Mays: synthesizers
Steve Rodby: acoustic bass

Recorded

Mountain Studios, Montreux: Autumn 1984
Odyssey Studios, London (overdubs): Autumn 1984

Technical Team

Producers: David Bowie, Pat Metheny
Sound Engineer: David Richards
Mixing: Bob Clearmountain

SIDE A: *This Is Not America* / 3:51
SIDE B: *This Is Not America (Instrumental)* / 3:51

David Bowie and Pat Metheny in 1984.

Genesis

In the autumn of 1984, jazz guitarist Pat Metheny was looking for a performer for the main song on the original soundtrack that he was in the process of composing for *The Falcon and the Snowman*, directed by John Schlesinger. This was an important choice, as the singles from soundtracks often achieved considerable success, and provided significant promotional material for the film. The producer himself suggested David Bowie. "I [...] was really not that aware of Bowie in general," said Metheny. "When Mr Schlesinger suggested him, I went out and bought a few records and realised that actually I was a big fan, and I agreed he was absolutely the perfect person to sing that song."[1] A viewing of the film was arranged without delay for the Englishman, who fell under the spell of this espionage film. "It's a magnificent piece of film-making," he commented with enthusiasm, "the best Schlesinger movie I've seen in years."[139] The singer took notes, and, when the screening was completed, suggested a list of titles to Pat Metheny for the song that they would soon be recording together, all of which were taken from the film's dialogue. One of these titles particularly caught Metheny's attention: "This Is Not America."

Production

After completing the recording of the original soundtrack at Odyssey Studios in London, Metheny joined Bowie at Mountain Studios in Montreux.

One day was allocated for the recording of the instrumental portions, and a second day was allotted for the vocals. As with Chuck Hammer on "Ashes to Ashes," Pat Metheny was an enthusiastic exponent of the Roland GR-300 Guitar Synthesizer, which he used to color the song with soaring layers. A Synclavier synthesizer (which cost £60,000, or $107,000, at the time!), whose sound was broadcast backward during the mixing, was also used. Bowie—as was his usual practice—recorded his vocals in only a few takes, and then called upon Pat Metheny and his musicians to provide the backing vocals. "He asked if any of us could sing," the guitarist remembers, "and as we couldn't, he did all the background vocals himself, kind of transforming into what seemed to be two or three different people as he did each part. That was pretty amazing."[1]

Dancing in the Street / Dancing in the Street (Instrumental)

UK Release on EMI America: August 12, 1985 (ref. EA 204) / Best UK Chart Ranking: 1
US Release on EMI America: August 12, 1985 (ref. B-8288) / Best US Chart Ranking: 7

David Bowie and Mick Jagger

DANCING IN THE STREET

William Stevenson, Ivory Joe Hunter, Marvin Gaye / 3:07

Musicians

David Bowie: vocals
Mick Jagger: vocals
Kevin Armstrong: electric guitar
G. E. Smith: electric guitar
Earl Slick: electric guitar
Matthew Seligman: bass
John Regan: additional bass
Neil Conti: drums
Steve Nieve: synthesizers
Pedro Ortiz: percussion
Jimmy Maelen: percussion
Mac Gollehon: trumpet
Stan Harrison: saxophone
Lenny Pickett: saxophone
Helena Springs: backing vocals
Tessa Niles: backing vocals

Recorded

Abbey Road Studios, London: June 1985
Power Station Studios, New York: July 1985

Technical Team

Producers: Clive Langer, Alan Winstanley
Additional Production: Nile Rodgers, Mick Jagger, Steve Thompson, Michael Barbiero
Sound Engineers: Bob Clearmountain, Mark Saunders, Stephen Benben
Assistant Sound Engineers: Steve Boyer, Ira McLaughlin, Richard Sullivan
Mixing: Bob Clearmountain

SIDE A: *Dancing in the Street* / 3:07
SIDE B: *Dancing in the Street (Instrumental)* / 3:17

Genesis

On July 13, 1985, a massive concert organized by Bob Geldof, the Boomtown Rats singer, and ex-Visage member Midge Ure was to take place simultaneously on the stages of Wembley Stadium in London and John F. Kennedy Stadium in Philadelphia. The aim: fund-raising for the relief of the famine in Africa. For this event, which brought together more than seventy artists on both sides of the Atlantic, the organizers planned a collaboration between David Bowie—who was invited to play at Wembley—and Mick Jagger, who was in Philadelphia. Initially they envisaged a song performed as a duet using the magic of direct broadcasting, but the inevitable seconds of lag time did not enable the synchronization of singers located on separate continents. The idea of a video recording was therefore adopted. Having previously considered a cover of "One Love / People Get Ready" by Bob Marley, this was abandoned in favor of the 1964 hit "Dancing in the Street" by vocal trio Martha and the Vandellas. Filmed in just a couple of hours at Millennium Mills, a defunct flower mill located at the London Royal Victoria Docks, the video was broadcast several times over the course of the sixteen hours of Live Aid, which gave the duo a nice summer success.

Production

The "Dancing in the Street" recording session took place at Abbey Road Studios on the evening following the recording of "That's Motivation" and "Absolute Beginners," both numbers composed by David Bowie for the original soundtrack of the film *Absolute Beginners*, directed by Julien Temple. The recording was completed at lightning speed, between 7:00 and 11:30 that same evening, thanks to the professionalism of Bowie's musicians, including Kevin Armstrong on guitar and Neil Conti on drums, with support from backup singers Helena Springs (co-writer of many of Bob Dylan's songs in 1978) and Tessa Niles, a lady with a golden voice who had been the hidden force behind collaborations with a plethora of artists, ranging from Eric Clapton to the Police. Clive Langer and Alan Winstanley, already responsible for the original soundtrack of *Absolute Beginners*, served as the song's producers. Mick Jagger and David Bowie recorded their parts in a single take.

Absolute Beginners / Absolute Beginners (Dub Mix)
UK Release on Virgin: March 3, 1986 (ref. VS. 838) / Best UK Chart Ranking: 2
US Release on Virgin: March 3, 1986 (ref. B-8308) / Best US Chart Ranking: 53

Bowie embodied a cynical
businessman in the film
Absolute Beginners.

Single

ABSOLUTE BEGINNERS
David Bowie / 5:35

Musicians
David Bowie: vocals
Kevin Armstrong: electric guitar
Matthew Seligman: bass
Neil Conti: drums
Steve Nieve: synthesizers
Rick Wakeman: synthesizers
Luís Jardim: percussion
Don Weller: saxophone
Gary Barnacle: tenor saxophone
Paul Weimer: tenor saxophone
Willie Garnett: tenor saxophone
Andy Mackintosh: baritone saxophone
Gordon Murphy: baritone saxophone
Janet Armstrong: backing vocals

Recorded
Abbey Road Studios, London (music): June 1985
Westside Studios, London (vocals): August 18, 1985
Mountain Studios, Montreux (overdubs): 1985

Technical Team
Producers: David Bowie, Clive Langer, Alan Winstanley
Sound Engineer: Mark Saunders

SIDE A: *Absolute Beginners* / 5:35
SIDE B: *Absolute Beginners (Dub Mix)* / 5:37

Genesis

When he launched into the filming of *Absolute Beginners*, his first feature film, Julien Temple already had a prestigious résumé. As a producer of videos for all the big names in music since the 1970s, he was the person behind the videos of "God Save the Queen" by the Sex Pistols (1977), "Rock This Town" by the Stray Cats (1980), and "Come On Eileen" by Dexys Midnight Runners in 1982. No one was really surprised to see David Bowie in the cast of this musical adaptation of the 1959 novel by Colin MacInnes; Bowie plays the part of Vendice Partners, an unscrupulous advertising agent.

Bowie suggested to Temple (who had directed the mini-film *Jazzin' for Blue Jean* in 1984) the idea of recording a number for the original soundtrack: "That's Motivation." At the end of the session, which took place in June at Abbey Road Studios, Bowie told the guitarist Kevin Armstrong that he had a new idea, and a few chords later, the musicians had laid down the instrumental score for "Absolute Beginners."

The song, whose lyricism takes us back to the great days of Bowie in the seventies, was a success in the United Kingdom when the single was released in March 1986. We often read that this was the singer's best piece during his relatively thankless 1980s. It actually is one of his finest compositions, quite simply, and it deserves to be ranked alongside "Quicksand," "Changes," and "Time." "Absolute Beginners" was also included on the album *Tonight* when it was rereleased by Virgin in 1995.

Production

A few weeks after the Abbey Road sessions, Bowie joined producers Clive Langer and Alan Winstanley in their Westside Studios in London, where he recorded the vocal line of his future single. The sound engineer Mark Saunders recalls: "The day Bowie was first due to show up at Westside, we were all a bit nervous—Bowie was the biggest star client for Clive and Alan at that point in time. We kept looking out the windows, waiting for a stretch limo to show up and an entire entourage to walk in, but then a black cab showed up and out popped the unaccompanied Bowie. He walked in, announced [...]: 'Hi, I'm David Bowie.'"[141]

To provide the female backing vocals, the singer wanted the voice of an amateur performer rather than a professional

backing singer. Guitarist Kevin Armstrong, who worked on the arrangements of the song (arrangements that, according to him, were wrapped up in twenty minutes), suggested calling on his sister Janet for this challenge. "He just went, 'Right, get her in.'"[130] Having been presented to the musicians at the end of the day, the song was introduced in a fragmentary manner. "By not knowing the whole song, it totally forced you out of your comfort zone,"[53] bassist Matthew Seligman later testified.

"Absolute Beginners" was released in four different formats: a 5:35 single version; a 4:46 promotional version; an instrumental version called "Dub Mix" for the B-side of the single; and finally an 8:01 version, called the "Full Length Version," which included the introduction of "That's Motivation" and a solo combining percussion and saxaphone.

Bowie performs "That's Motivation" in Julian Temple's musical comedy, which tells the story of the tumultuous loves of a fashion designer and a photographer at the beginning of the 1960s.

THAT'S MOTIVATION

David Bowie / 4:14

Musicians: David Bowie: vocals / **Kevin Armstrong:** electric guitar / **Matthew Seligman:** bass / **Neil Conti:** drums, electric guitar / **Steve Nieve, Rick Wakeman:** synthesizers / **Luís Jardim:** percussion / **Don Weller:** saxophone / **Gary Barnacle, Paul Weimer, Willie Garnett:** tenor saxophone / **Andy Mackintosh, Gordon Murphy:** baritone saxophone / **Janet Armstrong:** backing vocals / **Recorded:** Abbey Road Studios, London (music): June 1985 / Westside Studios, London (vocals): August 18, 1985 / **Technical Team:** Producers: David Bowie, Clive Langer, Alan Winstanley / **Sound Engineer:** Mark Saunders / **Arrangements:** Gil Evans

"That's Motivation" appeared with "Volare (Nel Blu Dipinto Di Blu)" and three versions of "Absolute Beginners" on a disc called *Absolute Beginners EP*, issued by Virgin on May 25, 2007.

With its guitar riff made in homage to "Material Girl," Madonna's hit released in January 1985 and produced by Nile Rodgers, "That's Motivation" adheres to the codes of musical comedy followed in the film. Here, the cynical advertising agent Vendice Partners, played by David Bowie, lavishes advice on the young Colin, a young idealistic photographer played by Eddie O'Connell: *"Welcome to the world of your dreams, Colin / Where you can be what you want / Commit horrible sins / And get away with it / Lust, gluttony, pride, anger, sloth, avarice and jealousy."*

When the musicians were recruited by Hugh Stanley-Clarke, EMI's project manager, for the recording session of "That's Motivation," they had no idea which artist they would be playing for. The session was booked in the name of "Mr X." They discovered only upon arrival that they would be accompanying the great David Bowie.

An iconic image from Julian Temple's film: Bowie performing some dance steps on the keyboard of a giant typewriter.

VOLARE (NEL BLU DIPINTO DI BLU)

Franco Migliacci, Domenico Modugno / 3:13

Musicians: David Bowie: lead and backing vocals / Erdal Kizilçay: programming, bass, piano, electric guitar, synthesizer, percussion, marimba / **Recorded:** Abbey Road Studios, London (?): June 1985 / Mountain Studios, Montreux (?): Summer 1985 / **Technical Team:** Producers: David Bowie, Erdal Kizilçay

The number of artists who have performed "Nel Blu Dipinto Di Blu" is now too many to count, though the song is better known by the name "Volare," as sung by Domenico Modugno in 1958 at the Eurovision song contest. This Italian hit reached number one on the American *Billboard* charts five times during the summer of 1958 and enjoyed massive worldwide success. Accompanied by Erdal Kizilçay, the musician who had already contributed to the demos of "Let's Dance" and "Modern Love" in December 1982, Bowie decided to deliver a new interpretation of this classic song for the soundtrack to *Absolute Beginners*. It was not the first time that Bowie had tried out foreign languages, as he had already recorded an Italian version of "Space Oddity" and German versions of "Love You Till Tuesday" and "Heroes," the latter of which was also recorded in French! The official David Bowie Facebook moderator stated in a post dated April 30, 2020, that "Volare (Nel Blu Dipinto Di Blu)" was recorded at the same time as "Absolute Beginners" and "That's Motivation," during the June 1985 session at the Abbey Road Studios. This is a relatively surprising piece of information, since Erdal Kizilçay was not involved in the first two numbers. It is difficult to imagine Kizilçay producing the entire instrumental score of "Volare" in so little time. More likely—and this is the option supported by many observers—the number was produced in the calm of Mountain Studios in Montreux during the summer of 1985.

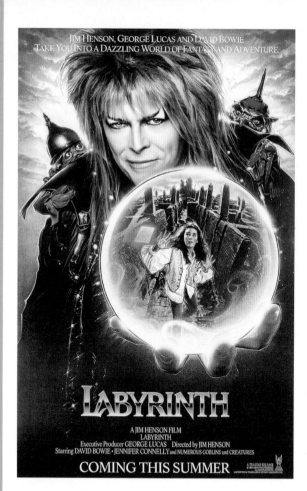

Labyrinth (1986)

1. Opening Titles Including Underground
2. Into the Labyrinth
3. Magic Dance*
4. Sarah
5. Chilly Down*
6. Hallucination
7. As the World Falls Down*
8. The Goblin Battle
9. Within You*
10. Thirteen O'Clock
11. Home at Last
12. Underground*

UK Release on EMI America: June 23, 1986 (ref. AML 3104)
US Release on EMI America: June 23, 1986 (ref. SV-17206)
Best UK Chart Ranking: 38
Best US Chart Ranking: Did Not Chart

* Only these songs, written and sung by David Bowie, are
covered here. The remaining tracks are instrumentals composed
by Trevor Jones for the *Labyrinth* original soundtrack.

KING OF THE GOBLINS:
BOWIE'S ULTIMATE AVATAR

Still basking in the glow of the success of his heroic fantasy film *Dark Crystal*, co-created with Frank Oz in 1982, Jim Henson repeated the experience in 1985 with *Labyrinth*, in which actors and animated characters co-exist on-screen. The film tells the story of the adventures of an adolescent girl, Sarah, who has only a few hours in which to find her little brother, Toby, who is lost in a labyrinth populated by fantastical creatures. Captured by Jareth, king of the goblins, the baby is otherwise condemned to become one of his subjects unless his sister can save him. In the end, it is only the courage of the young girl (played by 2001 Oscar-winning actress Jennifer Connelly) that can save him. From the outset of his project, Henson had only one intention: to entice David Bowie into taking a featured role. It was not difficult to convince the singer, as the idea of appearing in a film co-produced by George Lucas was very appealing to him. "We wrote the film for David. And we tailored a number of scenes around what he could do musically," said Henson. "We worked with David throughout all that beginning time of the film and that was fun."[142] Once the production had been launched at Elstree Studios in London, Bowie was able to focus on the second part of his task: composing some songs for the film, including a single that would appeal to the press. His involvement related to five new songs: "Magic Dance," "Chilly Down," "As the World Falls Down," "Within You," and "Underground."

Despite its many winning qualities, the film did not enjoy the same level of success as other popular fantasy films of the day like *The NeverEnding Story* (Wolfgang Petersen, 1984) and *Legend* (Ridley Scott, 1985). It was actually one of the greatest flops in the history of British cinema. This did not prevent *Labyrinth* from going on to become a cult classic beloved by a generation of movie fans, and the disquieting image of David Bowie, with his frowning eyebrows and hairstyle borrowed from *The Hunter*–era Debbie Harry, made quite an impression. At the time, most of Bowie's fans hated this period in their idol's career, but *Labyrinth* and its original soundtrack single remain an audacious and impressive moment in Bowie's catalog of work. If nothing else, one has to be impressed by the singer's willingness to constantly embrace new and interesting challenges.

MAGIC DANCE

David Bowie / 5:09

Musicians: David Bowie: lead and backing vocals / Dann Huff: electric guitar / Will Lee: bass, backing vocals / Steve Ferrone: drums / Robbie Buchanan: synthesizers, programming / Diva Gray: backing vocals / Fonzi Thornton: backing vocals / **Recorded:** Atlantic Studios, New York: October 1985 / **Technical Team:** Producers: David Bowie, Arif Mardin / **Sound Engineer:** Lew Hahn / **Assistant Sound Engineer:** Michael O'Reilly / **Mixing:** Jeremy Smith

Scorned by the music press and detested by the fans, "Magic Dance" is nonetheless a success in many respects. Bowie, who had been navigating along the vagaries of musical trends since 1968, never ceased to question himself and to pick out influences here and there to create a unique kind of music. Here, too, he was experimenting with a new musical genre, synthpop, which seemed to be a constant presence on MTV. This song illustrates a scene from the film in which Jareth, played by Bowie, sings while surrounded by his restless goblins and lots of chickens ("Working with a baby had its problems," said Jim Henson, "but then I tried directing chickens..."[143]). The baby, who was at the center of the film's intrigue, had an important role to play in this sequence, because he was about to become a goblin if his sister failed to find him. The song begins with a dialogue between Jareth and one of his subjects, borrowed from the film *The Bachelor and the Bobby-Soxer* (1947), directed by Irving Reis. In that earlier film, actors Cary Grant and Shirley Temple were the focus of a misunderstanding that has since became legendary:

– *You remind me of a man.*
– *What man?*
– *The man with the power.*
– *What power?*
– *The power of hoodoo.*
– *Hoodoo?*
– *You do.*
– *Do what?*
– *Remind me of a man...*

This number, which would have been an ideal single to promote the film, only appeared in a 12-inch-single format, under the name of "Magic Dance (A Dance Mix)," in the United States in January 1987, and it was stretched out to 7:11 for use in nightclubs (a nightmare for its detractors!). In 2007, EMI offered a *Magic Dance EP* as a download, combining four versions of the song and intended for the very rare fans of this track, which in spite of all its detractors is actually very catchy, and which works like a Proustian madeleine, taking the listener right back to the 1980s.

FOR BOWIE ADDICTS

During production, it was suggested that some baby noises should be inserted into "Magic Dance." Diva Gray's baby was given the chance to shine, but the little one categorically refused to perform when set in front of the microphone. So it was Bowie himself who obliged, at 0:46. "I never thought in twenty years I'd come back to working with gnomes,"[143] the singer commented in a bemused reference to his 1967 single, "The Laughing Gnome."

ON YOUR HEADPHONES

David Bowie was transfixed by Prince's performance in *Purple Rain*, which was released in theaters in 1984. There is a hat tip to this in the middle of each couplet of "Magic Dance" (especially at 0:20), which is a synthesizer riff that is curiously reminiscent to the one in "Sex Shooter" by Apollonia 6, one of the hits taken from the Albert Magnoli–directed film.

CHILLY DOWN

David Bowie / 3:43

Musicians: Charles Augins: vocals / Richard Bodkin: vocals / Kevin Clash: vocals / Danny John-Jules: vocals / Kevin Armstrong: electric guitar / Neil Conti: drums / Matthew Seligman: bass / Nick Plytas: synthesizers / **Recorded:** Abbey Road Studios, London: June 1985 / Atlantic Studios, New York: October 1985 / **Technical Team:** Producers: David Bowie / **Sound Engineer:** Tony Clark / **Mixing:** Michael O'Reilly /

For "Chilly Down," the credits incorrectly state that David Bowie is behind the microphone. In fact, it is the singers Charles Augins, Richard Bodkin, Kevin Clash, and Danny John-Jules (credited as backing singers) who perform this number, which is sung on the film by the Fire Gang, a band of amusing creatures who play basketball with their own heads, which come off like light bulbs on a lamp. They are also astonished that the young heroine of the film, Sarah, does not have the same self-decapitation abilities. ("*Her head don't come off!*"[144] cries one of them in the film.) On January 13, 2016, a video was posted on the official YouTube page of KMBA Productions, Danny John-Jules's company. In it, viewers will find the original demo of this number, which was originally called "Wild Things." The video is embellished with a multitude of photos taken during the recording sessions, and YouTube is the place to find this precious unreleased item!

The disquieting king of the goblins on the set inspired by the work of M. C. Escher.

AS THE WORLD FALLS DOWN

David Bowie / 4:46

Musicians: David Bowie: lead and backing vocals / Nicky Moroch: electric guitar / Jeff Mironov: electric guitar / Will Lee: bass / Steve Ferrone: drums / Robbie Buchanan: synthesizers, programming / Robin Beck: backing vocals / **Recorded:** Atlantic Studios, New York: October 1985 / **Technical Team:** Producers: David Bowie, Arif Mardin / Sound Engineer: Lew Hahn / Assistant Sound Engineer: Michael O'Reilly / **Mixing:** Lew Hahn, Michael O'Reilly

This love song accompanies a waltz between David Bowie and the (very) young Jennifer Connelly, and it feels like a very strange idea, especially in a film whose subtext, borrowed from *Alice's Adventures in Wonderland* by Lewis Carroll, is transparent: the transition from childhood to adulthood. The disconcerting scene is embellished by "As the World Falls Down," which is not all that far removed from the saccharine ballads of the period, including "Every Time You Go Away" by Paul Young and "Ballerina Girl" by Lionel Richie. Outside of this context, the song is on a level with the other impressive compositions of the film. Bowie even considered releasing this track as a single to be promoted by a video created by Steve Barron (the filmmaker behind Michael Jackson's "Billie Jean" video), but he abandoned this project at the last minute to focus on the production of his new album. Fans were eventually able to enjoy this unreleased video in 1993 on the VHS *Bowie: The Video Collection*, issued by Ryko Vision.

WITHIN YOU

David Bowie / 3:28

Musicians: David Bowie: vocals / Will Lee: bass / Steve Ferrone: drums / Robbie Buchanan: synthesizers, programming / Robin Beck: backing vocals / **Recorded:** Atlantic Studios, New York: October 1985 / **Technical Team:** Producers: David Bowie, Arif Mardin / Sound Engineer: Lew Hahn / Assistant Sound Engineer: Michael O'Reilly / Mixing: Lew Hahn

"Within You" appears during the most memorable scene in the film, in which David Bowie, Jennifer Connelly, and little Toby Froud appear in a set inspired by *Relativity*, an engraving by the Dutch artist M. C. Escher that depicts a maze of stairs, none of which seem to lead anywhere specific, and all of which defy the laws of gravity. Although this scene, with its very effective special effects, terrified a generation of young audiences, the song was not of the same stature. Furthermore, the lyrics (*"Everything I've done / I've done for you / I move the stars for no one"*) once again underline a troublingly amorous link between Jareth and Sarah.

Arif Mardin (left), in midproduction with gospel singers on "Underground." On the right are backing singers Luther Vandross, Chaka Khan, and Cissy Houston.

UNDERGROUND

David Bowie / 5:54

Side A: *Underground (Edited Version)* / 4:25 / **Side B:** *Underground (Instrumental)* / 5:54 / **UK Release on EMI America:** June 9, 1986 (ref. EA 216) / **US Release on EMI America:** June 9, 1986 (ref. B-8323) / **Best UK Chart Ranking:** 21 / **Best US Chart Ranking:** Did Not Chart

Musicians: David Bowie: lead and backing vocals / Albert Collins, Nicky Moroch: electric guitar / Robbie Buchanan: synthesizers, programming / Andy Thomas: additional programming / Richard Tee: piano, Hammond B-3 organ / Steve Ferrone: drums / Bob Gay: alto saxophone / Cissy Houston, Chaka Khan, Luther Vandross, Fonzi Thornton, Marcus Miller, Marc Stevens, Daphne Vega, Garcia Alston, Mary Davis Canty, Beverly Ferguson, A. Marie Foster, James Glenn, Eunice Peterson, Renelle Stafford: backing vocals / **Recorded:** Atlantic Studios, New York: October 1985 / **Technical Team:** Producers: David Bowie, Arif Mardin / **Sound Engineer:** Michael O'Reilly / **Assistant Sound Engineer:** Eddie Garcia / **Arrangements:** David Bowie, Robbie Buchanan, Arif Mardin / **Mixing:** Jeremy Smith

The only single taken from the original soundtrack of *Labyrinth*, "Underground" is a quality recording, supported by a video from Steve Barron in which Bowie, without his goblin king costume, encounters all kinds of creatures from the film. The video contains a clever mixture of live action and illustration. Filmed between the twenty-first and twenty-fifth of February 1986, in the warehouses of the freezer company Frigoscandia, in London, the video was a good companion piece to this single, which had high potential but which, unfortunately, did not drive the film's original soundtrack or the feature film itself to great success. The melody to "Underground" also appears in the film's introductory credits.

Already present for some of the arrangements for *Tonight*, Arif Mardin knew how to provide a discreet but high-quality contribution for the productions in which he was involved. He decided, with Bowie, to give "Underground" a gospel tinge, which suits it perfectly—and which might have inspired "Like a Prayer" by Madonna in 1989. A crack team of backing artists was recruited: the singer Chaka Khan, for whom Mardin had just written the arrangements for the hit "I Feel for You"; Cissy Houston, mother of the young Whitney (whose first opus topped the sales charts); and friend Luther Vandross, who had disappeared from Bowie's phonographic productions after *Young Americans*. The choir of the New Hope Baptist Church was invited to join the trio, providing its powerful support to the backing vocals of the song. "The film essentially deals with a girl's emotions and what she's going through [...]," explained David Bowie. "So I wanted something very emotional, and for me the most emotional music I can think of is gospel."[143] The famous blues guitarist Albert Collins took part in the session, but his incredible Fender Telecaster rhythms have unfortunately disappeared in the mixing, covered over by multiple layers of synthesizers.

Side A

WHEN THE WIND BLOWS

David Bowie, Erdal Kizilçay / 3:32

Musicians
David Bowie: lead and backing vocals
Erdal Kizilçay: electric guitar, bass, synthesizers, programming, trombone, trumpet, violon, percussion

Recorded
Mountain Studios, Montreux: 1985

Technical Team
Producers: David Bowie, David Richards
Sound Engineer: David Richards
Mixing: Bob Clearmountain

Side A: *When the Wind Blows* / 3:32
Side B: *When the Wind Blows (Instrumental)* / 3:32

Genesis

Concluding the long list of collaborations in which David Bowie was involved during the *Tonight* period, "When the Wind Blows" is the title song of an animated feature film directed by Jimmy T. Murakami and adapted from the eponymous graphic novel by Raymond Briggs, which was originally published in 1982. Inspired by the subject—the survival of an elderly couple following a nuclear attack on Great Britain by the USSR—and the poetry of Murakami's images, Bowie decided to compose a four-handed song with jack-of-all-trades Erdal Kizilçay, whom he greatly admired and regularly visited. "He started coming to my place twice a week, on Tuesdays and Thursdays, working in my studio," the musician remembered in 2020. "We started to compose."[119] During one of these sessions, Kizilçay had the singer listen to one of his new compositions, which combined gentleness with a symphonic explosion. David left with a copy, and the following week he asked the musician if he could take inspiration from it for the title song of the animated film. So it was that "When the Wind Blows" saw the light of day. Amazed by Kizilçay's expertise, Bowie went as far as recommending him to Iggy Pop to play the bass, drums, and synthesizer on *Blah-Blah-Blah*, for which he would also provide most of the arrangements.

Production

Recorded at Mountain Studios in Montreux under the attentive eye—and ears—of David Richards, "When the Wind Blows" is really Erdal Kizilçay's work, since he plays all the instruments in the piece, including the trumpet, trombone, and violin. The power of these instruments is perfectly suited to the nuclear explosion that occurs in the film. The multi-instrumentalist Kizilçay is dazzling in his virtuosity. From the introduction, the guitar riff, mixed with layers of synthesizers, is astonishing in its accomplishment. Coupled with a modern production method that anchors the song firmly in its period, "When the Wind Blows" is a track of effective lyricism, which is mostly due to its charming refrain. The song really should have been a success, but the public, alas, was not there to support it.

NEVER LET ME DOWN

ALBUM

NEVER LET ME DOWN

Day-In Day-Out . Time Will Crawl . Beat of Your Drum . Never Let Me Down .
Zeroes . Glass Spider . Shining Star (Makin' My Love) . New York's in Love .
'87 and Cry . Too Dizzy . Bang Bang

RELEASE DATES
United Kingdom: April 27, 1987
Reference: EMI America—AMLS 3117 (33 rpm); CDP 7 46677 2 (CD)
United States: April 27, 1987
Reference: EMI America—PJ-17267 (33 rpm); CDP 7 46677 2 (CD)
Best UK Chart Ranking: 6
Best US Chart Ranking: 34

THE ULTIMATE POP ALBUM

At the beginning of 1986, David Bowie was feeling encouraged by his continuing collaboration with the multi-instrumentalist Erdal Kizilçay, so the "Thin White Duke" turned away from acting work to concentrate on his friend Iggy Pop's new album, *Blah-Blah-Blah*. Recording began in February at Mountain Studios in Switzerland, and the proceedings took place under an atmosphere of friendly cooperation. David Richards and David Bowie produced, and the multi-talented Kizilçay played synthesizer and bass while also taking charge of programming and even providing some sporadic backing vocals. To say that Kizilçay, nicknamed "the invincible Turk" by Bowie, thoroughly understood the fundamentals of '80s rock would be an understatement, but the popular digital rhythm boxes and soulless synthesizers of the day created an icy patchwork, a lifeless hodgepodge of sound that did not always suit Iggy's style, despite the presence of Steve Jones, former guitarist from the Sex Pistols.

This collaboration with Kizilçay, together with pressure from EMI America, who were hoping to cash in on the phenomenal success of "Dancing in the Street," all encouraged Bowie to return to the studio at the end of September 1986 to record a follow-up to *Tonight*.

Iggy Pop's new album was well-received when it came out on October 23, riding on the back of the single "Real Wild Child (Wild One)," and marking an upturn in the Iguana's career. (Despite their undeniable merit, several of his earlier discs had come and gone without much notice from the public or the media.) The warm reception for Iggy's album boosted David Bowie's own ambitions for his next record.

The Arrival of Peter Frampton

Accompanied by Kizilçay and Richards, David Bowie arrived at Mountain Studios with some twelve songs ready to go.

The singer had laid down earlier demos of the tracks using a recently acquired Fostex sixteen-track recorder, which gave the musicians who were brought in to help record the backing tracks a precise road map to follow. Bowie explained in an interview: "I made demos of everything before we went in, and I played them to everybody [Erdal and David Richards] and I said, 'I want it to sound exactly like this but better.' Because I played everything. I programmed drum machines and then played bass and guitar, keyboards and synthesizer parts. [...] The demos are not dissimilar from this final album—except, of course that it's played much better."[145] Erdal Kizilçay played a major role in the creation of the album, working as a programmer, keyboard player, even a trumpeter...He left his mark everywhere.

Two weeks later, the trio was joined in Switzerland by Carlos Alomar, soon to be followed by Peter Frampton, another talented guitarist. A childhood friend of Bowie's, Frampton's mastery of the six-string guitar was immortalized on the double album *Frampton Comes Alive* in 1976. Like many of the great performers of the 1970s, by the mid-1980s it seemed as if Frampton's career was drying up. Shortly before the release of *Never Let Me Down*, Bowie said: "It really gives him a chance to showcase his talents as a guitarist, and then inevitably he'll go out on his own next year, and with a bit of luck people will know him for what he is— which is a great guitarist. And a very good songwriter and singer, as it happens."[145] In 2019, Frampton paid tribute to Bowie: "David reintroduced me as Peter Frampton the guitar player, in stadiums around the world. For that I thanked him so much whilst he was here with us. In fact I thank him all of the time simply because that rejuvenated my career. That completely turned everything around for me."[146]

At the end of November, Bowie and Richards flew to New York and set themselves up in Power Station Studios to

1987

put the finishing touches on the album. They added some brass tracks played by the Borneo Horns and backing vocals to help support the lead vocal line, and they concluded the recording by including an interesting mix of invited guests—including the actor Mickey Rourke, who added a rap to "Shining Star (Makin' My Love)." Mixing on the album was carried out by the talented Bob Clearmountain, who had also been responsible for mixing "Dancing in the Street."

1987

A Popular Success Despite an Avalanche of Bad Reviews

Like Bowie's previous album, when *Never Let Me Down* was released on April 27, 1987, it was panned by the musical press. Critics disliked the deluge of synthesizers and found the production overblown, and in almost every case, they denounced what they felt was the overall weakness of the songs. Challenged to justify himself every time he was interviewed, Bowie brushed off these criticisms, knowing that the public adored the album. Bowie was proven right by the sales numbers, especially in the UK, where *Never Let Me Down* eventually became the third most popular album of the artist's career. American fans, by contrast, mostly ignored the new record. Bowie said of this period: "I wanted something I could tour with on a very ground roots level. I wanted something that would work well with a small band. So it had to logistically be a five-piece band kind of music. I wrote small but energetically."[147]

Whether his critics agreed or not, the overly produced tracks do not in any way detract from their coherence as impressive rock songs. It is obvious that we are light-years away from the artistic triumphs achieved with *Hunky Dory*, *Aladdin Sane*, and *Low*. With *Never Let Me Down*, Bowie is adapting to the prevailing tastes of the times, sometimes

enthusiastically, and sometimes unconvincingly. Perhaps David Bowie's greatest regret on this album might be the excessive use of the Linn 9000 drum machine. This sound, considered by many to be the worst thing to come out of the 1980s, pervades the disc with a cold and impersonal monotony. Many years later, this album was entirely rearranged by producer Mario J. McNulty as part of the box set *Loving the Alien (1983–1988)*, which came out in 2018.

The "Glass Spider Tour"

As soon as *Never Let Me Down* was released, Bowie embarked on a spectacular tour that was announced in a

series of press conferences given across Europe in March of 1987. Thanks in part to the extravagant visual effects created by set designer Mark Ravitz and Toni Basil's choreography, the "Glass Spider Tour" was to mark an aesthetic high point in Bowie's career, even as critics continued to savage his latest album. A huge spider, forty-five feet high and covered with lights, hung over the stage at each show, providing the framework for some spectacular acrobatics. Performances began with a futuristically dressed Carlos Alomar playing a painfully discordant guitar solo punctuated by repeated shouts of "Shut up" coming from an invisible Bowie. The effect of this repetition usually made the joke fall flat with audiences. Recorded for posterity by the movie director David Mallet in Sydney in November 1987, the concert contained a number of outstanding pop numbers ("Time," "Absolute Beginners," "Modern Love"), but the overall performance was sadly lacking in spontaneity.

When this spectacular adventure—more indicative of Bowie's artistic past than of his future ambitions—came to an end, the singer found himself having to take a long look at where he wanted to go next. He chose to return to the basics of rock 'n' roll with his follow-up album, *Tin Machine.*

Carlos Alomar used the tapping technique on his Kramer guitar at the introduction to each concert of the "Glass Spider Tour."

DAY-IN DAY-OUT

David Bowie / 4:38

Side A: *Day-In Day-Out (Single Version)* / 4:10 / **Side B:** *Julie* / 3:40 /
UK Release on EMI America: March 23, 1987 (ref. EA 230) /
US Release on EMI America: March 23, 1987 (ref. B-8380) /
Best UK Chart Ranking: 17 / **Best US Chart Ranking:** 21

Musicians: David Bowie: lead and backing vocals, synthesizers, tambourine / Carlos Alomar: electric guitar, guitar synthesizer, tambourine, backing vocals / Peter Frampton: electric guitar / Sid McGinnis: electric guitar / Erdal Kizilçay: bass, synthesizers, programming, backing vocals / Carmine Rojas: additional bass / Philippe Saisse: piano / Lenny Pickett: tenor saxophone / Stan Harrison: alto saxophone / Steve Elson: baritone saxophone / Earl Gardner: trumpet, bugle / Laurie Frink: trumpet / Robin Clark: backing vocals / Loni Groves: backing vocals / Diva Gray: backing vocals / Gordon Grody: backing vocals / **Recorded:** Mountain Studios, Montreux: September–October 1986 / Power Station Studios, New York: November–December 1986 / **Technical Team: Producers:** David Bowie, David Richards / **Sound Engineer:** David Richards / **Assistant Sound Engineers:** Jon Goldberger, Justin Shirley-Smith, Andre Gauchat / **Mixing:** Bob Clearmountain

Genesis

Despite its radio-friendly sound, this first single has a serious intent, with words speaking to the socially marginalized via the story of a young woman forced into prostitution in order to feed her child. The finger of blame is pointed at President Reagan's social policies: *"First thing she learns is she's a citizen / Some things they turn out right / When you're under the USA / Something rings a bell and it's all over."* Created jointly by Julien Temple and Bowie, the video, which emphasizes the insecurity of life in the street and the brutality of the American authorities, was banned by the BBC because of its violent images. Bowie reacted to this censorship by saying, "I was pissed off because it was for the wrong reasons. Can you tell me if Madonna is being played on TV? [...] I find [her videos have] something a lot more perverse about it than anything in my video. Mine was very straight ahead street violence and it was quite obvious..."[147] Interestingly, this song was extremely well received in Spain, where a Spanish-language version of the track with the title "Al Alba" (At Dawn) was broadcast to promote the "Glass Spider Tour" concerts given in Madrid and Barcelona in July 1987.

Production

Bowie's artistic about-face is evident from the first few bars of "Day-In Day-Out." Omar Hakim's drum kit has been replaced by a Linn 9000 drum machine typical of the time and featured on innumerable hits from the record-producing trio Mike Stock, Matt Aitken, and Pete Waterman (who worked with Kylie Minogue, Rick Astley, Bananarama, and others). The drum machine can also be heard in Michael Jackson's "Bad," which appeared a few months later. Despite the many insults hurled at "Day-In Day-Out" in the press, it is nevertheless a powerful piece that's able to hold its own against the great hits of the period, even if Bowie's track does not equal the pop excellence of newcomers like Depeche Mode or Orchestral Manoeuvres in the Dark.

TIME WILL CRAWL

David Bowie / 4:18

Side A: *Time Will Crawl (Single Version)* / 4:03 / **Side B:** *Girls (Single Edit)* / 4:16 / **UK Release on EMI America:** June 1987 (ref. EA 237) / **US Release on EMI America:** June 1987 (ref. B-43020) / **Best UK Chart Ranking:** 33 / **Best US Chart Ranking:** Did Not Chart

Musicians: David Bowie: lead and backing vocals, synthesizers, tambourine / Carlos Alomar: acoustic guitar, guitar-synthesizer, tambourine, backing vocals / Peter Frampton: electric guitar / Sid McGinnis: electric guitar / Erdal Kizilçay: bass, electric guitar, synthesizers, programming, trumpet, backing vocals / Carmine Rojas: additional bass / Philippe Saisse: synthesizers / Robin Clark: backing vocals / Loni Groves: backing vocals / Diva Gray: backing vocals / Gordon Grody: backing vocals / **Recorded:** Mountain Studios, Montreux: September–October 1986 / Power Station Studios, New York: November–December 1986 / **Technical Team:** Producers: David Bowie, David Richards / **Sound Engineer:** David Richards / **Assistant Sound Engineer:** Jon Goldberger, Justin Shirley-Smith, Andre Gauchat / **Mixing:** Bob Clearmountain

Genesis

In David Bowie's words: "One Saturday afternoon in April 1986, along with some other musicians, I was taking a break from recording at Montreux Studios in Switzerland. It was a beautiful day and we were outside on a small piece of lawn facing the Alps and the lake. Our engineer, who had been listening to the radio, shot out of the studio and shouted: 'There's a whole lot of shit going on in Russia.' The Swiss news had picked up a Norwegian radio station that was screaming [...] that huge billowing clouds were moving over from the Motherland and they weren't rain clouds. This was the first news in Europe of the satanic Chernobyl."[56] This dramatic event led to David Bowie's swiftly composed song "How We War," a manifesto against the reaction of world leaders in the face of this disaster. Reworked into "Time Will Crawl," the song dwells on the

anguish felt by the composer who sings: "*I felt a warm, warm breeze / That melted metal and steel.*" But despite his bitterness toward those at the top, Bowie also offered surprising support to the Soviet leader of the day, Mikhail Gorbachev: "Right now, the person I admire ambivalently is Gorbachev, [...] because of what he's trying to do. [...] He is part of a new regime in Russia, the like of which they've never seen before, and I think it's knocking everything sideways. If he survives I think he'll bring about some very interesting changes to that country."[147]

Production

In the video made by Tim Pope for "Time Will Crawl," guitarist Peter Frampton cuts a lonely figure from the corner of a stage occupied by Bowie and a group of dancers. In the studio, the typically '80s-sounding guitar solo featured in this track was played by Sid McGinnis, who was also the soloist on "Day-In Day-Out" and "Bang Bang." This session guitarist, known for his contribution to the 1980 Dire Straits album *Making Movies*, is even more famous for his membership in The World's Most Dangerous Band, the group that appeared alongside Paul Shaffer on the *Late Show with David Letterman* every weeknight on CBS.

BEAT OF YOUR DRUM

David Bowie / 4:32

Musicians: David Bowie: lead and backing vocals, synthesizers, tambourine / Carlos Alomar: electric guitar, guitar-synthesizer, tambourine, backing vocals / Erdal Kizilçay: bass, synthesizers, programming, trumpet, backing vocals / Carmine Rojas: additional bass / Lenny Pickett: tenor saxophone / Stan Harrison: alto saxophone / Steve Elson: baritone saxophone / Earl Gardner: trumpet, bugle / Laurie Frink: trumpet / Robin Clark, Loni Groves, Diva Gray, Gordon Grody: backing vocals / **Recorded:** Mountain Studios, Montreux: September–October 1986 / Power Station Studios, New York: November–December 1986 / **Technical Team:** Producers: David Bowie, David Richards / **Sound Engineer:** David Richards / **Assistant Sound Engineer:** Jon Goldberger, Justin Shirley-Smith, Andre Gauchat / **Mixing:** Bob Clearmountain

Along with some fairly explicit sexual metaphors ("*I'd like to beat on your drum / I like the smell of your flesh*"), with this song Bowie has also composed a true declaration of love. Set against a pop-rock rhythm, the singer tells the object of his affections that he thinks of them despite the passing of time. "*Seasons may change, weather blows, but you still leave a mark on me.*" It is tempting to think that this song, with its memorable refrain, was written for Bowie's ex-wife. When producer Mario J. McNulty created the new version of *Never Let Me Down* for the box set *Loving the Alien (1983–1988)* in 2018, "Beat of Your Drum" came out as the B-side of the single "Zeroes (2018)," which was produced and sold as a beautiful vinyl picture disc.

David Bowie and the loyal
Coco Schwab, at the Live Aid
concert at Wembley Stadium
on July 13, 1985.

NEVER LET ME DOWN

David Bowie, Carlos Alomar / 4:03

Musicians

David Bowie: lead and backing vocals, synthesizers, harmonica, tambourine, Mellotron
Carlos Alomar: electric guitar, guitar synthesizer
Peter Frampton: electric guitar
Erdal Kizilçay: bass, programming, synthesizers
Carmine Rojas: additional bass
Crusher Bennett: percussion

Recorded

Power Station Studios, New York: December 1986

Technical Team

Producers: David Bowie, David Richards
Sound Engineer: David Richards
Assistant Sound Engineer: Jon Goldberger
Mixing: Bob Clearmountain

SIDE A: *Never Let Me Down (Single Version)* / 4:04
SIDE B: *'87 and Cry (Single Version)* / 3:52
UK Release on EMI America: August 17, 1987 (ref. EA 239)
US Release on EMI America: August 17, 1987 (ref. B-43031)
Best UK Chart Ranking: 34
Best US Chart Ranking: 27

The video for "Never Let Me Down," featured scenes of couples in a dance competition and was made by Jean-Baptiste Mondino. Bowie said of him: "He's like a craftsman and that's what he's trying to perfect, this craft of making his five minutes work."[149]

Genesis

In December 1986, when recording sessions for the album were finished at Power Station Studios, and while Bob Clearmountain was occupied with mixing, Bowie told David Richards that he had a tune in his head that was obsessing him. Eventually, he asked Carlos Alomar to get together with him to work on a new song. "The only thing that he had was the chorus,"[119] Alomar recalled, and suggested one of his own compositions: "I'm Tired." David Bowie wrote lyrics that were a tribute to Corinne "Coco" Schwab, his personal assistant, who had come to his rescue so many times when he was sinking into his personal hell of drug addiction—and who was to remain at his side until he died in 2016: "*When I needed soul revival I called your name / When I was falling to pieces I screamed in pain / Your soothing hand that turned me round / A love so real swept over me.*" "It's platonic," Bowie would later say. "But there is a romance in it, I guess, inasmuch as it's hard for two people to [be] prepared to be there if the other one needs someone, you know? There's not many people you find in life that you can do that with, or feel that way with."[148]

Production

Recorded in just a few hours at Power Station Studios, "Never Let Me Down" urgently needed David Richards's presence. He recalled: "Studio A just happened to be free. So we flew down the elevator to start recording in the other room, leaving Bob on the third floor to mix 'Zeroes.'"[149]

For the basic rhythm, Richards and Bowie used an old drum machine track left over from the Mountain Studios sessions, over which Carlos Alomar added his guitar lines and Crusher Bennett added some percussion effects, including güiro and castanets. The vocals were recorded in the evening, and by eleven that night everything was in the can, ready for mixing the next day. David Richards recalled: "It was so exciting to have the two studios going at once, and to have that kind of creativity happening all around us. It's something I will never forget."[149]

A gentle hat tip to Prince's "Little Red Corvette" was inserted into "Zeroes." Bowie was a great admirer of the so-called Kid from Minneapolis.

ZEROES

David Bowie / 5:46

Musicians: David Bowie: lead and backing vocals, synthesizers / Carlos Alomar: acoustic guitar, backing vocals / Peter Frampton: electric guitar, electric sitar / Erdal Kizilçay: bass, synthesizers, programming, backing vocals / Carmine Rojas: additional bass / Robin Clark, Loni Groves, Diva Gray, Gordon Grody, the Coquettes: backing vocals / **Recorded:** Mountain Studios, Montreux: September–October 1986 / Power Station Studios, New York: November–December 1986 / **Technical Team:** Producers: David Bowie, David Richards / Sound Engineer: David Richards / **Assistant Sound Engineer:** Jon Goldberger, Justin Shirley-Smith, Andre Gauchat / **Mixing:** Bob Clearmountain

Referencing 1977's *"Heroes,"* "Zeroes" paints the portrait of an imaginary rock group. With a spoken introduction recalling *"This ain't rock 'n' roll, this is genocide"* from "Diamond Dogs," "Zeroes" pays homage to the rock stars that influenced Bowie since his youth. "I wanted to put in every cliché that was around in the Sixties. [...] But it was done with affection—it's not supposed to be a snipe."[148] Bowie also gives a nod to the only singer he considered a true rival in 1987: Prince, who was riding on the success of his worldwide hit "Kiss," released in February 1986. With the words *"Me my little red Corvette,"* Bowie is quoting explicitly from Prince's 1982 hit "Little Red Corvette." At a press conference held on March 20, 1987, at the Players' Theatre in London announcing the forthcoming "Glass Spider Tour," a journalist referred to the theatrical and provocative aspects of Bowie's behavior in the 1970s, asking whether Prince could be viewed as an '80s version of him. Bowie's response was this: "I've moved on to a different area now, and I don't think anybody else could handle the job better."[47]

With its rhythmical acoustic guitar—a sound almost entirely absent from the rest of Bowie's 1980s repetoire—"Zeroes" is an approachable pop track, the melody sometimes recalling the Ziggy Stardust years.

Despite pompous staging and cumbersome accessories, the version of "Time" performed during the "Glass Spider Tour" was a great success with fans.

GLASS SPIDER

David Bowie / 4:56

Musicians: David Bowie: lead and backing vocals, synthesizers / Carlos Alomar: electric guitar, guitar synthesizer, backing vocals / Peter Frampton: electric guitar / **Erdal Kizilçay:** bass, synthesizers, programming, backing vocals / **Carmine Rojas:** additional bass / Robin Clark, Loni Groves, Diva Gray, Gordon Grody: backing vocals / **Recorded:** Mountain Studios, Montreux: September–October 1986 / Power Station Studios, New York: November–December 1986 / **Technical Team:** Producers: David Bowie, David Richards / **Sound Engineer:** David Richards / **Assistant Sound Engineer:** Jon Goldberger, Justin Shirley-Smith, Andre Gauchat / **Mixing:** Bob Clearmountain

The creature at the center of this cold and anguished track is *Thwaitesia argentiopunctata*, better known as the glass or sequined spider. Only a few millimeters in size, the abdomen of this spider is covered with extraordinary silver patches. It has the habit, according to Bowie's song, of weaving the skeletons of its devoured prey into its web ("*Having devoured its prey / It would drape the skeletons over its web*"). Bowie here develops a symbol that appears over and over again in the history of psychoanalysis. He sees the spider as a maternal figure, both protecting and consuming, and from whom children must eventually break free. "Spiders keep coming up in my references all the time," Bowie explained. "[...] I don't know what the Jungian aspects of it are. [...] It's kind of the pivotal song of the album and it's the idea [that] there's a point in every child's life when it realizes its parents are really not something they can depend on for everything, they are kind of on their own."[150] In a tribute to the singer's passion for these creatures, arachnologist Peter Jäger named a new species discovered in Malaysia in 2008 after the singer: *Heteropoda davidbowie*.

Mickey Rourke had to have his arm twisted to appear on "Shining Star (Makin' My Love)."

SHINING STAR (MAKIN' MY LOVE)

David Bowie / 4:05

Musicians: David Bowie: lead and backing vocals / Mickey Rourke: rap / Carlos Alomar: electric guitar, guitar synthesizer / Peter Frampton: electric guitar / Erdal Kizilçay: bass, synthesizers, programming / Carmine Rojas: additional bass / Crusher Bennett: percussion / Robin Clark, Loni Groves, Diva Gray, Gordon Grody: backing vocals / **Recorded:** Mountain Studios, Montreux: September–October 1986 / Power Station Studios, New York: November–December 1986 / **Technical Team:** Producers: David Bowie, David Richards / Sound Engineer: David Richards / Assistant Sound Engineer: Jon Goldberger, Justin Shirley-Smith, Andre Gauchat / Mixing: Bob Clearmountain

Performed in a high-pitched voice borrowed from Smokey Robinson, Bowie's pop track is a hymn to solidarity in a world gone astray. Already tackled in "Time Will Crawl" and "Day-In Day-Out," the themes of this track are anchored in a period of violence dominated by the media endlessly pointing out the diseased nature of society. In explaining the lyrics, Bowie said: "Again, it reflects back-to-street situations, and how people are trying to get together in the face of so many disasters and catastrophes, socially around them, never knowing if they're going to survive it themselves. The one thing they have got to cling on to is each other; [...] it's the only thing that they've got."[149]

A famous and surprising name is credited as making a guest appearance on this track, lending his support to Bowie in his quest for social justice. This was actor Mickey Rourke, then at the peak of his career after the success of *Year of the Dragon* (Michael Cimino, 1985) and *9½ Weeks* (Adrian Lyne, 1986). In the bridging passage of the song, the actor raps with Bowie, his stiff and hesitant voice combining extraordinarily well with the assurance of the lead singer. Rourke posted a comment on Instagram in 2019: "I

told David several times I can't sing at all, when we got to the studio I was terrified. [...] He just wanted me on the album, just cuz he loved me so much. I really miss him, he was one of a kind and most of all he was his own man."[151]

NEW YORK'S IN LOVE

David Bowie / 3:55

Musicians: David Bowie: lead and backing vocals, electric guitar / Carlos Alomar: electric guitar, guitar synthesizer / Peter Frampton: electric guitar / Erdal Kizilçay: bass, synthesizers, programming, backing vocals / Carmine Rojas: additional bass / Crusher Bennett: percussion / Robin Clark: backing vocals / Loni Groves: backing vocals / Diva Gray: backing vocals / Gordon Grody: backing vocals / **Recorded:** Mountain Studios, Montreux: September–October 1986 / Power Station Studios, New York: November–December 1986 / **Technical Team:** Producers: David Bowie, David Richards / Sound Engineer: David Richards / Assistant Sound Engineer: Jon Goldberger, Justin Shirley-Smith, Andre Gauchat / Mixing: Bob Clearmountain

There has always seemed to be something romantic about Bowie's relationship with New York. Many key moments in his career happened here. It was here that he first met Carlos Alomar and so many other musicians who were ready to follow him in his crazy explorations of soul and funk. It was also in New York that Bowie gave his last concert, and it's the city where David Bowie passed away on January 10, 2016. Back in 1986, Bowie's words carried more than a hint of sarcasm when he described New York as a city of blatant inequality where many people still felt financially insecure: *"Pretty as a picture / New York, New York / Ugly on each side."* In a press conference in August 1987, he said: "[Big cities are] so pompous and big and in love with themselves."[152] The Big Apple did not hold his words against him. On Wednesday, January 20, 2016, New York City's mayor, Bill de Blasio, proclaimed the date "David Bowie Day."[153]

1987

'87 AND CRY

David Bowie / 3:53

Musicians: David Bowie: lead and backing vocals, electric guitar, synthesizers, tambourine / **Carlos Alomar:** electric guitar, guitar synthesizer, backing vocals / **Peter Frampton:** electric guitar / **Erdal Kizilçay:** bass, synthesizers, programming, backing vocals / **Carmine Rojas:** additional bass / **Crusher Bennett:** percussion / **Lenny Pickett:** tenor saxophone / **Stan Harrison:** alto saxophone / **Steve Elson:** baritone saxophone / **Earl Gardner:** trumpet, bugle / **Laurie Frink:** trumpet / **Robin Clark, Loni Groves, Diva Gray, Gordon Grody:** backing vocals / **Recorded:** Mountain Studios, Montreux: September–October 1986 / **Power Station Studios, New York:** November–December 1986 / **Technical Team:** Producers: David Bowie, David Richards / **Sound Engineer:** David Richards / **Assistant Sound Engineer:** Jon Goldberger, Justin Shirley-Smith, Andre Gauchat / **Mixing:** Bob Clearmountain

After his implicit attack on President Ronald Reagan in "Day-In Day-Out," David Bowie here points the finger at the Iron Lady, Margaret Thatcher, who was the prime minister of Great Britain from 1979 to 1990, and who became notorious for her ruthlessly libertarian policies. Bowie explained in an interview published in the *New York Times* that "'87 and Cry" was a reflection of "Thatcherite England, where there's such a separation between a high, authoritative governmental force and the ordinary people, the 'dogs.' But I don't use a didactic kind of politicism; I tend to create an ambiance rather than a polemic."[154] The introductory guitar riff on this track is somewhat reminiscent of the Kinks' "You Really Got Me," and it plunges the listener into a world of powerful rock intonations, especially in the refrain, which verges on sounding almost like a heavy metal song.

TOO DIZZY

David Bowie, Erdal Kizilçay / 3:58

Musicians: David Bowie: lead and backing vocals / **Carlos Alomar:** electric guitar, guitar synthesizer, backing vocals / **Peter Frampton:** electric guitar / **Erdal Kizilçay:** bass, synthesizers, programming / **Carmine Rojas:** additional bass / **Philippe Saisse:** piano / **Crusher Bennett:** percussion / **Lenny Pickett:** tenor saxophone / **Stan Harrison:** alto saxophone / **Steve Elson:** baritone saxophone / **Earl Gardner:** trumpet, bugle / **Laurie Frink:** trumpet / **Robin Clark:** backing vocals / **Loni Groves:** backing vocals / **Diva Gray:** backing vocals / **Gordon Grody:** backing vocals / **Recorded:** Mountain Studios, Montreux: September–October 1986 / **Power Station Studios, New York:** November–December 1986 / **Technical Team:** Producers: David Bowie, David Richards / **Sound Engineer:** David Richards / **Assistant Sound Engineer:** Jon Goldberger, Justin Shirley-Smith, Andre Gauchat / **Mixing:** Bob Clearmountain

"Too Dizzy" was the result of a few David Bowie and Erdal Kizilçay recording sessions in 1985. For a long period, the two men met up every Tuesday and Thursday at the studio inside Erdal's home to fine-tune new songs. This collaboration would eventually lead to the album *Never Let Me Down*.

Recorded partly in Montreux and partly in New York, the character in this song is a jealous lover: *"Is it love or is it what? / Who's this guy I'm gonna blow away, hey / What kind of love is he giving you?"* Bowie would eventually disown this track, to the extent that after 1995, he had it taken off the track listings for all the reissued versions of the album. He once said dismissively: "It's a throwaway! I always thought it was better for Huey Lewis! I was unsettled with that song, but it's on the album anyway. It's one of the first songs that Erdal Kizilçay and I wrote together, a sort of try-out to see how we sparred together as writers. I thought a real Fifties subject matter was either love or jealousy, so I thought I'd stick with jealousy because it's a lot more interesting."[149]

BANG BANG

Iggy Pop, Ivan Král / 4:02

Musicians: David Bowie: lead and backing vocals / **Carlos Alomar:** electric guitar, guitar synthesizer / **Peter Frampton:** electric guitar, electric sitar / **Sid McGinnis:** electric guitar / **Erdal Kizilçay:** bass, synthesizers, programming, violin / **Carmine Rojas:** additional bass / **Robin Clark:** backing vocals / **Loni Groves:** backing vocals / **Diva Gray:** backing vocals / **Gordon Grody:** backing vocals / **Recorded:** Mountain Studios, Montreux: September–October 1986 / **Power Station Studios, New York:** November–December 1986 / **Technical Team:** Producers: David Bowie, David Richards / **Sound Engineer:** David Richards / **Assistant Sound Engineer:** Jon Goldberger, Justin Shirley-Smith, Andre Gauchat / **Mixing:** Bob Clearmountain

"Bang Bang" was composed by punk rocker Iggy Pop and his guitarist, Ivan Král, and it originally appeared on Iggy's 1981 album, *Party*. Like the other tracks by the Iguana that appeared on Bowie's *Tonight* album, the reason for this number's appearance on *Never Let Me Down* may have been that Bowie wanted to share some of his royalties with his friend.

The electric sitar heard on this track (as also on "Zeroes") is played by the virtuosic Peter Frampton. The instrument was a Coral Electric Sitar made by Danelectro that the guitarist acquired in 1977 while he was in New York recording his album *I'm in You*. Frampton related the story in 2019 as follows: "It was in a cupboard at the Electric Lady recording studios. [...] We pretty much lived there for six months and when we left on the very last day, the manager of the studios came out with this guitar and he said 'We have loved having you here, this is something that I have found that has been here for years, and no one has taken it or claimed it.' He then looked at me and said, 'I think that Jimi would like you to have it.'"[146] Jimi Hendrix, the first person to record at the Electric Lady Studios, had left the instrument there shortly before his death in 1970. A few notes played on this precious piece of rock 'n' roll history can be heard on *Never Let Me Down*.

Tina Turner and David Bowie backstage at the National Exhibition Centre in Birmingham, England, in March 1985.

GIRLS

David Bowie, Erdal Kizilçay / 4:16

Musicians: David Bowie: lead and backing vocals, synthesizers / **Carlos Alomar:** electric guitar, guitar synthesizer / **Peter Frampton:** electric guitar / **Erdal Kizilçay:** bass, synthesizers, programming, backing vocals / **Carmine Rojas:** additional bass / **Philippe Saisse:** piano / **Crusher Bennett:** percussion / **Lenny Pickett:** tenor saxophone / **Stan Harrison:** alto saxophone / **Steve Elson:** baritone saxophone / **Earl Gardner:** trumpet, bugle / **Laurie Frink:** trumpet / **Robin Clark:** backing vocals / **Loni Groves:** backing vocals / **Diva Gray:** backing vocals / **Gordon Grody:** backing vocals / **Recorded:** Mountain Studios, Montreux: September–October 1986 / Power Station Studios, New York: November–December 1986 / **Technical Team:** Producers: David Bowie, David Richards / **Sound Engineer:** David Richards / **Assistant Sound Engineer:** Jon Goldberger, Justin Shirley-Smith, Andre Gauchat / **Mixing:** Bob Clearmountain

Written by the Bowie-Kizilçay duo during their sessions in Montreux, "Girls" was offered to Tina Turner, who recorded it for her sixth solo album, *Break Every Rule*, which was released on September 5, 1986. Bowie recorded it himself during the *Never Let Me Down* sessions but quickly took it off the album's final track list. The style of the song is straightforward and meant for pop-radio airplay, which was something Bowie had been flirting with for a while without properly taking the plunge. Instead, it was issued on the B-side of "Time Will Crawl" in June 1987. Tina Turner's live version appeared on her *Live in Europe* CD in August 1988, in a version perfectly adapted to the very commercial style she was now pursuing. As he had done with "All the Young Dudes" in 1972, Bowie tried to reappropriate one of his own songs, but without much success.

JULIE

David Bowie / 3:40

Musicians: David Bowie: lead and backing vocals, tambourine / Carlos Alomar: acoustic guitar, guitar synthesizer / **Peter Frampton:** electric guitar / **Erdal Kizilçay:** bass, synthesizers, programming, backing vocals / **Carmine Rojas:** additional bass / **Robin Clark (?), Loni Groves (?), Diva Gray (?), Gordon Grody (?):** backing vocals / **Recorded:** Mountain Studios, Montreux: September–October 1986 / Power Station Studios, New York: November–December 1986 / **Technical Team:** Producers: David Bowie, David Richards / **Sound Engineer:** David Richards / **Assistant Sound Engineer:** Jon Goldberger, Justin Shirley-Smith, Andre Gauchat / **Mixing:** Bob Clearmountain

David Bowie seems to be casting himself as a criminal lover in this excessively pop-influenced track. If passion is at the heart of the song, the recurring presence of a gun rather takes the buoyant shine off the scene. The song can be added to the list of titles devoted to crimes of passion, including Johnny Hallyday's "Requiem pour un fou" (1976) or the wonderful "Where the Wild Roses Grow" (1995), sung by Nick Cave and Kylie Minogue. Driven by the rhythm of the Linn 9000 drum box and a tambourine, "Julie" is a simple but well-made song that deserved a place on *Never Let Me Down*. Instead, it was shunted to a spot on the B-side of the single "Day-In Day-Out," which came out on March 23, 1987, and eventually reappeared on the reissue of the album by Virgin Records in 1995, along with "Girls" and "When the Wind Blows."

CHINE TI
NE TIN
NE TIN M
MACHIN
TIN MAC
N MACH

ALBUM

TIN MACHINE

Heaven's in Here . Tin Machine . Prisoner of Love . Crack City .
I Can't Read . Under the God . Amazing . Working Class Hero . Bus Stop .
Pretty Thing . Video Crime . Run (on CD version only) .
Sacrifice Yourself (on CD version only) . Baby Can Dance

RELEASE DATES

United Kingdom: May 22, 1989
Reference: EMI USA—MTLS 1044 (33 rpm); CDP-7-91990-2 (CD)
United States: May 22, 1989
Reference: EMI USA—E1-91990 (33 rpm); CDP-7-91990-2 (CD)
Best UK Chart Ranking: 3
Best US Chart Ranking: 28

WORKING AS A TEAM AGAIN

Although the biggest stadiums and concert halls in the world had been packed for David Bowie's "Glass Spider Tour," he was now forty-one years old and starting to feel that his career was changing course. This is not to say that Bowie was thinking of taking early retirement from his musical life, but he was aware that he was not an up-and-coming star any longer. The dance routines and multicolored costumes used on his recent tour no longer seemed appropriate. Also, working as part of a team, like he'd done in the groups formed for *Spiders from Mars,* and the epic *Young Americans* and *Station to Station*, was something he was beginning to miss. It was also during this transitional moment in his career that Bowie would have a chance encounter with a talented musician who would further revive his desire to return to the friendly, collegiate atmosphere of his earlier Haddon Hall years.

Reeves Gabrels, a New Brother-in-Arms

Sara Terry had worked as the press officer on the "Glass Spider Tour" and she brought along her husband, Reeves Gabrels. Gabrels was an artist but also worked as a guitarist in an amateur group called the Dark. Gabrels did not advertise his talents as a musician, but a common interest in architecture and art drew him to Bowie. When the singer was finishing up his last series of concerts in Australia in November 1987, Sara Terry passed him a demo cassette from the Dark. Bowie was impressed by Gabrels's incisive and experimental guitar playing, which apparently reminded him of the brilliant technique of Earl Slick and the bold rock flavorings of Robert Fripp. At the beginning of 1988, Bowie suggested that he and Gabrels work together, thus beginning an artistic collaboration that was to prove productive and revitalizing for the singer. Gabrels later recalled: "David was 10 years older than me. I have no siblings, so he functioned like an older brother for me. When I started working with him, I was in my late twenties, early thirties. He showed me how the music industry worked."[155]

Although mostly attracted to jazz, Gabrels introduced David Bowie to the new wave of independent rock music emerging in America. Synonymous with a cultural revolution, young bands like the Pixies, Sonic Youth, and Dinosaur Jr. all proclaimed their rejection of drum boxes and other types of synthesizers, instead raising the banner for a new brand of rock music that was simple, honest, and without artifice. A few years later, this indie rock movement would eventually morph itself into the grunge movement, which insisted even more strongly on adhering to these core values of playing rock music without any excessive ornamentation or gimmicks.

In June 1988, Bowie invited Reeves Gabrels to participate in an unusual project: a collaboration with the Québécois dance group La La La Human Steps, who were preparing to appear in a show being put on to raise money for urgent renovation work at the Institute of Contemporary Arts in London. Bowie's idea was for Gabrels to work on a new version of the "Look Back in Anger" single from the *Lodger* album. Their task was completed after only two days, during which time the two musicians bonded as friends. A few weeks later, Bowie made up his mind: He would change his way of composing and form a creative, collaborative group that would work together to return to the fundamentals of rock. Reeves Gabrels would be one of the group's members.

An Experiment in Democracy

In August 1988, Bowie and Gabrels installed themselves at Mountain Studios in Montreux, Switzerland, and set to work producing new songs. Shortly after they started production, they were joined by the Sales brothers (Hunt on drums and Tony on bass), who were musicians Bowie had first met in

Tin Machine and their prestigious frontman, David Bowie, at the Paradiso in Amsterdam, on June 24, 1989.

1977 during the recording of Iggy Pop's *Lust for Life*. The band came together in an atmosphere that was friendly and collegial, providing the team spirit that Bowie had been so sorely missing in his professional life. Guitarist Kevin Armstrong, who had played on "Dancing in the Streets" and "Absolute Beginners," was also invited to contribute some lines with his six-chord guitar even though he was not officially part of the group. Armstrong did receive a warm acknowledgment from Bowie in the disc's sleeve notes. And so Tin Machine—now the album's official name—was born.

On the production side of things, young Tim Palmer brought a breath of fresh air to the quartet's music. This hire proved to be another prescient choice on Bowie's part, when two years later, in 1991, Palmer did the mixing for one of the greatest albums in the history of grunge: Pearl Jam's *Ten*.

A Muted Reception

When *Tin Machine* was released on May 22, 1989, music critics dismissed the songs, saying that their poor composition was disguised by overly energetic playing. In contrast, the British public greeted the album enthusiastically, sending the disc to number three on the charts (it went only to number twenty-eight in the United States). The three singles taken from the album—"Under the God," "Tin Machine," and "Prisoner of Love"—all disappeared from the airwaves pretty much without a trace. The album art featured a restrained photo taken by Masayoshi Sukita, which showed the four musicians dressed in elegant black suits. The album release was followed up with a tour that was intended to reconnect Bowie with his public. About fifteen concerts were put on, all in venues holding no more than two thousand spectators: the Roxy in Los Angeles, the Paradisio in Amsterdam, and the Cigale in Paris. Tony Sales recalled, "When we played the Roxy in LA, there were over a thousand people on Sunset Boulevard and tickets were going for $600 apiece. It was crazy, people were climbing up all over the building. But that was the idea—to play small places and cause a riot."[155] Not a single song from any of Bowie's previous albums appeared on the set lists for this more intimate series of concerts. During this summer of 1989, only songs from *Tin Machine* and covers of other artists' works were performed. This was not the most celebrated epoch of Bowie's career, but it did represent an important and necessary period of creative renewal.

LOOK BACK IN ANGER (1988 VERSION)

David Bowie / 6:58

Musicians

David Bowie: lead and backing vocals, synthesizers
Reeves Gabrels: electric guitar
Erdal Kizilçay: synthesizer, bass, programming

Recorded

Mountain Studios, Montreux: June 1988

Technical Team

Producers: David Bowie, David Richards
Sound Engineer: David Richards

First Collaboration with Reeves Gabrels

In the spring of 1988, the Canadian modern dance group La La La Human Steps asked David Bowie to take part in a show called *Intruders at the Palace*, which was to take place on July 1 at the Dominion Theatre in London. Working under the direction of choreographer Édouard Lock, the dancers were staging the show in order to raise funds for much-needed repairs to the roof of the Institute of Contemporary Arts in London.

Bowie decided on a version of his 1979 song "Look Back in Anger," but rearranged so as to make it more aggressive and violent. He asked guitarist Reeves Gabrels, whom he had met on the "Glass Spider Tour," to come and join him in Montreux. With the addition of Erdal Kizilçay on bass and programming, the team created a wild version of the song with a wall of guitars filling up all the available space in the mix. It was this collaboration that would eventually lead to the beginning of the *Tin Machine* experiment. The guitarist would later recall: "We both had that art school background. David would say to me, 'We need a Lichtenstein guitar solo there, rather than a Jackson Pollock.' I'd know exactly what he meant."[102]

Onstage at the Dominion Theatre

David Bowie threw himself heart and soul into this unique experiment with La La La Human Steps. His eight-minute contribution convinced those people lucky enough to be able to get a ticket that he was a multifaceted artist capable of creating great work in a variety of different mediums. As guitarists Reeves Gabrels and Kevin Armstrong and bass player Erdal Kizilçay played the instrumental introduction of the new version of "Look Back in Anger" from the back of the stage, Bowie executed a dance alongside the extraordinary Louise Lecavalier. He then went back to the mic and picked up his headless six-chord guitar, leaving Lecavalier to dance with her regular partner, Marc Béland. Louise Lecavalier would remember this occasion with strong emotion: "We arrived separately, each coming from our own different worlds, and our eyes met. His presence was so intense, he completely inhabited the moment during the performance. His stage presence was entirely concentrated in his eyes while his eyes were in turn entirely concentrated on me! I'll never forget it."[157]

HEAVEN'S IN HERE

David Bowie / 6:04

Musicians: David Bowie: lead vocals, electric guitar/ Reeves Gabrels, Kevin Armstrong: electric guitar / Tony Sales: bass, backing vocals / Hunt Sales: drums, backing vocals / **Recorded:** Mountain Studios, Montreux: August 1988 / Compass Point Studios, Nassau: November– December 1988 / **Technical Team:** Producers: Tin Machine, Tim Palmer / Sound Engineers: Justin Shirley-Smith, David Richards

There is something reminiscent of "The Jean Genie" in the very blues-heavy sound of "Heaven's in Here." Unlike the tracks that follow on *Tin Machine*, this track doesn't sound heavily influenced by repeated listening to Sonic Youth. Reeves Gabrels explained later how blues music had been one of the many inspirations for the album, listing a pretty wide-ranging group of artists who influenced the album: "Coltrane, the Pixies, Sonic Youth, Glenn Branca, Stravinsky, John Lee Hooker, Buddy Guy, Junior Wells and Muddy Waters. Put all that in a blender and you got Tin Machine."[53]

Right from the start of this album, the wide and powerful sound of the big hall at the Montreux Casino, situated above Mountain Studios, is very apparent. The musicians had installed themselves here, and Tim Palmer put mics in the room's gallery so they could capture the natural reverberation of the space.

TIN MACHINE

David Bowie, Reeves Gabrels, Tony Sales, Hunt Sales / 3:36

45 rpm version: Side A: *Prisoner of Love (Edit)* / 4:05 / **Side B:** *Baby Can Dance (Live)* / 6:19 / **CD single version:** 1. *Prisoner of Love (Edit)* / 4:05; 2. *Baby Can Dance (Live)* / 6:19; 3. *Crack City (Live)* / 5:15; 4. *Prisoner of Love (LP Version)* / 4:50 / **UK Release on EMI USA:** October 1989 (ref. 45 rpm: MT 76 / ref. CD single: CDMT 76) / **Best Chart Ranking:** 77

Musicians: David Bowie: lead vocals, electric guitar/ Reeves Gabrels, Kevin Armstrong: electric guitar / Tony Sales: bass, backing vocals / Hunt Sales: drums, backing vocals / **Recorded:** Mountain Studios, Montreux: August 1988 / Compass Point Studios, Nassau: November– December 1988 / **Technical Team:** Producers: Tin Machine, Tim Palmer / Sound Engineers: Justin Shirley-Smith, David Richards

It was a strange choice to pick this rock track, situated somewhere between rockabilly and punk, as the second single on the album. Its spontaneity and energy help make up for the lack of an effective melody, and it's a good example of Bowie's desire to return to the basics of rock 'n' roll. A few years later, the early standard bearers of the nascent grunge movement would follow a similar path. In hindsight, it seems unfair that "Tin Machine" has never been fully recognized as one of the precursors of this musical style. And Gabrels underlined this sentiment in 2020: "I remember at the time it being thought of as a harbinger of the '90s, because people always like to put that on David anyway, that he was anticipating the next thing. And strangely enough, other than the fact that we all wore suits, there was a lot of what became grunge."[119]

PRISONER OF LOVE

David Bowie, Reeves Gabrels, Tony Sales, Hunt Sales / 4:50

45 rpm version: Side A: *Prisoner of Love (Edit)* / 4:05 / **Side B:** *Baby Can Dance (Live)* / 6:19 / **CD single version:** 1. *Prisoner of Love (Edit)* / 4:05; 2. *Baby Can Dance (Live)* / 6:19; 3. *Crack City (Live)* / 5:15; 4. *Prisoner of Love (LP Version)* / 4:50 / **UK Release on EMI USA:** October 1989 (ref. 45 rpm: MT 76 / ref. CD single: CDMT 76) / **Best Chart Ranking:** 77

Musicians: David Bowie: lead vocals, acoustic guitar/ Reeves Gabrels, Kevin Armstrong: electric guitar / Tony Sales: bass, backing vocals / Hunt Sales: drums, backing vocals / **Recorded:** Mountain Studios, Montreux: August 1988 / Compass Point Studios, Nassau: November– December 1988 / **Technical Team:** Producers: Tin Machine, Tim Palmer / Sound Engineers: Justin Shirley-Smith, David Richards

Many critics and fans believed that the title "The Jean Genie" was a barely concealed reference to the French writer Jean Genet, and those suspicions were confirmed on this track. *Prisoner of Love* is the English title of Genet's last work, *Un captif amoureux*, which was published posthumously in 1986. The book describes the everyday lives of soldiers at the clandestine bases of the PLO (Palestinian Liberation Organization) that were visited by Genet. The message of the song on *Tin Machine*, its composition attributed to all four of the band, is very different. In simple phrasing, the narrator declares his love: *"I might take any highway / To be there with you / Even the best men shiver in their beds / I'm loving you above everything I have."* It is hard to believe

that these words were co-written with rock 'n' roller Tony Sales, better known for his colorful language and straight talking than for his poetry. "We sat in the studio throwing shit back and forth, and I enjoyed the experience very much. It was a highlight of my career really,"[47] said the drummer in 2016. This was the same man who came to recording sessions wearing a T-shirt that read "Fuck you! I'm from Texas" and who walked around proudly displaying a dagger on his belt. "Prisoner of Love" came out as a single in the UK, but in the United States it was offered only as a maxi 45 rpm; the single version was produced as a promotional item only.

CRACK CITY

David Bowie / 4:37

Musicians: David Bowie: lead vocals, electric guitar / Reeves Gabrels: electric guitar / Kevin Armstrong: electric guitar / Tony Sales: bass, backing vocals / Hunt Sales: drums, backing vocals / **Recorded:** Mountain Studios, Montreux: August 1988 / Compass Point Studios, Nassau: November–December 1988 / **Technical Team:** Producers: Tin Machine, Tim Palmer / Sound Engineers: Justin Shirley-Smith, David Richards

Like Serge Gainsbourg who, in his 1988 single "Aux enfants de la chance," denounces the dealers and the harm caused by drugs—"*Je dis dites-leur et dis-leur / De casser la gueule aux dealers / Qui dans l'ombre attendent leur heure*" (I'm telling you to tell them / To smash the faces of the dealers / Who wait in the shadows for their moment)—David Bowie is here denouncing those who sell crack, saying of it, "[The song] was unfortunately based on just walking around the streets of Nassau. You think it's bad here in New York—well, it is, but the crack situation down there was just trouble on legs, it was hateful. It may seem like a naive kind of story, but it made an impression on me as a writer."[156]

For the introduction, David Bowie looked to "Wild Things" by the Troggs for inspiration and particularly the Hendrix version, with its instantly recognizable power chord. But the similarities stop after two chords; "Crack City" is a piece of genuine rock that moves easily away from the Troggs' hit.

ON YOUR HEADPHONES
In a nod to Andy Warhol, who maintained that every human being would one day be famous, at the 3:30 mark Bowie asks the icon of pop art: "Andy, where's my fifteen minutes?"

1989

I CAN'T READ

David Bowie, Reeves Gabrels / 4:53

Musicians: David Bowie: lead vocals, electric guitar / **Reeves Gabrels, Kevin Armstrong:** electric guitar / **Tony Sales:** bass, backing vocals / **Hunt Sales:** drums, backing vocals / **Recorded:** Compass Point Studios, Nassau: December 1988 / **Technical Team: Producers:** Tin Machine, Tim Palmer / **Sound Engineer:** Tim Palmer

Soon after the gang of friends had set down their bags at Compass Point Studios in Nassau, Bowie was visited by another friend, the actor Gary Oldman. In a break between recording sessions, Oldman, Bowie, and Gabrels went aboard Bowie's yacht, the *Deneb Star C*, for a voyage that was supposed to take them all the way to Venezuela. The ocean was particularly rough that day and, because Gary Oldman was laid low with seasickness, the friends decided to stop at the Grenadine islands. On the journey, the group found time to record a demo for a new song using a four-track tape recorder. This song, "I Can't Read," would subsequently be recorded in a single take. An undervalued but remarkable piece, it suffers from the musicians' extremely casual rendering. Its refrains, nevertheless, are excellent and "I Can't Read" could have made a good single for the group. Irritated by criticism of the *Tin Machine* album, in 1995 Bowie let rip in an interview with journalist Steven Wells: "Tell you what, you do me a favour, when you go back to your record player, try and find a copy of *Tin Machine* and listen to a tune called 'I Can't Read,' listen to that one, will you? I don't ask you to listen to any of the rest, just listen to that one song because I think that song is one of the best I have ever written. I really do!"[158] And to do true justice to this piece, he re-recorded it as an acoustic version in 1996 while working on the *Earthling* album.

UNDER THE GOD

David Bowie / 4:06

45 rpm version: Side A: *Under the God* / 4:06 / **Side B:** *Sacrifice Yourself* / 2:08 / **CD single version:** 1. *Under the God* / 4:06; 2. *Sacrifice Yourself* / 2:08; 3. *The Interview* / 12:24 / **UK Release on EMI USA:** June 1989 (ref. 45 rpm: MT 68 / ref. CD single: CDMT 68) / **Best UK Chart Ranking:** 51

Musicians: David Bowie: lead vocals, electric guitar / **Reeves Gabrels, Kevin Armstrong:** electric guitar / **Tony Sales:** bass, backing vocals / **Hunt Sales:** drums, backing vocals / **Recorded: Mountain Studios, Montreux:** August 1988 / **Compass Point Studios, Nassau:** November–December 1988 / **Technical Team: Producers:** Tin Machine, Tim Palmer / **Sound Engineers:** Justin Shirley-Smith, David Richards

The first single to be released from *Tin Machine*, "Under the God" denounces hatred between different groups arising from skinhead, racist violence that was affecting cities from Washington to London. Bowie said of this song: "I wanted something that had the same simplistic, naive, radical, laying it down [as *Crack City*] about the emergence of a new Nazi."[159] The title "Under the God" brings to mind the "Under His Eye" mantra of Margaret Atwood's dystopian novel of 1985, *The Handmaid's Tale*. Like the Canadian author, Bowie refers to a god whose eye seems to be turned away from the horrors of our modern world. The song was issued as a single in the UK but only as a maxi 45 rpm in the United States. A promotional CD single version was also produced from the David Bowie Convention held on October 1, 1989, in the German city of Essen. This was an occasion where fans could get together to exchange collectors' items and rare discs. Limited to one hundred copies, this CD is much sought-after by collectors of Bowie memorabilia.

AMAZING

David Bowie, Reeves Gabrels / 3:04

Musicians: David Bowie: lead vocals, acoustic guitar / **Reeves Gabrels, Kevin Armstrong**: electric guitar / **Tony Sales**: bass, backing vocals / **Hunt Sales**: drums, backing vocals / **Recorded: Mountain Studios, Montreux**: August 1988 / **Compass Point Studios, Nassau**: November–December 1988 / **Technical Team**: Producers: Tin Machine, Tim Palmer / **Sound Engineers**: Justin Shirley-Smith, David Richards

During the last months of 1988, David Bowie was in love with Melissa Hurley, a dancer whom he had gotten to know during the "Glass Spider Tour." She was with him onstage when he performed in songs like "Bang Bang," "Absolute Beginners," and "Never Let Me Down," and he had been immediately attracted to the twenty-two-year-old. "Amazing" is a midtempo ballad in which he proclaims his love in words that take on a touching simplicity: "*Life's still a dream / Your love's amazing / Since I found you / My life's amazing.*" We can forgive the infatuated David Bowie for these fairly adolescent lyrics, because in May 1989 he announced the couple's engagement. He defended himself against comments about their age difference, saying: "The fact that my girlfriend is young, very naive and kind of straight is, for me, something I just would like her to retain for as long as she can. Cause there is so much crap out there, you know, and there's nothing wrong with being like that."[47] But love affairs can be short-lived in the world of rock 'n' roll, and their short-lived engagement was broken off in 1990. All that remains of this love story is the song "Amazing," which the group performed onstage during the "Tin Machine Tour."

WORKING CLASS HERO

John Lennon / 4:38

Musicians: David Bowie: lead vocals, electric guitar / **Reeves Gabrels:** electric guitar / **Kevin Armstrong:** electric guitar / **Tony Sales:** bass, backing vocals / **Hunt Sales:** drums, backing vocals / **Recorded:** Mountain Studios, Montreux: August 1988 / **Compass Point Studios, Nassau:** November–December 1988 / **Technical Team:** Producers: Tin Machine, Tim Palmer / **Sound Engineers:** Justin Shirley-Smith, David Richards

Perhaps the most famous song from John Lennon's first solo album of 1970, *John Lennon / Plastic Ono Band,* "Working Class Hero" belongs to that category of classic folk numbers wherein the lyrics denounce the system that crushes personalities and forces individuals to get in line; it's a song that is almost anarchist in feeling. *"When they've tortured and scared you for twenty-odd years / Then they expect you to pick a career"* are just some of the lines from Lennon's powerful ballad. Many artists have done versions of this song, including Marianne Faithfull, Marilyn Manson, and Green Day.

When Tin Machine had completed the recording of their first album at Compass Point Studios in Nassau, Sean, the son of John Lennon and Yoko Ono, came on a visit to see Duncan, Bowie's son, who, now aged seventeen, refused to be called Zowie any longer. The thirteen-year-old Sean paid close attention to what was going on in the studio, particularly watching the precise and adventurous guitar playing of Reeves Gabrels. Bowie explained how this cover version was added to the album's track list: "That's always been a really favourite song of mine. I like that first John Lennon album a hell of a lot. I think all the songs are really beautifully written and, again, very straight from the shoulder. There's an honesty in the lyrics there. And that particular song, I thought, would sound great as a rock song. It seemed very worth doing. [...] I think [Sean] likes it a lot."[140] Lennon's acoustic guitar is replaced by a violent and unrelenting rock vibe that only partially suits this legendary song. Its original, pure sound needs no rearranging, however accomplished it may be.

BUS STOP

David Bowie, Reeves Gabrels / 1:41

Musicians: David Bowie: lead vocals, acoustic guitar / **Reeves Gabrels:** electric guitar / **Kevin Armstrong:** electric guitar, Hammond B-3 organ / **Tony Sales:** bass, backing vocals / **Hunt Sales:** drums, backing vocals / **Recorded:** Mountain Studios, Montreux: August 1988 / **Compass Point Studios, Nassau:** November–December 1988 / **Technical Team:** Producers: Tin Machine, Tim Palmer / **Sound Engineers:** Justin Shirley-Smith, David Richards

For this short piece, Bowie and his friends set aside the American indie rock sound of the Pixies and Sonic Youth, opting instead to return to the essence of 1967. We rediscover here the David Bowie of "Love You Till Tuesday" in this pop number, which is placed midway through the album as if to show the emerging Britpop artists who the real boss is. The mocking words are addressed to a person who claims to have had a vision: *"Now Jesus he came in a vision / And offered you redemption from sin / I'm not sayin' that I don't believe you / But are you sure that it really was him / I've been told that it could've been blue cheese / Or the meal that we ate down the road."* For this lighthearted number, Bowie assumes his best Anthony Newley accent, while Hunt Sales hits the snare drum at the beginning of every bar in the style of John Eager in "Rubber Band." The group then packs away this sixties sound to return to a more typical Tin Machine energy. "Bus Stop" provides a brief interlude on the album, offering relief from the deluge of high-powered electric rock.

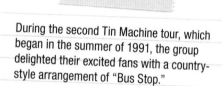

During the second Tin Machine tour, which began in the summer of 1991, the group delighted their excited fans with a country-style arrangement of "Bus Stop."

1989

PRETTY THING

David Bowie / 4:39

Musicians: David Bowie: lead vocals, acoustic guitar / Reeves Gabrels, Kevin Armstrong: electric guitar / Tony Sales: bass, backing vocals / Hunt Sales: drums, backing vocals / **Recorded:** Mountain Studios, Montreux: August 1988 / Compass Point Studios, Nassau: November–December 1988 / **Technical Team:** Producers: Tin Machine, Tim Palmer / Sound Engineers: Justin Shirley-Smith, David Richards

It would be an understatement to say that this crudely executed version of "Pretty Thing" is pretty off-putting. Bowie himself admitted that "it's a throwaway."[140] Even if we forgive the group for their apparently misguided punk-rock intentions, the text remains confusingly heavy-handed. Bowie may have wanted to ape the irreverence of the Sex Pistols, but his efforts fall flat in the ugliest of ways: *"Oh you pretty thing / Feel that pretty thing / Suck that pretty thing."* And our unease is confirmed when the words continue: *"Tie you down, pretend you're Madonna,"* aiming directly at the singer of "La Isla Bonita." Called upon to justify himself, Bowie mentioned a conversation with Madonna's ex-husband, actor Sean Penn: "[...] We were hanging out with Sean and he told us a few things! You know what I mean? [...] I was just trying to think of a... it's such a silly song anyway."[140]

From the production point of view, we find here again that all the energy is generated by Tim Palmer, giving the group the raw violence characteristic of the rock sound prevalent in studios in 1989: "From a production point [David] was a real eye-opener. I'd set up all these expensive mikes, but when he sang through them, it didn't sound like David Bowie, so we used a Shure SM57, which is the cheaper mike you can find. He opened his mouth and it was amazing. [...] Hunt Sales was amazing, too. In the middle of a take he'd be pushing all the mikes out of his way and carrying on playing."[159]

VIDEO CRIME

David Bowie, Hunt Sales, Tony Sales / 3:52

Musicians: David Bowie: lead vocals, electric guitar / Reeves Gabrels, Kevin Armstrong: electric guitar / Tony Sales: bass, backing vocals / Hunt Sales: drums, backing vocals / **Recorded:** Mountain Studios, Montreux: August 1988 / Compass Point Studios, Nassau: November–December 1988 / **Technical Team:** Producers: Tin Machine, Tim Palmer / **Sound Engineers:** Justin Shirley-Smith, David Richards

The unapologetic rock-centric sound of "Video Crime," fronted by a frenetic Bowie, can without a doubt be seen as a precursor of the grunge movement. In this track we can detect the seeds of that germinating movement, originating in Seattle but influenced by multiple other styles of music. We only have to listen to early works by Soundgarden, Temple of the Dog, Alice in Chains, or Stone Temple Pilots to be convinced that 1988's *Tin Machine* was already paving the way to this new moment in music.

Reeves Gabrels uses his guitar to produce sounds borrowed from noise rock, backed by the Sales brothers' rhythm section and supported by a guitar riff played by Kevin Armstrong in the background of the final mix. The result is an aggressive number to which lyrics with frequent references to violence are added. A recurring theme on this album, once again the notorious New York of the 1980s, is central to this track. In it, Bowie mentions the serial killer Ted Bundy who, shortly before his execution in 1989, confessed to the murder of more than thirty young women. It may be significant that one of Bowie's friends, Blondie lead singer Debbie Harry, claimed to have come across Ted Bundy in 1972 when she was trying to hail a cab in the streets of New York. A man drew up next to her and offered to give her a lift, something she accepted without hesitation. Much later, she described what happened: "I got in the car, and it was summertime and the windows were all rolled up except about an inch and a half at the top. [...] Automatically, I sort of reached to roll down the window and I realized there was no door handle, no window crank, no nothing. The inside of the car was totally stripped out. [...] I got very nervous. I reached my arm out through the little crack and stretched down and opened the car from the outside. As soon as he saw that, he tried to turn the corner really fast, and I spun out of the car and landed in the middle of the street."[160]

RUN

David Bowie, Kevin Armstrong / 3:20

Musicians: David Bowie: lead vocals, electric guitar / Reeves Gabrels: electric guitar / Kevin Armstrong: electric guitar / Tony Sales: bass, backing vocals / Hunt Sales: drums, backing vocals / **Recorded:** Mountain Studios, Montreux: August 1988 / Compass Point Studios, Nassau: November–December 1988 / **Technical Team:** Producers: Tin Machine, Tim Palmer / **Sound Engineers:** Justin Shirley-Smith, David Richards

Since one side of a 33 rpm vinyl disc can't hold more than thirty minutes of content, two numbers—"Run" and "Sacrifice Yourself"—appear only on the CD version of *Tin Machine*. (The compact disc was a new technology just taking off at the time.) It's a pity, because "Run" is an effective song with a memorable refrain that would have been perfect for the airwaves. Over a four-square rhythm supported by a catchy riff, Bowie sings of his need to be loved: "*And it's cold in here / Without your love / Trouble in here, trouble out there.*" This excellent number sums up the philosophy of the *Tin Machine* project, where the emphasis was placed on spontaneity, with the musicians committing their ideas to tape in no more than one or two takes, and without going back over them. Proud of their work, the joker of the group, drummer Tony Sales, said: "I think if there's anything that we could change, that might be our socks."[161]

As usual, Hunt Sales put all of his energy into the drum score for "Run," much to the chagrin of guitarist Kevin Armstrong. "He's the loudest drummer I've ever worked with," the guitarist said. "I almost went deaf those first two days. The power and volume were superhuman."

Iman in character as Martia, a shape-shifting "chameloid" in the film *Star Trek VI: The Undiscovered Country.*

In "Sacrifice Yourself," the central character is "married to a Klingon," an extraterrestrial being well known to fans of *Star Trek*. In an amusing coincidence, Iman, who was to become Bowie's wife two years later, appeared in the role of an extraterrestrial in the 1991 movie *Star Trek VI: The Undiscovered Country.*

SACRIFICE YOURSELF

David Bowie, Tony Sales, Hunt Sales / 2:08

Musicians: David Bowie: lead vocals, electric guitar / Reeves Gabrels, Kevin Armstrong: electric guitar / Tony Sales: bass, backing vocals / Hunt Sales: drums, backing vocals / **Recorded:** Mountain Studios, Montreux: August 1988 / Compass Point Studios, Nassau: November–December 1988 / **Technical Team:** Producers: Tin Machine, Tim Palmer / Sound Engineers: Justin Shirley-Smith, David Richards

On the thirteenth track on the album's CD version (omitted from the vinyl version because of space issues) *Tin Machine* offers listeners two minutes and eight seconds of a rock sound verging on the thrash metal popularized by the Californian group Metallica. Despite his background in jazz, Reeves Gabrels plays the guitar here in the style of Metallica's virtuoso guitarist, Kirk Hammett. Gabrels seems to be growing increasingly comfortable as the songs on *Tin Machine* progress, developing new ideas with each new bar. In the early days of their collaboration, this fine musician had some difficulty working with the hyperactive Sales brothers, saying a few years later: "I was in the studio doing a guitar thing and the Sales brothers kept getting on the talkback mic: 'No, you should play that more like B. B. King. No, play it more like Hendrix...' Every time I did a take it was a different, diametrically opposed instruction. I finally had enough. I stepped up to the closed-circuit camera and said, 'Look, I appreciate your input, but I've got a bunch of ideas of my own that I'm going to try first. So just shut the fuck up!' When the talkback came back up, they were laughing hysterically. Everything was fine after that. They just wanted to see how far they could push me."[155]

BABY CAN DANCE

David Bowie / 4:57

Musicians: David Bowie: lead vocals, electric guitar / Reeves Gabrels: electric guitar / Kevin Armstrong: electric guitar / Tony Sales: bass, backing vocals / Hunt Sales: drums, backing vocals / **Recorded:** Mountain Studios, Montreux: August 1988 / Compass Point Studios, Nassau: November–December 1988 / **Technical Team:** Producers: Tin Machine, Tim Palmer / Sound Engineers: Justin Shirley-Smith, David Richards

The last track on the album, "Baby Can Dance" sums up the *Tin Machine* experiment. Over the powerful sound of the Sales brothers, Reeves Gabrels, now fully liberated from the constraints of his classic musical background, adds an entirely improvised line on the guitar. In the lyrics, Bowie speaks of himself as "the shadow man," in seeming contrast with "the Rainbow Man," the character he assumed onstage at a London concert in February 1970. Despite working conditions that were sometimes difficult, producer Tim Palmer gave this album all the impact it needed, even if that meant going above and beyond the call of duty. He later described one interest problem he faced during production: "The other studio in Compass Point had Status Quo in it, great guys. The sad part was they'd stolen all the fucking mic stands, so I just grabbed some string and attached the microphones to the roof. Sometimes you'd come out of the control room and see Francis Rossi or Rick Parfitt trying to sneak a listen to what we were doing."[119]

ALBUM

TIN MACHINE II

Baby Universal . One Shot . You Belong in Rock 'n' Roll . If There Is Something .
Amlapura . Betty Wrong . You Can't Talk . Stateside . Shopping for Girls . A Big Hurt .
Sorry . Goodbye Mr. Ed . Hammerhead (hidden track)

RELEASE DATES
United Kingdom: September 2, 1991
References: London Records/Victory—828 272-1 (LP); 828 272-2 (CD)
United States: September 2, 1991
Reference: PolyGram/Victory—314 511 216-2 (CD)
Best UK Chart Ranking: 23
Best US Chart Ranking: 126

TIN MACHINE'S SWAN SONG

While he was still in the middle of the *Tin Machine* tour in the spring of 1989, David Bowie chose Rykodisc to reissue his catalog in CD format because the digitization work done by the label for other artists had greatly impressed him. The singer threw himself into the project and looked for all kinds of rarities to offer to album buyers as bonuses to the original albums. Alongside this vast undertaking, a boxed set entitled *Sound + Vision* was also released. It consisted mostly of lesser-known titles, B-sides, and other live versions. To promote the reissue campaign, Bowie announced the launch of the *Sound + Vision* tour, which he presented as a farewell world tour, and during which time (March to September of 1990) he planned to perform all his greatest hits. But before setting off on the road, Bowie gathered together the members of Tin Machine in Sydney to work on a new album.

Split Sessions between Sydney and Los Angeles

"I keep telling people that if they want to start their lives over again, go over to Australia to do it,"[162] Bowie declared in 2003. A huge fan of the country, Bowie had owned an apartment in Sydney since 1983. The apartment was located on Elizabeth Bay Road, just opposite the harbor where his yacht, the *Deneb Star C*, was moored. It was here in this idyllic setting that Tin Machine set about recording their second album at Studios 301 in September 1989. Supported by the in-house sound engineer, Guy Gray, the band recorded most of the backing tracks in a relaxed atmosphere, which inspired the rockers to write calmer lyrics than those that appeared on the first album. The sessions lasted until December, at which point Bowie interrupted them in order to prepare for the *Sound + Vision* tour. Producer Tim Palmer joined the venture solely for the second part of the recording, which would eventually begin

after the tour and which was conducted in a split format through March 1991. "On the first album, it was more a band feel," he would later explain. "Everyone was shipping in. On the second album, I was working primarily with Reeves Gabrels, putting the finishing touches on the songs at Eel Pie Studios in London. And we were sending mixes out to David for his approval. I don't think I saw Hunt and Tony much later on, when the album was almost complete."[163]

The *Sound + Vision* Tour, a False Farewell

Promoted as the singer's last tour, the *Sound + Vision* tour began in March 1990, running in parallel with the recording of the *Tin Machine II* album. In order to avoid confusion between the Tin Machine venture and Bowie's solo career, the Sales brothers and Reeves Gabrels refused to participate. Bowie responded by calling on Erdal Kizilçay to play bass, as well as by bringing in Adrian Belew, the guitarist on *Lodger*, and two of his friends: drummer Michael Hodges and keyboard player Rick Fox. Fox was also responsible for launching the samples and the sequences synchronized with the videos that were playing in the background during the tour. In these images viewers would occasionally see the dancer Louise Lecavalier, who had become one of Bowie's loyal collaborators. The choreography was done by Édouard Lock, and the overall set design for the tour was created by two other members of the La La La Human Steps company, Luc Dussault and Lyne Lefebvre.

The tour, which visited every continent except Australia, was a huge triumph. All of the artist's hits were performed, to the huge satisfaction of the audiences. After what was supposed to have been his last concert in Buenos Aires on September 29, 1990, Bowie changed his mind and declared that he would return to the stage, but would no longer play his old songs. In reality, he would never give up performing the hits that had made him an international star.

PolyGram, the distributor of *Tin Machine II* in the United States, took serious offense at the fact that the genitals of Greek statues were visible on the cover and decided to airbrush them out, which triggered Bowie's fury, as he later explained: "We thought the whole thing was ridiculous and childish. I suppose I should be grateful that at least they didn't put little surf shorts on the kouroi."[164]

An Album That Went Unnoticed

Tin Machine's second studio album, *Tin Machine II*, was released on September 2, 1991. The album cover was the work of Edward Bell, who had already produced the cover for *Scary Monsters (And Super Creeps)* in 1980. David Bowie having insisted that he did not want to appear on the cover, Bell suggested using four photographs of kouroi (Greek statues of naked young men whose virility was intended to underline that of the musicians), which would symbolize the equality that reigned within Tin Machine. In terms of distribution and promotion, after having amicably parted ways with EMI (who were delighted not to have to risk another failure), David Bowie enlisted the services of the young label Victory Music, which was owned by the Japanese brand JVC. This new label was highly motivated when it came to promoting *Tin Machine II*. In spite of its best efforts, Victory Music could do nothing to counter the poor reception the album received.

Tired of chronic misunderstandings within the team and disappointed by the bad reception of the disc, David Bowie convinced himself that the time had come to put an end to Tin Machine. Before that, the band embarked on a marathon tour and played more than sixty dates. The tour was called "It's My Life Tour," and it was named after the phrase that Hunt Sales had tattooed on his back. The live album *Live: Oy Vey, Baby* was released in July 1992, and it would prove to be the last manifestation of the Tin Machine adventure.

Adrian Belew and David Bowie during the *Sound + Vision* tour in 1990.

Single

Adrian Belew (featuring David Bowie)

PRETTY PINK ROSE

David Bowie / 4:43

Vinyl Single Version (UK): Side A: *Pretty Pink Rose (Edit)* / 4:07 / **Side B:** *Heartbeat* / 3:57 / **CD Single Version (UK):** 1. *Pretty Pink Rose* / 4:44; 2. *Heartbeat* / 4:00; 3. *Oh Daddy* / 3:06 / **CD Single Version (USA):** 1. *Pretty Pink Rose* / 4:44; 2. *Neptune Pool* / 3:01; 3. *Shoe Salesman* / 1:49; 4. *Oh Daddy* / 3:06 / **UK Release on Atlantic:** May 1990 (ref. vinyl single: A 7904T / ref. CD single: A 7904 CD; 7567-86173-2) / **US Release on Atlantic:** May 1990 (ref. CD single: 7 86200-2; 86200-2) / **Best UK Chart Ranking:** 89 / **Best US Chart Ranking:** Did Not Chart

Musicians: Adrian Belew: vocals, electric guitar, bass, drums / **David Bowie:** vocals / **Recorded:** Royal Recorders Studios, Lake Geneva, Wisconsin (music): November 11, 1989 / Right Track Studios, New York (vocals): January 15, 1990 / **Technical Team:** Producer: Adrian Belew / **Sound Engineer:** Rich Denhart

David Bowie recorded a first demo of "Pretty Pink Rose" with American musicians, including Bryan Adams's guitarist, Keith Scott, in Los Angeles in 1988. Set aside during the first work sessions of Tin Machine, the song was offered one year later to Adrian Belew, the guitarist on *Lodger*, whom the singer had recently asked to participate in the *Sound + Vision* tour. Belew was not immediately convinced by the duet that his friend had created for his fifth solo album, *Young Lions*, as he later revealed in 2016: "David's office sent a cassette. Excitedly I opened it and played it. 'Oh gawd,' it was awful! Imagine how I felt. Here I was on the verge of touring for a year with David Bowie and thinking we might produce a duet of perhaps a 'hit' song of David's, only to be confronted with something which sounded lifeless, limp, and plodding. I didn't know quite what to do."[165] Faithful to his established way of working, Belew then locked himself away in Royal Recorders Studios in Lake Geneva, Wisconsin, and rerecorded the instrumental part, playing all the instruments himself. The vocal portions were recorded at Right Track Studios in New York on January 15, 1990, with Belew and Bowie singing side by side into the same microphone. "Pretty Pink Rose" was released as a single in May 1990 and credited as "Adrian Belew (featuring David Bowie)," but the song did not meet with the success the guitarist had hoped for.

Adrian Belew (featuring David Bowie)

GUNMAN

Adrian Belew, David Bowie / 3:51

Musicians: David Bowie: vocals / Adrian Belew: electric guitar, bass, drums / **Recorded:** Royal Recorders Studios, Lake Geneva, Wisconsin (music): November 1989 / Right Track Studios, New York (vocals): January 15, 1990 / **Technical Team:** Producer: Adrian Belew / **Sound Engineer:** Rich Denhart

"Gunman" was recorded by accident when Adrian Belew and David Bowie were in the middle of rehearsals for the *Sound + Vision* tour and working on the vocal parts of "Pretty Pink Rose." "We went to record that in New York," as Belew later recalled, "and because we'd been rehearsing for the tour, his voice was shot. He said 'I'm sorry, but I can't sing it today.' I said 'okay,' I'd work on another song that hadn't got vocals and he could go home and rest. But he said, 'let me hear that.' He began writing lyrics and about half an hour later, he'd finished a song called 'Gun Man.' I was amazed. He then went in and sang it two or three times and that was it."[166]

Queen Latifah is a talented actress and a famous hip-hop star with eight successful studio albums to her name.

FAME 90

David Bowie, Carlos Alomar, John Lennon / 3:36

Technical Team
Remixes: Mark Plati, Jon Gass, DJ Mark the 45 King, Ron Fair, Arthur Baker, David Barratt

Vinyl Version (UK)
Side A: Fame 90 (Gass Mix) / 3:36
Side B: Fame 90 (Queen Latifah's Rap Version) / 3:10

CD Single Version (UK)
1. *Fame 90 (House Mix)* / 5:58
2. *Fame 90 (Hip Hop Mix)* / 5:58
3. *Fame 90 (Gass Mix)* / 3:36
4. *Fame 90 (Queen Latifah's Rap Version)* / 3:10

CD Maxi Single Version (USA)
1. *Fame 90 (Queen Latifah's Rap Version)* / 3:10
2. *Fame 90 (House Mix)* / 5:58
3. *Fame 90 (Gass Mix)* / 3:36
4. *Fame 90 (Hip Hop Mix)* / 5:58
5. *Fame 90 (Absolutely Nothing Premeditated Mix)* / 14:25

UK Release on EMI USA: March 26, 1990 (ref. vinyl single: FAME 90 / ref. CD single: CDFAME 90; 20 3805 2)
US Release on Rykodisc: March 26, 1990 (ref. maxi CD single: RCD5 1018)
Best UK Chart Ranking: 28
Best US Chart Ranking: Did Not Chart

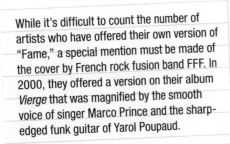

While it's difficult to count the number of artists who have offered their own version of "Fame," a special mention must be made of the cover by French rock fusion band FFF. In 2000, they offered a version on their album *Vierge* that was magnified by the smooth voice of singer Marco Prince and the sharp-edged funk guitar of Yarol Poupaud.

Genesis
Like so many other songs before it (e.g., "Space Oddity," "John, I'm Only Dancing," "Look Back in Anger"), it was now the turn of "Fame"—the 1975 hit from *Young Americans*—to benefit from the rejuvenation treatment when Rykodisc reissued all of Bowie's previous albums, each in a CD format that was enhanced with rare bonuses. The *Sound + Vision* promotional tour, slotted in between two recording sessions for the *Tin Machine* LP, was accompanied by the release of the *ChangesBowie* compilation album, whose name refers to two previous greatest hits collections: *ChangesOneBowie* from 1976 and *ChangesTwoBowie* from 1981.

To sell this new record, which admittedly felt a little stale, Rykodisc asked Jon Gass to remix the hit, thus offering buyers at least some semblance of novelty. Gass had just made a big name for himself as a talented sound engineer alongside producer L.A. Reid on the first two Babyface albums. Thus, "Fame 90" was born, and it was accompanied by a video from famed director Gus Van Sant.

Production
As usual, David Bowie proved himself to be a clever trend forecaster when he released a series of remixes of "Fame." Over the next decade, all the great pop singles would be released in multiple formats as CD singles, maxi-CD singles, Digipaks, and other limited editions...and all at overinflated prices. This was mainly to fill the coffers of the record companies, who took full advantage of the strategy at every opportunity. With the arrival of the MP3 format and illegal-download sites in the early 2000s, the record companies eventually faced a reckoning of sorts, but in 1990 Bowie offered us the perfect example of this new trend when he created no less than six versions of "Fame" and made them available in a variety of formats. "House Mix," "Hip Hop Mix," "Absolutely Nothing Premeditated Mix," "Bonus Beat Mix"—any pretext was good enough for creating a different edition. The only version that offered real novelty was "Queen Latifah's Rap Version," where the flow of the talented rapper Queen Latifah (who found international success with her hit "Ladies First") struck a perfect chord within the contemporary hip-hop movement.

BABY UNIVERSAL

David Bowie, Reeves Gabrels / 3:18

Vinyl Single Version (UK): Side A: *Baby Universal (New Mix)* / 3:06 / **Side B:** *You Belong in Rock 'n' Roll* / 3:30 / **CD Single Version (UK):** 1. 3:25; 4. *Heaven's in Here* / 6:41 / **CD Single Version (USA):** 1. *Baby Universal (Radio Edit)* / 3:07; 2. *Baby Universal (Extended Version)* / 5:35; 3. *Baby Universal (BBC Live Version)* / 3:04; 4. *Stateside (BBC Live Version)* / 6:35 / **UK Release on London Records / Victory:** October 1991 (ref. vinyl single: LON 310 / ref. CD single: LOCDT 310) / **USA Release on Polygram / Victory:** October 1991 (ref. CD single: CDP 588) / **Best UK Chart Ranking:** 48 / **Best US Chart Ranking:** Did Not Chart

Musicians: David Bowie: lead vocals, electric guitar / **Reeves Gabrels:** electric guitar / **Tony Sales:** bass, backing vocals / **Hunt Sales:** drums, backing vocals, tambourine / **Recorded:** Studios 301, Sydney: September–December 1989 / **Unknown Studio, Miami:** April–May 1990 / **Eel Pie Studios, London:** October–November 1990 / **A&M Recording Studios, Los Angeles:** March 1991 / **Technical Team: Producers:** Tin Machine, Tim Palmer / **Sound Engineers:** Guy Gray, Simon Vinestock, Eric Schilling, Ruggie Simkins, Chuck Ferry, Mark O'Donoughue (remix)

"Baby Universal" clearly announces the change of direction brought about by Tin Machine in 1989. Naturalness and spontaneity make a big comeback here, to the extent that you would swear the band had put aside their punk and indie rock nature in order to fully submerge themselves into the singer's unique universe. Indeed, Bowie's lyrics seem to contain a number of allusions to his past career, like the phrase "*Hello humans, can you feel me thinking?*" which has the distinct flavor of "Space Oddity" or "Starman." A powerful production and a crystal-clear sound underline the change of direction: We are a world away from the "garage" sound of the band's first album.

The song was released as a single to general indifference in October 1991. This failure proved to be a great disappointment for Bowie, who later declared: "I thought 'Baby Universal' was a really good song and I don't think it got heard. I didn't really want that to happen to it."[167]

Producer Hugh Padgham recorded a new version of "One Shot" with a view to releasing the track as a single.

ONE SHOT

David Bowie, Reeves Gabrels, Hunt Sales, Tony Sales / 5:11

CD single version: 1. *One Shot* / 4:02; 2. *Hammerhead* / 3:16 / **UK Release on London Records / Victory:** November 1991 (ref. CD single: 869 574-2) / **Best UK Chart Ranking:** Did Not Chart

Musicians: David Bowie: lead vocals, electric guitar / **Reeves Gabrels:** electric guitar / **Tony Sales:** bass, backing vocals / **Hunt Sales:** drums, backing vocals / **Recorded:** A&M Recording Studios, Los Angeles: March 1991 / **Technical Team: Producer:** Hugh Padgham / **Sound Engineer:** Hugh Padgham

First recorded with Tim Palmer in Sydney in late 1989, "One Shot" was given special treatment during sessions at A&M Recording Studios in Los Angeles eighteen months later. Victory Music, which was doing everything in its power to ensure the success of *Tin Machine II*, asked Hugh Padgham to rerecord the track and to remix it according to the radio standards of the time. The sound engineer, who had worked on *Tonight* in 1984, was by

---

FOR BOWIE ADDICTS

Bowie, who regularly played "Baby Universal" during the "Outside Summer Festivals Tour" in 1996, later rerecorded the track for the album *Earthling* in 1997. Eventually, the song was removed from the track listing of that record and a new version reappeared in 2020 on the *Is It Any Wonder?* EP under the name "Baby Universal '97."

then a world-renowned producer. His work on albums by Genesis (*Invisible Touch*, 1986), Sting (*...Nothing Like the Sun*, 1987), and Phil Collins (*...But Seriously*, 1989) had made him a star of the recording studios. "At that time, Hugh was a very successful producer/engineer," recalled Tim Palmer, "and the idea that his name would be on this particular song may encourage radio stations to give it more airplay."[163] But the strategy was to prove a failure, and the song, which did not make it onto the British charts, had a short-lived existence. In the United States it was released only as a promotional CD.

YOU BELONG IN ROCK N' ROLL

David Bowie, Reeves Gabrels / 4:07

Vinyl Single Version: Side A: *You Belong in Rock N' Roll* / 3:30 / **Side B:** *Amlapura (Indonesian Version)* / 3:47 / **CD Single Version:** 1. *You Belong in Rock N' Roll* / 3:30; 2. *Amlapura (Indonesian Version)* / 3:47; 3. *Stateside* / 5:38; 4. *Hammerhead* / 3:15 / **UK Release on London Records / Victory:** August 1991 (ref. vinyl single: LON 305; 869 402-7 / ref. CD single: LONCD 305) / **Best UK Chart Ranking:** 33

Musicians: David Bowie: lead vocals, acoustic guitar, saxophone / Reeves Gabrels: electric guitar / Tony Sales: bass, backing vocals / Hunt Sales: drums, backing vocals / **Recorded:** Studios 301, Sydney: September–December 1989 / Unknown Studio, Miami: April–May 1990 / Eel Pie Studios, London: October–November 1990 / A&M Recording Studios, Los Angeles: March 1991 / **Technical Team:** Producers: Tin Machine, Tim Palmer / **Sound Engineers:** Guy Gray, Simon Vinestock, Eric Schilling, Ruggie Simkins, Chuck Ferry

This extremely effective track dances along as light as a feather! The lyrics were almost certainly written for dancer Melissa Hurley, who at the time was sharing Bowie's life: "*Hand in hand in love with love / I love the cheap things that you say.*" But by then, the relationship between the two lovebirds was already in its final stages, and when Bowie finally ended things a few months later, he explained that their age difference was becoming an issue.

In terms of production, an unusual new instrument made its appearance during the recording sessions of Tin Machine's second album, and particularly on "You Belong in Rock N' Roll." Reeves Gabrels was now using a vibrator, which he placed on the guitar strings to make them vibrate. While the musician might have gotten away with using it during the band's appearance on the BBC's *Paramount City* in August 1991, the channel's watchdogs were more vigilant a few days later when Tin Machine appeared on a *Top of the Pops* broadcast. They formally banned Gabrels from brandishing the offending object on set, and the guitarist had to play without his new gadget.

IF THERE IS SOMETHING

Bryan Ferry / 4:45

Musicians: David Bowie: lead vocals, electric guitar / Reeves Gabrels: electric guitar / Tony Sales: bass, backing vocals / Hunt Sales: drums, backing vocals / Kevin Armstrong: electric guitar / **Recorded:** Mountain Studios, Montreux: August 1988 / Compass Point Studios, Nassau: November–December 1988 / A&M Recording Studios, Los Angeles: March 1991 / **Technical Team:** Producers: Tin Machine, Tim Palmer / **Sound Engineers:** Guy Gray, Simon Vinestock, Justin Shirley-Smith, Eric Schilling, Ruggie Simkins, Chuck Ferry

With Hunt Sales hammering away on his Ludwig drum set, Tin Machine presents an interesting reworking of this originally country-tinged track from Roxy Music's 1972 eponymous debut album. Reeves Gabrels unleashes a formidable guitar solo, mixing all sorts of techniques, including the use, at 1:15, of the revolutionary Whammy real-time harmonization pedal. The pedal was launched in 1989 by the American company DigiTech. Gabrels's score is without a doubt the most striking element of this cover, his virtuosity matched only by his creativity during the entirety of the track's 4:45 runtime.

Although "If There Is Something" benefits from the same mix as the other tracks on the record, it was actually recorded earlier, as Bowie explained to journalist Robin Eggar in 1991: "To take the wind out of those sails, the Roxy Music track was done for the first album, the second track we made, and we included it to show the cohesiveness of what we were doing then and now. We did it because after 'Heaven's In Here' we were so exhausted that we didn't have it in us to write another song so we used an old song to show how we as a band would approach someone else's material. [...] When we were mixing this album, I remembered we'd done the Roxy song, pulled it out to see how it sounded. We really got off on it."[168]

AMLAPURA

David Bowie, Reeves Gabrels / 3:46

Musicians: David Bowie: lead vocals, acoustic guitar / Reeves Gabrels: electric guitar / Tony Sales: bass, backing vocals / Hunt Sales: drums, backing vocals / **Recorded:** Studios 301, Sydney: September–December 1989 / Unknown Studio, Miami: April–May 1990 / Eel Pie Studios, London: October–November 1990 / A&M Recording Studios, Los Angeles: March 1991 / **Technical Team:** Producers: Tin Machine, Tim Palmer / **Sound Engineers:** Guy Gray, Simon Vinestock, Eric Schilling, Ruggie Simkins, Chuck Ferry

Bowie wrote the lyrics for this rock ballad in memory of his many trips to the island of Bali. "*I dream of Amlapura / Never saw in all my life a more shining jewel,*" the British star sings, having voyaged all around Southeast Asia on his yacht while accompanied by a crew of eight. In this moving track he pays tribute to a region where, in 1963, 1,600 people lost their lives during the eruption of the Agung volcano. Bowie even recorded a version of the song in Indonesian, which appeared on the B-side of the single "You Belong in Rock N' Roll."

As Tim Palmer would later reveal, after delivering what seemed to be a flawless vocal performance, Bowie inexplicably decided to give it a second try: "Everybody wanted to know why he wanted to do it again, because it was so good and so well performed. But he said that he felt the vocal could be sadder."[163]

BETTY WRONG

David Bowie, Reeves Gabrels / 3:48

Musicians: David Bowie: lead vocals, acoustic guitar, saxophone / Reeves Gabrels: electric guitar / Tony Sales: bass, backing vocals / Hunt Sales: drums, backing vocals, percussion / **Recorded:** Studios 301, Sydney: September–December 1989 / **Technical Team:** Producers: Tin Machine, Tim Palmer / **Sound Engineers:** Guy Gray, Simon Vinestock, Eric Schilling, Ruggie Simkins, Chuck Ferry

Who is the Betty Wrong to whom Bowie sings "*I'll be your light / When the shadows fall down the walls*"?

No one knows for sure, but most listeners agree that the singer was actively trying to return to a more commercial writing style on this second Tin Machine album. "Betty Wrong" is the proof, and Gabrels's repetitive (and heady) riff works wonderfully overlaid with the percussive rhythm executed with metronome precision by Hunt Sales. To discover the combo's exceptional energy, just listen to the version they played on the "It's My Life Tour." The musicians are in perfect harmony in an improvisation that falls somewhere between jazz and rock, and when Gabrels occasionally opts to stop his incessant flow of powerful solos—delivered on his white Steinberger M Series headless guitar—Bowie steps in with a few scales on saxophone. The young Eric Schermerhorn lent a hand to the rhythm section by playing backup guitar throughout the tour. Entirely recorded at Sydney's Studios 301, "Betty Wrong" also appeared on the soundtrack to Australian director George Ogilvie's movie *The Crossing* (1990).

YOU CAN'T TALK

David Bowie, Reeves Gabrels, Hunt Sales, Tony Sales / 3:09

Musicians: David Bowie: lead vocals, electric guitar, piano, saxophone / Reeves Gabrels: electric guitar, organ / Tony Sales: bass, backing vocals / Hunt Sales: drums, backing vocals, percussion / **Recorded:** Studios 301, Sydney: September–December 1989 / Unknown Studio, Miami: April–May 1990 / Eel Pie Studios, London: October–November 1990 / A&M Recording Studios, Los Angeles: March 1991 / **Technical Team:** Producers: Tin Machine, Tim Palmer / **Sound Engineers:** Guy Gray, Simon Vinestock, Eric Schilling, Ruggie Simkins, Chuck Ferry

After "I Can't Read" on the previous album, and a few months before Genesis largely won the public vote with their hit "I Can't Dance," Tin Machine graced us with "You Can't Talk." The writing of the track immediately strikes the listener as completely Bowian in style, despite the fact that it is credited to all four musicians. Hunt Sales's percussion accompanies Reeves Gabrels's multiple guitar tracks, the effects of which, cleverly placed in stereo, toy with the ears of the fans, whom we can easily imagine listening with their Sony Walkman Auto Reverse headphones glued to their ears. A rock song with a crystalline and powerful sound, "You Can't Talk" deserves to be (re)discovered as soon as possible!

STATESIDE

David Bowie, Hunt Sales / 5:38

Musicians: Hunt Sales: lead and backing vocals, drums / David Bowie: electric guitar, saxophone, backing vocals / Reeves Gabrels: electric guitar, organ / Tony Sales: bass, backing vocals / **Recorded:** Studios 301, Sydney: September–December 1989 / Unknown Studio, Miami: April–May 1990 / Eel Pie Studios, London: October–November 1990 / A&M Recording Studios, Los Angeles: March 1991 / **Technical Team:** Producers: Tin Machine, Tim Palmer / Sound Engineers: Guy Gray, Simon Vinestock, Eric Schilling, Ruggie Simkins, Chuck Ferry

Drummer Hunt Sales provides the lead vocals on this classic blues track, whose misogynistic lyrics refer to Marilyn Monroe as the *"blonde with no brain."* Biographer Nicholas Pegg, who is definitely no fan of Tin Machine, doesn't mince words in his description of the song: "Having taken one look at this undignified monstrosity, Bowie should have elected to stuff democracy. Instead, he capitulated to Mr. Sales and in doing so compromised the album."[47] Nevertheless, we can still appreciate the references to the American songbook, to which Sales alludes in the second verse, first citing "Home on the Range," an 1872 western classic that has become the official song of Texas. He next references the hit song "Summertime" by George and Ira Gershwin, when he slips in a discreet *"where the living is easy,"* and then finally he evokes the band America's hit, "A Horse with No Name" (1972). It would appear that Tin Machine's indomitable drummer was feeling homesick in 1991. It was Reeves Gabrels who summed up the power that lay dormant in this curious character, whose precise and spirited playing was too often overshadowed by his unruly antics: "In the best possible way, playing with Hunt in Tin Machine was a cross between riding a bronco and aerial combat."[169]

SHOPPING FOR GIRLS

David Bowie, Reeves Gabrels / 3:44

Musicians: David Bowie: lead vocals, acoustic guitar / Reeves Gabrels: electric guitar / Tony Sales: bass, backing vocals / Hunt Sales: drums, backing vocals, percussion / Kevin Armstrong: piano / **Recorded:** Mountain Studios, Montreux: August 1988 / Compass Point Studios, Nassau: November–December 1988 / A&M Recording Studios, Los Angeles: March 1991 / **Technical Team:** Producers: Tin Machine, Tim Palmer / Sound Engineers: Guy Gray, Simon Vinestock, Justin Shirley-Smith, Eric Schilling, Ruggie Simkins, Chuck Ferry

In 1987, Sara Terry and Kristin Helmore published a series of reports on the exploitation of children around the world in the Canadian newspaper the *Monitor*. Entitled "Children in Darkness: The Exploitation of Innocence," the investigation was illustrated by photographer Melanie Stetson Freeman. Sara Terry had met David Bowie during the "Glass Spider Tour," on which she was a press agent (she had also introduced him to her partner, guitarist Reeves Gabrels). The singer then discovered her work, which was focused on child slaves working in the silver mines of South Africa, as well as on very young child soldiers in Uganda and on child prostitution in Thailand. This last theme in particular inspired Bowie, who took several years to write the lyrics to this song, which was recorded between 1988 and 1991. "The song came about because we were talking about it one evening," Bowie later explained. "I'd been to Thailand and witnessed the same sort of thing going on. Approaching that as a subject was pretty hard because one didn't want to make it a sensational kind of thing. It was hard to stop it being finger-wagging so it ended up as pure narrative."[168]

A BIG HURT

David Bowie / 3:40

Musicians: David Bowie: lead vocals, electric guitar / Reeves Gabrels: electric guitar / Tony Sales: bass, backing vocals / Hunt Sales: drums, backing vocals / **Recorded:** Studios 301, Sydney: September–December 1989 / Unknown Studio, Miami: April–May 1990 / Eel Pie Studios, London: October–November 1990 / A&M Recording Studios, Los Angeles: March 1991 / **Technical Team:** Producers: Tin Machine, Tim Palmer / Sound Engineers: Guy Gray, Simon Vinestock, Eric Schilling, Ruggie Simkins, Chuck Ferry

Probably the weakest song on the album, "A Big Hurt" is also the only one credited solely to David Bowie. Fortunately, Gabrels's playing is remarkably ingenious, allowing listeners to discover just how much the guitarist has influenced subsequent generations of musicians, including Muse's brilliant Matthew Bellamy, who is known for his six-string experimentation. Just listen to the violent Whammy and vibrato stem detuning at 1:18 on "A Big Hurt" and compare it with the introduction of Muse's "Plug In Baby," on the *Origin of Symmetry* album, which the band released some twenty years after *Tin Machine II*. To give credit where credit is due, Reeves Gabrels was undeniably a step ahead of his contemporaries when it came to guitar innovation.

Hunt Sales performing onstage with Tin Machine in 1991.

SORRY

Hunt Sales / 3:29

Musicians: Hunt Sales: lead and backing vocals, drums, tambourine / David Bowie: acoustic guitar, saxophone / Reeves Gabrels: acoustic guitar, electric guitar / Tony Sales: bass, backing vocals / **Recorded:** Studios 301, Sydney: September–December 1989 / Unknown Studio, Miami: April–May 1990 / Eel Pie Studios, London: October–November 1990 / A&M Recording Studios, Los Angeles: March 1991 / **Technical Team:** Producers: Tin Machine, Tim Palmer / **Sound Engineers:** Guy Gray, Simon Vinestock, Eric Schilling, Ruggie Simkins, Chuck Ferry

A ballad whose melody is somewhere between the Eagles' "Hotel California" (1977) and the Scorpions' hit "Still Loving You" (1984), "Sorry" is the only song entirely written by Hunt Sales, the drummer with Tin Machine. It is also the second song on which he performs vocally. The musician appears to have a long list of things to make up for, since his text is limited to the following statements: *"Didn't mean to hurt you but I always do," "I wouldn't do for me what I would do for you,"* and finally *"Didn't mean to do it that way."* Behind its blatant and somewhat clumsy naiveté, the song is nevertheless very effective with its acoustic guitar and reverb-drenched backing vocals. We are a long way from the perfection of Guns N' Roses' "Don't Cry," which was recorded during the same period and became one of the flagship songs of the decade. But given that the writing of a quality ballad was an inevitable exercise for any self-respecting rock band, we can acknowledge that Tin Machine takes up the challenge here with flying colors.

track remained buried on this unloved album. For owners of the vinyl edition, be careful not to raise the arm of the turntable too quickly at the end of this track, because after a second of silence a rock flourish suddenly ends the album just as it began, with rage and fury.

GOODBYE MR. ED

David Bowie, Hunt Sales, Tony Sales / 3:24

Musicians: David Bowie: lead vocals, acoustic guitar, saxophone / Reeves Gabrels: acoustic guitar, electric guitar / **Tony Sales:** bass, backing vocals / **Hunt Sales:** drums, backing vocals / **Recorded:** Studios 301, Sydney: September–December 1989 / Unknown Studio, Miami: April–May 1990 / **Eel Pie Studios, London:** October–November 1990 / **A&M Recording Studios, Los Angeles:** March 1991 / **Technical Team:** Producers: Tin Machine, Tim Palmer / **Sound Engineers:** Guy Gray, Simon Vinestock, Eric Schilling, Ruggie Simkins, Chuck Ferry

After the powerful "Under the God" and "Video Crime" of the previous album and after older tracks such as "Day-In Day-Out" and "'87 and Cry," David Bowie paints a new picture of the United States during the presidency of George H. W. Bush. The delicate "Goodbye Mr. Ed" is an acerbic critique of the country the singer loved so much, and in particular of New York, which had seen an extremely high crime rate over the past decade. *Mister Ed* was a family TV series broadcast in the 1960s, and its slightly moralistic tone was traditional for television at the time. By titling his song "Goodbye Mr. Ed," Bowie wanted to suggest that the values conveyed by the series had been abandoned in favor of generalized violence and selfishness. Curiously placed at the end of the album, the song, with its touching and effective melody, is in fact the highlight of the album and might have had real potential as a single. Sadly, the

HAMMERHEAD

David Bowie, Hunt Sales / 1:50

Musicians: David Bowie: lead vocals, acoustic guitar / **Reeves Gabrels:** electric guitar / **Tony Sales:** bass, backing vocals / **Hunt Sales:** drums, backing vocals / **Recorded:** Studios 301, Sydney: September–December 1989 / **Unknown Studio, Miami:** April–May 1990 / **Eel Pie Studios, London:** October–November 1990 / **A&M Recording Studios, Los Angeles:** March 1991 / **Technical Team:** Producers: Tin Machine, Tim Palmer / **Sound Engineers:** Guy Gray, Simon Vinestock, Eric Schilling, Ruggie Simkins, Chuck Ferry

By offering listeners "Hammerhead" as a hidden track on the record, the musicians of Tin Machine were the initiators of a fashion that would last as long as the CD medium itself. Admittedly, the Beatles were the first to do this when they slipped a discreet "Her Majesty" in after a few seconds of silence at the end of *Abbey Road* in 1969, but this practice only really began to develop with the advent of the compact disc. For those who aren't familiar with these silver discs, the hidden track is a title absent from the official track listing of the album, which the listener usually accesses by continuing to listen after last track of the CD has supposedly ended. Placed after long moments of silence at the end of the last song, or sometimes on a separate track whose number isn't mentioned, hidden tracks were like a surprise gift offered by the artist. Throughout the 1990s, a large number of these ghost tracks appeared to set the fans' tongues wagging. Some of the most memorable iterations include "Your House" by Alanis Morissette (*Jagged Little Pill*, 1995), "Can't Be Stopped" by Janet Jackson (*The Velvet Rope*, 1997), and Coldplay's "The Escapist" (*Viva la Vida*, 2008).

In this hidden track, David Bowie presents his listeners with a high-speed account of his relationship with a woman he describes as a hammerhead shark. Like a fighter going head-to-head with his sweetheart, Bowie compares himself with famous boxers when he sings *"Have you felt like Dixon, and Ray, and Ali?"* This is, of course, a nod to George Dixon, Sugar Ray Robinson, and Muhammad Ali, three superstars of the ring who were well accustomed to taking hard blows from their adversaries.

NEEDLES ON THE BEACH

David Bowie, Reeves Gabrels, Hunt Sales, Tony Sales / 5:00

Musicians
David Bowie: electric guitar
Reeves Gabrels: electric guitar
Tony Sales: bass, backing vocals
Hunt Sales: drums, backing vocals

Recorded
Studios 301, Sydney: September–December 1989

Technical Team
Producer: Tin Machine
Sound Engineer: Guy Gray

Genesis

When the American label Upstart Records was putting together the compilation *Beyond the Beach* in 1992, a host of psycho-rock, surf music, and rockabilly bands flocked to participate, including the Daytonas, the Aqua Velvets, and the Falcons. But at the end of the album there is also a little-known Tin Machine track, which seems to have gotten lost among all the other offerings. As the album liner note asks: "What's David Bowie doing on this record, you might ask? Well as part of Tin Machine, of course."[170] It must be said that the members of Upstart were proud of their compatriot Reeves Gabrels for accompanying an international rock star of Bowie's stature. What's more, Tin Machine had agreed to part with one of their studio outtakes for the occasion, entitled "Needles on the Beach." The fledgling label was hugely excited and took advantage of this exclusive track to help promote the compilation.

With the help of a metaphor, Reeves Gabrels explained the process of selecting songs for an album, which sometimes leads artists to set certain songs aside: "I learned how to care for an idea. It's like trying to build a fire out of kindling and flint—you have to crowd around it and protect the flame and nurture it until you've got something you can use. And then you can decide: 'We got the flame going but the meal we cooked sucked.' And then you don't put that song on the album."[163]

Production

The influence of Australia, where this instrumental track was immortalized in the fall of 1989, can be felt in this surf music track that feels heavily inspired by the spirit of Hank Marvin's band, the Shadows. Listening to Gabrels's guitar score, whose tremolos and long reverb fill the entire sound spectrum, it's easy to imagine the musicians with surfboards in hand on Bondi Beach, just outside Sydney. The reality, according to Tin Machine's guitarist, was not quite so romantic: "The title came as a reference to surf music combined with the fact that we kept finding used needles on the beaches. Simple explanation really."[47]

Children in Narrabeen with syringes they collected along the beach.

TIE NO
BLACK
K TIE W
WHITE
NOISE
BLACK

ALBUM

BLACK TIE WHITE NOISE

The Wedding (on CD and cassette only) . You've Been Around . I Feel Free .
Black Tie White Noise . Jump They Say . Nite Flights . Pallas Athena . Miracle Goodnight . Don't
Let Me Down and Down . Looking for Lester (on CD and cassette only) .
I Know It's Gonna Happen Someday . The Wedding Song .
Jump They Say (Alternate Mix) (on CD and cassette only) .
Lucy Can't Dance (Bonus Track) (on CD only)

RELEASE DATES
United Kingdom: April 5, 1993
References: Savage/Arista/BMG—74321 13697 1 (33 rpm); 74321 13697 2 (CD)
United States: April 6, 1993
Reference: Savage/Arista/BMG—74785-50212-2 (CD)
Best UK Chart Ranking: 1
Best US Chart Ranking: 39

THE HYMN TO IMAN

The end of the Tin Machine "It's My Life Tour" in February 1992 spelled the end of the band. After four years of fruitful collaboration, the quartet disbanded without even making an official announcement to the press. "Tin Machine sort of disappeared," recalled Reeves Gabrels. "We didn't have a meeting about it, but it just collapsed. There were a few personality issues, and I think at one point David realized that he could just go back to being David Bowie. [...] After Tin Machine he got back together with Nile, because even though we sold something like two million records, we were a failure."[1] The end of Tin Machine also coincided with a radical change in David Bowie's life. In the spring of 1992, freshly released from the encumbrance of his rock combo, David Bowie left Europe for Los Angeles alongside his second wife, Iman Mohamed Abdulmajid.

David Bowie's Last Muse

Bowie originally met Iman in 1990 during the filming for Richard Shepard's film, *The Linguini Incident*, in which Iman had a small part. A star of the American modeling scene, Iman was born in Mogadishu, Somalia, in 1955, and she had recently decided to embrace an acting career. It was love at first sight between the singer and the budding actress, so much so that Iman accompanied Tin Machine on their European gigs in the autumn of 1991. David Bowie proposed to Iman in Paris at the end of October 1991. The couple flew to Lausanne on April 24, 1992, and tied the knot in a private religious ceremony. Later, British photographer Brian Aris took exclusive pictures of the pair's public nuptials for *Hello!* magazine. The event took place at Italy's Florence American Episcopal church on June 6,

1992, and including Brian Eno, Yoko Ono, and Bono, several stars, were all present. The couple remained together until the singer's death, on January 10, 2016, and they had a daughter together, Alexandria Zahra Jones, who was born in New York on August 15, 2000.

In the Heart of the Los Angeles Riots

After their civil marriage, Bowie and Iman flew off on their honeymoon to Los Angeles. Just as their plane landed in California on April 29, 1992, the city ignited following the acquittal of four police officers at the center of the infamous Rodney King trial. On March 3, 1991, the officers had been filmed severely beating King following a car chase through the streets of Los Angeles. Bowie, who could see the city in flames from his hotel room, was profoundly affected by the riots, triggered as they were by inequalities that lie deep in the heart of American society. The images went all round the world. These events inspired the singer to write lyrics in which he highlighted the peaceful co-existence of various communities living in America: *Black Tie White Noise*.

"The Wedding Album," a Present for Iman

David Bowie's first solo album since 1987's *Never Let Me Down* is almost entirely dedicated to his union with Imam. Having decided in 1991 to resume his solo career while still in the final stages of the Tin Machine tour, David Bowie reestablished contact with Nile Rodgers, the producer of *Let's Dance*. Confusingly, *Let's Dance* was an album Bowie famously repudiated, and this return to grace for Rodgers grows even stranger once one considers the

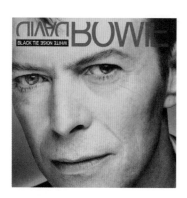

Sterling Campbell, who shares drumming duties with Poogie "Pugi" Bell on *Black Tie White Noise*, first discovered David Bowie in 1978. At the time, Campbell's neighbor was none other than Dennis Davis. One evening, Campbell offered to help Davis load his drum set into a van in exchange for tickets to an upcoming David Bowie concert at Madison Square Garden. Sterling had no way of knowing that he would one day be accompanying the megastar around the world on sold-out tours.

fact that Bowie implemented a diametrically opposed artistic direction for this new record than the one he had used on *Let's Dance*. Bowie's sole objective on this new album was to write personal songs that were very far removed from the FM hits he and Rodgers created together during the previous decade.

Work began on the "Wedding Album" in the summer of 1992, with demos recorded at Mountain Studios in Montreux and with sessions taking place at 38 Fresh Recording Studios in Los Angeles and at The Hit Factory in New York City. Despite the returning producer's commitment to the project—Rodgers engaged in multiple overdub sessions to refine this new opus—the collaboration between the two artists was not as rewarding as their original venture in 1982. "The difference between *Black Tie White Noise* and *Let's Dance* is night and day," reported Rodgers. "When we did *Black Tie White Noise*, I felt my hands were tied to a large extent. It was like, 'Hey, David, let's try this.' 'No, I don't wanna do this.' 'Hey, David, let's try this, then.' 'No, I don't want to do that either. This record is really about my wedding.' I'd say, 'But David, no one cares about your wedding. Let's make a hit!'"[29] The producer was wasting his breath, and he did not even mention this album in his biography, *Le Freak*, which was published in 2011.

Bowie Version 2.0

When it was released on April 5, 1993, *Black Tie White Noise* caused a stir with is modern, synthetic sounds and aesthetic. Leaving behind the pop-rock sonorities of the 1980s, Rodgers's production gave way to the use of full-on electronics that overwhelmed the music from the early 1990s. A few special guests, however, were invited to take part on the disc, such as the new jack swing singer Al B. Sure! on "Black Tie White Noise," guitarist Tony "Wild T" Springer on "I Know It's Gonna Happen Someday," and trumpet player Lester Bowie on a large number of the tracks. Old acquaintances of the singer also reappeared, such as Mike Garson on "Looking for Lester" and Mick Ronson on "I Feel Free," a cover of the Cream number that the Spiders from Mars often performed onstage when they accompanied the "Ziggy Stardust" Bowie persona. Signed to the new Savage label, Bowie's latest venture would mark the label's end. The company, which was distributed by BMG, declared bankruptcy straight after the release of the album and its attendant singles. The album marked a change in creative direction for the artist, who permanently departed from the mainstream in order to focus on a highly individual, refined, and demanding approach to production, which effectively meant that he would be appearing on the charts only intermittently from this point forward.

COLLABORATION

Single

REAL COOL WORLD
David Bowie / 4:14

Musicians
David Bowie: lead and backing vocals, electric guitar, saxophone
Nile Rodgers: electric guitar, backing vocals
John Regan (?), Barry Campbell (?): bass
Poogie "Pugi" Bell (?), Sterling Campbell (?): drums
Richard Hilton: synthesizers

Recorded
Mountain Studios, Montreux: April–July 1992
38 Fresh Recording Studios, New York: July–November 1992
The Hit Factory, New York: July–November 1992

Technical Team
Producer: Nile Rodgers
Sound Engineers: John Goldberger, Gary Tole, Andrew Grassi, Louis Alfred III, Lee Anthony, Neil Perry, Andy Smith

45 RPM VERSION (EUROPE)
Side A: Real Cool World (Album Edit) / 4:14
Side B: You've Been Around (Instrumental Version) / 4:29

MAXI CD SINGLE VERSION
1. *Real Cool World (Album Edit)* / 4:14
2. *Real Cool World (Radio Remix)* / 4:24
3. *Real Cool World (Cool Dub Thing #1)* / 7:23
4. *Real Cool World (12" Club Mix)* / 5:29
5. *Real Cool World (Cool Dub Overture)* / 9:10
6. *Real Cool World (Cool Dub Thing #2)* / 6:56

Europe Release on Warner: August 10, 1992 (45 rpm ref.: 5439-18808-7 / Maxi CD single ref.: 74321 148682)
US Release on Warner: August 10, 1992 (Maxi CD single ref.: 9 40575-2)
Best UK Chart Ranking: 53
Best US Chart Ranking: Did Not Chart

Genesis
After the recording sessions for *Black Tie White Noise* had already begun, David Bowie also agreed to contribute to the original soundtrack of the Ralph Bakshi film *Cool World*, which combined animation with live action. Hoping for a success on the scale of *Who Framed Roger Rabbit?* which had followed a similar visual process, the director gave the film a first-rate cast. Gabriel Byrne, Kim Basinger (an indisputable star following her role as Vicki Vale in Tim Burton's *Batman*, in 1989), and a young Brad Pitt (after his notable performance in Ridley Scott's *Thelma and Louise*) all appeared on the call sheet. The film received a particularly lackluster critical reception, but its original soundtrack did incorporate some of the greatest hitmakers from the new American electro scene, including Moby, as well as one of the leading groups coming out of the emerging industrial rock movement, Ministry. Bowie had a nose for emerging trends, and so it was that he contributed unreleased material from the *Black Tie White Noise* sessions to the soundtrack. Soon enough, Bowie was flirting with electronic music and another cult group from the industrial metal scene: Nine Inch Nails.

Production
The song selected for Bakshi's film has all the ingredients featured on the demos created in Montreux: rhythms combining drum machines and acoustic patterns, and FM synthesizers used at all levels. Bowie's contribution to the soundtrack is still far removed from the darker world of the other musicians who had work featured in the film. The song was reworked and released under the name of "Real Cool World." Its single release passed without much notice from the general public, even though it was an appetizer for fans who were waiting impatiently to find out what their idol had in store for them after his two albums with Tin Machine. "Real Cool World" was later included on the rerelease of *Black Tie White Noise*.

HOLLI WOULD IF SHE COULD
...AND SHE WILL

COOL WORLD

PARAMOUNT PICTURES PRESENTS FRANK MANCUSO, JR. A PRODUCTION OF RALPH BAKSHI KIM BASINGER COOL WORLD GABRIEL BYRNE BRAD PITT MUSIC MARK ISHAM

THE WEDDING

David Bowie / 5:04

Musicians: David Bowie: vocals, saxophone, programming / **Nile Rodgers:** electric guitar / **John Regan (?), Barry Campbell (?):** bass / **Poogie "Pugi" Bell (?), Sterling Campbell (?):** drums / **Michael Reisman:** tubular bells / **Richard Hilton (?), David Richards (?), Philippe Saisse (?), Richard Tee (?):** synthesizers / **Gerardo Velez:** percussion / **Recorded:** Mountain Studios, Montreux: April–July 1992 / 38 Fresh Recording Studios, New York: July–November 1992 / The Hit Factory, New York: July–November 1992 / **Technical Team: Producers:** David Bowie, Nile Rodgers / **Sound Engineers:** John Goldberger, Gary Tole, Andrew Grassi, Louis Alfred III, Lee Anthony, Neil Perry, Andy Smith

As its name suggests, "The Wedding" is a reworked version of the theme Bowie wrote for his wedding to Iman. The couple really hated Wagner's "Wedding March," so instead they chose a traditional Bulgarian tune, "Kalimankou Denkou," to be played during the bride's entrance into the church. For the next part of the service, the husband-to-be composed this instrumental theme. "I had to write music that represented for me the growth and character of our relationship," the singer confided in 1993. "It really was a watershed. It opened up a wealth of thoughts and feelings about commitment and promises and finding the strength and fortitude to keep those promises. It all came tumbling out of me while I was writing this music for church. And I thought: 'I can't stop here. There's more that I have to get out.' [...] It triggered the album."[171]

A drum machine and acoustic drum kit were combined in a syncopated rhythm that is typical of the electronic music of the early 1990s, accompanied by multiple layers of synthesizers and announcing an artistic direction that was in direct opposition of the brutal rock Bowie created with Tin Machine. The contributions of David Richards, with whom Bowie had recorded the first demos of the album at Mountain Studios, are particularly recognizable here—such was the extent that the technician had become a master in the production of modern sounds, particularly through the massive use of the full range of synthesizers and drum machines.

Those who own the vinyl edition of the album will note that the first track from the original album, "The Wedding," is missing, but they will appreciate the sung version now appearing at the end of the album and titled "The Wedding Song."

YOU'VE BEEN AROUND

David Bowie, Reeves Gabrels / 4:45

Musicians: David Bowie: lead and backing vocals, saxophone / **Nile Rodgers:** electric guitar, backing vocals / **Reeves Gabrels:** electric guitar / **John Regan (?), Barry Campbell (?):** bass / **Poogie "Pugi" Bell (?), Sterling Campbell (?):** drums / **Richard Hilton (?), David Richards (?), Philippe Saisse (?), Richard Tee (?):** synthesizers / **Gerardo Velez:** percussion / **Lester Bowie:** trumpet / **Fonzi Thornton, Tawatha Agee, Curtis King Jr., Dennis Collins, Brenda White-King, Maryl Epps:** backing vocals / **Recorded:** Mountain Studios, Montreux: April–July 1992 / 38 Fresh Recording Studios, New York: July–November 1992 / The Hit Factory, New York: July–November 1992 / **Technical Team: Producers:** David Bowie, Nile Rodgers / **Sound Engineers:** John Goldberger, Gary Tole, Andrew Grassi, Louis Alfred III, Lee Anthony, Neil Perry, Andy Smith

Written by Reeves Gabrels and David Bowie for the first Tin Machine album, "You've Been Around" had not found its place in the band's repertoire, despite being added to the set list on the group's first tour. Featuring couplets that many believe provided the inspiration for "Bachelorette" by Björk in 1997, the number's coldness presages the industrial rock sounds that Bowie would soon be wholeheartedly embracing. "What I like about it is the fact that for the first half of the song there's no harmonic reference," the singer explained later. "It's just drums, and the voice comes in out of nowhere, and you're not sure if it's a melody line or a drone."[47] The presence of Nile Rodgers—whose discreet funk rhythms can be heard behind the mixing—does confer upon the piece a pop-inflected tone that is supported by the soul-inspired vocals supplied by the backing singers. A distinguished guest also makes an entry on "You've Been Around" in the person of Lester Bowie, jazz trumpet player and founder of the Art Ensemble of Chicago, an instrumental band formed in 1967. "I knew Lester was in town," explained Bowie, "so gave him a buzz to appear on one track, but he was such a gas he ended up on about half of them."[172] Also noteworthy is the singer's nod to one of this first successes, when, at 2:44, he sings *You've changed me / Ch-ch-ch-ch-ch-ch-change!*" a thinly disguised reference to "Changes" from 1971.

The members of Cream—drummer Ginger Baker, guitarist Eric Clapton, and bassist-singer Jack Bruce—in London circa 1966.

I FEEL FREE

Jack Bruce, Pete Brown / 4:52

Musicians: David Bowie: lead and backing vocals, saxophone / Nile Rodgers: electric guitar, backing vocals / Mick Ronson, Reeves Gabrels: electric guitar / John Regan (?), Barry Campbell (?): bass / Poogie "Pugi" Bell (?), Sterling Campbell (?): drums / Richard Hilton: synthesizers / David Richards (?), Philippe Saisse (?), Richard Tee (?): synthesizers / Fonzi Thornton, Tawatha Agee, Curtis King Jr., Dennis Collins, Brenda White-King, Maryl Epps: backing vocals / **Recorded:** Mountain Studios, Montreux: April–July 1992 / 38 Fresh Recording Studios, New York: July–November 1992 / The Hit Factory, New York: July–November 1992 / **Technical Team:** Producers: David Bowie, Nile Rodgers / Sound Engineers: John Goldberger, Gary Tole, Andrew Grassi, Louis Alfred III, Lee Anthony, Neil Perry, Andy Smith

Originally intended for *Pin Ups* in 1973, then for *Scary Monsters (And Supers Creeps)* in 1980, this Cream cover was regularly played by Bowie and his Spiders from Mars on the *Ziggy Stardust* tour in 1972 and 1973. Also performed in rehearsal by Tin Machine, this song was destined to join the list of classic rock numbers revisited by David Bowie.

To immortalize the piece, Bowie called upon his old friend Mick Ronson, who was at that time seriously ill with liver cancer. Although drowned under multiple layers of synthesizers, Ronson's guitar part sealed the reunion between the two artists, who were to appear onstage together at Wembley on April 20, 1992, for the Freddie Mercury Tribute Concert. Mick Ronson died on April 29, 1993, a few weeks after the release of *Black Tie White Noise*. Although Bowie paid homage to him on numerous occasions, David was notable in his absence from the Mick Ronson Memorial Concert, which was given on April 29, 1994, at the London Hammersmith Odeon. That evening, Tony Visconti, Roger Daltrey, Ian Hunter, Roger Taylor, and Dana Gillespie came together to honor the guitarist's memory, whose contribution to Bowie's career is indisputable. "We were all hoping he would come," Trevor Bolder, bassist with the Spiders, said regretfully, "but he said [...] he was too upset that Mick has died to turn up for a memorial concert. But when Freddie Mercury died, Bowie was straight on stage because it was in front of millions of people. He got there for Freddie Mercury's concert, but he wouldn't get there for Mick Ronson's because it wasn't a big enough audience for him. [...] It was a shame because it was a great evening."[29]

A scene from the April 1992 riots in Los Angeles, following the acquittal of four policeman charged with using excessive force against Rodney King.

BLACK TIE WHITE NOISE

David Bowie / 4:52

1993

Musicians

David Bowie: lead and backing vocals, saxophone
Al B. Sure!: vocals
Nile Rodgers: electric guitar, backing vocals
John Regan (?), Barry Campbell (?): bass
Poogie "Pugi" Bell (?), Sterling Campbell (?): drums
David Richards (?), Philippe Saisse (?), Richard Tee (?): synthesizers
Richard Hilton: synthesizers, piano
Lester Bowie: trumpet
Fonzi Thornton, Tawatha Agee, Curtis King Jr., Dennis Collins, Brenda White-King, Maryl Epps: backing vocals

Recorded

Mountain Studios, Montreux: April–July 1992
38 Fresh Recording Studios, New York: July–November 1992
The Hit Factory, New York: July–November 1992

Technical Team

Producers: David Bowie, Nile Rodgers
Sound Engineers: John Goldberger, Gary Tole, Andrew Grassi, Louis Alfred III, Lee Anthony, Neil Perry, Andy Smith

45 rpm Version (Europe)

Side A: Black Tie White Noise (Radio Edit) / 4:10
Side B: You've Been Around (Dangers Remix) / 4:24

Maxi CD Single Version (Europe)

1. *Black Tie White Noise (Radio Edit)* / 4:10
2. *Black Tie White Noise (Extended Remix)* / 8:12
3. *Black Tie White Noise (Urban Mix)* / 4:03
4. *You've Been Around (Dangers Remix)* / 4:24

Maxi CD Single Version (USA)

1. *Black Tie White Noise (Waddell's Mix)* / 4:12
2. *Black Tie White Noise (3rd Floor Mix)* / 3:43
3. *Black Tie White Noise (Al B. Sure! Mix)* / 4:03
4. *Black Tie White Noise (Dangers Remix)* / 4:24
5. *Black Tie White Noise (Club Mix)* / 7:33
6. *Black Tie White Noise (Digi Funky's Lush Mix)* / 5:44
7. *Black Tie White Noise (Supa Pump Mix)* / 6:36

Europe Release on Savage/Arista/BMG: May 31, 1993 (45 rpm ref.: 74321 148687 / Maxi CD single ref.: 74321 148682)
US Release on Savage/BMG: May 31, 1993 (Maxi CD single ref.: 74785-50045-2)
Best UK Chart Ranking: 36
Best US Chart Ranking: Did Not Chart

Genesis

In spring 1992, David Bowie and Iman flew off for their honeymoon in the Los Angeles sun. On April 29, just as their plane was landing, the city ignited following the acquittal of four police officers who had been caught on film severely beating Rodney King. The City of Angels suffered unprecedented violence, caused by the injustices against American monitories. "It was an extraordinary feeling," Bowie explained in 1993. "I think the one thing that sprang to our minds was that it felt like a prison riot more than anything else. It felt as if innocent inmates of some vast prison were trying to break out—break free from their bonds. I don't think they've succeeded in doing that, by any means. The whole thing has been forgotten: I don't see any real change in Los Angeles."[173] The events were the singer's immediate inspiration for the number "Black Tie White Noise," which emphasizes the antagonism of communities sharing the same social difficulties. "Black Tie" is a reference to the suits worn by the artists that the young David Jones used to listen to as an adolescent: Little Richard, John Coltrane, and the Motown singers. On the other hand, "White Noise" is an allusion to the muffled sounds that synthesizers, amongst others, can generate. "'Black Tie White Noise' refers to the very obvious—the radical boundaries that have been put up in most of the Western World," said Bowie. "It also has a lot to do with the black and white sides of one's thinking."[173]

Production

David Bowie shares the vocal line in "Black Tie White Noise" with singer Al B. Sure!, the rising star of new jack swing, a style incorporating elements of hip-hop, contemporary R&B, and soul. With a less serious message than the statements of the rappers of Public Enemy or N.W.A.—including the famous Dr. Dre, Ice Cube, and Eazy-E—the leading figures in the new jack swing style mostly sing about the joys and torments of love. Al B. Sure! does not have the aura of Babyface or Bobby Brown, but his talent and high standards provide the song with the sound Bowie was looking for. "I've never worked longer with any artist than Al B. I had a particular thing that I wanted to do with this song, and he spent a long time working through it. He's really dedicated to what he does. I don't think I've ever seen anybody work harder. He's a really great guy. He understands very much what I'm trying to do, and his contribution to this album is not lightly given."[173]

Single

JUMP THEY SAY

David Bowie / 4:22

1993

Musicians

David Bowie: lead and backing vocals, saxophone
Nile Rodgers: electric guitar, backing vocals
John Regan (?), Barry Campbell (?): bass
Poogie "Pugi" Bell (?), Sterling Campbell (?): drums
**Richard Hilton (?), David Richards (?), Philippe Saisse (?),
Richard Tee (?):** synthesizers
Lester Bowie: trumpet
**Fonzi Thornton, Tawatha Agee, Curtis King Jr., Dennis Collins,
Brenda White-King, Maryl Epps:** backing vocals

Recorded

Mountain Studios, Montreux: April–July 1992
38 Fresh Recording Studios, New York: July–November 1992
The Hit Factory, New York: July–November 1992

Technical Team

Producers: David Bowie, Nile Rodgers
Sound Engineers: John Goldberger, Gary Tole, Andrew Grassi, Louis
Alfred III, Lee Anthony, Neil Perry, Andy Smith

45 rpm Version (Europe)

Side A: Jump They Say (Radio Edit) / 3:53
Side B: Pallas Athena (Don't Stop Praying Remix) / 5:36

CD Single Version (Europe)

1. *Jump They Say (7" Version)* / 3:53
2. *Jump They Say (Hard Hands Mix)* / 5:40
3. *Jump They Say (Jae-E Remix)* / 5:32
4. *Pallas Athena (Don't Stop Praying Mix)* / 5:36

Maxi CD Single Version (United States)

1. *Jump They Say (Album Version)* / 4:23
2. *Jump They Say (Radio Edit 1)* / 4:04
3. *Jump They Say (Club Hart Remix)* / 5:03
4. *Jump They Say (Leftfield Remix)* / 7:42
5. *Pallas Athena (Album Version)* / 4:41
6. *Pallas Athena (Don't Stop Praying Remix)* / 5:36

Europe Release on Savage/Arista/BMG: March 5, 1993 (45 rpm
ref.: 74321 13696 7 / CD single ref.: 74321 139422)
US Release on Savage/BMG: March 15, 1993 (Maxi CD single ref.:
74785-50034-2)
Best UK Chart Ranking: 9
Best US Chart Ranking: Did Not Chart

Genesis

On January 16, 1985, Terry Burns, David Bowie's half brother, killed himself by throwing himself under a train at Coulsdon South Station, near Cane Hill Hospital, where he had been an inpatient for many years. Concerning this tragic event, which the singer took many years to invoke in his work, the lyrics of "Jump They Say" have a very particular resonance: *"My friend, don't listen to the crowd / They say 'jump.'"* When the album was released, the artist detailed the other sources of inspiration for the piece: "'Jump They Say' is semi-based on my impression of my step-brother and probably, for the first time, trying to write about how I felt about him committing suicide. It's also connected to my feeling that sometimes I've jumped metaphysically into the unknown and wondering whether I really believed there was something out there to support me, whatever you wanna call it; a God or a life-force?"[174]

Production

Upon his arrival at 38 Fresh Recording Studios in New York, the keyboard player Richard Hilton faced a unique situation. He was presented with the demos of the songs he would be working on, and the first thing he heard was a collection of strange sounds that would be difficult to reproduce, even with the best synthesizers. "How am I going to get those sounds?"[163] he wondered. In fact, these noises that we hear from the song's introduction were recorded in Montreux with David Richards and were intended to be played backward in the mixing. The refrains of "Jump They Say" include a gimmick played by David Bowie on saxophone. Although the accuracy of his playing is somewhat lax, his individual character comes through. "I think David would be the first to admit that he's not a saxophonist in the traditional sense," confided Nile Rodgers. "I mean, you wouldn't call him up to do gigs. He uses his playing as an artistic tool. He's a painter. He hears an idea, and he goes with it. But he absolutely knows where he's going." [171]

Scott Walker (Noel Scott Engel), John Walker (John Maus), and Gary Walker (Gary Leeds) of the band the Walker Brothers.

NITE FLIGHTS

Scott Engel / 4:30

Musicians: David Bowie: lead and backing vocals / Nile Rodgers: electric guitar / John Regan (?), Barry Campbell (?): bass / Poogie "Pugi" Bell (?), Sterling Campbell (?): drums / Richard Hilton (?), David Richards (?), Philippe Saisse (?), Richard Tee (?): synthesizers / **Recorded:** Mountain Studios, Montreux: April–July 1992 / 38 Fresh Recording Studios, New York: July–November 1992 / The Hit Factory, New York: July–November 1992 / **Technical Team:** Producers: David Bowie, Nile Rodgers / **Sound Engineers:** John Goldberger, Gary Tole, Andrew Grassi, Louis Alfred III, Lee Anthony, Neil Perry, Andy Smith

When, in 1978, the Walker Brothers released their final album, *Nite Flights*, David Bowie had fallen under the spell of their dark music and songwriting style, which was very close to his own songs. The rather strange "Fat Mama Kick" shared some similarities with *Diamond Dogs*, and the saxophone notes that appear here and there added to the resemblance between the two artistic worlds. It is the title song from this opus that David Bowie decided to use on *Black Tie White Noise*. "The song has cut-up lyrics of the kind we were doing," he explains, "and he's a very good writer, I like to do an homage to people whose work I admire—I've done Lennon and Bryan Ferry songs in the past—and this was a chance to put Scott's beautiful song on an album."[172]

PALLAS ATHENA

David Bowie / 4:40

Musicians: David Bowie: vocals, saxophone / John Regan (?), Barry Campbell (?): bass / Poogie "Pugi" Bell (?), Sterling Campbell (?): drums / Richard Hilton (?), David Richards (?), Philippe Saisse (?), Richard Tee (?): synthesizers / Gerardo Velez: percussion / Lester Bowie: trumpet / Unidentified Musicians: strings / **Recorded:** Mountain Studios, Montreux: April–July 1992 / 38 Fresh Recording Studios, New York: July–November 1992 / The Hit Factory, New York: July–November 1992 / **Technical Team:** Producers: David Bowie, Nile Rodgers / **Sound Engineers:** John Goldberger, Gary Tole, Andrew Grassi, Louis Alfred III, Lee Anthony, Neil Perry, Andy Smith / **String Arrangements:** Michael Riesman

In this number David Bowie revives the ghosts of Hérouville and Berlin, providing a quasi-instrumental number that takes us back to the obscure but nonetheless very danceable "A New Career in a New Town" from *Low*, and "The Secret Life of Arabia" from *"Heroes."* It would appear that the singer paid particular attention to the clienteles at clubs, because over the years he produced numerous remixes of this number, releasing a *Pallas Athena* EP in 2010. He plays the saxophone on this piece, as seen in the playback appearance from *The Arsenio Hall Show* on May 6, 1993. Jazz trumpeter Lester Bowie also appears, although his trumpet playing is very understated on this piece.

Bowie in the video for
"Miracle Goodnight" directed
by Matthew Rolston.

MIRACLE GOODNIGHT

David Bowie / 4:14

45 rpm version (Europe): Side A: *Miracle Goodnight* / 4:14 / **Side B:** *Looking for Lester* / 5:36 / **CD single version (Europe):** 1. *Miracle Goodnight (Album Version)* / 4:14; 2. *Miracle Goodnight (12" 2 Chord Philly Mix)* / 6:22; 3. *Miracle Goodnight (Maserati Blunted Dub)* / 7:40; 4. *Looking for Lester (Album Version)* / 5:36 / **Europe Release on Savage/Arista/BMG:** October 1993 (45 rpm ref.: 74321 162267 / CD single ref.: 74321 16226 2) / **Best UK Chart Ranking:** 40

Musicians: David Bowie: lead and backing vocals / Nile Rodgers: electric guitar / John Regan (?), Barry Campbell (?): bass / Poogie "Pugi" Bell (?), Sterling Campbell (?): drums / Richard Hilton (?), David Richards (?), Philippe Saisse (?), Richard Tee (?): synthesizers / Fonzi Thornton, Tawatha Agee, Curtis King Jr., Dennis Collins, Brenda White-King, Maryl Epps: backing vocals / **Recorded:** Mountain Studios, Montreux: April–July 1992 / **38 Fresh Recording Studios, New York:** July–November 1992 / **The Hit Factory, New York:** July–November 1992 / **Technical Team:** Producers: David Bowie, Nile Rodgers / **Sound Engineers:** John Goldberger, Gary Tole, Andrew Grassi, Louis Alfred III, Lee Anthony, Neil Perry, Andy Smith

"*I love you in the morning sun / I love you in my dreams,*" sings David Bowie to his wife, Iman, in this third single from *Black Tie White Noise*. Surprising in its lightness, "Miracle Goodnight" is a pure product of the 1990s: synthesizer gimmicks at each corner of the stereo, and takes with drums mixed with an insipid drum machine were the key features for these mass-produced hits. "I loved that song […]," confided Nile Rodgers. "I thought it was incredible. If he'd released that as the first single, he would have had a smash."[29] The producer, when recording his guitar solo, was even instructed by the singer as to how he was supposed to play it: "When I played the solo […] he [David] even told me how I should approach it. […] He said, 'Nile, I want you to play this solo as if the 50s never existed.' No Blue Note, no Chuck Berry, no Little Richard, no James Brown. So I played like Les Paul."[1] And this is exactly how the virtuoso's score sounds, when, at 2:59 he produces some playing that is worthy of one of the greatest guitarists of the twentieth century—Lester William Polsfuss—better known as Les Paul.

DON'T LET ME DOWN AND DOWN

Tahra, Martine Valmont / 4:55

Musicians: David Bowie: lead and backing vocals / Nile Rodgers: electric guitar / John Regan (?), Barry Campbell (?): bass / Poogie "Pugi" Bell: drums / Richard Hilton (?), David Richards (?), Philippe Saisse (?), Richard Tee (?): synthesizers / Gerardo Velez: percussion / Lester Bowie: trumpet / Fonzi Thornton, Tawatha Agee, Curtis King Jr., Dennis Collins, Brenda White-King, Maryl Epps: backing vocals / **Recorded:** Mountain Studios, Montreux: April–July 1992 / **38 Fresh Recording Studios, New York:** July–November 1992 / **The Hit Factory, New York:** July–November 1992 / **Technical Team:** Producers: David Bowie, Nile Rodgers / **Sound Engineers:** John Goldberger, Gary Tole, Andrew Grassi, Louis Alfred III, Lee Anthony, Neil Perry, Andy Smith

Iman introduced her husband to the music of Tahra Mint Hembara, a Mauritanian singer living in Paris who was a good friend of hers. *Yamen Yamen*, the young artist's first album, appeared in 1989. Iman insisted on Bowie listening to one of the songs, "T'Beyby," which Tahra also sang in English under the title "Don't Let Me Down and Down." Won over by this romantic ballad, the singer decided to cover it on his new album. He also recorded a version that included several couplets in Indonesian, renamed for this occasion "Jangan Susahkan Hatiku." This curiosity was added to the bonus tracks for the album's rerelease in 2003.

Lester Bowie, the talented jazz trumpet player photographed by David Redfern in 1986.

LOOKING FOR LESTER

David Bowie, Nile Rodgers / 5:36

Musicians: David Bowie: saxophone / **Nile Rodgers:** electric guitar / John Regan (?), Barry Campbell (?): bass / Poogie "Pugi" Bell (?), Sterling Campbell (?): drums / Richard Hilton (?), David Richards (?), Philippe Saisse (?), Richard Tee (?): synthesizers / Mike Garson: piano / Lester Bowie: trumpet / **Recorded:** Mountain Studios, Montreux: April–July 1992 / 38 Fresh Recording Studios, New York: July–November 1992 / **The Hit Factory**, New York: July–November 1992 / **Technical Team:** Producers: David Bowie, Nile Rodgers / **Sound Engineers:** John Goldberger, Gary Tole, Andrew Grassi, Louis Alfred III, Lee Anthony, Neil Perry, Andy Smith / **Arrangements:** Chico O'Farrill

The Lester in question on this track is, of course, Lester Bowie, the trumpet player present throughout *Black Tie White Noise*. The turbulent musician made an indelible mark on this instrumental track arranged by Chico O'Farrill. "He's crazy in the studio," reported David on the subject of Lester Bowie, "and doesn't stand still when he's playing. He also doesn't like to hear the track [he's playing on] beforehand until he starts playing. You roll the tape and he jumps in. Sometimes he's madly out of tune but then there are these great slabs that work brilliantly because it is so spontaneous."[172]

Mike Garson, a pianist who had survived from the *Aladdin Sane* era, laid down a fiendish solo on this song, which left him questioning himself years later: "I wish I had played it better. I was trying to aspire to an Aladdin Sane kind of level and I couldn't get there."[163] Bowie had no such qualms about the status of Garson's talent: "He really has a gift. [...] He kind of plops those jewels in the track and they're quite [...] extraordinary, eccentric pieces of piano playing."[173]

I KNOW IT'S GONNA HAPPEN SOMEDAY

Morrissey / 4:14

Musicians: David Bowie: lead and backing vocals / Tony "Wild T" Springer: electric guitar / John Regan (?), Barry Campbell (?): bass / Poogie "Pugi" Bell (?), Sterling Campbell (?): drums / Richard Hilton: synthesizers, piano, programming / David Richards: synthesizers, programming / Fonzi Thornton, Tawatha Agee, Curtis King Jr., Dennis Collins, Brenda White-King, Maryl Epps, Frank Simms, George Simms, David Spinner, Lamya Al-Mugheiry, Connie Petruk, Nile Rodgers: backing vocals / Unidentified Musicians: strings / **Recorded:** 38 Fresh Recording Studios, New York: July–November 1992 / **The Hit Factory**, New York: July–November 1992 / **Technical Team:** Producers: David Bowie, Nile Rodgers / **Sound Engineers:** John Goldberger, Gary Tole, Andrew Grassi, Louis Alfred III, Lee Anthony, Neil Perry, Andy Smith / **Orchestral Arrangements:** Chico O'Farrill

When Morrissey released his third solo album, *Your Arsenal*, on July 27, 1992, Bowie discovered the song "I Know It's Gonna Happen Someday," which, in every respect resembled his "Rock 'n' Roll Suicide" track from *The Rise and Fall of Ziggy Stardust and the Spiders from Mars* album in 1972. Just listening to the finale of the song, it is obvious that the ex-Smiths singer did indeed intend to produce an homage to his colleague, especially as the number—like the rest of the opus—was produced by...Mick Ronson, former guitarist for the Spiders from Mars. As the good sport that he was, David Bowie decided to cover the song and remove from it all the references to "Rock 'n' Roll Suicide": "It occurred to me when I first heard Morrissey's latest album that he was possibly spoofing one of my earlier songs, and I thought, I'm not going to let him get away with that. I do think he's one of the best lyricists in England, and an excellent songwriter, and I thought his song was an affectionate spoof. [...] Anyway, I thought, I'll take that song he's done and I'll do it my way, so we'll have David Bowie doing Morrissey doing David Bowie!"[173] To add the final touch to his cover version, Bowie invited blues guitarist Tony "Wild T" Springer to add a six-string solo, which provided a fantastic accompaniment to the gospel choir that had formed for the occasion. This is the best song on *Black Tie White Noise*.

THE WEDDING SONG

David Bowie / 4:29

Musicians: David Bowie: lead and backing vocals, saxophone / Nile Rodgers: electric guitar / John Regan (?), Barry Campbell (?): bass / Poogie "Pugi" Bell (?), Sterling Campbell (?): drums / Richard Hilton (?), David Richards (?), Philippe Saisse (?), Richard Tee (?): synthesizers / Michael Reisman: tubular bells / Fonzi Thornton, Tawatha Agee, Curtis King Jr., Dennis Collins, Brenda White-King, Maryl Epps: backing vocals / Unidentified Musicians: strings / **Recorded:** Mountain Studios, Montreux: April–July 1992 / 38 Fresh Recording Studios, New York: July–November 1992 / The Hit Factory, New York: July–November 1992 / **Technical Team:** Producers: David Bowie, Nile Rodgers / Sound Engineers: John Goldberger, Gary Tole, Andrew Grassi, Louis Alfred III, Lee Anthony, Neil Perry, Andy Smith / **String Arrangements:** Michael Riesman

A vocal version of the opening theme of the album, "The Wedding Song" is explicitly a homage to Iman. "I was naming the children the night we met," confided Bowie "I knew that she was for me, it was absolutely immediate."[171] The instrumental score is identical to that of the first track on the disc, but this second version is supported by six talented backing singers, and it provides a vibrant finish to an album that is dedicated to love. "It's a very emotionally-charged album," explained Bowie. "[...] That's why it's got such a saccharine ending. [...] It should have been called 'The Wedding Cake,' because it really is all icing with a couple on top."[175]

JUMP THEY SAY (ALTERNATE MIX)

David Bowie / 3:58

Musicians: David Bowie: lead and backing vocals, saxophone / Nile Rodgers: electric guitar, backing vocals / John Regan (?), Barry Campbell (?): bass / Poogie "Pugi" Bell (?), Sterling Campbell (?): drums / Richard Hilton (?), David Richards (?), Philippe Saisse (?), Richard Tee (?): synthesizers / Lester Bowie: trumpet / Fonzi Thornton, Tawatha Agee, Curtis King Jr., Dennis Collins, Brenda White-King, Maryl Epps: backing vocals / **Recorded:** Mountain

Studios, Montreux: April–July 1992 / 38 Fresh Recording Studios, New York: July–November 1992 / The Hit Factory, New York: July–November 1992 / **Technical Team:** Producers: David Bowie, Nile Rodgers / Sound Engineers: John Goldberger, Gary Tole, Andrew Grassi, Louis Alfred III, Lee Anthony, Neil Perry, Andy Smith / **Remix and Additional Production:** JAE-E / **Sound Engineer (remix):** Stephen Hart

Offered as a bonus track for purchasers of the CD and cassette versions of *Black Tie White Noise*, this remix of "Jump They Say" is the work of a mysterious JAE-E. Behind this pseudonym is James Earley, the same producer who worked on the international success of *Please Hammer Don't Hurt 'Em*, the first album by rapper MC Hammer, whose singles "U Can't Touch This" and "Pray" both hit the Billboard charts in 1990. That James Earley was a master technician was very much in evidence in 1992; nevertheless, this highly talented producer has often gone unsung in the annals of music history.

LUCY CAN'T DANCE (BONUS TRACK)

David Bowie / 5:45

Musicians: David Bowie: lead and backing vocals / Nile Rodgers: electric guitar, backing vocals / John Regan (?), Barry Campbell (?): bass / Poogie "Pugi" Bell (?), Sterling Campbell (?): drums / Richard Hilton (?), David Richards (?), Philippe Saisse (?), Richard Tee (?): synthesizers / Gerardo Velez: percussion / Fonzi Thornton, Tawatha Agee, Curtis King Jr., Dennis Collins, Brenda White-King, Maryl Epps: backing vocals / **Recorded:** Mountain Studios, Montreux: April–July 1992 / 38 Fresh Recording Studios, New York: July–November 1992 / The Hit Factory, New York: July–November 1992 / **Technical Team:** Producers: David Bowie, Nile Rodgers / **Sound Engineers:** John Goldberger, Gary Tole, Andrew Grassi, Louis Alfred III, Lee Anthony, Neil Perry, Andy Smith

In 1992 David Bowie fled the mainstream like the plague. The word *mainstream* encompassed all the artistic productions created with the general public in mind, such as the much-maligned *Let's Dance* from 1983. Nile Rodgers even tried to convince Iman to ask Bowie to trust him on this particular song, but there was nothing doing, as she took her husband's side, and her husband basically did whatever he wanted. When the singer refused to include the very pop-sounding "Lucy Can't Dance" in his new opus, this caused great consternation. "'Lucy Can't Dance' [...] was a guaranteed Number 1 record," Rodgers commented with regret, "and everyone around him was totally perplexed when it only appeared as a bonus track on the CD. He was running from success and running from the word 'dance.' Imagine David Bowie and Nile Rodgers together, and we come out with a song 'Lucy Can't Dance.' Smokin'!! I was already accepting my Grammy. But he was not budging. It was an exercise in futility—no matter who I tried to call, it fell on deaf ears."[29]

OF SUBU

A THE B

BUDDH

A OF SU

SUBURB

THE BU

ALBUM

THE BUDDHA OF SUBURBIA

Buddha of Suburbia . Sex and the Church . South Horizon . The Mysteries .
Bleed Like a Craze, Dad . Strangers When We Meet . Dead Against It . Untitled No. 1 .
Ian Fish, U.K. Heir . Buddha of Suburbia (featuring Lenny Kravitz on guitar)

RELEASE DATES
Europe: November 8, 1993
Reference: Arista/BMG—74321 170042 (CD)
United States: October 24, 1995
Reference: Virgin—7243 8 40988 2 7 (CD)
Best UK/US Chart Ranking: Did Not Chart

A LITTLE-KNOWN BUT INSPIRED ALBUM

In the period when *Black Tie White Noise* was being promoted—the launch was expected in April 1993—David Bowie agreed to appear in *Interview* magazine, the monthly publication started by Andy Warhol in 1969. Bowie appeared in a column where each month a well-known personality in the artistic world asked a famous person a set of questions. For the forthcoming May edition, David Bowie was to be questioned by Hanif Kureishi, the British writer. Son of an English mother and a Pakistani father, Kureishi's name was, at that time, becoming increasingly well-known. Kureishi was the screenwriter for two well-received movies directed by Stephen Frears (*My Beautiful Laundrette* in 1985 and *Sammy and Rosie Get Laid* in 1987), and he won a prize with his first novel, *The Buddha of Suburbia*, when it was published in 1990. This semi-autobiographical book narrates the adventures of a young man, Karim Amir, in 1970s London. Pulled in two directions by religious tradition on the one hand and the lure of adolescent pleasure and illegal substances on the other, he struggles to find his place in society. It is likely that David Bowie recognized himself in this young man of the suburbs, with his dreams of escaping from his narrow background to become a famous actor living a life of unbridled sexuality. The novel's themes echo those of David (Bowie) Jones's song from 1966, "The London Boys," most especially because Kureishi grew up in Bromley and studied at Bromley Tech just like Bowie! The action of the book takes place partly in the suburbs of London and includes references to the college.

Soundtrack of the 1970s

A few weeks after the article for *Interview*, Hanif Kureishi asked a mutual friend, Alan Yentob, to arrange another meeting with Bowie. The writer and the singer met at the River Cafe in Hammersmith to talk about a possible collaboration.

Kureishi was at this time working on a four-episode adaptation of his novel for the BBC, to be directed by the South African filmmaker Roger Michell. For the televised version, both the director and the scriptwriter wanted a soundtrack made up of some of the key songs of the 1970s. They asked David Bowie for permission to use some of his classic numbers. He agreed willingly, but then suggested he compose a new musical soundtrack for the project.

Since no special promotion events had been arranged for *Black Tie White Noise* (apart from a few interviews and a noteworthy appearance on *The Arsenio Hall Show*), Bowie was able to meet up with David Richards in July at Mountain Studios to work on some forty instrumental pieces for the upcoming BBC production. Arriving in Montreux, Kureishi was not entirely convinced by Bowie's compositions and tactfully explained why they were not suitable for the series. He said later: "When he was composing this, and I expressed fear that some of the music was either too fast or slow, [...] he hurried back to his pad [...], spending the night redoing everything."[176] Bowie was eventually able to satisfy both the director and the screenwriter, and some of his compositions were included in the series. By now totally immersed in the new project, Bowie decided to develop it into a new album called, naturally enough, *The Buddha of Suburbia*.

Bowie and Kizilçay: A Productive Collaboration

The recording of this album in its entirety—which is to say, not just the soundtrack of the TV series—took place over a period of six days in August 1993. Erdal Kizilçay was once again asked to come and play the guitar, bass, drums, trumpet, and keyboards. The talented David Richards, an expert in many kinds of synthesizers and programming, joined the two men as a co-producer. Worked up from short pieces of instrumental music composed for Kureishi, the new songs made a surprisingly modern and ambitious

The British writer, screenwriter, and dramatist Hanif Kureishi shown at home in February 1991.

Naveen Andrews and Jemma Redgrave, two actors who appeared in *The Buddha of Suburbia*.

body of work, taking us back to the universe of *Low* or *"Heroes"* ("The Mysteries," "Ian Fish, U.K. Heir"), and at other moments venturing into the fields of pop ("Buddha of Suburbia") or dance music ("Sex and the Church"). Bowie also looked back to the instrumental experiments carried out with Brian Eno. He wrote of this in the album notes: "I took each theme or motif from the play and initially stretched or lengthened it to a five- or six-minute duration. [...] I experimented with various rhythmic elements, drums, percussion, temple blocks, et al until I found a sense of companionship to the primary motif. Then, having noted which musical key I was in and having counted the number of bars, I would often pull down the faders leaving just the percussive element with no harmonic information to refer to. Working in layers I would then build up reinforcements in the key of the composition totally blind so to speak. When all faders were pushed up again a number of clashes would make themselves evident. The more dangerous or attractive ones would then be isolated and repeated at varying intervals so giving the impression of forethought."[177]

A Forgotten but Spectacular Album

For David Bowie, the adventures of Kureishi's hero revived many different memories, some of which he described in the album notes. He also listed, in no particular order, the numerous influences at play in the composing of the music: Kraftwerk, T. Rex, The O'Jays, and the Beach Boys' album *Pet Sounds*, but also the Berlin Wall, his travels in Russia, and even his mother. Fresh and spontaneous, David Bowie's nineteenth studio album is full of good things. Unfortunately, it was labeled by BMG as the original soundtrack from the TV series, and so it did not receive the promotion it deserved. As a result, its UK release in November 1993 went entirely unnoticed. Overshadowed by the success of the compilation album *Bowie: The Singles Collection*, which was brought out at the same time by EMI, *The Buddha of Suburbia* instantly disappeared off the radar.

David Bowie (back row), David Richards (sitting on a chair), and Erdal Kizilçay (on the ground) pose with the members of 3D Echo in front of Mountain Studios in Switzerland.

BUDDHA OF SUBURBIA

David Bowie / 4:28

Musicians: David Bowie: lead and backing vocals, synthesizers, acoustic guitar, saxophone / **Erdal Kizilçay:** synthesizers, electric guitar, acoustic guitar / **Rob Clydesdale:** electric guitar / **Paul Davidson:** bass / **Isaac Prevost:** drums / **Recorded: Mountain Studios, Montreux:** July–August 1993 / **Technical Team: Producers:** David Bowie, David Richards / **Sound Engineer:** David Richards / **Assistant Sound Engineer:** Dominik Tarqua

Written during the first sessions working on the soundtrack for the TV series *The Buddha of Suburbia*, this piece, a surprisingly simple and effective pop number, is a thousand miles away from the furious rock of *Tin Machine* and the synthetic sounds of *Black Tie White Noise*. The lyrics gradually reveal the angst experienced by the hero, Karim Amir, who is coming to terms with his sexual orientation. "*Screaming along in South London / Vicious but ready to learn / Sometimes I fear that the whole world is queer*":

the words composed by Bowie, himself a one-time Bromley adolescent, reveal the particular connection he must have felt with Karim, Hanif Kureishi's semi-autobiographical hero. The members of 3D Echo, the rock trio brought in to provide the rhythmic backing for the track "Bleed Like a Craze, Dad," are not credited on this cut but they are certainly playing, as guitarist Rob Clydesdale would later testify: "We started to record [...] 'Buddha of Suburbia.' We weren't credited, but we definitely did that."[163] A second version of the track, issued as a single on November 22, 1993, can be heard at the end of the album with Lenny Kravitz on the guitar, and without the momentary buzzing sound at the beginning.

ON YOUR HEADPHONES

At 3:43 on "Buddha of Suburbia," when he sings his famous phrase "Zane, Zane, Zane, ouvre le chien," Bowie takes us back to the period of "All the Madmen," on *The Man Who Sold the World*.

SEX AND THE CHURCH

David Bowie / 6:25

Musicians: David Bowie: lead vocals, synthesizers, saxophone, programming / **Erdal Kizilçay:** synthesizers, trumpet, bass, electric guitar / **David Richards:** programming / **Recorded:** Mountain Studios, Montreux: July–August 1993 / **Technical Team:** Producers: David Bowie, David Richards / Sound Engineer: David Richards / Assistant Sound Engineer: Dominik Tarqua

The narrator of "Sex and the Church" (or perhaps Bowie himself?) refers explicitly to the problems haunting the hero of Kureishi's novel about the relationship between the pleasures of the flesh and religious faith of whatever persuasion. Bowie sings, or rather speaks, the words: *"I think there is a union between the flesh and the spirit / Sex and the church."* His voice is passed through a vocoder, a studio effect that can modify the pitch of the notes and, when pushed to the extreme, can also create a robotic sound. Bowie is impressive on this imposing track with its persistently repeating synthesizer motif, seemingly destined for nightclubs. It's a shame that dance music fans seem to have passed this song by, despite its similarity to the electronic beat of One O One Electric Dream and their 1989 hit, "Rock to the Beat."

SOUTH HORIZON

David Bowie / 5:26

Musicians: David Bowie: synthesizers, saxophone, programming, electronic percussion / **Erdal Kizilçay:** synthesizers, trumpet, double bass (?), drums / **Mike Garson:** piano / **David Richards:** programming / **Recorded:** Mountain Studios, Montreux: July–August 1993 / O'Henry Sound Studios, Burbank, California (piano): Autumn 1993 / **Technical Team:** Producers: David Bowie, David Richards / Sound Engineers: David Richards, Rick Ruggieri (O'Henry Sound Studios) / Assistant Sound Engineer: Dominik Tarqua

Jazz and electronic textures are mingled in this instrumental track that gives free rein to pianist Mike Garson. Garson recorded his contributions at O'Henry Sound Studios in Burbank, California, alongisde sound engineer Rick Ruggieri (and not Mick Ruggieri as the album credits incorrectly indicate). In the album notes, Bowie explains: "On my favorite piece, 'South Horizon,' all elements [...] were played both forwards and backwards. The resulting extracts were then intercut arbitrarily giving Mike Garson a splendidly eccentric backdrop upon which to improvise. I personally think Mike gives one of his best-ever performances on this piece and it thrills on every listening, confirming to me at least, that he is still one of the most extraordinary pianists playing today."[177] This dreamlike track has elements of the nu jazz or jazztronica of the late 1990s, which was developed by groups like Innerzone Orchestra, Jazzanova, and the French musician St Germain.

THE MYSTERIES

David Bowie / 7:12

Musicians: David Bowie: synthesizers, piano / **Erdal Kizilçay:** synthesizers / **Recorded:** Mountain Studios, Montreux: July–August 1993 / **Technical Team:** Producers: David Bowie, David Richards / Sound Engineer: David Richards / Assistant Sound Engineer: Dominik Tarqua

"The Mysteries" takes us back to David Bowie's so-called Berlin period. One of his most creatively productive periods, it was notable particularly for contributions from Brian Eno, with whom Bowie was to collaborate again on his *1. Outside* album. What we hear in "The Mysteries" is very much in the spirit of "Subterraneans," the track from *Low* that featured many-layered synthesizers, a sweet melody, and an unsettling drone-like undertow. Bowie confesses in the sleeve notes of *The Buddha of Suburbia* that "many of my working forms are taken in whole or in part from my collaborations with Brian Eno (who in my humble opinion occupies a parallel position in late 20th century popular music that [critic] Clement Greenberg in the 40's or [painter] Richard Hamilton in the 60's had to visual art)."[177]

BLEED LIKE A CRAZE, DAD

David Bowie / 5:22

Musicians: David Bowie: lead vocals, synthesizers, electric guitar / **Erdal Kizilçay:** synthesizers, electric guitar, percussion / **Rob Clydesdale:** electric guitar / **Paul Davidson:** bass / **Isaac Prevost:** drums / **Mike Garson:** piano / **Recorded:** Mountain Studios, Montreux: July–August 1993 / O'Henry Sound Studios, Burbank, California (piano): Autumn 1993 / **Technical Team:** Producers: David Bowie, David Richards / Sound Engineers: David Richards, Rick Ruggieri (O'Henry Sound Studios) / Assistant Sound Engineer: Dominik Tarqua

When Bowie arrived at Mountain Studios in Montreux in the summer of 1993, the rock group 3D Echo was there recording a new EP under the guidance of David Richards. Mixing pop, punk, and grunge, bass player Paul Davidson, guitarist Rob Clydesdale, and drummer Isaac Prevost had to make room for the newly arrived star. During the recording sessions, Bowie decided that the song "Bleed Like a Craze, Dad" would gain intensity if interpreted by a real group without the use of rhythm boxes and a preprogrammed bass. 3D Echo's manager, an acquaintance of David Richards's, suggested that they come along to a rehearsal in the grand salon of the Casino de Montreux. Perhaps the star would happen to hear them. Their manager's hunch paid off, and David Bowie hired the group on the spot. Erdal Kizilçay then added a guitar lick that paid tribute to "Shine On You Crazy Diamond (Part One)," the 1975 hit by Pink Floyd.

STRANGERS WHEN WE MEET

David Bowie / 4:58

Musicians: David Bowie: lead and backing vocals, electric guitar, synthesizers / Erdal Kizilçay: bass, drums, electric guitar, synthesizers / **Recorded:** Mountain Studios, Montreux: July–August 1993 / **Technical Team:** Producers: David Bowie, David Richards / **Sound Engineer:** David Richards / **Assistant Sound Engineer:** Dominik Tarqua

In January 1993, Angela Bowie published her second autobiography, *Backstage Passes: Life on the Wild Side with David Bowie*. Along with revelations about a considerable number of artists, including Mick Jagger, Iggy Pop, and Elton John, her book is also an exposé of her ex-husband's drug use during the California years, as well as his wild sex life (she mentions orgies with men and women) and the general environment of debauchery that was widespread in the music business in the 1970s. Nothing and no one was spared from this onslaught—something that Bowie found distasteful. Taking as his starting point a trial track recorded at Montreux in preparation for *Black Tie White Noise*, he composed the lyrics to "Strangers When We Meet." In an elegant rebuke, he wrote *All our friends / Now seem so thin and frail / Slinky secrets / Hotter than the sun.*

The riff at the beginning of the track is instantly recognizable as coming from "Gimme Some Lovin'" (1966) by the Spencer Davis Group, the same song that Bowie had already used in the middle of "Join the Gang" on his first album from 1967. No doubt believing that this title deserved to be better known, Bowie rerecorded "Strangers When We Meet" in 1994 for the *1. Outside* album.

DEAD AGAINST IT

David Bowie / 5:48

Musicians: David Bowie: lead vocals, synthesizers, programming / Erdal Kizilçay: synthesizers, bass, electric guitar / David Richards: programming / **Recorded:** Mountain Studios, Montreux: July–August 1993 / **Technical Team:** Producers: David Bowie, David Richards / **Sound Engineer:** David Richards / **Assistant Sound Engineer:** Dominik Tarqua

David Bowie here plunges into the new wave of the 1980s with its layers of saturated guitars drowned in reverb. Think the Cure on "Push" from their *The Head on the Door* album (1985), or the synthetic textures of groups like Orchestral Manoeuvres in the Dark ("Enola Gay," "Electricity") and Alphaville ("Forever Young"). But even taking these similarities into account, we're reminded yet again that Bowie resembles no one so much as Bowie, and in "Dead Against It" we find the singer looking back more to some of his

so-called Berlin recordings, such as "Breaking Glass" and "What in the World" from *Low* in 1977.

"Dead Against It" also appears on the B-side of the single "Buddha of Suburbia." This is only fair, since both these titles deserve to be remembered by posterity.

UNTITLED NO. 1

David Bowie / 5:01

Musicians: David Bowie: lead and backing vocals, synthesizers, saxophone, programming, piano / Erdal Kizilçay: synthesizers, bass, electric guitar / David Richards: programming / **Recorded:** Mountain Studios, Montreux: July–August 1993 / **Technical Team:** Producers: David Bowie, David Richards / **Sound Engineer:** David Richards / **Assistant Sound Engineer:** Dominik Tarqua

The instrumental portion of "Untitled No. 1" is supported by a repeating refrain of unclear words: "Shimmy Kapoor," "See me Kapoor," or even "Shammi Kapoor" (paying homage to the famous Indian actor and moviemaker)—it will never be known exactly what Bowie meant with these lyrics. The reference to Hanif Kureishi's book is, nevertheless, explicit in Bowie's use of the very common Indian and Pakistani surname Kapoor. To write the text of this song, David Bowie used his cut-up technique, producing lyrics without any apparent meaning: *In mornings she's so regal that the valley sighs / In the chilly sea that killed her real slows.* Bowie confessed in the album's sleeve notes that "Fifty percent of the lyrical content [in this album] is used just because I like the sound of the word."[177] The text may be mysterious but it has its own poetry, making it a wonderful match for the song's melody.

IAN FISH, U.K. HEIR

David Bowie / 6:27

Musicians: David Bowie: lead vocals, synthesizers / Erdal Kizilçay: synthesizers, classical guitar / **Recorded:** Mountain Studios, Montreux: July–August 1993 / **Technical Team:** Producers: David Bowie, David Richards / **Sound Engineer:** David Richards / **Assistant Sound Engineer:** Dominik Tarqua

Like "The Mysteries," this piece was put together from backing tracks initially recorded for the TV series and then slowed down for use on the album. Bowie returns here to the textures of the instrumental tracks found on *Low*, accompanied this time by his right-hand man, Erdal Kizilçay, who here and there slips in a few notes on the classical guitar—an instrument very rarely used in Bowie's repertoire, and here reminiscent of the koto melodies in "Moss Garden" on the *"Heroes"* album. The equally strange title of this mysterious and dreamlike piece is in fact an anagram of the name Hanif Kureishi.

In September 1991, Lenny Kravitz surfed the waves of Malibu and enjoyed massive success with his second album, *Mama Said*.

BUDDHA OF SUBURBIA (FEATURING LENNY KRAVITZ ON GUITAR)

David Bowie / 4:19

45 rpm version: Side A: *Buddha of Suburbia* / 4:24 / **Side B:** *Dead Against It* / 5:48 / **Maxi CD Single Version:** 1. *Buddha of Suburbia* / 4:24; 2. *South Horizon* / 5:25; 3. *Dead Against It* / 5:48; 4. *Buddha of Suburbia (Rock Mix)* / 4:21 / **Europe Release on Arista/BMG:** November 22, 1993 (45 rpm ref.: 74321 177057 / Maxi CD single ref.: 74321 177052) / **Best UK Chart Ranking:** 35

Musicians: David Bowie: lead vocals, synthesizers, acoustic guitar, saxophone / Erdal Kizilçay: synthesizers, electric guitar / Rob Clydesdale: electric guitar / Paul Davidson: bass / Isaac Prevost: drums / Lenny Kravitz: electric guitar / **Recorded:** Mountain Studios, Montreux: July–August 1993 / **Technical Team:** Producers: David Bowie, David Richards / **Sound Engineer:** David Richards / **Assistant Sound Engineer:** Dominik Tarqua

In the summer of 1993, when David Bowie was recording *The Buddha of Suburbia*, one of the most famous international rock stars of the day was Lenny Kravitz. After his first album, *Let Love Rule* (1989), amazed critics all over the world with its remarkable songwriting and virtuosic playing, the dreadlocked rocker took his place in the pop pantheon with his second LP, *Mama Said* (1991). His third album, the fully orchestrated *Are You Gonna Go My Way*, came out in March 1993, and there seemed to be nothing stopping the ongoing ascent of this genius. It's not surprising, then, that David Bowie asked Kravitz to add a guitar line to "Buddha of Suburbia," the plan being to bring the resulting song out as a single. The opening solo on track number one of the album, played by Kizilçay, is here replaced by the guitar of Kravitz, to the great displeasure of the ousted musician. Kizilçay was to say: "Lenny Kravitz [...] didn't come in, we just sent the tapes over to Los Angeles, he recorded and sent the tapes back. My solo was better, and David said to me: 'I love your solo, man, it's very oriental and the way you express it is just beautiful.'"[163] Nevertheless, the collaboration with the rising star of American rock continued.

Despite its undeniably great qualities (the lyrics are particularly good), and the fact that this song accompanied the trailers and the credits for the TV series, the track did not get taken up by the public. No sooner had the single come out than the *Buddha of Suburbia* interlude came to an end for Bowie, and its songs were mostly forgotten. For his part, Bowie continued to assert that this was one of his best albums, and one of his favorites out of his entire discography.

TSIDE 1.

DE 1.OU

OUTSID

SIDE 1.0

1.OUTS

IDE 1.0

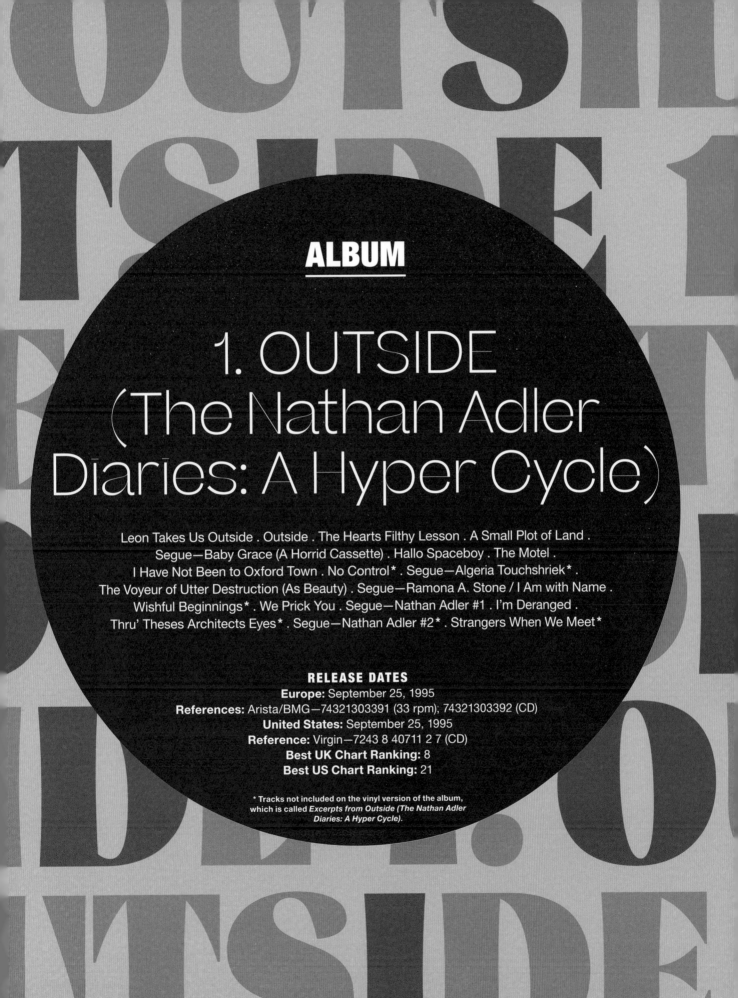

ALBUM

1. OUTSIDE (The Nathan Adler Diaries: A Hyper Cycle)

Leon Takes Us Outside . Outside . The Hearts Filthy Lesson . A Small Plot of Land .
Segue—Baby Grace (A Horrid Cassette) . Hallo Spaceboy . The Motel .
I Have Not Been to Oxford Town . No Control* . Segue—Algeria Touchshriek* .
The Voyeur of Utter Destruction (As Beauty) . Segue—Ramona A. Stone / I Am with Name .
Wishful Beginnings* . We Prick You . Segue—Nathan Adler #1 . I'm Deranged .
Thru' Theses Architects Eyes* . Segue—Nathan Adler #2* . Strangers When We Meet*

RELEASE DATES
Europe: September 25, 1995
References: Arista/BMG—74321303391 (33 rpm); 74321303392 (CD)
United States: September 25, 1995
Reference: Virgin—7243 8 40711 2 7 (CD)
Best UK Chart Ranking: 8
Best US Chart Ranking: 21

*Tracks not included on the vinyl version of the album,
which is called *Excerpts from Outside (The Nathan Adler
Diaries: A Hyper Cycle)*.

IN THE SHOES OF DETECTIVE NATHAN ADLER

While a guest at David Bowie's wedding ceremony in Florence on June 6, 1992, Brian Eno renewed his own bonds of friendship with the singer. The former keyboard player with Roxy Music and co-producer of the so-called Berlin Trilogy won international renown thanks to the colossal success of *Achtung Baby*, the U2 disc that he co-produced with Daniel Lanois and Steve Lillywhite in 1991. The brutal, industrial sounds of this work, along with its irresistible melodies, seduced Bowie, who brought up the idea of a new collaboration, the first since the great period of *Low*, *"Heroes,"* and *Lodger*. While writing the album *Black Tie White Noise*, Bowie shared some song ideas with Eno, but they had to wait until the release of *The Buddha of Suburbia* to bring their ideas to fruition.

Following a number of projects that were soon abandoned, such as a work commemorating the twelve hundredth anniversary of the town of Kyoto, in 1994 the two artists decided to start work on a new David Bowie album that would combine visual arts, literature, music, and sound experimentations of all kinds.

Outsider Music and Art / Art Brut

The art brut, or "outsider art," created by the painter Jean Dubuffet and bequeathed to the town of Lausanne, was installed in 1976 in the château of Beaulieu, which was not far from where David Bowie lived at the time. This was a source of inspiration for the singer. Sometimes thought of as a form of art created by the mentally ill, outsider art also encompasses works by self-taught creators and marginal individuals—a catch-all category that included prisoners, the mentally ill, or simply people with an original frame of mind who disregard social norms. Bowie was fascinated by these works, which were often naive and sometimes tortured, and in which, according to Dubuffet, "is manifested the only function of invention, rather than the

constants in cultural art, namely the chameleon and the monkey." David Bowie forged a link between outsider art and other artistic forms, also echoing the performance art of Chris Burden that he had previously evoked in the song "Joe the Lion." He was also interested in body art, as well as the work of Damien Hirst, who made death the central theme in his work. There was a combined interest in paganism and occult beliefs, as well as an obsession with the minotaur, a symbol of virility and power in Greek mythology. Bowie tried to combine all these influences into a cohesive framework.

In early 1994, at the invitation of the Austrian artist André Heller, Bowie and Eno went to the suburbs of Vienna to visit the Haus der Künstler ("artist's house") of the Maria Gugging psychiatric clinic, which makes a creative arts workshop available to its patients. "Brian and I took a couple of days there before we started working on this album," he explained, "to get some notion of what it must be like to be an artist who paints and works without feeling there is anything like judgement being made on him. [...] And what he's expressing is not for anybody other than the compulsion to make this work. [...] We tried to take some of that ambience when we went into the studio to work."[178] Not currently under any contractual obligations with a record company, Bowie set about creating a "free" work, somewhat tortured and labyrinthine, in which the listener could lose him- or herself. The English term generally used for art brut—"outsider art"—was the source of the album's name.

The Return of *Oblique Strategies*

Starting in March, the musician met his closest collaborators at Mountain Studios in Montreux. David Richards was at the controls, but he was credited as co-producer along with Brian Eno and David Bowie. Reeves Gabrels was equipped with his brand-new Parker Fly guitar, Erdal

Kizilçay provided bass and keyboards, Sterling Campbell was on drums, and the brilliant Mike Garson added his piano accompaniment throughout the disc. Eno and Bowie both played synthesizer now and again.

The musicians regularly met between March and November to record long swaths of instrumental material, often originating from the randomized instructions of Brian Eno, who had a new set of cards for his *Oblique Strategies* (see page 250). "He said to our drummer," as Bowie explained, "'You are the disgruntled ex-member of a South African rock band. Play the notes that you were not allowed to play.' And then the pianist was told, 'You are the morale booster of a small rag-tag terrorist operation. You must keep spirits up at all costs.'"[179] They all went along with this and improvised for many hours in accordance with these instructions. The producer then allocated a pseudonym to each of the musicians. Sterling Campbell became P. Maclert Singbell, a fictitious character: "He is said to have the only surviving recording of the shot that struck down the legendary 20th-century dictator John Kennedy, and another of the Swiss assassin Hud Helvetica cracking his knuckles prior to the brutal murder of the diminutive expeditor (v.i.) Roni Bean."[180] "I was trying to find some new ways of making improvisations go somewhere they wouldn't otherwise," explained Eno in 1996. "[...] I had been thinking about game-playing a lot. It was an approach that Roy Ascott had pioneered at Ipswich Art School during my time there, and I had most recently seen it working with my wife's family. At Christmas and other times the whole family play quite elaborate games which allow normally retiring people to become suddenly enormously extroverted and funny. Watching them, it occurred to me that the great thing about games is that they in some sense free you from being yourself: you are 'allowed' forms of behaviour that otherwise would be gratuitous, embarrassing or completely irrational. Accordingly, I came up with these role-playing games for musicians."[180]

The sessions were recorded and filmed with cameras pointing at each musician. Some of the images appeared in a promotional video interspersed with interviews featuring Bowie on his own. During these sessions, the singer painted tirelessly in a corner of the studio and nodded in agreement when something caught his attention. Richards then took notes in order to extract from these jam sessions the instrumental parts that would eventually be transformed into a distinct track. The songs created in Montreux were, for the most part, the work of all the musicians present.

Birth of the "Outside" Concept

In November 1994, for its one hundredth issue, the magazine *Q* suggested to David Bowie that he should write a diary of ten days of his life. The singer had a better idea. While his musicians were involved in the final session of improvisations for the future album, he went off and wrote a short story, which took the form of the diary of Nathan Adler, detective of Art Crime Inc. The police department in which he operated specialized in so-called art crimes, a new artistic movement that had elevated murder to an art form. Adler investigated the assassination of the young Baby Grace Belew, who was found in an abominably staged crime scene in front of the Museum of Modern Parts in Oxford Town. A number of disturbing characters were involved in the story, such as

Ramona A. Stone, who made jewelry from human body parts, and Artist Minotaur, the bloody murderer of the young Baby Grace.

By the time "The Diary of Nathan Adler—A non-linear Gothic Drama Hyper-Circle" appeared in the pages of *Q* in its January 1995 issue, Bowie had also decided to use his story to create a new concept album.

Every stage of the investigation forms part of a song, and the main characters are each allowed interludes that are distributed throughout the disc. The texts are conceived according to the cut-up technique, this time with the assistance of an application created for Apple Macintosh computers by Ty Roberts, of which a more highly developed version was called the Verbasizer. Bowie inserted phrases into it, which the machine cut up and randomly mixed together. The ideas were blended together to create an artistic patchwork that the artist had trouble selling to the record companies, despite his fame.

The Aborted Trilogy

Bowie's ultimate ambition was to sell three different albums based on this new material, but the record companies weren't biting. In the face of rejection by a large number of labels, he had to resign himself to returning to the studio in January 1995 to record some more accessible songs that would hopefully enable him to find a distributor.

At the Hit Factory Studios in New York, Bowie, Eno, and Richards created tracks such as "Hallo Spaceboy" and "We Prick You." The singer called upon his friend Carlos Alomar to provide some six-string scores, and on bassist Yossi Fine and drummer Joey Baron. The new songs won over Virgin, who distributed the disc in America, while Arista/BMG took care of the sales in Europe. The concept album, called *1. Outside*, with the number 1 indicating a trilogy in the making, was subtitled "The Nathan Adler Diaries: A Hyper Cycle."

The sleeve was illustrated with a self-portrait done in acrylics under the title *Head of DB*, and the album booklet contained a large number of pictures by photographer John

Scarisbrick, in which the singer plays the role of various characters from his story, the text of which is reproduced in full. The only modification: the surname of the young victim, which becomes Baby Grace Blue. Rumor has it that Adrian Belew did not appreciate the idea of the macabre murder of someone called Baby Grace Belew, whom he potentially associated with his then-eighteen-year-old daughter, Audie.

When the disc appeared on September 25, 1995, its dark and anguished "end of millennium" sounds struggled to win over the critics and the general public alike. The idea of giving this album any follow-up was therefore abandoned, something that the singer regretted in 2003: "We did record an awful lot of stuff, and there really is every intention of going through it and putting out Part II and Part III. The

second title was *Contamination*, and boy was that accurate. And it would have been nice to have somehow done it as a theatrical trilogy. I just don't have the patience."[181]

The *Outside* Tour

In 1995, despite the failure of *1. Outside*, David Bowie achieved a certain level of fame in the United States due to Nirvana and the success of the album *MTV Unplugged in New York*, which appeared in November of the previous year and included an unforgettable cover of "The Man Who Sold the World." While the young fans of Kurt Cobain did not know who wrote this hit, the musicians of the industrial rock scene, including Trent Reznor of Nine Inch Nails and his protégé, Marilyn Manson, affirmed their love of Bowie. The

David Bowie and Trent Reznor (Nine Inch Nails) onstage during the *Outside* tour in 1995.

David Bowie as Andy Warhol alongside Jeffrey Wright as Jean-Michel Basquiat, in Julian Schnabel's 1996 film, *Basquiat*.

Englishman, in return, appreciated the very singular music of Nine Inch Nails, and the cold and mechanical sonorities of the albums *Pretty Hate Machine* (1989) and *Broken* (1992). Bowie suggested that Nine Inch Nails could take part in his new tour of the United States, which was operating under the title "*Outside* Tour." The group provided the first part of the show; then Bowie joined them to interpret a set list consisting of numbers from both bands: "Subterraneans," "Scary Monsters (And Super Creeps)," "Reptile," "Hallo Spaceboy," "Hurt," and "The Voyeur of Utter Destruction (As Beauty)." Finally, Bowie's own musicians replaced Reznor's group to play the rest of the concert. Amongst them was a newcomer, who later played an important role in the world of the artist: bassist Gail Ann Dorsey.

Ten days of filming were sufficient for Bowie to leave his mark on the film *Basquiat*. In this feature film from 1996, Julian Schnabel retraces the life of the American artist Jean-Michel Basquiat. In it, David Bowie transformed into the role of the master of pop art, Andy Warhol. "I only had 7000 words, and once I got them in the right order, it was a doddle,"[182] recalled the singer with amusement.

LEON TAKES US OUTSIDE

David Bowie, Brian Eno, Reeves Gabrels, Erdal Kizilçay, Sterling Campbell, Mike Garson / 1:25

Musicians: David Bowie: spoken word / Reeves Gabrels: electric guitar / **Brian Eno, Erdal Kizilçay:** synthesizers / **Mike Garson:** piano / **Recorded:** Mountain Studios, Montreux: March–November 1994 / Westside Studios, London: November 1994–January 1995 / **Technical Team: Producers:** David Bowie, Brian Eno, David Richards / **Sound Engineer:** David Richards / **Assistant Sound Engineers:** Ben Fenner, Jon Goldberger, Dominik Tarqua

The fleeting introduction, "Leon Take Us Outside," plunges the listener into the album's singular world. On top of a musical background in which we recognize the signature of Brian Eno, the narrator sets out a series of dates and events without any obvious connection between them. In case there is any doubt, the instrument played by Reeves Gabrels is not a folk guitar, but rather a Parker Fly electric guitar provided with two microphones. This is what gives the instrument this bright and warm sound. The piece leads directly into the song "Outside," and the descent into darkness begins.

OUTSIDE

David Bowie, Kevin Armstrong / 4:04

Musicians: David Bowie: lead and backing vocals / Reeves Gabrels, Carlos Alomar: electric guitar / Yossi Fine: bass / Joey Baron: drums / **Brian Eno, Erdal Kizilçay:** synthesizers / **Recorded:** Mountain Studios, Montreux: March–November 1994 / **The Hit Factory, New York:** January–February 1995 / **Technical Team: Producers:** David Bowie, Brian Eno, David Richards / **Sound Engineer:** David Richards / **Assistant Sound Engineers:** Ben Fenner, Jon Goldberger, Dominik Tarqua

In 1981, Kevin Armstrong, at that time a member of the group Local Heroes SW9, recorded a song called "Love Is Essential" for the album *New Opium*, which was covered in 1983 by the British post-punk combo the Passions on their album *Sanctuary*. The piece haunted the guitarist, who sometimes played it during the levels testing sessions on the *Tin Machine* tour in 1989. David Bowie took an interest and asked if he could use it. The result was a number called "Now." It was played at some of the Tin Machine concerts but never recorded. When, at the beginning of 1995, Bowie recorded the vocals for his new album at Westside Studios in London, he suggested that Kevin Armstrong should come and lay down some guitar tracks for "Thru' These Architects Eyes," and he took this opportunity to let Armstrong hear his own version of "Now." "He must have taken a snapshot of that and worked on his

own," explained the guitarist, "because the next thing I heard of it was that he had called it 'Outside' and it was to be the title track of a new album. As for 'knowing where to stop,' it's an age-old question. I don't have a good answer except to say that you go with your gut feeling."[183]

FOR BOWIE ADDICTS

On January 11, 2016, the Czech website idnes.cz published an interview given by Pavel Karlik to the journalist Ondřej Bezr. Karlik, a sound engineer at Sono Records in Prague, revealed that in June 1997, during his *Earthling* tour, David Bowie had recorded a new version of "Outside" there, which still remains unreleased to this day.

THE HEARTS FILTHY LESSON

David Bowie, Brian Eno, Reeves Gabrels, Erdal Kizilçay, Sterling Campbell, Mike Garson / 4:57

Maxi Single CD Version (Europe): 1. *The Hearts Filthy Lesson (Radio Edit)* / 3:32; 2. *I Am with Name (Album Version)* / 4:06; 3. *The Hearts Filthy Lesson (Bowie Mix)* / 4:56; 4. *The Hearts Filthy Lesson (Alt. Mix)* / 5:19 / **Maxi Single CD Version (US):** 1. *The Hearts Filthy Lesson (LP Version)* / 4:57; 2. *The Hearts Filthy Lesson (Simenon Mix)* / 5:01; 3. *The Hearts Filthy Lesson (Alt. Mix)* / 5:20; 4. *Nothing to Be Desired* / 2:15 / **Europe Release on Arista/BMG:** September 11, 1995 (Maxi CD single ref.: 74321 30338 2) / **US Release on Virgin:** September 11, 1995 (Maxi CD single ref.: 7243 8 38518 2 9) / **Best UK Chart Ranking:** 35 / **Best US Chart Ranking:** 92

Musicians: David Bowie: vocals / Reeves Gabrels: electric guitar / Erdal Kizilçay: bass, synthesizers / **Sterling Campbell:** drums / **Mike Garson:** piano / **Brian Eno:** synthesizers / Bryony, Josey, Lola, and Ruby Edwards: backing vocals / **Recorded:** Mountain Studios, Montreux: March–November 1994 / **Westside Studios, London:** November 1994–January 1995 / **Technical Team: Producers:** David Bowie, Brian Eno, David Richards / **Sound Engineer:** David Richards / **Assistant Sound Engineers:** Ben Fenner, Jon Goldberger, Dominik Tarqua

Conceived during the long improvisation sessions in Montreux, "The Hearts Filthy Lesson," whose narrator is the detective Nathan Adler, is the first *1. Outside* single. It was released two weeks before the album, and the song takes the listener down into a world similar to that of the films of David Lynch. Bowie was a fan of Lynch, having portrayed an FBI agent in the movie *Twin Peaks: Fire Walk with Me*. "Oh,

Ramona / If there was only something between us," sings Adler, who seems to regret his liaison with a character who makes jewelry from human body parts and who becomes one of the suspects in his investigations. In 1995, "The Hearts Filthy Lesson" was used for the credits in the David Fincher film *Seven*, whose atmosphere is as morbid as Bowie's album. "When I heard it in the movie, I almost got scared to death,"[29] confided pianist Mike Garson, who provided a memorable score for the film.

The main element in the piece is without doubt the guitar leitmotif played by Reeves Gabrels. With his Parker Fly, the musician recorded the riff for the first time with the microphone for electric guitar. The six-string guitar is connected to a Univox Uni-Tron 5 pedal, which delivers a filter that is difficult to manage, as Gabrels explained: "It was just horrific, uncontrollable, but you could dial it in and get it to do some things."[184] The musician then recorded a second track with a microphone for acoustic guitar, thus giving this number a powerful riff with an inimitable sound.

Another curiosity on this track is the sound of children's voices that confront the listener from the start of the number, at 0:15.

Sabrina Guinness, a famous British television producer, took four brothers and sisters to Westside Studios as part of the Youth Cable Television group, which worked to introduce disadvantaged children to careers in television. The children had to interview the musicians and film the session. Brian Eno took an interest in the apprentice journalists and asked them to record some vocals before they left, which contributed to the somber and disconcerting atmosphere of this number.

A SMALL PLOT OF LAND

David Bowie, Brian Eno, Reeves Gabrels, Erdal Kizilçay, Sterling Campbell, Mike Garson / 6:34

Musicians: David Bowie: vocals / Reeves Gabrels: electric guitar / Erdal Kizilçay: bass, synthesizers / Sterling Campbell: drums / Brian Eno: synthesizers / Mike Garson: piano / **Recorded:** Mountain Studios, Montreux: March–November 1994 / Westside Studios, London: November 1994–January 1995 / **Technical Team:** Producers: David Bowie, Brian Eno, David Richards / Sound Engineer: David Richards / Assistant Sound Engineers: Ben Fenner, Jon Goldberger, Dominik Tarqua

In October 1994, the magazine *Q* published an internet conversation between David Bowie and Brian Eno, about the singer's album. "I forgot to tell you that I did a new beginning to that song which I like very much," wrote Eno.

"It's an atmospheric piece about 90 seconds long using your 'poor soul' phrase played very slowly and forming long drifting overlays. [...] I think it's lovely and you should get the tape soon."[185] This piece was to become "A Small Plot of Land," and it described the population of Oxford Town, the place where Bowie's story took place, and which is the origin of this concept album.

Starting with a jazz-influenced rhythm skillfully led by the virtuoso drummer Sterling Campbell and pianist Mike Garson, this number came from the improvisation sessions in Montreux. Rearranged for the 1996 film *Basquiat*, directed by Julian Schnabel, the song illustrates the state of mind of the painter following the death of Andy Warhol, who was played in the film by...Bowie himself.

FOR BOWIE ADDICTS

Donny McCaslin, the saxophonist and flautist on ★ (*Blackstar*), Bowie's last album, covered "A Small Plot of Land" on his own album *Beyond Now*, which was released on October 14, 2016, a few months after the singer's death.

SEGUE - BABY GRACE (A HORRID CASSETTE)

David Bowie, Brian Eno, Reeves Gabrels, Erdal Kizilçay, Sterling Campbell, Mike Garson / 1:39

Musicians: David Bowie: spoken word / Reeves Gabrels: electric guitar / Erdal Kizilçay: bass, synthesizers / Brian Eno: synthesizers / Mike Garson: piano / **Recorded:** Mountain Studios, Montreux: Autumn 1994 / Brondesbury Villas Studio, London (lyrics editing): January 1995 / **Technical Team:** Producers: David Bowie, Brian Eno, David Richards / Sound Engineer: David Richards / Assistant Sound Engineer: Dominik Tarqua / Lyrics Editing: Brian Eno

Recorded in one day at Montreux, the spoken interludes on the album were simply called "Segue," and they give voice to the characters of the story that Bowie wrote for *Q*. In this case, Baby Grace describes the ordeal suffered before her killing. "*Now they just want me to be quiet / And I think something is going to be horrid.*" It is of course Bowie's own voice featured here (and on all of the "Segue" tracks), and altered by that alchemist of sound, Brian Eno, from his Kilburn studio in London.

Single

HALLO SPACEBOY

David Bowie, Brian Eno / 5:14

Musicians
David Bowie: spoken word, lead and backing vocals, synthesizers
Reeves Gabrels: electric guitar, programming
Carlos Alomar: electric guitar
Yossi Fine: bass
Joey Baron: drums
Brian Eno: synthesizers, programming
Mike Garson: piano

Recorded
The Hit Factory, New York: January–February 1995

Technical Team
Producers: David Bowie, Brian Eno, David Richards
Sound Engineer: David Richards
Assistant Sound Engineer: Andy Grassi

SINGLE VERSION
Remix / Voice Recordings
Mayfair Studios, London: December 11–15, 1995

Technical Team
Producers: Chris Lowe, Neil Tennant
Sound Engineer: Bob Kraushaar
Programming: Pete Gleadall

MAXI CD SINGLE VERSION (EUROPE)
1. *Hallo Spaceboy (Remix)* / 4:25
2. *Under Pressure (Live Version)* / 4:07
3. *Moonage Daydream (Live Version)* / 5:35
4. *The Hearts Filthy Lesson (Radio Edit)* / 4:56

Europe Release on RCA/BMG: February 19, 1996 (Maxi CD single ref.: 74321353842)
Best UK Chart Ranking: 12

Genesis

In the summer of 1994, Reeves Gabrels and David Bowie worked on a new song, which the singer provisionally called "Moondust Will Cover You." A few months later, when he joined Bowie and Eno in New York for the final session of the album recording, Reeves Gabrels discovered that Bowie had reworked their joint track on his own and added it to the track listing of *1. Outside.* "He and Brian were in New York before I came," he reported, "and Brian doubled the tempo and added a drum machine. I thought, 'Cool, that's great!' but somehow my writing credits fell off. I didn't find out I didn't have writing credit until the album came out. [...It was] a lesson!"[184] Brian Eno, for his part, did not hesitate to take credit for the very successful production of this number: "I wrote some lightning chords and spaces [...] and suddenly, miraculously, we had something, Carlos and Joey at their shining best. Instantly D. came up with a really great vocal strategy (something about a Spaceboy), delivered with total confidence and certainty. When he's on, he's really on."[180]

Production

With Joey Baron on snare drums, in addition to drum machine programming, "Hallo Spaceboy" borrowed from Marilyn Manson's formula for his powerful industrial rock sound. Discovered by Trent Reznor—another influence on Bowie—Manson, whose real name is Brian Hugh Warner, released his debut album in 1994, *Portrait of an American Family*, in which he makes reference, among other cheerful subjects, to the killers Charles Manson and Richard Ramirez and the film *Poltergeist 2*. Bowie, harboring an obsession about death during the production of *1. Outside*, found in Manson and Reznor some formidable allies. With this in mind, it should be said that "Hallo Spaceboy" is just as surprising for how danceable it is. It was quite a bold and major departure for David Bowie to entrust the remix of this number to the Pet Shop Boys, the kings of nineties synthpop, when a maxi CD single release was set into motion. Neil Tennant and Chris Lowe took just a few days to give life to a completely new version of "Hallo Spaceboy" at Mayfair Studios in London in December 1995. Bowie rerecorded his vocals so that the single could become a duet with Neil Tennant, and the result was a success, eventually hitting twelfth place in the British charts.

THE MOTEL

David Bowie / 6:49

Musicians: David Bowie: vocals / Reeves Gabrels: electric guitar, programming / Erdal Kizilçay: bass, synthesizers / Sterling Campbell: drums / Brian Eno: synthesizers, programming / Mike Garson: piano / **Recorded:** Mountain Studios, Montreux: March–November 1994 / Westside Studios, London: November 1994–January 1995 / **Technical Team:** Producers: David Bowie, Brian Eno, David Richards / Sound Engineer: David Richards / Assistant Sound Engineers: Ben Fenner, Jon Goldberger, Dominik Tarqua

The piano is the key element in this splendid number from the Mountain Studios sessions. Mike Garson produces a remarkable improvisation here, which is mixed in with Reeves Gabrels's furious guitar playing. "That's my favorite track," confirmed the pianist. "I didn't compose it with him, but I mixed in a few harmonies that made it stronger. It's probably in his top-ten songs ever."[29] The meaning of the lyrics, written with the help of Eno's cut-up software, is unfathomable, but its poetry fits marvelously well with the music, whose melody and atmosphere were significantly inspired by "The Electrician," by the Walker Brothers, from their album *Nite Flights* (1978). Bowie had already covered this trio's title song on *Black Tie White Noise* in 1993.

I HAVE NOT BEEN TO OXFORD TOWN

David Bowie, Brian Eno / 3:47

Musicians: David Bowie: spoken word, lead and backing vocals / Reeves Gabrels: electric guitar / Carlos Alomar: electric guitar / Yossi Fine: bass / Joey Baron: drums / Brian Eno: synthesizers / **Recorded:** The Hit Factory, New York: January–February 1995 / **Technical Team:** Producers: David Bowie, Brian Eno, David Richards / Sound Engineer: David Richards / Assistant Sound Engineer: Andy Grassi

The main suspect in the case of the murder of Baby Grace Blue, Leon Blank claimed that he was never even at the scene of the crime. Imprisoned until the facts of the horrible assassination emerge, he claims his innocence in this pop-tinged track that would have been a great first choice for a single: "*I fear my days are numbered / Lord get me out of here.*"

The song, whose working title was "Toll the Bell," was recorded in New York in early 1995, when Bowie was struggling to convince the record companies to distribute his new work. The record companies felt his new material was too dark and experimental, so he had to compose some catchier tracks. That mission was accomplished with "I Have Not Been to Oxford Town," which shows the singer in a brighter light than do the other songs on *1. Outside.*

NO CONTROL

David Bowie, Brian Eno / 4:33

Musicians: David Bowie: lead and backing vocals / Reeves Gabrels: electric guitar, programming / Carlos Alomar: electric guitar / Yossi Fine: bass / Joey Baron: drums / Brian Eno: synthesizers, programming / **Recorded:** The Hit Factory, New York: January 20, 1995 / **Technical Team:** Producers: David Bowie, Brian Eno, David Richards / Sound Engineer: David Richards / Assistant Sound Engineer: Andy Grassi

On this ninth track of the album, the detective Nathan Adler has to face facts: He is losing control of the case and has found himself leading an investigation that he is unable to solve. Bowie pays homage to the musical comedies of Broadway by exaggerating his vocals in the style of Anthony Newley. As usual, an hour of recording time was sufficient to wrap up Bowie's contribution. Brian Eno remembers this New York recording session: "Watching him tune it to just the right pitch of sincerity and parody was one of the most fascinating things I've ever seen in a studio. I wonder if he realizes how good an artist he is at that kind of thing. People often take their own talents for granted. It's funny that the song is called 'No Control,' because this performance by him is a paradigm of control."[180]

SEGUE - ALGERIA TOUCHSHRIEK

David Bowie, Brian Eno, Reeves Gabrels, Erdal Kizilçay, Sterling Campbell, Mike Garson / 2:03

Musicians: David Bowie: spoken word / Reeves Gabrels: electric guitar / Erdal Kizilçay: bass, synthesizers / Sterling Campbell: drums / Brian Eno: synthesizers / Mike Garson: piano / **Recorded:** Mountain Studios, Montreux (lyrics recording): Autumn 1994 / Brondesbury Villas Studio, London (lyrics editing): January 1995 / **Technical Team:** Producers: David Bowie, Brian Eno, David Richards / Sound Engineer: David Richards / Assistant Sound Engineer: Dominik Tarqua / Lyric Editing: Brian Eno

The character of Algeria Touchshriek is a seventy-eight-year-old drug dealer who lives in Rail Yard, in Oxford Town. David Bowie brings this character to life in this short interlude, in which he announces that he wants to rent out the room underneath his shop to a certain Walloff Domburg: "*It would be nice to have company / We could have great conversations / Lookin' through windows for demons.*" In order to add color to this individual, Bowie gives him a cockney accent that is reminiscent of the toy seller in "Come and Buy My Toys," on his first album in 1967.

Artist Paul Reid's 2005 painting, *Minotaur*. The mythological creature was an inspiring figure for David Bowie as he wrote *1. Outside*.

focused on the creation of sound textures as his top priority: "Even though there's a very strong narrative and characters in this new piece, *Outside*, it really isn't what the album's about. The album is about atmosphere. It's about the sound of 1995. The narrative and the characters are really a kind of a skeleton. The content of the album is what's put on that skeleton, which is the musical texture. That's the flesh and the blood."[186] In this worthy descendant of "Look Back in Anger" (the drum patterns in particular have undeniable similarities), there is an addictive energy that plunges the listener right into the heart of the morbid motivations of Artist Minotaur.

SEGUE – RAMONA A. STONE / I AM WITH NAME

David Bowie, Brian Eno, Reeves Gabrels, Erdal Kizilçay, Sterling Campbell, Mike Garson / 4:01

Musicians: David Bowie: spoken word, lead and backing vocals / **Reeves Gabrels:** electric guitar / **Erdal Kizilçay:** bass, synthesizers / **Sterling Campbell:** drums / **Brian Eno:** synthesizers / **Mike Garson:** piano / **Bryony Edwards, Josey Edwards, Lola Edwards, Ruby Edwards:** backing vocals / **Recorded:** Mountain Studios, Montreux: March–November 1994 / **Westside Studios, London:** November 1994–January 1995 / **Brondesbury Villas Studio, London (lyrics editing):** January 1995 / **Technical Team:** Producers: David Bowie, Brian Eno, David Richards / **Sound Engineer:** David Richards / **Assistant Sound Engineers:** Ben Fenner, Jon Goldberger, Dominik Tarqua / **Lyrics Editing:** Brian Eno

Divided into two distinct parts, this track is introduced by a spoken-word segment in which Brian Eno (using a procedure that alters the pitch of the recorded sound) modifies David Bowie's voice to give it a more feminine aspect. This is Ramona A. Stone, one of the suspects in the case, who introduces herself in this interlude, which is followed by the number "I Am with Name," in which the computerized cut-up produces phrases of surreal poetry such as *"It'll end in chrome,"* or *"I am Ramona A. Stone / A person who loses a name / [...] Left at the crossroads / Between the centuries."* For the second time, we meet the youthful amateur backing vocalists Bryony, Josey, Lola, and Ruby Edwards, who first appeared on "The Hearts Filthy Lesson."

THE VOYEUR OF UTTER DESTRUCTION (AS BEAUTY)

David Bowie, Brian Eno, Reeves Gabrels / 4:21

Musicians: David Bowie: lead and backing vocals / **Reeves Gabrels:** electric guitar / **Erdal Kizilçay:** bass, synthesizers / **Sterling Campbell:** drums / **Brian Eno:** synthesizers / **Mike Garson:** piano / **Recorded:** Mountain Studios, Montreux: March–November 1994 / **Westside Studios, London:** November 1994–January 1995 / **Technical Team:** Producers: David Bowie, Brian Eno, David Richards / **Sound Engineer:** David Richards / **Assistant Sound Engineers:** Ben Fenner, Jon Goldberger, Dominik Tarqua

In this number, driven by Reeves Gabrels's heady guitar riff, the character of Artist Minotaur describes the full atrocity of his murders. While this narrative plays an important part in the album, Bowie was still heavily

If Camille Paglia's assistant had taken David Bowie's call seriously, the writer could have appeared on "We Prick You"!

WISHFUL BEGINNINGS

David Bowie, Brian Eno / 5:08

Musicians: David Bowie: vocals / Erdal Kizilçay: bass, synthesizers / Sterling Campbell: drums, tambourine / Brian Eno: synthesizers / **Recorded:** Mountain Studios, Montreux: March–November 1994 / Westside Studios, London: November 1994–January 1995 / **Technical Team:** Producers: David Bowie, Brian Eno, David Richards / Sound Engineer: David Richards / Assistant Sound Engineers: Ben Fenner, Jon Goldberger, Dominik Tarqua

In this number, Artist Minotaur tells the body of his young victim that he had little hope for the outcome of their relationship: *"We had such wishful beginnings / But we lived unbearable lives / I'm sorry little girl."*

The musicians were continually filmed during the Montreux sessions. While these sessions were never used to make an officially edited film, some images did appear on the EPK of *1. Outside.* An EPK (Electronic Press Kit) is a digital press file, and on the file that was created for this album we see David Bowie at 20:03 along with David Richards and assistant sound engineer Dominik Tarqua, all looking for the most suitable texture for the recorded voice sounds, like the one we hear from the introduction of "Wishful Beginnings." Hopefully one day these images will be released in DVD format, as they are such a testimony to the genesis of this fascinating concept album. The song was withdrawn from track listing of *1. Outside Version 2*, a reissue released by Arista/BMG in 1996, and replaced by the remix of "Hallo Spaceboy."

WE PRICK YOU

David Bowie, Brian Eno / 4:33

Musicians: David Bowie: lead and backing vocals / Reeves Gabrels: electric guitar, programming / Carlos Alomar: electric guitar / Yossi Fine: bass / Joey Baron: drums / Brian Eno: synthesizers, programming / **Recorded:** The Hit Factory, New York: January 14, 1995 / **Technical Team:** Producers: David Bowie, Brian Eno, David Richards / Sound Engineer: David Richards / Assistant Sound Engineer: Andy Grassi /

Recorded on January 14, 1995, at the Hit Factory Studios in New York, "We Prick You" depicts the trial of Leon Blank for the murder of Baby Grace Blue. With its pop rhythm and refrain, which is reminiscent of "Gloria" (1964) by Them, this track shows Bowie's aim to provide his album with some widely accessible songs so that he could find a willing record label. The recurrent phrase *"You show respect, even if you disagree"* comes from the American feminist Camille Paglia, who uttered the phrase during a televised debate. Initially David Bowie had sampled this phrase. He then tried to contact Paglia in the hope of obtaining her approval; after leaving quite a few messages with her assistant, Bowie never heard back. Apparently, the assistant thought this was some kind of prank being played by a random stranger. "I just gave up! So I replaced her line with me." "Sounds pretty much like her,"[187] added his accomplice Brian Eno.

David Lynch's 1997 film *Lost Highway* featured the song "I'm Deranged," taken from *1. Outside*.

SEGUE – NATHAN ADLER

David Bowie, Brian Eno, Reeves Gabrels, Erdal Kizilçay, Sterling Campbell, Mike Garson / 1:00

Musicians: David Bowie: spoken word / Reeves Gabrels: electric guitar / Erdal Kizilçay: bass / Sterling Campbell: drums / **Recorded:** Mountain Studios, Montreux: Autumn 1994 / Brondesbury Villas Studio, London (lyrics editing): January 1995 / **Technical Team:** Producers: David Bowie, Brian Eno, David Richards / Sound Engineer: David Richards / Assistant Sound Engineers: Ben Fenner, Jon Goldberger, Dominik Tarqua / Lyrics Editing: Brian Eno

In this short, one-minute interlude, it is detective Nathan Adler of Art Crime Inc. who delivers a rapid description of the three main suspects in the Baby Grace Blue case—Algeria Touchshriek, Ramona A. Stone, and Leon Blank—before addressing the listener: "*Oh wait, I'm getting ahead of myself / Let me take you back to when it all began.*" In this fleeting segment, Adler speaks over an instrumental score that was created at the Montreux sessions. Gabrels, Kizilçay, and Campbell play a slightly funky track, which is very reminiscent of Carlos Alomar on his six-string guitar. The very characteristic sound of Reeves Gabrels's Parker Fly is there to remind us that this is an entirely new musical moment.

I'M DERANGED

David Bowie, Brian Eno / 4:31

Musicians: David Bowie: vocals, saxophone / Reeves Gabrels: electric guitar, programming / Carlos Alomar: electric guitar / Yossi Fine: bass / Joey Baron: drums / Brian Eno: synthesizers, programming / Erdal Kizilçay: synthesizers / Mike Garson: piano / **Recorded:** Mountain Studios, Montreux: March–November 1994 / Westside Studios, London: November 1994–January 1995 / The Hit Factory, New York: January–February 1995 / **Technical Team:** Producers: David Bowie, Brian Eno, David Richards / Sound Engineer: David Richards / Assistant Sound Engineers: Ben Fenner, Andy Grassi, Jon Goldberger, Dominik Tarqua

"I'm Deranged" immerses the listener in the jungle world that Bowie was soon to develop on *Earthling*. Although Joey Baron was the drummer on the tracks recorded in New York at the beginning of 1995, and his presence on the backing tracks of this number was confirmed by Brian Eno's records, his playing here is hard to recognize. One would almost say that it sounds like there's a drum machine being used on this track, but there is nothing to support this theory. One element that is sufficiently rare to be worthy of note: the funk guitar rhythm played with the wah-wah pedal (doubtless by Carlos Alomar). This sound takes us back to the introduction of the monumental "1984," on *Diamond Dogs*. "I'm Deranged" was chosen by director David Lynch to play over the opening credits of his film *Lost Highway*, released in 1997.

THRU' THESE ARCHITECTS EYES

David Bowie, Reeves Gabrels / 4:22

Musicians: David Bowie: vocals / Reeves Gabrels: electric guitar / Kevin Armstrong: electric guitar, programming / Carlos Alomar: electric guitar / Yossi Fine: bass / Joey Baron: drums / Brian Eno: synthesizers, programming / Erdal Kizilçay: synthesizers / Mike Garson: piano / **Recorded:** Mountain Studios, Montreux: Autumn 1994 / Westside Studios, London: November 1994–January 1995 / The Hit Factory, New York: January–February 1995 / **Technical Team:** Producers: David Bowie, Brian Eno, David Richards / Sound Engineer: David Richards / Assistant Sound Engineer: Andy Grassi

While he was in London to finish off the mixing of the first numbers on the album and also to record the vocal tracks, Bowie called on Kevin Armstrong, who was the guitarist on "Dancing in the Street" and "Absolute Beginners," as well as on the two albums by Tin Machine. He suggested that Armstrong could contribute some six-string guitar notes on "Thru' These Architects Eyes." "It was the first time I met Brian Eno," recalled Armstrong in 2019. "Five minutes after being introduced to him I found myself standing next to him at the console with a guitar round my neck and being asked to play along to 'Architects' without ever having heard it before with Bowie looking on. [...] That was the last session I did with Bowie but I have since become friends with Brian and we still meet up."[183]

SEGUE – NATHAN ADLER

David Bowie, Brian Eno / 0:28

Musicians: David Bowie: spoken word / Brian Eno: synthesizers / Sterling Campbell: drums / **Recorded:** Mountain Studios, Montreux (lyrics recording): Autumn 1994 / Brondesbury Villas Studio, London (lyrics editing): January 1995 / **Technical Team:** Producers: David Bowie, Brian Eno, David Richards / Sound Engineer: David Richards / Assistant Sound Engineers: Ben Fenner, Jon Goldberger, Dominik Tarqua / Lyrics Editing: Brian Eno

In this twenty-eight-second interlude, Nathan Adler describes the rupture between Ramona A. Stone and Leon Blake. The characters in his investigation are linked, and Adler relates the discussion between the two lovers, who seem to have parted on bad terms: *"When she broke it off with Leon / She said, 'The ring is enough / I don't wanna see his face again.'"*

STRANGERS WHEN WE MEET

David Bowie / 5:07

45 rpm version (UK): Side A: *Strangers When We Meet (Edit)* / 4:19 / **Side AA:** *The Man Who Sold the World (Live Version)* / 3:32 / **CD single version (Europe):** 1. *Strangers When We Meet (Edit)* / 4:21; 2. *The Man Who Sold the World (Live Version)* / 3:34 / **Maxi CD single version (US):** 1. *Strangers When We Meet (Outside Album Version)* / 5:07; 2. *Strangers When We Meet (The Buddha of Suburbia Album Version)* / 4:58; 3. *The Man Who Sold the World (Live Version)* / 3:35 / **UK Release on RCA:** November 20, 1995 (45 rpm ref.: 74321329407) / **Europe Release on Arista/BMG:** November 20, 1995 (CD single ref.: 7432133236 2) / **US Release on Virgin:** November 20,1995 (CD single ref.: 7243 8 38530 2 1; V25D-38530) / **Best UK Chart Ranking:** 39 / **Best US Chart Ranking:** Did Not Chart

Musicians: David Bowie: vocals / Reeves Gabrels, Carlos Alomar: electric guitar / Yossi Fine: bass / Brian Eno: synthesizers, programming / Joey Baron: drums, tambourine / Mike Garson: piano / **Recorded:** The Hit Factory, New York: January–February 1995 / **Technical Team:** Producers: David Bowie, Brian Eno, David Richards / Sound Engineer: David Richards / Assistant Sound Engineer: Andy Grassi

There can be no doubt as to Bowie's ambitions with this cover of "Strangers When We Meet," which had already appeared on *The Buddha of Suburbia* and whose title is taken from a classic American film directed by Richard Quine and released in 1960. Given the initially skeptical response of the record companies to his other tracks, Bowie decided to record some more accessible songs for this album. This included a new version of this pop song, which was the least convincing number on his previous album. Completely out of step with the dark world of *1. Outside*, the track isn't served much better by this new iteration, especially given that the lyrics have no link whatsoever with the concept of the disc. David Bowie unveiled this second single for British television audiences with a performance on *Top of the Pops* on November 10, 1995. Shaking off the macabre concept of *1. Outside*, he sang this song with genuine emotion, also taking the opportunity to introduce his new bassist, the talented Gail Ann Dorsey, to British audiences. The video of the single, colored in sepia, was the work of Samuel Bayer, director of videos for "Smells Like Teen Spirit" by Nirvana (1991), "Doll Parts" by Hole (1994), and "Zombie" by the Cranberries (1994).

David Bowie knew how to use digital technology to reach a wider audience.

GET REAL

David Bowie, Brian Eno / 2:51

Musicians: David Bowie: vocals, saxophone / **Brian Eno:** synthesizers, programming / **Reeves Gabrels:** electric guitar, programming / **Erdal Kizilçay:** bass, synthesizers / **Sterling Campbell:** drums / **Recorded:** Mountain Studios, Montreux: March–November 1994 / Westside Studios, London: November 1994–January 1995 / **Technical Team:** Producers: David Bowie, Brian Eno, David Richards / **Sound Engineers:** David Richards / **Assistant Sound Engineers:** Ben Fenner, Andy Grassi, Jon Goldberger, Dominik Tarqua

In this pop song recorded between Montreux and London, use of the cut-up method makes it difficult for the listener to grasp the exact meaning of the lyrics. But Bowie's "exquisite corpse" phrases form a cohesive whole with the strangeness that predominates in *1. Outside.* *"You can't stop meaningful teenage cries / From deep behind fifty-year-old eyes,"* sings Bowie, undoubtedly in the character of one of the personalities from his short story "The Diary of Nathan Adler—A non-linear Gothic Drama Hyper-Circle." The song was released only as a bonus track on the Japanese version of the album, then on the rerelease from Columbia in 2004.

NOTHING TO BE DESIRED

David Bowie, Brian Eno, Reeves Gabrels, Erdal Kizilçay, Sterling Campbell, Mike Garson / 2:16

Musicians: David Bowie: vocals / **Reeves Gabrels:** electric guitar / **Erdal Kizilçay:** bass, synthesizers / **Sterling Campbell:** drums / **Brian Eno:** synthesizers, programming / **Mike Garson:** piano / **Bryony Edwards (?), Josey Edwards (?), Lola Edwards (?), Ruby Edwards (?):** backing vocals / **Recorded:** Mountain Studios, Montreux: March–November 1994 / Westside Studios, London: November 1994–January 1995 / **Technical Team:** Producers: David Bowie, Brian Eno, David Richards / **Sound Engineers:** David Richards / **Assistant Sound Engineers:** Ben Fenner, Andy Grassi, Jon Goldberger, Dominik Tarqua

This is a curiosity that one can readily attribute to the improvisation sessions in Montreux that took place between March and November 1994. The childlike backing vocals also suggest that the Edwards sisters, who sing on "The Hearts Filthy Lesson" and "I Am with Name," were involved in the London sessions during which Bowie recorded the first vocal lines on *1. Outside.* Present on the American maxi single of "The Hearts Filthy Lesson," this intriguing track concludes with lyrics in German. Some claim that this is an extract from the text of "Helden," the German version of "Heroes," recorded by Bowie in 1977, but the very rapid fade-out on this track does not allow more than an approximate understanding of the German lyrics.

Mick Ronson featuring David Bowie

LIKE A ROLLING STONE

Bob Dylan / 4:21

Mick Ronson, Heaven and Hull / **Europe Release on Epic:** May 10, 1994 (CD ref.: 474742 2) / **US Release on Epic:** May 10, 1994 (CD ref.: EK 53796) / **Did Not Chart**
Musicians: David Bowie: vocals / Mick Ronson, Keith Scott: electric guitar / Rene Wurst: bass / Mark Curry: drums / **Recorded:** Unknown Studio, Los Angeles (original track): 1988 / **Unknown Studio, New York** (additional guitars, vocals): 1992 / **Technical Team:** Producer: Bruce Fairbairn / **Additional Production:** Mick Ronson, Suzanne Ronson, Sam Lederman, Steve Popovich / **Sound Engineer:** Erwin Musper /

In 1992, David Bowie learned of the state of health of his old friend Mick Ronson, who had inoperable cancer of the liver. Bowie suggested that Ronson might like to contribute some notes on his six-string guitar for "I Feel Free." At that same time, the guitarist was launching the production of his new album, for which Bowie sent him some tapes with a view to a possible collaboration. Among the tapes was a recording with producer Bruce Fairbairn and Bryan Adams's musicians which caught the musician's attention. These sessions gave rise to the first version of "Pretty Pink Rose" (which Adrian Belew recovered in 1989) and a cover of the Bob Dylan hit "Like a Rolling Stone." Ronson used this number, added some guitars to it, and asked Bowie to sing it. Mick Ronson died on April 29, 1993. *Heaven and Hull*, his posthumous album, appeared a year later, on May 10, 1994.

Reeves Gabrels featuring David Bowie

THE KING OF STAMFORD HILL

David Bowie, Reeves Gabrels / 4:56

Musicians: David Bowie: lead and backing vocals / Gary Oldman: spoken word, backing vocals / Reeves Gabrels: electric guitar / Matt Gruenberg: bass / Milt Sutton: drums / **Recorded:** Mountain Studios, Montreux: 1988 / Playtime Music Studio, Boston: 1995 / **Technical Team:** Producer: Reeves Gabrels / Sound Engineers: David Richards, Justin Shirley-Smith, Tim Palmer, Matt Yelton, Reeves Gabrels

In 1978, a few years before playing Victor Maitland, Eddie Murphy's nemesis in *Beverly Hills Cop,* actor Steven Berkoff (who was a playwright in his spare time) had written *West,* a short piece detailing urban life through the tormented existence of a number of characters. Following their collaboration with the band La La La Human Steps in July 1988, David Bowie and Reeves Gabrels had thoughts of creating a

musical comedy derived from the work of Berkoff, which had already been adapted for British television in 1984. The two musicians started to work on outlines for songs, which were composed in their respective home studios. "I had a Tascam Porta 1 cassette, he had a Tascam Porta 1 cassette," recalls Gabrels. "So we would fly back and forth, I was living in London at that point, [and] he was living in Switzerland. He would grab his box of cassettes and come over to my house, and I would grab my box of cassettes and go over [to] his house, and those were our master tapes."[188] Although the project was soon abandoned in favor of the formation of Tin Machine, some demos did eventually see the light of day at Mountain Studios in Montreux, including "The King of Stamford Hill," which had been saved by Reeves Gabrels. Performed with a Cockney accent, which Bowie was particularly good at doing, the song included a star guest appearance by actor Gary Oldman, a close friend of the singer. In 1995, for his first album, *The Sacred Squall of Now*, Gabrels unearthed the recording, retained only the vocal tracks, and added guitar, bass, and drums, with arrangements that were borderline thrash metal. The result is a studio concoction of limited value, but certainly of interest to devoted Bowie fans.

Reeves Gabrels featuring David Bowie

YOU'VE BEEN AROUND

David Bowie, Reeves Gabrels / 2:55

Musicians: David Bowie: lead and backing vocals / Gary Oldman: vocals / Tom Dube: lead and backing vocals / Reeves Gabrels: electric guitar, percussion / Matt Gruenberg: bass / Hunt Sales: drums / **Recorded:** Mountain Studios, Montreux: 1988 / Playtime Music Studio, Boston: 1995 / **Technical Team:** Producer: Reeves Gabrels / Sound Engineers: David Richards, Justin Shirley-Smith, Tim Palmer, Matt Yelton, Reeves Gabrels

Written at the time of *Tin Machine*, "You've Been Around" remained unreleased until 1992, when Bowie decided to rerecord it for *Black Tie White Noise*. In 1995, Reeves Gabrels reworked the demo recorded by Bowie in 1988 and asked Gary Oldman to add some additional vocal lines so that the number could be included in his first solo album, *The Sacred Squall of Now*. The only interest of this new version is the discovery of the vocal timbre of the actor from *True Romance* and *Léon: The Professional*, who acquits himself very creditably alongside his friend, the great David Bowie.

ALBUM

EARTHLING

Little Wonder . Looking for Satellites . Battle for Britain (The Letter) .
Seven Years in Tibet . Dead Man Walking . Telling Lies . The Last Thing You Should Do .
I'm Afraid of Americans . Law (Earthlings on Fire)

RELEASE DATE
Europe: February 3, 1997
References: Arista/BMG—74321 43077-1 (33 rpm); 7432143077 2 (CD)
United States: February 3, 1997
Reference: Virgin—7243 8 42627 2 3 (CD)
Best UK Chart Ranking: 6
Best US Chart Ranking: 39

A FORAY INTO METAL, JUNGLE, AND DRUM 'N' BASS

The *Outside* tour came to an end on February 20, 1996; it was an immense undertaking with almost seventy concerts given across the world. In April of the same year, before going back on the road for the "Outside Summer Festivals Tour," which lasted from June 4 to July 21, David Bowie returned to Mountain Studios in Montreux to record a demo of "Telling Lies," a song he had started work on two years earlier during a session with Brian Eno in New York. Pleased with the results, he flew to New York with Reeves Gabrels and spent the month of May in the Looking Glass Studios polishing up a final version of the track. He hired Mark Plati, the studio sound engineer, to work for a few days on the song. A friend of Junior Vasquez, who was a well-known DJ at the Sound Factory, the young technician already had a number of successful songs to his name. His mastery of computers and computer software, which were becoming an increasingly important element in music recording, had earned him a reputation as a great sound engineer. He had notably collaborated with Prince in 1990 on some of the numbers from his album *Graffiti Bridge* ("Thieves in the Temple," "Round and Round," "The Latest Fashion"). More recently, Plati had worked on a number one hit called "Spaceman" with Babylon Zoo in January 1996. Plati had mixed the track himself, after taking care of the programming and playing keyboards.

The Influence of a New Generation of DJs

This collaboration gave David Bowie the confidence to abandon the industrial rock influences that colored so much of *1. Outside* and to experiment with new and more electronic sounds. This was a time when, despite the Britpop songs by Pulp, Blur, and Oasis that still featured heavily in the charts, a wind of innovation was sweeping Europe. Bowie was instantly attracted to trends like drum 'n' bass and jungle, which were being adopted by artists like Goldie and Photek. Massive Attack, Portishead, Pigeonhed, and Tricky (himself formerly a member of Massive Attack) contributed a darker, more sensual and more relaxed sound to the trip-hop influences that were all the rage. Groups like the Chemical Brothers and Underworld were taking off in the UK, attracting attention particularly with Underworld's hit "Born Slippy .NUXX," which appeared on the soundtrack of Danny Boyle's popular movie, *Trainspotting*. David Bowie became a passionate fan of this new electronic music. Asked by journalist Linda Laban about his views on drum 'n' bass, a style derived from breakbeat and so-called jungle music, he replied: "Who could not be influenced by it? It's the most exciting rhythm of the moment."[189]

Bowie was intrigued not only by the effect that listening to these new sounds had on him, but also by the all-powerful influence of DJs. Back in 1979, with his single "DJ" from the album *Lodger*, he had painted a rather dire picture of these trendsetters hiding behind their turntables. Nevertheless, the DJ phenomenon would only become more important as time went by. Now working as remixers and also as producers, and often hugely talented, these artists attracted a never-ending buzz in the UK. They appeared at festivals, electrifying increasingly large crowds. In 1997, when Daft Punk was about to launch the "French Touch" movement, which featured a tendency to combine disco and house music, British pop fans were being carried away by another group called the Prodigy. Prodigy's first two albums, *Experience* and *Music for the Jilted Generation*, were notable successes. Their third album, the hugely popular *The Fat of the Land*, was studded with hit singles ("Firestarter," "Smack My Bitch Up," "Breathe") and became the culminating moment of the electro movement in the UK.

Mark Plati: The Magician at the Looking Glass Studios

It was in the ferment of this period that Bowie tried to find a path for himself. A trendsetter in the 1970s, Bowie now found himself reduced to following trends set by others. But, as always, his characteristic talent led him to use the inspiration of this new musical moment to renew himself artistically. In July 1996, he bumped into Mark Plati at a concert in Berlin and invited him along on his tour. "It was a wonderful experience—I rode on the band bus, hung out in the dressing room with David and Iggy Pop, spent the gig at the front-of-house mix position, asked for my thoughts after the show. They also comped me a hotel room for the night. A fan's dream, for sure."[190] Almost immediately, David Bowie invited the young technician to be part of the production team for his next album, which was to be called *Earthling*.

Since the summer tour, Bowie's group had settled down as a band, now consisting of guitarist Reeves Gabrels, bass player Gail Ann Dorsey, drummer Zachary Alford, and pianist Mike Garson. Each of these musicians left their mark on the new album, even though the greater part of the production was done by Bowie, Gabrels, and Plati, the latter making use of his knowledge of MAO (computer-assisted music). In this way, it was possible to simplify the procedures of sampling and rhythm loops recorded by Alford on the drums before speeding them up and delivering them to Plati, who could then duplicate them as needed. Gabrels used a MIDI keyboard to enter many different types of sequences, inserting them into the tracks on the album wherever he thought appropriate. Bowie, in the meantime, relied more than ever on the cut-up technique of writing lyrics, focusing heavily on the use of Verbasizer, a computer program created by the American digital innovator Ty Roberts.

An Important Birthday

Earthling was released on February 3, 1997, and it's a skillful synthesis of the rock textures developed since the Tin Machine days, and the electronic effects that Bowie was now seeking. The album cover features a photo by Frank Ockenfels that was retouched by Davide De Angelis. It shows a back view of the singer, looking out over the English countryside and dressed in a coat designed by Alexander McQueen featuring the colors of the Union Jack. A genuine declaration of love for his country! Even though he was living in Switzerland purely for tax reasons, Bowie seemed to be watching over his native land, returning there with the *Earthling* tour, which began in the summer of 1997, six months after he celebrated his fiftieth birthday

Zachary Alford, Reeves Gabrels, David Bowie, Gail Ann Dorsey, and Mike Garson: a dynamic team on the Earthling tour.

Right and next page

For his fiftieth birthday, which celebrated on the stage of Madison Square Garden in New York on January 9, 1997, Bowie performed four songs with Lou Reed: "Queen Bitch," "I'm Waiting for the Man," "Dirty Blvd.," and "White Light / White Heat."

in grand style at Madison Square Garden in New York. That evening, none of the musicians who had featured so heavily in Bowie's career were invited onto the stage, with one exception: Lou Reed. Bowie used the extraordinary evening to call on the new guard of rock music, rather as a father would show off his children of the next generation. Sonic Youth, Dave Grohl of the Foo Fighters, Frank Black of the Pixies—all came forward to sing with him. "David is generally more about the present than the past,"[29] was how Reeves Gabrels explained it after the event. His remark could aptly be applied to *Earthling*, a powerfully modern album very much in touch with the times.

FOR BOWIE ADDICTS

On September 14, 1996, during a concert at the Roseland Ballroom in New York, David Bowie asked the audience about the title of his forthcoming album: "Earthling" or "Earthlings"? The crowd liked the first option best, and Bowie took their advice!

LITTLE WONDER

David Bowie, Reeves Gabrels, Mark Plati / 6:02

Musicians
David Bowie: lead and backing vocals, samples, saxophone, electric guitar
Reeves Gabrels: electric guitar, electronic guitar, synthesizers, programming
Gail Ann Dorsey: bass, backing vocals
Zachary Alford: drums, programming, samples, electronic percussion
Mike Garson: synthesizer
Mark Plati: synthesizers, loops, programming, samples

Recorded
Looking Glass Studios: August and October 1996
Right Track Recording Studios (mixing): October–November 1996

Technical Team
Producers: David Bowie, Reeves Gabrels, Mark Plati
Sound Engineer: Mark Plati
Assistant Sound Engineers: Dante DeSole, Matt Curry
Mixing: Mark Plati

CD SINGLE VERSION (EUROPE)
1. *Little Wonder (Edit)* / 3:40
2. *Telling Lies (Adam F Mix)* / 3:58

MAXI CD SINGLE VERSION (US)
1. *Little Wonder (Album Version)* / 6:02
2. *Little Wonder (Junior Vasquez Ambient Mix)* / 9:55
3. *Little Wonder (Junior Vasquez Club Dub)* / 8:10
4. *Little Wonder (Danny Saber Dance Mix)* / 5:30

Europe Release on Arista/BMG: January 27, 1997 (CD single ref.: 74321 44778 2)
US Release on Virgin: January 27, 1997 (Maxi CD single ref.: 7243 8 38585 2 1; V25G-38585)
Best UK Chart Ranking: 14
Best US Chart Ranking: Did Not Chart

Genesis
One evening in August 1996, when Bowie was absent from the studio and Mark Plati had to go home to look after his three-year-old daughter, Reeves Gabrels stayed behind with assistant sound engineer Dante DeSole. The two men spent the whole evening recording an unbelievable number of samples onto DAT (digital audio tape) cassettes. Gabrels, who swore by his MIDI Roland VG-8, which he used to transform his Parker Fly into an impressive electronic guitar, tried out all sorts of sound experiments. The next day, Plati and Gabrels worked on the jungle-style rhythm that introduced "Little Wonder," inserting the samples they'd made the previous evening. Bowie and his guitarist also added a few chords played on their Fernandes Series ZO (guitars recognizable by their small size), and the piece began to sound extraordinarily like "Firestarter," the hit by the Prodigy that had come out on March 18, 1996. Gabrels remembered with amusement: "We used to argue who was better—Underworld or Prodigy. I was the Underworld guy and he was the Prodigy guy."[163] But the song, which was nine minutes long, soon moved away from this model. The song was five minutes too long, according to Bowie, who later asked Plati to reduce it to 3:40 for issue on a single (for the album, an edited version lasting 6:02 was chosen).

Production
After this first session, Zachary Alford and Gail Ann Dorsey added their drum and bass parts, respectively. Dorsey was unaware that she was being recorded as she tried out her instrument to test the effects pedals. Plati, who kept all the tapes, including rehearsal tapes, inserted this improvised fragment into the song at 3:09. Some of the lyrics were also recorded, based on numerous sticky notes on which Bowie had written words. He used the sticky notes to compose phrases according to the cut-up method. The lead singer's vocals did not require any polishing, much to the amazement of Mark Plati, who had never before seen a singer that was able to nail a part in a single take. The video for "Little Wonder" was made by Floria Sigismondi, creator of the magnificent but very disturbing video for Marilyn Manson's "The Beautiful People."

Maxim Reality, Liam Howlett, Leeroy Thornhill, and Keith Flint formed the Prodigy, a seminal group in the British techno wave of the late 1990s.

LOOKING FOR SATELLITES

David Bowie, Reeves Gabrels, Mark Plati / 5:21

Musicians: David Bowie: lead and backing vocals, samples / **Reeves Gabrels:** electric guitar, electronic guitar, synthesizers, programming / **Gail Ann Dorsey:** bass, backing vocals / **Zachary Alford:** drums, programming, samples, electronic percussion / **Mike Garson:** synthesizer / **Mark Plati:** synthesizers, loops, programming, samples / **Recorded:** Looking Glass Studios: August and October 1996 / **Right Track Recording Studios (mixing):** October–November 1996 / **Technical Team:** Producers: David Bowie, Reeves Gabrels, Mark Plati / Sound Engineer: Mark Plati / Assistant Sound Engineers: Dante DeSole, Matt Curry / **Mixing:** Mark Plati

On June 13, 1996, Bowie and his musicians were preparing to leave Japan after their concert at Fukuoka Sunpalace, the last Japanese booking of their "Outside Summer Festivals Tour." While they were waiting to embark for the United States, where their tour was to continue, Garuda Indonesia Flight 865 had an engine failure while taking off and ended up in a ditch alongside the airport. Of the 275 passengers and crew on board, three died in the accident. Reeves Gabrels, in his hotel room at the airport when all of this was happening, saw the smoke rising up from the DC-10-30. This scene inspired the guitar line he used a few months later in "Looking for Satellites."

While the song draws its energy from the loops created by magician Mark Plati, Bowie insisted that his guitarist use only one string in his solo, with one concession: He graciously allowed Gabrels to move from one string to another at the chord change. The result, audible from 3:12, is an extended passage of wild slides.

BATTLE FOR BRITAIN (THE LETTER)

David Bowie, Reeves Gabrels, Mark Plati / 4:49

Musicians: David Bowie: lead and backing vocals, samples / **Reeves Gabrels:** electric guitar, electronic guitar, synthesizers, programming / **Gail Ann Dorsey:** bass, backing vocals / **Zachary Alford:** drums, programming, samples / **Mike Garson:** piano / **Mark Plati:** synthesizers, loops, programming, samples / **Recorded:** Looking Glass Studios: August and October 1996 / **Right Track Recording Studios (mixing):** October–November 1996 / **Technical Team:** Producers: David Bowie, Reeves Gabrels, Mark Plati / Sound Engineer: Mark Plati / Assistant Sound Engineers: Dante DeSole, Matt Curry / **Mixing:** Mark Plati

"Battle for Britain (The Letter)," a mixture of jungle and jazz influences, was created from an initial drum loop played by Zachary Alford that was then sped up to 160 bpm (beats per minute), thereby creating an earsplitting drum 'n' bass pattern. Alford later recorded this part live for inclusion in the final version of the song. With the rhythmic basis established, Bowie, Gabrels, and Plati got down to work.

Plati described the process later: "Reeves would be coming up with guitar parts and sounds, I'd be at the computer recording him or working on the arrangement, and David would be on the couch listening to the track over and over, writing the lyric. At days' end he'd do a vocal."[191] When it was time to record the piano part, Bowie asked Mike Garson to improvise in the style of Ragtime for Eleven Instruments, a jazz-influenced work by Igor Stravinsky that was first performed at the Aeolian Hall in London on April 27, 1920. Mike Garson, who had not been happy with his performance on "Looking for Lester" in 1992, now had adequate time to prepare for this recording session. The result is an extraordinary section of free jazz in the middle of a storm of electronic sound that is quite simply amazing—this song is one that merits revisiting as soon as possible.

SEVEN YEARS IN TIBET

David Bowie, Reeves Gabrels / 6:22

Maxi CD single version (Europe): 1. *Seven Years in Tibet (Edit)* / 4:01; 2. *Seven Years in Tibet (Mandarin Version)* / 3:58; 3. *Pallas Athena* / 8:18 / **Europe Release on Arista/BMG:** August 18, 1997 (Maxi CD single ref.: 74321512552) / **Best UK Chart Ranking:** 61

Musicians: David Bowie: lead and backing vocals, saxophone, samples / **Reeves Gabrels:** electric guitar, electronic guitar, synthesizers, programming / **Gail Ann Dorsey:** bass / **Zachary Alford:** drums, programming, samples, electronic percussion / **Mike Garson:** Farfisa organ / **Mark Plati:** synthesizers, loops, programming, samples / **Recorded:** Looking Glass Studios: August and October 1996 / **Right Track Recording Studios (mixing):** October–November 1996 / **Technical Team:** Producers: David Bowie, Reeves Gabrels, Mark Plati / Sound Engineer: Mark Plati / Assistant Sound Engineers: Dante DeSole, Matt Curry / **Mixing:** Mark Plati

Although the group did not perform in the Belgian capital during the "Outside Summer Festivals Tour," it was at this time that Reeves Gabrels composed "Brussels." With its guitar line clearly inspired by Fleetwood Mac's instrumental single "Albatross," released in November 1968, the song begins with nothing more than a series of chords played over drum loops created by Mark Plati. The verses came into being at the Looking Glass Studios and, upon the arrival of Dorsey, Alford, and Garson, an entire wall of sound was constructed. The sound featured massive and powerful choruses capable of blowing off the heads of even the most dedicated headbanger.

Bowie onstage at Radio City Music Hall in New York for the closing performance of the GQ Men of the Year Awards in 1997.

For the lyrics, Bowie returned to a theme he had already used back in 1967 in "Silly Boy Blue." Inspired by the book *Seven Years in Tibet,* an account of the travels of the Austrian mountaineer and explorer Heinrich Harrer, Bowie here pays tribute once more to Tibet, which was annexed by China in 1949. A movie version of Harrer's book was also released in the same year as *Earthling,* with Brad Pitt in the role of the writer.

On October 15, 1997, during a performance at the GQ Awards at Radio City Music Hall in New York, Bowie introduced this song with the words "Free Tibet!" Initially called "Are You Okay?" the words of the first verse of "Seven Years in Tibet" are taken from an anecdote that couldn't be further from the subject of Chinese imperialism. While Bowie, Plati, and Gabrels were in the recording studio with the instrumental part of the song almost completed, the guitarist saw a news item on the internet. An American woman who had left her groceries in the car during a heat wave had her skull cracked by a box of biscuits that exploded as a result of the extreme temperature. Screaming that she had been shot, she clutched at her head thinking her brains were spilling out. A passerby who had come to her aid began shouting to her: "Are you okay? Are you okay?" Bowie found this unlikely story quite striking, to say the least, and included a reference to it at the beginning of the song.

FOR BOWIE ADDICTS

Keen to have his pro-Tibet message heard by the Chinese authorities, Bowie recorded a version of "Seven Years in Tibet" in Mandarin. Renamed "A Fleeting Moment," the song came out as a single only in Hong Kong in 1997. Fortunately for curious fans, it can also be found on the maxi single released in Europe the same year, with the title "Seven Years in Tibet (Mandarin Version)."

Single

DEAD MAN WALKING

David Bowie, Reeves Gabrels / 6:50

Musicians
David Bowie: lead and backing vocals, samples, electric guitar
Reeves Gabrels: electric guitar, electronic guitar, synthesizers, programming
Gail Ann Dorsey: lead and backing vocals, bass
Zachary Alford: drums, programming, samples, electronic percussion
Mike Garson: piano, synthesizer
Mark Plati: synthesizers, loops, programming, samples

Recorded
Looking Glass Studios: August and October 1996
Right Track Recording Studios (mixing): October–November 1996

Technical Team
Producers: David Bowie, Reeves Gabrels, Mark Plati
Sound Engineer: Mark Plati
Assistant Sound Engineers: Dante DeSole, Matt Curry
Mixing: Mark Plati

CD SINGLE VERSION (EUROPE)
1. *Dead Man Walking (Moby Mix 1)* / 7:31
2. *Dead Man Walking (Album Version)* / 6:50
3. *I'm Deranged (Jungle Mix)* / 7:00

Europe Release on Arista/BMG: April 14, 1997 (Maxi CD single ref.: 74321474802)
Best UK Chart Ranking: 32

> **ON YOUR HEADPHONES**
> Gail Ann Dorsey had not intended to sing on "Dead Man Walking." Recorded unawares by Mark Plati while warming up, she ended up being a backing singer for this track.

Genesis

The title of this song, with its techno rhythm calibrated to 138 bpm, was taken from the movie *Dead Man Walking*, directed by Tim Robbins and starring Susan Sarandon and Sean Penn. Bowie's initial idea was to write lyrics paying tribute to Sarandon, with whom gossips say he had a brief affair during the 1982 filming of *The Hunger* (1983). These plans were scrapped when, in October 1996, he took part in a charity concert given in aid of the Bridge School in Hillsborough, California—a school for children with speech and physical impairments. Bowie heard Neil Young give an acoustic performance accompanied by two musicians from his group Crazy Horse, and the alchemy between these two artists awakened unusual feelings of respect. He described the occasion "They would slowly dance in a tight tribal circle. It was so moving, so poignant, they seemed to evoke and bring to life all that their youthful dreams. [...] The song owes a considerable amount to that performance."[192] "Dead Man Walking," for which Floria Sigismondi directed the video, was issued as a single in the UK and as a maxi 45 rpm in the United States.

Production

While most of the tracks on *Earthling* come from fragments of songs sketched out at various times during the preceding year, "Dead Man Walking" came from Mark Plati's computer at the Looking Glass Studios. The only requirement Bowie gave him was to create a song with the most techno-sounding rhythm possible, like Underworld's "Born Slippy .NUXX." The process of creating the track followed the usual pattern: Plati made a drum loop, Gabrels experimented with his effects pedals, and then they recorded layer upon layer of synthesizer (much of which was later simplified during the mixing). At this point, Bowie intervened with his guitar in hand, contributing a riff given to him by Jimmy Page in 1965, when the future Led Zeppelin guitarist was a session musician for the Manish Boys. Already used in 1970 for "The Supermen" on *The Man Who Sold the World*, the six-chord gimmick fit perfectly into this new song's techno rhythm.

Nothing stops Neil Young and his group Crazy Horse (Frank Sampedro, Ralph Molina, and Billy Talbot), not even the passing of the years.

Single

TELLING LIES

David Bowie / 4:50

Album version: Musicians: David Bowie: lead and backing vocals, electric guitar, samples / **Reeves Gabrels:** electric guitar, electronic guitar, synthesizers, programming / **Gail Ann Dorsey:** bass / **Zachary Alford:** drums, programming, samples, electronic percussion / **Mike Garson:** piano, synthesizers / **Mark Plati:** synthesizers, loops, programming, samples / **Recorded:** Looking Glass Studios: August and October 1996 / **Right Track Recording Studios (mixing):** October–November 1996 / **Technical Team:** Producers: David Bowie, Reeves Gabrels, Mark Plati / **Sound Engineer:** Mark Plati / **Assistant Sound Engineers:** Dante DeSole, Matt Curry / **Mixing:** Mark Plati

Single version: Maxi CD single version (Europe): 1. *Telling Lies (Feelgood Mix)* / 5:07; 2. *Telling Lies (Paradox Mix)* / 5:10; 3. *Telling Lies (Adam F Mix)* / 3:58 / **Digital Release on davidbowie.com:** September 11, 1996 / **Europe Release on Arista/BMG:** November 4, 1996 (Maxi CD single ref.: 74321 39739 2) / **Best UK Chart Ranking:** 76

Musicians: David Bowie: lead and backing vocals, synthesizers / **Reeves Gabrels:** electric guitar, synthesizers / **Zachary Alford:** drums, programming, samples / **Mark Plati:** synthesizers, loops, programming, samples / **Recorded:** Looking Glass Studios: May 1996 / **Technical Team:** Producers: David Bowie, Reeves Gabrels, Mark Plati / **Remixes:** Mark Plati

"Telling Lies" was first worked on with Eno in 1994, then sketched out by Bowie at the Mountain Studios in Montreux at the beginning of 1996. This song marked the beginning of Bowie's collaboration with Mark Plati. Newly recruited, Plati took over the tapes and carried out a remix with the title "Feelgood Mix." He also roped in DJs A Guy Called Gerald and Adam F, who came up with the very jungle-style "Paradox Mix" and the more melodic "Adam F Mix." These three versions were made available to download from the davidbowie.com site on September 11, 1996, making "Telling Lies" one of the first songs in history to be sold online. In November 1996, BMG, via its Arista label, brought out these three remixes on a maxi single to make it more accessible to the ordinary fan. In point of fact, the downloadable version was a huge success, receiving more than ten thousand downloads a day, according to the press release for the forthcoming album, and more than three hundred thousand in total, according to the official Bowie website. These numbers encouraged Bowie to rerecord "Telling Lies" during the recording sessions for *Earthling*. This time, the song was given more of a rock-centric vibe.

THE LAST THING YOU SHOULD DO

David Bowie, Reeves Gabrels, Mark Plati / 4:58

Musicians: David Bowie: lead and backing vocals, electric guitar, samples / **Reeves Gabrels:** electric guitar, electronic guitar, synthesizers, programming / **Gail Ann Dorsey:** bass / **Zachary Alford:** drums, programming, samples, electronic percussion, tambourine / **Mike Garson:** synthesizer / **Mark Plati:** synthesizers, loops, programming, samples / **Recorded:** Looking Glass Studios: August and October 1996 / **Right Track Recording Studios (mixing):** October–November 1996 / **Technical Team:** Producers: David Bowie, Reeves Gabrels, Mark Plati / **Sound Engineer:** Mark Plati / **Assistant Sound Engineers:** Dante DeSole, Matt Curry / **Mixing:** Mark Plati

During the *Earthling* recording sessions, Bowie and Plati took time out from creating breakbeat patterns and harsh electric guitars to record some acoustic versions of old numbers, including "Baby Universal" and "I Can't Read," two tracks from the Tin Machine era. Struck by the emotional power of their new rendering of "I Can't Read," Mark Plati insisted that it should be included on the new album. Instead, Bowie chose a song that was to end up as the B-side of a later single: "The Last Thing You Should Do." "*Last Thing* fit in better conceptually. I think time has shown him to be correct,"[191] Mark Plati would later concede.

Although David Bowie was infatuated with drum 'n' bass and jungle styles during this period, only four numbers on *Earthling* fall into those categories. After "Little Wonder," "Battle for Britain (The Letter)," and "Telling Lies," it was on "The Last Thing You Should Do" that Zachary Alford was able to show off his skill in setting up these ingenious rhythmical patterns. Once the loop was incorporated into the sequencer of Mark Plati's Logic software, Alford recorded a new, live track, improvising at will and adding all kinds of rolls and breaks. The combination of the two inputs was highly effective, highlighting Bowie's desire to set human creativity alongside machine-generated sounds. As he explained: "What I really wanted to do was not so very dissimilar to what I did in the '70s—and something I've repeatedly done—which is to take the technological and combine it with the organic. It was very important to me that we didn't lose the feel of real musicianship working in conjunction with anything that was sampled or looped or worked out on the computer."[193]

Music House

UNIT F 36 John Grove, Holloway, London, N7
NT: 071 - TRUNGDOGG 463 349

Single

I'M AFRAID OF AMERICANS

David Bowie, Brian Eno / 5:00

ALBUM VERSION

Musicians

David Bowie: lead and backing vocals, samples
Reeves Gabrels: electric guitar, electronic guitar, synthesizers, programming
Gail Ann Dorsey: bass
Zachary Alford: drums, programming, samples, electronic percussion, tambourine
Mike Garson: piano, synthesizer
Mark Plati: synthesizers, loops, programming, samples

Recorded

Looking Glass Studios: August and October 1996
Right Track Recording Studios (mixing): October–November 1996

Technical Team

Producers: David Bowie, Reeves Gabrels, Mark Plati
Sound Engineer: Mark Plati
Assistant Sound Engineers: Dante DeSole, Matt Curry
Mixing: Mark Plati

SINGLE VERSION (REMIX)

Additional Musicians (remix)

Ice Cube: rap ("I'm Afraid of Americans" [V3] only)

Recorded (remix)

Nothing Studios, New Orleans: 1997

Technical Team (remix)

Producers: Trent Reznor, Charlie Clouser, Keith Hillebrandt, Dave Ogilvie, Danny Lohner
Sound Engineer: Brian Pollack
Additional Production: Photek ("I'm Afraid of Americans" [V5] only)
Mixing: Dave "Rave" Ogilvie

MAXI CD SINGLE VERSION (US)

1. *I'm Afraid of Americans (V1)* / 5:31
2. *I'm Afraid of Americans (V2)* / 5:31
3. *I'm Afraid of Americans (V3)* / 6:18
4. *I'm Afraid of Americans (V4)* / 5:25
5. *I'm Afraid of Americans (V5)* / 5:38
6. *I'm Afraid of Americans (V6)* / 11:18

US Release on Virgin: October 14, 1997 (Maxi CD single ref.: 7243 8 38618 2 8)
Best US Chart Ranking: 66

Genesis

During recording sessions for *1. Outside* that took place between January 11 and January 13, 1995, Brian Eno and David Bowie shut themselves up in the Hit Factory Studios in New York to work on a piece with the provisional title of "Dummy." Over the course of these three days, Bowie polished his lyrics, transforming them into a diatribe against the American cultural imperialism that he came up against each time he traveled there. "I'm Afraid of Americans," with its uncompromising title, was not kept for the album but made its appearance instead on the soundtrack of a new movie by Paul Verhoeven called *Showgirls.*

The song surfaced once again in the summer of 1996 while *Earthling* was being recorded. As so often happened with Bowie, the text of the song is obscure in parts, but interviews with the singer make it clear that he did not mind upsetting American sensibilities, saying: "I was sick of travelling the world and seeing a McDonald's everywhere I went. US culture can be so reductive."[1] Elsewhere, he clarified that "it's not as truly hostile about Americans as say [Bruce Springsteen's] 'Born In The USA': it's merely sardonic. I was traveling in Java when the first McDonald's went up: it was like, 'for fuck's sake.' The invasion by any homogenized culture is so depressing."[192]

Production

Almost as soon as this weighty, accusatory number was captured on tape, Bowie thought it would make a good single. Instead of simply using the album version, he handed the piece over to his friend Trent Reznor. The digital scissors wielded by Reznor and his colleagues produced five versions of the song. A sixth version was remixed by Photek, one of the godfathers of jungle and drum 'n' bass and famous for his highly successful remixes. On "V3" there is also a vocal contribution from the rapper Ice Cube, famous as a founding member of N.W.A., as well as for his successful solo career.

Despite its sharp composition and powerfully modern sound, when the maxi single was released on October 14, 1997, the title did not meet with a warm reception from the public. Columbia's 2004 reissue of *Earthling* in Digipak format includes the three main versions of this song: the original version plus the "Show Girls OST" and the "Nine Inch Nails V1 Mix."

Reeves Gabrels relaxing at the console at London's Looking Glass Studios in October 1999.

LAW (EARTHLINGS ON FIRE)

David Bowie, Reeves Gabrels / 4:48

Musicians: David Bowie: lead and backing vocals, samples / **Reeves Gabrels:** electric guitar, electronic guitar, synthesizers, programming / **Mark Plati:** synthesizers, loops, programming, samples / **Recorded:** Looking Glass Studios: August and October 1996 / Right Track Recording Studios (mixing): October–November 1996 / **Technical Team: Producers:** David Bowie, Reeves Gabrels, Mark Plati / **Sound Engineer:** Mark Plati / **Assistant Sound Engineers:** Dante DeSole, Matt Curry / **Mixing:** Mark Plati

The last track on the album is a techno anthem, and a perfect number for clubs in the winter of 1997. Based on a riff by Reeves Gabrels, "Law (Earthlings on Fire)" was the first song to be worked on in the August 1996 recording sessions. It starts out with a voice sample quoting the famous words from mathematician and philosopher Bertrand Russell: "What men really want is not knowledge, but certainty," an idea that appealed to David Bowie. Justifying the recurring use of this sample, he asserted: "To me, it's the avenue of insanity to presume that if you keep studying you'll find the answers."[47] The song, with its mixture of techno and electronic sounds and powerful guitar chords played with palm muting, makes a fine ending for the album. This strange alchemy, which combined two seemingly opposed worlds of sound, was to be exploited with great success by groups like Orgy, on their magnificent version of New Order's "Blue Monday" from 1998. Future exponents of the genre were similarly destined for fame, including the German group Rammstein and their July 1997 hit "Du Hast." It is worth noting that "Law (Earthlings on Fire)" is the only cut on the album for which Reeves Gabrels used an amplifier on his guitar. On all the other tracks, his famous Parker Fly is plugged into his Roland VG-8 guitar processor with its digital amp simulator connected to the console.

ON YOUR HEADPHONES

At 1:02 on "Law (Earthlings on Fire)," it sounds as if Bowie is singing into the receiver of an old-style telephone. To obtain this lo-fi sound (with no low sounds), he is in fact singing through an empty glass bottle with a mic inside it, specially rigged up by Mark Plati.

I CAN'T READ

David Bowie, Reeves Gabrels / 4:40

Musicians
David Bowie: lead and backing vocals
Reeves Gabrels: acoustic guitar
Gail Ann Dorsey: bass
Mark Plati: synthesizers, acoustic guitar

Recorded
Looking Glass Studios: Autumn 1996

Technical Team
Producers: David Bowie, Reeves Gabrels, Mark Plati
Sound Engineer: Mark Plati
Mixing: Mark Plati

CD SINGLE VERSION (EUROPE)
1. *I Can't Read (Short Version)* / 4:30
2. *I Can't Read (Long Version)* / 5:24
3. *This Is Not America (with Pat Metheny Group)* / 3:46

Europe Release on ZYX Music / Velvel: December 1, 1997 (Maxi CD single ref.: ZYX 8757-8)
Best UK Chart Ranking: 73

Genesis

During the *Earthling* sessions, Bowie decided to record acoustic versions of two Tin Machine songs, "I Can't Read" and "Baby Universal." "I guess he just wanted to try doing them again in this updated style to see what they'd be like,"[194] Mark Plati said later. Bowie had thought of including this reworking of "I Can't Read" on the album, but changed his mind in favor of "The Last Thing You Should Do," a number that was more in keeping with the general tone of the album.

Why was Bowie now tempted by acoustic music when he had until this point refused to take part in the *Unplugged* program made so popular by MTV? It seems clear that he was motivated by the success of many of the live recordings bearing the *MTV Unplugged* insignia, including Eric Clapton, Alice in Chains, and Bob Dylan, not to mention Nirvana and their cover of "The Man Who Sold the World." All of these releases did extremely well, with live albums debuting in the marketplace soon after each artist or group's appearance on the popular program. The idea was for artists to play their hits in pared-down versions, using only acoustic instruments. Bowie never appeared on the MTV program, but nevertheless he recorded his own unplugged versions of his songs. He released "I Can't Read" as a single on December 1, 1997, on the back of its use on the soundtrack of Ang Lee's movie *The Ice Storm*.

Production

With the single "I Can't Read" (later retitled "I Can't Read '97"), Bowie proved that he could do without rhythm boxes and furious guitars. Here, he returned to what had made him a star in the first place: well-written songs supported by stripped-down arrangements. His rendering of this underrated number is superb. Accompanied by Gabrels and Plati on acoustic guitars, the whole piece is bound together with something sounding like a Mellotron but created on a synthesizer in the studio and added during the overdubbing sessions, to which Bowie also added backing vocals. A few mistakes in the performance give the piece a feeling of welcome authenticity and make us regret all the more that a Bowie episode of *MTV Unplugged* was never produced.

DJ Goldie and his metal plated teeth in London circa 2001.

David Bowie and Gail Ann Dorsey

PLANET OF DREAMS

David Bowie, Gail Ann Dorsey / 4:37

Compilation *Long Live Tibet* / **UK Release on EMI:** June 23, 1997 (33 rpm ref.: EMC 3768 / CD ref.: 7243 8 33140 2 7) / **Did Not Chart**

Musicians: David Bowie: lead vocals, synthesizers / **Gail Ann Dorsey:** lead vocals, bass / **Reeves Gabrels :** electric guitar, acoustic guitar / **Zachary Alford:** drums / **Mike Garson:** piano / **Mark Plati:** synthesizers / **Recorded:** (?) / **Technical Team:** Producer: David Bowie / **Sound Engineer:** Mark Plati / **Mixing:** Mark Plati

Bowie's affection for the people of Tibet is well known; "Silly Boy Blue" and "Seven Years in Tibet" are examples of his ongoing interest in a country annexed by China in 1949. In 1997, when EMI decided to issue a compilation bringing together the cream of British pop music in aid of the Tibet House Trust, a British charity raising money for Tibet, David Bowie naturally agreed to be included. With Gail Ann Dorsey, he came up with this pop ballad that was set alongside previously unheard versions of hits by Blur, Radiohead, Pulp, and Björk. Bowie's song has a number of musical hints or quotes: at 2:50, Dorsey gives us the bass line from the Hendrix version of "Hey Joe"—previously used by Bowie in 1967 on "She's Got Medals"; the humming sounds at the end of this track are also reminiscent of Lou Reed's "Walk on the Wild Side"; and the chord sequences are not too far removed from those found in George Michael's "Freedom '90." Produced for a good cause, the artists involved in the compilation all agreed to donate their royalties to the Tibet House Trust.

Goldie featuring David Bowie

TRUTH

Goldie / 5:16

Goldie, *Saturnz Return* / Europe Release on FFRR Records: February 1, 1998 (CD ref.: 828990.2) / **US Release on FFRR Records:** February 1, 1998 (CD ref.: 422-828-983-2) / **Best UK Chart Ranking:** 15 / **Best US Chart Ranking:** 178

Musicians: David Bowie: lead vocals / Goldie: programming, synthesizers / Mark Sayfritz: programming / **Recorded:** Manic One Studio, London: 1997 / Jacobs Studios, Farnham: Spring 1997 / Trident Studios, London: Spring 1997 / **Technical Team:** Producer: Goldie / **Sound Engineer:** Will O'Donovan / **Arrangements:** Goldie

When the Metalheadz label organized its first evenings at the Blue Note Club in Hoxton Square, London, in the mid-1990s, the public seemed reluctant to turn out. The venue was tiny, but the atmosphere was extraordinary, and word soon spread that the extra effort was worth it. Among those present, Michael-Lee Bock, aka DJ Lee, remembered: "The DJ booth was so small. [...] The crowd was literally on you."[195] Storm, aka Jane Conneely, an influential DJ and important member of the Metalheadz team, agreed: "You could touch the DJ and you could stand right next to the MC."[195] These evenings soon became the place to be, and they were the vehicle for new artists, including Goldie. Basking in the success of his first work, *Timeless*, released in September 1995, Goldie was soon to become the king of British drum 'n' bass music.

It was at one of these "Metalheadz at Blue Note" evenings that Bowie, then deeply involved in jungle and drum 'n' bass, met Goldie. Goldie's work interested Bowie, and he soon began thinking about a collaboration. The DJ agreed without knowing exactly how they might work together. One morning, Goldie woke up and found a scribbled text by his side. His explanation followed: "I wrote it on a five-day drug binge, but I woke up with a beautiful piece of writing next to me. And he [Bowie] loved it. It was a beautiful record, macabre."[196] The collaboration was short-lived but productive. "Truth" was perfect for Goldie's second album, the legendary *Saturnz Return*, which was released in 1998.

American composer Angelo Badalamenti worked with David Bowie on the compilation *Red Hot + Rhapsody (The Gershwin Groove)*.

David Bowie and Angelo Badalamenti

A FOGGY DAY (IN LONDON TOWN) / SUITE FOR A FOGGY DAY

Ira Gershwin, George Gershwin, Angelo Badalamenti / 5:24

Compilation, *Red Hot + Rhapsody (The Gershwin Groove)* / Europe Release on Antilles/Polygram: October 6, 1998 (CD ref.: 557 815-2) / US Release on Antilles/Polygram: October 6, 1998 (33 rpm ref.: 314 557-788-1 / CD ref.: 314 557 788-2)

Musicians: David Bowie: lead singer / Al Regni: alto saxophone / Todd Coolman: double bass / Grady Tate: drums / John Campo: bassoon / Andre Badalamenti: clarinet / Angelo Badalamenti: keyboards / Steve Badalamenti: trumpet / Sherry Sylar: oboe / The String Orchestra at SoHo: strings / **Recorded:** National Edison Studios, New York: July 1998 / Excalibur Sound Productions, New York: July 1998 / **Technical Team:** Producer: Paul Heck / **Sound Engineers:** Artie Freeman, Art Pohelmis / **Assistant Sound Engineers:** Yvonne Yedbelian, Jim Murray / **Conductor:** Angelo Badalamenti / **Arrangements:** Angelo Badalamenti

Genesis

Established in 1989, the Red Hot Organization promoted cultural projects that raised money for research into AIDS. The "Red Hot" series of compilations, each one featuring artists grouped together by style of music, became hugely successful in the United States. *Red Hot + Dance* (1992) and *Red Hot + Country* (1994) were warmly received and when, in 1998, the idea of *Red Hot + Rhapsody* based around the music of George Gershwin was suggested, artists including Morcheeba, Sinéad O'Connor, and the Roots were quick to sign up. There was one unusual condition however: the contributions for this album all had to be duets. American composer Angelo Badalamenti, famous for the unforgettable theme he composed in 1990 for David Lynch's TV series *Twin Peaks*, was also one of the people invited to contribute to the disc. He settled on recording

his own version of "A Foggy Day (In London Town)", made famous by Fred Astaire in 1937's *A Damsel in Distress*.

Production

Once Badalamenti had done his part, the Antilles label, which handled the compilations, circulated the tape. David Bowie heard it and expressed an interest. The two men had already collaborated indirectly when Bowie made a cameo in the movie *Twin Peaks: Fire Walk with Me*, and his song "I'm Deranged" had been used the previous year in Lynch's mysterious neo-noir movie, *Lost Highway*, which included a soundtrack composed by Badalamenti.

So it made sense for Bowie to get the job, beating out U2 singer Bono in the process. According to Badalamenti, after he made his decision, Bono called him from Ireland and begged him to change his mind, saying: "Angelo, this is Bono. I'm in my limousine in Ireland doing my album and touring, so this track is the last thing I wanted to hear because it's so beautiful. Can you let me be the singer?"[197] Bowie's impressive performance makes this one more rarity for fans to discover and enjoy.

ALBUM

'HOURS...'

Thursday's Child . Something in the Air . Survive . If I'm Dreaming My Life . Seven .
What's Really Happening? . The Pretty Things Are Going to Hell . New Angels of Promise .
Brillant Adventure . The Dreamers

RELEASE DATES
Digital: September 21, 1999
Reference: davidbowie.com (download)
Europe: October 4, 1999
Reference: Virgin—7243 8 48157 2 1 (CD)
United States: October 4, 1999
Reference: Virgin—7243 8 48157 0 7 (CD)
Best UK Chart Ranking: 5
Best US Chart Ranking: 47

Bowie once again adapted to
his era, opting for elegance
over glitz on *'Hours…'*

THE POP RENAISSANCE

Between May and November 1997, the eighty-three dates of the *Earthling* tour enabled David Bowie to reconnect with a public that had an affection for his previous successes of the 1970s, which he had mostly neglected to perform in his preceding tour. Ten days before the end of this adventure, the charitable fund-raising single "Perfect Day '97" was released. It was a Lou Reed cover, in which Bowie was in the company of a myriad of stars, including Bono, Elton John, Suzanne Vega, and Shane MacGowan. The artist thus initiated a string of quality artistic collaborations involving the gold-plated backing vocalist services for Keith Moon, the fiery drummer with the Who, who also called upon Ringo Starr (drums), Klaus Voormann (bass), Ron Wood (guitar), Lee Ritenour (guitar), and Booker T. Jones (Hammond organ), with a view to making a subsequent solo album. This legendary session gave birth to three numbers: "Real Emotion," "Naked Man," and "Do Me Good," which, in the end, only appeared on a re-release of the drummer's first work, *Two Sides of the Moon*, released by BMG in 1997.

A Return to Simple, Effective Writing

In the spring of 1998, Bowie spent some months in Bermuda with Iman. They rented a prestigious residence called Sea View. That autumn, Reeves Gabrels joined them, equipped with an acoustic guitar and a basic eight-track tape recorder so they could work on some song ideas. Having explored industrial rock repertoire for *1. Outside*, and then drum 'n' bass and techno for *Earthling*, the singer wanted to go back to his roots and compose using some simple chords with the guitar and vocal melody, as he had done in 1971, when he was ensconced in Haddon Hall for the creation of his album *Hunky Dory*. This was done much to the annoyance of Gabrels, who swore by his heavily saturated guitar sounds, which were laced with effects of all kinds!

Omikron: The Nomad Soul: A Pixelized Bowie

A while after this fruitful writing session, David Bowie was called upon by the developer of the Quantic Dream video game. The video game creator David De Gruttola—alias David Cage—suggested that Bowie write a song for his forthcoming game, *Omikron: The Nomad Soul*. "We met in London at the offices of Eidos, producer of this game," recalled Cage. "The meeting was supposed to last thirty minutes, which turned into two and a half hours! In the end, he had decided to compose a complete album dedicated to the world of [*The Nomad Soul*]."[199] It should be said that the esoteric aspect of the game had all the ingredients required to win over David Bowie: in Omikron, a futuristic city subject to a totalitarian regime, the player's avatar—who can be reincarnated in the body of thirty different characters—must investigate murders perpetrated by a demon.

The singer spent a number of weeks in Paris in order to work with Cage on the project's development. He had such a good relationship with the studio that he, Iman, and Gabrels all agreed to appear in the game in the form of an avatar, to the enhanced enjoyment of the players. At certain points in *Omikron*, the player can attend concerts given by a clandestine group called the Dreamers, with Bowie, alias Boz, on vocals; Reeves Gabrels on guitar; and even a very approximate version of Gail Ann Dorsey shown as a pixelized dancer behind the singer. The fruits of a close collaboration between Quantic Dream and the musicians, these motion-capture film sequences piqued Bowie's interest in other digital technologies, which he in turn developed and launched his own website. In addition to recording some lyrics, in particular for the trailers of *The Nomad Soul*, Bowie worked on writing a series of songs for the game itself, which he ended up retaining for his new album. Some of these

FOR BOWIE ADDICTS

During their meeting with the singer in London, David Cage and the managers of Eidos Interactive presented him with one of the secrets to their game: the transmigration of souls from one character to another. While Iman agreed to allow a player to inhabit the character for which she served as a model, David refused to allow this for his own avatar. The team reassured him that he wouldn't be forced to do anything like that. Bowie later said: "[I told them,] 'Yes, you're absolutely correct.' I'm not lettin' anybody climb inside of me!"[200]

pieces did appear, however, in *Omikron: The Nomad Soul*, in remixed versions.

Introspection As the Common Thread

As was the case for *The Buddha of Suburbia* in 1993, Bowie was inspired by his work on *Omikron: The Nomad Soul* for the material in his new album. When he began the recording sessions, he also kept in mind his initial aim: to write simple and effective songs. The artist, who was in an introspective mood, declared that all he had been listening to for the past year was his own music. He wanted to reach an older listener, someone who was closer to his own generation, rather than the younger audiences whom he had tried to seduce with the *Outside* tour. From the winter of 1999 until May of the following year, David Bowie completed the recording of ten numbers of his future opus (as well as a number of outtakes), working in both London and New York. The use of the cut-up technique was less frequent on this album, giving way to a more literary narration that flirted with autobiography. The structure of the pieces was also more traditional, like those on *Hunky Dory*. Mark Plati, who joined the recording in New York in May 1999, assisted the singer in the production of an accessible pop album, which was far removed from the tormented *1. Outside* and *Earthling*.

BowieNet and the Digital Revolution

Launched on September 1, 1998, the davidbowie.com website (more commonly referred to as BowieNet) helped the singer form a direct link with the fans. In exchange for an annual subscription, users could download unreleased content and communicate with each other via a dedicated chat space, in which Bowie regularly appeared, although he was

often hidden behind a variety of pseudonyms. It was therefore unsurprising that his new album, 'Hours...', should appear as a download on the American version of the site. The album sleeve for this release features photography by Tim Bret-Day that shows Bowie with long hair, holding in his arms his double, from the *Earthling* period. The staging, inspired by Michelangelo's *Pietà*, is explicit in this context: Bowie is making way for a new version of himself.

In the handful of promotional concerts that were given for the album, the singer's objective to reconnect with his past is clear, as testified to by his interpretation of "Can't Help Thinking About Me" on the set of *VH1 Storytellers* on August 23, 1999. Mark Plati, inspired by this reworking of the single, also suggested to Bowie the idea of re-recording his classic sixties numbers with a more modern production. Collected on *Toy*, a disc that would never actually be released by Virgin, the songs "Baby Loves That Way," "I Dig Everything," "Silly Boy Blue," and "In the Heat of the Morning" are all given a new lease on life. This is an album that would warrant an official release some time in the future.

Singer Eartha Kitt was an object of fantasy and a source of inspiration for the young David Jones.

THURSDAY'S CHILD

David Bowie, Reeves Gabrels / 5:24

CD single version (Europe): 1. *Thursday's Child (Edit)* / 4:25; 2. *Thursday's Child (Rock Mix)* / 4:27; 3. *We Shall Go to Town* / 3:56; 4. *1917* / 3:27 / **Europe Release on Virgin:** September 20, 1999 (CD single ref.: 7243 8 96268 2 7) / **Best UK Chart Ranking:** 16

Musicians: David Bowie: lead and backing vocals, synthesizers, programming / **Reeves Gabrels:** electric guitar, synthesizers, programming / **Mark Plati:** bass, synthesizers, programming / **Mike Levesque:** drums / **Holly Palmer:** backing vocals / **Recorded:** Sea View, Bermuda: Autumn 1998 / The Instrument Studio / Mute Records, London: February 1999 / Looking Glass Studios, New York: April–May 1999 / Chung King Studios, New York: April–May 1999 / **Technical Team:** Producers: David Bowie, Reeves Gabrels / Remix: Marius de Vries / Sound Engineers: Mark Plati, Kevin Paul / Assistant Sound Engineers: Jay Nicholas, Ryoji Hata / Mixing: Mark Plati

On this track David Bowie pays homage to Eartha Kitt, who in 1956 gave an unforgettable performance of "Thursday's Child," the title song from the jazz singer's album and autobiography, which were both published in the same year. Bowie revealed this influence on the set of *VH1 Storytellers*

on August 23, 1999. "When I was about fourteen, Eartha Kitt and D. H. Lawrence was some of my favorite bedtime reading,"[201] the singer said with amusement, stressing that the sensual portrait of the singer on the cover was not entirely disconnected with his interest in the book. He did specify, however, that this song was not written for Kitt, even though the singer was one of the inspirations for *'Hours...'*.

Imbued with a certain melancholy, the number is surprising in its simplicity and its sincerity, and it reveals a Bowie who is at peace with himself, and wiser after years of experience as a performer. The presence of Holly Palmer, a young backing singer with a very pleasant voice, devoid of any harshness, is the result of long discussions during the New York sessions. Bowie wanted the three singers of TLC, an internationally successful R&B group, to provide the backing vocals. Reeves Gabrels, unmoved by the music of this trio, which had just produced *FanMail*, one of the greatest albums of this genre, was against the idea. So the idea occurred to Bowie to have the line "Monday, Tuesday..." sung by Mark Plati's daughter, Alice, who was six years old and had accompanied her father to the studio at that time. But the little girl flatly refused. So Palmer took the job, then joined Bowie's tour group in the following months.

SOMETHING IN THE AIR

David Bowie, Reeves Gabrels / 5:46

Musicians: David Bowie: lead and backing vocals, saxophone, synthesizers, programming / **Reeves Gabrels:** electric guitar, synth guitar, synthesizers, programming / **Mark Plati:** bass, synthesizers, programming / **Mike Levesque:** drums / **Recorded:** Sea View, Bermuda: Autumn 1998 / **The Instrument Studio / Mute Records, London:** February 1999 / **Looking Glass Studios, New York:** April–May 1999 / **Chung King Studios, New York:** April–May 1999 / **Technical Team:** Producers: David Bowie, Reeves Gabrels / **Additional Production:** Mark Plati / **Sound Engineers:** Mark Plati, Kevin Paul / **Assistant Sound Engineers:** Jay Nicholas, Ryoji Hata / **Mixing:** Mark Plati

On first hearing the infinite melancholy exuded from "Something in the Air," one may be convinced that David Bowie was experiencing an unhappy breakup, whereas, in reality, he was experiencing a passionate period with his wife, Iman: *"We lay in each other's arms / But the room is just an empty space."* "When I'm really happy, I don't want to hear happy albums, and when I'm really sad, I don't want to hear happy albums," he explained. "So for me personally, there's not much place in my life for them."[29] "Something in the Air," which the director Christopher Nolan chose for the end credits on his tortured film *Memento*, in 2000, presents a convincing argument for this. The song conceals a number of curiosities, including Bowie's synthesized voice, processed with the Ring Modulator filter by Mark Plati. Reeves Gabrels's guitar has a very surf music feel on the couplets and is reminiscent of the arpeggios carefully executed in "Needles on the Beach," a number rescued from the *Tin Machine II* sessions. There follows a refrain whose harmonic descent is evocative of the—mythical—equivalent in "Hotel California" by the Eagles, which appeared in 1977. Breaking the calm of the song in its finale, the guitar solo is a real success, both in its ingenious writing and in its energy, which contributes to the track's refined pop climax. This is an essential track that ranks among Bowie's finest ballads.

SURVIVE

David Bowie, Reeves Gabrels / 4:11

Album Version: Musicians: David Bowie: lead and backing vocals, saxophone, synthesizers, twelve-string acoustic guitar, programming / **Reeves Gabrels:** electric guitar, acoustic guitar, synthesizers, programming / **Mark Plati:** bass, synthesizers, programming, Mellotron / **Mike Levesque:** drums / **Recorded:** Sea View, Bermuda: Autumn 1998 / **The Instrument Studio / Mute Records, London:** February 1999 / **Looking Glass Studios, New York:** April–May 1999 / **Chung King Studios, New York:** April–May 1999 / **Technical Team (Album Version):** Producers: David Bowie, Reeves Gabrels / **Additional Production:** Mark Plati / **Sound Engineers:** Mark Plati, Kevin Paul / **Assistant Sound Engineers:** Jay Nicholas, Ryoji Hata / **Mixing:** Mark Plati

CD Single Version: 1. *Survive (Marius de Vries Mix)* / 4:18; 2. *Survive (Album Version)* / 4:11 / **Europe Release on Virgin:** January 24, 2000 (CD single ref: 7243 8 96486 21) / **Best UK Chart Ranking:** 28

Technical Team (Single Version): Producers: David Bowie, Reeves Gabrels / **Remix:** Marius de Vries / **Sound Engineer:** Marius de Vries / **Assistant Sound Engineer:** Chris James Ryan

The album that Bowie created in 1999 was indisputably very calm in tone, as is evidenced by this third ballad, which is not without a certain charm. Here, fans find the singer playing his two favorite instruments: the saxophone and a twelve-string acoustic guitar. Initially written by Reeves Gabrels for his second album, the work on this song was completed in Bermuda.

With a judicious balance between the electronic and the human—the trademark of the albums *Earthling* and *'Hours...'*—Mike Levesque provided the drums, completing the Roland TR-707 drum machine programming. In the spring of 1999, the drummer (who shared duties with Sterling Campbell on cymbal) had been hired for five days to record the drum parts in New York for these pieces, and he wrapped up the first five numbers in just a few hours. "I'm not gonna let you tell everyone you did my record in [a] day,"[163] Bowie told him at the time. "So, I'm like, 'OK, I can slow down now,'" recalls Levesque, "and after that it would be like one a day, very relaxed lunch break, dinner breaks."[163]

IF I'M DREAMING
MY LIFE

David Bowie, Reeves Gabrels / 7:04

Musicians: David Bowie: lead and backing vocals, synthesizers / **Reeves Gabrels:** electric guitar, synthesizers, programming / **Chris Haskett:** electric guitar / **Mark Plati:** bass, synthesizers, programming / **Mike Levesque:** drums / **Recorded:** Sea View, Bermuda: Autumn 1998 / The Instrument Studio / Mute Records, London: February 1999 / Looking Glass Studios, New York: April–May 1999 / Chung King Studios, New York: April–May 1999 / **Technical Team:** Producers: David Bowie, Reeves Gabrels / **Additional Production:** Mark Plati / **Sound Engineers:** Mark Plati, Kevin Paul / **Assistant Sound Engineers:** Jay Nicholas, Ryoji Hata / **Mixing:** Mark Plati

We find Bowie at his most romantic in "If I'm Dreaming My Life," which incorporates alternatingly slow and surging rock passages. *"Was she never there/here? / Was she ever? / Was it air she breathed?"* sings the artist, without doubt inspired by the melancholy of love. This number has the benefit of the presence of Chris Haskett, a guitarist from the Rollins Band. In 2018, the musician, a friend of Gabrels, recalled his involvement in the sessions: "They were finishing the *'Hours...'* record...and to be fair, if you have Reeves Gabrels in your band, you don't need another guitar player. But Reeves is a very nice person and he insisted that he wanted to [record] a track in a certain way, like having irregular pauses. [...] The ironic thing [is] that growing up, David Bowie was one of my heroes. And getting to hang out with him was like, an amazing time in my life. And the irony is that when I finally get to play with him—I played terribly! (laughs) Fortunately the engineer—Mark Plati, was able to help me to clean it up."[202]

SEVEN

David Bowie, Reeves Gabrels / 4:04

Album Version: Musicians: David Bowie: lead and backing vocals, saxophone, synthesizers, twelve-string acoustic guitar / **Reeves Gabrels:** electric guitar, synth guitar, synthesizers / **Mark Plati:** bass, synthesizers / **Sterling Campbell:** drums / **Everett Bradley:** shakers, tambourine, congas / **Recorded:** Sea View, Bermuda: Autumn 1998 / The Instrument Studio / Mute Records, London: February 1999 / Looking Glass Studios, New York: April–May 1999 / Chung King Studios, New York: April–May 1999 / **Technical Team:** Producers: David Bowie, Reeves Gabrels / **Additional Production:** Mark Plati / **Sound Engineers:** Mark Plati, Kevin Paul / **Assistant Sound Engineers:** Jay Nicholas, Ryoji Hata / **Mixing:** Mark Plati

Maxi CD single version (Europe): 1. *Seven (Marius de Vries Mix)* / 4:12; 2. *Seven (Remix by Beck)* / 3:44; 3. *Seven (Live)* / 4:04; 4. *Seven (Demo)* / 4:05; 5. *Seven (Album Version)* / 4:04 / **Europe Release on Virgin:** July 17, 2000 (Maxi CD single ref.: 7243 8 96931 0 2) / **Best UK Chart Ranking:** 32

Additional Musicians: Steve Balbi: backing vocals / **Technical Team:** Producers: David Bowie, Reeves Gabrels / **Remix:** Marius de Vries

In 1999, the open conflict between the members of Oasis and Blur was no longer of any relevance. Oasis had not released an album of note for some time, and Blur had released a string of unforgettable discs that demonstrated limitless creativity and a capacity for reinventing themselves year after year. "When we used to argue about who was better, Oasis or Blur, there wasn't much argument; David and I both came up on the Blur side,"[63] recalled Reeves Gabrels. It was no coincidence that this "Seven" track has an element about it of "Coffee & TV," a successful single from *13*, Blur's sixth album, which was released in March 1999. The first version of the number was provided with a drum track from the start, like "Coffee & TV." But Bowie asked Mark Plati to try out the song without Sterling Campbell's track and opted to retain this version, where the drums come in only at the end of the piece.

When asked by David Quantick of *Q* magazine about the lyrics *"I got seven days to live my life / Or seven ways to die,"* and, more generally about this song with its slightly maudlin overtones, Bowie said: "Seven days to live, seven ways to die...I'd actually reduce that further to twenty-four hours to live. I'm very happy to deal and only deal with the existing twenty-four hours I'm going through. I'm not inclined to even think too heavily about the end of the week. [...] The present is really the place to be."[112]

Reeves Gabrels and David Bowie on either side of Alex Grant, the lucky winner of the "Cyber Song Contest," whose vocals were recorded on May 24, 1999, at Looking Glass Studios.

WHAT'S REALLY HAPPENING?

David Bowie, Reeves Gabrels, Alex Grant / 4:10

Musicians: David Bowie: lead and backing vocals, synthesizers, programming / **Reeves Gabrels:** electric guitar, synth guitar, synthesizers, programming / **Mark Plati:** bass, synthesizers, programming / **Mike Levesque:** drums / **Alex Grant:** backing vocals / **Larry Tressler:** backing vocals / **Recorded: Sea View, Bermuda:** Autumn 1998 / **The Instrument Studio / Mute Records, London:** February 1999 / **Looking Glass Studios, New York:** April–May 1999 / **Chung King Studios, New York:** April–May 1999 / **Technical Team: Producers:** David Bowie, Reeves Gabrels / **Additional Production:** Mark Plati / **Sound Engineers:** Mark Plati, Kevin Paul / **Assistant Sound Engineers:** Jay Nicholas, Ryoji Hata / **Mixing:** Mark Plati

On October 8, 1998, David Bowie announced the launch of a competition called "Cybersong Contest." Regardless of nationality, budding writers could submit lyrics consisting of three couplets for "What's Really Happening?" The winner would be chosen by David Bowie in person, from a preselection performed by the subscribers to Bowie's own website. The prize: a $15,000 publishing contract with Bug Music, a trip to New York to attend the recording of the number's vocal track, and a three-year subscription to the magazine *Rolling Stone*, which partnered in the operation, and a gift voucher for $500. The competition was a success, with more than eighty thousand entries submitted to BowieNet from November 2, 1998. The winner, Alex Grant, was named on January 20, 1999. The young American was invited to take part in the recording, which was broadcast in full on the singer's site, and took place on May 24, 1999, at the Looking Glass Studios. Grant and his friend Larry Tressler, who came with him that day, recorded the backing vocals for the number, and they were treated to an exceptional experience. The song, with its melody reminiscent of "You Keep Me Hangin' On" by the Supremes, fit perfectly in Bowie's repertoire. This adventure was a testimony to the singer's interest in the internet, which was still in its early days. Reeves Gabrels, the co-composer of "What's Really Happening?" sold his second album, *Ulysses (Della Notte)*, exclusively as a digital version on his own website. This digital release was a small revolution in the music world, which, three years later, was in major crisis due to the onset of illegal downloading. As for Alex Grant, he disappeared off the radar after his moment of glory.

THE PRETTY THINGS ARE GOING TO HELL

David Bowie, Reeves Gabrels / 4:40

Musicians: David Bowie: lead and backing vocals, synthesizers / **Reeves Gabrels:** electric guitar, synth guitar, synthesizers / **Mark Plati:** bass, synthesizers / **Mike Levesque:** drums, tambourine, cowbell / **Recorded:** Sea View, Bermuda: Autumn 1998 / The Instrument Studio / Mute Records, London: February 1999 / **Looking Glass Studios, New York:** April–May 1999 / **Chung King Studios, New York:** April–May 1999 / **Technical Team:** Producers: David Bowie, Reeves Gabrels / **Additional Production:** Mark Plati / **Sound Engineers:** Mark Plati, Kevin Paul / **Assistant Sound Engineers:** Jay Nicholas, Ryoji Hata / **Mixing:** Mark Plati

Originally intended for a future Reeves Gabrels album, this very rock-sounding piece is driven by Mike Levesque, who is in top form. "The drums [...] were anything but simple," explained Mark Plati. "Mike Levesque had been reading a biography of Keith Moon around this time, so I think he saw an opening to rise to the occasion. I think he's the instrumental star of that track."[29] The number makes reference to the Pretty Things, a group to which Bowie had paid homage in *Pin Ups* by covering "Rosalyn" and "Don't Bring Me Down." "Oh! You Pretty Things," the second track on *Hunky Dory*, also comes to mind. Another inspiration may have been "Your Pretty Face Is Going to Hell" by Iggy and the Stooges, from the album *Raw Power*, whose mixing was done by Iggy Pop and...David Bowie!

After being lightly remixed, "The Pretty Things Are Going to Hell" appeared in the film *Stigmata* (1999), directed by Rupert Wainwright.

While Mike Levesque was looking for the ideal drum motif to conclude "The Pretty Things Are Going to Hell," Reeves Gabrels asked him to use "We're an American Band" by Grand Funk Railroad as a reference. The introductory roll on the song inspired Levesque, who reproduced it at the end of his own track, at the same time borrowing the idea of the staccato cowbell rhythm from Grand Funk drummer Don Brewer.

NEW ANGELS OF PROMISE

David Bowie, Reeves Gabrels / 4:35

Musicians: David Bowie: lead and backing vocals, synthesizers / **Reeves Gabrels:** electric guitar, synth guitar, synthesizers / **Mark Plati:** bass, synthesizers / **Sterling Campbell:** drums / **Recorded:** Sea View, Bermuda: Autumn 1998 / The Instrument Studio / Mute Records, London: February 1999 / **Looking Glass Studios, New York:** April–May 1999 / **Chung King Studios, New York:** April–May 1999 / **Technical Team:** Producers: David Bowie, Reeves Gabrels / **Additional Production:** Mark Plati / **Sound Engineers:** Mark Plati, Kevin Paul / **Assistant Sound Engineers:** Jay Nicholas, Ryoji Hata / **Mixing:** Mark Plati

While finalizing the *Omikron: The Nomad Soul* game, David Cage and the Quantic Dreams team wondered about the introduction music. "New Angels of Promise" was chosen to be played just after the instrumental theme created by composer Xavier Despas, who composed the sound design for the game as well as the additional soundtrack. With its lyrics reminding players that they would encounter souls seeking a new body to inhabit during gameplay, this David Bowie song was a good choice. *"New angels of promise / We despair / We are the dead dreams / We take the blame,"* sings Bowie, sending us back to the tortured world of *1. Outside* and *Diamond Dogs* with this dark and powerful number.

BRILLIANT ADVENTURE

David Bowie, Reeves Gabrels / 1:54

Musicians: David Bowie: synthesizers, programming / **Reeves Gabrels:** synth guitar, synthesizers, programming / **Mark Plati:** synthesizers, programming / **Recorded:** Sea View, Bermuda: Autumn 1998 / The Instrument Studio / Mute Records, London: February 1999 / **Looking Glass Studios, New York:** April–May 1999 / **Chung King Studios, New York:** April–May 1999 / **Technical Team:** Producers: David Bowie, Reeves Gabrels / **Additional Production:** Mark Plati / **Sound Engineers:** Mark Plati, Kevin Paul / **Assistant Sound Engineers:** Jay Nicholas, Ryoji Hata / **Mixing:** Mark Plati

For this short interlude, which is perfectly suited to the visual world of *Omikron: The Nomad Soul*, David Bowie reconnects with the Japanese-influenced sonorities of "Moss Garden," from 1977's *"Heroes."* The use of the koto, which in this case is simulated using a synthesizer, transports us to the peaceful gardens of Tokyo. This fleeting track has little cohesion with rest of the album and is ultimately pretty dispensable.

David Cage, the visionary director of the Paris computer game studio Quantic Dream.

A pixelized David Bowie appears in one of the trailers for *Omikron: The Nomad Soul*.

THE DREAMERS

David Bowie, Reeves Gabrels / 5:14

Musicians: David Bowie: lead and backing vocals, synthesizers, programming / **Reeves Gabrels:** electric guitar, synth guitar, synthesizers, programming / **Mark Plati:** bass, synthesizers, programming / **Sterling Campbell:** drums / **Recorded:** Sea View, Bermuda: Autumn 1998 / The Instrument Studio / Mute Records, London: February 1999 / Looking Glass Studios, New York: April–May 1999 / Chung King Studios, New York: April–May 1999 / **Technical Team:** Producers: David Bowie, Reeves Gabrels / **Additional Production:** Mark Plati / **Sound Engineers:** Mark Plati, Kevin Paul / **Assistant Sound Engineers:** Jay Nicholas, Ryoji Hata / **Mixing:** Mark Plati

In the game *Omikron: The Nomad Soul*, David Bowie and Reeves Gabrels appeared as the singer and guitarist in the rock group the Dreamers, accompanied by a dancer resembling Gail Ann Dorsey. For the best gamers, being able to access one of the group's three concerts was a real prize. During the concerts, players could see Bowie and Gabrels performing "Something in the Air," "The Pretty Things Are Going to Hell," and "Survive." "What I am proudest of, are the virtual concerts in *The Nomad Soul*, the places in the city where the player could come, at a given time, to attend a concert by Bowie's underground band," said David Cage. "The animations were recorded in motion capture, and everything was filmed using a tool that we had developed to place the cameras and create the montage."[203] The guitar in "The Dreamers" is discreet, as is also the case on the whole album, whereas it was very much in evidence on *Earthling*. Reeves Gabrels later provided the explanation for this: "Because the album was taking a decidedly more introspective turn, it meant that I needed to approach the guitar-playing in a different way in order to wrap around the vocals. [...] As co-writer and co-producer I had to be extra careful that the guitar player in me was responding to the lyric content of the song."[29]

"The Dreamers" was intended to be the title of the album until Gabrels asked Bowie if his inspiration came from Freddie and the Dreamers, the British pop group famous for their singer, who performed wacky antics onstage.

FUN

David Bowie / 3:13

Musicians: David Bowie: vocals, synthesizers, saxophone / **Reeves Gabrels:** electric guitar, programming / **Gail Ann Dorsey:** bass, backing vocals / **Zachary Alford:** drums, programming, samples / **Mark Plati:** programming / **Recorded:** Looking Glass Studios: January 1998 / **Technical Team:** Producers: David Bowie, Reeves Gabrels, Mark Plati / Sound Engineer: Mark Plati

At the beginning of 1998, David Bowie and his guitarist Reeves Gabrels wanted to have some record of the *Earthling* tour. Many of the concerts were recorded with a view to creating a live album, which the singer hoped to have released with Virgin, but the record company backed out of this project, and only one new title, "Fun" (Gabrels often referred to it as "Funhouse" in interviews), appeared in 1998 on a CD-ROM accessible only to members of BowieNet. In 2000, these internet fans were able to acquire a copy of the album *LiveAndWell.com*, derived from the live editing sessions in 1998, in which "Fun" (Dillinja Mix) appeared. This version, remixed with its drum 'n' bass sound by Danny Saber, appeared on the EP *Is It Any Wonder?* released on March 20, 2020.

1917

David Bowie, Reeves Gabrels / 3:29

Musicians: David Bowie: vocals, synthesizers, programming / **Reeves Gabrels:** electric guitar, synth guitar, synthesizers, programming / **Mark Plati:** bass, synthesizers, programming / **Sterling Campbell (?), Mike Levesque (?):** drums / **Recorded:** Sea View, Bermuda: Autumn 1998 / The Instrument Studio / Mute Records, London: February 1999 / Looking Glass Studios, New York: April–May 1999 / Chung King Studios, New York: April–May 1999 / **Technical Team:** Producers: David Bowie, Reeves Gabrels / **Additional Production:** Mark Plati / **Sound Engineers:** Mark Plati, Kevin Paul / **Assistant Sound Engineers:** Jay Nicholas, Ryoji Hata / **Mixing:** Mark Plati

David Bowie pays heartfelt homage to Jimmy Page in this number, which combines furious playing on synth guitar by Gabrels, ultra-saturated and totally incomprehensible vocals, and synthesizer notes straight out of the early 1990s. Reeves Gabrels described this song best, as "a sort of psychotic update of the riff from Led Zeppelin's 'Kashmir.' [It] was one of the best things under the Bowie name from the 1990s, but its lack of conventionality saw it released as a 'B' side only."[29] In fact the number appeared on the maxi CD single of "Thursday's Child," released on September 20, 1999, and on the Columbia limited-edition reissue of *'Hours...'* in 2004.

WE SHALL GO TO TOWN

David Bowie, Reeves Gabrels / 3:56

Musicians: David Bowie: lead and backing vocals, saxophone, synthesizers / **Reeves Gabrels:** electric guitar, acoustic guitar, synth guitar, synthesizers / **Mark Plati:** bass, synthesizers / **Sterling Campbell (?), Mike Levesque (?):** drums / **Recorded:** Sea View, Bermuda: Autumn 1998 / The Instrument Studio / Mute Records, London: February 1999 / Looking Glass Studios, New York: April–May 1999 / Chung King Studios, New York: April–May 1999 / **Technical Team:** Producers: David Bowie, Reeves Gabrels / **Additional Production:** Mark Plati / **Sound Engineers:** Mark Plati, Kevin Paul / **Assistant Sound Engineers:** Jay Nicholas, Ryoji Hata / **Mixing:** Mark Plati

Although one might be convinced that it is Sterling Campbell playing drums on this track, it is impossible to be sure that it is him. In fact, on the four outtakes drip-fed to the fans via various singles or maxi singles released, the credits never clarify this detail.

"We Shall Go to Town" would not have been out of place in *'Hours...'* Delicate and meticulously executed, its production reminds many listeners of Bowie's interest in trip-hop, a form of music viewed by many as being conducive to spiritual journeys.

FOR BOWIE ADDICTS

Presented as a new track under the incorrect title "We Shall All Go to Town," the song was included on the maxi CD single of "Thursday's Child," which was released on Virgin on September 20, 1999.

WE ALL GO THROUGH

David Bowie, Reeves Gabrels / 4:11

Musicians: David Bowie: lead and backing vocals, synthesizers, twelve-string acoustic guitar / **Reeves Gabrels:** electric guitar, acoustic guitar, synth guitar, synthesizers / **Mark Plati:** bass, synthesizers / **Sterling Campbell (?), Mike Levesque (?):** drums / **Recorded:** Sea View, Bermuda: Autumn 1998 / The Instrument Studio / Mute Records, London: February 1999 / Looking Glass Studios, New York: April–May 1999 / Chung King Studios, New York: April–May 1999 / **Technical Team:** Producers: David Bowie, Reeves Gabrels / **Additional Production:** Mark Plati / **Sound Engineers:** Mark Plati, Kevin Paul / **Assistant Sound Engineers:** Jay Nicholas, Ryoji Hata / **Mixing:** Mark Plati

Included in the Japanese version of *'Hours...'*, "We All Go Through" also appears in *Omikron: The Nomad Soul*. In this number, originally written by Gabrels for his album *Ulysses (Della Notte)*, Bowie handles the backing vocals elegantly, harmonized in the manner of a Lennon-McCartney duet from the "Strawberry Fields Forever" period. It should be stressed that there is a little nod in the direction of the vocal line of "Billy Jack Bitch" from Prince (1995), which we find played identically in Mark Plati's bass line, from 2:55 through to the end of the piece.

NO ONE CALLS

David Bowie, Reeves Gabrels / 3:50

Musicians: David Bowie: lead and backing vocals, synthesizers, programming / **Reeves Gabrels:** electric guitar, synth guitar, synthesizers, programming / **Mark Plati:** bass, synthesizers, programming / **Recorded:** Sea View, Bermuda: Autumn 1998 / The Instrument Studio / Mute Records, London: February 1999 / Looking Glass Studios, New York: April–May 1999 / Chung King Studios, New York: April–May 1999 / **Technical Team:** Producers: David Bowie, Reeves Gabrels / **Additional Production:** Mark Plati / **Sound Engineers:** Mark Plati, Kevin Paul / **Assistant Sound Engineers:** Jay Nicholas, Ryoji Hata / **Mixing:** Mark Plati

When *'Hours...'* went on sale as a download on BowieNet on September 21, 1999, the most loyal fans were rewarded for their purchase with a bonus track: "No One Calls." Once again flirting with the trip-hop sonorities of "Angel" (1998) by Massive Attack, "Mysterons" (1994) by Portishead, and "Nothing Else" (1996) by Archive, Bowie pays homage to this popular style to which he felt uniquely drawn. A real success, whose instrumental score is not unlike "Thirteen O'Clock" by Trevor Jones on the original soundtrack of the 1986 Jim Henson film, *Labyrinth*...featuring David Bowie.

Placebo in their golden era, before the 2007 departure of drummer Steve Hewitt. Left to right: Stefan Olsdal, Brian Molko, and Steve Hewitt.

On January 12, 2016, Placebo released a video filmed by Stefan Olsdal on their YouTube page. In the video, viewers see Molko and Bowie rehearsing "Without You I'm Nothing" one last time before going onstage at Irving Plaza in New York.

Single

Placebo featuring David Bowie

WITHOUT YOU I'M NOTHING

Placebo / 4:15

Placebo, "Without You I'm Nothing" (single) / Europe Release on Hut Recordings / Elevator Music / Virgin: August 16, 1999 (CD single ref.: FLOORCDE10; 7243 8 96260 2 5) / **Best UK Chart Ranking:** Did Not Chart

Musicians: Brian Molko: electric guitar, vocals / **David Bowie:** vocals / Stefan Olsdal: bass / Steve Hewitt: drums / **Recorded:** Real World Studios, Box (original): 1998 / Whitfield Street Studios, London (original): 1998 / Chung King Studios, New York (David Bowie vocals): March 29, 1999 / **Technical Team:** Producer: Steve Osborne / Sound Engineers: Adrian Bushby, Tony Visconti (voice of David Bowie)

Following a self-titled album that appeared in June 1996, the trio Placebo was a hit across Europe. Their spirited and pared-down sound, influenced among others by the tortured songs of the Pixies, was a little revolution in and of itself, and their singer, the very glam Brian Molko, excelled in both his songwriting and his stage presence. The task of recording a second album is always a difficult one, but in

October 1996 Placebo picked up this challenge with unerringly sound judgment, producing their irresistible masterpiece *Without You I'm Nothing*, which included hits like "Every You Every Me," "Pure Morning," "You Don't Care About Us," "Burger Queen," and the somber "Without You I'm Nothing." David Bowie had already been won over by the charm of these melancholic songs a year earlier, when the Smith's lead singer, Morrissey, sent him a demo from the band. The star offered Molko's group the opportunity to open for him in a number of the concerts on the *Outside* tour, the *Earthling* tour, and the *Heathen* tour. "He took us under his wing, and we became one of his favourite support bands,"[1] the leader of the combo proudly declared.

Following the release of Placebo's second album, David Bowie suggested to their leader that they rerecord "Without You I'm Nothing," one of the group's rare love songs at that time. This was what happened on March 29, 1999. That very evening, Bowie joined Placebo onstage at the Irving Plaza in New York to perform the song, as well as performing "20th Century Boy" by T. Rex, which the trio had just covered for the original soundtrack of the film *Velvet Goldmine*. The 1998 film, directed by Todd Haynes, was largely inspired by the life of David Bowie. The connections had come full circle.

Ping-Pong and skateboarding are key references for the musicians of the Rustic Overtones.

Reeves Gabrels featuring David Bowie, Frank Black, and Dave Grohl

JEWEL

David Bowie, Frank Black, Mark Plati, Reeves Gabrels / 5:01

Reeves Gabrels, Ulysses (Della Notte) / Digital Release on www.reevesgabrels.com: November 4, 1999

Musicians: David Bowie: vocals / Frank Black: vocals, electric guitar / Reeves Gabrels: electric guitar / Dave Grohl: vocals, drums / **Mark Plati:** bass / **Recorded:** Musegarden Recording, New York: 1999 / **Technical Team:** Producer: Reeves Gabrels / **Sound Engineer:** Mark Plati / **Mixing:** Mark Plati

For his fiftieth birthday on January 9, 1997, David Bowie invited a large number of rock stars to come and sing with him onstage at Madison Square Garden. Among them were Frank Black, leader of the Pixies, and Dave Grohl, drummer and singer with the Foo Fighters. With his characteristic humor, Grohl expressed his admiration for the English singer: "His first live album, *David Live*, was on regular rotation in my living room when I was a kid, and his classic track 'Suffragette City' was quite a hit at the backyard parties I played with my nerdy high school band in the early '80s."[204] In 1999, for his second album, *Ulysses (Della Notte)*, Reeves Gabrels decided to bring together Black, Grohl, and Bowie in the studio to record a sensational number, "Jewel," in which the former Nirvana drummer and his powerful voice are instantly recognizable. The album was offered on Gabrels's website before being given a CD release in 2000 on the E-Magine Entertainment label.

Rustic Overtones featuring David Bowie

SECTOR Z

Dave Gutter / 4:16

Rustic Overtones, ¡Viva Nueva! / Europe and US Release on Tommy Boy: June 5, 2001 (CD ref.: TBCD 1471) /

Musicians: David Bowie: lead and backing vocals / Dave Gutter: vocals, electric guitar / Spencer Albee: vocals, synthesizers / Tony McNaboe: drums / Jon Roods: bass / Ryan Zoidis, Jason Ward: saxophone / Scott Pederson: trumpet / **Recorded:** Avatar Studios, New York: May 1999 / Looking Glass Studios, New York: July 1999 / **Technical Team:** Producers: Tony Visconti, David Leonard, Rustic Overtones / **Sound Engineers:** Tony Visconti, David Leonard, Steve Drown, Roger Sommers, Jim Begley / **Assistant Sound Engineers:** Chris Mazer, Ryoji Hata, Alex Chan

At the end of this millennium, groups combining ska, punk rock (called "roller punk" at the time because of its exaltation of the skateboard), and sugar-coated pop, were all the rage. Save Ferris, Reel Big Fish, Smash Mouth, and Sugar Ray were the new, fashionable rock bands. One of these bands, Rustic Overtones, stands out with its judicious mix of hip-hop and Latin-infused sounds. Seduced by this band, in 1999 Tony Visconti agreed to produce a handful of songs for their album *¡Viva Nueva!*. It was right in the middle of the production of the number "Man without a Mouth," at Avatar Studios in New York, that the producer suggested a collaboration that would be impossible to refuse: a duet with David Bowie. Dave Gutter and his friends hastened to compose a new number, "Sector Z," on which Bowie would sing from start to finish. On the same occasion, he laid down some backing vocals for "Man without a Mouth." Listeners had to wait two years before the appearance of the album by this group from Maine. The news was relayed on BowieNet on May 23, 2001, with the title "Familiar Voice on Rustic Overtones Album."[205]

"Nature Boy," a jazz standard revisited by David Bowie and Massive Attack, was used as the opening song of the 2001 Baz Luhrmann musical *Moulin Rouge*.

David Bowie and Massive Attack

NATURE BOY

eden ahbez / 4:08

Compilation, Moulin Rouge (Music from Baz Luhrmann's Film) / Europe Release on Interscope Records / Bazmark / Fox Music: May 8, 2001 (CD ref.: 490 507-2) / **US Release on Interscope Records / Bazmark / Fox Music:** May 8, 2001 (CD ref.: 06949 3035 2) / **Best UK Chart Ranking:** Did Not Chart / **Best US Chart Ranking:** 3

Musicians: David Bowie: vocals / **Robert Del Naja, Neil Davidge:** synthesizers, programming / **Unidentified Musicians:** strings / **Nicole Kidman:** spoken word / **Recorded:** Unknown Studio, Bristol (music): 2001 / Unknown Studio, New York (vocals): 2001 / **Technical Team: Producers:** Robert Del Naja, Neil Davidge, Tony Visconti / **Sound Engineers:** Lee Shephard, Tony Visconti / **String Arrangements:** Craig Armstrong

David Bowie and the members of Massive Attack met in 1995. Although some kind of collaboration between the singer and the godparents of trip-hop seemed obvious, what was needed was an opportunity to bring them together. During the filming of Baz Luhrmann's new film, *Moulin Rouge*, which started production in 2000, a plan was put in place for the creation of a modern and offbeat soundtrack. The idea was to combine fashionable artists with covers of traditional variety, jazz, and pop numbers. While Christina Aguilera, Lil' Kim, Mýa, and Pink updated "Lady Marmalade" by LaBelle, Rufus Wainwright offered a splendid version of "La Complainte de la Butte" by Jean Renoir and Georges van Parys. Luhrmann, an immense fan of Bowie, inserted numerous references to his idol in his film. Here and there we hear extracts from *Diamond Dogs* and *"Heroes."* "All of *Moulin Rouge* was truly influenced by Bowie and his creative sensibility,"[1] said the Australian director. The two men met at the Four Seasons hotel in Los Angeles to launch a collaboration on the film's original soundtrack. "Nature Boy," a track written in 1947 by eden ahbez, a hippie known for camping out under one of the *L*s in the "Hollywood" sign that dominates the City of Angels, was chosen. Popularized by Nat King Cole in 1948, the song was a standard of American vocal jazz, and Bowie willingly agreed to perform it. For the version that appeared on the soundtrack, arrangements were made by Robert Del Naja, now the only master of the Massive Attack ship, and supported by the group's producer, Neil Davidge.

PICTURES OF LILY

Pete Townshend / 4:59

Compilation Substitute—The Songs of the Who / Europe Release on Edel Records: June 4, 2001 (CD ref.: 0126242ERE) / **US Release on Edel Records:** June 4, 2001 (CD ref.: ED183022) /

Musicians: David Bowie: lead and backing vocals, Dubreq Stylophone / **Mark Plati:** electric guitar, bass, backing vocals / **Sterling Campbell:** drums, tambourine, backing vocals / **Recorded:** Looking Glass Studios, New York: October 2000 / **Technical Team: Producer:** David Bowie, Mark Plati / **Sound Engineer:** Mark Plati / **Assistant Sound Engineer:** Hector Castillo

Bowie, Plati, and Campbell only needed a few hours to create this version of "Pictures of Lily," a single by the Who that appeared in April 1967, and which narrates the imaginings of a young man standing in front of a photograph of a young woman. What was the occasion for this cover? An album in homage to Pete Townshend's group that was produced by Bob Pridden, and featured Sheryl Crow, Pearl Jam, and Paul Weller. "We did the entire thing in an afternoon, complete with Stylophone solo, Ronson homage outro and football hooligan chanting courtesy of the three of us," said Mark Plati.[206] The result, which was tailored to appeal to stadiums full of people, was a successful homage to this group, many of whose numbers Bowie had also covered in the past.

NICOLE KIDMAN
EWAN McGREGOR
MOULIN ROUGE
TRUTH · BEAUTY
MOULIN ROUGE!
FREEDOM · LOVE

Toy

1. Uncle Floyd*
2. Afraid*
3. Baby Loves That Way**
4. I Dig Everything
5. Conversation Piece**
6. Let Me Sleep Beside You**
7. Toy (Your Turn to Drive)**
8. Hole in the Ground**
9. Shadow Man**
10. In the Heat of the Morning
11. You've Got a Habit of Leaving**
12. Silly Boy Blue
13. Liza Jane
14. The London Boys**

* These numbers are described in the section on the *Heathen* album.

** Only these tracks are described here. They have all appeared on singles or albums, with the exception of "Hole in the Ground," which is an unreleased track.

THE PHANTOM ALBUM

Between June and October of 2000, and under the impetus of Mark Plati, David Bowie recorded *Toy*, an album that combined new versions of some of his songs from the 1960s. The production of the album was a rejuvenation of sorts for the fifty-year-old, who was delighted to revisit the first singles of Davy Jones ("Baby Loves That Way") and Davie Jones & the King Bees ("Liza Jane"), as well as B-sides that had gone unnoticed at the time ("The London Boys"). This ambitious project seduced the fans and enabled Bowie to work with some new musicians, including multi-instrumentalist Lisa Germano, guitarist Gerry Leonard, and trumpet player Cuong Vu. The release of the album was planned for March 2001, but Virgin was increasingly skeptical of its commercial potential, and they finally opted to defer the album's release indefinitely. This decision caused Bowie's departure from the label. The singer set up his own label, ISO Records, in June 2001. He also called upon the services of Columbia for the international distribution of his catalogue, of which he now assumed sole control. Even though it had been leaked in its entirety on the internet in 2011, to this day *Toy* has never had an official release, much to the disappointment of fans everywhere, who dreamed of a worthy issue of this phantom album. Bowie on the other hand, did release some of these numbers in various formats over the years.

BABY LOVES THAT WAY

Davie Jones / 4:41

Musicians: David Bowie: lead and backing vocals / **Mark Plati:** acoustic guitar / **Earl Slick, Gerry Leonard (?):** electric guitar / **Gail Ann Dorsey:** bass / **Sterling Campbell:** drums / **Mike Garson:** piano / **Emm Gryner, Holly Palmer:** backing vocals / **Lisa Germano:** violin / **Recorded:** Sear Sound Studios, New York: July 2000 / **Mark Plati's home studio:** September 2000 / **Looking Glass Studios, New York:** October 2000 / **Technical Team:** Producers: David Bowie, Mark Plati, Tony Visconti / Sound Engineer: Mark Plati / Assistant Sound Engineer: Pete Keppler

Originally appearing as the B-side on the 1965 single "You've Got a Habit of Leaving," "Baby Loves That Way" lived again with the input of Mark Plati, this time played slower and accompanied by Lisa Germano on violin. One can also imagine that the title track, "Toy," was inspired by this song where David Bowie bemoans the lack of interest his girlfriend shows in him: *"She fools around with other boys and treats me like an unwanted toy."* As with every track on this phantom album, the song was recorded live before being treated to various overdubs. "The concept was to make a record like they used to back in the day," explained Mark Plati. "We'd rehearse the songs really well, then go into a studio and track them as a full band, capturing for the most part the energy of a live performance. [...] The idea was to keep it loose, fast, and not clean things up too much or dwell on perfection, and so we ended up tracking thirteen songs in around nine days." [207]

CONVERSATION PIECE

David Bowie / 3:52

Musicians: David Bowie: lead and backing vocals / **Mark Plati:** acoustic guitar / **Earl Slick:** electric guitar / **Gerry Leonard (?):** electric guitar / **Gail Ann Dorsey:** bass / **Sterling Campbell:** drums / **Mike Garson:** piano / **Emm Gryner :** backing vocals / **Holly Palmer:** backing vocals / **Lisa Germano:** violin, mandolin / **Unidentified Musicians:** orchestra / **Recorded:** Sear Sound Studios, New York: July 2000 / **Mark Plati's home studio:** September 2000 / **Looking Glass Studios, New York:** October 2000 / **Technical Team:** Producers: David Bowie, Mark Plati, Tony Visconti / Sound Engineer: Mark Plati / Assistant Sound Engineer: Pete Keppler / Strings Arrangements: Tony Visconti

This surprise cover of "Conversation Piece" first appeared on the B-side of the single "The Prettiest Star," released on March 6, 1970. Although the original version flirted with Americana folk, this reworking was a successful ballad with a pop direction in spite of the inclusion of a mandolin played by Lisa Germano. She intervened in the work when the sessions were interrupted following the birth of the singer's daughter, Alexandria Zahra Jones, on August 15, 2000. "We took a long break after the initial tracking sessions, and reconvened at my home studio in the East Village," said Plati. "The first order of business was to

incorporate a couple of new people to add a few alternate colours—multi-instrumentalist Lisa Germano and guitarist Gerry Leonard. Lisa brought along her bag of toys—violin, mandolin, accordion, etc.—and we let her have a go on everything." [207] "Conversation Piece" appeared on the Japanese reissue of *Heathen* in 2007.

LET ME SLEEP BESIDE YOU

David Bowie / 3:11

Musicians: David Bowie: lead and backing vocals / **Mark Plati:** acoustic guitar / **Earl Slick, Gerry Leonard (?):** electric guitar / **Gail Ann Dorsey:** bass / **Sterling Campbell:** drums / **Mike Garson:** synthesizers / **Emm Gryner, Holly Palmer:** backing vocals / **Recorded:** Sear Sound Studios, New York: July 2000 / **Mark Plati's home studio:** September 2000 / **Looking Glass Studios, New York:** October 2000 / **Technical Team:** Producers: David Bowie, Mark Plati / Sound Engineer: Tony Visconti / Assistant Sound Engineer: Pete Keppler

"Let Me Sleep Beside You" was written in 1967 with a view to seducing the record companies, and ultimately producing a hit. Bowie did not wish to perform this song himself, but provided the material to his manager, Kenneth Pitt, so it could be offered to other artists. It would take until 1971, and the success of "Oh You Pretty Thing," as performed by Peter Noone, for Bowie to really attract the attention of the record labels. The presence of "Let Me Sleep Beside You" on *Toy* is very symbolic, because this was one of Bowie's first numbers (with "Karma Man," which was done during the same session) produced by Tony Visconti. This new version appeared on the compilation *Nothing Has Changed* in 2014.

YOUR TURN TO DRIVE

David Bowie / 4:56

Musicians: David Bowie: lead and backing vocals, Dubreq Stylophone / **Mark Plati:** acoustic guitar / **Earl Slick, Gerry Leonard (?):** electric guitar / **Gail Ann Dorsey:** bass / **Sterling Campbell:** drums / **Mike Garson:** piano / **Emm Gryner, Holly Palmer:** backing vocals / **Cuong Vu:** trumpet / **Recorded:** Sear Sound Studios, New York: July 2000 / **Mark Plati's Home Studio:** September 2000 / **Looking Glass Studios, New York:** October 2000 / **Technical Team:** Producers: David Bowie, Mark Plati, Tony Visconti / Sound Engineer: Mario J. McNulty / Assistant Sound Engineer: Pete Keppler

While the version of *Toy* that had leaked onto the net in March 2011 presented this unreleased song under the name of "Toy (Your Turn to Drive)," Columbia, with Bowie's approval, opted for a simpler title—"Your Turn to Drive"—when it appeared on the compilation *Nothing Has*

Changed in 2014. Although slightly repetitive, "Your Turn to Drive" has a charm of its own through its slightly hippie-tinged sound; it's not dissimilar in sound to "Hole in the Ground." The notable presence of the Stylophone is also no surprise in this return to Bowie's roots.

HOLE IN THE GROUND

David Bowie, George Underwood / 3:33

Musicians: David Bowie: lead and backing vocals, synthesizers / **Mark Plati:** acoustic guitar, synthesizers / **Earl Slick, Gerry Leonard (?):** electric guitar / **Gail Ann Dorsey:** bass / **Sterling Campbell:** drums / **Lisa Germano:** recorder / **Recorded: Sear Sound Studios, New York:** July 2000 / **Mark Plati's home studio:** September 2000 / **Looking Glass Studios, New York:** October 2000 / **Technical Team:** Producers: David Bowie, Mark Plati / **Sound Engineer:** Tony Visconti / **Assistant Sound Engineer:** Pete Keppler

A demo recorded with George Underwood—probably at Trident Studios in 1969—gives some indication as to the genesis of this unreleased blues number. The original version of this track includes slide guitar played in a surprising but very pleasant folk-country register. The reworking of the number for the *Toy* sessions is much more punchy but retains a hippie color to it because of the use of the recorder. Bowie's use of the Stylophone appears here as a distinct reference to 1969, when "Space Oddity"was created. That hit significantly contributed to the success of this little instrument.

SHADOW MAN

David Bowie / 4:46

Musicians: David Bowie: lead and backing vocals, synthesizers / **Mark Plati:** acoustic guitar / **Earl Slick, Gerry Leonard (?):** electric guitar / **Gail Ann Dorsey:** bass / **Mike Garson:** piano / **Unidentified Musicians:** orchestra / **Recorded: Sear Sound Studios, New York:** July 2000 / **Mark Plati's home studio:** September 2000 / **Looking Glass Studios, New York:** October 2000 / **Technical Team:** Producers: David Bowie, Mark Plati, Tony Visconti / **Sound Engineer:** Mark Plati / **Assistant Sound Engineer:** Pete Keppler / **Strings Arrangement:** Tony Visconti

The genesis of this number, written right at the beginning of the 1970s, remains a mystery. Various Bowie biographers attribute it to numerous incarnations, most of which are derived from recording sessions for the albums *The Man Who Sold the World* and *The Rise and Fall of Ziggy Stardust and the Spiders from Mars*. One thing is certain: The song had never progressed further than the demo stage. So it was a big surprise that Bowie decided to include it on *Toy*. This new reading of "Shadow Man" appears on the single "I've Been Waiting for You," released in Canada.

YOU'VE GOT A HABIT OF LEAVING

Davie Jones / 4:48

Musicians: David Bowie: lead and backing vocals / **Mark Plati:** acoustic guitar / **Earl Slick, Gerry Leonard (?):** electric guitar / **Gail Ann Dorsey:** bass / **Sterling Campbell:** drums / **Mike Garson:** piano / **Emm Gryner, Holly Palmer:** backing vocals / **Recorded: Sear Sound Studios, New York:** July 2000 / **Mark Plati's home studio:** September 2000 / **Looking Glass Studios, New York:** October 2000 / **Technical Team:** Producers: David Bowie, Mark Plati, Tony Visconti / **Sound Engineer:** Mark Plati / **Assistant Sound Engineer:** Pete Keppler

Frustrated not have seen *Toy* appear in March 2001 with Virgin, Bowie decided to issue his songs at the same pace as the maxi CD singles for *Heathen*. This time "You've Got a Habit of Leaving," a Davie Jones–era single, gets the rejuvenation treatment. Earl Slick offered the number a blistering guitar line, and the backing vocals of Emm Gryner and Holly Palmer send us back to the Bowie of the sixties, to the great appreciation of the fans of his early days. Upon listening to this surprising cover, one must wonder once more why Virgin, and then the singer, deprived us of the release of *Toy*, as the disc is such a unique and majestic work. "You've Got a Habit of Leaving" appeared in 2002 on the maxi CD single "Slow Burn."

THE LONDON BOYS

David Bowie / 3:45

Musicians: David Bowie: vocals / **Mark Plati:** acoustic guitar / **Earl Slick, Gerry Leonard (?):** electric guitar / **Gail Ann Dorsey:** bass / **Sterling Campbell:** drums / **Mike Garson:** Hammond organ / **Cuong Vu:** trumpet / **Unidentified Musicians:** orchestra / **Recorded: Sear Sound Studios, New York:** July 2000 / **Mark Plati's home studio:** September 2000 / **Looking Glass Studios, New York:** October 2000 / **Technical Team:** Producers: David Bowie, Mark Plati, Tony Visconti / **Sound Engineer:** Mark Plati / **Assistant Sound Engineer:** Pete Keppler / **Arrangements:** Tony Visconti

Much loved by the fans, "The London Boys" is one of David Bowie's essential tracks, even though it only appeared on the B-side of "Rubber Band" in December 1966. The version performed by Bowie onstage for *VH1 Storytellers* in August 1999 undoubtedly led Plati and the musicians to add it to *Toy*. This piece narrates the adventures of a young suburbanite heading for the British capital. He hangs out with the local youths, discovers drugs, and has numerous experiences that change him forever. Probably one of David Bowie's most autobiographical songs, this revised track retains its initial integrity. Although this new version was never issued in full, BowieNet issued two extracts from it for subscribers to the site in the summer of 2002.

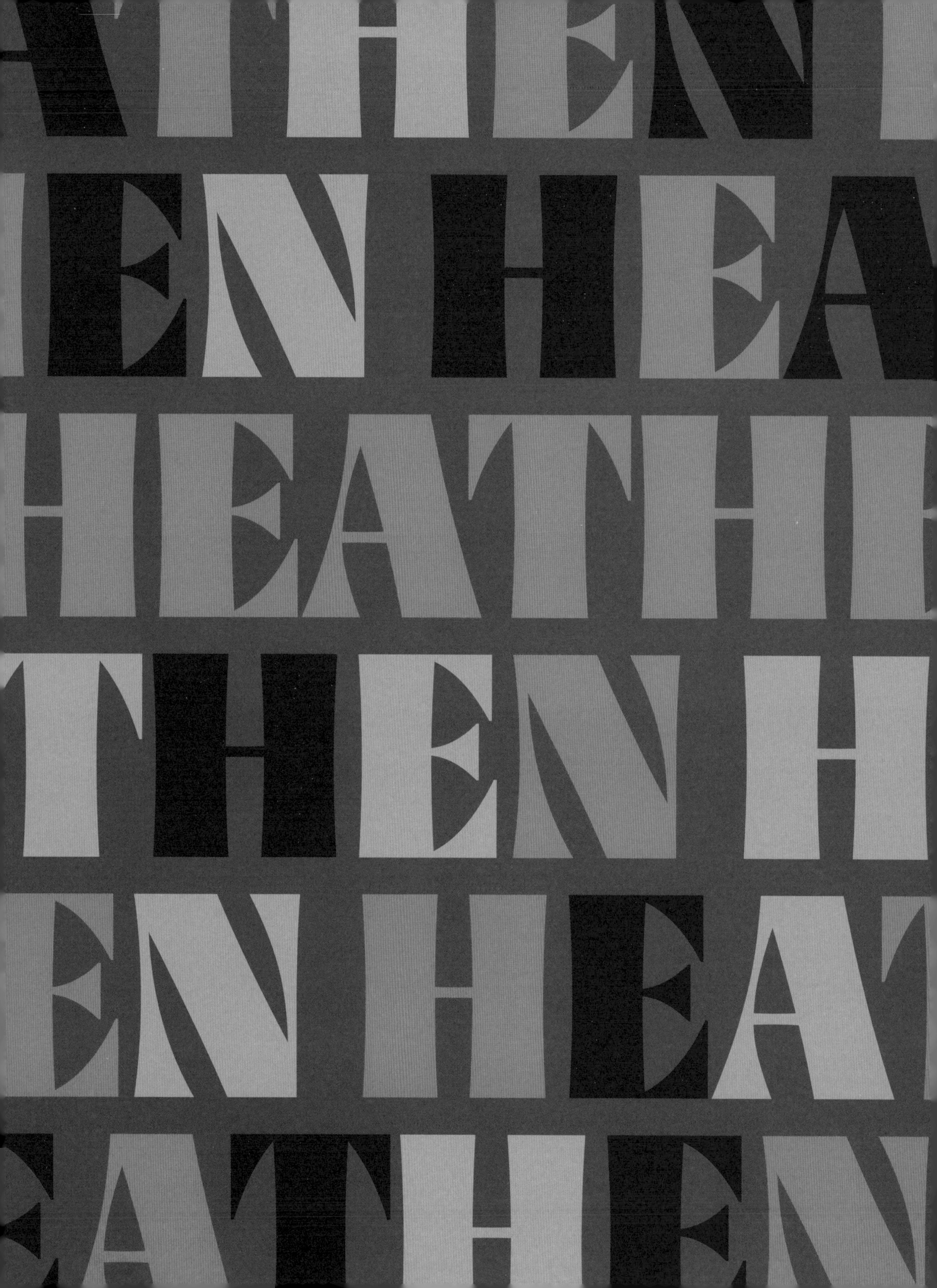

ATHEN H
EN HEA
HEATHE
THEN H
EN HEAT
EATHEN

ALBUM

HEATHEN

Sunday . Cactus . Slip Away . Slow Burn . Afraid . I've Been Waiting for You .
I Would Be Your Slave . I Took a Trip on a Gemini Spaceship . 5:15 The Angels Have Gone .
Everyone Says "Hi" . A Better Future . Heathen (The Rays)

RELEASE DATES

Europe: June 10, 2002

References: ISO Records / Columbia—508222 1 (33 rpm); 508222 2 (CD)

United States: June 11, 2002

References: ISO Records / Columbia—C 86630 (33 rpm); CK 86630 (CD)

Best UK Chart Ranking: 5

Best US Chart Ranking: 14

AN ALBUM WITH PROPHETIC UNDERTONES

In 1998, David Bowie renewed contact with his old friend Tony Visconti for the recording of a new song called "Safe," which was intended for the original soundtrack of the animated film *The Rugrats Movie*. Bowie and Visconti had not worked together since 1981's EP *David Bowie in Bertolt Brecht's Baal*. After their successful outing on "Safe," Bowie also entrusted Visconti with the string arrangements for his 2000 cover compilation album, *Toy*. At the same time, he also brought Visconti in to work on a new studio album. This reunion coincided with Bowie's becoming a father for the second time when little Alexandria Zahra Jones (nicknamed Lexi) was born on August 15, 2000. These events inspired the singer to write many new songs, which led to him producing a solo demo in 2001.

A few months later, following a day spent working at Visconti's personal studio in Manhattan, the two men discussed the idea of visiting Allaire Studios in Shokan, New York, a small town located in the state's Catskills region. Constructed in a 1928 residence overlooking the town of Woodstock and the Ashokan Reservoir, this residential studio had bay windows that provided a breathtaking view and helped keep the creative juices flowing. "The circumstances, the environment, everything about it was just perfect for us to find out if we still had a chemistry that was really effective," said Bowie. "And it worked out. It was perfect, not a step out of place, as though we had just come from the previous album into this one. It was quite stunningly comfortable to work with each other again."[208]

A Spiritual Retreat in the Catskills

During the first sessions at Allaire, David Bowie sorted through dozens of songs that he had brought with him. From August 2001, Visconti had a tightly knit team brought up to the studio to work on new tracks. He played bass, guitar, and recorder, and provided some of the backing vocals, and Bowie played synthesizer, guitars, and even some drums on "Cactus," a cover of a Pixies song. The use of analog instruments such as the Stylophone and the theremin signaled a return to Bowie's roots—a process that had already begun during the writing of *'Hours...'*. Drummer Matthew Chamberlain, formerly of Pearl Jam, took part in the first working sessions. He was joined later by guitarist David Torn and many other guests, including the members of the Scorchio Quartet, who embellished the disc with string scores written by Visconti. The atmosphere was not unlike a spiritual retreat, as described by the producer in his 2007 autobiography: "We had a schedule that we followed daily. David would awake at the crack of dawn and write. After we exercise[d] (Matt jogged, I did Tai Chi) Matt Chamberlain [and] I would meet him in the studio around 10:30 and we'd learn the songs of the day (usually two)."[35] By the beginning of September, the lyrics for twenty songs selected for the new opus had been written. One of these gave the album its title: *Heathen*.

Songs with Visionary Lyrics

As the lyrics for *Heathen* were being finished, the whole world was shocked by the attack on the Twin Towers on September 11, 2001. Bowie and Visconti, who had just finished recording the backing tracks at Allaire Studios, watched from their mountain retreat as the smoke rose from lower Manhattan. "For that whole day we lost contact with our loved ones. Iman was very close to it. He got hold of her for 10 minutes and the phones went down. My son lived very close. [...] All of us have stories like that. Did it influence the album? Undoubtedly, but a lot of those lyrics

are very prophetic. I swear to you only a few lines were amended after September 11."[209] Whether it was a harbinger of things to come, or inspired by the aftermath of tragic events, *Heathen* remains an album that is marked by a specific moment in time.

Back to the Top of the Charts

Finishing touches on *Heathen* were completed at Looking Glass Studios in New York in early January 2002. The album was released on June 10, 2002, in the United Kingdom via ISO Records, and it was released on June 11, 2002, in the United States. The album reached fifth place on the British charts, and it was unanimously commended by the critics, who seemed eager to announce a major return to form for the prolific artist. Bowie was delighted to be back with his group, from whom he had been separated while the disc was being recorded. "They were very understanding," he declared. "They've worked

Onstage at the Roseland Ballroom in New York on June 11, 2002, during the *Heathen* tour. Left to right: Earl Slick, Mike Garson, Mark Plati, Sterling Campbell, David Bowie, Gail Ann Dorsey, Catherine Russell, and Gerry Leonard.

with me long enough to know that we would be back together again before long."[210] On June 11, 2002, the *Heathen* tour was launched at the Roseland Ballroom in New York, with a concert given exclusively to members of BowieNet. The tour lasted through to October 23, 2002; David Bowie crisscrossed Europe and the United States, providing his audiences with a deluge of hits, but also sometimes complete performances of the albums *Low* and *Heathen*.

In 2001, David Bowie worked with the producer P. Diddy on the original soundtrack for the film *Training Day*. A new version of the song "This Is Not America" (1985) was recorded under the title "American Dream."

SUNDAY

David Bowie / 4:45

Musicians: David Bowie: lead vocals, synthesizers, Dubreq Stylophone / **Gerry Leonard, David Torn:** electric guitar / **Tony Visconti:** bass, electric guitar, backing vocals / **Matt Chamberlain:** drums, programming / **Recorded:** Allaire Studios, Shokan: August 6–September 14, 2001 / Looking Glass Studios, New York: January 2002 / **Technical Team:** Producers: David Bowie, Tony Visconti / **Sound Engineer:** Tony Visconti / **Assistant Sound Engineers:** Brandon Mason (Allaire Studios), Todd Vos (Allaire Studios), Hector Castillo (Looking Glass Studios), Christian Rutledge (Looking Glass Studios)

From the opening moments of *Heathen*, the omens of imminent catastrophe are glaringly obvious: "*Nothing remains / We could run / When the rain slows / Look for the cars or signs of life.*" David Bowie said later that the album was never meant to sound apocalyptic in tone, although it came to take on that meaning after the events of September 11, 2001. He certainly could not have imagined the dramatic situation into which the United States would be plunged while he and his team were hard at work on the album, but his lyrics proved to be disconcerting in their prescience. "'Sunday' is absolutely stunning," said Tony Visconti. "It took a long time to make and every time we added a layer of sound from either us or a visiting musician, the song grew to be more and more of an emotional experience."[104] To provide the singer's voice with a natural echo, the producer used a technique that had proved its worth on *"Heroes"* from 1977. He took advantage of the space in Allaire Studios to set up three microphones, which were triggered in sequence according to the power of the voice produced by the singer. Visconti played bass on "Sunday" and he also sang. "One of my passions is singing in a counter-tenor voice, or falsetto. My name, when I sing falsetto, is Shirley, because I copied the voice of Shirley in Shirley and Lee ('Let the Good Times Roll'). On 'Sunday' I got to sing in my newly acquired throat singing technique. That buzzy synth sound in the instrumental passage is actually me singing overtones."[211]

CACTUS

Black Francis / 2:54

Musicians: David Bowie: lead and backing vocals, electric guitar, acoustic guitar, EMS Synthi AKS synthesizer, piano, saxophone, drums / **David Torn:** electric guitar / **Tony Visconti:** bass, backing vocals / **Recorded:** Allaire Studios, Shokan: August 6–September 14, 2001 / Looking Glass Studios, New York: January 2002 / **Technical Team:** Producers: David Bowie, Tony Visconti / **Sound Engineer:** Tony Visconti / **Assistant Sound Engineers:** Brandon Mason (Allaire Studios), Todd Vos (Allaire Studios), Hector Castillo (Looking Glass Studios), Christian Rutledge (Looking Glass Studios)

David Bowie had been an avid admirer of the Pixies since the end of the 1980s. "I never could get over the fact that the Pixies formed, worked and separated without America taking them to its heart or even recognizing their existence for the most part," he declared in 2002. "It was a downright disgrace."[210] After an initial collaboration onstage at Madison Square Garden in January 1997, as well as a collaboration on Reeves Gabrels's second album ("Jewel," in 1999), Bowie decided to cover "Cactus," from *Surfer Rosa*, the group's first album. Bowie played the drums on this track and he also added some synthesizer embellishments via Brian Eno's famous EMS Synthi AKS, which a friend obtained for him. "It was up for auction, and I got it for my fiftieth birthday. We've put that back into service again, most obviously on 'Cactus.'"[210] Black Francis (who became Frank Black after he launched a solo career in 1992) was delighted with this cover: "How do you feel when David Bowie covers one of your songs? [...] You know. It's like having Jesus Christ come out of the clouds and say, 'You have done well, my son.' It doesn't get any bigger than that."[212]

FOR BOWIE ADDICTS

In homage to "T - R - E - X!" which was spelled out by T. Rex in their song "The Groover," the Pixies had inserted "P - I - X - I - E - S!" into their version of "Cactus," which assumed cult status. Bowie did the same, calling out "D - A - V - I - D!" in the middle of his cover version.

2002

SLIP AWAY

David Bowie / 6:05

Musicians

David Bowie: lead and backing vocals, acoustic guitar, piano, Dubreq Stylophone
David Torn: electric guitar
Gerry Leonard: electric guitar
Matt Chamberlain: drums
Tony Levin: bass
Jordan Rudess: synthesizers, piano
Gregor Kitzis (Scorchio Quartet): violin
Meg Okura (Scorchio Quartet): violin
Martha Mooke (Scorchio Quartet): viola
Mary Wooten (Scorchio Quartet): cello

Recorded

Allaire Studios, Shokan: August 6–September 14, 2001
Looking Glass Studios, New York: January 2002

Technical Team

Producers: David Bowie, Tony Visconti
Sound Engineer: Tony Visconti
Assistant Sound Engineers: Brandon Mason (Allaire Studios), Todd Vos (Allaire Studios), Hector Castillo (Looking Glass Studios), Christian Rutledge (Looking Glass Studios)
String Arrangements: Tony Visconti

Genesis

Although the concept of the album *Toy*—recorded two years earlier—was a reworking of old numbers from his catalog, David Bowie had taken advantage of a collaboration with Mark Plati to rerecord an old demo ("Hole in the Ground") and three new songs: "Toy (Your Turn to Drive)," "Afraid," and "Uncle Floyd." Eventually, Bowie decided to redo the last two songs for inclusion on *Heathen*.

"Uncle Floyd" is a reference to TV's *The Uncle Floyd Show*, hosted by Floyd Vivino between 1974 and 1998. "Back in the late '70's, everyone that I knew would rush home at a certain point in the afternoon to catch the Uncle Floyd show," recalled the singer. "[...] I knew so many people of my age who just wouldn't miss it. [...] I just loved that show."[210] Renamed "Slip Away," this is without doubt one of David Bowie's finest songs, and it deserves to be placed on the same level as "Quicksand," "Time," and "Something in the Air" among the artist's most moving ballads.

Production

For this number, David Bowie once again brings out the famous Stylophone that contributed to the success of "Space Oddity" in 1969. "It only plays one note at a time and you have to use a stylus to get at the keyboard," he explained. "Like using a pen. It has no volume control so you do that by putting your hand over the speaker."[210]

For the recording of the piano, Tony Visconti called upon Jordan Rudess, keyboard player with the prog-rock group Dream Theater. The immense cabin at Allaire Studios had an upright piano and a Steinway grand. As he was warming up on the Steinway, Rudess was summoned by Bowie and Visconti, who asked him to use the upright piano instead, before eventually changing their minds once again: "We want you to play the grand piano, but we want to take the lid off the upright piano and take the sustain pedal down from the upright piano, and then put the mics right next to the strings of the upright and let it capture the resonance of the upright while you play the grand."[213] In this manner, David Bowie and Tony Visconti reconnected with the methods previously used by Brian Eno on the so-called Berlin Trilogy!

2002

A symbol of bygone years, Floyd Vivino, aka Uncle Floyd, is the central character in "Slip Away."

Single

SLOW BURN

David Bowie / 4:41

45 rpm version, Europe: Side A: *Slow Burn* / 4:43 / **Side B:** *Wood Jackson* / 4:48 / **Maxi CD single version, Europe**: 1. *Slow Burn* / 4:43; 2. *Wood Jackson* / 4:48; 3. *Shadow Man* / 4:48; 4. *When the Boys Come Marching Home* / 4:46; 5. *You've Got a Habit of Leaving* / 4:51 / Europe release on ISO Records / Columbia: June 3, 2002 (45 rpm ref.: COL 672744 7; maxi CD single ref.: COL 672744 2) / **Best UK Chart Ranking:** 94

Musicians: David Bowie: lead and backing vocals, synthesizers / David Torn, Gerry Leonard, Pete Townshend: electric guitar / Tony Visconti: bass, backing vocals / Sterling Campbell: drums, tambourine / Kristeen Young: piano / Lenny Pickett (Borneo Horns): tenor saxophone / Stan Harrison (Borneo Horns): alto saxophone / Steve Elson (Borneo Horns): baritone saxophone / **Recorded:** Allaire Studios, Shokan: August 6–September 14, 2001 / Looking Glass Studios, New York: January 2002 / **Technical Team:** Producers: David Bowie, Tony Visconti / **Sound Engineer:** Tony Visconti / **Assistant Sound Engineers:** Brandon Mason (Allaire Studios), Todd Vos (Allaire Studios), Hector Castillo (Looking Glass Studios), Christian Rutledge (Looking Glass Studios)

On June 3, 2002, the maxi CD single "Slow Burn" heralded the imminent release of David Bowie's new album, which would go on sale a week later. Created by Markus Klinko, the cover photograph for the single showed the singer resolutely walking forward and carrying a very young child in one arm, as though to save the child from some past or future catastrophe. Catastrophe was a recurring theme on *Heathen*, and the threat of the extinction of the human race permeates this photograph, which is powerfully disconcerting. Despite the presence of Pete Townshend, this single did not find a big audience. The famous guitarist from the Who had already contributed some notes to "Because You're Young" in 1980, and here he provides a six-string guitar score for a track that was initially recorded in London and then emailed to Visconti and Bowie. Guitarist Gerry Leonard, who had taken part in various stages of the recording of *Heathen*, remembered: "I went into the studio maybe four or five times and they'd throw a few songs at me, like 'Have a go at this part' or 'Do a solo here.' I did a solo on ['Slow Burn']; I think I got booted off by Pete Townshend, but that's OK. I'll get out of the way for Pete any day."[163]

During an interview given to *New Musical Express* in November 2013, the lead singer of the Killers, Brandon Flowers, talked about the creation of one of his band's biggest hits, "All These Things That I've Done." He confessed to borrowing from Bowie: "We [...] took the bassline from a David Bowie song called 'Slow Burn' [...], although enough time has probably passed now that I think he probably won't sue us!"[214]

After leaving Nirvana, Dave Grohl and his band Foo Fighters became one of the most celebrated groups of the twenty-first century.

AFRAID

David Bowie / 3:28

Musicians: David Bowie: lead and backing vocals, electric guitar, acoustic guitar, synthesizers / **Mark Plati:** electric guitar / **Tony Visconti:** bass, backing vocals / **Sterling Campbell:** drums / **David Torn:** electric guitar, Suzuki Omnichord / **Lisa Germano, Gregor Kitzis, Meg Okura (Scorchio Quartet):** violin / **Martha Mooke (Scorchio Quartet):** viola / **Mary Wooten (Scorchio Quartet):** cello / **Recorded:** Looking Glass Studios, New York: October–November 2000 (original production), January 2002 (overdubs) / **Allaire Studios, Shokan:** September 14, 2001 (strings) / **Technical Team (Original Version): Producers:** David Bowie, Mark Plati / **Sound Engineer:** Mark Plati / **Assistant Sound Engineer:** Hector Castillo / **Technical Team (Additional Production): Producers:** David Bowie, Tony Visconti / **Sound Engineer:** Tony Visconti / **Assistant Sound Engineers:** Brandon Mason (Allaire Studios), Todd Vos (Allaire Studios), Hector Castillo (Looking Glass Studios), Christian Rutledge (Looking Glass Studios) / **String Arrangements:** Tony Visconti

The second surviving song from the *Toy* album to end up on *Heathen*, "Afraid" appears here in a version that is almost identical to the original. Motivated by the success of an acoustic session broadcast on BowieNet on November 2, 2000, the singer decided to keep this track much as it had been when it was recorded by Mark Plati, who added some guitar overdubs to it in 2002. However, Gail Ann Dorsey's bass part was replaced by a new one written by Tony Visconti. Plati had this to say about writing the lyrics for "Afraid": "At the time, David was reading a book by Andrew Loog Oldham called *Stoned*, where he described locking up Jagger and Richards until they came up with a decent tune. So...I sent David off to the lounge in the Looking Glass Studios, and told him to stay there until he was done! Of course, we were just kidding—sort of (he did stay there until he was done)."[207]

I'VE BEEN WAITING FOR YOU

Neil Young / 3:00

Musicians: David Bowie: lead and backing vocals, synthesizers / **David Torn, Gerry Leonard, Dave Grohl:** electric guitar / **Tony Visconti:** bass, backing vocals / **Matt Chamberlain:** drums / **Recorded:** Allaire Studios, Shokan: August 6–September 14, 2001 / Looking Glass Studios, New York: January 2002 / **Technical Team: Producers:** David Bowie, Tony Visconti / **Sound Engineer:** Tony Visconti / **Assistant Sound Engineers:** Brandon Mason (Allaire Studios), Todd Vos (Allaire Studios), Hector Castillo (Looking Glass Studios), Christian Rutledge (Looking Glass Studios)

For this track, Bowie covered a song from Neil Young's self-titled first album, which was originally released in November 1968. "When I got that album in 1969, I was dazzled by the overall complexity of sound," Bowie explained. "It was so majestic but aloft or lonely sounding at the same time. A real yearning. And I'd always wanted to do that song on stage or someplace."[210] Here, Bowie gives the song a new lease on life with a very rockcentric sound, on which Dave Grohl (of Foo Fighters and Nirvana fame) adds a guitar line with full power bends. Like Pete Townshend did on "Slow Burn," Grohl recorded his part separately and then emailed the finished product to Bowie and Visconti. Gerry Leonard, who had already completed his string portion, saw himself once again ousted from the mix. "That was another one where I played a bunch of stuff on it but Grohl ended up on the end of it. [...] I need to do a bit more shouting, a bit more argy-bargy, I guess!"[163] he added with amusement.

The Legendary Stardust
Cowboy, upside down, with his
Airline acoustic guitar in hand.

I WOULD BE YOUR SLAVE

David Bowie / 5:14

Musicians: David Bowie: lead vocals, electric guitar, synthesizers / David
Torn: electric guitar / **Tony Visconti:** bass / **Matt Chamberlain:** drums /
Gregor Kitzis, Meg Okura (Scorchio Quartet): violin / Martha Mooke
(Scorchio Quartet): viola / **Mary Wooten (Scorchio Quartet):** cello /
Recorded: Allaire Studios, Shokan: August 6–September 14, 2001 /
Looking Glass Studios, New York: January 2002 / **Technical Team:**
Producers: David Bowie, Tony Visconti / **Sound Engineer:** Tony Visconti /
Assistant Sound Engineers: Brandon Mason (Allaire Studios), Todd Vos
(Allaire Studios), Hector Castillo (Looking Glass Studios), Christian Rutledge
(Looking Glass Studios) / **String Arrangements:** Tony Visconti

On September 11, 2001, the whole world was shocked by
the al-Qaeda attacks on American soil. The next morning,
Bowie and Visconti—who had just added the final touches
to the backing tracks of *Heathen*—wondered if the string
recording session planned at Allaire Studios should still go
ahead. The arrangements devised by Visconti were based
on ideas that Bowie had been toying with on his Korg
Trinity synthesizer, and they were ready to record. The
members of the Scorchio Quartet were supposed to leave
Manhattan for Shokan on September 14 in order to meet
with Bowie and Visconti and get to work. But the National
Emergencies Act had been invoked in the United States,
and it seemed that the musicians would not be able to
make the trip. Finally, everyone decided to keep the session on the schedule, mostly in an attempt to make a return
to normalcy. "We called for [...] the Scorchio Quartet to see
if they felt like recording [...]," recounted Visconti. "Of
course, it was the best thing to do, to try doing something
to make life seem normal again. They braved all the check-
points out of the city crammed into violist Martha Mooke's
car and arrived a little shaken but anxious to make
music."[211] Bowie and Visconti then decided to record each
instrument by plugging a microphone into a guitar amp in
order to give extra bite to the overall sound of the quartet.
"It all worked so well," remembered Visconti. "We had a
great day, a much-needed day."[211]

I TOOK A TRIP ON A GEMINI SPACESHIP

The Legendary Stardust Cowboy / 4:04

Musicians: David Bowie: lead vocals, synthesizers, saxophone,
theremin / **David Torn:** electric guitar, Suzuki Omnichord / **Tony Visconti:**
bass, electric guitar / **Matt Chamberlain:** drums, programming / Gregor
Kitzis, Meg Okura (Scorchio Quartet): violin / Martha Mooke (Scorchio
Quartet): viola / **Mary Wooten (Scorchio Quartet):** cello / **Recorded:**
Allaire Studios, Shokan: August 6–September 14, 2001 / Looking
Glass Studios, New York: January 2002 / **Technical Team:**
Producers: David Bowie, Tony Visconti / **Sound Engineer:** Tony Visconti /
Assistant Sound Engineers: Brandon Mason (Allaire Studios), Todd Vos
(Allaire Studios), Hector Castillo (Looking Glass Studios), Christian Rutledge
(Looking Glass Studios)

David Bowie never concealed the fact that he was inspired
by the Legendary Stardust Cowboy for the name of his most
famous avatar: Ziggy Stardust. In this number, he pays homage to the American singer who is not well known outside
his own country—a sort of Johnny Cash on LSD, and the
author of a handful of albums and singles since the end of
the 1960s. Here, Bowie covers one of the Legendary Stardust
Cowboy's classics: "I Took a Trip on a Gemini Spaceship,"
which tells the story of an astronaut traveling in space and
thinking of his beloved. "When I read on his site that he
thought that because I'd borrowed his name that, at least I
should sing one of his songs," confided Bowie, "I got guilty
and wanted to make amends immediately. So I covered one
of his best songs, 'I Took a Trip on a Gemini Spaceship'
although he sings '*spacecraft*' on the record." [210]

The singer gives the song a new flavor, leaving behind the
ballad styling of the original in favor of a sound closer to
what Bowie and his team produced on *Earthling*.
Interestingly, Matt Chamberlain recorded rhythmic patterns
played out on all kinds of objects (oil cans, pieces of metal,
etc.), and then played his drums over the top of this cacoph-
ony of sound. From 0:57 David Bowie plays an instrument
that perfectly illustrates the outer space and futuristic atmosphere of the song: the theremin. To be more specific, he
uses two of them: an older model belonging to Visconti (who
had introduced this instrument to Bowie during the sessions) and a more recent digital model made by Longwave.

2002

5:15 THE ANGELS
HAVE GONE

David Bowie / 5:00

Musicians: David Bowie: lead vocals, electric guitar, synthesizers /
David Torn: electric guitar / Tony Visconti: bass, backing vocals / Matt
Chamberlain: drums / Jordan Rudess: piano / **Recorded:** Allaire
Studios, Shokan: August 6–September 14, 2001 / **Looking Glass
Studios**, New York: January 2002 / **Technical Team:** Producers:
David Bowie, Tony Visconti / **Sound Engineer:** Tony Visconti / **Assistant
Sound Engineers:** Brandon Mason (Allaire Studios), Todd Vos (Allaire
Studios), Hector Castillo (Looking Glass Studios), Christian Rutledge
(Looking Glass Studios)

On "5:15 The Angels Have Gone," we encounter the delicate playing of Jordan Rudess, the keyboard player with
Dream Theater. He gives the track a discreet score with a
slightly dissonant nuance to it, not unlike the unforgettable solo by Mike Garson on "Aladdin Sane (1913-1938-
197?)" in 1973. Every day before recording began, Rudess
received precise (more or less) instructions from Bowie.
"Every time before a track, David would paint a verbal
picture to me of what the song was about, so I would get
in the mood," recalled the musician. "There was one song
['5:15 The Angels Have Gone'] where I was playing the
piano, and he painted this picture of me in an old dusty
restaurant/cafe at a place in France, and by the time he
finished the story, I was deeply in it. So when I did the
track, I was really in the mood."[213]

EVERYONE SAYS 'HI'

David Bowie / 3:59

Maxi CD Single Version, Europe: 1. *Everyone Says "Hi" (Radio Edit)* /
3:29; 2. *Safe* / 4:44; 3. *Baby Loves That Way* / 4:44; 4. *Sunday (Tony
Visconti Mix)* / 4:57 / **Europe Release on ISO Records / Columbia:**
September 16, 2002 (Maxi CD single ref.: COL 673076 2) / **Best UK
Chart Ranking:** 20

Musicians: David Bowie: lead and backing vocals / Carlos Alomar:
electric guitar / Gary Miller: electric guitar, acoustic guitar, synthesizers,
programming / John Read: bass / Brian Rawling: programming / Dave
Clayton: synthesizers, piano / Solá Ákingbolá: percussion / Philip
Sheppard: electric cello / Tony Visconti: acoustic guitar, backing vocals /
Recorded: Looking Glass Studios, New York: January 2002 / **Sub
Urban Studios**, London: January 2002 / **Technical Team:** Producers:
Brian Rawling, Gary Miller, Tony Visconti (acoustic guitar and
voice) / **Mixing:** Gary Miller

In January 2002, after Bowie and Visconti recorded an
acoustic version of "Everyone Says 'Hi'" at Looking Glass
Studios in New York, the tracks were sent to London so that
Gary Miller could add a personal touch to the track. Miller
was a producer and lyricist famous for numerous collaborations with the trio Stock Aitken Waterman during the 1980s.
He retained only the vocals created by Bowie and Visconti,
opting instead to create a completely new structure.

Numerous musicians contributed to the piece, including Carlos Alomar and keyboard player David Clayton, who had famously been involved in the production of Bob Marley's posthumous single "Iron Lion Zion" in 1992. "It started off like a remix, but ended up as a fully-fledged production,"[215] Miller said in 2002. "Everyone Says 'Hi'" was then offered as a single for the United Kingdom and in Europe, where it received a fairly lukewarm reception.

A BETTER FUTURE

David Bowie / 4:11

Musicians: David Bowie: lead and backing vocals, acoustic guitar, synthesizers / **David Torn, Gerry Leonard:** electric guitar / **Tony Visconti:** bass, electric guitar / **Matt Chamberlain:** drums, programming / **Recorded:** Allaire Studios, Shokan: August 6–September 14, 2001 / **Looking Glass Studios, New York:** January 2002 / **Technical Team: Producers:** David Bowie, Tony Visconti / **Sound Engineer:** Tony Visconti / **Assistant Sound Engineers:** Brandon Mason (Allaire Studios), Todd Vos (Allaire Studios), Hector Castillo (Looking Glass Studios), Christian Rutledgc (Looking Glass Studios)

Heathen earned its reputation as a prophetic album because of tracks like "A Better Future," which was actually created a few days before the attacks on the World Trade Center. "I think *Heathen* was a very spiritual album," confided Tony Visconti. "David wrote some great lyrics, wore his heart on his sleeve for that album."[104] The singer, who composed these words with his one-year-old daughter, Lexi, in mind, gave way to a naiveté that one can readily forgive: "*Give my children sunny smiles / Give them warm and cloudless skies / I demand a better future.*" Having written the song "Kooks" for his son in 1971, here Bowie gives his little girl a song full of despair, which he described as follows: "It's a very simple song that says

'[...] What are you doing to us? Why have you allowed my daughter to come into a world of such chaos and despair? I demand a better future or I'm not gonna like you anymore.' It's a threat to God!"[47]

HEATHEN (THE RAYS)

David Bowie / 4:16

Musicians: David Bowie: lead vocals, synthesizers, saxophone / **David Torn:** electric guitar, Suzuki Omnichord / **Tony Visconti:** bass, backing vocals / **Matt Chamberlain:** drums, tambourine / **Gregor Kitzis, Meg Okura (Scorchio Quartet):** violin / **Martha Mooke (Scorchio Quartet):** viola / **Mary Wooten (Scorchio Quartet):** cello / **Recorded:** Allaire Studios, Shokan: August 6–September 14, 2001 / **Looking Glass Studios, New York:** January 2002 / **Technical Team: Producers:** David Bowie, Tony Visconti / **Sound Engineer:** Tony Visconti / **Assistant Sound Engineers:** Brandon Mason (Allaire Studios), Todd Vos (Allaire Studios), Hector Castillo (Looking Glass Studios), Christian Rutledge (Looking Glass Studios)

The first lyrics of "Heathen (the Rays)" should be reread to take into account the troubling coincidence between Bowie's writing, and the tragic events that occurred a few days later: "*Steel on the skyline / Sky made of glass / Made for a real world / All things must pass.*" "Strangely, some songs you really don't want to write," confided David Bowie. "I didn't like writing 'Heathen.' There was something so ominous and final about it. It was early in the morning, the sun was rising and through the windows I could see two deer grazing down below in the field. In the distance a car was driving slowly past the reservoir and these words were just streaming out and there were tears running down my face. But I couldn't stop, they just flew out. It's an odd feeling, like something else is guiding you, although forcing your hand is more like it."[210]

SAFE

David Bowie, Reeves Gabrels / 4:42

Musicians: David Bowie: lead and backing vocals, synthesizers / **David Torn:** electric guitar / **Tony Visconti:** bass, electric guitar / **Matt Chamberlain:** drums, programming / **Unidentified Musicians:** orchestra / **Recorded:** Sear Sound Studios, New York (strings): August 1998 / **Allaire Studios, Shokan:** August 6–September 14, 2001 / **Looking Glass Studios, New York:** January 2002 / **Technical Team:** Producers: David Bowie, Tony Visconti / **Sound Engineer:** Tony Visconti / **Assistant Sound Engineers:** Brandon Mason (Allaire Studios), Todd Vos (Allaire Studios), Hector Castillo (Looking Glass Studios), Christian Rutledge (Looking Glass Studios)

At the request of Karyn Rachtman, the musical supervisor for the animated film *The Rugrats Movie*, Bowie was commissioned to write a song for the original soundtrack. He turned to a number called "(Safe in This) Sky Life," which he had composed previously with Reeves Gabrels. Bowie decided to call upon Tony Visconti for the new arrangements. Following a rupture in their friendship that had lasted nearly two decades, this track actually marked a reunion for Bowie and his co-producer.

The song had been recorded in August 1998 with an all-star lineup. Clem Burke, from Blondie, was on drums; Richard Barone, of the Bongos, provided backing vocals, and Jordan Rudess, at that time an intermittent member of Dream Theater, played keyboards. Tony Visconti wrote the string arrangements. But the scene in which the number appeared was cut out during the editing of the film, much to the disappointment of Karyn Rachtman, who declared: "I have always wanted to work with David Bowie and I finally had my chance. He delivered a song far beyond my wildest dreams and now I can't even use it. The song is beautiful."[216] Visconti decided to rerecord the number, now renamed "Safe," during the *Heathen* sessions, retaining only the string section from the original recording. The song was not incorporated into the album's track listing, but it was offered as a bonus track to purchasers of the "Everyone Says 'Hi'" single in September 2002. It was also included on the second CD of the limited edition reissue of *Heathen*, which appeared in Japan in 2007.

WOOD JACKSON

David Bowie / 4:45

Musicians: David Bowie: lead vocals, synthesizers / **David Torn:** electric guitar, acoustic guitar / **Tony Visconti:** bass, recorder, backing vocals / **Matt Chamberlain:** drums, percussion / **Jordan Rudess:** Hammond organ / **Recorded:** Allaire Studios, Shokan: August 6–September 14, 2001 / **Looking Glass Studios, New York:** January 2002 / **Technical Team:** Producers: David Bowie, Tony Visconti / **Sound Engineer:** Tony Visconti / **Assistant Sound Engineers:** Brandon Mason (Allaire Studios), Todd Vos (Allaire Studios), Hector Castillo (Looking Glass Studios), Christian Rutledge (Looking Glass Studios)

Among the three outtakes derived from the *Heathen* sessions, "Wood Jackson" includes the sounds of the Hammond organ, played by Jordan Rudess at Allaire Studios. Appearing on the single releases of "Slow Burn" and "Everyone Says 'Hi,'" this song is somewhat of a rarity, and it has a certain interest in its own right. Its languor, marked by Matt Chamberlain's rhythms, was pleasing for the fans from Bowie's early days. This song contains much of the midtempo pop coloring that is very much in evidence on *Space Oddity* and *Hunky Dory*.

FLY

David Bowie / 4:10

Musicians: David Bowie: lead and backing vocals, synthesizers / **Gerry Leonard, Carlos Alomar:** electric guitar / **Tony Visconti:** bass, electric guitar, backing vocals / **Matt Chamberlain:** drums, programming / **Lisa Germano:** violin, backing vocals / **Recorded:** Allaire Studios, Shokan: August 6–September 14, 2001 / **Looking Glass Studios, New York:** January 2002 / **Technical Team:** Producers: David Bowie, Tony Visconti / **Sound Engineer:** Tony Visconti / **Assistant Sound Engineers:** Brandon Mason (Allaire Studios), Todd Vos (Allaire Studios), Hector Castillo (Looking Glass Studios), Christian Rutledge (Looking Glass Studios)

Originating during the *Heathen* recording sessions, this rare track made its first appearance on the double limited edition release of *Reality* in 2003. It includes Lisa Germano as a backing vocalist and violinist, and guitarist Carlos Alomar also makes a guest appearance. The track has a contagious energy to it, which would probably not have been in keeping with the very spiritually inspired sounds of *Heathen*.

Tony Visconti's incisive bass is complemented by an addictive synthesizer riff, and Matt Chamberlain's drums cut a path through a deluge of sound information, steering their way through multiple layers of guitars, synthesizers, and surging lyrics. A rock song with great potential, "Fly" unfortunately only ever reached the status of a bonus track.

The American musician Lisa Germano added her multi-instrumentalist talents to *Heathen*.

WHEN THE BOYS COME MARCHING HOME

David Bowie / 4:44

Musicians: David Bowie: lead and backing vocals / **David Torn, Carlos Alomar**: electric guitar / **Tony Visconti**: bass, backing vocals / **Matt Chamberlain**: drums, percussion / **Jordan Rudess**: piano / **Gregor Kitzis, Meg Okura (Scorchio Quartet)**: violin / **Martha Mooke (Scorchio Quartet)**: viola / **Mary Wooten (Scorchio Quartet)**: cello / **Recorded:** Allaire Studios, Shokan: August 6–September 14, 2001 / **Looking Glass Studios, New York**: January 2002 / **Technical Team: Producers:** David Bowie, Tony Visconti / **Sound Engineer:** Tony Visconti / **Assistant Sound Engineers:** Brandon Mason (Allaire Studios), Todd Vos (Allaire Studios), Hector Castillo (Looking Glass Studios), Christian Rutledge (Looking Glass Studios) / **String Arrangements:** Tony Visconti

Although the introduction of "When the Boys Come Marching Home" is not dissimilar to "My Lady Blue" by Éric Serra (the synthesizer... the chord sequence... the bass glissandos...), the comparison stops there. In this song, Bowie wrote lyrics that referred to soldiers returning from the front, but he was very far from imagining that his adopted country was about to launch a war in Iraq. This song can be appreciated for its melancholy and profound subject matter, supported by the very gentle rhythm provided by Matt Chamberlain. Bowie was so taken by Chamberlain's drum playing that he sampled it and used it again on the song "Bring Me the Disco King," which appeared on his next album, *Reality*. "When the Boys Come Marching Home" appears among the bonus tracks on the Japanese reissue of *Heathen* that was released in 2007.

ALBUM

REALITY

New Killer Star . Pablo Picasso . Never Get Old . The Loneliest Guy .
Looking for Water . She'll Drive the Big Car . Days . Fall Dog Bombs the Moon .
Try Some, Buy Some . Reality . Bring Me the Disco King

RELEASE DATES
Europe: September 15, 2003
Reference: ISO Records / Columbia—COL 512555 9 (CD)
United States: September 16, 2003
Reference: ISO Records / Columbia—CK 90576 (CD)
Best UK Chart Ranking: 3
Best US Chart Ranking: 29

THE LAST ALBUM OF THE 2000s

With the *Heathen* tour over, it was not long before David Bowie was back in the recording studio. He was keen to get to work on his new album, taking advantage of the excellent relations between him and the other members of his group. At the end of October 2002, Bowie announced to the rest of the group, who had been touring with him for months across Europe and the United States, that their services would soon be required for a new round of recording sessions.

Reality: Concept-Free Pop Music

In January 2003, Bowie arrived at New York's Looking Glass Studios with Tony Visconti and sound engineer–musician Mario J. McNulty. In the course of this creative phase, the three men recorded a significant number of early demos, with Bowie on guitar, Visconti on bass, and McNulty on drums. Their aim was to compose new songs in a rapid and spontaneous way, writing lyrics that were less esoteric than what made it onto *Heathen*, which was a fairly spiritual, searching album. Tony Visconti jealously guarded the recorded demos, convinced that they would be suitable for the album. As it turned out, many of the backing tracks did not need to be rerecorded. The musicians from the *Heathen* tour then arrived to perfect the sketched-out pieces, with Sterling Campbell adding the drums, Gerry Leonard and Earl Slick incorporating their six-string guitars, and Gail Ann Dorsey taking up a backing singer role alongside Catherine Russell. Pianist Mike Garson was invited along as well.

Recording on the album continued intermittently until May 2003. *Reality* was officially released on September 15, 2003, in the UK (and on the following day in North America) with album art designed by graphic designer Rex Ray and based on a photo of Bowie taken by Frank W. Ockenfels.

A *Reality* Tour

A new world tour was announced in October, and Bowie asked his musicians to learn and rehearse almost eighty songs so that there could be a different set list each evening. In this way, the public would be surprised, and Bowie's group would have to be constantly on the ball, artistically speaking. All Bowie's classic numbers were performed during the tour, which was referred to simply as "A Reality Tour."

On June 23, 2004, while performing onstage at the T-Mobile Arena in Prague, David Bowie appeared to be suffering from worrying signs of discomfort just as he was about to sing "Reality." He left the stage briefly, leaving the group to play "A New Career in a New Town," which was an instrumental track, followed by "Be My Wife," sung by Catherine Russell. Bowie returned to perform "China Girl," but after a few more songs he had to admit defeat. His inability to perform was attributed to extreme fatigue and a pinched nerve in his shoulder, but no one seemed particularly concerned. On June 25, the whole team took part in the Hurricane Festival in Scheeßel, Germany. As he left the stage, Bowie collapsed in the wings, seemingly in the grip of a heart attack. He was rushed to St. Georg Hospital in Hamburg, where an angioplasty was carried out to unblock an artery. The rest of the tour was canceled. David Bowie would never again perform in concert with his group.

His last appearance onstage took place in November 2006, at the Black Ball, a charity gala in New York. Bowie sang "Wild Is the Wind" and "Fantastic Voyage" for the event, and he also performed a duet of "Changes" with Alicia Keys. The Black Ball was an occasion that would prove especially poignant for Mike Garson: "'Changes' was the song I auditioned with for Mick Ronson and David in '72, so it was my opening thing and the last thing I did with him and the last thing he ever did live."[163]

The Twin Towers of the World Trade Center were targeted by al-Qaeda during the attacks carried out on September 11, 2011. In the foreground, *The Sphere*, a work by the German artist Fritz Koenig (1971)

NEW KILLER STAR

David Bowie / 4:41

UK CD Single Version: 1. *New Killer Star* / 3:44; 2. *Love Missile F1 Eleven* / 4:14 / **US CD Single Version:** 1. *New Killer Star (Radio Edit)* / 3:44 / **Europe Release on ISO Records / Columbia:** September 29, 2003 (CD single ref.: COL 674275 1) / **US Release on ISO Records / Columbia:** September 29, 2003 (CD single ref.: CSK 56555) / **Best Chart Ranking:** Did Not Chart

Musicians: David Bowie: lead and backing vocals, electric guitar, synthesizers, tambourine / **Earl Slick, Gerry Leonard, David Torn:** electric guitar / **Tony Visconti:** bass, backing vocals / **Sterling Campbell:** drums / **Gail Ann Dorsey, Catherine Russell:** backing vocals / **Recorded: Looking Glass Studios, New York:** January–May 2003 / **Allaire Studios, Shokan:** May 2003 / **Technical Team: Producers:** David Bowie, Tony Visconti / **Sound Engineer:** Tony Visconti / **Assistant Sound Engineer:** Brandon Mason (Allaire Studios)

Bowie always denied that he had composed *Reality* as a tribute to the city of New York, which was still reeling from the 2001 attack on the World Trade Center. And yet this album seems haunted by memories of that day, the very first words of the album recalling the appearance of the Financial District where the Twin Towers once stood: "*See the great white scar / Over Battery Park / Then a flare glides over / But I won't look at that scar.*" Bowie is referring here to Battery Park City, where he once lived, with its green spaces that were much loved by people living in Tribeca and the Financial District. Lying in the southern area of Manhattan, this district was, like many others, covered by ash and debris when the World Trade Center fell. "[It's] about the fact that for the last five years I've been living in New York, and as a family we were greatly affected, fairly traumatized by what happened. And this, I guess, is just the resonance of living in this particular area, because I'm literally down the road."[217]

Despite the sad memories of that terrible day, "New Killer Star" is actually a fairly cheerful pop song, conveying David Bowie's renewed sense of optimism. "The ghost of the tragedy that happened there is reflected in the song, but I'm trying to make something more positive out of it. The birth of a new star."[36] Bowie keeps the rhythm going on guitar, Tony Visconti's bass line—recorded as part of the earlier demos during their first working sessions—was preserved in the mixing. Guitarist David Torn adds liveliness to the song with some strong chorus effect chords, notably at 1:29. "New Killer Star" is the only single from the *Reality* album to appear in both the UK and the US.

Jonathan Richman, singer and guitarist of the Modern Lovers, wrote the song "Pablo Picasso."

PABLO PICASSO

Jonathan Richman / 4:06

Musicians: David Bowie: lead and backing vocals, electric guitar, synthesizers, saxophone / Earl Slick: electric guitar / Gerry Leonard: acoustic guitar / Mark Plati: bass / Sterling Campbell: drums / Tony Visconti: programming, backing vocals / **Recorded:** Looking Glass Studios, New York: January–May 2003 / Allaire Studios, Shokan: May 2003 / **Technical Team:** Producers: David Bowie, Tony Visconti / **Sound Engineer:** Tony Visconti / **Assistant Sound Engineer:** Brandon Mason (Allaire Studios)

Recorded in 1972 by its composer, Jonathan Richman, this song did not have its official launch until the first album by Modern Lovers was released in 1976 (not counting the cover version recorded by the song's original producer, John Cale, which he released on his solo album in 1975). Bowie gives us a greatly modified version here, moving away from the very repetitive harmonic structure of the original. Bowie said at the time: "Apologies now to Jonathan Richman, but I took the lyrics and made a song that is completely different. The original is a little dirge-like, and it's all on one note. It doesn't move much, which gives it a power, but it gives it the power of another era. I wanted to change the era and give it a more contemporary feel."[47]

The introduction and concluding solos are notable for the acoustic guitar passages from Gerry Leonard, which create a flamenco feeling that fits well with the title of the song. Performing onstage, Leonard was able to reproduce the acoustic sound from the recording by plugging his electric guitar into a Kaoss Pad—a revolutionary multi-effect touch pad made by Korg.

NEVER GET OLD

David Bowie / 4:25

Musicians: David Bowie: lead and backing vocals, electric guitar, synthesizers, Dubreq Stylophone / **Earl Slick:** electric guitar, acoustic guitar / **Gerry Leonard:** electric guitar / **Mark Plati:** bass, electric guitar / **Tony Visconti:** mandolin, backing vocals / **Sterling Campbell:** drums / **Mike Garson:** piano / **Gail Ann Dorsey, Catherine Russell:** backing vocals / **Recorded:** Looking Glass Studios, New York: January–May 2003 / The Hitching Post Studio, Bell Canyon: April–May 2003 / Allaire Studios, Shokan: May 2003 / **Technical Team:** Producers: David Bowie, Tony Visconti / Sound Engineers: Tony Visconti, Bill Jenkins (Hitching Post Studio) / Assistant Sound Engineer: Brandon Mason (Allaire Studios)

"There's never gonna be enough sex / And I'm never ever gonna get old," proclaims the fifty-six-year-old rocker in this effective pop-rock number. Bowie was to confess that he could not envisage the day when he would have to give up: "I could imagine at a certain age, when I have no vocal cords left, that I would find a young man who could sing my parts for me. But I don't see why I would stop. Fortunately, I've retained much of the stubbornness and curiosity I always had as a teenager. [...] As long as I have it, that interest, I don't think it will stop."[218]

"Never Get Old" came out as a single only in Japan (in February 2004) but beginning in June 2003, the song was used for international promotion for the forthcoming album when it appeared in an advertising campaign mounted by the mineral water brand Vittel. The ad shows David Bowie at home, encountering—sometimes with amusement, sometimes seemingly annoyed—the different personalities adopted by himself over the years. These personalities are acted out by David Brighton, one of Bowie's most well-known impersonators. The song "Never Get Old," which boasts of the singer's eternal youthfulness, was used to illustrate Vittel's slogan: "A new life every day."

Mark Plati played guitar on this track, and later remarked: "I wanna do this really simple bass part, like from Sly's Stone's 'Everyday People.' [...] That was bingo from the first go."[163]

Earl Slick, David Bowie, Gail Ann Dorsey, and Gerry Leonard perform "Never Get Old" at Rockefeller Plaza in New York on September 18, 2003.

An American soldier in Kuwait during Operation Desert Storm in January 2003.

THE LONELIEST GUY

David Bowie / 4:12

Musicians: David Bowie: lead vocals / Gerry Leonard: electric guitar / Tony Visconti: bass / Mike Garson: piano / **Recorded:** Looking Glass Studios, New York: January–May 2003 / The Hitching Post Studio, Bell Canyon: May 2003 / **Technical Team:** Producers: David Bowie, Tony Visconti / **Sound Engineers:** Tony Visconti, Bill Jenkins (Hitching Post Studio)

During the recording sessions for *Reality* at Looking Glass Studios, pianist Mike Garson played on a digital Yamaha piano equipped with a dual-function MIDI controller. The audio signal coming from the instrument (here, the sound of a piano) was recorded by Visconti, who then passed the digital information (the "MIDI") to a computer. In this way, the piano portion of the song is preserved, but its sound can be changed according to the mixing. Standardized in 1983, this device was to become invaluable to musicians around the world. Garson returned to his studio in Bell Canyon, California, with the MIDI files, which allowed him to redo his parts on a grand piano. His sound engineer, Bill Jenkins, then recorded the new versions and sent them back to Visconti. The producer was thus able to bring the depth and power of a concert piano to "The Loneliest Guy." By contrast, Visconti opted for the colder sound of the digital Yamaha for another song in the album, "Bring Me the Disco King." As Visconti said: "So, we had a mixture in terms of Mike's piano contributions."[208] Unfortunately, Mike Garson's personal studio burned down on November 9, 2018, as California was being ravaged by wildfires. Although no one died, the musician lost all of his instruments, recordings, and mementos from a life spent on the road and in the studio.

LOOKING FOR WATER

David Bowie / 3:28

Musicians: David Bowie: lead and backing vocals, electric guitar, synthesizers, tambourine / **Earl Slick, Gerry Leonard:** electric guitar / Mark Plati: bass / Sterling Campbell: drums / **Recorded:** Looking Glass Studios, New York: January–May 2003 / Allaire Studios, Shokan: May 2003 / **Technical Team:** Producers: David Bowie, Tony Visconti / **Sound Engineer:** Tony Visconti / **Assistant Sound Engineer:** Brandon Mason (Allaire Studios)

The United States invaded Iraq at the beginning of 2003, and this event had a great effect on Bowie, who purportedly had in mind a man crawling across the desert in search of water when he wrote the lyrics to this song. This led Bowie to designate the song as an implicit rallying call to people all over the world who denounced the US's involvement in the war: "That made me think, well, the only thing he *would* be looking at would be the oil pumps. And the oil pumps seem to be working, but there is no water."[47]

To give more body to the guitar and drum tracks recorded in New York, David Bowie and Tony Visconti decided to travel to Allaire Studios, two hours outside of Manhattan, to make use of the natural reverb of recording spaces. Visconti placed the studio's two ATC SCM 150 speakers in the very spot where, in August 2001, Matt Chamberlain had set up his drum kit. Visconti then played the recorded tracks one by one at maximum volume, capturing the sound with a pair of Earthworks mics suspended from the ceiling. To obtain the desired resonance, he then added a new drumming sound to the mix. Pleased with the result, he commented that "it sounds as if the drum kit was at Allaire. [...] It's got a nice one-second decay [*sic*] in there, which is ideal for drums."[208]

SHE'LL DRIVE
THE BIG CAR

David Bowie / 4:35

Musicians: David Bowie: lead and backing vocals, electric guitar, synthesizers, harmonica, saxophone, tambourine / **Earl Slick, Gerry Leonard:** electric guitar / **Mark Plati:** bass / **Sterling Campbell:** drums / **Tony Visconti:** programming, backing vocals / **Gail Ann Dorsey, Catherine Russell:** backing vocals / **Recorded: Looking Glass Studios, New York:** January–May 2003 / **Allaire Studios, Shokan:** May 2003 / **Technical Team: Producers:** David Bowie, Tony Visconti / **Sound Engineer:** Tony Visconti / **Assistant Sound Engineer:** Brandon Mason (Allaire Studios)

On September 8, 2003, David Bowie gave a concert at Riverside Studios in London. Broadcast by satellite to eighty-six cinemas in twenty-six different countries, this event was an indication of how up-to-date Bowie was when it came to the new frontier of digital distribution. Introducing "She'll Drive the Big Car," Bowie remarked: "This one is a tragic little story about a lady and her family. And she lives in the wrong part of town, but she wants to live in an even badder, wronger part of town—but her would-be affair, her boyfriend, doesn't turn up."[219] The song presents a picture of the ideal American family, but with a darker side bubbling underneath the surface. A fine pop song that features Bowie playing his harmonica to the delight of fans still hankering for the halcyon days of "Cracked Actor" and "The Jean Genie."

DAYS

David Bowie / 3:19

Musicians: David Bowie: lead and backing vocals, acoustic guitar, synthesizers, saxophone, percussion, Dubreq Stylophone / **Earl Slick, Gerry Leonard:** electric guitar / **Tony Visconti:** bass, backing vocals / **Sterling Campbell:** drums / **Mike Garson:** synthesizers / **Recorded: Looking Glass Studios, New York:** January–May 2003 / **Allaire Studios, Shokan:** May 2003 / **Technical Team: Producers:** David Bowie, Tony Visconti / **Sound Engineer:** Tony Visconti / **Assistant Sound Engineer:** Brandon Mason (Allaire Studios)

After a country-infused introduction, this pop number emerges with some fairly naive lyrics. The narrator is haltingly apologizing to his lover: *"All I've done / I've done for me / All you gave / You gave for free / I gave nothing in return."* Here again, Tony Visconti has preserved the bass line of the demo version rather than using what was recorded by Mark Plati. The sound of this instrument, heard also on "New Killer Star" and "The Loneliest Guy," is truly amazing! Visconti used a Fender Precision bass dating from 1967, to which Roger Giffin—guitar maker to the stars—added two DiMarzio mics on the bridge, along with a Telecaster guitar mic near the neck. "Days" might really have taken off if Bowie and Visconti had not decided to overlay the lyrics with the oppressively heavy sounds of a rhythmical synthesizer.

Bowie and his famous Supra-Tone Supro guitar—which was equipped with a Bigsby vibrato installed by American luthier Flip Scipio—performing with bassist Gail Ann Dorsey.

The infamous producer Phil Spector and former Beatle George Harrison shown here in the early 1970s

FALL DOG BOMBS THE MOON

David Bowie / 4:04

Musicians: David Bowie: lead and backing vocals, electric guitar, synthesizers / **Earl Slick, Gerry Leonard:** electric guitar / **Tony Visconti:** bass, backing vocals / **Mario J. McNulty:** drums / **Recorded:** Looking Glass Studios, New York: January–May 2003 / Allaire Studios, Shokan: May 2003 / **Technical Team:** Producers: David Bowie, Tony Visconti / **Sound Engineers:** Tony Visconti, Mario J. McNulty / **Assistant Sound Engineer:** Brandon Mason (Allaire Studios)

That David Bowie took only thirty minutes to write the lyrics of "Fall Dog Bombs the Moon" can be explained by his use of the so-called cut-up technique. Asked in a 2003 interview with journalist Bill DeMain about his use of this technique when composing *Reality*, Bowie was quite open about his process: "I find it incredibly useful as a writer's tool. And I'm amazed these days at the amount of cut-up sites that are now on the Internet. It's quite phenomenal. There are at least ten, and two or three of them are excellent. I've used them, too—I've put a bunch of pieces of text into the thing, then hit the 'cut-up button,' and it slices it up for me."[36] The sound engineer Mario J. McNulty is credited as playing the drums on this track, as once again Tony Visconti kept the original version recorded for the album's demos.

TRY SOME, BUY SOME

George Harrison / 4:25

Musicians: David Bowie: lead and backing vocals, electric guitar, synthesizers / **Earl Slick, Gerry Leonard:** electric guitar / **Mark Plati:** bass / **Sterling Campbell:** drums / **Tony Visconti:** synthesizers / **Recorded:** Looking Glass Studios, New York: January–May 2003 / Allaire Studios, Shokan: May 2003 / **Technical Team:** Producers: David Bowie, Tony Visconti / **Sound Engineer:** Tony Visconti / **Assistant Sound Engineer:** Brandon Mason (Allaire Studios)

George Harrison recorded the first version of "Try Some, Buy Some" for his album *All Things Must Pass* in 1970. Dissatisfied with the result, he put the song away until he co-produced a version for Ronnie Spector, formerly the main lead singer of the Ronettes and also married to producer Phil Spector. Released by Apple Records, the Beatles' record label, the single struggled its way to the seventy-seventh spot on the *Billboard* charts in May 1971. It was rerecorded by Harrison in 1972 for his new album *Living in the Material World* (1973). Bowie gives us a version that is close to the original, but with synthesizers replacing the mandolin—a strange choice because Tony Visconti played the mandolin on other songs off the *Reality* album. As Bowie later explained: "It never really occurred to me that I was actually covering a George Harrison song. I was kind of doing an homage to Ronnie because I've adored her for years. I think it's really rather fitting and quite lovely that in fact, it is an unwitting tribute to George."[220] On the same occasion, Bowie referred to his love of cover songs: "Over the years I've had many songs that I put onto a list because one day I'll do a *Pin Ups 2* album of covers."[220] Sadly, this project was never brought to fruition.

REALITY

David Bowie / 4:24

Musicians: David Bowie: lead and backing vocals, electric guitar, synthesizers, tambourine / **Earl Slick:** electric guitar, acoustic guitar / **Gerry Leonard (?):** electric guitar / **Mark Plati:** bass / **Sterling Campbell:** drums / **Gail Ann Dorsey, Catherine Russell:** backing vocals / **Recorded: Looking Glass Studios, New York:** January–May 2003 / **Allaire Studios, Shokan:** May 2003 / **Technical Team: Producers:** David Bowie, Tony Visconti / **Sound Engineer:** Tony Visconti / **Assistant Sound Engineer:** Brandon Mason (Allaire Studios)

In 1999, Bowie declared: "I like reality a lot! I'm hungry for it."[221] Did this interview with journalist Chris Roberts give Bowie the idea for the name for his new album? Who knows? We do know, at least, that his life in his fifties was more peaceful than it had been in previous decades. In 2003, he said: "My marital life, domestic life, personal life,

whatever you want to call it is just wonderful, and my work has been going so well. So I'm a really lucky guy, you know, in that way. When I was in my twenties, I'd never thought for one second that my life would be this good in fact. This age didn't exist for me when I was twenty. 'Fifty-six? Are you kidding me? I'm never going to make it there.' You know, all these romantic, nihilistic dreams that teenagers have."[222]

Instead of relying on the wall of Marshall amps generally used onstage and in the studio to create his guitar's unusual sound, Earl Slick made use of a small device released in 1998 by the American firm Line 6. This small, red, bean-shaped unit—called the Pod—contained a vast array of amplifier types, effects, and settings (including choice of speaker, user memories, etc.) and it provided a toolbox adopted for studio use by a fair number of musicians, even if it could never be as good as a tube amp. Earl Slick used the tool discreetly but effectively on this track, and only a trained ear could tell the difference.

David Bowie and Earl Slick
onstage at the Change Theater
in Poughkeepsie, New York,
on August 19, 2003.

Kate Beckinsale starred in 2003's
Underworld. The film's original
soundtrack included a Danny Lohner
remix of "Bring Me the Disco King."

BRING ME
THE DISCO KING

David Bowie / 7:45

Musicians: David Bowie: lead and backing vocals / Matt Chamberlain:
drums / Mike Garson: piano / **Recorded:** Allaire Studios, Shokan:
August 6–September 14, 2001 (drums), May 2003 (reamping) / **Looking
Glass Studios, New York:** January–May 2003 / **Technical Team:**
Producers: David Bowie, Tony Visconti / **Sound Engineer:** Tony Visconti /
Assistant Sound Engineers: Brandon Mason, Todd Vos (Allaire Studios)

"Bring Me the Disco King" is a perfect illustration of the
creative process behind certain songs that might have
taken different forms before finally appearing on an album.
Composed by Bowie while he was writing *Black Tie White
Noise* in 1992, the first version of "Bring Me the Disco
King" was recorded by musician-producer Nile Rodgers.
With a disco rhythm box, synthesizers, and a piano contribution from Mike Garson, Bowie thought the original version was farily banal, and so he decided to drop it. A few
years later, in the *Earthling* period, Bowie and Reeves

Gabrels tried to resuscitate the track by adding a powerful
guitar. This time, the energy of the guitar overwhelmed the
melody, which was the most important feature to the song
in Bowie's opinion. Opting to make one last attempt at getting the song right in 2003, Bowie decided to go for a minimalist approach, featuring nothing more than his voice,
Garson's piano, and a drum track already recorded by Matt
Chamberlain for "When the Boys Come Marching Home"
in 2001. The result allowed the vocals to assert themselves
at the forefront of the track, thereby providing a magnificent conclusion to *Reality*.

It is an unfortunate truth that many remixes are actually
inferior reworkings of an original song, but the Danny
Lohner mix of "Bring Me the Disco King," which appeared
on the soundtrack of the movie *Underworld* (directed by
Len Wiseman, 2003), is the exception that confirms the
rule. Thanks to polished production from Danny Lohner,
bass player and clarinetist with Nine Inch Nails, the track
works wonderfully. Supported by the subtle guitars of John
Frusciante (Red Hot Chili Peppers) and keyboards from
Lisa Germano, the remix works wonderfully.

Sterling Campbell, one of the driving forces in David Bowie's discography.

Bowie and Ray Davies backstage at the fifteenth annual Tibet House Benefit Concert at New York's Carnegie Hall on February 28, 2003.

WATERLOO SUNSET

Ray Davies / 3:28

Musicians: David Bowie: lead and backing vocals, electric guitar, synthesizer, claps / **Earl Slick:** electric guitar, acoustic guitar / **Gerry Leonard:** electric guitar / **Tony Visconti:** bass, claps, backing vocals / **Sterling Campbell:** drums / **Recorded:** Looking Glass Studios, New York: January–May 2003 / **Technical Team:** Producers: David Bowie, Tony Visconti / **Sound Engineer:** Tony Visconti

On February 28, 2003, David Bowie took part for the third year in a row in the Tibet House Benefit Concert. The Tibet House is an association established in 1987 to protect Tibetan culture. On this occasion, other performers included Angélique Kidjo, Ziggy Marley, and Lou Reed. Another musician who participated in these concerts was Ray Davies, formerly of the Kinks. Together with Bowie, Davies performed one of the Kinks' most famous numbers, "Waterloo Sunset," which hit number two on the UK charts in May 1967. As a result, Bowie decided to record his own version.

Offered as a bonus track for purchasers of the Japanese edition of *Reality*, this song also came out as a single with "Never Get Old," but it was only made available in Japan.

QUEEN OF ALL THE TARTS (OVERTURE)

David Bowie / 2:53

Musicians: David Bowie: lead and backing vocals, electric guitar, synthesizers / Earl Slick, Gerry Leonard: electric guitar / Tony Visconti: bass, synthesizers, backing vocals / Sterling Campbell: drums / Gail Ann Dorsey, Catherine Russell: backing vocals / **Recorded:** Looking Glass Studios, New York: January–May 2003 / **Technical Team:** Producers: David Bowie, Tony Visconti / **Sound Engineer:** Tony Visconti

This is a strange piece, seemingly written for a musical. The words of the title are repeated over and over again while the instrumental part is similarly repetitive. For most of the concerts of "A Reality Tour," "Queen of All the Tarts (Overture)" was played before Bowie and his musicians came onto the stage. Much to the delight of Bowie fans everywhere, this previously unpublished track was included in the limited edition release of *Reality* in 2003.

LOVE MISSILE F1 ELEVEN

Martin Degville, Neal Whitmore, Anthony James / 4:14

Musicians: David Bowie: lead and backing vocals, electric guitar, synthesizer / Earl Slick, Gerry Leonard: electric guitar / Tony Visconti: bass, synthesizers / Sterling Campbell: drums / **Recorded:** Looking Glass Studios, New York: January–May 2003 / Allaire Studios, Shokan: May 2003 / **Technical Team:** Producers: David Bowie, Tony Visconti / **Sound Engineer:** Tony Visconti / **Assistant Sound Engineer:** Brandon Mason (Allaire Studios)

Released as a single with "New Killer Star," this is a cover version of Sigue Sigue Sputnik's "Love Missile F1-11," which was originally produced by Giorgio Moroder. The original track went to number three on the UK charts when it came out in March 1986. Bowie's version is almost identical to the original. Neal Whitmore, guitarist with Sigue Sigue Sputnik, described his reaction to Bowie's tribute: "We were absolutely thrilled when David covered us. What a compliment! The single biggest influence on my life and career had heard of us, and liked our work enough to do his own version."[47]

COLLABORATIONS

The original soundtrack for the 2003 film *Charlie's Angels: Full Throttle* featured a brilliant version of "Rebel Rebel."

REBEL REBEL

David Bowie / 3:10

Compilation *Charlie's Angels: Full Throttle—Music from the Motion Picture* / UK Release on Columbia / Sony Music: June 24, 2003 (CD ref.: 5123062000) / **US Release on Columbia / Sony Music:** June 24, 2003 (CD ref.: CK 90132) / **Best UK Chart Ranking:** Did Not Chart / **Best US Chart Ranking:** 12

Musicians: David Bowie: lead vocals / Earl Slick, Mark Plati, Gerry Leonard: electric guitar / Tony Visconti: bass, synthesizers / Sterling Campbell: drums / Mike Garson: piano / Gail Ann Dorsey, Catherine Russell: backing vocals / Mario J. McNulty: percussion / **Recorded:** Looking Glass Studios, New York: January 2003 / **Technical Team:** Producer: Tony Visconti / **Sound Engineers:** Tony Visconti, Brandon Mason / **Assistant Sound Engineer:** Mario J. McNulty

After the success of Joseph McGinty Nichol's 2000 movie *Charlie's Angels*, in 2003 a sequel, *Charlie's Angels: Full Throttle,* was about to hit the world's cinema screens. The explosive soundtrack for this second installment of the adventures of Cameron Diaz, Lucy Liu, and Drew Barrymore is made up partly of vintage hit songs ("Surfer Girl" by the Beach Boys, Bon Jovi's "Livin' on a Prayer"), but also of new pieces by Pink ("Feel Good Time") and Nickelback featuring Kid Rock ("Saturday Night's Alright [For Fighting]"). While busy promoting *Reality*, David Bowie was able to surprise his fans with an announcement in the pages of *Performing Songwriter*: "There's a new recording of ['Rebel Rebel'] that they're using in the *Charlie's Angels* movie. It's the version that we've been playing on the shows this last year. I hadn't done it in quite a few years, so we restructured it and made it more minimal, and it works really well."[36] This new version of the hit song was produced by Tony Visconti and featured all the musicians of Bowie's group. It was highly successful, a combination of power and melody. The song was a surprise for Bowie's fans and an introduction to his music for younger people flocking to see the thrilling, stunt-filled super-production with its three female protagonists. The new version of "Rebel Rebel" appeared on the limited edition of *Reality* that was released in September 2003. It was also included in the thirtieth-anniversary rerelease of *Diamond Dogs*, which came out from Virgin in 2004.

Lou Reed featuring David Bowie

HOP FROG

Lou Reed / 1:47

Lou Reed, *The Raven* / Europe Release on SIRE / Reprise Records: January 28, 2003 (CD ref.: 9362-48372-2) / **US Release on SIRE / Reprise Records:** January 28, 2003 (CD ref.: 48372-2) / **Best Chart Ranking:** Did Not Chart

Musicians: David Bowie: lead and backing vocals / Lou Reed: lead vocals, electric guitar / Mike Rathke: electric guitar / Fernando Saunders: bass / Tony Smith: drums / Friedrich Paravicini: keyboards / **Recorded:** Sear Sound Studios, New York: 2002 / Clinton Recording, New York: 2002 / Cove City Sound Studios, Long Island: 2002 / Looking Glass Studios, New York: 2002 / **Technical Team:** Producers: Lou Reed, Hal Willner / **Sound Engineer:** Tim Latham

"Hop Frog," with its powerful guitar riff, marks the meeting of two great performers. At the time of recording, Lou Reed was busy composing a double-disc concept album inspired by the works of Edgar Allan Poe, and he suggested that Bowie choose a song to collaborate on for the new album. Bowie's choice was "Hop Frog," the name of a Poe short story that was originally published in 1849. The story tells of the vengeance taken by a dwarf on a king who had terrorized him since childhood. The song is a real novelty highlighting the rapport between two of the most influential rockers of the twentieth century. "Hop Frog" was released on Lou Reed's ambitious album *The Raven* on January 28, 2003.

Kristeen Young onstage in 2007.

Kristeen Young featuring David Bowie

SAVIOUR

Kristeen Young / 5:23

Kristeen Young, *Breasticles* / US Release on Test Tube Baby: November 1, 2003 (ref. CD: [?]) / **Best Chart Ranking:** Did Not Chart

Musicians: Kristeen Young: lead and backing vocals, synthesizers, piano / **David Bowie:** lead vocals / **Richard Fortus:** electric guitar / **Tony Visconti:** electric guitar / **Brian Ion:** bass / **Jeff White:** drums / **Recorded:** Looking Glass Studios, New York: 2003 / **Technical Team:** Producer: Tony Visconti / **Sound Engineer:** Tony Visconti / **Assistant Sound Engineer:** Mario J. McNulty

Bowie first met singer Kristeen Young in the early 2000s. Bowie was impressed by the young singer's energetic rock 'n' roll style, and when she sent him a demo and asked him to sing a duet, he accepted immediately. Coincidentally, Young's third album was also going to be produced by Bowie's friend and longtime collaborator, Tony Visconti. The song "Saviour" was duly recorded and released as part of an LP entitled *Breasticles* in 2003. Unfortunately, the track was met with complete indifference. On October 24, 2020, which also happened to be Record Store Day—an annual worldwide event bringing together fans, artists, and independent record stores—Kristeen Young launched "American Landfill," a new single partly based on track she recorded with Bowie in 2003. Explaining the reasoning behind this reworking of "Saviour," Young cited the misogyny and ageism she felt she had been subjected to when she tried to promote the song in 2003: "People [...] didn't know 'what to do with the song,' as it didn't fit a genre. As for Bowie they would say, 'Why is he still making music? He's irrelevant.' I love the song. Bowie loved the song."[223]

Earl Slick and David Bowie

ISN'T IT EVENING (THE REVOLUTIONARY)

Earl Slick, David Bowie / 4:55

Earl Slick, Zig Zag / US Release on Sanctuary Records: December 9, 2003 (CD ref.: 06076-84671-2) / **Best Chart Ranking:** Did Not Chart

Musicians: David Bowie: lead and backing vocals / **Earl Slick:** electric guitar, acoustic guitar / **Mark Plati:** bass, synthesizers, programming / **Recorded:** Looking Glass Studios, New York: February 2003 / **Technical Team:** Producer: Mark Plati / **Sound Engineers:** Mark Plati, Pete Keppler, Jack Schell, Keith Uddin / **Assistant Sound Engineers:** Hector Castillo, Christian Rutledge, Chris Martin

Earl Slick, Bowie's faithful guitarist, already had six solo albums to his name when he began work on *Zig Zag* in 2003. Robert Smith of the Cure joined Slick to sing "Believe" (a less satisfactory performance than Smith's duet with Blink-182 on "All of This," which came out in the same year), and Bowie appeared to sing on "Isn't It Evening (The Revolutionary)" alongside the versatile Mark Plati, who was also in charge of programming on the album, in addition to playing the synthesizer and the bass. Unfortunately, this track isn't terribly memorable, but it is interesting for the obvious rapport between the singer and his guitarist, who had been at his side since 1975 and *Station to Station*.

Kashmir featuring David Bowie

THE CYNIC

Kasper Eistrup / 4:23

Kashmir, *No Balance Palace* / Europe Release on Columbia / Sony BMG: October 10, 2005 (33 rpm ref.: 82876 72767 1 / CD ref.: 82876 72767 2) / **Best Chart Ranking:** Did Not Chart

Musicians: David Bowie: lead vocals / **Kasper Eistrup:** lead vocals, electric guitar / **Henrik Lindstrand:** electric guitar, synthesizer / **Asger Engholm Techau:** drums / **Mads Tunebjerg:** bass / **Recorded:** Sun Studios, Copenhagen: March–April 2005 / **Looking Glass Studios, New York:** 2005 / **Technical Team:** Producers: Tony Visconti, Kashmir / **Sound Engineers:** Tony Visconti, Mario J. McNulty / **Assistant Sound Engineer:** Andreas Hviid

In the winter of 2005, Tony Visconti was producing a new album by Danish rockers Kashmir at Sun Studios in Copenhagen. One of Kashmir's songs particularly attracted Visconti's attention. "The Cynic" seemed tailor-made for David Bowie, who was always on Visconti's mind even though the singer's career was currently on hold for health reasons. Visconti asked the Danish musicians' permission to send Bowie an early mix of the song to see if he'd be interested in joining them on the track. The band agreed enthusiastically. In his book, *The Autobiography*, Visconti writes: "We waited for days for David to send back an e-mail. When he said yes, the band whooped for joy and each of them had to read the e-mail to be convinced."[35]

David Bowie and BT

(SHE CAN) DO THAT

David Bowie, Brian Transeau / 3:15

Compilation *Stealth—Music from the Motion Picture* / Europe Release on Epic: July 12, 2005 (CD ref.: 520420 2) / **US Release on Epic:** July 12, 2005 (CD ref.: EK 94475) / **Best Chart Ranking:** Did Not Chart

Musicians: David Bowie: lead vocals / **BT:** programming, synthesizers / **Kristeen Young:** lead vocals / **Recorded:** Looking Glass Studios, New York (lead singer): 2005 / **Unknown Studio, Los Angeles (music):** 2005 / **Technical Team:** Producers: Brian "BT" Transeau, Tony Visconti / **Sound Engineers:** Brian "BT" Transeau, Tony Visconti

In 2005, David Bowie collaborated with Brian Transeau—better known by his stage name BT—on a song for the soundtrack of Rob Cohen's futuristic thriller, *Stealth*. Bowie met up with his team at Looking Glass Studios in New York to record a demo of the song, which was produced by Tony Visconti with Mario J. McNulty at the console, and with Kristeen Young providing the robotic vocals. This recording was sent to BT in Los Angeles, who

converted it into a rather more effective techno-rock remix for the movie. In August 2016, Kristeen Young put the original version of "(She Can) Do That" on Facebook, posting a message alluding to the close relationship she shared with Bowie: "This is something maybe 6 people at most have heard. It's a David Bowie vocal demo (with me singing also) for a song for the film *Stealth* [...] recorded about 10 years ago? I was new to New York. [...] What ended up on the soundtrack sounds very different to this and I didn't get credited (not Bowie's fault) even tho' my voice is on it. P.S. David wrote all the vocals on this. I just sang what he told me to. I. was. a. ro. bot."[224]

TV on the Radio featuring David Bowie

PROVINCE

Kyp Malone, David Andrew Sitek / 4:37

TV on the Radio, *Return to Cookie Mountain* / Europe Release on 4AD: June 30, 2006 (33 rpm ref.: CAD 2607 / CD ref.: CAD 2607 CD) / **US Release on Interscope:** June 30, 2006 (33 rpm ref.: ORG 002 / CD ref.: B0007466-02) / **Best UK Chart Ranking:** 90 / **Best US Chart Ranking:** 41

Musicians: David Bowie, Kyp Malone, Tunde Adebimpe: vocals / **David Andrew Sitek:** sampler, electric guitar, bass, claviers / **Jaleel Bunton:** drums / **Gerard Smith:** piano / **Recorded:** Stay Gold Studio, Brooklyn: 2005 / **Head Gear Studio, Brooklyn:** 2005 / **Technical Team:** Producer: David Andrew Sitek / **Sound Engineers:** Chris Coady, Chris Moore / **Assistant Sound Engineer:** Matt Littlejohn

In 2004, during yet another photo session, David Bowie heard the EP *Young Liars* by the American group TV on the Radio, who happened to be good friends of the stylist working on the photoshoot. Bowie got the group's contact information from the stylist and managed to get David Andrew Sitek on the phone. Sitek, the guitarist and producer for the group, was in the middle of unloading a truck full of equipment for a concert when he picked up Bowie's call. Thinking it was his friend Julian Gross of the Liars having a joke, Sitek hung up. Undeterred, Bowie soon arranged to meet Sitek in person. Listening to the demos for the group's forthcoming album, Bowie was impressed: "I really love this 'Province' track, the lyrics and the strange choice of sounds. This is really incredible."[225] Sitek, seizing his chance, quickly suggested a collaboration, and Bowie agreed!

It's impossible to refuse an appearance by David Bowie, even when your name is Scarlett Johansson!

Scarlett Johansson

FALLING DOWN

Tom Waits / 4:55

Scarlett Johansson, *Anywhere I Lay My Head* / Europe Release on ATCO Records: May 16, 2008 (CD ref.: 8122 79925 8) / **US Release on ATCO Records:** May 16, 2008 (33 rpm ref.: R1 454588 / CD ref.: R2 454524) / **Best UK Chart Ranking:** 64 / **Best US Chart Ranking:** 126

Musicians: Scarlett Johansson: lead vocals / David Bowie: backing vocals / David Andrew Sitek: sampler, electric guitar / Jaleel Bunton: acoustic guitar / Nick Zinner: slide guitar / Ryan Sawyer: drums, tambourine, vibraphone / Sean Antanaitis: organ, Guitorgan, banjo, piano, bells, tambourine, synthesizers / **Recorded:** Dockside Studios, Maurice, Louisiana: Spring 2007 / Stay Gold Studio, Brooklyn (David Bowie vocals): May 2007 / **Technical Team: Producer:** David Andrew Sitek / **Sound Engineers:** Colin Suzuki, David Farrell, Korey Richey, Rick Kwan

In the mid-2000s, actress and (occasional) singer Scarlett Johansson was offered a contract with ATCO Records, a subsidiary of Atlantic Records, with conditions stating that she could fulfill the terms of her deal whenever she felt she had enough good songs for an album. As a great admirer of Tom Waits, in 2007 she decided to record a disc of covers of Waits's songs under the artistic direction of David Andrew Sitek, guitarist for and producer of TV on the Radio. Sitek booked five weeks at Dockside Studios in Maurice, Louisiana. The studio occupied an old, New Orleans–style house in a beautiful natural setting. The magical atmosphere of the place lent a particular color to the album—a combination of Americana and melancholy folk music. A few days before recording started, Scarlett Johansson bumped into David Bowie at a party, and Bowie said: "Hey, I hear you're working with Dave Sitek."[226] The conversation started there but no collaboration was suggested at the time. A little while later, when the album was in its mixing stage, Sitek called Johansson to tell her that Bowie had come by to add backing vocals to two of the tracks: "Falling Down" and "Fannin Street." Johansson was delighted: "It was the best phone call I ever got."[226]

Scarlett Johansson

FANNIN STREET

Tom Waits / 4:55

Scarlett Johansson, *Anywhere I Lay My Head* / Europe Release on ATCO Records: May 16, 2008 (CD ref.: 8122 79925 8) / **US Release on ATCO Records:** May 16, 2008 (33 rpm ref.: R1 454588 / CD ref.: R2 454524) / **Best UK Chart Ranking:** 64 / **Best US Chart Ranking:** 126

Musicians: Scarlett Johansson: lead vocals / David Bowie: backing vocals / David Andrew Sitek: sampler, electric guitar, synthesizers / Jaleel Bunton: acoustic guitar / Nick Zinner: electric guitar / Ryan Sawyer: tambourine / Sean Antanaitis: electric guitar, piano, bells, tambourine, synthesizers / **Recorded:** Dockside Studios, Maurice, Louisiana: Spring 2007 / Stay Gold Studio, Brooklyn (voice David Bowie): May 2007 / **Technical Team: Producer:** David Andrew Sitek / **Sound Engineers:** Colin Suzuki, David Farrell, Korey Richey, Rick Kwan

Tom Waits's melancholy song describes a street in Boston, the eponymous Fannin Street. In this version, produced by David Andrew Sitek, the song is perfectly adapted for Scarlett Johansson's voice, and it takes the listener on a journey into the depths of the America that Tom Waits loved to evoke in his compositions. If forced to choose the best track to come out of all of Bowie's artistic collaborations during the first decade of the twenty-first century, "Fannin Street" would be a clear front runner. The sublime poetry of the lyrics are beautifully enhanced by Bowie's vocals.

ALBUM

THE NEXT DAY

The Next Day. Dirty Boys. The Stars (Are Out Tonight). Love Is Lost.
Where Are We Now?. Valentine's Day. If You Can See Me. I'd Rather Be High.
Boss of Me. Dancing Out in Space. How Does the Grass Grow?.
(You Will) Set the World on Fire . You Feel So Lonely You Could Die. Heat

RELEASE DATES
World Digital Release on iTunes: February 28, 2013
United Kingdom: March 11, 2013
References: ISO Records / Columbia / Sony Music—88765 461861 (33 rpm);
88765 46186 2 (CD)
United States: March 12, 2013
References: ISO Records / Columbia—88765461861 (33 rpm);
88765 46186 2 (CD)
Best UK Chart Ranking: 1
Best US Chart Ranking: 2

A TRIUMPHANT RETURN

It had been seven years since David Bowie had released an album, and his life had been restricted to just a few artistic collaborations here and there, mostly in film. Bowie played the role of Nikola Tesla in *The Prestige* (2006), directed by Christopher Nolan, and he subsequently took part in two much less celebrated films—*August* (2008), directed by Austin Chick, and *Bandslam* (2009) by Todd Graff—before disappearing once more. If one believed the speculations of many journalists at the time, David's state of health was deteriorating by the end of the decade. The reality was quite different. The singer was devoting himself to his family and was enjoying time with his wife, Iman, and their daughter, Lexi, who he wanted to see grow up. But he also wrote many song sketches in the privacy of his home studio, which was equipped with a digital multitrack recorder, some acoustic guitars, and his faithful Korg Trinity synthesizer. During the summer of 2010, he suggested to his old friend Tony Visconti—at that time in the midst of production for *The Future Is Medieval,* the new Kaiser Chiefs album—that they meet and work on some ideas for songs, just for the enjoyment of playing music together. Surprised by this proposal, the producer assured Bowie that he would make himself available once he had completed his work on the Kaiser Chiefs album. Thus, in the autumn of 2010, the adventure of *The Next Day* officially began.

Initial New York Reunions

From November 2010, Bowie discreetly gathered together some of his most loyal colleagues at a surprising location: the tiny "6/8:" rehearsal and recording studios located in New York City's East Village. For five days, Bowie played synthesizer, Tony Visconti played bass, Sterling Campbell played drums, and Gerry Leonard played guitar. "[It was] a tiny little room really off the radar," recalled Leonard. "It's the kind of place you could get locked into and be in some horror movies. Definitely the last place you'd look for a rock star."[163] The singer wanted to preserve an air of secrecy around these recording sessions so as to avoid any pressure from record companies or from the fans. In four days, a dozen different tracks took shape, and Bowie recorded them all on his multitrack recorder. The musicians said goodbye and returned to their other work. Bowie did not issue any more news for several months.

A Recording Carried Out Under Close Supervision

At the end of April 2011, work began in earnest. David Bowie sent some emails to his musicians to invite them to take part in a recording. Bassist Gail Ann Dorsey, guitarists David Torn and Gerry Leonard, and drummer Zachary Alford all joined Bowie and got to work. Zachary Alford replaced Sterling Campbell at the last minute because Campbell was on tour with the B-52s. On May 2, 2011, everyone came together under conditions of strict secrecy at the Magic Shop studio, where they were asked to sign a confidentiality agreement. "The sheet music that was handed out as each new song was introduced was always meticulously and purposefully collected from our music stands at the end of the day," recalled Dorsey, "so that there wasn't even a chance of a piece of paper with some chords scribbled on it being leaked or entering into the world. It was something from a spy movie."[227] Recording began under the watchful eye of producer Visconti, Mario J. McNulty, and assistants Brian Thorn and Kabir Hermon, who were on the controls. The recording sessions that took place between May 2011 and October 2012 saw a number of musicians coming and going, including Tony Levin on bass, Earl Slick on guitar, and Steve Elson on saxophone.

2013

While he was sitting in on an audition for *The Next Day* at Human Worldwide Studios in December 2012, Rob Stringer (the president of Sony Music) asked Bowie what was planned for the promotional campaign, one month before the launch of the first single. To which the singer answered firmly: "There is no PR campaign. We're just going to drop it on [the] eighth of January. That's it."[227]

David Bowie remained a fan of the Legendary Stardust Cowboy throughout his career, and he's shown here posing with some ephemera at the High Line Ballroom in New York.

Tony Visconti, David Bowie, and Brian Thorn are in front of the console at the Magic Shop sound studios during a recording session for *The Next Day*.

Tony Visconti's son, Morgan, also took part in the recording sessions. At the time, Morgan owned Human Worldwide Studios, which was where the vocals and various overdubs were recorded and mixing on the album took place. After the album was released, other sessions were scheduled in order to refine some of the abandoned tracks in time for a rerelease of the disc in November 2013. This entire little working world was subjected to the same secrecy: Never discuss the recording as it was in progress. "I was on the cover of *Guitar Player* magazine. It was the Christmas issue," revealed Earl Slick, "the one you want to be on the cover of, the one that's on the newsstands twice as long. And I'm making a new Bowie album and I can't tell them anything."[228]

The Shock of *Where Are We Now?*

January 8, 2013, five o'clock in the morning, New York time. While Bowie was celebrating his sixty-sixth birthday, his new single was released online on iTunes, as well as a music video on the Vevo and YouTube platforms. This was a complete surprise, as no one was aware of the artist's plans for a comeback. Even Sony Music, the distributor of the new album via their Columbia label, was notified only a month in advance. The music world, reeling from the shock of it all, gave *The Next Day* a very warm reception in March 2013; it went to the top of the charts worldwide. Bowie gave no interviews and left everything to his colleagues. The singles "Where Are We Now?" "The Stars (Are Out Tonight)," "The Next Day," and also "Valentine's Day" were the only promotional vehicles for this LP that had been so long awaited by the fans. "Basically, [Bowie] saying nothing is almost promoting the record itself," explained Zachary Alford. "In this day and age, people are so distracted that it's hard to show them anything they'll pay attention to. By actually giving them nothing, they want to know more."[229] Created by Jonathan Barnbrook, the enigmatic cover design for *The Next Day* reuses the visual from *"Heroes"* (1977), masked by a white square. "Often the most simple ideas can be the most radical," confided the graphic designer. "We understand that many would have preferred a nice new picture of Bowie but we believed that would be far less interesting."[230]

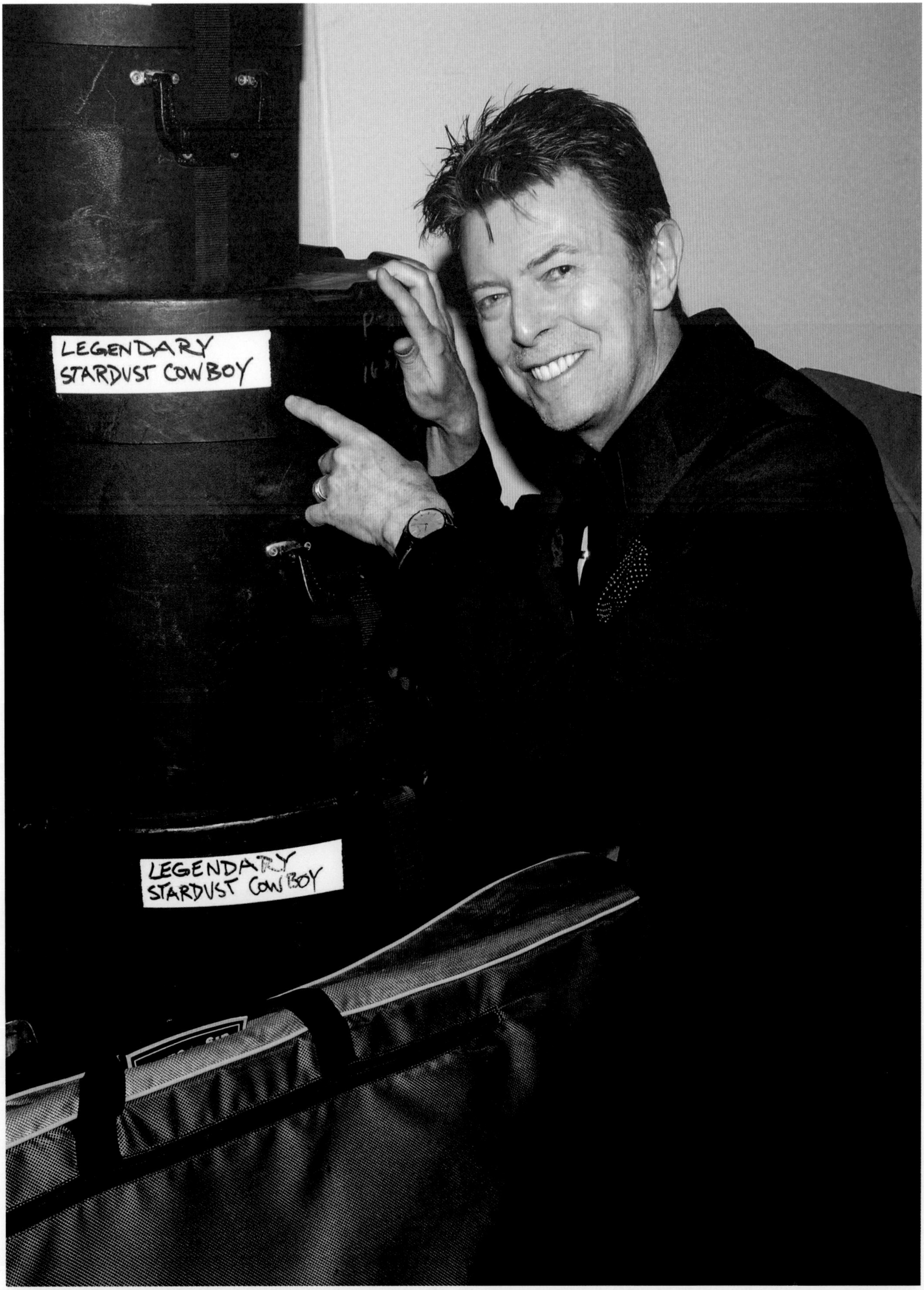
LEGENDARY
STARDUST COWBOY
LEGENDARY
STARDUST COWBOY

Floria Sigismondi directed the music videos for "The Next Day" and "The Stars (Are Out Tonight)."

THE NEXT DAY

David Bowie / 3:26

There is no side A or side B on the 45 rpm single. The two sides are identical, with no label or description. / **Single Version:** *The Next Day* / 3:26 / **World Digital Release on iTunes:** June 17, 2013 / **Europe Release on ISO Records / Columbia:** June 17, 2013 (45 rpm ref.: 88883741287) / **Best Chart Ranking:** Did Not Chart

Musicians: David Bowie: lead and backing vocals, electric guitar / **Gerry Leonard:** electric guitar / **David Torn:** electric guitar / **Gail Ann Dorsey:** bass / **Zachary Alford:** drums, tambourine / **Antoine Silverman:** violin / **Maxim Moston:** violin / **Hiroko Taguchi:** viola / **Anja Wood:** cello / **Recorded:** The Magic Shop, New York: May 2, 2011 (backing tracks), March 2012 (vocals, overdubs) / **Human Worldwide Studios, New York:** September 2011 (overdubs) / **Technical Team:** Producers: David Bowie, Tony Visconti / **Sound Engineers:** Mario J. McNulty, Tony Visconti / **Assistant Sound Engineers:** Brian Thorn, Kabir Hermon / **String Arrangements:** David Bowie, Tony Visconti

Genesis

When the music video for "The Next Day" appeared during the night of May 7–8, 2013, on YouTube, the result was simultaneous consternation and panic. In barely a few hours, the video of the third single from the eponymous album was taken down from the platform by its moderators, who then rereleased it with a notice stating that eighteen was the minimum age for viewing. It should be stated that the song's lyrics paint an accusatory portrait of the Catholic Church. *"They live upon their feet and they die upon their knees / They can work with Satan while they dress like the saints,"* sings a Bowie who is clearly operating at the top of his game. The music video, which features actors Marion Cotillard and Gary Oldman, was created by filmmaker Floria Sigismondi. In it we see priests frolicking with prostitutes before the video concludes in a bloodbath. The references to religious iconography (such as the eyeballs presented on a platter, which evoke the martyrdom of Saint Lucy of Syracuse) were too numerous for the taste of William A. Donohue, chairman of the Catholic League. On May 8 he issued a statement on the association's website, in which he wrote: "David Bowie is back, but hopefully not for long. The switch-hitting, bisexual, senior citizen from London has resurfaced."[231]

Production

By opening the album with a cheery pop number, Bowie creates an element of surprise, since the first single, "Where Are We Now?" could be construed as promising a disc with an ethereal and a melancholic atmosphere. The song was recorded on May 2, 2011, which happened to be the first day of work at the Magic Shop studios. The recording process followed a routine established by the singer: Bowie was already at the controls, with his slippers on and listening to the tracks scheduled for that day, when the musicians arrived at about 10:30. He presented the pieces to them, which were then rehearsed and recorded in a maximum of one or two takes, before being set to one side and ready for the overdubs.

DIRTY BOYS

David Bowie / 2:58

Musicians: David Bowie: vocals / Earl Slick, Gerry Leonard, Tony Visconti: electric guitar / **Tony Levin:** bass / **Zachary Alford:** drums / **Steve Elson:** baritone saxophone / **Recorded:** The Magic Shop, New York: September 17, 2011 (backing tracks), March 2012 (overdubs), May 8, 2012 (vocals), July 2012 (overdubs) / **Technical Team:** Producers: David Bowie, Tony Visconti / **Sound Engineers:** Mario J. McNulty, Tony Visconti / **Assistant Sound Engineers:** Brian Thorn, Kabir Hermon

From the second number, the atmosphere takes a heavy turn, very midtempo, led by the incisive guitars of Earl Slick, Gerry Leonard, and Tony Visconti. It is good to see Steve Elson, from the Borneo Horns, providing a high-quality baritone saxophone score, especially on the end solo. "'Dirty Boys,' the second song on the album, is very sleazy," said Tony Visconti. "[…] It's dark and it's sexy. There's a fantastic sax solo. [Steve Elson is] a little guy, and he's got a huge baritone sax, and he plays this dirty solo in it that sounds like stripper music from the 1950s. Old bump-and-grind stripper music…It wouldn't be out of place on *Young Americans*."[232]

Following no news from Bowie for years, Earl Slick was convinced that he owed his presence on *The Next Day* to a car accident. In May 2012, after a concert in Montclair, New Jersey, the guitarist was returning to New York in an AC Cobra driven by a friend. Suddenly the car caught fire and the two passengers barely had time to get out. The incident made it into one of the local papers, and the next day, the guitarist received a call from the singer: "He asks me if I was OK, and then he asks me to come and play on the record."[1]

play a couple living in a wealthy suburb, pursued by stars who have escaped from a magazine. The singer considers that his anonymity, cultivated over many years, is a precious commodity, which his wife, Iman, would confirm: "We went this summer [to London]. And no one knew we were there! [...] We went and did different things and the press never knew! It's absurd this idea that celebrities can't be anonymous. We even went on the London Eye."[233] It is quite surprising, with its catchy refrains, that this song was not met with a warm reception by the public, as its writing gives it a very special place in David Bowie's later discography: as one of the artist's last pop singles. It also appeared on the three-disc version of the compilation *Nothing Has Changed* in 2014.

Single

THE STARS (ARE OUT TONIGHT)

David Bowie / 3:56

Single Version: 1. The Stars (Are Out Tonight) / 3:56 / 2. Where Are We Now? / 4:08 / **World Digital Release on iTunes:** February 26, 2013 / UK Release on ISO Records / Columbia / Sony Music: April 20, 2013 (45 rpm ref.: 88883705557) / **US, Canada, and Europe Release on ISO Records / Columbia / Sony Music:** April 20, 2013 (45 rpm ref.: 88883704917) / **Best Chart Ranking:** Did Not Chart

Musicians: David Bowie: lead and backing vocals, acoustic guitar, claps / Gerry Leonard, David Torn: electric guitar / Tony Visconti: recorder, claps / Gail Ann Dorsey: bass, backing vocals / Zachary Alford: drums, tambourine / Steve Elson: baritone saxophone, contrabass clarinet / Antoine Silverman, Maxim Moston: violin / Hiroko Taguchi: viola / Anja Wood: cello / Janice Pendarvis: backing vocals / **Recorded:** The Magic Shop, New York: May 9, 2011 (backing tracks), March 2012 (overdubs) / **Human Worldwide Studios, New York:** October 2011 (vocals, overdubs) / **Technical Team:** Producers: David Bowie, Tony Visconti / Sound Engineers: Mario J. McNulty, Tony Visconti / **Assistant Sound Engineers:** Brian Thorn, Kabir Hermon / **String Arrangements:** David Bowie, Tony Visconti

This number is a virulent attack on the excesses of the star culture of the early 2010 decade. Coming from one of the artists who was constantly in the limelight for the previous forty years because of his androgynous looks, his indiscretions, and irreverential outpourings in the magazines, such a manifesto might appear a bit rich. But the singer handles the content with good grace: "*Stars are never sleeping / Dead ones and the living / [...] / They watch us from behind their shades / Brigitte, Jack and Kate and Brad / From behind their tinted window stretch.*"

When it appeared, the single "The Stars (Are Out Tonight)" was accompanied by a music video by Floria Sigismondi in which Bowie and the actress Tilda Swinton

LOVE IS LOST

David Bowie / 3:57

Musicians: David Bowie: lead and backing vocals, synthesizers / Gerry Leonard: electric guitar / Gail Ann Dorsey: bass / Zachary Alford: drums / **Recorded:** The Magic Shop, New York: September 13, 2011 (backing tracks), March 2012 (overdubs) / **Human Worldwide Studios, New York:** November 19, 2011 (vocals, overdubs) / **Technical Team:** Producers: David Bowie, Tony Visconti / **Sound Engineers:** Mario J. McNulty, Tony Visconti / **Assistant Sound Engineers:** Brian Thorn, Kabir Hermon

Before its release as a single in a remixed version in December 2013, "Love Is Lost" appeared in an initial, much more rock-sounding incarnation, on *The Next Day*. Although Bowie's Korg Trinity synthesizer reigns supreme, with its Hammond organ sonorities, Gerry Leonard's guitar also has pride of place. "I loved doing 'Love Is Lost' [...]," reported the guitarist. "I mean, it's such a great moody piece. I'd been listening to a lot of Peter Green's Fleetwood Mac, and how he used that reverb kind of bluesy lead, and you can hear I'm channelling a lot of that stuff."[234] Tony Visconti, for his part, takes us back to *Low* and the drums processed with an Eventide H910 Harmonizer rack. This effect, which is perceptible on some of the snare drum beats in the number's introduction, conveys a nostalgia for the Berlin years, which Bowie would develop more extensively in "Where Are We Now?"

In 2017, as a final tribute to David Bowie, bassist Tim Lefebvre recorded a very successful cover of "Love Is Lost" for *When It Falls*, an album by his jazz pianist wife, Rachel Eckroth, which he produced.

Single

WHERE ARE WE NOW?

David Bowie / 4:08

Musicians:
David Bowie: vocals, synthesizers, acoustic guitar, piano
Gerry Leonard, David Torn: electric guitar
Tony Levin: bass
Zachary Alford: drums
Henry Hey: piano
Tony Visconti: synthesizer

Recorded:
The Magic Shop, New York: September 13, 2011 (backing tracks),
March 2012 (overdubs)
Human Worldwide Studios, New York: October 2011 (vocals, overdubs)

Technical Team:
Producers: David Bowie, Tony Visconti
Sound Engineers: Mario J. McNulty, Tony Visconti
Assistant Sound Engineers: Brian Thorn, Kabir Hermon

SINGLE VERSION
Where Are We Now? / 4:08
World Digital Release on iTunes: January 8, 2013
Best UK Chart Ranking: 6
Best US Chart Ranking: Did Not Chart

2013

Genesis

When the music video for "Where Are We Now?" went online on the Vevo and YouTube platforms on January 8, 2013, at five o'clock in the morning, this was a double surprise for the Bowie fans. Of course, no one had heard about the artist's comeback, but above all, one question tantalized the observers: was this exceptionally melancholic number the shape of things to come in the forthcoming album? The appearance of *The Next Day* that March would reassure the public and the critics. "When he said this was the first single, it did surprise me, but I should know better," confided Tony Visconti. "He's always going to do something you don't expect him to do, even me."[235] This song, which is deeply nostalgic, evokes memories of the years spent in Berlin. There is the Dschungel Club, a mythical Berlin night spot, located in the Neukölln district, the Potsdamer Platz, a place that is emblematic of the division of the two parts of the city, and KaDeWe (a contraction of Kaufhaus des Westens), the city's most famous shopping center. Created by Tony Oursler, the music video parades images of Berlin behind two dolls, on which are embedded the faces of Bowie and the painter Jacqueline Humphries, Oursler's companion. The singer appears in the video dressed in a T-shirt blazoning "M/S Song of Norway," the name of the famous ship built in the early 1970s. The fans would easily be able to work out the thinly disguised reference to his painful separation in 1969 from Hermione Farthingale, who left to join the tour of the Andrew L. Stone musical....*Song of Norway*.

Production

For "Where Are We Now?" Bowie asked Zachary Alford to emphasize the first beat of each bar. For the recording of this drums sound, Tony Visconti coupled the Alford microphones with those on the other instruments (guitar, bass, voice, etc.) distributed throughout the room. The sound captured at a given distance thereby provided a natural reverb, which was well suited to the atmosphere of the piece. The presence of pianist Henry Hey should also be noted. Visconti mixed his score, delivered on his first day at the Magic Shop, with the one that Bowie had previously recorded, but for the final mixing he retained only Hey's track, leaving out the studio experimentations in favor of a homogeneous sound.

Celebrated multimedia artist Tony Oursler directed the music videos for "Where Are We Now"
and the edited version of "Love Is Lost (Hello Steve Reich Mix by James Murphy for the DFA)."

The St. Valentine's Day massacre occurred on February 14, 1929. Seven members of Chicago's North Side Gang were murdered.

Single

VALENTINE'S DAY

David Bowie / 3:01

Single Version: 1. *Valentine's Day* / 3:01 / 2. *Plan* / 2:02 / **World Digital Release on iTunes:** August 19, 2013 / **Europe Release on ISO Records / Columbia:** August 19, 2013 (45 rpm ref.: 88883756667) / **Best Chart Ranking:** Did Not Chart

Musicians: David Bowie: lead and backing vocals, claps / **Earl Slick:** electric guitar / **Tony Visconti:** bass / **Sterling Campbell:** drums / **Recorded:** The Magic Shop, New York: July 24, 2012 (backing tracks), September 18, 2012 (vocals) / **Technical Team: Producers:** David Bowie, Tony Visconti / **Sound Engineers:** Mario J. McNulty, Tony Visconti / **Assistant Sound Engineers:** Brian Thorn, Kabir Hermon

A severe critique of the free sale of guns in the United States, "Valentine's Day" contains multiple references to the dramas that have punctuated the history of this country. Marked by a recent event that occurred in Oakland, California, on April 2, 2012, when a man shot seven people at the University of Oikos, here Bowie delivers poignant and moving lyrics. The title has a dual meaning. Firstly, it refers to the Saint Valentine's Day Massacre in 1929, where

seven people were killed, victims of the gang warfare between Al Capone and his rival, Bugs Moran. It also refers to the character in the song, a murdered school pupil, whose daily life is described by Bowie. Among the targets referred to is the school's football coach. One might say that Bowie was prescient: In 2018, the shootings at Marjory-Stoneman Douglas High School in Parkland, Florida, killed seventeen people, including the school's football coach. This drama took place on February 14, Valentine's Day.

The music video by Indrani and Markus Klinko is marked by a symbolic gesture. In the final seconds, the singer raises his bloodred headless guitar to the sky, reminiscent of the speech by Charlton Heston during the annual convention of the National Rifle Association, on May 20, 2000. The actor, who was president of the gun lobbying association, brandished his gun skyward, addressing the crowd and his main rival, Democratic presidential candidate Al Gore: "As we set out this year to defeat the divisive forces that would take freedom away, I want to say those fighting words for everyone within the sound of my voice to hear and to heed, and especially for you, Mr. Gore: 'From my cold, dead hands!'"[236]

2013

Exceptional bassist and backing vocalist Gail Ann Dorsey worked with Bowie from 1995 to 2003.

IF YOU CAN SEE ME

David Bowie / 3:16

Musicians: David Bowie: lead and backing vocals, synthesizers / **Gerry Leonard, David Torn:** electric guitar / **Tony Levin:** bass / **Zachary Alford:** drums, percussion / **Gail Ann Dorsey:** backing vocals / **Recorded: The Magic Shop, New York:** May 4, 2011 (backing tracks), March–April 2012 (vocals, overdubs) / **Technical Team:** Producers: David Bowie, Tony Visconti / **Sound Engineers:** Mario J. McNulty, Tony Visconti / **Assistant Sound Engineers:** Brian Thorn, Kabir Hermon

Although Gail Ann Dorsey, who provides the backing vocals on "You Can See Me," declared that she played fretless bass on this number, it was probably the line recorded by Tony Levin that was retained in the mixing. All wrapped up during the third working day at the Magic Shop, the backing tracks of this indomitable free jazz–influenced piece are reminiscent of the energy deployed by Bowie and Alford on *Earthling* fourteen years earlier. Maybe the drummer had been endowed with eternal youth—his drum patterns, which are very complex, seem to be played out with a disconcerting ease. For the best description of this unidentified sound object, with its somber, almost seedy atmosphere, one has only to quote biographer Nicholas Pegg, who wrote in 2016: "This is among [...] the most frightening three minutes you'll ever spend in David Bowie's company."[47]

I'D RATHER BE HIGH

David Bowie / 3:44

Musicians: David Bowie: lead and backing vocals / **Gerry Leonard:** electric guitar, acoustic guitar / **Tony Levin:** bass / **Zachary Alford:** drums / **Recorded: The Magic Shop, New York:** September 15, 2011 (backing tracks), March 2012 (overdubs), May 9, 2012 (vocals) / **Technical Team:** Producers: David Bowie, Tony Visconti / **Sound Engineers:** Mario J. McNulty, Tony Visconti / **Assistant Sound Engineers:** Brian Thorn, Kabir Hermon

On this track, Bowie sings about a young man of seventeen, returning from the front and devastated by his years of combat. The ghosts of the war in Afghanistan, which had already lasted ten years, soar overhead in this number, denouncing the woes of a youth broken by this interminable conflict. The narrator states that he would be better off under the influence of drugs than reliving the years spent in the field. "He's just burnt out," explains Visconti, "and rather than becoming a human being again, I think he laments, 'I'd rather be high / I don't want to know / I'm trying to erase these thoughts from my mind.'"[232] Bowie made multiple takes of the backing vocals to obtain a Beatles-like feel.

BOSS OF ME

David Bowie, Gerry Leonard / 4:09

Musicians: David Bowie: lead and backing vocals / **Gerry Leonard:**
electric guitar / **Tony Visconti:** recorder / **Tony Levin:** Chapman stick /
Zachary Alford: drums, shaker / **Gail Ann Dorsey, Janice Pendarvis:**
backing vocals / **Steve Elson:** baritone saxophone / **Recorded:** The
Magic Shop, New York: September 14, 2011 (backing tracks), March
2012 (overdubs) / **Human Worldwide Studios, New York:** November 26,
2011 (vocals, overdubs) / **Technical Team:** Producers: David Bowie,
Tony Visconti / **Sound Engineers:** Mario J. McNulty, Tony Visconti /
Assistant Sound Engineers: Brian Thorn, Kabir Hermon

In the summer of 2011, Gerry Leonard suggested that Bowie
join him at his house in Woodstock, New York, to work on
some new compositions, including "Boss of Me" and "I'll
Take You There." In conditions of utmost secrecy, the guitarist had to get hold of some equipment, including a drum
machine. He called on one of his friends, who owned an old
Roland TR-808: "Ed, I'm borrowing your drum machine. I
can't tell you what for, but I need to take it right now."[237]

There has been much conjecture as to the significance of
the title "Boss of Me." The singer was probably influenced by
a television program that his daughter, Lexi, liked to watch—
as did millions of young adolescents throughout the world in
the 2000s decade—broadcast on FX until 2011: *Malcolm in
the Middle*, whose theme tune was "Boss of Me," performed
by the group They Might Be Giants. Journalist Chris O'Leary
suggests an alternative source, emphasizing the use by Gerry
Leonard of the Boss ME-80 pedal. This is plausible, as the
guitarist, at that time in partnership with the Roland brand,
the parent company of Boss, was an ambassador for the
ME-80 multi-effects pedal in 2014.

On September 14, 2011, while recording the song,
Zachary Alford suggested that Tony Levin should play the
number on a Chapman stick rather than on bass. This
instrument, which is played using the tapping technique,
enables the combination of the high harmonics of a guitar
at the bass frequency of a four-string bass. "Tony wasn't
thrilled with that," explained Alford, "because there were a
lot of chord changes. He doesn't like to do songs with
chord changes on the Stick, but everybody thought it
sounded great."[229]

DANCING OUT IN SPACE

David Bowie / 3:24

Musicians: David Bowie: lead and backing vocals, synthesizers / **Gerry
Leonard, David Torn:** electric guitar / **Gail Ann Dorsey:** bass / **Zachary
Alford:** drums / **Recorded:** The Magic Shop, New York: May 4 and 7,
2011 (backing tracks), March 2012 (overdubs), October 8, 2012 (vocals) /
Technical Team: Producers: David Bowie, Tony Visconti / **Sound
Engineers:** Mario J. McNulty, Tony Visconti / **Assistant Sound Engineers:**
Brian Thorn, Kabir Hermon

The soaring notes of this bouncy piece owe much to guitarists Gerry Leonard and David Torn, both specialists in
meticulously crafted textures. While Torn uses a large
number of modern digital effects to produce his riffs,
Leonard was very open to trying out new approaches. An
enthusiast for the Boss effects, for whom he was a product
ambassador, he was also open to exploring vintage equipment. He is very skillful in performing on this disc with
one of the machines most prized by collectors: the Synthi
Hi-Fli, created in 1972 by the company EMS, of which only
150 were made. This analog multieffects equipment incorporates a myriad of tools for guitarists seeking sound
effects. Behind their cheesy names—Treble Booster, Pitch
Shifter, Ring Modulator, or Sustain Fuzz—there are so
many effects lurking inside this white box to light up the
eyes of seasoned musicians such as David Gilmour of Pink
Floyd and Steve Hackett of Genesis. With this device, Gerry
Leonard treats himself to all sorts of guitar experimentations on *The Next Day*. "It's just crazy, completely crazy
sound on that track,"[232] confirmed producer Tony Visconti.

2013

Sister Rosetta Tharpe was an American singer, songwriter, and guitarist who achieved notoriety for her unique mixture of soul and gospel music with electric guitar. Bowie was inspired by her work on the track "(You Will) Set the World on Fire."

HOW DOES THE GRASS GROW?

David Bowie, Jerry Lordan / 4:33

Musicians: David Bowie: lead and backing vocals, synthesizers / **Gerry Leonard, David Torn:** electric guitar / **Gail Ann Dorsey:** bass, backing vocals / **Zachary Alford:** drums / **Recorded:** The Magic Shop, New York: May 3, 2011 (backing tracks), January 16, 2012 (vocals, overdubs), March 2012 (overdubs) / **Technical Team: Producers:** David Bowie, Tony Visconti / **Sound Engineers:** Mario J. McNulty, Tony Visconti / **Assistant Sound Engineers:** Brian Thorn, Kabir Hermon

Recorded on the second day of the Magic Shop sessions, on May 3, 2011, this number has all the qualities of a single that one tends to hum as soon as you hear it on the radio. Its "ya-ya-ya-ya" refrain was also borrowed from "Apache" by the Shadows (which went to number one on the British charts in July 1960), hence the sharing of the credits with Jerry Lordan, that song's writer. After "I'd Rather Be High," Bowie again sings of the drama of warfare, this time referring to the battlefields: *How does the grass grow / Blood blood blood.*" The singer uses what is perhaps a less dramatic musical register, but his denunciation of the armed conflicts breaking out all over the world is just as strong.

(YOU WILL) SET THE WORLD ON FIRE

David Bowie / 3:30

Musicians: David Bowie: lead and backing vocals / **Earl Slick, Gerry Leonard:** electric guitar / **Tony Visconti:** bass / **Sterling Campbell:** drums, tambourine / **Gail Ann Dorsey, Janice Pendarvis:** backing vocals / **Recorded:** The Magic Shop, New York: July 25, 2012 (backing tracks) / Human Worldwide Studios, New York: September 27, 2012 (vocals) / **Technical Team: Producers:** David Bowie, Tony Visconti / **Sound Engineers:** Mario J. McNulty, Tony Visconti / **Assistant Sound Engineers:** Brian Thorn, Kabir Hermon

In this number, Bowie mixes very powerful guitar chords on the couplets and a very Motown rhythm on the refrains to conjure up the portrait of a female vocalist trying to make a name for herself. He includes a number of references to Greenwich Village in New York, where the American folk scene emerged in the 1960s, with artists such as Pete Seeger, Joan Baez, and, of course, Bob Dylan, referred to here as Bobby. The question arises, however, of the identity of this African-American singer who, armed with her guitar, will soon have the world at her feet. Bowie has never given a specific indication, but one might envisage that he is honoring Sister Rosetta Tharpe in this song, queen of the blues and gospel, who handled the Gibson SG like no other female musician had ever done, and who tried to forge a career in the New York folk scene before moving to Europe for a better life. This is a fitting homage for the very considerable talent of this artist underrated by the general public.

Henry Hay collaborated with Bowie on *The Next Day* and *Lazarus*.

YOU FEEL SO LONELY YOU COULD DIE

David Bowie / 4:41

Musicians: David Bowie: lead and backing vocals, acoustic guitar / **Gerry Leonard, David Torn, Tony Visconti:** electric guitar / **Gail Ann Dorsey:** bass, backing vocals / **Zachary Alford:** drums / **Janice Pendarvis:** backing vocals / **Henry Hey:** piano / **Antoine Silverman, Maxim Moston:** violin / **Hiroko Taguchi:** viola / **Anja Wood:** cello / **Recorded:** The Magic Shop, New York: May 3, 2011 (backing tracks), March 2012 (vocals, overdubs) / **Human Worldwide Studios, New York:** March 2012 (overdubs) / **Technical Team:** Producers: David Bowie, Tony Visconti / **Sound Engineers:** Mario J. McNulty, Tony Visconti / **Assistant Sound Engineers:** Brian Thorn, Kabir Hermon / **String Arrangements:** Tony Visconti

With its delicate guitar arpeggios, this piece is reminiscent of "Rock 'n' Roll Suicide" (1972) also given the interest that the singer had always had in the music of Otis Redding and soul in general. The string quartet emphasizes the melancholy exuded by the song itself, as does the gentle playing of pianist Henry Hey, a newcomer to the sessions for *The Next Day*, and with whom Tony Visconti had had a fruitful collaboration on *Hooked!*, Lucy Woodward's third album. "I loved his versality and flawless technique," said the producer. "He played on several other small projects for me."[47] The musician's playing, although it does not have the grandiloquence of Mike Garson, is notable, and contributes a welcome plenitude among the more powerful numbers of the album.

HEAT

David Bowie / 4:25

Musicians: David Bowie: lead and backing vocals, acoustic guitar / **Gerry Leonard, David Torn:** electric guitar / **Gail Ann Dorsey:** bass / **Zachary Alford:** drums / **Antoine Silverman, Maxim Moston:** violin / **Hiroko Taguchi:** viola / **Anja Wood:** cello / **Recorded:** The Magic Shop, New York: May 6, 2011 (backing tracks), March 2012 (overdubs) / **Human Worldwide Studios, New York:** November 5, 2011 (vocals, overdubs) / **Technical Team:** Producers: David Bowie, Tony Visconti / **Sound Engineers:** Mario J. McNulty, Tony Visconti / **Assistant Sound Engineers:** Brian Thorn, Kabir Hermon / **String Arrangements:** Tony Visconti

Bowie performs "Heat" with a deep and profoundly disconcerting voice, like the one that would characterize the song "Blackstar" three years later. The tessitura he chose is so low that one can barely recognize his powerful timbre when he vocalizes, almost sobbing, *My father ran the prison / My father ran the prison.* The text is not the most transparent, as Tony Visconti commented in the pages of *Rolling Stone* in 2013: "I'm not quite sure what he's singing about on it, but it's a classic Bowie ballad. [...] And I can't give too much away about it because honestly, I don't know exactly what it's about, if it's about being in a real prison or being imprisoned in your mind. Again, it's certainly not about him; he's singing as the voice of somebody."[232] This has been a constant source of discussions among the fans concerning this mysterious and elusive conclusion to the album.

On November 4, 2013, ISO Records and Columbia published *The Next Day Extra*, a collector's edition of *The Next Day*, consisting of the original album, a second disc with eight previously unissued songs and two remixes, and a DVD containing the music videos for the album's four singles.

A digital version of the new disc was also offered, called *The Next Day Extra EP*, but it lacked three tracks: "Plan," "I'll Take You There," and "So She," which were already available as bonus tracks on the deluxe digital edition of *The Next Day*, which was released in March 2013.

World Digital Release on iTunes: November 4, 2013 / **Europe Release on ISO Records / Columbia / Sony Music:** November 4, 2013 (CD Box Set ref.: 88883787812) / **Best UK Chart Ranking:** 89 / **Best US Chart Ranking:** Did Not Chart

ATOMICA

David Bowie / 4:08

Musicians: David Bowie: lead and backing vocals, synthesizers, programming, piano / **Earl Slick, Gerry Leonard, David Torn:** electric guitar / **Gail Ann Dorsey:** bass / **Zachary Alford:** drums / **Alex Alexander:** percussion / **Erin Tonkon:** backing vocals / **Recorded: The Magic Shop, New York:** May 2, 2011 (backing tracks), March 2012 (overdubs), July 2012 (overdubs), August 26, 2013 (vocals), August 2013 (overdubs) / **Human Worldwide Studios, New York:** August 2013 (overdubs) / **Technical Team:** Producers: David Bowie, Tony Visconti / **Sound Engineers:** Mario J. McNulty, Tony Visconti / **Assistant Sound Engineers:** Brian Thorn, Kabir Hermon

This is a number that would have had the fans dancing if it had been given a single release in spring 2013. Although its backing tracks were recorded on day one at the studio, on May 2, 2011, "Atomica" was in its definitive form when the track listing for *The Next Day* was posted. Also, Bowie delivered his vocal line only in the summer of 2013, for the release of *The Next Day Extra*. "Some songs, like 'Atomica,' needed more work and were assigned to the back burner intentionally for future releases,"[47] explained Tony Visconti. A good start for this album rerelease, which recalls another disco rhythm number performed by a rock group: "Atomic" by Blondie, which appeared on *Eat to the Beat* in 1979.

LOVE IS LOST (HELLO STEVE REICH MIX BY JAMES MURPHY FOR THE DFA)

David Bowie / 10:26

Single Version: / 4:07 / **World Digital Release on iTunes:** December 16, 2013 / **Best Chart Ranking:** Did Not Chart

Musicians: David Bowie: lead and backing vocals, synthesizers / **Gerry Leonard:** electric guitar / **Gail Ann Dorsey:** bass, backing vocals / **Zachary Alford:** drums / **Roy Bittan:** piano / **James Murphy:** programming, synthesizers, claps / **Matthew Thornley, Hishan Bharoocha, Jordan Hebert:** claps / **Recorded: The Magic Shop, New York:** September 13, 2011 (backing tracks), March 2012 (overdubs) / **Human Worldwide Studios, New York:** November 19, 2011 (vocals, overdubs) / **Plantain Studios, New York (remix):** 2013 / **Technical Team:** Producers: David Bowie, Tony Visconti, James Murphy (remix) / **Sound Engineers:** Mario J. McNulty, Tony Visconti, Matthew Shaw (remix) / **Assistant Sound Engineers:** Brian Thorn, Kabir Hermon

While the Canadian group Arcade Fire was recording its new album, *Reflektor*, at Electric Lady Studios in New York, during the summer of 2013, a star guest made an appearance: David Bowie. The band had already met the singer in September 2005, at Radio City Music Hall in New York, during a "Fashion Rocks" fund-raising soiree for victims of Hurricane Katrina, where they performed three songs together. As a close acquaintance of James Murphy, producer of this opus (and incidentally, also the former leader of LCD Soundsystem), Bowie was charmed by the song being recorded that day, "Reflektor," and recorded a few phrases that would be discreetly inserted into the final mixing of the song. Somewhat later, he offered James Murphy the opportunity of remixing "Love Is Lost," one of the high

A three-track live EP featuring David Bowie and Arcade Fire was recorded at the Fashion Rocks event on September 8, 2005.

points in *The Next Day*. Murphy constructed a spectacular version lasting ten minutes and twenty-six seconds, which included scoring of applause borrowed from "Clapping Music" (1972) by Steve Reich—hence the appearance of the composer's name in the extended remix number. He also introduced a piano line by Roy Bittan that was recorded for "Ashes to Ashes" in 1980. This reworking of "Love Is Lost" appeared on *The Next Day Extra* in November 2013, as well as in single format on December 16, 2013. The long version is accompanied by a magnificent music video from Barnaby Roper, which includes—as a new homage to "Ashes to Ashes"—an almost subliminal image of Bowie as clown at 6:44. The "edit" version of the number was shortened to 4:07, and it was included in the compilation *Nothing Has Changed*, where it was accompanied by a video filmed in one night at David Bowie's offices, for a total cost of $12.99, the price of the USB drive onto which the video was loaded. The growing interest in vinyl at the time meant that "Love Is Lost (Hello Steve Reich Mix by James Murphy for the DFA)" was also released in a twelve-inch-record format, which the older among us are still allowed to refer to as a maxi single.

PLAN

David Bowie / 2:02

Musicians: David Bowie: electric guitar, synthesizers, percussion / Zachary Alford: drums / **Recorded:** The Magic Shop, New York: September 14, 2011 (drums), January 2012 / Human Worldwide Studios, New York: January 2012 / **Technical Team:** Producers: David Bowie, Tony Visconti / **Sound Engineers:** Mario J. McNulty, Tony Visconti / **Assistant Sound Engineers:** Brian Thorn, Kabir Hermon

If this instrumental curiosity seems familiar upon first listening, it is because it introduced the music video of "The Stars (Are Out Tonight)," when the single was released in February 2013. Recorded solely by David Bowie on January 19 and 20, 2012, and based on a drum line by Zachary Alford for "The Informer," "Plan" was offered as a bonus track on the deluxe digital and vinyl editions of *The Next Day*. The guitar played by the singer is the Fender Stratocaster that rocker Marc Bolan gave him after his appearance on the *Marc* broadcast in 1977.

THE INFORMER

David Bowie / 4:32

Musicians: David Bowie: lead and backing vocals / Gerry Leonard, David Torn: electric guitar / Gail Ann Dorsey: bass / Zachary Alford: drums / Henry Hey: piano / **Recorded:** The Magic Shop, New York: September 14, 2011 (backing tracks), March 2012 (overdubs), August 2013 (overdubs) / Human Worldwide Studios, New York: September 21, 2011 (vocals, overdubs), August 2013 (overdubs) / **Technical Team:** Producers: David Bowie, Tony Visconti / **Sound Engineers:** Mario J. McNulty, Tony Visconti / **Assistant Sound Engineers:** Brian Thorn, Kabir Hermon

As was the case for several numbers from the album, the recording sessions for "The Informer," which started in September 2011, after the summer Leonard-Bowie duo sessions, were spread out over nearly two years. The hardest task would therefore have been to maintain cohesion in the sound takes. This was where the shadow man Brian Thorn came in, assistant sound engineer present throughout all the sessions. "There was actually an effort to make a similar-sounding recording for each band," explained sound engineer Mario J. McNulty, "and that was one of Tony's requests. I would have our assistant Brian Thorn recall everything for every song, and Brian did so in great detail. I could always reference an EQ setting from a previous month, for example."[238]

I'D RATHER BE HIGH (VENETIAN MIX)

David Bowie / 3:50

Musicians: David Bowie: lead and backing vocals, synthesizers / Gerry Leonard: electric guitar / Tony Levin, Tony Visconti: bass / Zachary Alford: drums / Henry Hey: synthesizer (?), harpsichord (?) / **Recorded:** The Magic Shop, New York: September 15, 2011 (original version), March 2012 (overdubs), August 2013 (additional takes) / **Technical Team:** Producers: David Bowie, Tony Visconti / **Sound Engineers:** Mario J. McNulty, Tony Visconti / **Assistant Sound Engineers:** Brian Thorn, Kabir Hermon

During the summer of 2013, Bowie invited Tony Visconti and Henry Hey to work on a new version of "I'd Rather Be High." Hey suggested the inclusion of a harpsichord sound, probably played on a synthesizer in this case. Tony Visconti rerecorded the bass line in his own style, and a new mixing was applied. The song was used for a Louis Vuitton advertisement created by Romain Gavras, in which Bowie also performed. The song's use of the harpsichord married well with the visuals of the Venetian ball filmed for the luxury brand's ad, which suggests that this collaboration was already planned at the time of the song's recording in August 2013. The song appeared on the B-side of the maxi 45 rpm single of "Love Is Lost (Hello Steve Reich Mix by James Murphy for the DFA)" in December 2013.

LIKE A ROCKET MAN

David Bowie / 3:28

Musicians: David Bowie: lead and backing vocals, acoustic guitar, synthesizers / Gerry Leonard, David Torn: electric guitar / Gail Ann Dorsey: bass, backing vocals / Zachary Alford: drums / Janice Pendarvis: backing vocals / **Recorded:** The Magic Shop, New York: May 2, 2011 (backing tracks), March 2012 (vocals, overdubs), August 2013 (overdubs) / Human Worldwide Studios, New York: August 2013 (overdubs) / **Technical Team:** Producers: David Bowie, Tony Visconti / **Sound Engineers:** Mario J. McNulty, Tony Visconti / **Assistant Sound Engineers:** Brian Thorn, Kabir Hermon

Despite its title citing one of Elton John's greatest hits ("Rocket Man" in 1972) and its couplets that recall those of "Help!" (1965) by the Beatles, "Like a Rocket Man" is most definitely a true David Bowie original. Recorded between May 2011 and August 2013, this piece emphasizes the pop spirit that is more in evidence on *The Next Day Extra* than on the original version of the album.

BORN IN A UFO

David Bowie / 3:04

Musicians: David Bowie: lead and backing vocals / Earl Slick: electric guitar / Tony Visconti: bass / Sterling Campbell: drums / Henry Hey: synthesizers / **Recorded:** The Magic Shop, New York: July 23, 2012 (backing tracks), September 26, 2012 (vocals), August 2013 (overdubs) / Human Worldwide Studios, New York: August 2013 (overdubs) / **Technical Team:** Producers: David Bowie, Tony Visconti / **Sound Engineers:** Mario J. McNulty, Tony Visconti / **Assistant Sound Engineers:** Brian Thorn, Kabir Hermon

"Born in a UFO" was initially written and recorded during the sessions for *Lodger*, between 1978 and 1979. As he was not happy with the result, Bowie put the song to one side, and then brought it back out for *The Next Day* in May 2011. He recorded a new version at that time with Gail Ann Dorsey, Zachary Alford, and Gerry Leonard, which he still did not like. On July 23, 2012, he was determined to sort out this number once and for all. Sterling Campbell was on drums and Earl Slick on six-string guitar. The bass was rerecorded by Tony Visconti, and after a number of final overdubs by Henry Hey in August, Bowie was able to record his vocals on September 26. A year later, in August 2013, the final touches were applied to the number, which was released on *The Next Day Extra*, after a gestation period of thirty-five years. Of particular note are the refrains in this third recording, which are a hat tip to "Born in the USA" (1984) by Bruce Springsteen, of whom Bowie was always a great admirer and a loyal friend.

I'LL TAKE YOU THERE

David Bowie, Gerry Leonard / 2:44

Musicians: David Bowie: lead and backing vocals, acoustic guitar, synthesizers / Gerry Leonard, David Torn, Tony Visconti: electric guitar / Gail Ann Dorsey: bass, backing vocals / Zachary Alford: drums / Alex Alexander: percussion / Janice Pendarvis: backing vocals / **Recorded:** The Magic Shop, New York: September 12, 2011 (backing tracks), March 2, 5, 14, 2012 (vocals, overdubs) / **Technical Team:** Producers: David Bowie, Tony Visconti / **Sound Engineers:** Mario J. McNulty, Tony Visconti / **Assistant Sound Engineers:** Brian Thorn, Kabir Hermon

Appearing on the deluxe digital edition of *The Next Day*, and on the vinyl version of the album, "I'll Take You There" only borrows the title from the soul anthem by the Staples Singers, which was released in 1972. This is a resolutely rock piece, whose lyrics narrate the worries of Sophie and Lev, a migrant couple arriving in the United States. *"What will be my name in the USA?"* asks Sophie. *"Hold my hand and I'll take you there,"* answers Lev. Bowie once again stalks the darker aspects of America in this deep and moving song, taken at a lively pace with its refrains played with metronomic precision by Zachary Alford. The song was written at Woodstock, in collaboration with Gerry Leonard, in August 2011, and immortalized that September.

GOD BLESS THE GIRL

David Bowie / 4:11

Musicians: David Bowie: lead and backing vocals, synthesizers, claps / Gerry Leonard: electric guitar / Morgan Visconti: acoustic guitar / Tony Levin: bass / Zachary Alford: drums / Alex Alexander: percussion, claps / Gail Ann Dorsey, Janice Pendarvis: backing vocals / Henry Hey: piano / **Recorded:** The Magic Shop, New York: September 12, 2011 (backing tracks), 2012 (overdubs) / Human Worldwide Studios, New York: November 2, 2011 (vocals, overdubs) / **Technical Team:** Producers: David Bowie, Tony Visconti / **Sound Engineers:** Mario J. McNulty, Tony Visconti / **Assistant Sound Engineers:** Brian Thorn, Kabir Hermon

An initial candidate for inclusion in the track listing of *The Next Day*, in the end "God Bless the Girl" was included only in the Japanese edition of the album in March 2013. Logically added to *The Next Day Extra*, the song in its own right confers legitimacy to this high-quality collector's edition. The voice of Gail Ann Dorsey is relegated to backing vocalist as Tony Levin (who played bass on this number), injects genuine emotion into the track. Henry Hey also contributes, and in doing so confirms his entente cordiale with Bowie, who chose him as musical director for his musical, *Lazarus*, in 2015. Morgan Visconti—son of the producer and the owner of Human Worldwide Studios—provides the acoustic guitar rhythm on this number. This was effectively a reprise for him in the David Bowie discography, having previously played three piano notes on "Warszawa" in 1976!

Bassist Tony Levin worked with Bowie, King Crimson, and Peter Gabriel, among others.

SO SHE

David Bowie / 2:31

Musicians: David Bowie: lead and backing vocals, acoustic guitar, synthesizers / Gerry Leonard: electric guitar, synthesizers / David Torn: electric guitar / Tony Visconti: bass, electric guitar / Zachary Alford: drums / Antoine Silverman, Maxim Moston: violin / Hiroko Taguchi: viola / Anja Wood: cello / **Recorded:** The Magic Shop, New York: May 12, 2011 (backing tracks), October 2012 (vocals, overdubs) / **Technical Team:** Producers: David Bowie, Tony Visconti / **Sound Engineers:** Mario J. McNulty, Tony Visconti / **Assistant Sound Engineers:** Brian Thorn, Kabir Hermon / **String Arrangements:** David Bowie, Tony Visconti

With the quality of its writing and performance, "God Bless the Girl" would have been the ideal conclusion for the adventure of *The Next Day* if David Bowie had not opted to close this collector's disc with the short and rather superfluous "So She," which had already been heard on the deluxe digital and vinyl editions of the original album. *"She saw me smile / Feeling like I'd never been in love,"* sings a romantic Bowie in this studio remnant, reworked to provide the fans with another new song.

BLACK.
STAR)
R) ★ (BL
KSTAR)
★ (BLA
ACKST

ALBUM

★

(BLACKSTAR)

★ (Blackstar). 'Tis a Pity She Was a Whore. Lazarus. Sue (Or in a Season of Crime).
Girl Loves Me. Dollar Days. I Can't Give Everything Away

RELEASE DATE
Worldwide Digital Release: January 8, 2016
Europe and United States: January 8, 2016
Ref.: ISO Records / Columbia / Sony Music—88875173871 (33 rpm);
88875173862 (CD)
Best UK Chart Ranking: 1
Best US Chart Ranking: 1

FAREWELL

In 2013, after making only rare public appearances for more than a decade, David Bowie reappeared on the music scene. *The Next Day* leapt up the charts, while the exhibition "David Bowie Is" opened on March 23, 2013, at the Victoria and Albert Museum in London. The exhibition was visited by a record number of people. This retrospective, notable for its spectacular and immersive installations, provided an overview of Bowie's career through five hundred items selected from more than seventy-five thousand objects from his personal collection.

Reinvigorated by these successes, David Bowie planned to make 2014 a good year, and co-wrote a musical with the Irish playwright Enda Walsh. Called *Lazarus*, the musical was a mixture of autobiography and fable. Bowie composed several new pieces for this work: "No Plan," "Killing a Little Time," "When I Met You," and "The Hunger" (later to become "Lazarus"). But plans for a wonderful year were overshadowed by a diagnosis of liver cancer. Terrible as the news was, it did not interfere with his determination to finish *Lazarus*, and the musical had its premiere on December 7, 2015, at the New York Theatre Workshop. Bowie also managed to complete his final album, *Blackstar*, at the same time.

Maria Schneider and Jazz

In the spring of 2014, Bowie was in the audience for a concert given by the Maria Schneider Orchestra at Birdland, the famous New York jazz club. Intrigued by the fusion of genres that characterized the ensemble's music, he suggested to Maria Schneider that they work together. The result was "Sue (Or in a Season of Crime)," a jazz-inspired single released in November 2014 and included as part of Bowie's compilation album, *Nothing Has Changed*. Reconnecting with a style that he considered one of the pillars of his musical makeup, Bowie was keen to compose more

pieces with Maria Schneider. Busy with preparing her own new album, Schneider was reluctant to take on a new project, suggesting instead that Bowie use Donny McCaslin, her saxophonist, and the rest of his group. At the beginning of June 2014, she invited Bowie to one of their concerts at the 55 Bar, a jazz club in Greenwich Village as notable for its tiny size as for its great reputation. The performance by these outstandingly virtuosic musicians drew on music of many styles and influences, including jazz, electro, funk, and hip-hop. Impressed by the ease with which McCaslin manipulated these musical traditions, Bowie immediately invited the saxophonist to collaborate with him on his new album. A recording session was arranged for the beginning of 2015.

The first stage of the project began in the summer of 2014, at the same time as *Lazarus* was being composed. Bowie met with Tony Visconti, Zachary Alford, and guitarist Jack Spann—a friend of the producer's—at the Magic Shop recording studio to put together some demos. A small number of titles were recorded, confirming a style that was less rock influenced and more personal. Next, Bowie shut himself up in his studio for a few months, although he did remain in constant contact with Donny McCaslin and his group, sending them numerous demos in preparation for the sessions scheduled for January 3, 2015. A new, more polished version of "'Tis a Pity She Was a Whore" was also being worked on, following the demo used for the B-side of "Sue (Or in a Season of Crime)" in November.

Last Days at the Magic Shop

On January 3, 2015, the group set up at the Magic Shop with Donny McCaslin on saxophone, flute, and clarinet; Tim Lefebvre on bass; Mark Guiliana on drums; and Jason Lindner on piano, Wurlitzer, and synthesizers. Each

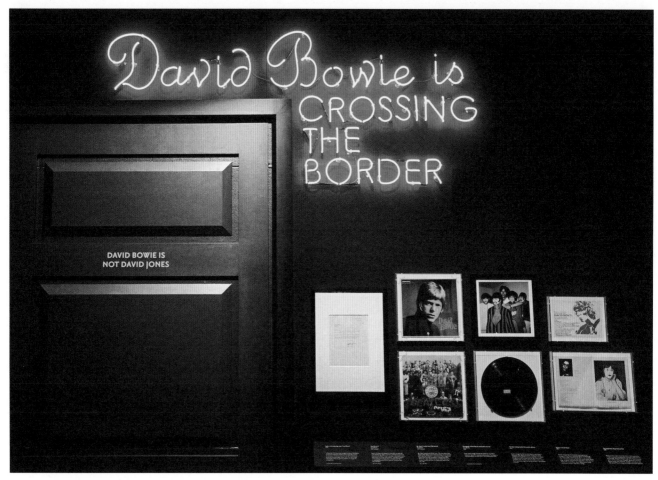

The traveling museum exhibition "David Bowie Is ..." originated at the Victoria and Albert Museum in London and was also shown at the Brooklyn Museum from March 2 to July 15, 2018.

musician signed a confidentiality clause relating to the album they were making as well as to David Bowie's state of health. Tony Visconti arranged the studio sessions so that the group worked for one week each month from January through April. Obsessed by the idea of fusing genres, Bowie was listening to the innovative music produced by Kendrick Lamar and D'Angelo, especially from their respective albums, *To Pimp a Butterfly* and *Black Messiah*, both of whom offered an alternative to traditional hip-hop via their integration of other musical styles. As Tony Visconti put it: "We wound up with nothing like that, but we loved the fact Kendrick was so open-minded and he didn't do a straight-up hip-hop record. He threw everything on there, and that's exactly what we wanted to do. The goal, in many, many ways, was to avoid rock & roll."[239]

With this aim in mind, producer James Murphy—who had done the remix of "Love Is Lost" at the end of 2013—met up with the team in February. Originally intended to participate as a co-producer, in the end Murphy did little more than give some advice and add some drum portions to the new version of "Sue (Or in a Season of Crime)" and "Girl Loves Me." In March 2015, Ben Monder contributed some sensitive additions on his six-string guitar. Some overdubs and the majority of the takes of Bowie's vocals were carried out in April at Human Worldwide Studios, and finally the disc was mixed at Electric Lady Studios by a new member of the team: Tom Elmhirst. This talented musician had already worked with Arcade Fire on *Reflektor*, to which Bowie had contributed some backing vocals. The disc was completed in June, leaving Bowie free to return to preparations for the musical *Lazarus*.

David Bowie's Musical Testament

When the new album came out on January 8, 2016, it was rapturously received, going to number one on the American Billboard chart—a first in Bowie's career. The lyrics contain numerous messages of farewell, and the disc as a whole forms a kind of last will and testament. The lyrics of both "Blackstar" and "Lazarus," together with the sonic landscape they inhabit, seem like a premature invitation to Bowie's funeral. The actual name of the album is the logo ★, but its unpronounceable character means that it has the more convenient title of *Blackstar*. Jonathan Barnbrook, who created the daring album art for the 2013's *The Next Day*, was asked to design the new album: a black star on a white background for the CD, and a black sleeve with the shape of a star cut out of it for the vinyl version, which allowed the grooves of the disc inside to show

Jason Lindner, Mark Guiliana, Donny McCaslin and Tom Lefebvre accepting the Grammy Award for Best Alternative Album for *Blackstar* on February 12, 2017.

through. In November 2015, the designer said of his art-work: "This was a man who was facing his own mortality. The *Blackstar* symbol [★], rather than writing 'Blackstar,' has a sort of finality, a darkness, a simplicity, which is a representation of the music."[240]

Two days after the launch of his twenty-sixth studio album, on January 10, 2016, Bowie died at his New York City home on Lafayette Street. The news shocked the whole world because Bowie had kept his illness a secret. But with *Blackstar*, he left an eloquent parting message. The first lines of "Lazarus" speak for themselves: *"Look up here, I'm in heaven / I've got scars that can't be seen / I've got drama, can't be stolen / Everybody knows me now."*

In keeping with the funereal mood of *Blackstar*, the Magic Shop studio, where the instrumentals for the disc had been recorded, closed permanently on March 16, 2016, unable to meet the rapidly rising New York rental costs. For Tony Visconti: "A part of my life just died. I will miss Magic Shop almost as much as I miss my friend David Bowie."[241]

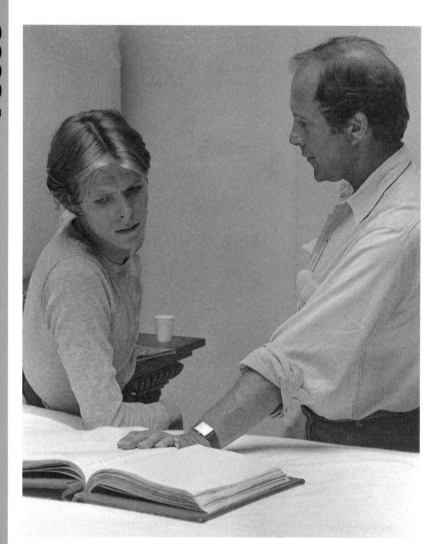

David Bowie and director Nicolas Roeg on the set of *The Man Who Fell to Earth* in 1976.

LAZARUS

Thomas Jerome Newton at Thirty Years On

In the summer of 2013, while on a week's holiday in London, David Bowie took the opportunity to have tea with an old friend, cinema and theater producer Robert Fox. Fox recalled the meeting: "I went to the hotel and within minutes he said he wanted to write a musical. All he knew at that time was that it would be called *Lazarus* and be based on the character, Thomas Newton, from *The Man Who Fell to Earth*."[242] To write the book, Fox suggested the Irish playwright Enda Walsh. Bowie was happy with the idea, although he planned to introduce numerous songs from his own repertoire into the piece. The Belgian director Ivo van Hove—whose version of Arthur Miller's play *A View from the Bridge* had greatly impressed Fox—together with his trusted colleague, production designer Jan Versweyveld, came to join the team. Thirty years after Nicolas Roeg's movie, *Lazarus* features

the character Newton, an extraterrestrial who finds himself stranded on a hostile Earth and, disillusioned, takes refuge in alcohol. A mysterious young woman comes to his aid, and Newton manages to build a rocket and so find a way of leaving Earth.

New Songs and Old

David Bowie threw himself heart and soul into this project, one of the most ambitious of his career. Among the numerous demos intended for his new album recorded in his home studio in August 2014, Bowie also recorded four new numbers for the musical: "The Hunger" (later becoming "Lazarus"), "Wistful" (later "No Plan"), "Killing a Little Time," and "When I Met You." These appeared together on the EP *No Plan*, released on January 8, 2017.

During 2015, despite the progressive worsening of his illness, Bowie was active on all fronts. He recorded

Late-night talk show host Seth Meyers poses with (clockwise, from top left) Cristin Milioti, Michael C. Hall, Michael Esper, and Sophia Anne Caruso, the stars of the American production of *Lazarus*.

Blackstar, co-wrote the book for the musical with Enda Walsh, and kept an eye on the musical supervision for the musical, which was undertaken by Henry Hey, the pianist on "The Next Day." A group made up of guitarists JJ Appleton and Chris McQueen, bass player Fima Ephron, drummer Brian Delaney, saxophonist Lucas Dodd, and trombonist Karl Lyden was to play live for the performances scheduled to take place at the New York Theatre Workshop, an intimate venue that's quite different from the bright lights of Broadway. Rehearsals began in October with the role of Thomas Jerome Newton taken by actor Michael C. Hall, unforgettable from his roles as David James Fisher in *Six Feet Under* and as the terrifying but also amiable serial killer Dexter Morgan in *Dexter*.

Curtain Up for the Last Time

On the evening of the musical's premiere on December 7, 2015, a fragile-looking David Bowie appeared onstage to receive the public's applause for the last time. Robert Fox recalls: "He looked beautiful and frail and behaved as always impeccably and despite being in great pain he took a curtain call with the cast and band to the delight of everyone in the building. Then he slipped home, whilst everyone else celebrated at the opening night party."[242] The venue was packed and all tickets for all dates sold out in just a few minutes.

On January 11, 2016, just a few hours after Bowie's death, the performers in *Lazarus* had to carry out a difficult task: recording the vocal lines for the cast album that was due to be released later that year. When *Lazarus: The Original Cast Recording to the Musical by David Bowie and Enda Walsh* came out on October 21, 2016, it was immediately successful, reaching number ten on the UK charts. "He was ill, and he said writing the musical was on his bucket list,"[243] remembers his friend Tony Visconti. David Bowie, like his character Newton, was to leave Earth with elegance and panache.

Sue (Or in a Season of Crime) / 'Tis a Pity She Was a Whore / Sue (Or in a Season of Crime) (Radio Edit)

Digital Release: November 17, 2014 (UK), November 28, 2014 (US) / UK Release on ISO Records / Parlophone: November 17, 2014 (45 rpm 10" ref.: 10RDB2014) / US Release on ISO Records / Columbia: November 28, 2014 (45 rpm 10" ref.: 88875028701) / Best UK Chart Ranking: 81 / Best US Chart Ranking: Did Not Chart

Side A

SUE (OR IN A SEASON OF CRIME)

David Bowie, Maria Schneider, Paul Bateman, Bob Bhamra / 7:24

Musicians

David Bowie: lead vocals
Ben Monder: electric guitar
Jay Anderson: double bass
Mark Guiliana: drums
Frank Kimbrough: piano
Donny McCaslin: tenor sax, soprano sax
Ryan Keberle: trombone
Jesse Han: flute
David Pietro: alto flute, soprano sax
Rich Perry: tenor sax
Scott Robinson: clarinet, bass clarinet, contrabass clarinet
Tony Kadleck: trumpet, bugle
Greg Gisbert: trumpet, bugle
Augie Haas: trumpet, bugle
Mike Rodriguez: trumpet, bugle
Keith O'Quinn: trombone
Marshall Gilkes: trombone
George Flynn: bass trombone, contrabass trombone

Recorded

Avatar Studios, New York: July 24, 2014

Technical Team

Producers: David Bowie, Tony Visconti
Sound Engineer: Kevin Killen
Conductor: Maria Schneider
Arrangements: Maria Schneider

45 rpm 10" Version (Europe and US)

Side A: *Sue (Or in a Season of Crime)* / 7:24
Side B1: *'Tis a Pity She Was a Whore* / 5:27
Side B2: *Sue (Or in a Season of Crime (Radio Edit)* / 4:01

Genesis

David Bowie dreamed for many years of a collaboration with Maria Schneider. Composer, arranger, conductor, and ardent defender of musicians' rights, she had been recognized as a fine jazz musician ever since the release of her first album, *Evanescence*, in 1994. Between May 8 and 10, 2014, alongside the Maria Schneider Orchestra, she gave a series of three concerts at the famous American jazz club Birdland, where Louis Armstrong, Billie Holiday, and Lester Young had performed in their time. Bowie, sitting in the audience, was intrigued by the originality of this music—dissonant, free, and mysterious, yet played with an unrivaled rigor and virtuosity—awakening in him long-buried memories of loved styles of music (jazz, big band, improvisation). A few days later, he asked Maria Schneider if she would work with him on one of his compositions. The two musicians got together at the piano keyboard, and it took no more than two sessions for Maria Schneider to find the right balance between the jazz writing of the song and the dark color that Bowie wanted. A recording session was organized at Euphoria Studios with the seventeen members of the orchestra and, on July 24, 2014, the song was immortalized at Avatar Studios in New York, formerly known as the Power Station (the name was revived in September 2017). When "Sue (Or in a Season of Crime)" came out as a single in November 2014, its 10-inch vinyl format was designed to recall the vintage jazz element Bowie was after, a perfect reproduction of one of the classic 78 rpm discs produced by Brunswick, Decca, and Parlophone. The song also opens the compilation album *Nothing Has Changed*, which stands as a true retrospective of Bowie's career.

Production

The Maria Schneider Orchestra required very few takes to complete "Sue (Or in a Season of Crime)." Almost seven and a half minutes of soaring jazz was something new for Bowie fans. Bowie sings like a crooner, his voice rising over the free improvisations of Donny McCaslin's saxophone against the dark layers of the orchestra's brass

Although she is absent from the recording, Maria Schneider's free spirit left its mark on Bowie's final album.

section. Tight playing by Mark Guiliana on drums is supported by the virtuosic double bass of Jay Anderson. With this piece, Maria Schneider won the Grammy Award for best arrangement, instruments, and voice in February 2016. Busy preparing for her new album, Maria Schneider was not able to pursue further collaboration, much to Bowie's disappointment. She did, however, point him toward Donny McCaslin and his quartet, sound advice that was to pay dividends on the astonishing *Blackstar*.

FOR BOWIE ADDICTS

Paul Bateman and Bob Bhamra are credited as co-composors of "Sue (Or in a Season of Crime)," because Bowie borrowed a chord sequence from "Brand New Heavy" (1997), a number performed by Plastic Soul, their drum 'n' bass group.

★ (BLACKSTAR)

David Bowie / 9:57

Musicians
David Bowie: lead and backing vocals, synthesizers
Ben Monder: electric guitar
Tim Lefebvre: bass
Mark Guiliana: drums
Jason Lindner: Wurlitzer, synthesizers
Tony Visconti: synthesizers
Donny McCaslin: saxophone, flute

Recorded
The Magic Shop, New York: March 20, 2015 (backing tracks and vocals)
Human Worldwide Studios, New York: April 2–3, May 15, 2015 (vocals and overdubs)

Technical Team
Producers: David Bowie, Tony Visconti
Sound Engineers: Kevin Killen (the Magic Shop), Tony Visconti (Human Worldwide Studios)
Assistant Sound Engineers: Kabir Hermon (the Magic Shop), Erin Tonkon (Human Worldwide Studios)
Arrangements: Tony Visconti, David Bowie
Final Mixing: Tom Elmhirst

Worldwide Digital Release: November 19, 2015
Best UK Chart Ranking: 61
Best US Chart Ranking: 78

Genesis

In the autumn of 2015, Swedish director Johan Renck was just finishing filming his series *The Last Panthers*. All he needed now was a piece of theme music to match the show's themes. A member of his team suggested approaching David Bowie, who appeared to be interested. Renck sent Bowie two unedited episodes and showed him a storyboard, saying later: "We discussed aspects of the show; the plot, but also the currents of guilt. We talked about the dark heart of Europe, biblical aspects of human nature. I showed him a concept board of the title sequence—images laced with demons from the worlds of Bosch and Grünewald. Then he said go—it all fits. Then he played me his new song, 'Blackstar.'"[244] Of this piece Renck said: "'Blackstar' was an extraordinary piece of music—it's like an anthem. It's really my cup of tea: it's dark, it's ominous, but it's also dreamy."[1] Following that, David Bowie asked Renck to make the video for the song that was to be released as a single on November 19, 2015. To give the director some artistic pointers, Bowie sent him a number of drawings, including one of a man with a bandage over his mouth and buttons placed on his eyes. This was the origin of Button Eyes, the inspiration for the character Bowie assumes in the video, a terrifying figure with bandaged eyes and buttons where the eyes should be. Another sketch shows a lifeless astronaut, and this, too, appeared in the video. Renck commented: "To me, it was a hundred percent Major Tom, a character that he had revisited and used over his career."[243] Even before the release of the song "Lazarus," with its explicit words, Bowie was letting drop little hints about his imminent death, like these barely concealed farewells to the mythical hero of "Space Oddity."

Production

"Blackstar" was recorded on March 20, 2015, in two distinct parts that were then put together by Tony Visconti and mixed by Tom Elmhirst in a single session that lasted ten hours. The flute and guitar segments were recorded during the overdubbing sessions in April 2015, along with Bowie's lead vocals. For the latter parts, Tony Visconti added a somewhat surprising effect: using the Automatic Double Tracking (ADT) system, he doubled Bowie's voice in fifths, giving it an unsettling robotic sound, *"I'm a blackstar, I'm a blackstar."*

David Bowie appears in the music video for "Blackstar" directed by Johan Renck.

Attempting to reproduce the demo that Bowie had made of "Blackstar," and for which he had programmed an electronic rhythm box, drummer Mark Guiliana plays a free-jazz rhythm on his fourteen-inch snare drum while Jason Lindner doubles some of the beats on the bass drum with a Moog synthesizer. Although played by the whole ensemble, the sound is more akin to a sample.

The end product lasted for more than ten minutes, meaning it did not conform to the format insisted on by the iTunes Store, which did not accept singles of that duration. Unwillingly, Visconti reduced it to 9:57, saying: "It's total bullshit. But David was adamant it be the single, and he didn't want both an album version and a single version."[239]

Actor Michael C. Hall delivered a
memorable performance of "Lazarus"
on the December 17, 2015, episode of
The Late Show with Stephen Colbert.

'TIS A PITY SHE WAS A WHORE

David Bowie / 4:52

Musicians: David Bowie: lead and backing vocals, synthesizers / **Ben Monder:** electric guitar / **Tim Lefebvre:** bass / **Mark Guiliana:** drums, programming Roland SPD-SX / **Jason Lindner:** piano, synthesizers / **Donny McCaslin:** saxophone / **Erin Tonkon:** backing vocals / **Recorded:** The Magic Shop, New York: January 5, 2015 (backing tracks) / **Human Worldwide Studios, New York:** April 20 and 22, 2015 (vocals and overdubs) / **Technical Team: Producers:** David Bowie, Tony Visconti / **Sound Engineers:** Kevin Killen (the Magic Shop), Tony Visconti (Human Worldwide Studios) / **Assistant Sound Engineers:** Kabir Hermon (the Magic Shop), Erin Tonkon (Human Worldwide Studios) / **Final Mixing:** Tom Elmhirst

Genesis

This strange title, "'Tis a Pity She Was a Whore," is borrowed from a play by the English playwright John Ford, *'Tis a Pity She's a Whore*, first put on in 1626 and published in 1633. This controversial piece, based around the incestuous love between Giovanni and his sister Annabella, is one of many literary references in *Blackstar*. The demo version of the song came out on the B-side of "Sue (Or in a Season of Crime)" on November 14, 2015. David Bowie subsequently decided to give it the respect it deserved and rerecorded it with McCaslin, Guiliana, Lindner, and Lefebvre so as to fit it in with the strange universe of the other demos.

Production

The saxophone part recorded by Bowie in August 2014 is replaced by that of Donny McCaslin, with a harmonized interpretation in two different keys. Jason Lindner adds his own personal touch, a few notes on a honky-tonk piano with thumbtacks on the hammers, giving a bright, metallic sound, and deliberately left out of tune to give the authentic feel of the seedy barrooms of the old days.

A guest appears on this track—Erin Tonkon, Tony Visconti's assistant at Human Worldwide Studios—taking part for the second time in a Bowie recording, having contributed some backing vocals for "Atomica" in 2013. As she said in an interview: "It was incredible. Unlike other projects, I was present from the very beginning to the end, from ideas to demos to recording, mixing and mastering. I even got to deliver the test pressings to David's house. [...] Watching him work was a masterclass of getting ego out of the way. Even though he was the boss and he had the final

say, he was cool and didn't discredit anyone's ideas based on their age or gender or experience level. He never got stuck in the past and was always willing to try something different and experimental."[245]

ON YOUR HEADPHONES

When the backing tracks were being recorded, the musicians were placed all together in the same room. Bowie was singing along with them. His voice can be heard, picked up by the mics of the instrumental players, and was sometimes retained in the final mixing along with his lead vocals that were recorded in April 2015. Examples of his voice can be found between 4:03 and 4:32 of "'Tis a Pity She Was a Whore."

Single

LAZARUS

David Bowie / 6:22

Musicians: David Bowie: lead vocals, electric guitar, synthesizers / **Ben Monder:** electric guitar / **Tim Lefebvre:** bass / **Mark Guiliana:** drums / **Jason Lindner:** Wurlitzer, synthesizers / **Donny McCaslin:** saxophone / **Recorded:** The Magic Shop, New York: January 3, 2015 (backing tracks) / **Human Worldwide Studios, New York:** April 23–24, May 7, 2015 (vocals and overdubs) / **Technical Team: Producers:** David Bowie, Tony Visconti / **Sound Engineers:** Kevin Killen (the Magic Shop), Tony Visconti (Human Worldwide Studios) / **Assistant Sound Engineers:** Kabir Hermon (the Magic Shop), Erin Tonkon (Human Worldwide Studios) / **Final Mixing:** Tom Elmhirst / **Worldwide Digital Release:** December 17, 2015 / **Best UK Chart Ranking:** 45 / **Best US Chart Ranking:** 40

Genesis

Sketched out by Bowie in August 2014 and given the working title "The Hunger," this dark ballad was then handed over to the pianist Henry Hey, musical director of the musical *Lazarus*. The poignant words of the song, written originally for the musical but soon made part of the singer's discography, reveal the last thoughts of a man at the end of his life and take on an undeniably autobiographical tone. Visconti

2016

recalled: "When I read the lyrics to 'Lazarus' and a few other songs, I knew what he was doing. I think it was clear in his mind that this could be his last album. He was putting all those messages in there. Like that first verse of "Lazarus"— *'Look up here, I'm in heaven.'* I heard that and I smiled. 'I know what you're saying David,' and he laughed."[246]

Directed by Johan Renck, the song's video is equally explicit. In what appears to be an abandoned hospital, a bedridden Bowie appears as Button Eyes, the character already seen in the "Blackstar" video with bandaged eyes and buttons where the eyes should be. Based on the Bible story of Jesus resurrecting Lazarus of Bethany, the song was released as a single on December 17, 2015. A month later, its mysterious text became prophetic: The singer, who had just died, would become immortal through his work.

Production

While Henry Hey had focused on the energetic demo of *Lazarus* recorded in August 2014 for the rehearsals of the musical, the version reworked with Donny McCaslin and his musicians in January 2015 brings out the darker aspects of the words. Hey commented on these differences, mostly too small and detailed for the less well-informed listener, but saying more generally: "The version that you hear in the show [...] is more direct, more aggressive, and actually fits the show better than David's version would."[163] For the album version, Tony Visconti retained some of the guitar lines recorded by Bowie on the original demo, adding those played by Ben Monder at the overdubbing stage. The backing tracks were added in on January 3, 2015, in what Bowie thought an overly restrained atmosphere. Drummer Mark Guiliana recalled: "I remember that we played a really nice first take—everyone played very musically, but politely. David said something like, 'Great, but now let's *really* do it.' He was always pushing us. The version on the record is the next take, where we are all taking a few more chances. The intro didn't exist on his demo, but after the first take we kept playing and Tim started playing this beautiful line with the pick, which David liked and thought it would make for a nice intro."[247]

Gifted drummer Mark Guiliana appears onstage at Ronnie Scott's Jazz Club on November 1, 2004.

SUE (OR IN A SEASON OF CRIME)

David Bowie, Maria Schneider, Paul Bateman, Bob Bhamra / 4:40

Musicians: David Bowie: lead vocals, electric guitar / **Ben Monder:** electric guitar / **Tim Lefebvre:** bass / **Mark Guiliana:** drums / **James Murphy:** percussion / **Jason Lindner:** Wurlitzer, synthesizers / **Donny McCaslin:** saxophone, flute, clarinet / **Recorded:** The Magic Shop, New York: February 2, 2015 (backing tracks) / **Human Worldwide Studios, New York:** April 23 and 30, 2015 (vocals) / **Technical Team: Producers:** David Bowie, Tony Visconti / **Sound Engineers:** Kevin Killen (the Magic Shop), Tony Visconti (Human Worldwide Studios) / **Assistant Sound Engineers:** Kabir Hermon (the Magic Shop), Erin Tonkon (Human Worldwide Studios) / **Final Mixing:** Tom Elmhirst

Genesis

Composed with Maria Schneider and originally played by her orchestra of seventeen virtuoso musicians, such a perfect rendering of "Sue (Or in a Season of Crime)" might have been hard to repeat. The original version of the song—impeccably played—was beautifully matched by Bowie's lyrics in which the narrator confesses to the murder of his woman. Bowie shed new light on the story in the new version, adding two final couplets to the "Radio Edit"

version of the original. The murderer, who has just discovered a note in which Sue tells him of her unfaithfulness, shouts out, in a furious tornado of music that finishes as abruptly as it had started: "*I'm such a fool / Right from the start / You went with that clown.*"

Production

For the new arrangements of the song, Bowie gives free rein to Donny McCaslin. Keen to move as far away as possible from the original version, McCaslin encourages the musicians to improvise to the maximum. Unsatisfied with the result, he decides to revise the part originally played by Maria Schneider, giving it a new color by concentrating on saxophone, flute, and clarinet. James Murphy, producer and lead singer of LCD Soundsystem, uses percussion to bring out the brutality of the verses, while Ben Monder supports the ensemble with a brilliant guitar riff. At the drum kit, Mark Guiliana gives a performance to match the fiercest of jungle rhythms hammered out by Zachary Alford on *Earthling* in 1997, further evidence of the freedom accorded to the musicians during these sessions. Guiliana said of this track: "For this version he wanted a bit more edge, a bit more urgency. We played it more stripped down and a little faster. The energy of this track is really special—again, David encouraged us to really go for it. Tim [Lefebvre] was free to go to what I call 'Tim World,' which is one of my favorite musical places."[247]

In addition to working with David Bowie on *Blackstar*, bassist Tim Lefebvre has also collaborated with celebrated artists Bill Evans, Jamie Cullum, and Empire of the Sun.

GIRL LOVES ME

David Bowie / 4:51

Musicians: David Bowie: lead and backing vocals, synthesizers / **Tim Lefebvre:** bass, electric guitar / **Mark Guiliana:** drums / **James Murphy:** tambourine / **Jason Lindner:** synthesizers / **Donny McCaslin:** flute / **Recorded:** The Magic Shop, New York: February 3, 2015 (backing tracks) / Human Worldwide Studios, New York: April 16 and May 17, 2015 (vocals) / **Technical Team: Producers:** David Bowie, Tony Visconti / **Sound Engineers:** Kevin Killen (the Magic Shop), Tony Visconti (Human Worldwide Studios) / **Assistant Sound Engineers:** Kabir Hermon (the Magic Shop), Erin Tonkon (Human Worldwide Studios) / **Final Mixing:** Tom Elmhirst

Genesis

It is not easy at a first listening to grasp the meaning of the lyrics of "Girl Loves Me" with its scattering of words from two different types of slang. Firstly, there is the occasional polari expression, a language used particularly in the eighteenth century in Great Britain by sailors and fairground performers. Later, in the 1950s and '60s, it became the secret language of the London homosexual community, which was hounded by legislation and discrimination.

David Bowie also uses nadsat, a language invented by Anthony Burgess for his novel *A Clockwork Orange*, published in 1962. A combination of syllables and Russian and English contractions, this jargon was popularized by Malcolm McDowell and his *droogies* ("friends" in nadsat) in Stanley Kubrick's movie adaptation of 1971. In "Girl Loves Me," *cheena* means "woman," *malchek* "boy," *rot* "mouth," and *rozz* "policeman." In Tony Visconti's judgment, "The lyrics are wacky, but a lot of British people, especially Londoners, will get every word."[239]

Production

The occasional guitar lines of "Girl Loves Me" are taken by bass player Tim Lefebvre, doubling his own bass line on the Fender Stratocaster given to Bowie by Marc Bolan in 1977. This song, one of Bowie's favorites, is also notable for Mark Guiliana's intricate drum playing. Using two interlinked rhythm boxes, he attempts to reproduce the pattern recorded by Bowie on the original demo. The quieter notes on the snare drum were picked up by a nearby mic while the counter-rhythm was recorded on Bowie's mic, which remained on during all the live takes. Tony Visconti was to take advantage of this arrangement to give a sense of space at the mixing stage. The use of two mics placed at a distance from one another has the effect of giving a subtle rhythmical mismatch recalling that of the song's original demo version.

Single

DOLLAR DAYS

David Bowie / 4:44

Musicians: David Bowie: lead and backing vocals, acoustic guitar, electric guitar, synthesizers / Ben Monder: electric guitar / Tim Lefebvre: bass / Mark Guiliana: drums, programming / Jason Lindner: piano, synthesizers / Donny McCaslin: saxophone / **Recorded:** The Magic Shop, New York: February 6, 2015 (backing tracks) / Human Worldwide Studios, New York: April 27, 2015 (vocals) / **Technical Team:** Producers: David Bowie, Tony Visconti / **Sound Engineers:** Kevin Killen (the Magic Shop), Tony Visconti (Human Worldwide Studios) / **Assistant Sound Engineers:** Kabir Hermon (the Magic Shop), Erin Tonkon (Human Worldwide Studios) / **Final Mixing:** Tom Elmhirst

Exceptionally, Bowie had not provided a demo recorded beforehand for this song. He finished it on his own on his acoustic guitar just a few minutes before presenting it to his musicians in the studio on February 6, 2015. Called on for his expertise, James Murphy advised Mark Guiliana on the drum pattern for the verses, played mainly on the toms. To this spontaneous take, Visconti and Bowie added some overdubs of synthesizers, guitars, and backing vocals. The musicians did not discover how the whole thing sounded until the disc was completed.

The mixing of "Dollar Days" and "I Can't Give Everything Away" carried out by Tom Elmhirst was done on the same day because one song leads into the next on the album, with a transition marked by four bars of rhythm box taken from the original demo of "I Can't Give Everything Away." In an interview in 2017, Elmhirst commented: "The vocals were there, the performances were there. I didn't have to do a lot of work. It was quite painless for me, the whole process, because it was recorded and produced so well."[248]

I CAN'T GIVE EVERYTHING AWAY

David Bowie / 5:47

Single Version: *I Can't Give Everything Away (Radio Edit)* / 4:26 / Worldwide Digital Release: April 6, 2016 / **Best Chart Ranking:** Did Not Chart

Musicians: David Bowie: lead and backing vocals, electric guitar, harmonica, synthesizers, programming / Ben Monder: electric guitar / Tim Lefebvre: bass / Mark Guiliana: drums / Jason Lindner: Wurlitzer, synthesizers / Donny McCaslin: saxophone, flute / **Recorded:** David Bowie's home studio, New York: August 2014 / The Magic Shop, New York: March 21, 2015 (backing tracks) / Human Worldwide Studios, New York: May 7, 2015 (vocals) / **Technical Team:** Producers: David Bowie, Tony Visconti / **Sound Engineers:** Kevin Killen (the Magic Shop), Tony Visconti (Human Worldwide Studios) / **Assistant Sound Engineers:** Kabir Hermon (the Magic Shop), Erin Tonkon (Human Worldwide Studios) / **Final Mixing:** Tom Elmhirst

In answer to those who describe *Blackstar* as a "experiment in jazz," David Bowie unleashes this number recalling the rhythms and textures of the 1992 album *Black Tie White Noise*. Introduced by a rhythm box loop taken from the demo recorded in August 2014, "I Can't Give Everything Away" rolls out the red carpet for the musicians who supported Bowie throughout this project. Ben Monder executes a magnificent concluding guitar solo on his Ibanez AS-50 de 1982, following on from the virtuosic tenor sax playing of Donny McCaslin. Tim Lefebvre gives body to his bass notes through his use of a 3Leaf Audio Octabvre, an analogue octave divider. The harmonica line was taken from the initial demo version of the song and given a central place in the mixing, bringing to mind two landmarks in Bowie's singing career: "A New Career in a New Town" on *Low* (1977) and "Never Let Me Down" on the 1987 album of the same name. "I Can't Give Everything Away" was released as a single on April 6, 2016, three months after Bowie's death, making the song a noble conclusion to the *Blackstar* adventure.

In the summer of 2017, Nine Inch Nails gave a number of concerts at various American festivals to promote their EP *Add Violence*, due for release on July 21, 2017. On their set list right from the first date—July 19 at the Rabobank Arena in Bakersfield, California—Trent Reznor performed a cover version of Bowie's "I Can't Give Anything Away" as a tribute to his friend who had died the year before.

2016

NO PLAN

1. Lazarus*
2. No Plan
3. Killing a Little Time
4. When I Met You

* This version is identical to the one on the album.

Worldwide Digital Release: January 8, 2017 / Europe Release on ISO Records / Columbia / Sony Music: January 8, 2017 (maxi 45 rpm ref.: 88985419651/ CD ref.: 88985419612) / **US Release on ISO Records / Columbia**: January 8, 2017 (maxi 45 rpm ref.: 88985419651/ CD ref.: 88985419612) / **Best UK Chart Ranking:** 92 / **Best US Chart Ranking:** 131

On January 8, 2017, exactly one year to the day after the release of David Bowie's last album, ISO Records and Columbia brought out the EP *No Plan*, consisting of the song "Lazarus" and three numbers from the *Blackstar* recording sessions. These four pieces had already been available on the soundtrack of the musical *Lazarus,* which had been released on October 21, 2016 as a double CD. The first CD was the version recorded by the performers in the musical; the second consisted of David Bowie's original versions.

Michael C. Hall and Sophie Anne Caruso appear in the final scene of David Bowie's stage musical, *Lazarus*.

NO PLAN

David Bowie / 3:40

Musicians: David Bowie: lead vocals / **Ben Monder:** electric guitar / **Tim Lefebvre:** double bass / **Mark Guiliana:** drums / **Jason Lindner:** Wurlitzer, synthesizers / **Donny McCaslin:** saxophone, flute / **Recorded:** The Magic Shop, New York: January 7 and 10, 2015 / **Technical Team:** Producers: David Bowie, Tony Visconti / **Sound Engineer:** Kevin Killen / **Assistant Sound Engineer:** Kabir Hermon

Originally called "Wistful," "No Plan" was quickly chosen for the musical *Lazarus* and was one of the pieces used for auditioning the performers. The emotional nature of the song and the long-held notes sung by Bowie made considerable demands on the actors who were not professional singers. Sophia Anne Caruso rose to the challenge, performing wonderfully both onstage and in the studio. From the production side, Henry Hey was later to confide: "David had made a demo of it and it was interesting and spooky. I had a demo that had no lyrics. I still have that demo; it will not see the light of the day unless I'm given permission to show that."[163]

Recorded during the *Blackstar* sessions, "No Plan" is notable particularly for Tim Lefebvre's performance on the double bass. Speaking of this delicate jazz instrument in 2018, he commented: "Upright is a physical instrument, and to master it is literally impossible due to the infinite fingerings, scales and techniques. BUT! It's a beautiful sounding thing to play upright. I love it. I'll never be a master but as long as I can play passably well I will continue to do so."[249]

KILLING A LITTLE TIME

David Bowie / 3:46

Musicians: David Bowie: lead vocals, electric guitar / Ben Monder: electric guitar / Tim Lefebvre: bass / Mark Guiliana: drums / Jason Lindner: piano, Wurlitzer / Donny McCaslin: saxophone, flute / **Recorded:** The Magic Shop, New York: March 23, 2015 (backing tracks) / Human Worldwide Studios, New York: May 19, 2015 (vocals) / **Technical Team:** Producers: David Bowie, Tony Visconti / **Sound Engineers:** Kevin Killen (the Magic Shop), Tony Visconti (Human Worldwide Studios) / **Assistant Sound Engineers:** Kabir Hermon (the Magic Shop), Erin Tonkon (Human Worldwide Studios)

Try as Tony Visconti and David Bowie might to deny the influence of rock on their work during the production of *Blackstar*, it comes back with a vengeance when it was time to record "Killing a Little Time," a wild number originally called "Black Man of Moscow." The last song to be recorded by David Bowie, it exposes an anger otherwise kept hidden behind the muted and often somber songs like "Lazarus" or "Blackstar." Michael C. Hall was the singer in the stage version and the studio recording of the soundtrack; his energetic rendering sticks close to the original demo, which was worked on by Bowie in his home studio in August 2014.

WHEN I MET YOU

David Bowie / 4:08

Musicians: David Bowie: lead and backing vocals, acoustic guitar, electric guitar, programming, synthesizers / Tim Lefebvre: bass / Mark Guiliana: drums / **Recorded:** David Bowie's home studio, New York: August 2014 / The Magic Shop, New York: January 3, 2015 (backing tracks) / Human Worldwide Studios, New York: May 5, 2015 (vocals) / **Technical Team:** Producers: David Bowie, Tony Visconti / **Sound Engineers:** Kevin Killen (the Magic Shop), Tony Visconti (Human Worldwide Studios) / **Assistant Sound Engineers:** Kabir Hermon (the Magic Shop), Erin Tonkon (Human Worldwide Studios)

Originally written for *Lazarus*, "When I Met You" was recorded by Bowie and his musicians on the first day of the *Blackstar* sessions at the Magic Shop. The acoustic electric guitars of the demo were retained for the final version of the song to which were added Tim Lefebvre on bass and Mark Guiliana on drums. Henry Hey, who adapted the song for the musical, recalled the demo sent by Bowie in late 2014: "[It] was so raw, and there was this strummy guitar that was kind of badly played and midrangey and I thought it was so perfect for the song that I went on to include it in the *Lazarus* arrangement and instruct the second guitarist to play like that."[163]

NEVER LET ME DOWN 2018

Included in the box set *Loving the Alien (1983–1988)*.

1. Day-In Day-Out
2. Time Will Crawl
3. Beat of Your Drum
4. Never Let Me Down
5. Zeroes
6. Glass Spider
7. Shining Star (Makin' My Love)
8. New York's in Love
9. '87 and Cry
10. Bang Bang

The talented Mario J. McNulty served as the producer on 2018's *Never Let Me Down.*

MARIO J. MCNULTY'S REVISION

Before his death, Bowie had left instructions with his accountant and friend Bill Zysblat about the management of his estate and immense musical legacy. The first instruction was to begin work on a reedited version of *Never Let Me Down*, an album that had left the singer (and the critics) unsatisfied, despite its many qualities. Released in 1987, it seemed as if the disc's production smacked too much of its time, with its low-quality rhythm boxes and eighties-style synthesizers. Bowie, who had never concealed his disappointment with regard to this album, had been very impressed by Mario J. McNulty's remix of "Time Will Crawl" in 2008 for the *iSelect* compilation. McNulty, award-winning sound engineer with a perfect ear for music, had already worked with Bowie on the recording of *Reality* in 2003. Now, at the beginning of 2018, he set out to produce a new version of *Never Let Me Down*, to be added to the box set *Loving the Alien (1983–1988)*, planned for release in the autumn. Mario J. McNulty's task was to remove the typically 1980s-sounding arrangements and replace them with more timeless instrumentation. The idea seemed extraordinary and even impossible; an album is a summation of the influences and sounds of its time. The project was nevertheless launched. Reeves Gabrels, a witness to Bowie's desire to revisit the disc, was to play an important part in the forthcoming adventure.

Bowie's Old Team Steps Up

For the remix of "Time Will Crawl" in 2008, the rhythm box had been replaced at Bowie's request by the impeccable playing of drummer Sterling Campbell. The same course was followed for the majority of tracks that had a makeover on *Never Let Me Down 2018*. In addition to David Bowie's vocal line, other elements retained from the 2008 version were the acoustic guitar played by Bowie on some of the numbers, Carlos Alomar's guitar parts, the harmonica tracks on "Never Let Me Down," and also the electric sitar played by Peter Frampton on "Zeroes." The introduction to this song was taken out in favor of an extended acoustic guitar passage. Some of the synthesizers in "Day-In Day-Out" were replaced with the original brass parts played by the Borneo Horns, which had been dropped at the mixing stage in 2008 and substituted with a more modern sound. Tim Lefebvre, bass player on *Blackstar*, joined the team, along with David Torn, guitarist on *The Next Day*. Singer Laurie Anderson replaced Mickey Rourke on "Shining Star (Makin' My Love)," while musician Nico Muhly composed the string arrangements included in the remixed "Beat of Your Drum," "Never Let Me Down," and "Bang Bang." The song "Too Dizzy"—one that Bowie had always hated—was not rerecorded and does not appear on the disc. While the minutely detailed work carried out by the talented Mario J. McNulty on this disc is to be admired, it has to be said that the spirit of the original album is totally missing, and the end result is strangely lacking in emotion. For those who loved *Never Let Me Down* in the mid-1980s—and they are many—a bit of advice: Give this a miss!

IS IT ANY WONDER?

1. Baby Universal '97
2. Fun (Clownboy Mix)
3. Stay '97
4. I Can't Read '97
5. Nuts
6. The Man Who Sold the World (Live Eno Mix)

UK and US Release on ISO Records / Parlophone: March 20, 2020 (maxi 45 rpm ref.: DB 80120, 0190295332358 / CD ref.: DBCD 80120, 0190295301378) / **Best UK Chart Ranking:** 10 / **Best US Chart Ranking:** Did Not Chart

On March 20, 2020, ISO Records/Parlophone released a new EP by David Bowie, bringing together a number of his songs revisited during the *Earthling* period, between 1995 and 1997. "Baby Universal '97" and "I Can't Read '97," two Tin Machine songs, are presented here in stripped-down versions. Recorded at Looking Glass Studios in October 1996 during an acoustic session with Reeves Gabrels, Gail Ann Dorsey, and Mark Plati, they are not entirely new, since "I Can't Read '97" had come out as a single in December 1997. Two reworked numbers, "Stay '97" and "Fun" (Clownboy Mix), offer something new, while "Nuts," recorded on the same day as "The Last Thing You Should Do," had never been issued before in any format. The EP concludes with a trip-hop version of "The Man Who Sold the World (Live Version)," remixed on October 30, 1995, by Brian Eno at Westside Studios in London.

FUN (CLOWNBOY MIX)

David Bowie, Reeves Gabrels / 3:12

Musicians: David Bowie: lead vocals / Reeves Gabrels: electric guitar / Gail Ann Dorsey: bass, backing vocals / Zachary Alford: drums, programming, samples / Mark Plati: programming, synthesizers / Mike Garson: piano / **Recorded:** Looking Glass Studios, New York: January 1998 / Ocean Way Recording, Los Angeles (remix): May 1998 / **Technical Team:** Producers: David Bowie, Reeves Gabrels, Mark Plati / Sound Engineers: Mark Plati, Steve Guest / **Additional Production:** Danny Saber (remix)

The American producer and musician Danny Saber could always be relied on to perform quality mixing, and this is no exception. The American group Garbage and the trip-hop group Ruby had already turned to this alchemist of sound for some of their pieces, and every time the collaboration led to a hit number. "Fun," circulating under various different titles—including "Is It Any Wonder"—since the beginning of 1998, is in fact a reworked version of "Fame." Familiar to fans from the early years of this century, the song underwent numerous remixes, including "Clownboy Mix 3," "Clownboy Mutant Mix," "Clownboy Mix Vocal Up," and "Clownboy Instrumental."

STAY '97

David Bowie / 7:32

Musicians: David Bowie: lead vocals / Reeves Gabrels: electric guitar, synthesizers / Gail Ann Dorsey: bass, backing vocals / Zachary Alford: drums / Mark Plati: programming / Mike Garson: programming, synthesizers / **Recorded:** The Factory Studios, Dublin: May 1997 / **Technical Team:** Producers: David Bowie, Reeves Gabrels, Mark Plati / Sound Engineers: Mark Plati, Steve Guest

Mark Plati was to say of this new version of a song originally featuring on *Station to Station* in 1975: "It has some crazy twists and turns in it. I hadn't heard it since we did it. We recorded it in Ireland, during the tour pre-production, and then mixed it in New York. Around then was also when I did the 'I'm Deranged' remix, which was part of the 'Dead Man Walking' single. It just didn't stop."[194]

On July 14, 2014, David Bowie's Takamine FP400SC guitar was auctioned off for $46,875 by Julien's Auctions in Beverly Hills, California.

NUTS

David Bowie, Reeves Gabrels, Mark Plati / 5:22

Musicians: David Bowie: lead vocals / Reeves Gabrels: electric guitar / Mark Plati: programming, synthesizers / **Recorded:** Looking Glass Studios, New York: November 1996 / **Technical Team:** Producers: David Bowie, Reeves Gabrels, Mark Plati/ **Sound Engineer:** Mark Plati

This unidentified piece of sound lost in the middle of Bowie's acoustic EP is nothing more than a mainly instrumental outtake from the recording sessions of *Earthling* in 1996. More precise, it comes from those moments of relaxation in the studios when Mark Plati would be tinkering with the rhythm box and synthesizers and Reeves Gabrels would be torturing his six-chord Parker Fly in search of unearthly sounds. Mark Plati recalled: "'Nuts' was done after the first mastering of *Earthling*. [...] We did a session where we did two songs. One of them was 'Last Thing You Should Do,' which ended up on the album. [...] And 'Nuts' was just the other."[194] Punctuated now and then by David Bowie shouting "Nuts," this drum 'n' bass track, interesting mainly because it was previously unreleased, is nevertheless a good example of the insatiable creativity of Bowie and his musicians.

THE MAN WHO SOLD THE WORLD (LIVE ENO MIX)

David Bowie / 3:35

Musicians: David Bowie: lead vocals / Reeves Gabrels, Carlos Alomar: electric guitar / Peter Schwartz: synthesizers, programming / Brian Eno: backing vocals / **Recorded:** Westside Studios, London (mixing): October 30, 1995 / **Technical Team:** Producer: David Bowie / **Sound Engineer:** Brian Eno

"The Man Who Sold the World (Live Version)" came out as the B-side of the single "Strangers When We Meet" in November 1995. A few days earlier, Brian Eno had collected together the recorded tracks and shut himself up in Westside Studios in London in order to do an ambitious remix, something very much of its time, somewhere between trip-hop and an atmospheric electro. Eno writes without false modesty in his logbook for 1995: "What a great version. It sounds completely contemporary, both the text and the music, and could easily have been included on *Outside*. In fact I wish it had been—it has a clarity (there are very few instruments) which a lot of that record could benefit from."[180]

Mother / Tryin' to Get to Heaven

Worldwide Digital Release: January 8, 2021 / UK and US Release on ISO Records / Parlophone: January 8, 2021 (45 rpm ref.: DB 80147) / Best Chart Ranking: Did Not Chart / Side A: Mother / 5:00 / Side AA: Tryin' to Get to Heaven (Single Edit) / 5:07

David Bowie and Bob Dylan shown together in the mid-1980s.

MOTHER

John Lennon / 5:00

Musicians: David Bowie: lead vocals / Reeves Gabrels: electric guitar / Tony Visconti: bass, backing vocals / Andy Newmark: drums / Jordan Rudess: piano / Richard Barone: backing vocals / **Recorded:** Sea View, Bermuda: 1997 / Sound on Sound Studios, New York: July–August 1998 / **Technical Team:** Producers: David Bowie, Tony Visconti, Mark Plati / **Sound Engineers:** Dave Amlen (Sound on Sound Studios), Zach Wind (Sound on Sound Studios), Reeves Gabrels (Sea View)

In 1997, Yoko Ono initiated preproduction for a compilation of cover versions of songs by John Lennon. Invited to take part in the project, David Bowie chose to do a new version of "Mother" from the 1970 *John Lennon / Plastic Ono Band*, the first solo album by the former Beatle. After an initial demo recorded at Sea View, Bermuda, Bowie took advantage of this reunion with his old friend Tony Visconti for the recording of "Safe" to add some overdubs to "Mother" and finish the mixing. Yoko Ono's compilation never saw the light of day, and so this very successful tribute to Lennon, a close friend of Bowie's, was to remain in the singer's archive. It eventually came out as a single with "Tryin' to Get to Heaven" on January 8, 2021. The sleeve of the 45 rpm is restrained, showing a black and white photograph of a baby's hand, that of Lexi, Bowie's daughter. Limited to 8,147 copies, 1,000 of which were in cream-colored vinyl, the disc sold out in just a few minutes on davidbowie.com and the online sales site Dig!

TRYIN' TO GET TO HEAVEN

Bob Dylan / 5:07

Musicians: David Bowie: lead vocals, acoustic guitar, saxophone / Reeves Gabrels: electric guitar, acoustic guitar, guitar pedal steel, synthesizers, backing vocals / Gail Ann Dorsey: bass, backing vocals / Zachary Alford: drums / Mark Plati: synthesizers, programming / **Recorded:** Looking Glass Studios, New York: February 1998 / **Technical Team:** Producers: David Bowie, Reeves Gabrels, Mark Plati / **Sound Engineer:** Mark Plati

To celebrate what should have been David Bowie's seventy-fourth birthday, the heirs to his estate decided to bring out, on January 8, 2021, two songs recorded in the 1990s. "Tryin' to Get to Heaven" was a Bob Dylan song, recorded with producer Daniel Lanois in January 1997, during the making of the *Time out of Mind* album. Bowie had done a cover of this song in January 1998 for *LiveAndWell.com*, an album supposedly linked to the *Earthling* tour but which never came about. The song remained on the shelf until it was broadcast in October 1999, without Bowie's knowledge, on DOS 84, a Spanish radio station that was offering the song for listeners to download. Once the Bowie clan had intervened to clamp down on the leak, the song returned to the archives, where it stayed until 2021, when it was released on this single.

CODA

LIVEALBUMS

David Live . Stage . Ziggy Stardust: The Motion Picture . Tin Machine Live: Oy Vey, Baby .
Arcade Fire & David Bowie Live Ep (Live at Fashion Rocks) . Live Santa Monica '72 .
Vh1 Storytellers . A Reality Tour . Live Nassau Coliseum '76 . Cracked Actor (Live Los Angeles '74) .
Live in Berlin (1978) . Welcome to the Blackout (Live London '78) . Serious Moonlight (Live '83) .
Glastonbury 2000 . Tin Machine at La Cigale in Paris 1989 . Glass Spider (Live Montreal '87) .
Brilliant Live Adventures: Ouvrez Le Chien (Live Dallas 95) . Changesnowbowie .
I'm Only Dancing (The Soul Tour 74) . Brilliant Live Adventures: No Trendy Rechauffe (Live Birmingham 95) .
Brilliant Live Adventures: Liveandwell.Com . Brilliant Live Adventures: Look at the Moon! (Live
Phoenix Festival 97) . Brilliant Live Adventures: Something in the Air (Live In Paris 99) .
Brilliant Live Adventures: At the Kit Kat Klub (Live New York 99)

COMPILATIONS

The World of David Bowie . Images 1966–1967 . Changesonebowie . Starting Point . The Best of Bowie .
Christiane F. Wir Kinder Vom Bahnhof Zoo . Another Face . Changestwobowie . Rare . Golden Years .
A Second Face . Love You Till Tuesday . Fame and Fashion . Changesbowie . Early On (1964–1966) .
The Singles Collection . The Deram Anthology (1966–1968) . The Best of Bowie 1969/1974 .
The Best of Bowie 1974/1979 . Bowie at the Beeb . Best of Bowie . Club Bowie . The Collection .
The Best of David Bowie (1980/1987) . iSelect . Nothing Has Changed . Legacy . Now

BOX SETS

Sound + Vision . The Platinum Collection (2005) . Zeit! 77–79 . Five Years (1969–1973) .
Who Can I Be Now? (1974–1976) . A New Career in a New Town (1977–1982) .
Loving the Alien (1983–1988) . Spying Through a Keyhole .
Clareville Grove Demos . The Mercury Demos .
Conversation Piece

There are no less than twenty-four live albums in David Bowie's official discography. Some of them appeared during his lifetime and on his own initiative. They include: *David Live, Stage,* and *Ziggy Stardust: The Motion Picture,* as well as recordings of, respectively, the *Diamond Dogs* tour (1974), the "Isolar II Tour" (1978), and the *Ziggy Stardust* tour (1972–1973). Other live albums appeared posthumously, giving us a taste of the magic of other triumphant Bowie tours, as in the case of *Live Nassau Coliseum '76,* recording during the "Isolar Tour" of 1976 but not brought out until 2017. Collectors will not be able to resist the six live albums released between 2020 and 2021, which give us epic versions of *1. Outside* (1995), *Earthling* (1997), and *'Hours...'* (1999). Packaged together in a limited edition, they are part of the box set *Brilliant Live Adventures,* which is the most recent tribute to the magic of an evening spent in the company of the great David Bowie.

DAVID LIVE

Recorded between July 8 and July 12, 1974, at the Tower Theater, Upper Darby, PA (United States).

Release Date: UK: October 29, 1974 / **Ref.:** RCA—APL 2-0771 (33 rpm) / **United States:** October 29, 1974 / **Ref.:** RCA—CPL 2-0771 (33 rpm) / **Best UK Chart Ranking:** 2 / **Best US Chart Ranking:** 8 / **Track Listing:** 1984 • Rebel Rebel • Moonage Daydream • Sweet Thing • Changes • Suffragette City • Aladdin Sane • All the Young Dudes • Cracked Actor • When You Rock 'n' Roll With Me • Watch That Man • Knock on Wood • Diamond Dogs • Big Brother • Width of a Circle • The Jean Genie • Rock 'n' Roll Suicide

STAGE

Recorded on April 28–29, 1978, at the Spectrum, Philadelphia, PA (United States); on May 5, 1978, at the Providence Civic Center, Providence, RI (United States); and May 6, 1978, at the Boston Garden, Boston, MA (United States).

Release Date: UK: September 8, 1978 / **Ref.:** RCA—PL 02913(2) (33 rpm) / **United States:** September 8, 1978 / **Ref.:** RCA—CPL2-2913 (33 rpm) / **Best UK Chart Ranking:** 5 / **Best US Chart Ranking:** 44 / **Track Listing:** Hang On to Yourself • Ziggy Stardust • Five Years • Soul Love • Star • Station to Station • Fame • TVC 15 • Warszawa • Speed of Life • Art Decade • Sense of Doubt • Breaking Glass • "Heroes" • What in the World • Blackout • Beauty and the Beast

ZIGGY STARDUST: THE MOTION PICTURE

Recorded on July 3, 1973, at the Hammersmith Odeon, London (UK).

Release Date: UK: October 1, 1983 / **Ref.:** RCA—PL 84862 (2) (33 rpm) / **United States:** October 1, 1983 • **Ref.:** RCA—CPL2-4862 (33 rpm) / **Best UK Chart Ranking:** 17 / **Best US Chart Ranking:** 89 / **Track Listing:** Hang On to Yourself • Ziggy Stardust • Watch That Man • Medley: Wild Eyed Boy from Freecloud / All the Young Dudes / Oh! You Pretty Things • Moonage Daydream • Space Oddity • My Death • Cracked Actor • Time • Width of a Circle • Changes • Let's Spend the Night Together • Suffragette City • White Light/White Heat • Rock 'n' Roll Suicide

TIN MACHINE LIVE: OY VEY, BABY

Comprised of various recordings made during the "It's My Life Tour" (1991–1992).

Release Date: UK: July 2, 1992 / **Ref.:** Victory—828 328-1 (33 rpm); 828 328-2 (CD) / **United States:** July 2, 1992 / **Ref.:** Polygram/Victory—383 480 004-2 (CD) / **Best Chart Ranking:** Did Not Chart / **Track Listing:** If There Is Something (recorded February 17, 1992, at the Budokan, Tokyo, Japan) • Amazing (recorded December 7, 1991, at the Riviera Theatre, Chicago, IL, United States) • I Can't Read (recorded November 20, 1991, at the Orpheum Theatre, Boston, MA, United States) • Stateside (recorded November 27 or 29, 1991, at the Academy of Music, New York, NY, United States) • Under the God (recorded February 10 or 11, 1992, at the Kouseinenkin Kaikan, Sapporo, Japan) • Goodbye Mr. Ed (recorded February 17, 1992, at the Budokan, Tokyo, Japan) • Heaven's in Here (recorded November 27 or 29, 1991, at the Academy of Music, New York, NY, United States) • You Belong in Rock 'n' Roll (recorded December 7, 1991, at the Riviera Theatre, Chicago, IL, United States)

ARCADE FIRE & DAVID BOWIE LIVE EP (LIVE AT FASHION ROCKS)

Recorded September 8, 2005, at Radio City Music Hall, New York, NY (United States).

Release Date: Worldwide Digital Release on iTunes: November 21, 2005 / **Best Chart Ranking:** Did Not Chart / **Track Listing:** Life on Mars? • Wake Up • Five Years

LIVE SANTA MONICA '72

Recorded October 20, 1972, at the Civic Auditorium, Santa Monica, CA (United States).

Release Date: Worldwide Digital Release: June 30, 2008 / **Europe:** June 30, 2008 / **Ref.:** EMI—50999-237663-2-7 (CD) / **United States:** June 30, 2008 / **Ref.:** Virgin/EMI—50999-237663-2-7 (CD) / **Best UK Chart Ranking:** 61 / **Best US Chart Ranking:** Did Not Chart / **Track Listing:** Introduction • Hang On to Yourself • Ziggy Stardust • Changes • The Supermen • Life on Mars? • Five Years • Space Oddity • Andy Warhol • My Death • The Width of a Circle • Queen Bitch • Moonage Daydream • John, I'm Only Dancing • Waiting for the Man • The Jean Genie • Suffragette City • Rock 'n' Roll Suicide

VH1 STORYTELLERS

Recorded August 23, 1999, at the Manhattan Center, New York, NY (United States).

Release Date: Worldwide Digital Release: July 6, 2009 / **UK:** July 6, 2009 / **Ref.:** EMI—5099996490921 (CD) / **United States:** July 6, 2009 / **Ref.:** Virgin/EMI—5099996490921 (CD) / **Best Chart Ranking:** Did Not Chart / **Track Listing:** Life on Mars? • Rebel Rebel (truncated) • Thursday's Child • Can't Help Thinking About Me • China Girl • Seven • Drive-In Saturday • Word on a Wing

A REALITY TOUR

Recorded November 22 and 23, 2003, at the Point Theatre, Dublin (Ireland).

Release Date: Worldwide Digital Release: January 25, 2010 / **Europe:** January 25, 2010 / **Ref.:** ISO Records / Columbia / Sony Music—88697588272 (CD) / **United States:** January 25, 2010 / **Ref.:** ISO Records / Columbia—88697588272 (CD) / **Best UK Chart Ranking:** 53 / **Best US Chart Ranking:** Did Not Chart / **Track Listing:** Rebel Rebel • New Killer Star • Reality • Fame • Cactus • Sister Midnight • Afraid • All the Young Dudes • Be My Wife • The Loneliest Guy • The Man Who Sold the World • Fantastic Voyage • Hallo Spaceboy • Sunday • Under Pressure • Life on Mars? • Battle for Britain (The Letter) • Ashes to Ashes • The Motel • Loving the Alien • Never Get Old • Changes • I'm Afraid of Americans • "Heroes" • Bring Me the Disco King • Slip Away • Heathen (The Rays) • Five Years • Hang On to Yourself • Ziggy Stardust • Fall Dog Bombs the Moon • Breaking Glass • China Girl

LIVE NASSAU COLISEUM '76

Recorded March 23, 1976, at the Nassau Veterans Memorial Coliseum, Uniondale, NY (United States).

Release Date: Worldwide Digital Release: February 10, 2017 / **UK:** February 10, 2017 / **Ref.:** Parlophone—0190295989774,—DB 74768 (33 rpm) / 0190295989781 (CD) / **United States:** February 10, 2017 / **Ref.:** Parlophone—0190295989774—DB 74768 (33rpm) / RP2-558572 (CD) / **Best Chart Ranking:** Did Not Chart / **Track Listing:** Station to Station • Suffragette City • Fame • Word on a Wing • Stay • Waiting for the Man • Queen Bitch • Life on Mars? • Five Years • Panic in Detroit • Changes • TVC 15 • Diamond Dogs • Rebel Rebel • The Jean Genie

CRACKED ACTOR
(LIVE LOS ANGELES '74)

Recorded September 5, 1974, at the Universal Amphitheatre, Los Angeles, CA (United States).

Release Date: Worldwide Digital Release: April 22, 2017 / **Europe:** April 22, 2017 / **Ref.:** Parlophone—DBRSD 7476 (33 rpm) / CDDBS 7476 (CD) • **United States:** April 22, 2017 / **Ref.:** Parlophone—CDDBS 7476 (CD) / **Best UK Chart Ranking:** 20 / **Best US Chart Ranking:** Did Not Chart / **Track Listing:** Introduction • 1984 • Rebel Rebel • Moonage Daydream • Sweet Thing / Candidate / Sweet Thing (Reprise) • Changes • Suffragette City • Aladdin Sane • All the Young Dudes • Cracked Actor • Rock 'n' Roll With Me • Knock on Wood • It's Gonna Be Me • Space Oddity • Diamond Dogs • Big Brother • Time • The Jean Genie • Rock 'n' Roll Suicide • John, I'm Only Dancing (Again)

LIVE IN BERLIN (1978)

Recorded May 16, 1978, at the Deutschlandhalle, West Berlin (West Germany).

Release Date: Sold exclusively at the Brooklyn Museum: March 2, 2018 / **Ref.:** Parlophone—DBISNY 20181 (33 rpm) / **Best Chart Ranking:** Did Not Chart / **Track Listing:** "Heroes" • Be My Wife • Blackout • Sense of Doubt • Breaking Glass • Fame • Alabama Song • Rebel Rebel

WELCOME TO THE BLACKOUT (LIVE LONDON '78)

Recorded June 30 and July 1, 1978, at the Earls Court Exhibition Centre, London (UK).

Release Date: Worldwide Digital Release: April 21, 2018 / UK and United States: April 21, 2018 / **Ref.:** Parlophone—DBRSD 7782 (33 rpm); CDDB 7782 (CD) / **Best UK Chart Ranking:** 16 / **Best US Chart Ranking:** Did Not Chart / **Track Listing:** Warszawa • "Heroes" • What in the World • Be My Wife • The Jean Genie • Blackout • Sense of Doubt • Speed of Life • Sound and Vision • Breaking Glass • Fame • Beauty and the Beast • Five Years • Soul Love • Star • Hang On to Yourself • Ziggy Stardust • Suffragette City • Art Decade • Alabama Song • Station to Station • TVC 15 • Stay • Rebel Rebel

SERIOUS MOONLIGHT (LIVE '83)

Recorded September 12, 1983, at the Pacific National Exhibition Coliseum, Vancouver, BC (Canada).

Release Date: Worldwide Digital Release: October 12, 2018 / **Europe:** October 12, 2018 / **Ref.:** Parlophone—0190295511180 (CD) / **Best Chart Ranking:** Did Not Chart / **Track Listing:** Look Back in Anger • "Heroes" • What in the World • Golden Years • Fashion • Let's Dance • Breaking Glass • Life on Mars? • Sorrow • Cat People (Putting Out Fire) • China Girl • Scary Monsters (And Super Creeps) • Rebel Rebel • White Light/White Heat • Station to Station • Cracked Actor • Ashes to Ashes • Space Oddity / Band Introduction • Young Americans • Fame • Modern Love

GLASTONBURY 2000

Recorded June 25, 2000, at the Glastonbury Festival, Pilton (UK).

Release Date: Worldwide Digital Release: November 30, 2018 / **UK and United States:** November 30, 2018 / **Ref.:** Parlophone/BBC—0190295570453 (33 rpm); 0190295568733 (CD) / **Best UK Chart Ranking:** 25 / **Best US Chart Ranking:** Did Not Chart / **Track Listing:** Introduction (Greensleeves) • Wild Is the Wind • China Girl • Changes • Stay • Life on Mars? • Absolute Beginners • Ashes to Ashes • Rebel Rebel • Little Wonder • Golden Years • Fame • All the Young Dudes • The Man Who Sold the World • Station to Station • Starman • Hallo Spaceboy • Under Pressure • Ziggy Stardust • "Heroes" • Let's Dance • I'm Afraid of Americans

TIN MACHINE AT LA CIGALE IN PARIS 1989

Recorded June 25, 1989, at La Cigale, Paris (France).

Release Date: Worldwide Digital Release: August 20, 2019 / **Ref.:** Parlophone / **Best Chart Ranking:** Did Not Chart / **Track Listing:** Amazing • Heaven's in Here • Sacrifice Yourself • Working Class Hero • Maggie's Farm • I Can't Read • Baby Can Dance • Under the God

GLASS SPIDER (LIVE MONTREAL '87)

Recorded August 30, 1987, at the Olympic Stadium, Montreal, Quebec (Canada).

Release Date: Worldwide Digital Release: February 15, 2019 / **UK:** February 15, 2019 / **Ref.:** Parlophone—0190295511135 (CD) / **Best Chart Ranking:** Did Not Chart / **Track Listing:** Up the Hill Backwards • Glass Spider • Day-In Day-Out • Bang Bang • Absolute Beginners • Loving the Alien • China Girl • Rebel Rebel • Fashion • Scary Monsters (And Super Creeps) • All the Madmen • Never Let Me Down • Big Brother • '87 and Cry • "Heroes" • Sons of the Silent Age • Time Will Crawl / Band Introduction • Young Americans • Beat of Your Drum • The Jean Genie • Let's Dance • Fame • Time • Blue Jean • Modern Love

BRILLIANT LIVE ADVENTURES : OUVREZ LE CHIEN (LIVE DALLAS 95)

Recorded October 13, 1995, at the Starplex Amphitheatre, Dallas, TX (United States).

Release Dates: Worldwide Digital Release: July 2020 / **UK:** October 30, 2020 / **Ref.:** ISO Records / Parlophone—DBBLALP 95991 (33 rpm); DBBLACD 95991 (CD) / **United States:** October 30, 2020 / **Ref.:** ISO Records / Parlophone—DBBLALP 95991 (33 rpm); DBBLACD 95991 (CD) / **Best UK Chart Ranking:** 32 / **Best US Chart Ranking:** Did Not Chart / **Track Listing:** Look Back in Anger • The Hearts Filthy Lesson • The Voyeur of Utter Destruction (As Beauty) • I Have Not Been to Oxford Town • Outside • Andy Warhol • Breaking Glass • The Man Who Sold the World • We Prick You • I'm Deranged • Joe the Lion • Nite Flights • Under Pressure • Teenage Wildlife

CHANGESNOWBOWIE

Recorded in November 1996 at Looking Glass Studios, New York, NY (United States).

Release Date: Worldwide Digital Release: April 17, 2020 / **UK:** April 17, 2020 / **Ref.:** ISO Records / Parlophone—CNBLP 2020 (33 rpm); CNBCD 2020 (CD) / **United States:** April 17, 2020 / **Ref.:** ISO Records / Parlophone—CNBLP 2020 (33 rpm); CNBCD 2020 (CD) / **Best UK Chart Ranking:** 17 / **Best US Chart Ranking:** 88 / **Track Listing:** The Man Who Sold the World • Aladdin Sane • White Light/White Heat • Shopping for Girls • Lady Stardust • The Supermen • Repetition • Andy Warhol • Quicksand

I'M ONLY DANCING (THE SOUL TOUR 74)

Recorded October 20, 1974, at the Michigan Palace, Detroit, MI (United States), and November 30, 1974, at the Municipal Auditorium, Nashville, TN (United States).

Release Date: Worldwide Digital Release: August 29, 2020 / **UK and United States:** August 29, 2020 / **Ref.:** Parlophone—DBRSDLP 2020 (33 rpm); DBRSDCD 2020 (CD) / **Best UK Chart Ranking:** 18 / **Best US Chart Ranking:** 104 / **Track Listing:** Introduction—Memory of a Free Festival • Rebel Rebel • John, I'm Only Dancing (Again) • Sorrow • Changes • 1984 • Moonage Daydream • Rock 'n' Roll With Me • Love Me Do / The Jean Genie • Young Americans • Can You Hear Me • It's Gonna Be Me • Somebody Up There Likes Me • Suffragette City • Rock 'n' Roll Suicide • Panic in Detroit • Knock on Wood • Foot Stompin' / I Wish I Could Shimmy Like My Sister Kate / Foot Stompin' • Diamond Dogs • It's Only Rock 'n' Roll (But I Like It) / Diamond Dogs

David Bowie's concert at the Élysée Montmartre in Paris on October 14, 1999, was immortalized on the record *Brilliant Live Adventures: Something in the Air (Live in Paris 99).*

BRILLIANT LIVE ADVENTURES: NO TRENDY RECHAUFFE (LIVE BIRMINGHAM 95)

Recorded December 13, 1995, at the Big Twix Mix Show, National Exhibition Centre, Birmingham (UK).

Release Dates: **Worldwide Digital Release:** March 12, 2021 / **UK and United States:** November 20, 2020 / **Ref.:** ISO Records / Parlophone—DBBLALP 95992 (33 rpm); DBBLACD 95992 (CD) / **Best UK Chart Ranking:** 86 / **Best US Chart Ranking:** Did Not Chart / **Track Listing:** Look Back in Anger • Scary Monsters (And Super Creeps) • The Voyeur of Utter Destruction (As Beauty) • The Man Who Sold the World • Hallo Spaceboy • I Have Not Been to Oxford Town • Strangers When We Meet • Breaking Glass • The Motel • Jump They Say • Teenage Wildlife • Under Pressure • Moonage Daydream • We Prick You • Hallo Spaceboy (Version 2)

BRILLIANT LIVE ADVENTURES: LIVEANDWELL.COM

Compiled from various recordings made during the *Earthling* tour (1997).

Release Dates: **First appearance for downloading on davidbowie.com:** September 13, 2000 / **Worldwide:** January 15, 2021 / **Ref.:** ISO Records / Parlophone—0190295253196, DBBLALP 95993 (33 rpm); 0190295253202, DBBLACD 95993 (CD) / **Best UK Chart Ranking:** 52 / **Best US Chart Ranking:** Did Not Chart / **Track Listing:** I'm Afraid of Americans (recorded October 15, 1997, at the Radio City Music Hall, New York, NY, United States) • The Hearts Filthy Lesson (recorded July 20, 1997, at the Phoenix Festival, Long Marston, UK) • I'm Deranged (recorded June 10, 1997, at the Paradiso, Amsterdam, Netherlands) • Hallo Spaceboy (recorded November 2, 1997, at the Metropolitan, Rio de Janeiro, Brazil) • Telling Lies (recorded June 10, 1997, at the Paradiso, Amsterdam, Netherlands) • The Motel (recorded June 10, 1997, at the Paradiso, Amsterdam, Netherlands) • The Voyeur of Utter Destruction (recorded November 2, 1997, at the Metropolitan, Rio de Janeiro, Brazil) • Battle for Britain (recorded October 15, 1997, at the Radio City Music Hall, New York, NY, United States) • Seven Years in Tibet (recorded October 15, 1997, at Radio City Music Hall, New York, NY, United States) • Little Wonder (recorded October 15, 1997, at Radio City Music Hall, New York, NY, United States) • Pallas Athena (bonus track, from the Tao Jones Index single, 1997) • V-2 Schneider (bonus track from the Tao Jones Index single, 1997)

BRILLIANT LIVE ADVENTURES: LOOK AT THE MOON! (LIVE PHOENIX FESTIVAL 97)

Recorded July 20, 1997, at the Phoenix Festival, Long Marston (UK).

Release Date: **Worldwide Digital Release:** February 12, 2021 / **UK and United States:** February 12, 2021 / **Ref.:** ISO Records / Parlophone—DBBLALP 95994 (33 rpm); DBBLACD 95994 (CD) / **Best UK Chart Ranking:** 16 / **Best US Chart Ranking:** Did Not Chart / **Track Listing:** Quicksand • The Man Who Sold the World • Driftin' Blues / The Jean Genie • I'm Afraid of Americans • Battle for Britain (The Letter) • Fashion • Seven Years in Tibet • Fame • Looking for Satellites • Under Pressure • The Hearts Filthy Lesson • Scary Monsters (And Super Creeps) • Hallo Spaceboy • Little Wonder • Dead Man Walking • White Light/White Heat • O Superman • Stay

BRILLIANT LIVE ADVENTURES: SOMETHING IN THE AIR (LIVE IN PARIS 99)

Recorded October 14, 1999, at the Élysée Montmartre, Paris (France).

Release Date: Worldwide Digital Release: March 12, 2021 / **UK and United States:** March 12, 2021 / **Ref.:** ISO Records / Parlophone—DBBLALP 95995 (33 rpm); DBBLACD 95995 (CD) / **Best UK Chart Ranking:** 16 / **Best US Chart Ranking:** Did Not Chart / **Track Listing:** Life on Mars? • Thursday's Child • Something in the Air • Word on a Wing • Can't Help Thinking About Me • China Girl • Always Crashing in the Same Car • Survive • Drive-In Saturday • Changes • Seven • Repetition • I Can't Read • The Pretty Things Are Going to Hell • Rebel Rebel

BRILLIANT LIVE ADVENTURES: AT THE KIT KAT KLUB (LIVE NEW YORK 99)

Recorded November 19, 1999, at the Kit Kat Klub, New York, NY (United States).

Release Date: Worldwide Digital Release: April 2, 2021 / **UK and United States:** April 2, 2021 / **Ref.:** ISO Records / Parlophone—0190295178024, DBBLALP 95996 (33 rpm), 0190295178017, DBBLACD 95996 (blue CD) / **Best UK Chart Ranking:** 20 / **Best US Chart Ranking:** Not Listed / **Track Listing:** Life on Mars? • Thursday's Child • Something in the Air • China Girl • Can't Help Thinking About Me • Always Crashing in the Same Car • Survive • Stay • Seven • Changes • The Pretty Things Are Going to Hell • I'm Afraid of Americans

Whether putting together singles, presenting some of the older recordings, or introducing rarities, there have been so many compilations of David Bowie's songs since he started out in 1964 that it would be impossible to provide an exhaustive list. In order to give a coherent picture of the singer's discography, we have opted to list only compilations published by Bowie's recording companies in Europe, the UK, and the United States. Some of these discs include quite unusual items. *Rare*, for example, was released by RCA in December 1982, and the recording company was hoping to extract the maximum profit from its protégé before he left for another label. The compilation album includes some little-heard tracks sung in Italian and German. Another valuable album is *Love You till Tuesday* (1984) consisting of songs intended for the movie of the same name, and including older songs such as the first version of "Space Oddity" with John Hutchinson speaking the famous countdown before Major Tom's rocket takes off, as well as new vocal contributions from Hutchinson and Hermione Farthingale on the magnificent "Sell Me a Coat." Whether you're new to Bowie's music or a lifelong fan, there are compilations here to suit all tastes.

THE WORLD OF DAVID BOWIE

Release Date: March 6, 1970 / **Ref.:** Decca—SPA 58 (33 rpm) / **Best Chart Ranking:** Did Not Chart / **Track Listing:** Uncle Arthur • Love You till Tuesday • There Is a Happy Land • Little Bombardier • Sell Me a Coat • Silly Boy Blue • The London Boys • Karma Man • Rubber Band • Let Me Sleep Beside You • Come and Buy My Toys • She's Got Medals • In the Heat of the Morning • When I Live My Dream

IMAGES 1966-1967

Release Date: February 1973 / **Ref.:** London Records—BP 628/9 (33 rpm) / **Best US Chart Ranking:** 144 / **Track Listing:** Rubber Band • Maid of Bond Street • Sell Me a Coat • Love You till Tuesday • There Is a Happy Land • The Laughing Gnome • The Gospel According to Tony Day • Did You Ever Have a Dream • Uncle Arthur • We Are Hungry Men • When I Live My Dream • Join the Gang • Little Bombardier • Come and Buy My Toys • Silly Boy Blue • She's Got Medals • Please Mr. Gravedigger • London Boys • Karma Man • Let Me Sleep Beside You • In the Heat of the Morning

CHANGESONEBOWIE

Release Date: UK: May 21, 1976 / **Ref.:** RCA—RS 1055 (33 rpm) / **United States:** May 21, 1976 / **Ref.:** RCA—APL1-1732 (33 rpm) / **Best UK Chart Ranking:** 32 / **Best US Chart Ranking:** 10 / **Track Listing:** Space Oddity • John, I'm Only Dancing • Changes • Ziggy Stardust • Suffragette City • The Jean Genie • Diamond Dogs • Rebel Rebel • Young Americans • Fame • Golden Years

STARTING POINT

Release Date: UK: 1977 / **Ref.:** Decca / London Records—LC 50007 (33 rpm) / **United States:** 1977 / **Ref.:** London Records: LC 50007 (33 rpm) / **Best Chart Ranking:** Did Not Chart / **Track Listing:** The Laughing Gnome • Love You till Tuesday • Please Mr. Gravedigger • We Are Hungry Men • The London Boys • Come and Buy My Toys • Karma Man • When I Live My Dream • Join the Gang • Silly Boy Blue

THE BEST OF BOWIE

Release Date: UK: December 15, 1980 / **Ref.:** K-Tel—NE 1111 (33 rpm) / **Best UK Chart Ranking:** 3 / **Track Listing:** Space Oddity • Life on Mars? • Starman • Rock 'n' Roll Suicide • John, I'm Only Dancing • The Jean Genie • Breaking Glass • Sorrow • Diamond Dogs • Young Americans • Fame • Golden Years • TVC 15 • Sound and Vision • "Heroes" • Boys Keep Swinging

CHRISTIANE F. WIR KINDER VOM BAHNHOF ZOO

Release Date: Europe: April 1981 / **Ref.:** RCA—BK 43606 (33 rpm) / **United States:** April 1981 / **Ref.:** RCA—ABL1-4239 (33 rpm) / **Best UK Chart Ranking:** Did Not Chart / **Best US Chart Ranking:** 135 / **Track Listing:** V-2 Schneider • TVC 15 • "Heroes"/"Helden" • Boys Keep Swinging • Sense of Doubt • Station to Station • Look Back in Anger • Stay • Warszawa

ANOTHER FACE

Release Date: UK: May 1981 / **Ref.:** Decca—TAB 17 (33 rpm) / **Best Chart Ranking:** Did Not Chart / **Track Listing:** Rubber Band • The London Boys • The Gospel According to Tony Day • There Is a Happy Land • Maid of Bond Street • When I Live My Dream • Liza Jane • The Laughing Gnome • In the Heat of the Morning • Did You Ever Have a Dream • Please Mr. Gravedigger • Join the Gang • Love You till Tuesday • Louie, Louie Go Home

CHANGESTWOBOWIE

Release Date: UK: November 16, 1981 / **Ref.:** RCA—BOWLP 3 (33 rpm) / **United States:** November 16, 1981 / **Ref.:** RCA—AFL1-4202 (33 rpm) / **Best UK Chart Ranking:** 24 / **Best US Chart Ranking:** Did Not Chart / **Track Listing:** Aladdin Sane (1913-1938-197?) • Oh! You Pretty Things • Starman • 1984 • Ashes to Ashes • Sound and Vision • Fashion • Wild Is the Wind • John, I'm Only Dancing (Again) 1975 • D.J.

RARE

Release Date: UK: December 1982 / **Ref.:** RCA—PL 45406 (33 rpm) / **Best UK Chart Ranking:** 34 / **Track Listing:** Ragazzo Solo, Ragazza Sola • Round and Round • Amsterdam • Holy Holy • Panic in Detroit • Young Americans • Velvet Goldmine • "Helden" • John, I'm Only Dancing (Again) (1975) • Moon of Alabama • Crystal Japan (Instrumental)

GOLDEN YEARS

Release Date: Europe: August 1983 / **Ref.:** RCA—PL 14792, BOWLP 4 (33 rpm) / **United States:** August 1983 / **Ref.:** Mainman/RCA—AFL1-4792 (33 rpm) / **Best UK Chart Ranking:** 33 / **Best US Chart Ranking:** 99 / **Track Listing:** Fashion • Red Sails • Look Back in Anger • I Can't Explain • Ashes to Ashes • Golden Years • Joe the Lion • Scary Monsters (And Super Creeps) • Wild Is the Wind

A SECOND FACE

Release Date: UK: 1983 / **Ref.:** Decca—TAB 71 (33 rpm) / **Best Chart Ranking:** Did Not Chart / **Track Listing:** Let Me Sleep Beside You • Sell Me a Coat • She's Got Medals • We Are Hungry Men • In the Heat of the Morning • Karma Man • Little Bombardier • Love You till Tuesday • Come and Buy My Toys • Silly Boy Blue • Uncle Arthur • When I Live My Dream

LOVE YOU TILL TUESDAY

Release Date: UK: May 1984 / **Ref.:** Deram—BOWIE 1, 820 083-1 (33 rpm) / **United States:** May 1984 / **Ref.:** London Records—820 083-1 R-1 (33 rpm) / **Best UK Chart Ranking:** 53 / **Best US Chart Ranking:** Did Not Chart / **Track Listing:** Love You till Tuesday • The London Boys • Ching-A-Ling • The Laughing Gnome • Liza Jane • When I'm Five • Space Oddity • Sell Me a Coat • Rubber Band • Let Me Sleep Beside You • When I Live My Dream

FAME AND FASHION

Release Date: Europe: May 1984 / **Ref.:** RCA—PL84919 (33 rpm); PD84919 (CD) / **United States:** May 1984 / **Ref.:** RCA—AFL1-4919 (33 rpm); PCD1-4919 (CD) / **Best UK Chart Ranking:** 40 / **Best US Chart Ranking:** 147 / **Track Listing:** Space Oddity • Changes • Starman • 1984 • Young Americans • Fame • Golden Years • TVC 15 • "Heroes" • D.J. • Fashion • Ashes to Ashes

CHANGESBOWIE

Release Date: UK: March 20, 1990 / **Ref.:** EMI—DBTV 1 (33 rpm); CDP 79 4180 2 (CD) / **United States:** March 20, 1990 / **Ref.:** Rykodisc—RALP 0171-2 (33 rpm); RCD 20171 (CD) / **Best UK Chart Ranking:** 1 / **Best US Chart Ranking:** 39 / **Track Listing:** Space Oddity • Starman • John, I'm Only Dancing • Changes • Ziggy Stardust • Suffragette City • Jean Genie • Life on Mars? • Diamond Dogs • Rebel Rebel • Young Americans • Fame '90 Remix • Golden Years • Sound and Vision • "Heroes" • Ashes to Ashes • Fashion • Let's Dance • China Girl • Modern Love • Blue Jean

EARLY ON (1964-1966)

Release Date: United States: 1991 / **Ref.:** Rhino Records—R2 70526 (CD) / **Best Chart Ranking:** Did Not Chart / **Track Listing:** Liza Jane • Louie, Louie Go Home • I Pity the Fool • Take My Tip • That's Where My Heart Is • I Want My Baby Back • Bars of the County Jail • You've Got a Habit of Leaving • Baby Loves That Way • I'll Follow You • Glad I've Got Nobody • Can't Help Thinking About Me • And I Say to Myself • Do Anything You Say • Good Morning Girl • I Dig Everything • I'm Not Losing Sleep

THE SINGLES COLLECTION

Release Date: Europe: November 16, 1993 / **Ref.:** EMI—EM1512, 7243 8 28099 1 3 (LP); 7243 8 28099 2 0 (CD) / **United States:** November 16, 1993 / **Ref.:** Rykodisc—RCD 10218/19 (CD) / **Best UK Chart Ranking:** 9 / **Best US Chart Ranking:** Did Not Chart / **Track Listing:** Space Oddity • Changes • Starman • Ziggy Stardust • Suffragette City • John, I'm Only Dancing • The Jean Genie • Drive-In Saturday • Life on Mars? • Sorrow • Rebel Rebel • Rock 'n' Roll Suicide • Diamond Dogs • Knock on Wood • Young Americans • Fame • Golden Years • TVC 15 • Sound and Vision • "Heroes" • Beauty and the Beast • Boys Keep Swinging • D.J. • Alabama Song • Ashes to Ashes • Fashion • Scary Monsters (And Super Creeps) • Under Pressure • Wild Is the Wind • Let's Dance • China Girl • Modern Love • Blue Jean • This Is Not America • Dancing in the Street • Absolute Beginners • Day-In Day-Out

THE DERAM ANTHOLOGY (1966-1968)

Release Date: Europe: June 9, 1997 / **Ref.:** Deram—844 784-2 (CD) / **United States:** June 9, 1997 / **Ref.:** Deram / A&M Records—P2-44784 (CD) / **Best Chart Ranking:** Did Not Chart / **Track Listing:** Rubber Band (Single Version) • The London Boys • The Laughing Gnome • The Gospel According to Tony Day • Uncle Arthur • Sell Me a Coat • Rubber Band • Love You till Tuesday • There Is a Happy Land • We Are Hungry Men • When I Live My Dream • Little Bombardier • Silly Boy Blue • Come and Buy My Toys • Join the Gang • She's Got Medals • Maid of Bond Street • Please Mr. Gravedigger • Love You till Tuesday (Single Version) • Did You Ever Have a Dream • Karma Man • Let Me Sleep Beside You • In the Heat of the Morning • Ching-A-Ling • Sell Me a Coat • When I Live My Dream • Space Oddity

THE BEST OF BOWIE 1969/1974

Release Dates: Europe: October 7, 1997 / **Ref.:** EMI—7243 8 21849 2 8 (CD) / **United States:** 1997 / **Ref.:** EMI–Capitol Entertainment Properties—72438-21683-2-4 (CD) / **Best UK Chart Ranking:** 11 / **Best US Chart Ranking:** Did Not Chart / **Track Listing:** The Jean Genie • Space Oddity • Starman • Ziggy Stardust • John, I'm Only Dancing • Rebel Rebel • Let's Spend the Night Together • Suffragette City • Oh! You Pretty Things • Velvet Goldmine • Drive-In Saturday • Diamond Dogs • Changes • Sorrow • The Prettiest Star • Life on Mars? • Aladdin Sane • The Man Who Sold the World • Rock 'n' Roll Suicide • All the Young Dudes

THE BEST OF BOWIE 1974/1979

Release Date: Europe: April 1998 / **Ref.:** EMI—7243 4 94300 2 0 (CD) / **United States:** April 1998 / **Ref.:** Virgin—7243 4 94300 0 6 (CD) / **Best UK Chart Ranking:** 39 / **Best US Chart Ranking:** Did Not Chart / **Track Listing:** Sound and Vision • Golden Years • Fame • Young Americans • John, I'm Only Dancing (Again) • Can You Hear Me • Wild Is the Wind • Knock on Wood • TVC 15 • 1984 • It's Hard to Be a Saint in the City • Look Back in Anger • The Secret Life of Arabia • D.J. • Beauty and the Beast • Breaking Glass • Boys Keep Swinging • "Heroes"

BOWIE AT THE BEEB

Release Date: Europe: September 26, 2000 / **Ref.:** EMI / BBC—7243 5 28629 2 4 (CD) / **United States:** September 26, 2000 / **Ref.:** Virgin—7243 5 28629 2 4 (CD) / **Best UK Chart Ranking:** 7 / **Best US Chart Ranking:** 181 / **Track Listing:** In the Heat of the Morning • London Bye Ta Ta • Karma Man • Silly Boy Blue • Let Me Sleep Beside You • Janine • Amsterdam • God Knows I'm Good • The Width of a Circle • Unwashed and Somewhat Slightly Dazed • Cygnet Committee • Memory of a Free Festival • Wild Eyed Boy from Freecloud • Bombers • Looking for a Friend • Almost Grown • Kooks • It Ain't Easy • The Supermen • Eight Line Poem • Hang On to Yourself • Ziggy Stardust • Queen Bitch • I'm Waiting for the Man • Five Years • White Light/White Heat • Moonage Daydream • Hang On to Yourself • Suffragette City • Ziggy Stardust • Starman • Space Oddity • Changes • Oh! You Pretty Things • Andy Warhol • Lady Stardust • Rock 'n' Roll Suicide

BEST OF BOWIE

Release Date: Europe: October 22, 2002 / **Ref.:** EMI—7243 5 39821 2 6 (CD) / **United States:** October 22, 2002 / **Ref.:** Virgin—7243 5 41929 2 0 (CD) / **Best UK Chart Ranking:** 1 / **Best US Chart Ranking:** 4 / **Track Listing:** Space Oddity • The Man Who Sold the World • Oh! You Pretty Things • Changes • Life on Mars? • Starman • Ziggy Stardust • Suffragette City • John, I'm Only Dancing • The Jean Genie • Drive-In Saturday • Sorrow • Diamond Dogs • Rebel Rebel • Young Americans • Fame • Golden Years • TVC 15 • Wild Is the Wind • Sound and Vision • "Heroes" • Boys Keep Swinging • Under Pressure (with Queen) • Ashes to Ashes • Fashion • Scary Monsters (And Super Creeps) • Let's Dance • China Girl • Modern Love • Blue Jean • This Is Not America (with Pat Metheny Group) • Loving the Alien • Dancing in the Street (with Mick Jagger) • Absolute Beginners • Jump They Say • Hallo Spaceboy (Pet Shop Boys Remix) • Little Wonder • I'm Afraid of Americans (V1) • Slow Burn (Radio Edit)

CLUB BOWIE

Release Date: UK: December 2, 2003 / **Ref.:** Virgin—VTCD591 (CD) / **Best Chart Ranking:** Did Not Chart / **Track Listing:** The Scumfrog vs. David Bowie: Loving the Alien • David Bowie: Let's Dance (Trifactor vs. Deeper Substance Remix) • David Guetta vs. Bowie: Just for One Day (Heroes) (Extended Version) • The Scumfrog vs. David Bowie: This Is Not America • Solaris vs. Bowie: Shout (Original Mix) • David Bowie: China Girl (Riff & Vox Club Mix) • David Bowie: Magic Dance (Danny S Magic Party Remix) • David Bowie: Let's Dance (Club Bolly Extended Mix) • David Bowie video: Let's Dance (Club Bolly Mix)

THE COLLECTION

Release Date: UK: May 3, 2005 / **Ref.:** EMI Gold—7243 4 77653 2 2 (CD) / **United States:** May 3, 2005 / **Ref.:** EMI—72434-77653-2-2 (CD) / **Best Chart Ranking:** Did Not Chart / **Track Listing:** Unwashed and Somewhat Slightly Dazed • The Width of a Circle • Andy Warhol • Soul Love • Cracked Actor • Sweet Thing • Somebody Up There Likes Me • Word on a Wing • Always Crashing in the Same Car • Beauty and the Beast • Repetition • Teenage Wildlife

THE BEST OF DAVID BOWIE (1980/1987)

Release Date: UK: March 19, 2007 / **Ref.:** EMI—00946 3 86478 2 9 (CD) / **United States:** March 19, 2007 / **Ref.:** Virgin—0946-3-86587-2-6 (CD) / **Best UK Chart Ranking:** 34 / **Best US Chart Ranking:** Did Not Chart / **Track Listing:** Let's Dance • Ashes to Ashes • Under Pressure • Fashion • Modern Love • China Girl • Scary Monsters • Up the Hill Backwards • Alabama Song • Drowned Girl • Cat People • This Is Not America • Loving the Alien • Absolute Beginners • When the Wind Blows • Blue Jean • Day-In Day-Out • Time Will Crawl • Underground

iSELECT

Release Dates: UK: free offer with *The Mail on Sunday*, June 29, 2008 / **Europe:** October 14, 2008 / **Ref.:** EMI—5099923664029 (CD) / **United States:** October 14, 2008 / **Ref.:** Astralwerks Records / EMI—ASW 36640, 5099923664029 (CD) / **Best Chart Ranking:** Did Not Chart / **Track Listing:** Life on Mars? • Sweet Thing / Candidate / Sweet Thing (Reprise) • The Bewlay Brothers • Lady Grinning Soul • Win • Some Are • Teenage Wildlife • Repetition • Fantastic Voyage • Loving the Alien • Time Will Crawl (MM Remix) • Introduction by B. Mitchel Reed from KMET / Hang On to Yourself (Live)

David Bowie appears in a clip from the music video for "Jump They Say" from 1993's *Black Tie, White Noise*.

NOTHING HAS CHANGED

Release Dates: Europe: November 14, 2014 / **Ref.:** Parlophone—825646205639, DBLP6414 (33 rpm) / 825646205745, DB64142 (double CD) / 825646205769, DB64143 (triple CD) / **United States:** November 2014 / **Ref.:** Legacy/Columbia—88875030991 (33 rpm) / 888750309723 (double CD) / 88875030982SC1 (triple CD) / **Best UK Chart Ranking:** 5 / **Best US Chart Ranking:** 57 / **Track Listing (33 rpm):** Let's Dance • Ashes to Ashes (Single Version) • "Heroes" (Single Version) • Changes • Life on Mars? • Space Oddity • Starman (Single Version) • Ziggy Stardust • The Jean Genie (Original Single Mix) • Rebel Rebel • Golden Years (Single Version) • Fame • Sound and Vision • Under Pressure (with Queen) • Sue (Or in a Season of Crime) • Hallo Spaceboy (PSB Remix) (with The Pet Shop Boys) • China Girl (Single Version) • Modern Love (Single Version) • Absolute Beginners (Single Version) • Where Are We Now? / **Track Listing (Double CD):** Space Oddity • The Man Who Sold the World • Changes • Oh! You Pretty Things • Life on Mars? • Starman (Original Single Mix) • Ziggy Stardust • Moonage Daydream • The Jean Genie (Original Single Mix) • All the Young Dudes • Drive-In Saturday • Sorrow • Rebel Rebel • Young Americans (Original Single Edit) • Fame • Golden Years (Single Version) • Sound and Vision • "Heroes" (Single Version) • Boys Keep Swinging • Fashion (Single Version) • Ashes to Ashes (Single Version) • Under Pressure (with Queen) • Let's Dance (Single Version) • China Girl (Single Version) • Modern Love (Single Version) • Blue Jean • This Is Not America (with the Pat Metheny Group) • Dancing in the Street (with Mick Jagger) • Absolute Beginners (Edit) • Jump They Say (Radio Edit) • Hallo Spaceboy (PSB Remix) (with the Pet Shop Boys) • Little Wonder (Edit) • I'm Afraid of Americans (V1) (Radio Edit) • Thursday's Child (Radio Edit) • Everyone Says 'Hi' (Edit) • New Killer Star (Radio Edit) • Love Is Lost (Hello Steve Reich Mix by James Murphy for the DFA Edit) • Where Are We Now? • Sue (Or in a Season of Crime) / **Track Listing (Triple CD):** Sue (Or in a Season of Crime) • Where Are We Now? • Love Is Lost (Hello Steve Reich Mix by James Murphy for the DFA Edit) • The Stars (Are Out Tonight) • New Killer Star (Radio Edit) • Everyone Says 'Hi' (Edit) • Slow Burn (Radio Edit) • Let Me Sleep Beside You (previously unreleased) • Your Turn to Drive • Shadow Man • Seven (Marius De Vries Mix) • Survive (Marius De Vries Mix) • Thursday's Child (Radio Edit) • I'm Afraid of Americans (V1) (Radio Edit) • Little Wonder (Edit) • Hallo Spaceboy (PSB Remix) (with the Pet Shop Boys) • The Hearts Filthy Lesson (Radio Edit) • Strangers When We Meet (Single Version) • Buddha of Suburbia • Jump They Say (Radio Edit) • Time Will Crawl (MM Remix) • Absolute Beginners (Single Version) • Dancing in the Street (with Mick Jagger) • Loving the Alien (Single Remix) • This Is Not America (with the Pat Metheny Group) • Blue Jean • Modern Love (Single Version) • China Girl (Single Version) • Let's Dance (Single Version) • Fashion (Single Version) • Scary Monsters (And Super Creeps) (Single Version) • Ashes to Ashes (Single Version) • Under Pressure (with Queen) • Boys Keep Swinging • "Heroes" (Single Version) • Sound and Vision • Golden Years (Single Version) • Wild Is the Wind (2010 Harry Maslin Mix) • Fame • Young Americans (2007 Tony Visconti Mix Single Edit) • Diamond Dogs • Rebel Rebel • Sorrow • Drive-In Saturday • All the Young Dudes • The Jean Genie (Original Single Mix) • Moonage Daydream • Ziggy Stardust • Starman (Original Single Mix) • Life on Mars? (2003 Ken Scott Mix) • Oh! You Pretty Things • Changes • The Man Who Sold the World • Space Oddity • In the Heat of the Morning (Stereo Mix) • Silly Boy Blue • Can't Help Thinking About Me (with the Lower Third) • You've Got a Habit of Leaving (Davy Jones and the Lower Third) • Liza Jane (Davie Jones and the King Bees)

LEGACY

Release Date: Europe: November 11, 2016 / **Ref.:** Parlophone—DBLP64161 (33 rpm); DB 64161, 190295919900 (CD); DB 64162, 190295919870 (double CD) / **United States:** November 11, 2016 / **Ref.:** Legacy/Columbia—88985376581 (33 rpm); 88985376592 (CD); 88985376602 (double CD) / **Best UK Chart Ranking:** 5 / **Best US Chart Ranking:** 78 / **Track Listing (33 rpm and CD Versions):** Let's Dance • Ashes to Ashes • Under Pressure (with Queen) • Life on Mars? (2016 Mix) • Changes • Oh! You Pretty Things (UK Version Only) • The Man Who Sold the World • Space Oddity • Starman • Ziggy Stardust • The Jean Genie • Rebel Rebel • Young Americans (US Version Only) • Golden Years • Dancing in the Street (with Mick Jagger on UK Version Only) • Modern Love (US Version Only) • China Girl • Fame • Sound and Vision • "Heroes" • Where Are We Now? • Lazarus / **Track Listing (Double CD):** Space Oddity • The Man Who Sold the World • Changes • Oh! You Pretty Things • Life on Mars? (2016 Mix) • Starman • Ziggy Stardust • Moonage Daydream • The Jean Genie • All the Young Dudes • Drive-In Saturday • Sorrow • Rebel Rebel • Young Americans • Fame • Golden Years • Sound and Vision • "Heroes" • Boys Keep Swinging • Fashion • Ashes to Ashes • Under Pressure (with Queen) • Let's Dance • China Girl • Modern Love • Blue Jean • This Is Not America (with the Pat Metheny Group) • Dancing in the Street (with Mick Jagger) • Absolute Beginners • Jump They Say • Hallo Spaceboy (with the Pet Shop Boys) • Little Wonder • I'm Afraid of Americans • Thursday's Child • Slow Burn • Everyone Says 'Hi' • New Killer Star • Where Are We Now? • Lazarus • I Can't Give Everything Away

NOW

Release Date: Europe and **United States:** April 21, 2018 / **Ref.:** Parlophone—0190295739645, DBNOW 77 (33 rpm) / **Best UK Chart Ranking:** 43 / **Best US Chart Ranking:** Did Not Chart / **Track Listing:** V-2 Schneider • Always Crashing in the Same Car • Sons of the Silent Age • Breaking Glass • Neuköln • Speed of Life • Joe the Lion • What in the World • Blackout • Weeping Wall • The Secret Life of Arabia

Bringing out a box set of a selection of songs by an artist is often an opportunity for recording companies to make quick and massive sales, but sometimes the intention is more praiseworthy. An example from the late 1980s is provided by Rykodisc who, with the album *Sound + Vision*, produced an exemplary collection of rare or hitherto unreleased songs by Bowie. Prompted by the same intentions,

in 2016 Parlophone produced a box of delights for fans with *Who Can I Be Now? (1974-1976)*, which included a number of outtakes, among which is a wonderful piece of soul music from the *Young Americans* period that gives the box set its title. There are treasures to be found in these box sets both for collectors and for fans of demos recorded by Bowie on a small tape recorder in the late 1960s.

SOUND + VISION

Release Date: United States: September 19, 1989 / **Ref.:** Rykodisc—RALP 0120/21/22-2 (33 rpm box set "Clear"); RCD 90120/21/22 (CD box set) / **Best US Chart Ranking:** 97 / **Track Listing Disc 1 "Sound + Vision I":** Space Oddity • Wild Eyed Boy from Freecloud • The Prettiest Star • London Bye Ta-Ta • Black Country Rock • The Man Who Sold the World • The Bewlay Brothers • Changes • Round and Round • Moonage Daydream • John, I'm Only Dancing • Drive-In Saturday • Panic in Detroit • Ziggy Stardust (Live) • White Light/White Heat (Live) • Rock 'n' Roll Suicide (Live) / **Track Listing Disc 2 "Sound + Vision II":** Anyway, Anyhow, Anywhere • Sorrow • Don't Bring Me Down • 1984/Dodo • Big Brother • Rebel Rebel • Suffragette City (Live) • Watch That Man (Live) • Cracked Actor (Live) • Young Americans • Fascination • After Today • It's Hard to Be a Saint in the City • TVC 15 • Wild Is the Wind / **Track Listing Disc 3 "Sound + Vision III":** Sound and Vision • Be My Wife • Speed of Life • "Helden" (1989 Remix) • Joe the Lion • Sons of the Silent Age • Station to Station (Live) • Warszawa (Live) • Breaking Glass (Live) • Red Sails • Look Back in Anger • Boys Keep Swinging • Up the Hill Backwards • Kingdom Come • Ashes to Ashes / **Track Listing Disc 4 "Sound + Vision Plus":** John, I'm Only Dancing (Live at the Music Hall, Boston October 1, 1972) • Changes (Live at the Music Hall, Boston October 1, 1972) • The Supermen (Live at the Music Hall, Boston October 1, 1972) • **Video:** Ashes to Ashes

THE PLATINUM COLLECTION (2005)

Release Date: Europe: November 7, 2005 / **Ref.:** EMI—0946 3 44076 2 5 (CD box set) / **United States:** November 7, 2005 / **Ref.:** Virgin/EMI: 09463-31304-2-5 (CD box set) / **Best UK Chart Ranking:** 53 / **Best US Chart Ranking:** 65 / **Track Listing Disc 1 "The Best of David Bowie 1969/1974":** The Jean Genie • Space Oddity • Starman • Ziggy Stardust • John, I'm Only Dancing • Rebel Rebel • Let's Spend the Night Together • Suffragette City • Oh! You Pretty Things • Velvet Goldmine • Drive-In Saturday • Diamond Dogs • Changes • Sorrow • The Prettiest Star • Life on Mars? • Aladdin Sane • The Man Who Sold the World • Rock 'n' Roll Suicide • All the Young Dudes / **Track Listing Disc 2 "The Best of David Bowie 1974/1979":** Sound and Vision • Golden Years • Fame • Young Americans • John, I'm Only Dancing (Again) • Can You Hear Me • Wild Is the Wind • Knock on Wood • TVC 15 • 1984 • It's Hard to Be a Saint in the City • Look Back in Anger • The Secret Life of Arabia • D.J. • Beauty and the Beast • Breaking Glass • Boys Keep Swinging • "Heroes" / **Track Listing Disc 3 "The Best of David Bowie 1980/1987":** Let's Dance • Ashes to Ashes • Under Pressure • Fashion • Modern Love • China Girl • Scary Monsters (And Super Creeps) • Up the Hill Backwards • Alabama Song • Drowned Girl • Cat People (Putting Out Fire) • This Is Not America • Loving the Alien • Absolute Beginners • When the Wind Blows • Blue Jean • Day-In Day-Out • Time Will Crawl • Underground

ZEIT! 77-79

Release Date: UK: May 3, 2013 / **Ref.:** EMI—DBZEIT7779 (CD box set) / **Best Chart Ranking:** Did Not Chart / **Track Listing Disc 1 "Low":** Speed of Life • Breaking Glass • What in the World • Sound and Vision • Always Crashing in the Same Car • Be My Wife • A New Career in a New Town • Warszawa • Art Decade • Weeping Wall • Subterraneans / **Track Listing Disc 2 "Heroes":** Beauty and the Beast • Joe the Lion • "Heroes" • Sons of the Silent Age • Blackout • V-2 Schneider • Sense of Doubt • Moss Garden • Neuköln • The Secret Life of Arabia / **Track Listing Disc 3 "Stage":** Warszawa • "Heroes" • What in the World • Be My Wife • Blackout • Sense of Doubt • Speed of Life • Breaking Glass • Beauty and the Beast • Fame • Five Years • Soul Love • Star • Hang On to Yourself • Ziggy Stardust • Art Decade • Alabama Song • Station to Station • Stay • TVC 15 / **Track Listing Disc 4 "Lodger":** Fantastic Voyage • African Night Flight • Move On • Yassassin • Red Sails • D.J. • Look Back in Anger • Boys Keep Swinging • Repetition • Red Money

FIVE YEARS (1969-1973)

Release Date: Europe and **United States:** September 25, 2015 / **Ref.:** Parlophone—DBXL 1 (33 rpm box set) / 0825646284085, DBX 1 (CD box set) / **Best UK Chart Ranking:** 45 / **Best US Chart Ranking:** Did Not Chart / **Track Listing Disc 1 "David Bowie A.K.A. Space Oddity":** Space Oddity • Unwashed and Somewhat Slightly Dazed • Don't Sit Down • Letter to Hermione • Cygnet Committee • Janine • An Occasional Dream • Wild Eyed Boy from Freecloud • God Knows I'm Good • Memory of a Free Festival / **Track Listing Disc 2 "The Man Who Sold the World":** The Width of a Circle • All the Madmen • Black Country Rock • After All • Running Gun Blues • Saviour Machine • She Shook Me Cold • The Man Who Sold the World • The Supermen / **Track Listing Disc 3 "Hunky Dory":** Changes • Oh! You Pretty Things • Eight Line Poem • Life on Mars? • Kooks • Quicksand • Fill Your Heart • Andy Warhol • Song for Bob Dylan • Queen Bitch • The Bewlay Brothers / **Track Listing Disc 4 "The Rise and Fall of Ziggy Stardust and the Spiders from Mars":** Five Years • Soul Love • Moonage Daydream • Starman • It Ain't Easy • Lady Stardust • Star • Hang On to Yourself • Ziggy Stardust • Suffragette City • Rock 'n' Roll Suicide / **Track Listing Disc 5 "Aladdin Sane":** Watch That Man • Aladdin Sane (1913-1938-197?) • Drive-In Saturday • Panic in Detroit • Cracked Actor • Time • The Prettiest Star • Let's Spend the Night Together • The Jean Genie • Lady Grinning Soul / **Track Listing Disc 6 "Pin Ups":** Rosalyn • Here Comes the Night • I Wish You Would • See Emily Play • Everything's Alright • I Can't Explain • Friday on My Mind • Sorrow • Don't Bring Me Down • Shapes of Things • Anyway, Anyhow, Anywhere • Where Have All the Good Times Gone! / **Track Listing Disc 7 "Live Santa Monica '72":** Introduction • Hang On to Yourself • Ziggy Stardust • Changes • The Supermen • Life on Mars? • Five Years • Space Oddity • Andy Warhol • My Death • The Width of a Circle • Queen Bitch • Moonage Daydream • John, I'm Only Dancing • Waiting for the Man • The Jean Genie • Suffragette City • Rock 'n' Roll Suicide / **Track Listing Disc 8 "Ziggy Stardust: The Motion Picture Soundtrack":** Introduction • Hang On to Yourself • Ziggy Stardust • Watch That Man • Wild Eyed Boy from Freecloud • All the Young Dudes • Oh! You Pretty Things • Moonage Daydream • Changes • Space Oddity • My Death • Introduction • Cracked Actor • Time • The Width of a Circle • Let's Spend the Night Together • Suffragette City • White Light/White Heat • Farewell Speech • Rock 'n' Roll Suicide / **Track Listing Disc 9 "The Rise and Fall of Ziggy Stardust and the Spiders from Mars (2003 Mix)":** Five Years • Soul Love • Moonage Daydream • Starman • It Ain't Easy • Lady Stardust • Star • Hang On to Yourself • Ziggy Stardust • Suffragette City • Rock 'n' Roll Suicide / **Track Listing Disc 10 "Re:Call 1":** Space Oddity (Original UK Mono Single Edit) • Wild Eyed Boy from Freecloud (Original UK Mono Single Version) • Ragazzo Solo, Ragazza Sola • The Prettiest Star (Original Mono Single Version) • Conversation Piece (Mono Version) • Memory of a Free Festival (Part 1) • Memory of a Free Festival (Part 2) • All the Madmen (Mono Single Edit) • Janine (Mono Version) • Holy Holy (Original Mono Single Version) • Moonage Daydream (The Arnold Corns Single Version) • Hang On to Yourself (The Arnold Corns Single Version) • Changes (Mono Single Version) • Andy Warhol (Mono Single Version) • Starman (Original Single Mix) • John, I'm Only Dancing (Original Single Version) • The Jean Genie (Original Single Mix) • Drive-In Saturday (German Single Edit) • Round and Round • John, I'm Only Dancing (Sax Version) • Time (US Single Edit) • Amsterdam • Holy Holy (Spiders Version) • Velvet Goldmine

WHO CAN I BE NOW? (1974-1976)

Release Date: Europe and **United States:** September 23, 2016 / **Ref.:** Parlophone—0190295989835, DBXL2 (33 rpm box set) / 0190295989842, DBX 2 (CD box set) / **Best UK Chart Ranking:** 21 / **Best US Chart Ranking:** 192 / **Track Listing Disc 1 "Diamond Dogs":** Future Legend • Diamond Dogs • Sweet Thing • Candidate • Sweet Thing (Reprise) • Rebel Rebel • Rock 'n' Roll With Me • We Are the Dead • 1984 • Big Brother • Chant of the Ever Circling Skeletal Family / **Track Listing Disc 2 "David Live (Original Mix)":** 1984 • Rebel Rebel • Moonage Daydream • Sweet Thing / Candidate / Sweet Thing (Reprise) • Changes • Suffragette City • Aladdin Sane (1913-1938-197?) • All the Young Dudes • Cracked Actor • Rock 'n' Roll with Me • Watch That Man • Knock on Wood • Diamond Dogs • Big Brother • The Width of a Circle • The Jean Genie • Rock 'n' Roll Suicide / **Track Listing Disc 3 "David Live (2005 Mix)":** 1984 • Rebel Rebel • Moonage Daydream • Sweet Thing / Candidate / Sweet Thing (Reprise) • Changes • Suffragette City • Aladdin Sane (1913-1938-197?) • All the Young Dudes • Cracked Actor • Rock 'n' Roll with Me • Watch That Man • Knock on Wood • Here Today, Gone Tomorrow • Space Oddity • Diamond Dogs • Panic in Detroit • Big Brother • Time • The Width of a Circle • The Jean Genie • Rock 'n' Roll Suicide / **Track Listing Disc 4 "The Gouster":** John, I'm Only Dancing (Again) • Somebody Up There Likes Me (Alternative Early Mix) • It's Gonna Be Me (Without Strings) • Who Can I Be Now? • Can You Hear Me (Alternative Early Version) • Young Americans • Right (Alternative Early Version) / **Track Listing Disc 5 "Young Americans":** Young Americans • Win • Fascination • Right • Somebody Up There Likes Me • Across the Universe • Can You Hear Me • Fame / **Track Listing Disc 6 "Station to Station":** Station to Station • Golden Years • Word on a Wing • TVC 15 • Stay • Wild Is the Wind / **Track Listing Disc 7 "Station to Station (2010 Harry Maslin Mix)":** Station to Station • Golden Years • Word on a Wing • TVC 15 • Stay • Wild Is the Wind / **Track Listing Disc 8 "Live Nassau Coliseum '76":** Station to Station • Suffragette City • Fame • Word on a Wing • Stay • Waiting for the Man • Queen Bitch • Life on Mars? • Five Years • Panic in Detroit • Changes • TVC 15 • Diamond Dogs • Rebel Rebel • The Jean Genie / **Track Listing Disc 9 "Re:Call 2":** Rebel Rebel (Original Single Mix) • Diamond Dogs (Australian Single Edit) • Rebel Rebel (US Single Version) • Rock 'n' Roll with Me (Live—Promotional Single Edit) • Panic in Detroit (Live) • Young Americans (Original Single Edit) • Fame (Original Single Edit) • Golden Years (Single Version) • Station to Station (Original Single Edit) • TVC 15 (Original Single Edit) • Stay (Original Single Edit) • Word on a Wing (Original Single Edit) • John, I'm Only Dancing (Again) (1975) (Single Version)

A NEW CAREER IN A NEW TOWN (1977-1982)

Release Date: Europe and **United States:** September 29, 2017 / **Ref.:** Parlophone—DBXL 3 (33 rpm box set) / 0190295843014, DBX 3 (CD box set) / **Best UK Chart Ranking:** 19 / **Best US Chart Ranking:** 151 / **Track Listing Disc 1 "Low":** Speed of Life • Breaking Glass • What in the World • Sound and Vision • Always Crashing in the Same Car • Be My Wife • A New Career in a New Town • Warszawa • Art Decade • Weeping Wall • Subterraneans / **Track Listing Disc 2 "Heroes":** Beauty and the Beast • Joe the Lion • "Heroes" • Sons of the Silent Age • Blackout • V-2 Schneider • Sense of Doubt • Moss Garden • Neuköln • The Secret Life of Arabia / **Track Listing Disc 3 "Heroes EP":** "Heroes"/"Helden" (German Album Version) • "Helden" (German Single Version) • "Heroes"/"Héros" (French Album Version) • "Héros" (French Single Version) / **Track Listing Disc 4 "Stage (Original)":** Hang On to Yourself • Ziggy Stardust • Five Years • Soul Love • Star • Station to Station • Fame • TVC 15 • Warszawa • Speed of Life • Art Decade • Sense of Doubt • Breaking Glass • "Heroes" • What in the World • Blackout • Beauty and the Beast / **Track Listing Disc 5 "Stage (2017)":** Warszawa • "Heroes" • What in the World • Be My Wife • The Jean Genie • Blackout • Sense of Doubt • Speed of Life • Breaking Glass • Beauty and the Beast • Fame • Five Years • Soul Love • Star • Hang On to Yourself • Ziggy Stardust • Suffragette City • Art Decade • Alabama Song • Station to Station • Stay • TVC 15 / **Track Listing Disc 6 "Lodger":** Fantastic Voyage • African Night Flight • Move On • Yassassin • Red Sails • D.J. • Look Back in Anger • Boys Keep Swinging • Repetition • Red Money / **Track Listing Disc 7 "Lodger (2017 Tony Visconti Mix)":** Fantastic Voyage • African Night Flight • Move On • Yassassin • Red Sails • D.J. • Look Back in Anger • Boys Keep Swinging • Repetition • Red Money / **Track Listing Disc 8 "Scary Monsters (And Super Creeps)":** It's No Game (Part 1) • Up the Hill Backwards • Scary Monsters (And Super Creeps) • Ashes to Ashes • Fashion • Teenage Wildlife • Scream Like a Baby • Kingdom Come • Because You're Young • It's No Game (Part 2) / **Track Listing Disc 9 "Re:Call 3":** "Heroes" (Single Version) • Beauty and the Beast (Extended Version) • Breaking Glass (Australian Single Version) • Yassassin (Single Version) • D.J. (Single Version) • Alabama Song • Space Oddity (1979 Version) • Ashes to Ashes (Single Version) • Fashion (Single Version) • Scary Monsters (And Super Creeps) (Single Version) • Crystal Japan • Under Pressure (Single Version) (with Queen) • Cat People (Putting Out Fire) (Soundtrack Album Version) • Peace on Earth / Little Drummer Boy (with Bing Crosby) • Baal's Hymn (*Bertolt Brecht's Baal*) • Remembering Marie A. (*Bertolt Brecht's Baal*) • Ballad of the Adventurers (*Bertolt Brecht's Baal*) • The Drowned Girl (*Bertolt Brecht's Baal*) • The Dirty Song (*Bertolt Brecht's Baal*)

LOVING THE ALIEN (1983-1988)

Release Date: Europe and **United States:** October 12, 2018 / **Ref.:** Parlophone 019025693527, DBXL4 (33 rpm box set) / 0190295693534, DBX 4 (CD box set) / **Best UK Chart Ranking:** 19 / **Best US Chart Ranking:** Did Not Chart / **Track Listing Disc 1 "Let's Dance":** Modern Love • China Girl • Let's Dance • Without You • Ricochet • Criminal World • Cat People (Putting Out Fire) • Shake It / **Track Listing Disc 2 "Serious Moonlight [Live '83]":** Look Back in Anger • "Heroes" • What in the World • Golden Years • Fashion • Let's Dance • Breaking Glass • Life on Mars? • Sorrow • Cat People (Putting Out Fire) • China Girl • Scary Monsters (And Super Creeps) • Rebel Rebel • White Light/White Heat • Station to Station • Cracked Actor • Ashes to Ashes • Space Oddity / Band Introduction • Young Americans • Fame • Modern Love / **Track Listing Disc 3 "Tonight":** Loving the Alien • Don't Look Down • God Only Knows • Tonight • Neighborhood Threat • Blue Jean • Tumble and Twirl • I Keep Forgettin' • Dancing with the Big Boys / **Track Listing Disc 4 "Never Let Me Down":** Day-In Day-Out • Time Will Crawl • Beat of Your Drum • Never Let Me Down • Zeroes • Glass Spider • Shining Star (Makin' My Love) • New York's in Love • '87 and Cry • Bang Bang / **Track Listing Disc 5 "Never Let Me Down [2018]":** Day-In Day-Out • Time Will Crawl • Beat of Your Drum • Never Let Me Down • Zeroes • Glass Spider • Shining Star (Makin' My Love) • New York's in Love • '87 And Cry • Bang Bang / **Track Listing Disc 6 "Glass Spider [Live Montreal '87]":** Up the Hill Backwards • Glass Spider • Day-In Day-Out • Bang Bang • Absolute Beginners • Loving the Alien • China Girl • Rebel Rebel • Fashion • Scary Monsters (And Super Creeps) • All the Madmen • Never Let Me Down • Big Brother • '87 and Cry • "Heroes" • Sons of the Silent Age • Time Will Crawl / Band Introduction • Young Americans • Beat of Your Drum • The Jean Genie • Let's Dance • Fame • Time • Blue Jean • Modern Love / **Track Listing Disc 7 "Dance":** Shake It (Re-mix aka Long Version) • Blue Jean (Extended Dance Mix) • Dancing with the Big Boys (Extended Dance Mix) • Tonight (Vocal Dance Mix) • Don't Look Down (Extended Dance Mix) • Loving the Alien (Extended Dub Mix) • Tumble and Twirl (Extended Dance Mix) • Underground (Extended Dance Mix) • Day-In Day-Out (Groucho Mix) • Time Will Crawl (Dance Crew Mix) • Shining Star (Makin' My Love) (12" Mix) • Never Let Me Down (Dub/Acapella) / **Track Listing Disc 8 "Re:Call 4":** Let's Dance (Single Version) • China Girl (Single Version) • Modern Love (Single Version) • This Is Not America (The Theme from "The Falcon and the Snowman") (with the Pat Metheny Group) • Loving the Alien (Re-mixed Version) • Don't Look Down (Re-mixed Version) • Dancing in the Street (Clearmountain Mix) (with Mick Jagger) • Absolute Beginners • That's Motivation • Volare • Labyrinth Opening Titles / Underground • Magic Dance • As the World Falls Down • Within You • Underground • When the Wind Blows (Single Version) • Day-In Day-Out (Single Version) • Julie • Beat of Your Drum (Vinyl Album Edit) • Glass Spider (Vinyl Album Edit) • Shining Star (Makin' My Love) (Vinyl Album Edit) • New York's in Love (Vinyl Album Edit) • '87 and Cry (Vinyl Album Edit) • Bang Bang (Vinyl Album Edit) • Time Will Crawl (Single Version) • Girls (Extended Edit) • Never Let Me Down (7" Remix Edit) • Bang Bang (Live—Promotional Mix) • Tonight (Live) (with Tina Turner) • Let's Dance (Live) (with Tina Turner)

SPYING THROUGH A KEYHOLE

Release Date: Europe: April 5, 2019 / **Ref.:** Parlophone—0190295495084 (45 rpm box set) / **Best UK Chart Ranking:** 55 / **Track Listing:** Mother Grey (Demo) • In the Heat of the Morning (Demo) • Goodbye 3D (Threepenny) Joe (Demo) • Love All Around (Demo) • London Bye Ta-Ta (Demo) • Angel Angel Grubby Face (Demo Version 1) • Angel Angel Grubby Face (Demo Version 2) • Space Oddity (Demo Excerpt) • Space Oddity (Demo w/Hutch)

CLAREVILLE GROVE DEMOS

Release Date: UK: May 17, 2019 / **Ref.:** Parlophone—0190295495060 (45 rpm box set) / **Best Chart Ranking:** Did Not Chart / **Track Listing:** Space Oddity (Clareville Grove Demo) • Lover to the Dawn (Clareville Grove Demo) • Ching-A-Ling (Clareville Grove Demo) • An Occasional Dream (Clareville Grove Demo) • Let Me Sleep Beside You (Clareville Grove Demo) • Life Is a Circus (Clareville Grove Demo)

THE MERCURY DEMOS

Release Date: Europe and **United States:** June 28, 2019 / **Ref.:** Parlophone—DBMD 1969 (33 rpm box set) / **Best Chart Ranking:** Did Not Chart / **Track Listing:** Space Oddity • Janine • Occasional Dream • Conversation Piece • Ching-A-Ling • I'm Not Quite • Lover to the Dawn • Love Song • When I'm Five • Life Is a Circus

CONVERSATION PIECE

Release Date: UK and United States: November 15, 2019 / **Ref.:** Parlophone—DBCP 6869, 0190295389291 (CD box set) / **Best Chart Ranking:** Did Not Chart / **Track Listing Disc 1 "Home Demos":** April's Tooth of Gold • The Reverend Raymond Brown (Attends the Garden Fête on Thatchwick Green) • When I'm Five • Mother Grey • In the Heat of the Morning • Goodbye 3D (Threepenny) Joe • Love All Around • London Bye Ta-Ta • Angel Angel Grubby Face (Version 1) • Angel Angel Grubby Face (Version 2) • Animal Farm • Space Oddity (Solo Demo Fragment) • Space Oddity (Version 1) • Space Oddity (Version 2) • Space Oddity (Version 3) • Lover to the Dawn • Ching-A-Ling • An Occasional Dream • Let Me Sleep Beside You • Life Is a Circus • Conversation Piece • Jerusalem • Hole in the Ground / **Track Listing Disc 2 "The 'Mercury' Demos":** Space Oddity • Janine • An Occasional Dream • Conversation Piece • Ching-A-Ling • I'm Not Quite (aka Letter to Hermione) • Lover to the Dawn • Love Song • When I'm Five • Life Is a Circus / **Track Listing Disc 3 "Conversation Pieces":** In the Heat of the Morning (Decca Mono Version) • London Bye Ta-Ta (Decca Alternative Version) / **"BBC** *Top Gear* **Radio Session with the Tony Visconti Orchestra, Recorded 13th May, 1968":** In the Heat of the Morning • London Bye Ta-Ta • Karma Man • When I'm Five • Silly Boy Blue • Ching-A-Ling • Space Oddity (Morgan Studios Version—Alternative Take) • Space Oddity (U.K. Single Edit) • Wild Eyed Boy from Freecloud (Single B-side—Mono Mix) • Janine (Mono Mix) • Conversation Piece / **"BBC** *Dave Lee Travis Show* **Radio Session, Recorded 20th October, 1969":** Let Me Sleep Beside You • Unwashed and Somewhat Slightly Dazed • Janine / **Track Listing Disc 4 "The David Bowie (aka Space Oddity) Album":** Space Oddity • Unwashed and Somewhat Slightly Dazed (inc. Don't Sit Down) • Letter to Hermione • Cygnet Committee • Janine • An Occasional Dream • Wild Eyed Boy from Freecloud • God Knows I'm Good • Memory of a Free Festival / **The Extras:** Wild Eyed Boy from Freecloud (Single B-side Stereo Mix) • Letter to Hermione (Early Mix) • Janine (Early Mix) • An Occasional Dream (Early Mix) • Ragazzo Solo, Ragazza Sola (Full Length Version) / **Track Listing Disc 5 "The Space Oddity Album":** Space Oddity • Unwashed and Somewhat Slightly Dazed • Letter to Hermione • Cygnet Committee • Janine • An Occasional Dream • Wild Eyed Boy from Freecloud • Conversation Piece • God Knows I'm Good • Memory of a Free Festival / **The Extras:** Wild Eyed Boy from Freecloud (Single Version) • Ragazzo Solo, Ragazza Sola

GLOSSARY

Backing band: a group of musicians accompanying an artist on stage or in the studio.

Backing tracks: instrumental or vocal (or sometimes simply rhythmical) tracks prerecorded to accompany a singer or group of players.

Bend: technique practiced by guitarists where one or more stings are pushed sideways, parallel to the neck. This causes the pitch of a sounded note to rise by a semitone or more.

Bottleneck: a glass or metal tube that the guitarist places on one finger and then slides over the strings to get a metallic sound. Blues players developed this way of playing using, as the name indicates, the neck of a bottle.

Bridge: transition between two passages of a song. It generally refers to the section between verse and refrain.

Click: a repeated sound made by an audio metronome. It is sent by the sound engineer to the musicians' headphones during a recording session so that all the players can be perfectly synchronized with one another.

Cocotte: a guitar-playing technique using one note that can be "open," "closed," or "skank-style," chiefly used in funk music. There is no English equivalent of this word.

Delay: an audio effect that creates an echo-like sound. Integrated into an effect pedal or a mixing console, it can be used for voices or instruments, and it can repeat a sound at different time intervals.

Detuning: modification of the pitch of one or more notes obtained by altering the tuning of an instrument or a recorded sound.

Easy listening: style of music similar to so-called ambient music, where the sounds have no harshness and are acceptable to all tastes.

Effects pedal: small electronic device used to transform the sound of an instrument while it is being played.

Electroacoustic (guitar): acoustic guitar with at least one microphone to amplify the sound in the same way as an electric guitar.

Fader: a control that slides up and down on a mixing board. It is used to control the volume of each individual track of a recording.

Fingerpicking: guitar-playing technique, particularly for acoustic guitars, typical of American folk music, blues, and bluegrass. The melody and the backing rhythm are played at the same time.

Front man: refers to the singer of a group, because he or she stands in front of the other musicians at the front of the stage.

Funkateer: in urban slang, a fan of funk music associating him- or herself with particular attitudes and a particular lifestyle.

Fuzz: audio effect producing a saturated, thick, and coarse sound, the notes being distorted by a fuzz box. Popularized by musicians such as the Rolling Stones and Jimi Hendrix, fuzz is principally used with electric guitars.

Gimmick: a short series of notes with an easily recognizable melody that attracts attention and remains in the listener's memory. Originally found in jazz, it has progressively been taken up by other musical genres.

Guitar hero: title given to a particularly brilliant and creative guitarist. Often applied to the great guitarists 1980s hard rock and heavy metal musicians.

Harmonization: technique of multiplying the vocal or instrumental line with the same notes in unison or an octave apart. If the line or lines added to the original are played or sung on other notes (thirds or fifths, for example), the term *polyphonic harmonization* is used.

Headless (guitar): type of guitar without a headstock where the strings are attached the opposite way around from usual, the tuners normally being placed behind the bridge.

Jam session: improvisatory session where several musicians get together informally for the simple pleasure of playing.

Lineup: list of musicians in a group.

Mash-up: song made up of elements of pre-existing numbers.

Midtempo: A song played at a moderate speed.

Mod: a subculture that emerged in London at the end of the 1950s, in opposition to traditional British culture. Rock music, fashionable clothes, and the use of Vespa scooters were characteristics of young mods in '60s England.

Noise music: characterized by the use of loud and often unpleasant sounds, the aim being to break away from traditionally constructed music where harmony is important.

Outtake: piece of music recorded in a studio or onstage that is omitted from the official version of an album. It can be an unreleased item or an alternative version of an existing title and is sometimes revived for inclusion in a compilation or new edition.

Overdubs: new sounds recorded (voice and/or instruments) and added to an already existing recording.

Palm muting: technique used with guitar and bass guitar where the notes are muffled by placing the palm of the hand (right hand for right-handers and left for left-handers) across the strings near the bridge. It is done to dampen the sound of the notes played with the plectrum.

Pattern: repeating rhythmical or melodic sequence in a piece of music.

Phasing: audio effect obtained by filtering a signal and creating a series of highs and lows in the frequency spectrum. Available as a pedal or a rack, the effect is often a sweeping, wavelike oscillation.

Reamping: a studio technique where a recorded audio signal is run through an external process (a guitar amplifier or sound system, for example) before being reinserted into the mixing. The engineer can thus adapt the sound as he or she wishes.

Reissue: rerelease of an album or a single.

Reverb: a natural or an artificial echo effect added to an instrument or a voice during recording or mixing.

Reverse: deliberate reversal of a sound on an audio track so that it is heard backward.

Ride cymbal: struck on the bow to give a powerful sound or on the bell in swing and jazz, the ride is often the largest cymbal in a drum kit, placed on the right-hand side for right-handers and on the left for left-handers.

Riff: an abbreviation of the expression *rhythmic figure*, a riff is a short fragment of a few notes that returns regularly during a piece and accompanies the melody.

Road manager: part of a musician's team, the road manager organizes and supervises tours.

Scat: vocal style used in jazz that utilizes nonsense syllables instead of comprehensible song lyrics.

Set list: list of numbers performed by an artist or a group at a concert.

Side project: artistic project pursued by an artist—often secretly—outside their professional work with a group or as a soloist.

Skiffle: a style of folk music popular in the UK in the 1950s. Influenced by jazz and blues, it was characterized by the use of homemade instruments.

Slap: technique used on an electric bass, chiefly in funk and disco music. The strings are struck by the side of the thumb, and the other fingers of the right hand then pull the strings upward.

Slide: technique used on the guitar consisting of a continuous and rapid sliding of a chord or of one note into another so that the intermediate notes can be heard.

Songwriter: the author of the words and/or music of a song.

Strumming: guitar technique where the right hand (or the left hand in the case of left-handed players) sweeps across all the strings from top to bottom.

Sustain: capacity of an instrument to prolong the sound of a note. This term is mainly used to describe the sound qualities of a guitar.

Swinging London: a phrase applied to London in the 1960s where music, fashion, and youth brought new energy to the capital of pop culture.

Talkback: an intercom in a recording studio that allows the sound engineer or producer in the control room to communicate with the musicians recording in the live room.

Test pressing: a sample version of a disc made and used to determine whether there are faults in the recording before the full-scale pressing. Test pressings by well-known artists are often much sought after by collectors.

Track listing: list of the songs featured on an album.

Trigger: sensor designed to digitize the sounds of a drum kit. Placed in contact with the instrument's batter head, it transforms the beats into electric signals, which are then sent to a module that produces the sounds.

Wah-wah: audio effect produced by the oscillation of the sound frequency between bass and treble, giving a sound that resembles a human voice repeating the onomatopoeic "wah." Mainly used with electric guitars, this effect can be achieved using the pedal of the same name.

BIBLIOGRAPHY

1 - Dylan Jones, *David Bowie: A Life*, London, Windmill Books, 2017.

2 - *Sound and Vision*, directed by Rick Hull, documentary, Prometheus Entertainment/ Foxstar, 2002.

3 - Kenneth Pitt, *Bowie: The Pitt Report*, London, Omnibus Press, 1985.

4 - *David Bowie: His Life on Earth 1947–2016*, New York, Time Inc. Books, 2016.

5 - James McCarthy, "Did Rogers Ferris' Injured Foot Really Help Launch David Bowie on the Road to Stardom?" Walesonline.co.uk, January 16, 2016.

6 - Kevin Cann, *Any Day Now, David Bowie: The London Years (1947–1974)*, Croydon (UK), Adelita Ltd., 2010.

7 - *David Bowie: Finding Fame*, directed by Francis Whately, documentary, BBC2, 2019, Vimeo, video, 16:25.

8 - *David Bowie: Origins of A Starman*, directed by Chrome Dreams, documentary, Chrome Dreams, 2004.

9 - Leslie Thomas, "For Those Beyond the Fringe," *Evening News and Star*, November 2, 1964.

10 - *Tonight*, BBC2, November 12, 1964, video, Youtube.

11 - Laura Snapes, "'Devoid of Personality': BBC Verdict on Early Bowie Audition Unearthed," *Guardian*, October 9, 2018.

12 - John Hutchinson, *Bowie & Hutch*, Bridlington (UK), Lodge Books, 2014.

13 - *Ultimate Record Collection: David Bowie, Part I*, London, Bandlab Technologies, 2020.

14 - Howard Massey, *The Great British Recording Studios*, Milwaukee, Hal Leonard Books, 2015.

15 - Interview with Bob Solly by Sophie de Rosée, *Daily Telegraph*, November 13, 2010.

16 - Andrew McGinn, "Springfield Graduate Has Connection to David Bowie," *Springfield News-Sun*, January 11, 2016.

17 - Jordan Runtagh, "David Bowie's 10 Greatest Davy Jones–Era Tracks," *Rolling Stone*, January 12, 2016.

18 - Phil Lancaster, *At the Birth of Bowie*, London, John Blake, 2019.

19 - *David Bowie—VH1 Storytellers*, documentary, Parlophone, 2009.

20 - Kevin Cann, "David's Deram Chronology," jacket notes for the re-release of the *David Bowie* album, UMC/Deram, 2018.

21 - Original jacket notes for the *David Bowie* album, Deram, 1967.

22 - *Bowie: The Ultimate Music Guide*, Deluxe Remastered Edition, London, Uncut / Time Inc. (UK) Ltd., 2018.

23 - Paul Trynka, "Uncle Arthur and Other Creations," interview with Derek Fearnley, Paul Trynka (website).

24 - Alan Sillitoe, "The Disgrace of Jim Scarfedale," in *The Loneliness of the Long Distance Runner*, London, HarperCollins, 2007.

25 - Michael Parkinson, interview with David Bowie, *Parkinson*, BBC1, September 21, 2002, YouTube.

26 - Richard Cromelin, "David Bowie: The Darling of the Avant Garde," *Phonograph Record*, January 1972, Bowie Golden Years.

27 - John Dingwall, "Before Ziggy Stardust There Was 'David McBowie' the Singing Sensation Who Faked a Scottish Accent," *Mirror*, January 11, 2016.

28 - Rod Meade Sperry, "That Time David Bowie Almost Became a Buddhist Monk—And What He Said (and Sang) About That Time," *Lion's Roar*, January 15, 2016.

29 - David Buckley, "Interview for Book *Strange Fascination*," Mark Plati (website), 1999.

30 - Interview with David Bowie by Paul Du Noyer, *Q* magazine, April 1990, Paul Du Noyer (website).

31 - Martin Hayman, "Outside David Bowie…Is the Closest You're Gonna Get," *Rock*, October 1973, Bowie Golden Years.

32 - Jackie, "Face to Face with David Bowie: The Secret of My Lost Year…," May 10, 1970, Bowie Wonderworld.

33 - Sylvain Siclier, "Haddon Hall, la maison où 'David inventa Bowie'" (Haddon Hall, The House Where "David Invented Bowie"), *Le Monde*, July 29, 2015.

34 - Simon Goddard, "The Starman Cometh," *Record Collector* no. 490, March 2019.

35 - Tony Visconti, *The Autobiography, Bowie, Bolan and The Brooklyn Boy*, London, HarperCollins, 2007.

36 - Bill DeMain, "The Sound and Vision of David Bowie," *Performing Songwriter*, September–October 2003.

37 - Penny Valentine, "David Bowie Says Most Things the Long Way Round," *Disc and Music Echo*, October 25, 1969, Bowie Wonderworld.

38 - George Tremlett, *David Bowie: Living on the Brink*, Da Capo Press, 1997.

39 - Paul Trynka, "A Letter from Hermione," trynka.net.

40 - "Paul Buckmaster," *The Music Aficionado*, February 27, 2019.

41 - *Beside Bowie: The Mick Ronson Story*, directed by Jon Brewer, documentary, Universal, 2018, video, 7:54.

42 - Russell Hall, "Producer's Corner: Tony Visconti," *Performing Songwriter*, November 2008.

43 - Woody Woodmansey, *Spider from Mars: My Life with Bowie*, London, Sidgwick & Jackson, 2016.

44 - Raymond Telford, "Hype and David Bowie's Future," *Melody Maker*, March 28, 1970, Bowie Golden Years.

45 - Nietzsche Friedrich Neitzsche, *Thus Spoke Zarathustra*, 1883.

46 - Frankie Neilson, "How Ralph Became a 'Spider from Mars,'" *Richmond News*, June 19, 2013.

47 - Nicholas Pegg, *The Complete David Bowie*, London, Titan Books, 2016.

48 - "David Bowie: 'Britain Could Benefit from a Fascist Leader,'" April 26, 1976, in The Bowie Bible.

49 - Unpublished interview with John Swenson for *Zygote Magazine*, January 1971, David Bowie Forever.

50 - Interview with Lulu, for BBC, October 15, 2011, Youtube, video, 2:34.

51 - Cameron Crowe, "The *Playboy* Interview with David Bowie," *Playboy*, September 1976.

52 - Tony Horkins, "A Close Shave with Mick Ronson," *Beat Instrumental*, March 1980, Mick Ronson (website).

53 - Paul Trynka, *Starman*, New York, Little, Brown, 2011.

54 - Ken Scott and Bobby Owsinski, *Abbey Road to Ziggy Stardust*, Van Nuys, CA, Alfred Music Publishing, 2012.

55 - Craig Copetas, "Beat Godfather Meets Glitter Mainman: William Burroughs Interviews David Bowie," *Rolling Stone*, February 28, 1974.

56 - Notes from the booklet accompanying the compilation disc *iSelect*, 2008.

57 - Publicity for *Hunky Dory*, *Melody Maker*, January 8, 1972.

58 - *Hunky Dory* jacket notes.

59 - Roger Griffin, *David Bowie: The Golden Years*, London, Omnibus Press, 2016.

60 - Michael Watts, "Oh You Pretty Thing," *Melody Maker*, January 22, 1972, The Ziggy Stardust Companion.

61 - Angie Bowie, *Free Spirit*, London, Mushroom Books, 1981.

62 - Valerie Siebert, "Jamming Good: Spiders Drummer Woody Woodmansey's Favourite Bowie Moments," *The Quietus*, February 22, 2017.

63 - Mike McGrath, "Bowie Meets Springsteen," *The Drummer*, November 26, 1974, Bowie Golden Years.

64 - Interview with Trevor Bolder by Dmitry M. Epstein, *Let It Rock*, dmme.net, October 2003.

65 - *David Bowie and the Story of Ziggy Stardust*, directed by James Hale, documentary, BBC 4, 2012.

66 - Interview with David Bowie by Russell Harty, *Plus Pop*, Granada TV, January 17, 1973, YouTube, video.

67 - Tina Brown, "The Bowie Odyssey," *Sunday Times Magazine*, July 20, 1975, Bowie Golden Years.

68 - "Bassist Trevor Bolder Discusses the Hit Song 'The Jean Genie,'" Classic Rock Network, YouTube, video.

69 - Robert Hilburn, "Bowie Finds His Voice," *Melody Maker*, September 14, 1974, Bowie Golden Years.

70 - Terry O'Neill, *When Ziggy Played the Marquee*, New York, ACC Editions, 2017.

71 - "David Bowie: l'été français qui changea sa vie," *Le Journal du Dimanche*, January 17, 2016.

72 - Marie Ottavi, "Ma minute Bowie: Dominique Blanc-Francard, producteur," Libération.fr, January 11, 2016.

73 - "David Bowie Pays Tribute to Syd Barrett," *New Musical Express*, July 11, 2006.

74 - Weird & Gilly, *Mick Ronson: The Spider with the Platinum Hair*, London, Music Press Books, 2017.

75 - David Sinclair, "Ziggy's Axeman," *Rolling Stone*, June 24, 1993, Mick Ronson (website).

76 - David Buckley, "'Bowie Was Like Orson Welles': Diamond Dogs at 40," *Mojo*, April 24, 2014.

77 - Caryn Rose, "Bruce Springsteen Pays Tribute to David Bowie with Live 'Rebel Rebel,'" UltimateClassicRock.com, January 17, 2016.

78 - Album booklet notes from the *Diamond Dogs* 30th Anniversary Edition, 2004.

79 - Neil Cossar, *David Bowie: I Was There*, Penryn, Red Planet Publishing, 2017.

80 - Ken Sharpe, "Traveling with Bowie," *Record Collector* no. 354, October 2008.

81 - Notes from the booklet in the box set *Who Can I Be Now? [1974–1976]*, May 2016.

82 - Martin Kirkup, "Diamond Dogs," *Sounds*, May 4, 1974, Bowie Golden Years.

83 - Chris Charlesworth, "Ringing the Changes," *Melody Maker*, March 13, 1976, Bowie Golden Years.

84 - Interview with Ava Cherry by SlyStoned, 'David Bowie was fascinated by soul music', funk-u.com, October 18, 2014.

85 - Stuart Grundy and John Tobler, *The Record Producers*, London, BBC, 1982.

86 - Johnny Black, "The Greatest Songs Ever! Young Americans," *Blender*, April 2004, Bowie Wonder World.

87 - David Bowie, "I Went to Buy Some Shoes, and I Came Back with 'Life on Mars,'" Daily Mail Online, June 28, 2008.

88 - Christian John Wikane, "Living the Dream: Robin Clark and Carlos Alomar Remember David Bowie and Luther Vandross," PopMatters, June 20, 2016.

89 - John Robinson, "Heart and Soul," *Uncut*, February 2015.

90 - Anthony O'Grady, "David Bowie: Watch Out Mate! Hitler's on His Way Back," *New Musical Express*, August 1975.

91 - Dave Thompson, *Moonage Daydream*, London, Plexus, 1987.

92 - John Earls, "David Bowie Abandoned Covering Bruce Springsteen After Meeting Him," *New Musical Express*, August 19, 2016.

93 - Andy Greene, "E Street's Roy Bittan on Collaborating with Bowie, Bob Seger, Stevie Nicks," *RollingStone*, January 15, 2015.

94 - *David Bowie—Planet Rock Profile,* VH1, December 3, 1998.

95 - Robert Hilburn, "Bowie: Now I'm a Businessman," *Melody Maker*, February 28, 1976.

96 - Jason Anderson, "The Ties That Still Bind," *Uncut*, April 2016.

97 - Richard Cromelin, "The Return of the Thin White Duke," *Circus*, March 2, 1976.

98 - Alan Light, "How David Bowie Helped Nina Simone Out of a Slump", Time.com, January 11, 2016.

99 - Hugo Wilcken, *Low,* New York, Bloomsbury, 2005.

100 - Stephen Dalton and Rob Hughes, "Trans-Europe Excess," *Uncut*, April 2001.

101 - *The Bowie Years, Volume 2, From Soul Boy to Berliner*, London, Anthem Publishing, 2018.

102 - *Mojo—The Collectors' Series: Bowie Changes 1976–2016*, Peterborough (UK), Bauer Consumer Media, 2018.

103 - Jon Pareles, "David Bowie, 21st-Century Entrepreneur," *New York Times*, June 9, 2002.

104 - "David Bowie's 30 Best Songs: Jimmy Page, Keith Richards, Tony Visconti, Johnny Marr and More Choose Their Favourites…," *Uncut*, February 19, 2015.

105 - Tim Lott, "The Thin White Duke Has Gone. Here's the New David Bowie," *Record Mirror*, September 24, 1977.

106 - Sleeve notes from the album *Ambient 1: Music for Airports*, 1978.

107 - John Orme, "Iggy's Lust Words," *Melody Maker*, August 13, 1977.

108 - Interview with David Bowie by Avi Lewis, Much Music, 1997, YouTube.

109 - *David Bowie: Five Years*, directed by Francis Whately, documentary, BBC, 2013, video, 29:56.

110 - "Q Writers Love 'Joe the Lion,'" David Bowie (website), December 28, 2000.

111 - Paul Farhi, "Bing and Bowie: An Odd Story of Holiday Harmony," *Washington Post*, December 20, 2006.

112 - David Quantick, "Now Where Did I Put Those Tunes?" *Q Magazine*, October 1999.

113 - Ted Scott, "AudioWise: Stories from Sound Control: Bing Crosby," www.tedscott.co.uk.

114 - Charles M. Young, "Bowie Plays Himself, Ziggy Returns to Earth," *Rolling Stone* no. 256, January 12, 1978.

115 - Interview with David Bowie, "David Bowie—Rock Report 1987," YouTube.

116 - Clive Young, "Producing David Bowie's Berlin Trilogy," Pro Sound News, April 6, 2018.

117 - Sean Mayes, *Life on Tour with Bowie*, London, Music Press Books, 2016.

118 - Michael Watts, "My Natural Response to Disco," *Melody Maker*, May 19, 1979.

119 - *Ultimate Record Collection: David Bowie, Part II,* London, Bandlab Technologies, 2020.

120 - Michael Watts, "Confession of an Elitist," *Melody Maker*, February 18, 1978.

121 - Paul Trynka, "An Idiot's Guide," Paul Trynka (website), July 8, 2005.

122 - Angus MacKinnon, "The Future Isn't What It Used to Be," *New Musical Express*, September 13, 1980, Bowie Golden Years.

123 - Robert Hilburn, "David Bowie: The View from the Top," *Los Angeles Times*, September 9, 1980.

124 - Kurt Loder, "Scary Monster on Broadway," *Rolling Stone* no. 130, November 13, 1980.

125 - "David Bowie," *Pete's Blog*, The Who (website), January 11, 2016.

126 - Robert Gourley, "Under Pressure: Gail Ann Dorsey on Playing Bass for David Bowie," PleaseKillMe.com, December 20, 2017.

127 - Kory Grow, "How David Bowie, Nile Rodgers Made 'Let's Dance' a Hit," *Rolling Stone*, April 14, 2016.

128 - Nile Rodgers, *Le Freak,* London, Sphere, 2011.

129 - Interview with Nile Rodgers by Benji B, Red Bull Music Academy, Madrid, 2011.

130 - Rob Hughes, "Dancing with the Big Boys," *Uncut* no. 258, November 2018, p. 60.

131 - Ken Kurson, "Steve Elson: David Bowie's Sax Appeal," *Rock & Roll Globe*, November 12, 2019.

132 - Kuêlan Nguyen, "David Bowie: l'été français qui changea sa vie," *Le Journal du Dimanche*, January 17, 2016.

133 - Tom Doyle, "Out of the Blue," *Mojo* no. 297, August 2018.

134 - "Nile Rodgers Tells the Story of 'Let's Dance,'" Fender Artist Check-In, Fender, June 22, 2020, YouTube.

135 - Dave Lifton, "Why David Bowie's 'Let's Dance' Video Angered Stevie Ray Vaughan," UltimateClassicRock.com, August 5, 2019.

136 - Talia Schlanger, "Nile Rodgers on Writing Smash Hits and Reworking David Bowie's 'Let's Dance,'" NPR, August 29, 2019.

137 - GBD, "1983…Le Jeune Youri Lenquette Assiste au Lancement du Serious Moonlight Tour de Bowie," Gonzo Music, February 13, 2016.

138 - Kevin Johnson, "The Story Behind David Bowie's 'Let's Dance' Bass Line," No Treble, February 17, 2020.

139 - Charles Shaar Murray, "Sermon from the Savoy," *New Musical Express*, September 29, 1984.

140 - Adrian Deevoy, "Boys Keep Swinging," *Q Magazine*, June 1989.

141 - James Gent, "'Absolute Beginners': The Story of David Bowie's Last Big Hit," We Are Cult, January 8, 2017.

142 - "*Labyrinth* Preview," *Starzone: The International Magazine of David Bowie*, no. 16, 1986.

143 - *Inside the Labyrinth*, directed by Des Saunders, documentary, Jim Henson Television, 1986, YouTube.

144 - *Inside the Labyrinth*, directed by Des Saunders, documentary, Jim Henson Television, 1986, YouTube.

145 - The Best of Vox Pop, "David Bowie: Raw & Uncut Interview from 1987," YouTube.

146 - Kevin Cooper, "Interview: Peter Frampton," UK Music Reviews, March 12, 2019.

147 - Tricia Jones, "David Bowie: Is the Lad Too Sane for His Own Good?" *i-D Magazine* no. 49, July 1987.

148 - Kurt Loder, "David Bowie: Stardust Memories," *Rolling Stone*, April 23, 1987.

149 - *Music & Sound Output*, The Bowie Bible, June 1987.

150 - "David Bowie—1987 London Press Conference 2/3" (for the launch of the "Glass Spider Tour"), Player's Theatre, London, March 20, 1987, YouTube.

151 - Mickey Rourke on Instagram, October 4, 2019.

152 - "Bowie! Back on the High Wire," *Musician*, August 1987.

153 - Twitter account of the office of the mayor of New York, Bill de Blasio, January 21, 2016.

154 - Jon Pareles, "David Bowie Mingles Glamour and Gloom," *New York Times*, April 26, 1987.

155 - Rob Hughes, "A Garage Band with a Budget!" *Uncut*, July 2019.

156 - Notes from the booklet in the *Tin Machine* box set, EMI (UK), May 1989, p. 5.

157 - Emmanuelle Bouchez, "David Bowie et Louise Lecavalier, duo de danse électrique," *Télérama*, January 13, 2016.

158 - Steven Wells, "The Artful Codger: An Interview with David Bowie," *New Musical Express*, November 25, 1995.

159 - "Bowie: The Return of the Tin White Duke," *Melody Maker*, July 1, 1989.

160 - Trey Taylor, "Obvious History: Did Debbie Harry Have a Near-Fatal Brush with Ted Bundy?" *Interview*, February 16, 2018.

161 - "David Bowie—Tin Machine—Interview & Rehearsal—1989," YouTube.

162 - Daisy Dumas, "Bowie Down Under: Star Hooked on Sydney," *Sydney Morning Herald*, January 16, 2016.

163 - *Ultimate Record Collection: David Bowie, Part III*, London, Bandlab Technologies, 2021.

164 - Jae-Ha Kim, "Tin Machine Gives Its Singer Power to Be Simply Bowie," *Chicago Sun-Times*, December 1 1991, Bowie Wonderworld.

165 - Reeves Gabrels, Facebook, January 26, 2016.

166 - Philip Bradley, "David Played Guitar," *International Musician and Recording World*, June 1990, Bowie Wonderworld.

167 - "Baby Universal '97 Available for Streaming Now," David Bowie (website), January 30, 2020.

168 - Sean Egan, *Bowie on Bowie,* Chicago, Chicago Review Press, 2015.

169 - David Barsalou, "Is Hunt Sales the Most Underrated Drummer in the USA?", Not So Modern Drummer, January 8, 2015.

170 - Liner notes for the compilation *Beyond the Beach*, Upstart Records, 1994.

171 - David Sinclair, "'Station to Station': An Interview by David Sinclair with David Bowie," *Rolling Stone*, June 10, 1993.

172 - Graham Reid, "David Bowie Interviewed (1993)," *New Zealand Herald*, 1993.

173 - "David Bowie—Back in Black (And White)," *Record Collector*, May 1993, Bowie Wonder World.

174 - Steve Sutherland, "Bowie and Brett 'Alias Smith And Jones' (Part Two) NME 27 March 1993," New Musical Express, March 27, 1993, Bowie and Brett.

175 - Steve Sutherland, "Bowie and Brett 'Alias Smith And Jones' (Part One) NME 27 March 1993," *New Musical Express*, March 20, 1993, Bowie and Brett.

176 - Hanif Kureishi, "My Friend David Bowie by Hanif Kureishi," *Guardian*, August 12, 2017.

177 - Album notes, *The Buddha of Suburbia*, Arista/BMG, 1993 and 2007.

178 - Larry Katz, "David Bowie (1995)," The Katz Tapes, March 9, 2016.

179 - Interview with David Bowie by Ingrid Sischy, *Interview*, September 1995.

180 - Brian Eno, *A Year with Swollen Appendices*, London, Faber and Faber, 1996.

181 - Ken Scrudato, "David Bowie—Life on Earth," *Soma*, July 2003, Bowie Wonder World.

182 - Chris Roberts, "Action Painting," *Ikon*, October 1995, Bowie Wonder World.

183 - Lisa Torem, "Kevin Armstrong—Interview," Pennyblackmusic, March 11, 2019.

184 - Ray McClelland, "The guitarguitar Interview: Reeves Gabrels," guitarguitar, October 23, 2020.

185 - "Internet Conversation Between Bowie and Eno," *Q*, October 26, 1994, Bowie Wonder World.

186 - "1.Outside EPK (Part 1)," 1995, Youtube.

187 - Dominic Wells, "Boys Keep Swinging," *Time Out*, September 6, 1995.

188 - "Reeves Gabrels on Songwriting with David Bowie," Reverb.com, July 25, 2018, Youtube.

189 - Linda Laban, "Bowie Retrospective," Mr. Showbiz, March 1997, Bowie Wonder World.

190 - Paul Trynka, "'I Will Not Make Product'—Mark Plati," Paul Trynka (website).

191 - David Buckley, "Interview for Book *Strange Fascination*," Mark Plati (website), 1999.

192 - Press release for *Earthling*, 1997, quoted in "Earthling," The Bowie Bible.

193 - Adam Budofsky, "David Bowie: A Different View," *Modern Drummer*, July 1997.

194 - Jeff Slate, "David Bowie in the 1990s: Producer Mark Plati Lifts Lid on New Archival Releases," *Rock Cellar Magazine*, April 14, 2020.

195 - Todd L. Burns, "Nightclubbing: Metalheadz at Blue Note," Red Bull Music Academy, April 2, 2013.

196 - Shauna Flaherty, "Bowie Taught Me the Power of Reinvention," *Mixmag*, June 22, 2017.

197 - Yelena Deyneko, "The Dream Man," *Spirit and Flesh*, March 30, 2015.

198 - Aaron J. Sams, "The Song Bono Lost to Bowie," U2 Songs, February 18, 2016.

199 - Stéphane Jarno, "'The Nomad Soul,' le jeu vidéo dans lequel 'David Bowie s'était impliqué à fond,' est téléchargeable gratuitement" ["The Nomad Soul" the video game in which "David Bowie was heavily involved," can be downloaded free of charge], Télérama, January 18, 2016.

200 - Robert Phoenix, "In Bowie's Head," *Getting It*, October 5, 1999, Bowie Wonder World.

201 - *VH1 Storytellers*, "David Bowie," aired October 18, 1999, on VH1.

202 - Dan Volohov, "Honest Creativity: An Interview with Chris Haskett of the Henry Rollins Band," Punk Globe, August 2018.

203 - "'The Nomad Soul': David Cage revient sur la création de son jeu précurseur" ["The Nomad Soul": David Cage reflects on the creation of his seminal game], CNC, May 26, 2020.

204 - Dave Grohl on Instagram, April 29, 2020.

205 - "Familiar Voice on Rustic Overtones Album," David Bowie (website), May 23, 2001.

206 - Chris O'Leary, "Pictures of Lily," Pushing Ahead of the Dame, February 27, 2014.

207 - "Interview in *Mojo*," Mark Plati (website).

208 - Richard Buskin, "David Bowie & Tony Visconti: Recording Reality," *Sound on Sound*, October 2003.

209 - Dave Simpson, "Ground Control," *Guardian*, June 5, 2002.

210 - "Rock's Heathen Speaks," Livewire's One on One, concertlivewire.com, June 16, 2002.

211 - "David Bowie: *Heathen* Part One," Visconti (website), 2002.

212 - Beth Peerless, "Rock Icon and Pixies Frontman Black Francis Will Perform Solo Among the Redwoods in Big Sur," *Monterey Herald*, August 13, 2009.

213 - Chris Cope, "Jordan Rudess of Dream Theater on Working with David Bowie and the New Album *The Astonishing*," Drowned in Sound, February 8, 2016.

214 - "Brandon Flowers on the Stories Behind the Killers' Greatest Hits," *NME Blog*, November 8, 2013.

215 - Sam Inglis, "Gary Miller," *Sound on Sound*, August 2002.

216 - "David Bowie Cut from *Rugrats* Soundtracks," David Bowie (website), October 6, 1998.

217 - Pat Pierson, "Conversation Piece," *Yeah Yeah Yeah* no. 22, 2003.

218 - George Varga, "Bowie's Impact on Popular Culture Is Almost Inestimable," *San Diego Union-Tribune*, January 11, 2016.

219 - David Bowie Live at Hammersmith Riverside, DVD, 60:00, ISO/Columbia, 2003.

220 - David Wilde, "David Bowie's *Reality*," press release, 2003, Bowie Wonder World.

221 - Chris Roberts, "David Bowie: 'I'm Hungry for Reality,'" *Uncut*, October 1999.

222 - Wes Orshoski, "David Bowie: Never Get Old," Steinway & Sons, 2003.

223 - Jesse Cline, "Kristeen Young Unearths David Bowie Collaboration for Her Forthcoming Record Store Day Release," *Flood Magazine*, October 13, 2020.

224 - Kristeen Young, Facebook, August 2016.

225 - David Sitek, "TV on the Radio's Dave Sitek on David Bowie's Message: 'Stay Strange,'" *Rolling Stone*, January 28, 2016.

226 - Andy Greene, "How Scarlett Johansson and David Bowie Got Together," *Rolling Stone*, February 13, 2008.

227 - Johnny Black, "How Bowie Stunned the World with *The Next Day*," Louder, January 7, 2021.

228 - Alexis Petridis, "Inside the Story of How David Bowie Made *The Next Day*," *Guardian*, January 12, 2013.

229 - Andy Greene, "David Bowie 'Likes the Struggle' of Winning Fans," *Rolling Stone*, February 1, 2013.

230 - Laurie Tuffey, "Jonathan Barnbrook Talks Bowie Artwork," *The Quietus*, January 8, 2013.

231 - "Bowie's 'Jesus' Video Is a Mess," Catholic League, May 8, 2013.

232 - Andy Greene, "David Bowie's *The Next Day* Album: A Track-by-Track Preview," *Rolling Stone*, January 15, 2013.

233 - Carole Cadwalladr, "Iman: 'I am the Face of a Refugee,'" *Guardian*, June 29, 2014.

234 - "Star Man—Exclusive Interview with Bowie Wingman, Gerry Leonard," Roland, 2013.

235 - "Roland Talk Exclusively with David Bowie Producer, Tony Visconti," Roland, 2013.

236 - NRA Convention, 2000, Youtube.

237 - Andy Greene, "David Bowie Guitarist Gerry Leonard: 'Odds of a Tour Are 50-50,'" *Rolling Stone*, February 20, 2013.

238 - David Weiss, "Engineering David Bowie's *The Next Day*—Inside the Magic Shop Sessions with Mario J. McNulty," SonicScoop, March 11, 2013.

239 - Andy Greene, "The Inside Story of David Bowie's Stunning New Album, *Blackstar*," *Rolling Stone*, November 23, 2015.

240 - Mark Sinclair, "Bowie, Barnbrook and the Blackstar Artwork," *Creative Review*, November 26, 2015.

241 - David Weiss, "The Magic Shop Is Closing: What It Means to NYC Audio," SonicScoop, February 23, 2016.

242 - Robert Fox, "Remembering David Bowie," *Vogue*, January 11, 2016.

243 - *David Bowie: Five Years*, directed by Francis Whately, documentary, BBC, 2013.

244 - Michael Bonner, "'Dark, Brooding, Beautiful': How Bowie's *Blackstar* Became the Theme for a TV Series," *Uncut* no. 224, January 2016.

245 - Jackie Smiley, "Erin Tonkon," Sonnox.

246 - Tony Visconti, "We All Thought He Had More Time," *Mojo*, March 2016.

247 - Ken Micallef, "Track by Track: Mark Guiliana on David Bowie's *Blackstar*," *Modern Drummer*, February 2016.

248 - Paul Zollo, "Remembering *Blackstar*: Bowie's Final Studio 'Experiment,'" Recording Academy Grammy Awards, May 15, 2017.

249 - "Exclusive Q&A with *Blackstar* Bassist Tim Lefebvre!" David Bowie News, February 23, 2018.

Additional Documentation

Clifford Slapper, *Bowie's Piano Man*, London, Fantom Publishing, 2014.

"'60s," *Mojo* no. 5, 2016.

Jean-Michel Guesdon and Philippe Margotin, *Pink Floyd La Totale*, E/P/A, Paris, 2017.

Matthieu Thibault, *David Bowie - L'Avant-Garde Pop*, Le Mot et le Reste, Marseille, 2013.

Matthieu Thibault, *La Trilogie Bowie-Eno*, Camion Blanc, Rosières-en-Haye, 2011.

Recording dates for the albums *The Next Day* and ★ (*Blackstar*) are from Nicholas Pegg's *The Complete David Bowie*, published by Titan Books in 2016.

Internet Sources

bowie-collection.de
bowie-singles.com
bowiebible.com
bowiegoldenyears.com
bowiesongs.wordpress.com
bowiewonderworld.com
brunoceriotti.weebly.com
davidbowie.com
davidbowienews.com
equipboard.com
memory-alpha.fandom.com
mickronson.co.uk
petshopboys.net
popmatters.com
reverb.com
thinwhiteduke.net

INDEX

The songs, albums, and singles analyzed in this book are emphasized in bold, along with portraits of specific performers.

ACKNOWLEDGMENTS

This book is the fruit of a collaboration with the indispensable Laurence Basset and Myriam Blanc. We would like to express our thanks for their patience during the formulation of this project.

Thanks also to Flavie Gaidon and to all the team at E/P/A, and to Sara Quémener and Zarko Telebak at ZS Studio.

Many thanks to Nathalie Lefebvre, and to the Clerc and Lefebvre families for their support.

Dedicated to Valérie Vie Le Sage

Copyright © 2021, Éditions E/P/A—Hachette Livre
Translation copyright © 2021 by Black Dog and Leventhal Publishers
Translation by Simon Burrows, Caroline Higgitt, and Paul Ratcliffe by arrangement with Jackie Dobbyne of Jacaranda Publishing Services Limited

Cover design by Katie Benezra
Cover copyright © 2021 by Hachette Book Group, Inc.

Front cover photograph © Michael Ochs/Getty Images
Back cover photograph © Lester Cohen/Getty Images

Original title: David Bowie, *La Totale*
Texts: Benoît Clerc
Published by Éditions E/P/A—Hachette Livre, 2021

Black Dog & Leventhal Publishers
Hachette Book Group
1290 Avenue of the Americas
New York, NY 10104

www.hachettebookgroup.com
www.blackdogandleventhal.com

First English-language Edition: November 2021

Black Dog & Leventhal Publishers is an imprint of Perseus Books, LLC, a subsidiary of Hachette Book Group, Inc. The Black Dog & Leventhal Publishers name and logo are trademarks of Hachette Book Group, Inc.

The publisher is not responsible for websites (or their content) that are not owned by the publisher.

The Hachette Speakers Bureau provides a wide range of authors for speaking events. To find out more, go to www.HachetteSpeakersBureau.com or call (866) 376-6591.

LCCN: 2021930882

ISBNs: 978-0-7624-7471-4 (hardcover), 978-0-7624-7472-1 (ebook)

Printed in China

10 9 8 7 6 5 4 3 2 1